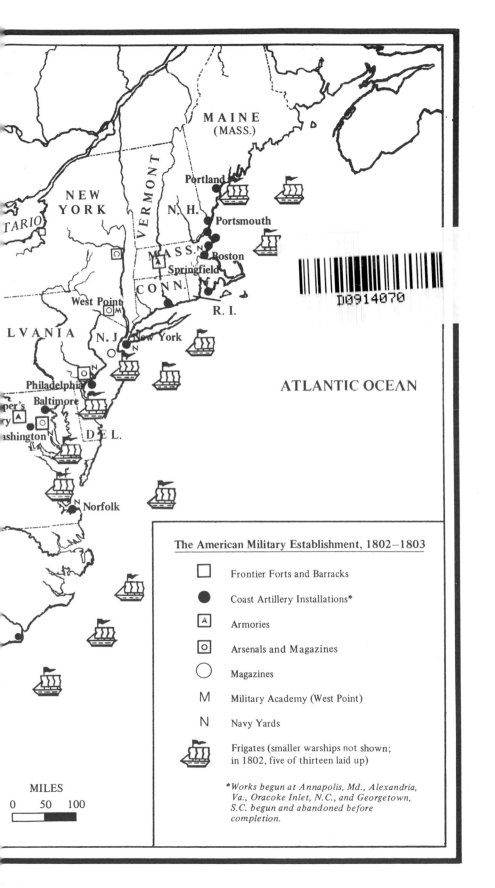

The American Military Establishment, 1802–1803

☐	Frontier Forts and Barracks
●	Coast Artillery Installations*
Ⓐ	Armories
⊙	Arsenals and Magazines
○	Magazines
M	Military Academy (West Point)
N	Navy Yards
⛵	Frigates (smaller warships not shown; in 1802, five of thirteen laid up)

*Works begun at Annapolis, Md., Alexandria, Va., Oracoke Inlet, N.C., and Georgetown, S.C. begun and abandoned before completion.

MILES

0   50   100

Eagle and Sword

★ ☆ ★ ☆ ★ ☆ ★ ☆ ★

Eagle and Sword

★ ☆ ★ ☆ ★ ☆ ★ ☆ ★

The Federalists and the Creation of the Military Establishment in America, 1783-1802

★

Richard H. Kohn

THE FREE PRESS
A Division of Macmillan Publishing Co., Inc.
NEW YORK
Collier Macmillan Publishers
LONDON

The Free Press
A Division of Macmillan Publishing Co., Inc.
866 Third Avenue, New York, N.Y. 10022

Collier Macmillan Canada, Ltd.

Library of Congress Catalog Card Number: 74-33092

Printed in the United States of America

printing number
1 2 3 4 5 6 7 8 9 10

Library of Congress Cataloging in Publication Data

Kohn, Richard H
    Eagle and sword.

    Bibliography: p.
    Includes index.
    1. Militarism--United States--History. 2. United
States. Army--History. 3. United States--History--
Constitutional period, 1789-1802. I. Title.
UA23.K737   355.021'3'0973   74-33092
ISBN 0-02-917551-8

Chapter 2 was published in different form as "The Inside History of the Newburgh
    Conspiracy: America and the Coup d'Etat," in the *William and Mary Quarterly*, 3d
    series, XXVII (1970), 187-220.
Part of Chapter 8 appeared previously as "The Washington Administration's Decision to
    Crush the Whiskey Rebellion," in the *Journal of American History*, LIX (1972), 567-584.
Portions of Chapter 9 appeared previously as "General Wilkinson's Vendetta with General
    Wayne: Politics and Command in the American Army, 1791-1796," *Filson Club History
    Quarterly*, XLV (1971), 361-372.

All are used by permission.

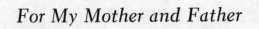
For My Mother and Father

Contents

Illustrations and Maps

following page 172

Preface

When I began this book about a decade ago, I intended to answer a relatively straightforward set of questions: how and why the American military establishment came into existence, when it became permanent, and why it assumed the shape it eventually did in the nineteenth century. From earlier investigation, it was clear that the traditional explanation was not very convincing. The origin of the peacetime army had been explained as a response to the Indian threat in the Northwest Territory in the 1780s and 1790s, and the rest of the military establishment—the storehouses, the arsenals at Springfield and Harpers Ferry, the coast artillery forts, the military academy at West Point, and the War Department and administrative apparatus governing the whole—were explained either as carry-overs from the Revolutionary war or as protection to meet the military threats from abroad in the 1790s. In other words, the creation of the United States military establishment was a functional response to military need.

This explanation left several unresolved puzzles. Why would a nation that began in 1783 with potent antimilitary traditions, with the almost universally held belief that standing armies posed an unacceptable danger to liberty and republican government, immediately begin to create a national army and actually possess a complete military establishment within twenty years of independence? Extensive plans for such an establishment were advanced in 1783 by George Washington, Alexander Hamilton, Henry Knox, Timothy Pickering, and other leading politicians and soldiers, but virtually rejected during the 1780s. Yet within another 15 years, by the time the Federalists left office in 1801, the United States possessed almost exactly the set of institutions proposed earlier. There did exist other alternatives, among them the state militias. It also occurred to me that military institutions are usually created or adopted by governments, and that to understand the birth of the military establishment one must first analyze the legislation and the decisions that brought the institutions into existence. First and foremost, then, the creation of the American military establishment was "political" in the purest sense of that term, given that a western society in the eighteenth century would adopt some form of military organization common to the age.

It quickly became apparent, also, that one of the chief forces behind a national establishment was a specific group of men: for the most part, veterans of the Continental Army, believers in a far stronger central government ("nationalists" in the 1780s), and founders and leaders of the Federalist party and the government after 1789. Several advocated a military establishment in 1783 and eventually impressed their military thinking on the party and on the government generally. Because such an institution was indistinguishable, at least in American thinking in the 1780s, from the classic European standing army, I was led into a second story: whether or not the Federalists were militarists wishing to engraft onto the young republic a standing army, with all that such an institution implied politically. During and after that era, Jeffersonian Republicans and many historians have accused the Federalists and their party of militarism, so I set out to test the interpretation by exploring the attitudes and actions of Federalists concerning peacetime armies, force, and military establishments from the beginning of the post revolutionary era.

What follows, then, could best be described as a study of the politics of the birth of the military establishment in America. It is far broader than the description implies, for I have attempted to provide an overall explanation of the creation of the military establishment, and I have pursued in depth the problem of Federalist militarism. But the following pages do not constitute a complete history of the beginning of the country's national military institutions. I have not traced the development of army or War Department internal structure, the procedures for supply, recruitment, promotion, or a variety of other facets of organizational life that characterize mature military institutions. In order to focus on the twin themes of militarism and the birth of an important institution, I have kept discussions of military operations, tactics, and strategy to a minimum. Nor have I attempted to relate military affairs directly to developments and practices during the War for Independence or in Europe, except when the relationship influenced directly the process by which the peacetime establishment came into existence. And I have not dealt in any substantive way with naval affairs; politically and militarily, eighteenth-century Americans considered navies and naval force so different from armies and military force that the two must logically be treated separately. Many of these and other important questions must await future historians of eighteenth-century military affairs.

When I began this study, I believed that the military was a minor issue after the Revolution, especially when compared to the Constitution, Hamilton's economic program, foreign relations, and the like. As I probed deeper, however, it became apparent that the military establishment was intimately involved in nearly every one of the great events and struggles which have for so long attracted the attention of historians. By the end, I became convinced that at no other time in American history— save perhaps the Reconstruction years and the era of the Cold War—had militarism so seriously threatened the United States. And at no other peacetime period in American history, with the same two exceptions of 1865–1877 and the post 1945 years, did military affairs exert more influence on national life than during the twenty years after independence when the American military establishment began.

Richard H. Kohn

Acknowledgments

It is a pleasure to thank publicly the many institutions and individuals who aided my work. Merrill Jensen first suggested a parallel topic while I was in graduate school, and throughout has given his guidance, help, and advice. I am indebted to him in ways that one can never repay. Edward M. Coffman introduced me to the fascinating world of armies and serious military history, and for a decade has given his counsel and friendship. Also at the University of Wisconsin, David W. Tarr of the political science department taught me the wider dimension of contemporary military affairs, and Jerald Hage of the sociology department opened up the mysteries of bureaucracy and complex organizations; both left their stamp on my thinking and on this book.

Carl E. Prince and George A. Billias shared their research and their thinking about post revolutionary American politics. In addition, Professor Billias showed me his biography of Elbridge Gerry in draft, offered good advice, and read the final manuscript at my and the publisher's request. Samuel Thomas allowed me to see his typescript edition of George Rogers Clark papers, and William B. Skelton shared his research on the army officer corps. All four men exchanged findings in the finest traditions of the scholarly community. While not in on the ground floor of this particular project, Gerald N. Grob critiqued the manuscript and helped immensely in many other ways. At a crucial point, Philip J. Greven, Jr. encouraged me to write a different kind of concluding chapter, and thereby materially improved the book. Stephen G. Kurtz and David Syrett read some of these chapters in dissertation form and furnished invaluable criticism. Gordon Payne, David L. Sallach, Mark E. Lender, Harry M. Klein, William A. Loveland, and Constance and Joseph Piellucci aided in research and verification. Jane Adas deserves special thanks for a virtuoso typing performance. And I want to express my gratitude to colleagues and friends, too numerous to list here, for conversations in which their ideas often stimulated and clarified my own thinking.

One of the greatest sources of aid were the editors, past and present, of documentary projects, many of whom shared their time, findings, and profound knowledge of this period. I wish especially to thank Harold C. and Patricia Syrett, Jacob E. and Jean G. Cooke, the late Cara-Louise Miller, Barbara Chernow, and the rest of the staff at The Papers of Alexander Hamilton; Mary-Jo Kline of The Adams Papers; Donald Jackson and Dorothy Twohig of The Papers of George Washington; Robert E. Rutland and Barbara D. Ripel of The Papers of James Madison; Richard B. Morris of The Papers of John Jay; Linda De Pauw and the staff at The Papers of the First Federal Congress; Paul H. Smith of the Library of Congress project on the correspondence of members of the Continental Congress; Herbert Johnson of The Papers of John Marshall; and Merrill Jensen and Gaspare J. Saladino of the Documentary History of the Ratification of the Constitution.

Grants from the American Philosophical Society (Penrose Fund), the Rutgers University Research Council, and the National Endowment for the Humanities defrayed many of my research costs, and in the last case underwrote an indispensable year away from teaching.

Without the collections of the great libraries and manuscript repositories in the eastern United States, it would have been impossible to learn enough about either the army or the politics of this era to write such a book. I owe a special debt to the staffs and especially the manuscript curators, and in some cases the staffs at print and map divisions, of the following institutions: Essex Institute; Massachusetts Historical Society; Harvard University Library; American Antiquarian Society; Rhode Island Historical Society; John Carter Brown Library, Brown University; Rhode Island State Archives; Connecticut Historical Society; Connecticut State Library; Yale University Library; New York State Library; United States Military Academy Library; City College of the City University of New York Library; Columbia University Library; New-York Historical Society; New York Society Library; Frick Art Reference Library; New York Public Library; New Jersey Historical Society; Rutgers University Library; Princeton University Library; Historical Society of Pennsylvania; Independence National Historical Park; American Philosophical Society; Philip and A. S. W. Rosenbach Foundation; Pennsylvania Historical and Museum Commission; Dickinson College Library; Carnegie Library of Pittsburgh; University of Pittsburgh Library; Western Pennsylvania Historical Society; Washington College (Pa.) Library; Maryland Historical Society; Library of Congress; National Archives; University of Virginia Library; Virginia State Library; Virginia Historical Society; College of William and Mary Library; Colonial Williamsburgh Foundation, Inc.; North Carolina Department of Archives and History; Southern Historical

Collection, University of North Carolina Library; Duke University Library; South Caroliniana Library, University of South Carolina; Filson Club; Kentucky Historical Society; University of Kentucky Library; Ohio Historical Society; Ohio State Library; Cincinnati Historical Society; Burton Historical Collection, Detroit Public Library; William L. Clements Library, University of Michigan; Indiana Historical Society; Indiana State Library; University of Indiana Library; Chicago Historical Society; University of Chicago Library; University of Wisconsin Library; and the State Historical Society of Wisconsin. My thanks go also to institutions and individuals, listed separately elsewhere, who graciously allowed the reproduction of maps, paintings, and other visual materials in their possession.

Three of my closest friends contributed so substantially that expressions of thanks at this point are almost superfluous. For ten years, Kenneth R. Bowling has freely shared his unparalleled knowledge of the source material for this era, exchanged notes, and criticized this work at every stage. George M. Curtis III added very able criticism of the final draft, and through his tough-minded thinking on the function of an historian, shaped the final product in ways he never knew. Robert C. Twombly painstakingly edited the entire book and contributed his skill in the craft of historical writing with the kind of care that only a close friend would give.

Last of all, Lynne Holtan Kohn lent not only her formidable literary eye, but by her patience, understanding, and encouragement imparted a special meaning to years of effort that might otherwise have been drudgery. Only she knows.

RHK

Abbreviations in Footnotes

The footnotes in this book contain two types of symbols for frequently cited works and places: first, manuscript repositories in plain caps; second, all other citations in italicized caps, almost all of which refer to published documentary collections. Below are the full bibliographic citations:

EI   James Duncan Phillips Library, Essex Institute, Salem, Massachusetts.

CHS   Connecticut Historical Society, Hartford, Connecticut.

HSP   Historical Society of Pennsylvania, Philadelphia, Pennsylvania.

LC   Manuscript Division, Library of Congress, Washington, D.C.

MHS   Massachusetts Historical Society, Boston, Massachusetts.

NA   National Archives, Washington, D.C.

NYHS   New-York Historical Society, New York, New York.

NYPL   Manuscripts and Archives Division, The New York Public Library, Astor, Lenox, and Tilden Foundations, New York, New York.

WLCL   William L. Clements Library, University of Michigan, Ann Arbor, Michigan.

AC   Joseph Gales and W. W. Seaton, compilers, *Debates and Proceedings in the Congress of the United States* [*Annals of Congress*] (Washington, 1834–1856).

ASP, IA   Walter Lowrie and Matthew Clarke, eds., *American State*
ASP, MA *Papers . . . Indian Affairs* and *Military Affairs* series (Washington, 1832–1861).

C S   Congress, Session [as in Fifth Congress, Second Session (5C 2S)].

JCC   Worthington C. Ford *et al.*, eds., *Journals of the Continental Congress, 1774–1789* (Washington, 1904–1937).

LCRK   Charles R. King, *The Life and Correspondence of Rufus King* (New York, 1894–1900).

LMCC   Edmund C. Burnett, ed., *Letters of Members of the Continental Congress* (Washington, 1921–1938).

MAWA   George Gibbs, *Memoirs of the Administrations of Washington and John Adams* . . . (New York, 1846).

PAH   Harold C. Syrett *et al.*, eds., *The Papers of Alexander Hamilton* (New York, 1961–date).

PJM   William T. Hutchinson *et al.*, eds., *The Papers of James Madison* (Chicago, 1962–date).

PTJ   Julian Boyd, ed., *The Papers of Thomas Jefferson* (Princeton, 1950–date).

RG   Record Group [in the National Archives].

WAH   Henry Cabot Lodge, ed., *The Works of Alexander Hamilton* (New York, 1904).

WGW   John C. Fitzpatrick, ed., *The Writings of George Washington* . . . (Washington, 1931–1944).

WJA   Charles Francis Adams, ed., *The Works of John Adams* (Boston, 1850–1856).

WKPM   Richard C. Knopf, ed., *Anthony Wayne, A Name in Arms . . . The Wayne-Knox-Pickering-McHenry Correspondence* (Pittsburgh, 1960).

WMQ   *The William and Mary Quarterly*, Third Series.

WTJ   Paul Leicester Ford, ed., *The Works of Thomas Jefferson* (New York, 1892–1899).

1

★ ☆ ★ ☆ ★ ☆ ★ ☆ ★

Introduction:
The Military Heritage
of the Founding Fathers

★

Mankind are divided into five states or conditions, the Soldier, the Gown-man [judge], the Merchant or trader, the Mechanic, and the husbandman—All necessary and useful to the public. The soldier toils to enlarge the dominions, disappoints the designs of enemies, and keeps the subjects in their obedience to the government and laws of the state.

*Compendium of Military Duty . . . for the Militia
of the United States, 1793.*[a]

In 1783 when Americans began to confront the problem of national security and what kind of military institutions to establish, they already possessed a rich and varied military past which extended back over a century and a half. Through many conflicts with the Indians and continual warfare with various European nations beginning in the 1680s, Americans developed their own military institutions and gained familiarity with those of Europe. Long before independence these institutions, the way in which they functioned, their place in society, and their relationship to the state had become fixed in American thinking. In addition, Americans read history that emphasized martial issues, and within their own memory, they had engaged in two long and shattering wars: the Seven Years' War (1755–1763) and the Revolution itself. From these experiences emerged assumptions, ideas, and traditions which were destined to shape and distort military issues in the two decades after independence, and make much of the creation of a military establishment into a struggle to grow beyond an unyielding set of popular truths about the world of war and the armies that peopled it.

1

Origins of the Prejudice Against Standing Armies

> A Standing Army, however necessary it may be at some times, is always dangerous to the Liberties of the People. Soldiers are apt to consider themselves as a Body distinct from the rest of the Citizens. They have their Arms always in their hands. Their Rules and their Discipline is severe. They soon become attached to their officers and disposed to yield implicit obedience to their Commands. Such a Power should be watched with a jealous Eye.
>
> Samuel Adams, 1776.[b]

No principle of government was more widely understood or more completely accepted by the generation of Americans that established the United States than the danger of a standing army in peacetime. Because a standing army represented the ultimate in uncontrolled and uncontrollable power, any nation that maintained permanent forces surely risked the overthrow of legitimate government and the introduction of tyranny and despotism. Composed of officers from the aristocracy and soldiers from the bottom of society brutalized by harsh discipline, isolated from the rest of society, loyal not to an ideal or to a government but to a commander and to its own traditions, the standing army could not be fettered by any of the traditional checks that preserved liberty. Even if it did not attempt an outright coup, armies could act to enforce the will of a dictatorial ruler, or harass and terrorize a people regardless of law or constitution. Because of its social composition, its discipline, and the rootless character of the rank and file, in idle times it threatened not only political institutions but religion, morals, life, private property—virtually the entire fabric of political and social life.[1]

The institution so dreaded by Americans in the eighteenth century was the professional army, developed in Europe during the hundred years preceding the Revolution. The armies of that era were tightly structured institutions, dependent on long training and hard discipline in order to control the soldiery and prepare it for the difficulties of combat and camp life. Since the basic weapon was a smooth-bore musket inaccurate and difficult to reload, battles could only be won at close range and commanders had to deploy their troops in closely packed ranks which wheeled and maneuvered until they were close enough to the enemy to loose a withering volley and then charge with the bayonet. The stress of battle, the violence, the complexity of march, and the movements to work the weapons required troops that were automatons. Most were the scum of society, sold or shanghaied into the service, rootless, lacking any class or national loyalties. To train them, to prevent desertion and violence against officers and civilians, and to push them into battle, eighteenth-century armies practiced savage discipline. The result was a brutalized soldiery under rigid authority that was obviously capable of wreaking havoc on a civilian population.

Because of the scarcity of recruits, the time necessary to mold them into a fighting force, the expense, and the carnage of battle, warfare in the eighteenth century tended to be limited and stylized, marked by endless marches and countermarches as generals searched for advantages of position or terrain. In addition, armies were encumbered by huge supply trains, by their storage magazines, and by the rudimentary character of transport and the road network. Armies were not the static institutions so often pictured by historians; when led by skillful generals, they could be capable of all kinds of complex operations, even amphibious assaults against defended shorelines. Yet due to limits in firepower and mobility, they could not pin down or pursue a shattered opponent and destroy him completely. Invariably the vanquished escaped to fight again. Thus, because of the nature of the weapons, the armies, the societies, and the international political system—princes related by kinship or marriage struggling mostly over borders, colonies, and empire—war was less a conflict to death between rival societies than a highly ritualized phenomenon with rules and commonly accepted practices. It began over small incidents, disrupted civilian life and property relatively little, and ended not by total victory or unconditional surrender but by labyrinthian negotiations between winners and losers over colonial possessions, trading rights, and the like. Yet limited and "civilized" as the warfare system seemed, it rested on armies of officer aristocrats and hard-bitten soldiers which posed obvious dangers to the political and social life of a newly founded republic. [2]

The origin of the implacable fear of standing armies lay in the conjunction of Americans' own colonial experience and the radical Whig political ideology which was so influential in the way the Revolutionary generation perceived events. The distrust of military power and the hostility to permanent standing armies were deeply rooted in British political and constitutional thought. Beginning in the 1620s, England experienced three-quarters of a century of wrenching political struggle over the existence of an army, its control by Parliament or the Crown, its internal governance, and its relationship to the English people and society. In the process, Parliament gained control over the military, and after the Glorious Revolution in 1689, Parliament instituted annual appropriations for the army and a yearly mutiny act defining the code of military justice in order to keep the army under its control. In the process of these struggles, there developed a fully articulated anti-army ideology which assumed that military power not only represented the ultimate power in society, but also that it constituted an acute and overbearing threat to liberty. To Englishmen attacking the Crown's forces, history gave the danger of standing armies the widest possible dimension and made it into the universal tool of despotism. According to the leading Whig pamphleteers, no nation could maintain its liberty and a standing army at the same time. The militia—yeomen and landholders armed and trained, men with a stake in society and a desire to preserve liberty, men who would never seize power or overturn legitimate political forms unless they were tyrannical—was the only safe and sensible military institution. Quoting respected political philosophers and adding lurid descriptions of how restless mercenaries corrupted a population, Whig pamphleteers like John Trenchard simplified the menace into one convenient slogan. After the great standing army debate of the late 1690s and the outpouring of radical tracts, generations of Englishmen and Americans were unable to distinguish the varieties of militarism and military interference in politics, or the differences in military institutions. Henceforth, Rome's legions, the Turkish janissaries, and Cromwell's New Model Army would all qualify as "standing armies," a powerful, emotional phrase so easily understood and so universally accepted that it needed no further definition.[3]

Americans absorbed the standing army literature eagerly, but while Trenchard, James Burgh, and other Whig publicists focused colonial reading and thinking on the subject, Americans read history for themselves.[4] At the same time, they also had firsthand experience with European military practices that reinforced political theory and identified the standing army in American minds as a foreign, anti-libertarian institution. The first settlers consciously changed the old British militia system in order to avoid the merging of political and military power. "How dangerous it might be," noted John Winthrop in his journal, "to erect a standing authority of military men, which might easily, in time, overthrow the civil power."[5] After 1660, more than half the royal governors sent to America were army officers with experience as the captains of the garrison in English towns, the enforcers of Crown authority, and as governors, they were authoritarian and quick to use force.[6] British regulars were sent to crush Bacon's Rebellion in Virginia in the 1670s, and again to put down Leisler's Rebellion in New York over a decade later. Time and again attempts at military cooperation between the British army and the colonies ended in friction, mutual disgust, and antagonism. Regular officers snubbed colonial officers, who in turn derided the hidebound, inconsistent regulars; to Americans, generals like Edward Braddock typified the British army at its inefficient and arrogant worst.

While most of these contacts were brief and infrequent, they occurred at crucial times in the history of the colonies, and during the Seven Years' War—within the memory of the Revolutionary generation—all the difficulties and antagonisms were replayed on a far wider scale than ever before.* Thousands of regulars debarked in America, marched through the colonies, and fought on the North American continent. Colonists by the thousands served in British regiments or as auxiliaries to the regulars in colonial units, viewing the brutal discipline, the fraud of recruiting parties, and the dictatorial methods of British officers. Civil-military conflict flared at all levels. Army recruiters plied country boys with rum, enlisted indentured servants and apprentices, and arrested colonial deserters despite protests and on more than one occasion riots by local townspeople. Troops were quartered in the homes of unwilling colonials; legislatures battled their governors, the British Commander-in-Chief, and Whitehall over strategy and manpower and money for military operations. "American Morals and Religion were never in so much danger as . . . in the present War," wrote Ezra Stiles; "the officers endeavor to restrain the vices of the private soldiers while on Duty, But I take it the Religion of the Army is Infidelity and Gratification of the Appetites."[7]

Yet in 1763, many Americans still liked the army for the protection it offered and for its boost to the local economy. For all the warnings of history, theory, and experience, many colonials were actually quite ambivalent towards the troops, especially the officers, to whom they were attracted socially and whom as a rule they treated with respect.[8] During the next decade all this changed. After 1763, for the first time the British government stationed several thousand soldiers in the mainland colonies, and as the agitation increased colonials focused much of their discontent on the army as the most visible, crude symbol of British authority. When redcoats suppressed tenant riots on some of the Hudson River manors in 1766, looting and destroying property, many Americans began to see the analogy between the British army and the standing army of classical theory.[9]

Incidents of civil-military friction after that increased steadily; colonial agitation continued and imperial officials called more and more often upon the military for protection and enforcement. Finally in Boston in 1770, after a long campaign in the local press by radical leaders warning of the danger of standing armies, after months of mounting tensions and frequent clashes between the soldiers and townspeople, the inevitable explosion occurred: regulars killed five civilians in the streets. Immediately the Boston Massacre became a *cause célèbre* up and down the seacoast. "Cato's Letters . . . and all the writings of Trenchard and

---

*John Adams remembered fifty years later: "The Treatment of the Provincial officers and soldiers by the British officers during that War [Seven Years' War], made my blood boil in my veins." John Adams to Benjamin Rush, May 1, 1807, Alexander Biddle, ed., *Old Family Letters: Copied from the originals for Alexander Biddle* (Philadelphia, 1892), 135.

Gordon, Mrs. Macaulay's History, Burgh's Political Disquisitions, Clarendon's History of the Civil War, and all the writings relative to the revolutions in England became fashionable reading," John Adams recalled in old age. "Not the battle of Lexington or Bunker's Hill, not the surrender of Burgoyne or Cornwallis were more important events in American history than the battle of King Street, on the 5th of March, 1770."[10] In annual orations for years afterward Boston revolutionary leaders made a legend of the "horrors of THAT DREADFUL NIGHT" when Americans saw the "ground crimsoned with the gore of hundreds of fellow citizens."[11] Like no other incident before or since, the Boston Massacre permanently embedded the prejudice against standing armies into the American political tradition. It was no accident that the Declaration of Independence repeatedly charged George III with militarism and referred to the abuses of a regular army. ("He has kept among us . . . standing armies"; "He has affected to render the military independent of and superior to the civil power"; "quartering large bodies of troops among us"; "protecting them, by a mock trial"; "transporting large armies of foreign mercenaries to compleat the works of death, desolation, and tyranny. . . .")

Hatred of the standing army thus became central to the Revolutionary tradition, deeply interwoven with the language of independence and birth of the United States as a nation. To Americans, warnings of radical political theory had been borne out. The British army represented that monstrous "CONSPIRACY against Liberty" which Americans saw emanating from the ministry in London; it was the agent of European corruption come to sap American virtue, the iron fist of customs regulation, the tyranny of trial without jury.[12] So old was the tradition, so familiar were the warnings, and so powerful was the experience with the British army in the 1760s and 1770s that by the winning of independence "standing army" had become a catch-phrase that automatically evoked a series of preconfirmed images and definitions. And because these images were charged with political meaning, and at the same time obscured fundamental differences between the varieties of military institutions, the prejudice against standing armies could not help but warp military policy in the United States for generations to come.

Counterpoint: Militia

From a well regulated militia we have nothing to fear; their interest is the same with that of the state. . . . [T]hey do not jeopard(ize) their lives for a master who considers them only as the instruments of his ambition. . . .

John Hancock, 1774.[c]

From the very beginning of settlement, war and military practices in the colonies diverged from those in Europe. During the first years, Americans lived in primitive societies ringed by potential enemies. Instead of a competition over borders or empire, war in America was a matter of survival, for settlers and Indians both a defense of home and family and life itself, a protracted series of desperate conflicts between rival societies marked often by the worst atrocities. With neither the manpower nor the resources to maintain permanent forces, the colonists adapted the old English militia system to their defense needs. [13]

The basis of the colonial militia was universal obligation: the charge to every able-bodied male (usually 16 to 60) to arm himself, enroll in his local unit, muster and train periodically, and march to war when called by his leaders. The militia laws usually established fines for absence from muster or failure to have the proper arms and equipment, defined the length and conditions of service, and set the structure and deployment of units according to military circumstances. [14] There were major differences among colonies in tactical structure and in the effectiveness of the institutions, but as settlement progressed and the Indian threat waned, the militia systems everywhere began to decay as viable fighting organizations. The frequency of company or regimental musters declined. As life became safer and colonial society more complex, the list of exemptions from service lengthened and militia began to serve more of a ceremonial and police function. In almost every colony in the eighteenth century, the signs of deterioration were evident: laws laxly enforced, efficiency down, arms and equipment in short supply, and morale at a low ebb. During emergencies, English officials complained bitterly about poor training, desertion, and unwillingness to serve. On the eve of the Seven Years' War, North Carolina showed officially a strength of 15,000 infantry and 400 cavalry, but typically many of the units lacked officers or equipment and the rolls were padded with men dead or long since moved away. [15]

Part of the reason for these endemic weaknesses during the colonial era was that the militia was not a system at all. In reality it was a concept of defense: the idea of universal obligation for defensive war, a people in arms to ward off an invader. Indeed in many colonies units could not legally serve outside provincial borders. Yet while defensive in theory, war in America usually necessitated tactical and strategic offensives. Except in dire local emergencies, no colony used the militia as it was organized on paper. Instead, the government usually called for volunteers or drafted quotas from various companies so as not to strip individual areas of all protection or totally disrupt the local economy. As early as the mid-seventeenth century, colonies were drafting and maintaining semi-regular forces—in New England in the 1690s men served a year or two in garrison posts and as scouting parties between towns during the raiding seasons; after the 1644 massacre in Virginia, a line of frontier forts was manned by selected militia and by the 1680s, volunteer or drafted rangers were scouting assigned areas to warn of attack. As warfare in North America in the eighteenth century became increasingly an extension of Britain's struggle for empire with European rivals, the trend toward using volunteers accelerated. British regulars bore most of the burden, with Americans serving in their own units as auxiliaries, but because most of the duty involved offensive expeditions or long stretches of garrison duty, the enrolled militia almost never served. "The Land must be tilled and Business Followed; every House and Plantation cannot be guarded, and on the Frontier [the militia] are Miles distant, and so can afford little Aid to one another," wrote Benjamin Franklin in explaining the "Provincial Troops" kept up by some colonies.[16] As an institution, the militia was a training and administrative shadow, a paper organization superimposed on the local governmental structure to implement the concept of universal obligation.

And yet within this institutional vagueness lay the real source of the militia's vitality, and Americans never questioned the ultimate worth or necessity of the militia system. Its amorphous nature made it flexible enough to meet a variety of military situations. Simple legislation could increase the number of cavalry units for patrols to control the slave population, or require frontier militiamen to equip themselves with snowshoes, or raise the fines, increase the training, or modify the table of organization.[17] Colonials could not conceive of discarding the institution, in part because standing troops were anathema and required consent from the Crown, in part because the militia was too ingrained an element in American culture, too closely identified with colonial history and with the colonial conception of warfare as a defense against invading savages. As he travelled around Europe in the 1780s, John Adams repeatedly cited "The Towns, Militia, Schools and Churches as the four Causes of the Growth and Defence of N[ew] England" and the source of "the Virtues and talents of the People"—"Temperance, Patience, Fortitude, Prudence, . . . Justice, . . . Sagacity, Knowledge, Judgment, Taste, Skill, Ingenuity, Dexterity, and Industry."[18]

Already by the Revolution, the militia was charged with political meaning; already it represented the very antithesis of the corrupting and tyrannical standing army. As John Trenchard had put it, in terms that John Hancock repeated almost exactly 75 years later, "There can be no danger where the Nobility and chief Gentry of *England* are the Commanders, and the Body [is] made up of the Freeholders, their Sons and Servants; unless we can conceive that the Nobility and Gentry will join in an unnatural Design to make void their own Titles to their Estates and Liberties: and if they could entertain so ridiculous a Proposition, they would never be obeyed by the Souldiers."[19] The political tradition which flowed from radical Whig theory in England, reinforced by tangible experience with British forces, strengthened American faith in the militia, confirmed the association in American minds of the militia with liberty, freedom, and colonial virtue—the standing army with European militarism, corruption, and tyranny. After 1783, the effort to create a national military establishment would entail a struggle to outgrow such revolutionary slogans and adapt one institution or the other to the military needs of the new nation.

The War for Independence

It is a favorite toast in the army, "A hoop to the barrel," or "Cement to the Union."

> Major General Henry Knox, February 1783.[d]

For the generation of the founders of the United States, the great laboratory for all things military was the War for Independence. During its course, Americans recruited a national army and a navy, licensed privateers, wrestled with the problems of supply and finance, appointed generals, made strategy, fought Indians, coordinated war plans with allies—in short for eight years, Americans waged eighteenth-century war in all its manifold complexity. It was almost inevitable that the leaders of the new nation, many themselves veterans of the conflict, would look to Washington's Continental Army as a model for virtually every detail of military organization. Yet the legacy of the war was ambiguous. The conflict encompassed every kind of combat and strategic and tactical situation known to eighteenth-century warfare as militia and regulars fought separately and together under all conceivable conditions. But unlike previous wars, the Revolution was a war for national independence, which often made a mockery of eighteenth-century strategy and tactics. Afterwards Americans could not agree on what had happened or on the comparative value of regulars and militia; the "lessons" for the future were too murky, too confused.

For one group, however, the lessons were clear. To most of the higher-ranking officers of the Continental Army, the heads of the special branches and administrative departments, and Washington's staff, the war proved that militia were unreliable and inefficient. As they worked to create a stable, disciplined force capable of defeating British regulars in open battle, Washington and other commanders rapidly concluded that long-service Continentals should replace the ill-organized and untrained citizen regiments. "[T]hey come in you cannot tell how, go, you cannot tell when; and act, you Cannot tell where," Washington wrote in exasperation at the militia, "consume your Provisions, exhaust your Stores, and leave you at last in a critical moment."[20] When asked by Congress in 1783 to consider the nation's future needs, Washington and the other leaders of the Continental Army unanimously recommended a national military establishment and a complete overhaul of the militia. Their proposals became crucial both to the nationalist program to strengthen the central government in the 1780s and to Federalist policy in the 1790s.

Federalist adoption of the Continental Army viewpoint on defense matters was not at all coincidental. Seeded throughout the Continental Army officer corps especially in the top ranks, the staff departments, and the coterie of officers who served Washington as aides and secretaries were many of the future leaders of the Federalist party. Rufus King, John Marshall, and Jonathan Dayton were all captains during the war. Arthur St. Clair (Governor of the Northwest Territory), Benjamin Lincoln (Collector for the port of Boston), Rufus Putnam (Judge of the Northwest Territory, Surveyor-General of the U.S.), Henry Knox (Secretary of War), Charles Cotesworth Pinckney (ambassador) had all been generals. The commissaries and contractors included such leading Federalists as Jeremiah Wadsworth and William Duer. From Washington's aides and secretaries alone came David Cobb and Richard Varick, Alexander Hamilton, Edmund Randolph (Attorney General and Secretary of State), Secretary of War James McHenry, Jonathan Trumbull, Jr. (congressman, Speaker, and Governor of Connecticut), and David Humphreys (diplomat in the 1790s). Young at the beginning of the war, for many of these men service in the Continental Army provided the first real taste of public life. Significantly enough, the experience was at the national level, fighting for the whole country, serving in the first large organization which threw citizens from the different states together. ("A century in the ordinary intercourse, would not have accomplished what the Seven Years' association in Arms did" in breaking down state loyalty, Washington remembered.)[21] At a formative stage in their lives they were exposed to military values; they learned the strength of executive leadership in contrast to the weakness of Congress under the Articles of Confederation. Some came of age in the Continental Army; others formed friendships and made contacts that meant much in later years; still others formed judgments about politics that would last a lifetime.

Henry Knox, a bluff, convivial six footer nearly 300 pounds in weight, a bookseller and minor political figure in his native Boston, was only 25 when the war began. As the colonies moved toward rebellion Knox read deeply in military science, and soon after entering the service Washington made him chief of artillery. Knox remained at the General's side throughout the war, during the years of despair—the retreat across Jersey, Valley Forge, Arnold's treason—as well as the moments of triumph and elation. By force of personality, by knowledge and administrative talent, Knox made the corps of artillery truly effective in spite of frequent lapses in transport and shortages of lead, powder, and other necessary matériel. Knox saw it all: the makeshift character of the army, deficiencies in supply, profiteering, apathy, inflation. "The vile water-gruel governments which have taken place in most of the States are totally disproportioned to the exigencies of the war," he told his brother on the eve of the Yorktown campaign.[22] By the end Knox was representing the officer corps in the agitation for half-pay pensions and had become a thoroughly committed nationalist. "America will have fought and bled to little purpose if the powers of government shall be insufficient to preserve the peace."[23]

Like Knox, Timothy Pickering struggled through the most dismal crises of the war. About 30 at the beginning, a Harvard graduate from a respectable farming family who had already begun a career in politics, Pickering fought the war from a succession of crucial administrative posts. For a year he served as Adjutant General, the executive agent of the Commander-in-Chief. In 1778 Pickering joined the Board of War, the congressional agency for supervising the army and all military matters, but a group which lacked the power to handle its huge administrative responsibilities. Pickering saw the weakness of government, the jealousy inherent in divided authority. Rampant inflation in 1778 and 1779 consumed his modest salary and crippled his efforts to procure supplies. In late 1780 Pickering became Quartermaster General. To keep the army's horses from starving he commandeered forage; to procure transport for the march to Yorktown he sold precious supplies—and used state money earmarked for the Massachusetts line. By war's end, arrested for debt because he had issued personal notes for supplies, the tall, humorless, aggressively independent, righteous New Englander had learned to despise the Confederation for its lack of power.[24]

For young Dr. James McHenry, a Scotch-Irish immigrant who settled in Baltimore four years before Lexington and Concord, the experience was nearly as personal. McHenry's wartime career has never been probed by scholars. His nationalism probably stemmed from two years as assistant secretary to Washington at the nadir of the army's fortunes (1778-1780), when—desperate for men and supplies, suffering the worst winter (1779-1780) of the conflict—the officer corps came near to revolt. McHenry made enough contacts—Washington, Hamilton, and influential Maryland leaders—to launch himself successfully in state and then national politics. In 1782 he advised his friend Hamilton not to enter Congress. "We have already immolated [ourselves] . . . on the altar of liberty," McHenry lamented. "If I had best served my family as faithfully as I have the public, my affairs would have been today in a very different order."[25]

Alexander Hamilton knew the story only too well. In 1777, Washington made the 22-year-old artillery captain from the West Indies his aide-de-camp, thereby beginning one of the most important confidential relationships in American history. Hamilton was brilliant, talented, ingratiating, and ambitious; rapidly he became trusted and then indispensable as secretary and agent for the Commander-in-Chief. Until the two quarreled four years later, only Washington was closer to the center or more knowledgeable about the army, Congress, or the war effort. When Hamilton left for Congress in 1782 he was already a national figure. But above all else he was a creature of the war: the intimacy with Washington ("he was an *Aegis very important to me*" admitted Hamilton in studied understatement after Washington's death), marriage into the potent Schuyler family in New York, and contacts with important national leaders. [26] Furthermore from his own reading and reflection Hamilton worked out ideas which guided his politics for the rest of his life. "The fundamental defect," he began in a long analysis of the state of the nation in 1780, when the war effort was on the verge of collapse, "is a want of power in Congress." [27] In long letters to influential congressmen, Hamilton sketched out a political and financial program that became the fundamental testament of nationalism and Federalism: sound public credit; the attachment of monied interests to government; a national bank; vigorous executive leadership in government policy and administration; and over all a strong national government with clearcut taxing authority, and diplomatic, military, and economic muscle ("[t]he confederation in my opinion should give Congress complete sovereignty"). [28]

Together these four men—three as Secretaries of War and the fourth as the author of the first peacetime report in Congress on the subject, as adviser to the President, and as leader of the Federalist party—along with George Washington became the spokesmen for a national military establishment. They recognized very quickly that questions of military policy had overarching political dimensions. To argue for a peacetime army after 1783 was to favor giving the national government added authority, a symbol of ultimate sovereignty—in eighteenth-century terms the power of the sword. But militias were state institutions; to rely on them for defense would weaken the union politically as well as militarily.

While most Federalists accepted this fact by the 1790s, for many the fascination and attraction with armies went much deeper. In social philosophy Federalists constantly emphasized order, tradition, the natural distinctions among men, and social harmony. Federalists viewed society as an integrated, stable organism in which individuals deferred to their superiors and subordinated and sacrificed interests and passions for the common good. Individuals should be guided by duty and principle, by virtue and courage, by independence of mind, but at the same time by deference. [29] Strikingly these same values personified the eighteenth-century military officer. The conjunction was not surprising; eighteenth-century armies drew their officers from the aristocracy and undoubtedly these values permeated the cultural setting into which Federalists were born and matured. The army reinforced these ideals and, for young men from different colonies, homogenized, codified, and connected the values with a critical experience at a peculiarly influential point in their lives. Significantly, in the only two states studied intensively, Pennsylvania and New York, the divisions over the Constitution in 1787–1788 followed along military service: Federalists were mostly veterans of the Continental Army officer corps, Antifederalists veterans of the militia. Social philosophy, interstate associations, nationalism in politics, respect for the effectiveness of regulars over militia—all came together in the Continental Army to give a cast and a character to the Federalist party which it retained for the entire span of its existence. [30]

By 1783 many officers sensed what had happened. In May, Knox and several other top officers organized the Society of the Cincinnati to perpetuate friendships and memories of their wartime service. Immediately the Society came under blistering attack as the embryo of a political pressure group or even a military aristocracy since it was modeled on the federal system (state societies and a national group), its members were identified by ceremonial badges, and the membership passed to the eldest son in each officer family. The Society appeared to be just the kind of semi-military organization that grew out of the classic standing army. In Europe, officers not on active duty nonetheless remained in government service on half-pay, able to be mobilized at the government's call, attached to the army interest, a kind of semi-standing army scattered throughout society. That is why the demands for a half-pay bonus by Continental Army officers during the war sparked such heated resistance, and why the Society of the Cincinnati—with its aristocratic trappings—generated such intense suspicion. The fears were never borne out, but there was a modicum of truth in the opposition's animosity. By maintaining the associations of the war, the Cincinnati provided an institutional and emotional bond between the Continental Army and the future Federalist party. [31]

Given the virulent prejudice against standing armies, so deeply rooted in American thinking, military experience, and political tradition, it was almost foreordained that Americans would choose the militia for security after the Revolution. Out of the war, however, there emerged a group of men who—from their own military service and for political reasons—believed in a national army and regular troops. For at least a decade after independence, they were the most dynamic element in American politics. The birth of the military establishment would in large part be the story of their effort to provide for the common defense and create a durable, lasting union.

PART ONE

★ ☆ ★ ☆ ★ ☆ ★ ☆ ★

Power of the Sword

★

*in which
the nationalists develop plans for a
military establishment, watch as those
plans are defeated in the Confederation
Congress, and then provide the
authority for a regular army in the
Constitution of 1787.*

★ ☆ ★ ☆ ★ ☆ ★ ☆ ★

2

★ ☆ ★ ☆ ★ ☆ ★ ☆ ★

The Newburgh Conspiracy:
Nationalism and Militarism
[1783]

★

The idea of a redress by force is too chimerical to have had a place in the
imagination of any serious mind in this Army. . . . The Army is a
dangerous instrument to play with.

George Washington, 1783[a]

At the close of the Revolution, after the preliminary articles of peace
had been signed but before knowledge of them had reached America,
there occurred at the Continental Army's Newburgh cantonment one of
the most bizarre and little understood events in the history of the United
States. At the very moment of victory, the officer corps responded to an
anonymous appeal from one of its members and met to consider mutiny
against constituted civilian authority. The Newburgh conspiracy was the
closest an American army has ever come to revolt or coup d'etat, and it
exposed the fragility of civil-military relations at the beginning of the
republic. Had the army cast off civilian control at the critical moment of
the nation's birth, a national military establishment might have been
impossible for generations afterward.

Behind the events at Newburgh in March 1783, lay a complex plot
which involved not only certain leaders of the army, but of Congress as
well, most importantly the very same men who would be responsible in
the following years for founding an American military establishment.
The willingness of these men to risk shattering the delicate bond of trust
between the army and the American people, in violation of the deep-
rooted tradition against direct military interference in politics and the
long-standing warnings about the dangers of an army, revealed a flaw
which would dog the Federalist party throughout its existence.

Nearly forty years later, Timothy Pickering received a letter from a stranger in New York asking for information about the anonymous addresses circulated at camp in 1783. Pickering had been there during those hectic days and his correspondent wanted the retired soldier's opinion of the origin of the addresses, their purpose, and the significance of the whole episode. "On comparing the accounts," Pickering read, three interpretations were possible, all of which implied some kind of conspiracy. The first suggested a coup d'etat: the addresses were "part of a deliberate and studied plan, to break down the civil authority and to erect on its ruins, a military despotism." Only the "vast influence" of Commander-in-Chief George Washington averted this "dreadful catastrophe." The second explanation theorized that the conspiracy was merely artificial, a drama contrived to give "a sort of political and moral finishing to the character of Washington and the Army." The last, and more realistic, view was that the whole business had been part of a more complex plot to use the officers "as auxiliaries to the fiscal measures of that day." Specifically, the army's discontent had been used to pressure first Congress, then the individual states, into accepting an amendment to the Articles of Confederation giving the national government power to tax imports. Both the first and second theories, Pickering's correspondent claimed, had little or no evidence in their support. But the third was intriguing, supported by some "highly important and acknowledged facts" and by others "less known."[1]

Pickering's correspondent was none other than John Armstrong, Jr., who as a young major and aide-de-camp to General Horatio Gates, had written the addresses.[2] Armstrong never provided a convincing explanation to Pickering for dredging up the Newburgh incident and it has never received much attention except among historians, who have generally accepted Armstrong's third interpretation. Some scholars have even argued that the nationalists were actually interested in a coup d'etat.[3] While much of the incident remains a mystery, the conspiracy did involve many of the most important political leaders of the generation after the Revolution, and it revealed that some of them were unprincipled and cynical enough to use the threat of a coup to achieve their political goals. But, whatever its ultimate political purpose, the Newburgh conspiracy had a vast and far-reaching influence on the American military establishment, an influence that is still felt today.[4]

Although the roots of the crisis went back several years, the first stage in the conspiracy began in late 1782. In the last week in December, Major General Alexander McDougall and Colonels John Brooks and Matthias Ogden rode into Philadelphia with a petition to Congress from the army encamped at Newburgh.* "We have borne all that men can bear—our property is expended—our private resources are at an end, and our friends are wearied out and disgusted with our incessant applications." The major grievance was pay. Officers and men had not received their salaries in months. More important, the officers were concerned about receiving the half-pay pensions promised by Congress in 1780. To the officers, half-pay was "an honorable and just recompense for several years hard service" during which their "health and fortunes" had been "worn down and exhausted." But they feared, and with good reason, that its general unpopularity might induce Congress to repudiate the promise. Therefore, they were willing to accept a commutation of half-pay to some equivalent lump sum payment. For all its moderation and plea for sympathy, however, the petition spoke in thinly veiled threats: "any further experiments on their [the army's] patience may have fatal effects."[5]

The petition capped almost six months of continual turmoil in the northern encampment, and within the officer corps, agitation which had surfaced over compensation five years earlier. Earlier efforts to settle the pay problem with state governments had failed, and when Congress considered the question of half-pay in the summer of 1782, the resurgence of all the old arguments in opposition only heightened the officers' desperation.[6] Pay and half-pay, however, were only symptoms of a deeper malaise in Newburgh. Most officers were apprehensive about returning to civilian life. Many had been impoverished by the war while friends at home had grown fat on the opportunities provided by the war. For all, the end of hostilities meant re-entering a society that had adjusted to their absence, and in traditionally antimilitary New England, a society that would accord none of the advantages or plaudits that returning veterans expect to receive. During those long, boring months of 1782, a growing feeling of martyrdom, an uncertainty, and a realization that long years of service might go unrewarded—or perhaps even hamper their future careers—made the situation increasingly explosive.

In mid-November, their patience exhausted, the officers decided to petition Congress once more. Major General Henry Knox drafted the address and, in correspondence with Secretary at War Benjamin Lincoln, carefully laid the groundwork for its reception in Philadelphia. On his part, Lincoln took the utmost pains to press the seriousness of the situation on delegates in Congress.[7] From Philadelphia General Arthur St. Clair explained the political situation to McDougall's committee, and

*Officially, the army at Newburgh consisted of about 550 officers and over 9,000 enlisted men. See William Barber, "Abstract of Musters for the Northern Army," Oct. 1782, Alexander McDougall Papers, New-York Historical Society, New York, N.Y. Secretary for Foreign Affairs Robert R. Livingston in Philadelphia estimated the size of the army at 12,000 (to John Jay, Aug. 9, 1782, Robert R. Livingston Papers, New-York Historical Society).

advised the officers to tell Congress "in the most express and positive terms" that unless action was immediate, it could expect "a convulsion of the most dreadful nature and fatal consequences."[8] Events were rapidly approaching a crisis. As one officer put it, "the Event of the Embassy *must* be agreeable" or the future could not be predicted.[9]

Although few in the army knew it, the petition's timing was perfect. The same week that McDougall journeyed from Newburgh to Philadelphia, political conditions shifted abruptly in Congress. On December 24, Congress was shocked to learn that Virginia had repealed her ratification of the Impost of 1781. Since Rhode Island had refused earlier to ratify, the measure was now dead.[10] Most shocked of all were Superintendent of Finance Robert Morris and the clique of nationalists under his leadership in Congress. Based chiefly in the Middle states but with pockets of strength in the South and New England, merchants and lawyers and planters and elements of the old colonial aristocracy, conservative on questions of finance and fearful of the excesses of popular rule, the nationalists had come to power in 1780 at the low point in the war. Immediately they embarked on reforms to rejuvenate the war effort, strengthen congressional authority, and administer public affairs more efficiently. Throughout the war, then as the guiding force behind the Constitution in 1787 and as the nucleus of the Federalist party, the nationalists drove persistently to add to the power and authority of the central government. In the early 1780s, the impost was the heart of their program, in the words of an opponent, "held out by them as the only means of restoring Public Credit, of preventing a Disunion of the States, and saving the Country from immediate ruin—in short . . . the infallible, grand Political Catholicon, by which every evil was to be avoided, and every advantage derived."[11] The significance of the impost followed naturally from the design of centralization. "Without certain revenues," Hamilton had declared in 1780, "a government can have no power; that power, which holds the purse strings absolutely, must rule."[12]

The nationalists were overjoyed by McDougall's petition ("new topics in favor of the Impost," concluded James Madison).[13] To pay any of the army's claims, Congress would have to find new sources of money. Paper money would no longer circulate, and nationalists could argue that new foreign loans could not be floated without some visible means to meet interest payments. The only alternative was a new funding system; to the nationalists, this meant a new impost amendment giving Congress the power to tax imports. "In this situation what was to be done?" asked Hamilton a few months later, recalling those critical days when the nationalists groped for some way to salvage their program. "It was essential to our cause that vigorous efforts should be made to restore public credit—it was necessary to combine all the motives to this end, that could operate upon different descriptions of persons in the different states. The necessity and discontents of the army presented themselves as a powerful engine."[14] The air of crisis and possible mutiny would bludgeon Congress into another impost. When Congress then presented it as a measure to repay its victorious army, the states and the public could not possibly refuse. "Depend on it," Gouverneur Morris wrote on January 1, 1783, "good will arise from the situation to which we are hastening."[15]

Within 24 hours of their arrival, McDougall and his officers conferred with Robert Morris.[16] Within another week, the nationalist leadership had convinced McDougall and his colleagues that the army's only hope for payment lay in a new funding system. But unless McDougall and the army cooperated fully, the nationalists threatened, "they would oppose" referring army claims to the states "till all prospect of obtaining Continental funds was at an end."[17] McDougall's first task was to gain the support of the whole officer corps. On January 9, he wrote Knox on the possibility of uniting "the influence of Congress with that of the Army and the public Creditors to obtain permanent funds for the United states." It would, he added, "promise [the] most ultimate Security to the Army."[18] McDougall's second duty was to buttonhole individual congressmen, spreading rumors of the army's uneasiness and the dire prospects if Congress refused satisfaction.

The nationalist leaders would take care of the rest. Certainly not all of the nationalists were involved—only Hamilton, financier Robert Morris, and assistant financier (but no relation) Gouverneur Morris for certain.[19] Others participated with varying degrees of enthusiasm. Some were uninformed of the machinations; others ignored them, willing to work for nationalist ends regardless of the means employed. Madison probably knew nothing directly of the manipulations behind the scenes. But he felt that without an increase in national authority, the union would collapse and the states would degenerate into small units warring with each other constantly.[20] In the weeks ahead, Madison's skill in debate and his incisive political understanding would perfectly complement the stratagems of the nationalist floor leaders, Hamilton and James Wilson. After the army had set the stage and spread the threats, the nationalists would forge an acceptable funding system and maneuver it through Congress.

On January 6, Congress received the army memorial and referred it to a grand committee of one delegate from each state. The next day this committee talked with Robert Morris. At a meeting marked by "loose conversation" on the "critical state of things," the financier stated "explicitly" that his office could not advance the army any pay, and could not even promise any "until certain funds should be previously established."[21] On January 13, McDougall and the army committee intensified the pressure. At a meeting with the grand committee, the officers depicted the resentment in camp in unmistakable terms. When a congressman asked them what, specifically, the army might do if not satisfied, one colonel replied that Congress could expect "at least a mutiny." McDougall added that however prudent the officers and men might be, they were extremely angry. Brooks declared that "the temper of the army was such that they did not reason or deliberate cooly on consequences, and therefore a disappointment might throw them blindly into extremities."[22] By the end of the conversation, the grand committee was convinced that a powder keg would explode in Newburgh unless Congress acted quickly. Therefore it appointed Hamilton, Madison, and John Rutledge of South Carolina to draft a report on the army's claims, after consulting with Robert Morris to determine the monetary resources at the Confederation's disposal. Pressure tactics were working. Soon the tense and solemn mood of the meeting with McDougall pervaded the halls of Congress.[23]

For the next ten days, while Hamilton and the committee prepared a report on the army's claims, Robert Morris and his associates maneuvered to bring consideration of a new revenue system before Congress. Using the full weight of his personal prestige and the authority of his office as arbiter of national finance, Morris delayed congressional efforts to refurbish the old Confederation taxing system and turned aside initiatives to seek new foreign loans.[24] On January 22, the grand committee submitted its report. In the midst of debate the financier suddenly tendered his resignation. In a bitter letter he declared that his own integrity and position as financier were "utterly unsupportable" because of the Confederation's financial distress. If "permanent provision for the public debts of every kind" was not established by the end of May, he threatened, Congress would have to find a new superintendent.[25]

In the wake of Morris's action, the strain of McDougall's scare campaign, and the urgency of the army's unquestioned discontent, the nationalists gained their first victory. On January 25, after three days of debate on Hamilton's report, Congress agreed to leave the first two claims of the army—present pay and the settlement of unpaid salaries—to Morris's discretion. To support his efforts, it promised to "make every effort in [its] power to obtain from the respective states substantial funds, adequate to the object of funding the whole debt of the United States."[26] Nationalist tactics had worked beautifully; a new revenue system was now before Congress under circumstances that made its adoption imperative.

But the nationalist victory was incomplete. The heart of the report was a provision for commuting half-pay into an outright grant, the one point which would solidly wed the army's interests to those of other public creditors. Twice on January 25, the nationalists tried to shove the measure through, but both times a coalition of New England and New Jersey delegates voted no. Rhode Island and Connecticut were bound by instructions from their legislatures to oppose half-pay in any form, and other eastern congressmen well knew the popular aversion to anything resembling pensions. The nationalists dropped the matter for the moment; Congress referred it to a committee of five, including Hamilton and Wilson, and then turned its attention to a new impost proposal.[27]

Despite this setback, the nationalist program seemed on the surface to be faring well. But in reality, the Morrises and Hamilton were stymied at several points. Knox's silence—it had been three weeks since Mc-Dougall had written to him—was ominous. Unless the officer corps cooperated, by keeping up or increasing the pressure from Newburgh and agreeing not to seek half-pay from the states, the whole nationalist design could collapse. A second problem was tactical. Even after a month of crisis politics, nationalist maneuvers were still masked. But to a man like Arthur Lee, an old hand at political infighting and anti-Morris for years, their stratagems were becoming obvious. He would not be bluffed. "A Majority of the Army at least," he told Samuel Adams, "will remember that they are Citizens, and not lend themselves to the tory designs, as I verily believe this is, of subverting the Revolution. . . ."[28] Lee and other antinationalists benefited mightily when Hamilton, overly excited in debate over the impost, openly suggested using the army claims to force national funds on the states. The opposition "smiled at the disclosure," noted Madison, saying "in private conversation that Mr. Hamilton had let out the secret."[29]

The greatest obstacle of all, however, was Congress's reluctance to adopt commutation of the pensions. Hamilton's committee of five, appointed in January to reshape the measure, recommended it again on February 4, but New England's opposition remained adamant and subsequent debate led nowhere. Commutation was critically important. The fear of a mutinous army might prod Congress into resolving national revenues, but the state legislatures, scattered over the continent far from the army's potential grasp, would not necessarily ratify such an amendment. The Confederation must be committed to paying the huge sums commutation entailed; then like it or not, the states would have to agree to the revenue system or abandon a long-standing promise to the new nation's army. For this reason, the Morrises and Hamilton were willing to use any tactic that could ram commutation down congressional throats.[30]

Overshadowing all these obstacles was the likelihood that news of a peace treaty would arrive at any moment. Peace was the one contingency that could not be manipulated by the nationalist leadership. Should definite word arrive, the crisis would be over, the need to buttress national authority lost, and the nightmares of mutiny dispelled in the euphoria of victory. Peace would also destroy the army's political leverage. No longer needed, it would be quickly demobilized to save money and allow the rank and file to return home. Nationalist leaders understood these possibilities all too well.[31] When commutation lost for the second time on February 4, they began the preparations to use force.

The second stage in the plot began on February 8, when Colonel Brooks left Philadelphia to corner Knox and commit the army to the nationalist program. In his dispatch pouch, Brooks carried two letters for Knox. One, from McDougall and Ogden, reported to the entire army in detail on the political situation and emphasized the dim prospects for commutation.[32] The other was a personal message from Knox's "dear friend" Gouverneur Morris, lamenting the state of the nation and pleading for a union of the officers with other public creditors to enact permanent taxes. "The army may now influence the Legislatures," intimated Morris, "and if you will permit me a Metaphor from your own Profession after you have carried the Post the public Creditors will garrison it for you."[33] Four days later a secret letter, more explicit, more conspiratorial, and more pressing, left Philadelphia for Knox. Under a prearranged pseudonym, McDougall wrote that the army might well have to mutiny in order to gain its just due—declare publicly that it would not disband until it could be paid and assured of commutation. Such a move would be very dangerous, he admitted; Knox should wait for definite instructions. Meanwhile their friends would decide whether to introduce a motion to this effect on the floor of Congress. "But the Army," McDougall added, "ought not to lose a moment in preparing for events."[34]

Although these overtures to Knox implied the use of force, nationalist leaders were not scheming counterrevolution. Any plans that even suggested a coup were unrealistic. Later Hamilton admitted that while some leaders entertained "views of coercion," most agreed with his assessment that the "ar[my] would moulder by its own weight and for want of the means of keeping together. The soldiery would abandon their officers. There would be no chance of success without having recourse to means that would reverse our revolution."[35] The British had tried for years to capture Congress, and failed. A country so dispersed geographically, with so many conflicting interests and groups, so many local sources of power and authority, could never be united by the bayonet, especially in the face of deeply rooted traditions of antimilitarism. The attempt would only bring on chaos and civil war, exactly the conditions the nationalists wished to avoid. The whole thrust of the nationalist effort was toward strengthening national authority. A coup would simply destroy it.

What the nationalists wished when they sent Brooks back to Newburgh was the active cooperation of Knox and the other leaders of the army's effort for redress.[36] Should all the rumors and parliamentary maneuvers in Philadelphia fail, a declaration by the army that it would not disband might frighten Congress into passing commutation, then passing another funding system to raise the money. Such a declaration, while constituting only a passive mutiny, would definitely convey overtones of more positive action in the future, perhaps even a military takeover. Congress would have no choice: accept commutation or risk the consequences. The dangers in the scheme were considerable. In the first place, a statement by the army that it would not lay down its arms would disgrace the national government. It would proclaim to the world that in its first breath of independence, the United States was unwilling to treat its victorious soldiery with justice. Secondly, it might lead to a wholly unpredictable chain of events. No one could possibly foresee the consequences of the military's declaring its independence from the civil power. Yet in the first week of February, anticipating the worst, the Morrises and Hamilton were willing to take the chance. Knox and the other leaders in Newburgh were responsible men, and could be depended upon to keep the situation in hand.[37]

The nationalists did have another alternative, one they eventually used, and one that historians of the conspiracy have never fully understood. If an incident had to be staged in Newburgh, they could foment a real mutiny among the officers. But it was even more risky since it would involve not only a confrontation with Congress, but also with the military's legitimate leadership. For some time Robert Morris and the others had known of a dissident element in camp which could be persuaded to force an explosion, though the manipulations required would be far more delicate than the rather direct approaches they were making to Knox. There was a group of young officers, a small extremist wing of the corps, which was angrier, more dogmatic and hotheaded, and which fumed at Washington's moderate leadership.[38] Unlike many older officers, these men had grown up in the army and had less to look forward to on returning to civilian life. They sensed more deeply the impending loss of their military status and privilege.[39] These Young Turks naturally gravitated to Horatio Gates, the "hero of Saratoga," an overbearing and sensitive general whose bad blood with Washington was long-standing. Gates's pretensions had suffered for years. For him the discontent in Newburgh could be used to recoup his reputation and, incidentally, to snatch the army away from his rival. Fed by disillusionment, frustration, and personal dreams of glory, Gates and his young zealots evidently lost all sense of reality and began planning a full-fledged coup d'etat. The exact nature of the group and its plans will probably never be known. But there are strong hints that they talked of replacing Congress and ruling themselves, either as individuals under a new form of government or through a military dictatorship.[40]

Apparently they approached Robert Morris in January.[41] The financier, recognizing in them another tool should an uprising in Newburgh prove necessary, cynically encouraged their hope for a coup.[42] It was far safer, of course, for the nationalists to rely on Knox. Under regular leadership, a declaration by the officers that they would not disband would represent the united voice of the whole army. The Gates group could never speak for all the officers, most of whom revered Washington. Yet Gates and his men, if handled with cunning, could be used to kindle an insurrection in camp that might very well scare Congress more, especially if the mutiny were partially directed against Washington's authority. The scheme, however, involved a desperate gamble. If Gates successfully snatched the army from Washington, the military takeover and civil war the nationalists were determined to avoid might become reality. Furthermore, the nationalists mistrusted Gates. Hamilton, for one, considered him a personal enemy since Gates and the young congressman's father-in-law, General Philip Schuyler, had been sworn enemies for years; Washington, Hamilton's other patron, looked on Gates with equal disdain.[43] But if they could not push their program through Congress, and if Knox would not cooperate, then Hamilton and the Morrises would have no choice but to use Gates.

In the first week of February, using Gates was only a last resort. Then on February 12, news arrived in Philadelphia that George III, in a speech to Parliament, had mentioned preliminary articles of peace signed between Great Britain and the United States. While the report was only hearsay, the nationalists thought peace was certain, even "hourly expected."[44] Haste was now imperative. Though Knox was yet to be heard from, the nationalists now felt that they must prepare to use Gates just as a safeguard. The plan was simple. Through him, they would incite a mutiny in the army—spark the explosion—then make certain it was immediately snuffed out.[45] It was a treacherous double game, fraught with uncertainty. But to the nationalists the whole future of the country was at stake. The only alternative to the disintegration of the confederacy was the impost or some other measure which could effectively shore up the central government. On the other hand, fomenting a mutiny might produce the same result: anarchy, civil war, and an end to the Confederation. The whole venture cut a fine line between parallel disasters.

The other side in the double game, the means by which the convulsion would be harnessed, was George Washington, the patient, persevering commander whom the nationalists knew would never brook direct military interference in politics. The day after the king's speech arrived, the nationalists readied Washington for the coming storm. Hamilton began his letter by pointing out the injustice the army felt and the possibility that the oncoming peace would justify its fears. In a political sense, however, the army might assure itself justice while at the same time easing the country's financial dilemma. "Urged with moderation," Hamilton argued, its claims could "operate on those weak minds which are influenced by their apprehensions more than their judgments; so as to produce a concurrence in the measures which the exigencies of affairs demand." This pressure might "add weight to the applications of Congress to the several states." The problem, however, would "be to keep a *complaining* and *suffering army* within the bounds of moderation." This would be Washington's duty, "*to take the direction*" of the army's anger, preserving its confidence in him without losing that of the nation. "This will enable you," added the commander's former aide, "in case of extremity to guide the torrent, and bring order perhaps even good, out of confusion." But Washington should prepare for the worst. He should know that there was a real danger of the army rejecting his leadership. Many officers, Hamilton noted, felt that "delicacy carried to an extreme prevents your espousing its interests with sufficient warmth." Although obviously false, this feeling tended "to impair that influence, which you may exert with advantage, should any commotions unhappily ensue."[46]

Brooks was already in Newburgh when Hamilton's letter arrived, trying to establish direct channels between the nationalists and Knox. His activities, however—with whom he spoke and what information was passed—remain clouded.[47] Undoubtedly he talked to Washington and to Knox, to whom he delivered McDougall's report and Gouverneur Morris's letter.[48] Knox was the pivot in the nationalist scheme. As the leader in all the agitation at Newburgh since mid-1782, as a friend of the most important officers, and as a respected member of Washington's military family, Knox could best influence the corps to cooperate. But Knox was also extremely cautious. While he sympathized deeply with nationalist goals, he was first and foremost a soldier, with his career tied to Washington's and to the reputation of the army. Not only were these plans risky, potentially damaging to the army's image, but they would throw him into direct conflict with his patron. The Massachusetts general would not risk a show of force. He undoubtedly said as much to Brooks, and on February 21, he wrote McDougall and Gouverneur Morris to the same effect. "I consider the reputation of the American Army as one of the most immaculate things on earth," he told McDougall; "we should even suffer wrongs and injuries to the utmost verge of toleration rather than sully it in the least degree."[49] The army could exert no pressure except when directed by the "proper authority."[50] Otherwise, its influence "can only exist in one point, and that to be sure is a sharp point which I hope in

God will never be directed than against the Enemies of the liberties of America."[51]

The final stage of the conspiracy began when Knox's rebuffs reached Philadelphia near the end of February. The nationalists acted without hesitation.[52] For the last three weeks their efforts in Congress had been losing momentum. The impost proposal was mired in violent arguments over detail. The nationalists could not muster enough votes without conceding both the appointment of collectors by the states and a limitation on the number of years the measure would be in effect. Even worse than the debates and interminable delays was the appearance of antinationalist counterattacks on the very foundations of the impost. On February 18, Rutledge and John Francis Mercer proposed that all the revenue from any impost be appropriated for the exclusive use of the army—for salaries and half-pay—rather than to provide generally for the restoration of public credit. The restriction cleverly reversed the chief nationalist argument—that permanent funds were needed to satisfy the army's claims—and thus attacked the whole concept of an impost as adding to the strength of the central government.[53]

Although nationalist leaders easily blocked these attacks, it was obvious that the impost would not pass strictly on its own merits. Immediately they shifted attention to commutation. Again, however, Congress deadlocked. New Englanders, still mindful of the unpopularity of pensions in their region, continued to vote in opposition. At one point the nationalists had to choke off an attempt to recommend half-pay back to the states.[54] Faced with such obstacles, the nationalists amplified their campaign of rumor. Washington, they hinted, was losing control of the officers; the army would not lay down its arms, would declare so soon, and had even made plans to support itself in the field.[55] By the end of the month, the Massachusetts delegation and Oliver Wolcott, Sr., of Connecticut had swung over to commutation. But threats were not enough. The air of crisis and the shaky coalition supporting commutation could evaporate at a moment's notice. It had been over two weeks since word of the king's speech. Now, with Knox's refusal to help, it was the last possible moment for action.

On February 26, the nationalists opened their final offensive. To incite the army, McDougall penned one last frenzied letter to Knox, suggesting that there was no hope left for the officers' claims and that the army might soon be split into separate detachments to prevent rebellion.[56] In a similar move, Robert Morris requested permission to make his resignation public, in order not to mislead those who had "contracted engagements" with him. The explanation sufficed, and "without dissent or observation" Congress agreed. News of his resignation, as he well realized, would rock the army and call into question the whole fabric of Confederation finance. After a short wait to let these maneuvers take effect, the nationalists alerted Gates.[57]

The emissary was Walter Stewart, a Pennsylvania colonel, former aide of Gates, and now inspector of the Northern Army.[58] His trip would arouse no suspicion, since illness had kept him home in Philadelphia and he would be rejoining the army by direct order of the Commander-in-Chief.[59] Stewart reached the cantonment on Saturday, March 8. If he followed custom, he called first on Washington, then rode the four miles southeast from Newburgh to Gates's headquarters at the Edmondson house.[60] Although there is no record of the meeting, Stewart undoubtedly pledged Morris's support for any action the officers might take and assured Gates and his followers that the public creditors were fully behind them. Apparently nothing passed that hinted of the nationalists' planned treachery; Stewart probably knew as little of their true intentions as Armstrong and Gates. The officers and their ambitious leader still thought that the first initiatives had been theirs, and that Morris was the unwitting tool, influenced by "hopes of future greatness, which he might promise himself in case of success, by having the sole direction and control of the Finances."[61] In any case, Gates had been waiting for the signal.[62] The die was cast.

Within hours rumor flew around camp that "it was universally expected the Army would not disband until they had obtained justice," that the public creditors would join the officers in the field, if necessary, to redress their grievances, and many in Congress looked favorably on the venture.[63] Then on Monday morning, the conspirators published anonymously a call for a meeting of all field officers and company representatives for Tuesday morning at 11 o'clock to consider McDougall's report of February 8 and to plan a new course of redress. Simultaneously, William Barber, Stewart's assistant in the inspector's department, took several copies of an unsigned address to the adjutant's office where officers from various lines gathered each morning to receive general orders.[64] When the officers saw it, and later, as copies circulated around the encampment, bedlam ensued.

Written by Armstrong and copied by Christopher Richmond, another of Gates's aides, the first of the famous Newburgh Addresses urged the officers to forget "the meek language of entreating memorials" and "change the milk-and-water style" of their last petition to Congress. In the most inflammatory rhetoric, Armstrong recalled the army's suffering and glory, comparing them with "the coldness and severity of government," and the country's ingratitude to the men who had placed it "in the chair of independency." Whom would peace benefit? Not the officers, who could look forward only to growing "old in poverty, wretchedness and contempt." Could they, he asked, "consent to wade through the vile mire of dependency, and owe the miserable remnant of that life to charity, which has hitherto been spent in honor?" If so, they would be pitied, ridiculed, for suffering this last indignity. They had bled too much. They still had their swords. "If the present moment be lost, every future effort is in vain; and your threats then, will be as empty as your entreaties now." In a menacing reference to Washington, Armstrong demanded that they "suspect the man who would advise to more moderation and longer forebearance." Draw up one last remonstrance, Armstrong argued, without "the sueing, soft, unsuccessful epithet of memorial," and send it to Congress as an ultimatum. If the terms of the December petition were met, the army would keep its faith. If not, the army would have its alternatives—"If peace, that nothing shall separate them [Congress] from your arms but death: if war, that courting the auspices, and inviting the direction of your illustrious leader, you will retire to some unsettled country, smile in your turn, and 'mock when their [Congress's] fear cometh on.'"[65]

Washington, shocked and dismayed, realized that the officers were about to plunge "themselves into a gulph of Civil horror."[66] But he had expected the explosion for some time. He had understood the hints Hamilton had dropped the previous month, even to the point of suspecting Gates—"the old le[a]ven"—of again working to undermine him "under the mask of the most perfect dissimulation and apparent cordiality."[67] Joseph Jones, Washington's friend from Virginia then sitting in Congress, had that very week reported rumors in Philadelphia that the army would not disband and that there were "dangerous combinations" working against the commander.[68]

Though not surprised, Washington still faced a "predicament" as "critical and delicate as can well be conceived," one he had fought throughout the war and which, at this point, never seemed closer to overwhelming him.[69] On the one hand, he could in no sense compromise Congress's jurisdiction over the military. On the other, the officers' temper had turned so ugly, and so directly in conflict with civil authority, that a refusal to stand on their side—perhaps any counsel of moderation—might cost him his position and authority. Yet Washington never wavered. He was certain that "the sensible, and discerning part of the army" could hardly "be unacquainted" with his faithful service, that by the sheer power of his personality and the officers' almost filial devotion to their commander, he could continue, as he wrote Hamilton, to hold them "within the bounds of reason and moderation."[70]

In his first move, Washington threw the conspirators on the defensive. On Tuesday morning, March 11, he issued general orders which objected to the address and invitation to a meeting as "disorderly" and "irregular." An assembly with his personal approval would take place at noon on Saturday to discuss McDougall's letter from Philadelphia. The senior officer present—undoubtedly Gates—would preside, and, implying his own absence, Washington requested a full report of its deliberation afterwards.[71] The ploy had possibilities. Five days hiatus might cool down passions. In any event, Washington planned to attend the meeting and confront the officers in person, with Gates in the chair, strictly circumscribed by procedure and unable to speak out or manipulate the proceedings.[72]

Gates and his men immediately countered with a second address designed to soften Washington's reproach. In fact, they claimed the general obviously approved of their actions. A meeting on Saturday hardly differed from one on Tuesday, since it would consider the same agenda. The "solemnity" of his order "sanctified" their appeals, added unanimity, and would "give system" to the proceedings. And, the officers were reminded, "it cannot possibly lessen the *independence* of your sentiments."[73]

On Saturday morning tension was high. Officers from every unit stationed near Newburgh filed up the low hill to the newly constructed log and board public meeting house which Washington had ordered built in December to encourage more intercourse and "sociability" among officers of different states. The "New Building" consisted chiefly of a large low-ceilinged room, about seventy by forty feet, with a small stage and lectern at one end.[74] As Gates opened the proceedings, the Commander-in-Chief entered and asked permission to address the gathering. Gates could hardly refuse, and Washington mounted the stage. Instead of pleading for delay, he took the offensive, denouncing the anonymity of the first summons to a meeting as "unmilitary" and "subversive of all order and discipline." Then he attacked Armstrong's first address directly, maligning its motives, its appeal to "feelings and passions" rather than "reason and good sense," and its "insidious purposes." "I have been a faithful friend to the army . . . ," Washington declared, "the constant companion and witness of your distresses." No one present could possibly suppose he was "indifferent to its interests." Yet either of the alternatives proposed in the address was simply a "physical impossibility." Would the officers leave wives and children and all their property to desert the country "in the extremest hour of her distress," to "perish in a wilderness with hunger, cold and nakedness?" Or worse, could the army actually contemplate "something so shocking" as turning its swords against Congress, "plotting the ruin of both, by sowing the seeds of discord and separation" between military and civil? "My God!" Washington exclaimed, "What can this writer have in view, by recommending such measures? Can he be a friend to the army? Can he be a friend to this country? Rather is he not an insidious foe?"

Again Washington raked the motives of the secret writer, especially the insinuation that strong, independent men should suspect the man of moderation. It was merely a trick, he said, to suppress open discussion, to take away freedom of speech so that "dumb and silent, we may be led, like sheep, to the slaughter." Then Washington reminded the officers of their duty and the disgrace that would follow any step that might sully the army's glory or tarnish its deserved reputation for courage and patriotism. Congress, like any large body "where there is a variety of different interests to reconcile," moved slowly. But ultimately it would justify the army's faith, and Washington pledged himself "in the most unequivocal manner" to press its case. With a final appeal to reason and virtue and a plea to reject any wicked "attempts to open the flood-gates of civil discord" and "deluge our rising empire in blood," Washington ended his formal speech.[75]

He then produced Joseph Jones's letter as proof of Congress's good intentions. After reading the first paragraph, Washington paused, fumbled in his vest, found the spectacles Dr. David Rittenhouse had sent him in February, and put them on. Unaffectedly, the tall general murmured that he had grown gray in the service of his country, and now found himself going blind. The assemblage was stunned. A year's frustration, a week's excitement and expectation, then the unbearable strain of confronting their beloved commander, seemed to hang suspended in that one moment. In his speech, Washington had stood them at the abyss, forced them to face the implications of rash action—civil war, treason, and the undoing of eight years' effort. The contrast with this simple dramatic gesture, an act that blended Washington's charismatic influence with the deepest symbolic patriotism, was overpowering. The tension, the imposing physical presence of the Commander-in-Chief, the speech, and finally an act that emotionally embodied the army's whole experience, combined all at once and shattered the officers' equanimity. Spontaneously they recoiled. Some openly wept.[76]

Gates's plans disintegrated. Sitting helpless on the podium, he watched the officers' resolve evaporate in a wave of emotion. In a moment Washington was gone, the meeting now firmly in the grasp of his lieutenants. First Knox moved to thank the commander for his speech. Then after the McDougall report and other documents were read, Rufus Putnam moved to appoint Knox, Brooks, and another officer to bring in resolutions. After a brief interval, Knox returned with motions that reaffirmed the army's "attachment to the rights and liberties of human nature" and its "unshaken confidence" in Congress, and asked the Commander-in-Chief to write Congress again on the army's behalf. The officers accepted these unanimously, declaring their "abhorrence" and "disdain" of the "infamous propositions" advanced in the addresses, and their "indignation [at] the secret attempts of some unknown persons to collect officers together, in a manner totally subversive of all discipline and good order."[77] Only Pickering, of all the men present, stood up and objected, angry at the officers' hypocrisy in damning "with infamy two publications which during the four preceding days most of them had read with admiration [and] talked of with rapture."[78] But the assemblage was too overwhelmed to respond, and the meeting adjourned.

Even as the officers left the hall, news of the incident was on the way to Philadelphia. Tuesday afternoon Washington had posted copies of the addresses and his general orders. Coming on the heels of other serious problems, the "alarming intelligence" according to Madison induced "peculiar awe and solemnity . . . and oppressed the minds of Cong[res]s with an anxiety and distress which had been scarcely felt in any period of the revolution."[79] Immediately the nationalists seized the initiative. As an embarrassment to the men involved, the committee appointed to consider Washington's dispatches consisted exclusively of opponents of commutation and the impost.[80] Both measures had languished for days. The explosion in Newburgh, properly represented, would add new urgency.

The one obstacle left to commutation was Eliphalet Dyer, a Connecticut delegate who reflected his constituents' dislike of pensions and felt bound by his instructions to oppose half-pay in any form. Earlier in March he had agreed that if his vote alone blocked the measure he would consent. But at the crucial moment, he had surprised everyone by voting no, quibbling over one insignificant provision.[81] When Congress heard from Washington on March 17, Dyer, though shaken, stubbornly refused to allow fear, instead of "great principles of right and justice" to stampede the proceedings.[82] Two more days of uncertainty, however, weakened him. Badgered by the nationalists and McDougall, told that only he prevented the measure, that he had become the focus of resentment from everyone in the army, that commutation was more publicly acceptable than half-pay, that it alone "would quiet and pacify the Army," Dyer caved in.[83] On March 20, he introduced a motion for passage, "extorted from him," said Madison, "by the critical state of our affairs."[84] Two days later, a committee of Hamilton, Dyer, and one other delegate submitted a report recommending five years full pay to all officers entitled to half-pay. With Connecticut now in agreement, commutation passed. The impact of Newburgh and the apprehension of something worse converted even such confirmed nationalist opponents as Arthur Lee and John Francis Mercer.[85]

Superficially, the nationalist intrigue had worked well, and within another month Congress approved a new impost amendment. But it was not a clearcut victory for the nationalists. The impost contained such a jumble of compromises, so many concessions to sectional jealousy and state sovereignty, that even Hamilton could not bring himself to vote for it. It was limited to 25 years, the revenues restricted to paying debts, and its enforcement uncertain since the states would appoint collectors. Yet it was all the nationalists could muster. News of peace had arrived on March 12, the army was disintegrating, and Robert Morris's resignation was public.[86] Even as they girded for the effort to sell the new funding measure to the states, the nationalists' political star was waning.

The same day that Congress voted its approval of commutation, it received Washington's speech and the proceedings of the March 15 meeting. Even though apprehension lingered over the army's mood, the news dissipated "the cloud" of fear and "afforded great pleasure" to the delegates.[87] Instead of arousing suspicion and distrust by its flirtation with mutiny, the army emerged from the Newburgh affair with enhanced prestige and honor. Few knew how close to calamity the officers had really come. The public record belied any conspiracy, showing only a loyal officer corps rejecting the seductions of despair despite deep and abiding grievances. "Though intended for opposite purposes," remarked Knox, the affair "has been one of the happiest circumstances of the war, and will set the military character of America in a high point of view."[88] Most officers were equally ecstatic and wanted the proceedings published. "The whole transaction ought to be *known*," crowed David Humphreys, Washington's young aide. "It will do honour to the Army . . . honour to the Country . . . honour to human Nature."[89]

Within two months, the addresses, Washington's speech, the resolutions of the March 15 meeting, and a few other documents were printed from one end of the country to the other.[90] But only a few people perceived the darker overtones of those hectic three months. Jedidiah Huntington, one of the leaders in the army's agitation, had predicted that "the Matter [would] wear as great a Variety of Guises as there may be Persons to tell the Story," but no one was talking.[91] It was Washington, standing in the eye of the storm, who deduced more than anyone. It occurred to him and to others at Newburgh, he told Hamilton, that the scheme had been hatched and matured in Philadelphia, that Robert Morris had very likely been the culprit, and that for selfish reasons the politicians had been toying with the army. With some evasion, Hamilton admitted almost every one of these accusations. He told Washington that the group under suspicion, the "most sensible the most liberal," the men "who think continentally," had been working to include the army with other public creditors "in order that the personal influence of some, the connections of others, and a sense of justice to the army as well as the apprehension of ill consequences might form a mass of influence in each state in favour of the measures of Congress." Physical coercion, he emphasized, was impossible, though at times the country's prospects seemed so hopeless that "could force avail" he would be sorely tempted.

With all these confessions, however, Hamilton knew the secret would be safe with Washington. In addition to his own sympathy for the nationalist effort to strengthen the central government, Washington had benefited too much from the incident ever to hurl public charges. Like the army itself, Washington's reputation for honesty and unshakable devotion to the government and to the Revolution had been enhanced enormously.* And in the final analysis, Hamilton noted wryly, those who could piece together the real story "would be puzzled to support their insinuations by a single fact."[92]

With the intrigue submerged beneath favorable public reaction, the army again became a nationalist tool, this time to gain ratification of the impost.[93] But in New England commutation sparked such a popular outcry that some states refused to ratify a revenue system that would finance military bonuses. The hubbub over commutation, and then over the Society of the Cincinnati, which New Englanders discovered in early winter, 1783, delayed ratification for months. Nationalist leaders had pulled off a daring stroke in early 1783. The impost might never have been revived without pressure from the army, pressure which they had applied with sinister precision. But in the end their strategy almost backfired. By joining the army to the impost through commutation, they furnished anti-impost forces with a popular issue that delayed the measure's ratification and took the momentum out of the campaign's first, and most crucial, phase.[94] Ironically the army, responsible for the passage of the impost, was in part responsible for its demise.

Much of the Newburgh affair will never be known. The questions are endless: how much of the plot Brooks or Stewart, the two messengers to the army, knew; whether or not others were involved with the Morrises,

---

*In late 1783, a British spy advanced the following interpretation of Washington: "A deep endless ambition, too thinly veiled to escape the penetration of some of those who saw him constantly in the various scenes of this Revolution [and] saw him behind the coulisse as well as upon the stage, makes the basis of the character of this man . . . ; great, not by shining talents, but by a happy concurrence of circumstances, a good useful understanding, an unwearied passive perseverance, the mediocrity of all his competitors and the *weakness or perfidy* of his antagonists. Genius it seems is not the growth of this Western world, and even when imported droops and dies under this unfavorable sky. May this be as it will; genius at least was not the lot of Washington. [W]ithout a spark of imagination, enthusiasm, or that torrent of talent that carries everything before it, cold[,] deliberate, slow, patient, persevering, he now finds himself elevated to a pitch of grandeur he never dreamed of, & would not even now grasp at the supreme power, if to obtain it he must as Cromwell surround the state house and tell them: 'begone; the Lord you seek has left this place.'" F. Michaelis to Major George Beckwith, Oct. 4, 1783, Bancroft Transcripts, New York Public Library, New York, N.Y.

Hamilton, and McDougall; or even how much McDougall himself understood of the complex maneuvering in Congress and at Newburgh. One fact, however, remains: the Morrises and Hamilton clearly understood the seditious nature of their undertaking. They, and quite likely others in the nationalist movement, did not share the American hatred of standing armies or fears of militarism. They were attracted to armies for their power and simplicity and were even willing to use them in ways totally antithetical to American political tradition and practice. It was a glaring flaw, one that would surface again twenty years later to shatter the Federalist party and doom it to ultimate oblivion.

At the same time the nationalists never intended a coup d'etat as some historians have claimed, although Hamilton did let slip that the possibility was discussed, a revealing fact in itself. Had they planned the military overthrow of the Confederation, they would have made the preparations in secret without spreading rumors and threats that could only warn Congress. Given Hamilton's feelings about Gates, they would have chosen a more reliable, popular, and personally acceptable military leader, and in no case would they have warned Washington of a coming upheaval in camp, as Hamilton did in the second week of February. Nationalist leaders were aware of the American attitude toward armies and military interference in politics. They hoped to strengthen national authority in the United States, not discredit and destroy it. That they were willing to risk destroying the government in order to enlarge its power speaks only for their methods and their desperation, not their ultimate goals.

Above all a coup was a practical impossibility in the America of 1783 and the nationalist leaders knew it. The army was not composed of the rootless, determined band of janissaries loyal only to a commander that such an adventure demanded. "Even among the officers, whose situations were similar," Brooks recalled forty years later, "there could have been no union in the pursuit of an object of ever doubtful legitimacy: Washington himself could not have effected it." Officers and soldiers alike had other loyalties, not only political but to "parents and other relations, perhaps wives and children, who were dear to them, and to whose society they were anxiously wishing to be restored." For the rank and file, a call to revolt "would have been but the watch word for them to abandon their veteran companions, and return to their friends and firesides."[95]

Nor were the conditions those that have typically spawned coups d'etat in modern times. Even though the Continental Congress was weak, there was no political vacuum in the country. State and local authorities were strong; the extremist groups or grinding class conflicts that precipitate chaos, revolution, and military interference were comparatively insignificant. Apparently the officer corps came by and large from the same social stratum which controlled the nation's political and social life, and the corps did not identify itself as a separate caste with its own traditions and loyalties, despite feelings of common danger and paranoia over half-pay. Unlike the armies of many new nations, America's military had no reason to intervene in the political process generally, no desire to veto a particular policy or interfere as the guardians of order or virtue in society, although most of the officers probably favored a strong union and fiscal measures that would assure their interests as ex-officers. The United States possessed legitimate political leaders and institutions, working within well-developed traditions that drew strength from a set of widely accepted beliefs. Most important of all, it had a tradition of legitimacy in governmental forms despite a recent revolution, and rigid, well-defined traditions of civilian dominance of the military.[96] It was this tradition of civilian supremacy and the prejudice against standing armies that assured that any coup, or even the attempt, would plunge the country into bitter civil war. And it is the presence of this tradition, unstained by any contrary experience, that has saved the United States from the coup d'etat ever since.

Although the composition of the army and the government and various political, geographic, and social conditions made a coup impossible, the country did face a crisis in early 1783, a crisis whose significance cannot be overstated. The traditions of civilian supremacy and antimilitarism were powerful and immediate, but they were still young. England's struggle with Cromwell and military interference was barely a century old. There the civil-military relationship had since developed without friction because the military drew its leadership from the same aristocracy that ran the government. The identity of interests between the leaders of the two organizations and the constant interchange of men from positions in one to those in the other made military interference almost irrelevant.[97] The United States, however, was a republic without a closed, sharply defined elite; given its political predispositions, it could never construct so vague a civil-military relationship, or allow its military institutions to become an extension of one particular group or class.

Furthermore, the traditions of civilian dominance and antimilitarism, while strongly entrenched attitudes, had been tested in a *national* political arena for only eight years. Throughout the war, the potential conflict between Congress and the army and the implications of such conflict worried leaders in both institutions. Both sides had striven mightily to preserve the form and the substance of military subordination. Each understood that while state political and civil-military traditions were strong, nationally there were few precedents, and those that did exist were weak. One false step could be disastrous. The tradition of military subordination to the civil, in terms of its origins and its implementation on the national level, was still raw in early 1783, in a sense untested, and, at a time when great precedents were being set, extremely vulnerable.

A full-fledged coup d'etat—in the modern sense of the military displacing the regular government and substituting itself or a set of men or a specific political system of its own choosing—was not the problem in 1783. But there are different degrees of intervention that can take a variety of different forms.[98] The Newburgh incident was a case of outside pressure on the normal political process, similar in its operation to modern lobbying. What distinguished it, however, was the threat of more direct intervention, and it could have resulted in more serious consequences. Had Washington not interceded, the officer corps might very well have taken Armstrong's advice. What followed would not have been the kind of venture that required the determination and the united action which Brooks and others knew was not possible. It would have been a passive mutiny, a declaration of independence from the nation by the military, and it would in all probability have precipitated a major political and constitutional crisis. Instead of a small, forgotten event at the close of the war, hidden in the outpouring of joy over independence and the return of peace, it would have become a major happening, widely known and remembered, affecting the politics of the whole period. Long into the future it would have cast a pall of suspicion on any military institution the new republic created, perhaps even making the establishment of a national army impossible for some time. In an oblique way, at a crucial point in the nation's development, it would have eroded the tradition of civilian control.

Once civilian control is violated, even by the most halting attempt, a certain purity is irretrievably lost. The bond of trust between the military and society at large evaporates. A new, corrupting element, something previously unthinkable partly because it has never been attempted, is injected into the political process. Once this happens, an aura of automatic rejection is shattered. The possibility of military overthrow then forever lurks in the background, corroding legitimate political activity until the very conditions that provoke its use become more real. No matter how sacred the tradition, how deep rooted the consensus, or how powerful and legitimate the governmental forms, direct military interference in politics makes the coup a political-constitutional alternative for generations to come.

The Newburgh affair was significant for what did not happen. No tradition was broken and no experience with direct military intervention occurred to haunt future American political and military life. The only precedent set, in fact, positively reaffirmed Anglo-American tradition: the first national army in American history explicitly rejected military interference and military independence from civilian control. The disbanding of the Continental Army without a damaging incident assured that civilian control of the military for the foreseeable future would be more an administrative than a political problem. America did stand at the crossroads in March 1783. Today, as one weighs an impossible number of variables and attempts to judge the alternatives without the certainty that hindsight normally offers, the significance of the event is vague and indistinct. Perhaps contemporaries understood the question more clearly. To them the shape of the country's political institutions, even whether or not the disparate sections could live together in union, was uncertain. Thomas Jefferson was describing a general feeling when he claimed "that the moderation and virtue of a single character has probably prevented this revolution from being closed as most others have been by a subversion of that liberty it was intended to establish."[99]

3

★ ☆ ★ ☆ ★ ☆ ★ ☆ ★

Visions of Security,
Nationalist Style
[1783]

★

There are those also among us who wish to keep up a large force, to have large Garrisons, to increase the navy, to have a large diplomatic Corps. . . . [I]t is easy to see where all this will lead us, and Congress I think is not yet prepared for such Systems.

Congressman Stephen Higginson, 1783.[a]

In the wake of the Newburgh conspiracy, as tension evaporated and the nation rejoiced in its stunning victory over the British, the Confederation demobilized its military forces and began the long, difficult process of forging a defense policy for the future. There never existed the slightest doubt, in the army or in the councils of the government, that the Continental Army would be disbanded at war's end. And in 1783, the pressures for immediate demobilization were intense: fears of a renewed outburst from dissatisfied officers; the seething discontent among rank and file eager to return home; the desperate financial plight of the government; nationalist desires to keep Robert Morris at the helm of the finance office, servicing accounts and paying off army salaries; and hopes that returning officers would, as Hamilton put it, "by their own solicitation . . . forward the adoption of funds [the impost] in the different states."[1] For the moment, British troops remained on American soil and Congress worried about paying off its own soldiers lest they march home, in Washington's words, "enraged, complaining of injustice—and committing enormities on the innocent Inhabitants in every direction."[2] As a result the army was released piecemeal during the summer, legally on furlough to guard against the chance that hostilities might resume. The men melted back into civilian society, quietly, without incident. By

40

January of 1784, all that remained of the army that had consummated the Revolution and established American independence was a small corps of artillery and one regiment of infantry, about 600 rank and file under Henry Knox's command, guarding leftover stores at West Point and Springfield, Massachusetts, and occupying New York City while civilian officials re-established American rule.[3]

The Continental Army disappeared, as a force in politics and as a prototype for American military institutions. Today the army is fond of tracing its origins back to the Revolution, depicting itself as the descendant of Washington's valiant Continentals. On the contrary, the Continental Army went out of existence permanently in 1783. During its lifetime it had been an *ad hoc* institution designed to oppose the British army in open eighteenth-century warfare. For a generation afterward it provided tradition and certain patterns organizationally—command relationships, logistics, drill, scales of forage and subsistence, and the like—but in a basic institutional sense it was never organized or constructed to provide a permanent solution to American security. To Americans in 1783, the Continental Army was a regular establishment, a standing army. The newly independent republic would create a very different institution: a small constabulary to police the frontier and serve as a nucleus for protection against foreign enemies. After every war in American history, leaders in the military, Congress, and the executive branch would consider and attempt to rethink the problems of national security and military organization, and the Revolution was no different. The labyrinthian legislative and political process by which the United States Army came into existence started in the spring of 1783, begun by men who never imagined that the edifice they built would be the progenitor of the gargantuan military establishment of mid-twentieth century America.

Congress first considered peacetime military problems in early April 1783, before hostilities with Great Britain were declared at a formal end, when the states of Pennsylvania and New York requested help in dealing with the Indians. Both had open frontiers inhabited by some of the most formidable, hostile tribes in America, and both had been devastated by bloody Indian conflict during the course of the war. Pennsylvania wanted Congress to begin peace negotiations with the tribes. New York asked permission (necessary since the Articles of Confederation prohibited state armies in peacetime) to send a part of her contingent in the Continental Army to occupy the forts held by the British, forts that dominated the territory of the Six Nations and which could not be allowed to fall into Indian hands when the British withdrew. New York's request startled the nationalists, who did not wish to see precedents established giving the states, not the Confederation, responsibility for defense. Hamilton and

William Floyd, the New York representatives, diverted the application, but it was obvious that Congress needed to act. Other delegates were receptive anyway. The West was considered by many to be the future of America's empire, the source of strength, of wealth, of power, and not coincidentally an area where land speculation was already a long-standing mania. Furthermore, no matter how deeply congressional leaders disagreed over the nation's foreign relations, they knew that military establishments and navies went with sovereignty, "necessary appendages," as Dr. Benjamin Rush said.[4] In American minds the governments of the *ancien régime* were naturally hostile to a republic; safety lay only in strength, in maintaining a viable military capability. A country destined to expand, to increase in population and in wealth, a nation of great agriculture and expanding commerce—such a nation must expect conflict in the eighteenth-century world. "That nations should make war against nations," wrote John Jay, a negotiator of the peace treaty and after 1784 the Confederation's Secretary for Foreign Affairs, "is less surprising than their living in uninterrupted peace and harmony."[5]

Prodded by the western problem and by the need "to carry into execution . . . other articles of the Confederation not attended to during the war," Congress on April 4 appointed a committee "to provide a system for foreign affairs, for Indian affairs, [and] for military and naval establishments."[6] The committee, chaired by Hamilton and dominated by nationalists, wrote immediately to Washington for a "general plan" including "such institutions . . . as may be best adapted to . . . security," "economy," and "the principles of our governments."[7] Like most good generals, Washington passed the request on to his principal advisors, to the army branch chiefs (Inspector General Steuben, Chief of Artillery Knox, and Quartermaster General Pickering, among others), and to George Clinton, the governor of strategically positioned New York. Within a week all replied and their position papers, together with Washington's final report to the committee, Secretary at War Benjamin Lincoln's ideas, and the committee's own recommendations provided the first comprehensive statements of national security needs in American history. Phrased in the broadest possible terms, the papers represented the final reflections of the nation's most experienced soldiers, men who had organized, led, supplied, and drilled regulars and militia for eight years. Significantly, almost every one of these officers came from the Continental Army and—except for George Clinton—was to become a Federalist in the late 1780s. Some were veteran politicians already, well aware of the political and ideological influences which shaped military policy.[8]

Without a dissenting voice every officer recommended the establishment of a national army—despite the existence of the militia, despite the Confederation's thin financial resources, despite the knowledge that geography made the United States relatively invulnerable to surprise attack. The most pressing military need lay on the frontier. The government must physically possess and police the West, and, given the presence of the Indians, that meant troops. Every officer spoke of Indians in terms of deterrence and retaliation—"awing savages" was a favorite expression. "The first measures with relation to them," predicted Brigadier General Jedidiah Huntington, "[w]ill make deep and lasting impressions."[9] The United States could neutralize British influence in the area and maintain peace only by occupying strategic points like Niagara Falls (Fort Niagara) or the source of the Ohio River (Fort Pitt), using the forts both to impress the tribes and to launch retaliatory expeditions. A chain of posts at these critical water junctions would also blunt attacks from neighboring British and Spanish colonies, another worry. West Point, controlling the Lake Champlain–Hudson River invasion corridor would have to be garrisoned for the same reason, and in fact several officers proposed making the Hudson bastion the physical focus for the whole establishment, with a magazine for storage of gunpowder and ordnance, an arsenal for manufacture of muskets and cannon, and a military academy.

For none of these functions would militia suffice. Because of the limitations of state law, militia would have to be rotated out of the garrisons at least yearly—clearly an inefficient and expensive proposition. Nor would militia be suitable for other defense duties. Troops were needed to guard and maintain arsenals, and for internal order—a point several officers emphasized. As Steuben put it, in recommending a horse guard to protect the government, "Congress and its followers should never be exposed to the Mad proceedings of a Mob."[10] The country also needed an institution to keep alive military art and skill, to study war, and to serve as a model organizationally for the militia, obviously no job for part-time soldiers. "To make any art a study," argued Steuben, "it should not only be a passion but a business."[11]

Supporting an army designed for frontier defense and as the nucleus for security in a general war, as well as a navy and a system of coastal fortresses to protect major seaports, required ancillary institutions for the storage of munitions and supplies, for the manufacture of weapons, and for professional education. Secretary at War Benjamin Lincoln, who was at the time pressing Congress for funds to store leftover equipment, advised Hamilton's committee that the country desperately needed magazines.[12] To lose the matériel then in the government's possession either through delay or lack of protection would be a waste, and neglecting future needs would be shortsighted since a truly independent nation must be able to mobilize its own resources without relying on foreign countries whose good will might be uncertain. Lincoln suggested five magazines, each consisting of an arms and cannon factory, a powder laboratory, and a storehouse, scattered the length of the country from Springfield, Massachusetts to Camden, South Carolina. The other officers agreed.

Furthermore, to back up the army, a military academy was necessary. Some of the officers doubted whether Congress would approve the idea, but all argued it strongly. Veterans of the war would soon age and the experience of fighting the British would be forgotten. Soldiering was too important and complex a subject for amateurs, especially in the technical branches of artillery and engineering. What Washington's officers wanted was a professional army composed of career officers trained in the science of warfare.

Yet in calling for a regular army all the officers understood the political implications perfectly. Knox, Lincoln, and Pickering knew that an army added prestige and solidity to the national government and interestingly enough George Clinton, although later a leading Antifederalist and the Republican nominee for Vice-President in 1792, stated explicitly that "the Support of the Federal Union" was "the first and Principal Object" of an army.[13] Furthermore every officer realized the difficulty involved in proposing a regular establishment. Several tried lamely to distinguish their own proposals from a standing army on the basis of numbers and in truth none of them wished to see the country commit its defense to the classic European military establishment. But they were caught in an uncomfortable dilemma that nationalists, and later the Federalist party, never entirely overcame: the standing army was politically unfeasible (and anathema to the public) yet some regular establishment was imperative because the militia was unquestionably unsound militarily.

In 1783 the solution that occurred to all Washington's advisers was a thoroughgoing overhaul of the entire militia system. Obviously the militia was the most congenial system for a republic ("the only palladium of a free people," intoned Pickering), and the only acceptable alternative politically and financially.[14] Every officer criticized it, however, for lax discipline, unreliability, weak training, and—most important—lack of uniformity. To strengthen it militarily required three basic changes, each of which not coincidentally implied strengthening the national government's control over militia affairs. First the states must make their systems uniform—in structure, arms, equipment, and training—so that various state forces could fight together effectively. Second, training must be upgraded through increased muster time and bivouac in the field for at least a week every year. Fines would need to be increased and the laws enforced, and to insure uniformity and standards several of the officers recommended a system of inspectors from the national government. Third, a number of the officers proposed classing. Pickering thought it ridiculous to expect men past fifty to serve in anything short of a total emergency. Attempting to train all able-bodied men dissipated scarce money, time, and effort. Men should be classed by age, the youngest being obligated for longer training and for instant combat readiness. After reaching their mid-twenties, these would pass out of the first class into a reserve corps responsible for less training and subject to call only in national crisis. Only Steuben dared attack the concept of the citizen-soldier directly and his contempt stemmed mostly from a disdain for amateurism. The German professional preferred a small, highly trained continental militia composed only of volunteers and modeled exactly on the proposed national army. If no country could mount an expeditionary force larger than the 40,000 Britain sent during the war, the United States did not need the 400,000 then enrolled in the militia. Properly organized, trained, and equipped, 25,000 would provide sufficient strength for a country safe from surprise attack because of the distance of potential foes.

When he received the recommendations of his officers near the end of April 1783, Washington collected them together, added his own ideas, and sent a long and learned report to Hamilton's committee. "Sentiments on a Peace Establishment" was virtually rediscovered in the 1920s by John McAuley Palmer, a brigadier general in the regular army involved intimately in military policy in the War Department and before Congress. Palmer and most historians since then have assumed that Washington's ideas were original with him, and that the report, one of the great state papers in American history, endorsed the citizen-soldier in national defense.[15] In reality Washington copied his subordinates, in form and substance, almost completely. And his final recommendations, although acknowledging the importance of militia, were designed to persuade an unwilling country of the necessity for a regular military establishment. George Washington understood the political climate even better than his leading officers. Hamilton had warned privately beforehand that Congress's "prejudices will make us wish to keep up as few troops as possible."[16] Washington began with a typical disclaimer against "a *large* standing Army" even while insisting that "a few Troops" were "not only safe, but indispensably necessary."[17] He proposed only what he considered to be the bare minimum, politically feasible army. In 1784, after reading Steuben's plan to abolish the militias as state organizations, Washington claimed he had "hinted the *propriety* of a Continental Militia" but had "glided almost insensibly into what I thought *would*, rather than what I conceived *ought* to be a proper peace Establishment for this Country."[18]

Washington advocated a regular force of four infantry regiments and one of artillery, in all slightly over 2,600 officers and men, distributed in forts stretching around the periphery of the country. One infantry regiment would shield New England from Canada; another would garrison a line along the Great Lakes from Fort Oswego on Lake Ontario to Mackinac Island at the juncture of lakes Huron, Superior, and Michigan; a third would wind along the Ohio River; and the fourth would cover the

Georgia and Carolina frontier. Admittedly the force was large. Yet Britain still controlled Canada, the frontier was extensive and filled with "numerous, soured and jealous" Indian tribes, and the Indians must be "awed" if peace were to be maintained and the fur trade secured. To garrison so many forts Washington decreased the regular Continental Army infantry regiment by one-third (to 400 rank and file). Proportionately the army would contain more companies and officers for detached commands and in an emergency each regiment could be enlarged quickly to field strength without adding officers or worrying about the leadership to train incoming recruits. This was originally William Heath's idea, antedating by nearly forty years John C. Calhoun's proposal for an army expansible in wartime.

Washington added all sorts of specifics for the new regular army. Promotion should depend on merit, not seniority. Commanding would be two generals, each responsible for a separate district and each reporting independently to the Secretary of War. They would visit the detachments regularly, accompanied by an engineer to check the condition of the forts. Enlistments must extend three years at a minimum to avoid "the danger and inconvenience of entrusting any important Posts to raw Recruits." Washington also commented on rations, recruiting, rotating the garrisons, and other necessary details of organizational life and structure.

Like his advisers Washington supported the establishment of arsenals, magazines, and a military academy, although he thought the country could survive with three large arsenals to store munitions and equipment instead of the five recommended by Benjamin Lincoln. An academy for training artillerists and engineers was also necessary—unless, noted the general sarcastically, "we intend to let the Science become extinct" or "depend entirely upon Foreigners for their friendly aid." As for the production of arms, cannon, powder, and other ordnance, Washington thought the nation should eventually establish the capability, but in the meantime attach small factories to each arsenal.

Likewise the Commander-in-Chief adopted the ideas of his staff on reorganizing the militia. All arms, equipment, organization, and training needed to become uniform among the states and, using Pickering's report, Washington wanted state adjutant generals appointed to inspect each militia twice yearly. Over them a national inspector general would "superintend the execution of the proposed regulations." Classing was essential. All citizens aged 18 through 50 owed service in the last extremity, but the 18 to 25-year-olds, those of "natural fondness for Military parade," the "Van and flower . . . ever ready for Action and zealous to be employed," should be separated out for increased training and duty. Washington even advocated a minutemen corps of special companies, enlisted for several years, chosen either by lot or organized as an elite unit, ready for any sudden invasion. The thrust of his advice was reform:

more practice, special units, enforcement of the laws, new provisions for inspection and reporting to the Confederation, national examinations for officers, national regulations for drill and structure, and above all uniformity. None of these changes could be accomplished without some form of national control over the state organizations. George Washington accepted the citizen-soldier, but he had no faith in militia as they then stood. "A peace establishment ought always to have two objects in view," Washington told Steuben a year later, "The one[,] present security of Posts, of Stores and the public tranquillity; the other, to be prepared, if the latter is impracticable, to resist . . . the sudden attempts of a foreign or domestic enemy."[19] And for this Washington wanted regulars.[20]

Washington's report reached the congressional committee on the peace establishment in mid-May 1783. Working from that document, a letter from Secretary Lincoln, and Steuben's plans for a military academy and for a national military establishment, Hamilton drafted recommendations for Congress. Buried in committee work and undoubtedly pleased by plans with such strong nationalist implications, Hamilton had neither the time nor the inclination to go much beyond Washington's blueprint.[21] On the crucial question of a national army, Hamilton agreed completely, even down to the number of regiments of infantry and artillery. To provide supplies and equipment, Congress must maintain five magazines as Secretary Lincoln suggested, each containing enough supplies and munitions to outfit 6,000 men. So that the country need not depend on foreign countries, foundries and factories for cannon, arms, and powder would have to be built. On grounds of expense Hamilton recommended against a military academy for the time being, but he made provision for professors to be attached to the artillery regiment, which he designated the Corps of Engineers (to include engineering as well as artillery officers), and he did not foreclose the possibility of an academy in the future.

In several ways, however, Hamilton went further than Washington, both in advocating regulars and in centralizing defense in the national government. First, not only would the Confederation command, pay, and supply the army, but Hamilton expected it to recruit the men and appoint the officers, something never sanctioned by the Articles of Confederation, which left those functions to the states. Hamilton's justification was expedience: since the forces would be assigned to the states in proportion to their population and none would furnish a complete regiment, apportionment and replacement of officers would "create endless perplexity" unless Congress made the appointments. Likewise allowing Congress to supervise recruiting would save money by preventing state competition for the men from jacking up enlistment bounties. Secondly, Hamilton's regiments were 20 percent larger than Washington's and the entire army numbered well over 3,000. Like John C. Calhoun later, Hamilton pressed for an expansible army; in wartime the rank and file would double so that regulars would bear the brunt of combat. Third, Hamilton in tone and substance downgraded the militia. Nowhere did he acknowledge that overall security depended on the militia. "Congress ought not to overlook" the subject, he said, since it was "a constitutional duty," and for uniformity, Congress would have to "adopt and recommend a plan." Hamilton urged uniformity, strengthened training, and classing, but the latter only halfheartedly. He divided up the men by marriage instead of by age; bachelors were liable to muster half again as often as the married men, but both groups would contain men old enough to make the military effectiveness of the units in the long run questionable. Hamilton thus wrote off the militia as a whole. In its place he suggested an elite corps of volunteer citizens enlisted from the cities for eight-year terms, to consist of not more than 2 percent of the rest of the militia, and to be armed, clothed, and paid (even for training) by the central government. This force, obligated to drill as often as 26 times annually, would be liable for service anywhere in the union or overseas. In organization and function these "train bands" corresponded more closely to the modern army reserve than to the colonial militia.[22]

Hamilton, Washington, and the leaders of the Continental Army all agreed that security for the new nation depended upon a small, tightly organized national army backed by magazines, arsenals, and educational facilities that would not only support the regulars but also provide the arms, equipment, supplies, and technical expertise for the larger forces sure to be needed in wartime. In peacetime regulars would man a system of frontier posts and seacoast fortresses to prevent the Indians from controlling the West and to blunt attacks along the most strategic avenues of invasion. Hamilton, Washington, and many of the officers also suggested a navy, but none discussed the matter in detail. Finally, in the absence of American willingness to maintain larger peacetime forces, because of the expense and the fear of standing armies in peacetime, the militia would have to continue. But without reorganization under national auspices its usefulness would remain marginal. Literally every facet of military policy and every element in the military establishment for the next decade and a half were foreshadowed in the plans written out in 1783; nearly every proposal in that year became an integral part of Federalist policy, including Hamilton's elite corps from the cities which surfaced in modified form in 1798 as the Federalist volunteer companies. By the time the Federalists left office in 1801, they had succeeded in creating the very peacetime establishment many of them first envisioned at the close of the Revolution.

The critical problem facing Hamilton and other men of similar political persuasion, both in 1783 and for the next decade or more, was how to implement a program of such vigorous nationalism, so similar to a standing army, in the face of a suspicious Congress and public. Militarily the United States in 1783 was complacent, ebullient, optimistic. Having just defeated one of the great military powers of the era without extensive preparations beforehand, most Americans confidently looked to the militia for their defense. And there existed, furthermore, specific and immediate stumbling blocks for the nationalists which, together with the swirl of Congressional infighting, conspired to prevent their military ideas from gaining a fair hearing.

Hamilton and Madison anticipated trouble at the beginning; the Articles of Confederation allowed Congress to raise land and naval forces but nowhere was it spelled out clearly whether the authority existed in peacetime. To argue that the Confederation's power would lapse unless there were a war, Hamilton pointed out in a long introduction to his report, would hamstring the nation's ability to defend itself. "[T]he United States would be obliged to *begin to create* at the very moment they would have occasion *to employ* a fleet and army." "[A] length of time is requisite to levy and form an army and still more to build and equip a navy, . . . a work of leisure and of peace requiring a gradual preparation of the means—there cannot be presumed so improvident an intention in the Confederation as that of obliging the United States to suspend all provision for the common defence 'till a declaration of war or an invasion.'" Furthermore, Hamilton insisted that for certain functions state forces would never do. Much of the frontier lay outside state jurisdictions. Relying on the individual states for defense would unfairly burden some and endanger the rest by giving "the keys of the United States" to one state and entrusting "the care of the safety of the *whole* to a *part*." Besides, for efficiency and economy the army and its ancillary agencies— posts, arsenals, the artillery regiment—needed "a general and well-digested system."²³

The arguments were lucid and valid. Hamilton would use them often in the next five years to justify a national military establishment, and they eventually merged into the underlying justifications for all Federalist military policy in the 1790s. But in 1783 the reasoning seemed weak and futile. Already opposition was beginning to surface as word leaked out concerning the contents of the report (the "professed view is to strengthen the hands of Government," sneered Stephen Higginson, "to make us respectable in Europe, and . . . to divide among themselves and their Friends, every place of honour and of profit").²⁴ The report also placed the nationalists in an uncomfortable political dilemma. With the authority in peacetime "at least subject to be called in question," Madison explained to Edmund Randolph, any decision by Congress to assume the prerogative might be vetoed by the states, especially given their "present paroxism of jealousy" over the impost. Worse yet the states might stiffen in their opposition to the funding plan, interpreting an impost and an army together as a power grab by the national government. Yet to deny congressional power would clearly jeopardize national security and might conceivably establish precedents for interpreting congressional powers narrowly, a position nationalists quite naturally wished to avoid. "The only expedient for this dilemma," Madison observed, "seems to be delay, but even that is pregnant with difficulties" since the arrival of the definitive treaty of peace would drive Congress into dismantling the whole wartime establishment.[25]

Hamilton did delay—until June 17 when he presented the report along with the proposals of Washington, Lincoln, Steuben, and Chief Engineer Louis Du Portail.[26] But Congress was mired in bitter disputes over foreign affairs and Virginia's cession of her western lands, over finance, and over a variety of other issues long bottled up by the war. The more Robert Morris and his allies applied pressure ("a Phalanx that attacks with great force," complained Arthur Lee), the more Congress seemed to balk, to resist decisions on difficult issues. "Congress have set to[o] long in a City where every man affects the politician," declared Lee. "They must remove to some Spot where they will have a better chance to act independently."[27] Four days after Hamilton's report was read, Lee got his wish. Angry recruits of the Pennsylvania line ("liberally served" with "spiritous drink from the tipling houses adjoining," according to Madison) surrounded Congress and demanded their pay.[28] For days the delegates had known of the coming mutiny but had been unable to head it off. Now, with arguments raging between factions over how to respond, and with the Pennsylvania government, its eye on the election next fall, unwilling to call out the militia, many saw no alternative to leaving Philadelphia. Amid a welter of charges and accusations over who was responsible, Congress moved to Princeton, New Jersey, where it immediately became embroiled in fresh debates over where to locate a permanent national capital. Morris stayed in Philadelphia, preferring state to congressional influence. His absence weakened further the chances for passing Hamilton's plan for a military establishment. "Things seem to be working right," smiled Higginson, noting he could carry motions at Princeton when in Philadelphia no one would support him. "The great man and his agents are very uneasy, they see their influence daily declining."[29]

In late July, the nationalists tried to revive the Hamilton report by inviting to Princeton George Washington, who "with little else to do, than to be teased with troublesome Applications and fruitless Demands" wanted to dispell "this distressing Taedium" with "some special recall."[30] In truth new pressures were building to deal with the frontiers. Worried that Britain might evacuate the key forts along the Great Lakes before American troops arrived to keep the works away from the Indians, Washington had sent Steuben to Canada to discuss the transfer with British commander General Frederick Haldimand. The Indian situation also seemed uncertain. The New York and Pennsylvania requests for a peace treaty with the tribes still lay on the table and in mid-August, Congress learned from Philip Schuyler that New York might initiate her own negotiations at any moment. If Congress wished to head off state interference and stabilize the area, it would have to send its own deputation, with troops as a guard to impress the tribes with American strength. From still other sources came news that the Indians wanted peace, that Congress should begin talks and that "great numbers" of squatters were crossing to the Ohio region, threatening sale of the lands by their occupation and blocking the potential revenue to the Confederation of the West—and providing the explosive tinder that could (in General William Irvine's judgment) "renew the Indian War."[31]

Washington arrived in Princeton on August 25 to a joyous public welcome from the town and from Congress, and immediately set to work with a committee appointed to confer with him about Hamilton's report. Most of the discussions centered on technical matters—the structure of the regiments, fortifications, pay scales—although Washington did object to Hamilton's elite militia corps because it concentrated defensive strength and military skills in the cities, discriminating against other areas. But, in general, Washington's modifications were minor; he supported the plan, stressing once more the need either for a completely revamped militia or a regular army, and preferably both. In conferences with the committee over Indian policy, Washington pointed specifically to the need for troops to chase off squatters and establish a governmental presence in areas outside state jurisdiction.[32]

The committee presented Washington's reflections on September 10 and Congress scheduled Hamilton's report for debate in late October. But, as everyone knew, the prospects for positive action were growing dimmer every day. Congress was bogged down in intense debate over where next to meet after the coming adjournment, whether to move periodically, whether to create a national capital at all. Attendance was dwindling; sometimes only eight or nine states were present on the floor when for any decision, seven states had to vote in the affirmative. Congress seemed to be foundering in exhaustion after eight years of war—tempers growing shorter, the old antagonism between the nationalists and their opponents as sharp as ever. It was not the atmosphere for making hard, long-range decisions for the future.[33] In September Steuben reported that the British in Canada had made no effort to cooperate in turning over the posts and quite likely intended to hold on along the southern edge of the Great Lakes for at least another year and perhaps two.[34] While Congress received several reminders that squatters continued to pour onto western lands, the real sense of urgency, the need to have forces to beat the Indians into those British forts, had disappeared.

Actually Congress would never have swallowed Hamilton's report. Even the "sunshine of the General's name," as David Howell labelled the nationalist ploy to use Washington's influence, could not do it.[35] Opponents fought the Hamilton plan every inch of the way. In order to invite Washington to Princeton, Congress had to remove all reference to the purpose of his visit from the resolution. Again in early August when the committee was appointed to confer with him, strenuous objections were voiced about Congress's authority to raise troops in peacetime, and after Washington's arrival, when some of the delegates sought clarification on the constitutional issue, the dissension had been so acute that Congress had been unable even to agree to "consider the question of a peace establishment."[36] The last effort came on October 23. For two days in committee of the whole the delegates argued over Hamilton's report. None of the disagreements had cooled and in the end, Congress could only accept, knowing the western situation could not be ducked forever, the necessity for "some garrisons . . . to be maintained in time of peace at the expence of the United States for their security and defense, under their present circumstances."[37]

On the surface the great obstacle appeared to be the Confederation's ill-defined power to create a military establishment. Yet for many congressmen the constitutional tangle served as cover for deeper political, sectional, or personal motives. Hamilton's proposals had been too nationalistic, too much like a standing army in peacetime. "If Congress have power to establish an army of 500," reasoned Howell, "they may of 5,000 men . . . and in time however good and virtuous the present members of Congress may be supposed, that body might degenerate into lordly aristocrats."[38] Howell and William Ellery of Rhode Island led the opposition; they saw behind Hamilton the hand of Robert Morris, merging the power of the purse and the power of the sword, "the Impost being necessary to pay off the standing army, and the standing army being so necessary to secure an effectual collection of the Impost." Nor could the two see any benefit for Rhode Island; "why," they demanded, should "Rhode Island, New Jersey, or Delaware, . . . be at the expence of maintaining a chain of forts from Niagara to the Mississippi to secure the fur trade of New York, or the back settlements of Virginia!"[39] Other New Englanders agreed wholeheartedly and, further, with their states convulsed that summer and fall over commutation and the Society of the Cincinnati, they dared not favor anything that appeared pro-military. In June the Massachusetts legislature had replaced its entire congressional delegation because it voted for commutation and then created a special committee of correspondence to keep watch over the new representatives. (The issue had real power; years later Eliphalet Dyer lamented that his vote for commutation in March 1783 destroyed his 25-year career in Connecticut politics.)[40] Elbridge Gerry, the tall, angular merchant from Marblehead, friend of the Adamses, a republican ideologue and an experienced patriot with a long career in politics, returned to Congress on that wave of anger in Massachusetts. For the next ten years his was the leading voice against a peacetime military establishment. In 1783, alive to any threats to republican principles, Gerry sensed that a peacetime army had to be viewed as part of a larger mosaic: attempts to increase central power, executive influence, the Society of the Cincinnati, the attempt to create an independent federal city "with such materials for an oligarchical influence as have been mentioned." To Gerry and to other New Englanders, to suspicious men like Arthur Lee who had watched the nationalists for years, these measures smelled of counter-revolution. "How easy the transition from a republican to any other form of Government, however despotic," Gerry warned John Adams. "And how ridiculous to exchange a British Administration, for one that would be equally tyrannical, perhaps much more so!"[41]

The end of the session in 1783 marked a turning point in the political history of the Confederation. The nationalist star had waned. Robert Morris was now a lame duck, his administration under investigation in Congress; nationalist congressmen scattered back to their home states even before the session closed, some because their terms had expired under the rule of three-year rotation in office, others because they realized that the climate had changed, still others like Hamilton out of sheer disgust with public life. Never again would they attempt to realize their program within the framework of the Articles of Confederation. Instead they turned to a reworking of the whole political system by means of a national convention, a strategy proposed several years earlier and one which would achieve spectacular results within another five years. Like the rest of their vision to create lasting, viable national institutions in an essentially urban and commercially-oriented society, the peacetime military establishment went underground in 1783, awaiting a constitutional structure which would make its legality unquestionable and an administration of the government which would be willing to fight, and if necessary pay the political price in opposition and unpopularity, for its adoption.[42]

4

★ ☆ ★ ☆ ★ ☆ ★ ☆ ★

The Military Policy
of the Confederation
[1784-1788]

★

As to the protection of our own frontiers, it would seem best to leave it to the people themselves, as hath ever been the case. . . . This will always secure to us a hardy set of men on the frontiers. . . . Whereas, if they are protected by regulars, security will necessarily produce inattention to arms, and the whole of our people becoming disused to War, render the Curse of a standing Army Necessary.

Richard Henry Lee, 1784.[a]

When Congress re-assembled at Annapolis late in 1783, freed for the first time in years from nationalist domination (not "the least tincture of *poisonous influence*," boasted David Howell), the delegates still had to confront thorny questions of national defense.[1] Pressured by the need to open the West and to stabilize relations with the Indians, Congress eventually overcame heated disagreements enough to raise a regiment of troops. It laid the foundation for a national military establishment in peacetime. But military policy was still entangled in sectional interests, still plagued by the web of constitutional, political, and ideological influences that had so distorted the debate earlier in the year. In order to implement western policy, Congress compromised, and in the process created an army so flawed in organization and leadership that it came to symbolize the weaknesses of government under the Confederation. The forging of that compromise provides a perfect case study of how military policy has been made in America, how purely military considerations have so often given way to politics, local interests, and fears of militarism.

As the delegates made their way to Annapolis in the winter of 1783–1784, the prospects for unraveling the disputes over a national army seemed dimmer than ever. Soundings from important constituents confirmed the unpopularity of anything resembling a standing army in peacetime, so much so that one congressman predicted no action in the coming session.[2] None of the issues which had blocked Hamilton's report were yet resolved. Nor did the setting in Annapolis promise to help. For weeks a quorum was impossible and then when enough delegates arrived, attention focused on ratifying the final peace treaty with Great Britain. The fast social pace in town also hampered serious work. Elbridge Gerry thought the atmosphere ideal "for transacting publick Business," but to dour David Howell, the "plays, Balls, Concerts, routs, hops, Fandangoes and fox hunting" were pure *"tedium."*[3]

And yet the pressures were beginning to build. By early 1784 it was apparent that the West would have to be opened for settlement. Congress and the states owed land to veterans which had been promised as bounties for enlistment during the war. Prominent citizens and speculators were beginning to talk eagerly of the vast tract of wilderness. Most telling of all, Congress saw in the West a huge financial reservoir for the Confederation, not only to meet yearly expenses and pay off the war debt, but to kill Robert Morris's impost schemes. Antinationalists like Gerry and Howell clearly understood that with Congress on its feet financially, the chief justifications for the impost collapsed. Near the beginning of March 1784, Congress accepted Virginia's cession of her claim to the old Northwest; immediately thereafter the delegates appointed negotiators to iron out a peace with the Indians and purchase from them large tracts of land. Further delay was now impossible.[4]

Most in Congress also understood that opening the West for settlement required armed forces. Troops must accompany the emissaries to the Indians as guards and to impress the tribes with American power. Squatters were pouring into the Ohio Valley, threatening to deter purchase of federal land by speculators and settlers. The Confederation needed forces merely to police the area, to protect its citizens, and to keep the peace. Furthermore in 1784 Congress still expected to occupy the British-held forts, at least Oswego, Niagara, Detroit, and Mackinac, and unless Americans were on the spot to replace British garrisons, the Indians might occupy or destroy the works. In December 1783, Philip Schuyler warned that if Congress meant to move soldiers up the Mohawk River toward Niagara when the river opened to navigation in the spring, construction of boats would have to begin in March.[5]

Forts Oswego and Niagara posed a special problem that confused and embittered the debates over military policy all through 1784. Both posts lay in western New York, dominating the region where the powerful Six Nations lived, and controlling the water route west along the Great Lakes. Important New Yorkers had speculative interests there; as early as the spring of 1783, considering negotiations of its own with the Indians for land, the state had asked Congress for permission to raise state forces to accompany a peace delegation and to occupy the two forts. Hamilton, who then represented the state, had refused to present the request formally to Congress; he realized the threat to a national army and to Confederation power in general inherent in the precedent of state forces negotiating peace with Indians and garrisoning two of the most strategic western forts. But New York persisted, with a single ulterior motive, in the opinion of the Massachusetts representatives in Congress. In 1783 Massachusetts had reopened an ancient land claim to the area from the Finger Lakes to Lake Erie, claiming the region as part of her territory. According to the Massachusetts congressmen, New York intended to strengthen its legal claims by purchasing part of the area from the Indians, or failing in that, by physically occupying the territory under the pretext of preventing the forts from falling into Indian hands. "They are really to[o] cunning for M[assachuse]tts in Matters of Land," complained one Bay State delegate.[6]

In January 1784, with little apparent prospect of Congress providing money for garrisons, Governor George Clinton asked the New York legislature to decide on a course of action. The Assembly and Senate responded by authorizing Clinton to ask Congress for information about the Confederation's intentions. Since New York had no representatives then in Annapolis, Clinton forwarded the resolution to the President of Congress and asked Edward Hand, Washington's former adjutant general and a delegate from Pennsylvania, to sponsor the New York request for information. "The Legislature seem anxiously desirous of being furnished with it," Clinton emphasized.[7] A few weeks later New York dispatched an emissary to the British in Canada to discuss the evacuation of Niagara and Oswego. New York was serving an ultimatum and Congress knew it: if Congress did not garrison the strongholds on lakes Erie and Ontario, New York would.[8]

Less than a week before New York delegates Epraim Paine and Charles DeWitt reached Annapolis, congressman David Howell proposed a committee to study the occupation of British-held posts in the Northwest and the possibility of a small force to guard and supply them. After seconding by Arthur Lee, Congress referred it to a committee of Howell, Lee, Gerry, and John Francis Mercer. All four were confirmed antinationalists, on record against a national military establishment and, in the case of Gerry and Howell, vociferous opponents of standing armies in peacetime. Yet the four all had reasons for supporting a Confederation army. As antinationalists they favored selling off western lands to scuttle the impost, then being considered for ratification by several state governments. Virginians Lee and Mercer, representing the state with the most extensive unguarded frontier, knew the benefit of putting the burden of western defense on the Confederation. And for Elbridge Gerry, the advantages outweighed the risks. Certainly Congress had to forestall New York from occupying the disputed western portion of the state with New York troops, even if he, like most New Englanders, wanted no part of a standing army. Massachusetts might even gain something. One last regiment remained in national service, stationed in and around West Point, under the command of Henry Knox, and composed mostly of men from Massachusetts and New Hampshire. It had been enlisted at more than double the pay and bounty of other Continental Army forces and the two states had been paying the extra amount. But if Congress could be induced to use these troops for peacetime duty, the states might escape those costs. And in the end, Gerry and the rest of the committee felt they had nothing to fear; they would decide what kind of forces would be proposed and on what terms. Hamilton's report need not be considered at all. "It will be judged necessary," predicted Howell's fellow Rhode Islanders, "to establish for a time some troops, at suitable posts in the Western territory, and to keep up a few men to guard our public stores, but no standing army."[9]

True to form, when the Howell committee presented a report on April 6, all the broader questions of national security and a peacetime military establishment were altogether omitted. In fact, to avoid the question of Congress's authority, the committee preferred to use Knox's regiment at West Point to garrison the British forts, but the extra expense of those troops, plus the fact that their terms of service expired within another year, made other forces necessary. To have men ready to replace the British garrisons, however, some New England troops, perhaps as many as 250 men, would have to be used; the only other forces at Congress's disposal were 100 men near Pittsburgh, enlisted under normal Continental Army pay scales. For the future protection of the frontier, the committee admitted that new men would have to be raised: a thousand-man army, three battalions of infantry and one of artillery, enlisted for three-year terms, and stationed in posts on the Great Lakes, Lake Champlain, and along the Ohio River. This was the bare minimum possible, proposed without a large staff or any of the supporting institutions like arsenals that nationalists had suggested the year before. Supplies would come from local contractors near each fort, unless necessity dictated the creation of government magazines. The report conceded to the Confederation only the authority to apportion quotas of men from each state, to appoint the officers (doubtful constitutionally under the Articles), and to command the army. All other questions about national security—a navy, coast defenses, arsenals and magazines to produce and store munitions, a military academy—would wait until "Congress determine on a Peace establishment, a subject which in the opinion of your committee should be considered as *entirely distinct** from the present measure."[10]

By limiting discussion to garrisons for the western posts and by recommending the smallest force possible, the report cleverly attempted to evade all the difficult questions raised by Hamilton in 1783. Most of these issues, however, could not be avoided. Congress's authority to raise troops in peacetime, which could be construed as the power to maintain a standing army, would certainly cause trouble once the delegates focused on wording a resolution. New Englanders, Gerry especially, viewed the whole subject with profound suspicion, partly because of their own personal hostility to standing armies and partly because of the political traps in any military issue, given the uproar over commutation and over the appearance of the Society of the Cincinnati then raging east of the Hudson. Evidently Gerry and the rest of the New England delegates were willing to allow the Confederation a small army, but not if the wording of the resolution established or acknowledged Congress's independent power to raise troops. And out of pure state self-interest (and probably as a defense at home for consenting to troops), the Massachusetts and New Hampshire delegations planned to force Congress into assuming the extra costs of Knox's regiment, or at least that portion the states had been paying after November 1783, when the rest of the Continental Army had been discharged.[11]

The best way for Congress to justify paying the regiment was to use it to garrison the British posts until new forces could be raised. But the New Yorkers boiled at the very thought, and became so furious by the end of the session that they tried to wreck all efforts to create a peacetime army. Paine and DeWitt had reached Annapolis in late March determined to force the issue of state soldiers for Oswego and Niagara. Shrewdly Congress had referred their first request to the Howell committee and added Paine to it, which seemed to satisfy the two delegates. But between early April when the committee reported and late May when debate finally began (the delay may have been a stratagem to steamroller the report through under the pressure of impending adjournment), Paine and DeWitt became more and more suspicious about Congress's motives. Twice more they demanded that New York's request be considered and each time Congress sidetracked the issue. "[T]he utmost chicanery was urged in the house to prevent such motion being made," growled Paine, having uncovered the plot to cheat New York out of the disputed territory. "[C]ongress are unwilling that we should garrison Oswego and Niagara, as I believe the design is for congress to garrison these two posts

*Emphasis added.

[with the Massachusetts troops], and that Massachusetts intends to cede a part of their country to the United States."[12] "[T]he chagrin was very visible," Paine added grimly, "when congress were told plainly that New York would not suffer Massachusetts troops to march into that country."[13]

When debate started in earnest on May 25, only ten days remained until adjournment, and the selfish personal and state interests, the transparent evasions in the committee report, the ideological fears of standing armies—all exploded into fierce conflict. The mood on the floor was already intense; "tumult and disorder," "caballing . . . and injustice reign almost perpetually," observed Paine in disgust, "even to the degree of challenging."[14] Discussion began harmlessly enough with an attempt by Howell and James Monroe to preserve the fragile sectional bargain first suggested in the committee report: enlist 450 new troops and use the leftover Massachusetts men for immediate service in the British posts.[15] But immediately Edward Hand proposed enlisting 896 men. Then Massachusetts interrupted with the question of congressional authority, and the fight was on.

As the battle intensified, day after day and roll call after roll call, every attempt at compromise broke down either over Congress's power to raise an army independently of the states, over the use of the Massachusetts troops, or over the New England demand that Congress shoulder the extra pay and bounties of the regiment. The South and Middle states—New York excepted—wanted a national army. These states lay closest to the Indians. Powerful local interests already owned large tracts of the wilderness, and demanding protection, southern and Middle states citizens would settle the West. If the Confederation underwrote the cost of security, so much the better. And yet with only 11 states present and voting, the South-Middle states coalition could not muster the necessary seven-state majority. Many of their delegates insisted that the power to requisition forces in peacetime was critical; as Dr. Hugh Williamson reasoned, "the very independence or safety of an Empire may depend on its arming in time of peace to prevent an invasion."[16] Massachusetts's demand for restitution of the pay and bounty money struck many southerners as blackmail. "[T]his single charge [the bounties] may amount to a Million," continued Williamson, and "open a field for extensive charges by that State against the United States. . . . New Hampshire has a similar claim."[17] Judging by their maneuvers during the floor fight, several southerners were willing to compromise on the money if New England would give in on Congress's power, that is on "requisitions"—requisitioning the troops from the states instead of merely "recommending" that they enlist the men.[18]

New England never relented. On the second day of debate, Elbridge Gerry delivered a long tirade against standing armies, against the "authority to make requisitions" which "must admit an unlimited power to extend . . . requisitions," against an army which must surely degenerate into the "coercive means" to implement Congress's financial programs. Entered into the *Journal* as preface to a motion (ironically an offer to trade the requisition question for the pay and bounty money), Gerry's doctrinaire speech solidified the New England delegates into a rigid bloc which no amount of argument or bargaining could shake. With New York voting to obstruct everything until she gained authority for a state force, the New Englanders possessed five votes. The South and Middle states had no choice but to capitulate. On June 2, Congress discharged the last regiment of the Continental Army, leaving only eighty men to guard stores at Fort Pitt and West Point, and thus dropping the expensive Massachusetts and New Hampshire soldiers from state and Confederation payrolls. On that subject, however, the southerners never surrendered; state claims for the money would be settled in exactly the same manner that other army accounts were handled. The next day, Congress "recommended" that the four states of Connecticut, New York, New Jersey, and Pennsylvania contribute militia to a 700-man force for 12 months of duty. The Secretary at War was to organize the units; pay, rations, and the Articles of War were to be the same as those of the Continental Army. The same day Congress ordered 300 of the new force to accompany the Indian negotiators, and then adjourned.[19]

The June 3 resolution created the first national peacetime military force in American history, the progenitor and lineal ancestor of the establishment that has continued until the present. Fittingly, as would often be the case for the next century and a half, politics overrode purely military considerations. Fashioning a military policy had been confusing, an irrational process as much dependent on land disputes, fears of standing armies, and state interests as on the defense needs of the nation. The end result was vague—a compromise force: not under state control, and enlisted for service out-of-state, so clearly not militia; not wholly under Confederation authority, not long-service regulars, and furnished obviously at the pleasure of the states, so certainly not a standing army. The Confederation's "army" was unique, undefinable, and as its history subsequently showed, the bastard child of quarrelsome, uncertain congressional parents. Indeed few congressmen left Annapolis fully satisfied about the outcome of the struggle. Monroe and Williamson claimed later that the only alternative left, given New England's intransigence, was militia, even though the result, in Williamson's estimation, was a "poor expedient."[20] For others, however, the implications were more foreboding. "[A] weak and blameable desire of popular Applause in

Members of Congress may wrest from the foederal Government a power essential to the safety of the Union," protested Thomas Stone to Monroe. "Government can neither be protected or supported without the power and . . . it's being even questioned by leading Men . . . will render the exercise of it impracticable."[21]

Only the New Englanders returned home with a sense of victory. Elbridge Gerry sincerely believed in the danger of standing armies. Almost singlehandedly he had dictated to Congress in 1784, and for another five years, in public and behind the scenes, he would lead the struggle to keep a military establishment out of the national government's hands. Gerry returned to Congress in 1783 in the midst of a tide of antimilitary hysteria in New England; he understood the explosiveness of the issue at home. (Boston, after all, annually celebrated the massacre of 1770.) In a long report to the state legislature in June 1784, he and Francis Dana justified their obstructionism on the ground that enabling "Congress to raise a few men for a Short period may extend their powers indefinitely both as to the number of men and term of inlistment." The measure was "altogether unnecessary" in a country possessed of militia and "remote from Nations which have standing armies." If Congress needed a small army for the frontier and to guard stores, its size "ought to be limited by an express article of the Confederation."[22] The General Court responded with approval, but Gerry felt compelled to press the issue again when he returned to Boston in October. "If a regular Army is admitted, will not the Militia be neglected, and gradually dwindle into Contempt? [A]nd where then are We to look for Defence of our Rights and Liberties?" "The Sense of the Legislature should be known," he announced.[23] Once more the General Court backed Gerry, this time with curt instructions to the state congressional delegation: "oppose, and by all ways and means . . . prevent the raising of a standing army of any number, on any pretence whatever, in time of peace."[24]

Gerry's actions in the summer and fall of 1784, sanctioned formally by Massachusetts, sounded the death knell for a viable military policy under the Confederation. In the spring of 1785, the expiration of the one-year enlistments forced Congress to reconsider the entire problem, but in the end little changed. The South and Middle states wanted requisitions, New England opposed them. This time southerners probably had the votes to compel requisitions, but no one relished another bitter battle. For one thing, everyone agreed that constitutionally a requisition meant drawing men proportionally from all 13 states (presumably as in tax matters, to protect individual states from discrimination by the central government). An order to all 13 was a complex, time-consuming process which undoubtedly meant the disbanding of the 700 militia raised before. And time had become precious. Congress now accepted an army as integral to western policy: to protect envoys to the Indians, to evict squatters, to neutralize British subversion of the Indians and the critically-positioned posts, which after another exchange of correspondence with Canada were obviously going to remain outside American control for the foreseeable future. Most of all Congress wanted land sales to begin immediately, and troops were needed to guard the surveyors. Under this pressure the South and Middle states gracefully accepted another 700-man "recommendation." In return, New England agreed to regulars instead of militia, enlisted for three-year terms. Otherwise, except on minor points, the 1785 resolution followed its predecessor exactly.[25]

That same session, with an ordinance defining the powers and duties of the Secretary at War, Congress completed arrangements for commanding and administering the new army. In March Henry Knox accepted the post and set to work surveying the state of the troops and the condition of the arms and other munitions left over from the war. As the administrative link between Congress and the new regiment, Knox kept the musters and returns, oversaw the magazines and storehouses, prepared estimates for pay and supplies, implemented congressional resolutions, and directed the army's units. He was perfect for the job. Few men in America possessed wider military experience or such familiarity with the mechanics of high command and civil-military relations. Slow, methodical, with an eye for detail—no innovator—Knox was loyal and conscientious, capable of executing a compromise policy under the weak and divided leadership of the Confederation even while disagreeing personally with that policy.[26] After 1785 the policy never changed; Congress under the Articles of Confederation did not again face the broader dimensions of national security, the questions of whether or not to establish a national army, and if so, what kind of institution to construct. Even divorced from Hamilton's nationalistic proposal in 1783, military policy was too complex a subject, too vulnerable to other state and sectional issues, and too entangled in the more important, and more volatile, issues of the prejudice against standing armies and the relative power of the states versus the national government.

Nowhere was the inadequacy of the Confederation's military policy more clearly revealed than in the activities of the small regiment established by Congress. From its beginning in 1784 the army faced formidable obstacles. None of the states mobilized existing militia; instead each went through the more involved process of recruiting their companies soldier by individual soldier. New York, angry over Congress's refusal to allow a state force, flatly refused to furnish her quota. In Connecticut, recruiting was delayed for months because the legislature had adjourned before Congress acted.[27] Pennsylvania and New Jersey acted within two months, but divided authority over the force caused trouble from the onset. Pennsylvania expected Congress to underwrite the expenses of recruiting and supply; the Superintendent of Finance would not assume the costs until the men were assembled and ready to act under national authority.[28] Pennsylvania's officers took oaths to both the state and the Confederation and, adding to the paperwork, Lieutenant-Colonel Commandant Josiah Harmar reported both to Congress and to the Supreme Executive Council, the state executive. Since she had the largest quota, Pennsylvania named the commanding officer. Harmar's war record was excellent and he was a personal friend of Thomas Mifflin, who was a popular state politician, a former major general in the Continental Army, and not coincidentally, the President of Congress in 1784. According to Harmar's friend and aide, Ebenezer Denny, the state "reserved" the command for Harmar, delaying appointments of the other officers until he returned from England where he had delivered the ratified final peace treaty.[29]

Harmar's first task was to find good men. The Council issued the typical recruiting instructions: enlist only men of high character without fits, ruptures, or other diseases; induct them sober, before a justice of the peace.[30] In the rush to march west, however, Harmar took whomever he could find. As one soldier remembered it, pay and bounty were so low "that it could not be a sufficient inducement to any man" who was not "inclined" to military life.[31] Late that fall, with his unit nearly filled, Harmar set out for Pittsburgh to begin duty as the guard to Indian commissioners Arthur Lee and Richard Butler. Desertion struck at once. In Bedford, Pennsylvania, where the detachment bivouacked for a few days, discipline broke down completely, the men drunk, disorderly, and destroying civilian property. One private ended a mad junket through town at the bottom of a twenty-foot well, where he stayed to sober up until help arrived. Four others, the so-called "Irish Mess," entered a store, waited for the proprietor to go to the back room, then dismantled the whole establishment, merchandise included. Harmar sprung them from jail, tried them at a drumhead court martial back at camp, and sentenced each to 100 lashes. The punishment had no deterrent effect.[32]

Desertion plagued Harmar continually, as it would the Indian-fighting army for another century. The commandant spent the winter of 1784–1785 at Indian negotiations and repairing Fort McIntosh, a small post about forty miles down the Ohio from Pittsburgh. Supplies were always short and the weather a constant burden. One boat loaded with flour caught in the ice and was freed only at the cost of frostbite (one man lost both legs) and near death among the enlisted men involved. The soldiers drank themselves into oblivion at every opportunity, so much so that Harmar finally banned liquor without written permission from an officer (investigation revealed that the whiskey came from stores brought along for the Indians). The officers themselves were hardly exemplary. During the long, boring, cold-weather months, isolated in the wilderness, they drank as heavily as the men. One night after Christmas, in a state of total inebriation, several of them mustered the McIntosh garrison, ordered the men around senselessly, began quarreling, and nearly came to blows. On another occasion a lieutenant for no apparent reason clubbed a soldier to death after the trooper innocently asked permission to buy a quart of rum. Spring was received gratefully by the army, which welcomed the opportunity to begin active operations. Already by May 1785, however, less than one year from its beginning, the army was owed more than $4,000 in back pay.[33]

In 1785 all the difficulties of beginning an army anew reappeared when Congress replaced the one-year militiamen with three-year regulars. This time New York and Connecticut arranged immediately for recruiting while Pennsylvania and New Jersey, their legislatures already adjourned by the time of the congressional resolution, had to delay enlisting until the fall. Harmar expected the transition to be easy, but to his horror only a handful of the Pennsylvania contingent could be induced to re-enlist, forcing him (in the midst of operations) to detach officers for the recruiting service. Ebenezer Denny for one hated such duty, and if the New York experience was at all typical, Denny had good cause. Cash for bounties and advance pay, as well as clothing of all kinds, was continually short at the recruiting stations. Good men—healthy, intelligent, and interested in service as well as the bounty—were hard to find. Some deserted immediately from the recruiting camps. Of the 27 enlisted at West Point in July 1785, one was disabled by a bad knee and two others had venereal disease. One "capable man" for "Sergeant" found the next month by Captain John Hamtramck, recruiting his company at the Point, also had "to get cure[d] of the clap."[34] Once the companies reached full strength, Knox rushed them west for the Indian negotiations and to deal with the increasingly vexing problem of squatters. Once again the trek across Pennsylvania was a travesty of desertion and destruction. At one point, discovering a plot by ten men to desert in a group, Hamtramck decided to execute one of the conspirators on the spot "to make an example." At the last moment, with the company lined up for the execution and the victim standing with one leg in his grave, half dead from fear, Hamtramck changed the order to 300 lashes. "Had I been in another service," sneered the French Canadian veteran of the Continental Army, just then beginning a twenty-year career in the peacetime military, "I would have certenly shot him. . . . No Man deserved it more."[35]

To some extent these were the problems that have always afflicted armies. For the next century and a half, as long as military life remained boring and unattractive and the army stayed isolated in lonely garrisons far from settlement, drunkenness and desertion would pervade the peace-time enlisted ranks. In the spring of 1785, Harmar's regiment began active operations and unhappily its record was one of unremitting failure in every important mission it undertook. In April Harmar sent Ensign John Armstrong down the Ohio River to clear out squatters. Armstrong returned after evicting several families but reported rumors of hundreds of families encroaching further west despite posted warnings against illegal farming. Harmar reported to Knox that the numbers were "immense" and that based at McIntosh in Pennsylvania, the army could not patrol more than 150 miles downstream. At Knox's urging Congress authorized the commandant to build a fort 140 miles farther down the river at the confluence of the Muskingum and Ohio. With two compa-nies, Major John Doughty moved to the site and spent the late summer and fall of 1785 dispossessing squatters in the neighborhood, constructing Fort Harmar, and establishing the first permanent government presence in the Northwest Territory.[36]

Every year for the next few years, the army slowly advanced into hostile territory, building new forts—Fort Finney at the falls of the Ohio (present-day Louisville) and Fort Steuben (Steubenville, Ohio) in 1786, Fort Knox at Vincennes on the Wabash and Fort Franklin on the Allegheny in 1787, Fort Washington at Cincinnati in 1789—as it went. But it never licked the squatters. "The most effectual method to convince these people that we were in earnest," Doughty observed, "was to burn and destroy all their houses and barns." Doughty suspected, however, that many had planned to resist and would plant again the next year since they had only "removed to the opposite shoure." Houses he had pulled down the previous spring were rebuilt by the fall, and since the army had no legal authority except to chase the squatters away, the game could continue indefinitely.[37] Two years later in 1787, the situation had wors-ened considerably. "All future attempts to remove intruders may be abortive," Knox warned Congress; "their numbers may be so great as to defy the power of the United States."[38] Optimistically, Knox claimed his soldiers could remove the squatters, but the Confederation never really solved the problem. By the end of the decade, the Indian menace had made farming away from protected settlements on the north side of the Ohio too dangerous anyway, and having sold huge tracts of land to the Symmes Associates and to the Ohio Company, Congress worried less and less about the consequences on land sales. The real challenge in the West, for the army and for Congress as everyone knew, was Indians.

In the 1780s a multitude of tribes inhabited present day Ohio and Indiana, living in small, scattered villages on the major rivers and their tributaries. Almost all had sided with the British during the Revolution, and despite signing treaties in 1784, 1785, and 1786, many continued to snipe across the Ohio River and around Pittsburgh. None of the horse

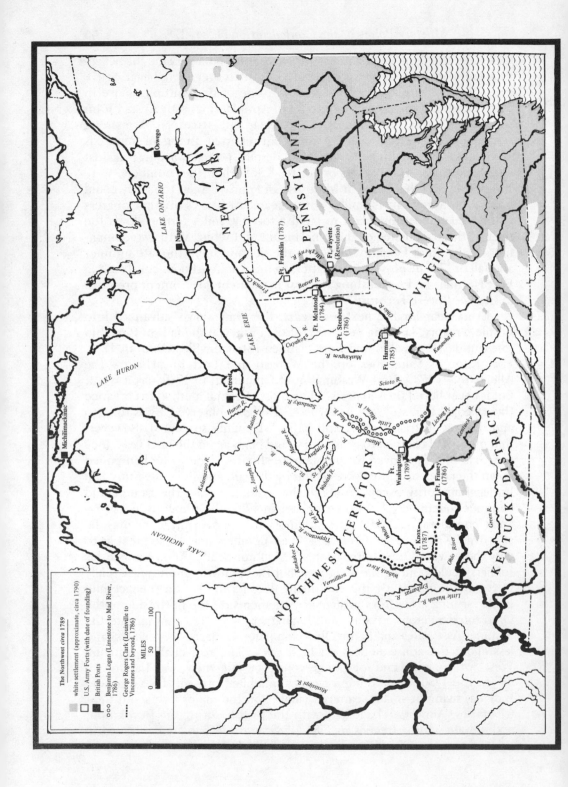

The Northwest circa 1789

white settlement (approximate, circa 1790)

U.S. Army Forts (with date of founding)

British Posts

Benjamin Logan (Limestone to Mad River, 1786)

George Rogers Clark (Louisville to Vincennes and beyond, 1786)

MILES

0   50   100

NEW YORK

PENNSYLVANIA

VIRGINIA

NORTHWEST TERRITORY

KENTUCKY DISTRICT

LAKE ONTARIO

LAKE ERIE

LAKE HURON

LAKE MICHIGAN

Oswego

Niagara

Detroit

Michilimackinac

Ft. Franklin (1787)

Ft. Fayette (Revolution)

Ft. McIntosh (1784)

Ft. Steuben (1786)

Ft. Harmar (1785)

Ft. Washington (1789)

Ft. Finney (1786)

Ft. Knox (1787)

French C.

Beaver R.

Allegheny R.

Ohio R.

Kanawha R.

Cuyahoga

Muskingum R.

Scioto R.

Licking R.

Kentucky R.

Green R.

Sandusky R.

Huron R.

Raisin R.

Kalamazoo R.

St. Joseph R.

St. Joseph R.

Maumee R.

Auglaize R.

St. Mary's R.

Wabash R.

Eel R.

Tippecanoe R.

Kankakee R.

Vermillion R.

White R.

Wabash River

Embarras R.

Little Wabash R.

Ohio River

Mad R.

Miami R.

Little Miami R.

Mississippi R.

stealing, the kidnappings, the murders, the torture and mulilation of prisoners really ended with the war. By the middle of the decade, in tempo and frequency, the violence began to increase, especially between the Kentuckians and tribes inhabiting the Miami, Maumee, and Upper Wabash river valleys. For ceremonial chores the army always seemed adequate. Units accompanied United States envoys and guarded the vast stores of food, drink, and presents the whites always brought to powwows. The soldiers paraded, fired salutes, and in general struck martial postures. But judging by the Indians' behavior in the ten years after the Revolution, they were not in the least impressed, much less "awed" (one of the army's major functions). For the most part the army had to stick to its small posts for its own protection. All six companies "would easily fall a sacrifice if the Savages were so disposed," Lieutenant Erkuries Beatty told his congressman brother in 1785. "[H]owever a soldier has no right to think, therefore I leave that to men in power and hope their penetrating genius's, will not suffer a handful of men to be sacrificed to their folly."[39] One of the army's active duties, especially in 1786, was to protect Geographer of the United States Thomas Hutchins while he and his surveyors marked off lands for sale and occupation. Between August and October 1786, Hamtramck commanded 200 men guarding Hutchins's party, which day and night, seven days a week, laid out four ranges near the Pennsylvania border. In mid-September, hearing that Indians were stalking them and skeptical of the army's effectiveness, the surveyors retreated to the Ohio River and refused to continue. Although Hutchins himself returned to work, the onset of cold weather prevented him from finishing the fifth range and by the next spring the Indians had become so menacing that further surveying was out of the question.[40]

Civilian and military observers invariably attributed Indian hostility in part to the forts along the Great Lakes from which British officials dispensed supplies of food and munitions, and advice which misled the tribes and egged them on to resist American expansion. "Villainous emissaries have been continually sallying from thence, poisoning the minds of the Savages—and depreciating the character of the Americans," declared Harmar.[41] Henry Knox passed the information to Congress and between his reports and letters from the West, some of which were printed in the newspapers, Americans became firmly convinced that Britain held the key to peace beyond the Alleghenies. But whatever the source (and the British were but one factor), the army was clearly powerless either to prevent Indian raids or retaliation by incensed Kentuckians. In 1786 the whites mounted two large forays across the Ohio into federal territory; Congress officially ignored the unauthorized intrusions and the army watched silently. Without doubt the frontier was drifting into war. In mid-1786 Knox gave Harmar permission to punish any insults to posts, troops, or legal settlers, but cautioned him to

distinguish outlaw bands from war parties acting under tribal orders and
to avoid precipitating a costly war. The next year a Wyandot party
captured a soldier within sight of the garrison at Fort Harmar. After
evading pursuit, the Indians took the man to their village, murdered him,
and carried the scalp through the Indian towns. It was the first military
casualty since the army's formation, and the men were angry. Knox told
Congress that the incident signalled a sharp change in Indian policy and
used it as an argument for renewing the army, whose three-year enlistments were due to expire legally in late 1787. But Congress, paralyzed
during the opening salvoes of the campaign to ratify the new constitution, would not permit any change in the army's defensive stance.[42]

The reasons for the army's ineffectiveness during the 1780s were
numerous and only in part within the power of Congress to remedy. First
and foremost the army lacked the manpower to carry out its duties. Had
the Confederation been able diplomatically to dislodge the British and
mount a sufficiently large army to envelop the Ohio area, from the south
along the river and north from Pittsburgh to Presque Isle (Erie, Pennsylvania) and then along the Great Lakes, the Indian wars of the 1790s might
have been avoided altogether. As it was, military power could only be
applied by slowly advancing down the Ohio River, then north from
Cincinnati to the Maumee River, a route vulnerable all along its northern
flank and—with the presence of the Six Nations in western New York and
northwestern Pennsylvania—a route totally exposed at the rear in Pittsburgh. A military solution to the Indian problem required not only
offensive operations, but the commitment of a force large enough to
occupy forts along the route and at the center of Indian territory. The
Confederation Congress, uncertain of its own authority to raise an army
and bankrupt for funds, in a country just emerged from a long, exhausting war and pervaded by intense antimilitarism, could never commit itself
to such a military policy. Interestingly enough it took George Washington's administration over two years to arrive at that policy, and, hampered by a similar political climate, a total of six years to implement it.

What distinguished the Confederation from its successor in military
affairs as much as anything else was money. The shaky financial picture
undermined every military program. In 1783, at Congress's request, the
Secretary at War attempted to establish permanent magazines to house
leftover munitions and equipment. But for lack of funds, Robert Morris
blocked construction in Virginia and South Carolina (Springfield was
finished and buildings at West Point almost constructed), even though
everyone understood that it would be cheaper to erect the buildings while
troops were still in service for labor.[43] In relative terms, the cost of the

military establishment every year was immense. Of the $435,000 for operating expenses in the 1785 rough budget estimate, over $187,000—43 percent—was earmarked for the army, the largest single expense. By Knox's calculations, rations alone for six months cost $42,000; clothing at the lowest contract price ran over $20 per soldier.[44] Unfortunately, the Confederation did not always have the money, and instead of borrowing it, Congress often obliged the army to do without.

The effect on the military establishment was debilitating. Most of the time the soldiers never received their pay and at one point Congress suspended regular distribution of money. On three different occasions between 1785 and 1789 regimental paymaster Erkuries Beatty travelled east to Congress where he was bandied from official to official, "put . . . off with vague answers," and then finally promised some settlement.[45] At the end of the decade the army was owed nearly $150,000 in pay and subsistence (the monthly pay of a private was $7). At various times the soldiers lived on short rations because supplies were lacking or went into the field with clothing in tatters, or without essential apparel. The result was low morale, continual desertion, habitual drunkenness, and mutinous behavior.[46]

In addition, the lack of funds limited army operations at every turn. In June 1786, even though the Indian situation began to deteriorate noticeably, Knox requested—and was refused—$1,000 to transport three tons of lead and powder to Fort Pitt for distribution to the frontier posts; the Board of Treasury, Congress's financial agency after Robert Morris retired, claimed the treasury was empty, lacking money even for "the public officers whose services are indispensibly necessary for the support of the mere form of civil government."[47] In order after order, Knox reminded Harmar of the Confederation's financial weakness and cautioned him to avoid any action that might lead to war. Near the end of 1786 Knox explicitly forbade offensive operations without specific orders from his office. As the head of the military establishment, however, Knox was subjected to pressure from below—an officer corps eager for action and frustrated by restraints—and from Congress above. Late the next year the Board of Treasury complained about the difficulty of supplying the army and hinted that the Confederation might dispense altogether with its small force. Knox exploded, blaming government poverty on the irresponsibility of the states and defending the army as essential. Without troops, squatters would overrun the West and Congress would never gain a revenue; without the army as a buffer, whites and Indians would drag the government into a full-scale war which would heighten the financial crisis. If land could be stolen and held "by the tenure of force and the temporary imbecility of the general government," Knox argued, the nation's dignity would be a joke. Westerners might even contemplate "obtaining security by association" with some other government "that may be able and willing to afford assistance."[48] In this case, the army's effectiveness was vastly overdrawn, but it was not the first time the Secretary had to stress the army's usefulness to the nation. Almost alone, operating his office and his forces at a bare minimum, Henry Knox nurtured the beginning of American military power through its most disheartening years.

But whatever limitations came from the outside, the army itself was so flawed internally as to compromise seriously its ability to function. Most of the army's internal operating procedures, for example, were developed on the spot or copied directly from the Continental Army experience, since Congress had specified the use of some wartime procedures and almost all officers were veterans of their respective state lines. There is no evidence that Knox or Harmar ever developed regulations for army activities like marching, encampment, tactical deployment, guard duty, parade, or any of the rules for everyday activities which armies use to standardize routine duty. Certainly some of the officers needed the guidance. Some, of course, were excellent, but as a rule the quality of leadership in the First Regiment was mediocre. Many of the officers tended to be harsh and dictatorial with their men, contemptuous of local civilians, and blind in their hatred for the Indians. (Significantly many of those still left in the army in 1792 resigned soon after Anthony Wayne assumed command.) Actually Congress exercised only partial authority over the officers or the army. The states controlled appointments, recruiting, and promotions. Sometimes the states provided the supplies for their own contingents. Questions of relative rank in the same grade, which caused some bitter disputes between officers, were not settled until the Confederation ceased to exist. "It is my ardent wish that the new government may speedily be adopted, and that all these State affairs may cease," wrote Harmar in exasperation. "We may then hope for order and regularity."[49]

In a basic institutional sense, Congress never prepared the army for peacetime. One incident illustrated the problem dramatically—in fact so spectacularly that Congress was finally moved to act. During the winter of 1785–1786, with desertion decimating the companies at Fort McIntosh, post commandant Major John Wyllys decided to try two recently apprehended deserters as an example to plug the drain. The Articles of War drawn up during the Revolution for the Continental Army, however, specified a panel of 13 officers for capital cases, obviously impossible in a peacetime army which contained less than 40 officers in toto. Therefore Wyllys convened a five-officer court which tried the men, convicted them, and (following normal procedure) forwarded the record and the decision to the war office for congressional approval before carrying out the sentence. As a deterrent Wyllys published the sentence at the post, whereupon three other soldiers immediately deserted.

Shocked by the new loss and fearing that discipline was near collapse, Wyllys apprehended the three and executed them immediately without trial. "[N]othing but such exemplary punishment could produce the desired effect," Wyllys explained to Knox in asking the Secretary's "approbation."[50] Knox was horrified. He informed Congress that under the circumstances, a court martial for the executed three was "almost impossible," but no commander could "supersede the laws . . . and annul the compact, which the public have made with their troops, that they shall be governed by the rules and articles of war," by summary execution. Congress agreed, and ordered Wyllys arrested, the two deserters convicted in the earlier court martial released, and a board of inquiry convened to investigate the incident.[51]

In July 1786, Knox related the results of the investigation to Congress along with his own recommendations. Wyllys had ordered the executions, Knox argued, "as a terror to the rest of the troops" because the situation at the post was approaching mutiny. "[T]he practice of all ages and countries" justified "inflicting instant death on . . . mutineers" and not waiting "until the smothered flame burst out into open mutiny." Caught "in one of those exigencies, which arise in the affairs of men," Wyllys had acted "for the public service," justifiably, "on military and political principles." He should be released and exonerated. Since the fort lay inside Pennsylvania, Congress should remain silent and let the state, if it wished, prosecute the major.[52] Obviously Knox was glossing over basic issues and most delegates must have realized it. To prevent such an atrocity from ever reoccurring, however, Congress revised the Articles of War, not only on the size of court martial panels but on several other points, and in the process took a giant step toward the creation of a military establishment truly designed for peacetime duty on the frontier.[53]

Although the First Regiment failed to police the frontier or to damp down the conflict between whites and Indians, it was by no means useless or inactive during the 1780s. Harmar and his officers functioned as the eyes and ears of the government in the West, relaying intelligence about the British and the Indians, monitoring the pace and direction of settlement, and exploring the wilderness.[54] At strategic points the army built forts which were indispensable stepping stones in the campaigns of the early 1790s. No one will ever know for certain what incidents were prevented by the existence of the army along the Ohio River. At the time, however, these were routine, almost trivial activities, the kind that could have been performed by any group of men the government wished to employ in the region. What stood out were the weakness and the pitiful condition of the force. Knowledgeable observers inside and outside the army agreed about the army's ineffectiveness and the Confederation's inability to project military strength. The troops "contribute nothing to the defence of the frontier inhabitants," asserted one writer, who wanted them disbanded in favor of offensives against the Indians by settlers, an argument that would rise to cacophonic proportions after army defeats in 1790 and 1791. "They are rather prisoners in that country, than in possession of it. . . . all they can do is take care of themselves."[55] In 1786 Congress discussed at length the possibilities of additional powers, and dealt directly with the difficulties of raising troops. Even opponents of increasing national power recognized that because of the uncertainty of the Confederation's power on the subject, and because of politics, Congress was hard pressed to confront the basic issues of national defense, much less resolve them.[56] By 1787 many Americans viewed the army and the defective policy which had created it as the very symbol of the inadequacy of government under the Articles of Confederation. Only after the writing and ratification of a new frame of government was the ability of the United States to provide for the common defense finally assured.

5

★ ☆ ★ ☆ ★ ☆ ★ ☆ ★

Militarism and
the Founding Fathers
[1787-1788]

★

An army is the strongest of all factions, and completely the instrument of a leader, skilful enough to enlist its sympathies, and inflame its passions. It is given to a president, and election is the only surety that he will not use it. . . . The precept, "that money should not be appropriated for the use of an army, for a longer term than two years," is like that which forbid Caesar to open the treasury.

John Taylor of Caroline, 1814.[a]

When the framers of the Constitution gathered in Philadelphia in 1787 to construct a new government for the United States, their military concerns were for national security in its broadest context: how to protect the nation against all manner of external and internal threats. With the Revolution and the bitter divisions in Congress in the early 1780s in mind, they purposely armed the government with explicit power to raise armies and navies in peacetime, to support and administer them effectively, to reform the militia, to wage war independently of the states, and to suppress any domestic threat to the law or established authority. Naturally the military sections of the Constitution provoked a searching debate, and out of that debate emerged the outlines of two conflicting theories of national security that went back to the seventeenth-century English standing army debates and which were destined to be adopted by the political parties soon to develop after the new government went into operation.

Late in the summer of 1786, in western Massachusetts hundreds of miles from the Ohio frontier, there erupted a rebellion that more than any Indian conflict underlined nationalist claims about the military weakness of the central government. Long burdened by heavy debts, mounting taxation, and a lack of hard currency, farmers and townspeople west of Worcester turned on the courts and the legal system with mob action and violence. On August 29, a mob of 1,500 seized the Northampton county courthouse. In the next six weeks, bands of self-styled "regulators" disrupted the legal process in five other counties, and at Springfield in September, 1,100 rebels bluffed the state supreme court into adjournment while 800 militiamen looked on helplessly. Shays's Rebellion was in full swing.[1]

Within another six months, the Massachusetts government mobilized enough militia and volunteers from the eastern part of the state to disperse the mobs and crush the regulator movement. But the rebellion sent shock waves throughout the country. Congress resolved unanimously to raise over 1,300 men of its own in New England, and while it needed the pretense of Indian conflict, and the vast majority of the men were never enlisted, it was the only decisive act in military affairs by the Confederation since the war. The man most responsible was Secretary at War Henry Knox. Twice he travelled to his native state, observing the rebellion firsthand and conferring with Massachusetts officials about how to suppress it and protect the federal arsenal at Springfield. Mistakenly Knox concluded that the rioters were bent on complete political and social revolution and that attempts to overthrow established order would likely spread far beyond state, and even New England, borders. To nationalist friends Knox painted lurid pictures of anarchy and imminent civil war. The rebels' "creed," he informed George Washington, was that "the property of the United States, had been protected from . . . Britain by the joint exertions of *all*, and therefore ought to be the *common property* of all."[2] Rumors of all sorts—of British intervention, of concerted plots against all authority—swept the nation. Washington, usually unruffled, almost came unnerved. "If there exists not a power to check [the rebels]," he exclaimed to James Madison, "what security has a man for life, liberty, or property?"[3]

Like no other single event of the decade, Shays's Rebellion dramatized the military impotence of the United States. Suddenly, with an urgency lacking before, the need to suppress insurrection and to guarantee domestic order was injected into the debate over the military powers of the central government. The maintenance of order had been a delicate problem throughout the eighteenth century, when permanent law enforcement agencies did not exist and when mob action often fulfilled a legitimate function, sanctioned to some extent in political theory, to protect the community or to check excesses of the magistracy or to redress grievances when the normal legal or political process offered no other recourse. But beginning in the early 1780s, popular tumult and extralegal action appeared to be growing, and state governments seemed unwilling or unable either to head it off or check its excesses. Precisely for this purpose many Americans wanted a government capable of applying force. As the rebellion so spectacularly revealed, Congress possessed neither the authority to intervene, not even to protect federal property at the arsenal in Springfield, nor the machinery to use force independent of the states, which under the Articles of Confederation enlisted all soldiers for national service. "[H]ere is felt the imbecility, the futility, the nothingness of the federal powers," growled nationalist Edward Carrington, formerly quartermaster of the Southern Army and in 1786 a congressman from Virginia. "[T]he U.S. have no troops, nor dare they call into action, what is called the only safeguard of a free government, the Militia of the State, it being composed of the very objects of the force."[4]

On May 29, 1787, Edmund Randolph of Virginia opened the formal sessions of the Constitutional Convention with a "long and elaborate" speech on the state of government in America. The Confederation, he asserted, was incompetent for every military object its framers had intended: it provided no security against invasion; it could not prevent individuals or states from starting a war; nor could it adequately wage war itself. Without authority to send troops into a member state, Congress could not maintain internal order. Furthermore, without adequate financial resources, it could not support the regular military establishment that defense demanded, volunteers being undependable and militia, which were hard to collect in large bodies anyway, lacking the perseverance for long campaigns. Congress under the Articles could not force member states to furnish their requisitions, whether of money or of soldiers. "The journals of Congress a history of expedients," noted James McHenry tersely, describing Randolph's statements.[5] In the Virginia plan which Randolph then offered ("Not . . . a federal government— . . . a strong *consolidated* union," Abraham Yates observed), a two-house Congress would have broad but vaguely defined powers of legislation including the ability to create a national military establishment.[6] That same day, Charles Pinckney, a South Carolina planter and lawyer who had led the effort to revise the Articles in Congress in 1786, proposed a similar framework in which Congress's power to raise military forces was defined explicitly.[7]

In the wide-ranging discussions that followed, and in fact throughout the convention, nearly every delegate acknowledged that a primary function of government was defense against foreign and domestic enemies.

Most of the framers viewed force as a process fundamental to the very nature of government itself. "[N]o government could be energetic on paper only, which was no more than straw," argued William Paterson in presenting the small state plan of union; "there must be a small standing force to give every government weight."[8] Edmund Randolph had used that same word in his opening remarks, and in a pamphlet published later in 1787 he proclaimed openly that no government "which hangs on human inclination alone" could be "stable" without the means of "coercion."[9]

Some in the convention reacted uneasily to so crude a definition of the ultimate basis of governmental authority. William Pierce of Georgia was uncertain "whether any government can have sufficient energy to effect its own ends without the aid of a military power" and he sensed wavering in others also.[10] George Mason had no doubt whatsoever. "What, would you use military force to compel the observance of a social compact," asked the Virginia lawyer incredulously when he heard Paterson's statement. "[Y]ou can no more execute civil Regulations by Military Force than you can unite opposite Elements, than you can mingle Fire with Water."[11] Alexander Hamilton and James Madison agreed that compulsion could not provide the foundation for a confederated system. "Force," Hamilton said, "may be understood [as] *a coertion of laws or coertion of arms*."[12] Law did not restrain another sovereignty; any member state could defy central authority indefinitely, and if the government then resorted to military force, that state, with soldiers of its own, would likely resist, creating in Hamilton's words "war and carnage" as the "only means" of compelling obedience.[13] If the government were national, however, acting from, through, and on the people instead of member states, law and force could indeed compel obedience without tearing society apart. Instead of bringing on civil war between sovereign entities, defiance would constitute a confrontation between individuals and the government, and thus become riot or rebellion, difficult problems to be sure, but well within the capability of the penal system and the courts, marshalls, posse comitatus, militia, or at last regular forces. Force then became functional—and fundamental to the day-to-day operations of the state if only as a threat hovering in the background. All government was "founded in force," Charles Pinckney told the South Carolina ratifying convention. "[T]he dignity of a government could [not] be maintained, its safety insured, or its laws administered without a body of regular forces to aid the magistrate in the execution of his duty."[14]

The convention then proceeded to write into the Constitution almost exactly the authority necessary for the government not only to create the military institutions first proposed by the nationalists in 1783, but also to use those institutions against any foe, foreign or domestic. In early August the convention considered a draft Constitution from the committee of detail, which had worked the resolutions of the committee of the whole and various plans into a coherent document. Under this draft, Congress could "raise armies" and "build and equip fleets." The national government guaranteed each state a "Republican form of Government" (thus allowing intervention to crush the twin dangers of anarchy and monarchism), and protection "against . . . foreign invasion, and, on the application of its Legislature, against domestic violence." If necessary, militia could be mobilized under national auspices to "execute the laws of the Union, enforce treaties, suppress insurrections, and repel invasions." Command of the army and navy, with power to commission all officers, belonged to the executive, who by virtue of being Commander-in-Chief of the militia in addition, controlled all the military forces in the nattion.[15]

There never existed the slightest doubt among the vast majority that the new government must be able to create a national military establishment. To assure supremacy over the states, the central authority might need its own forces, and enough authority over the militia to prevent a state from evading or checkmating the national will. Almost universally the framers believed in the superiority of regulars over militia in warfare. Charles Pinckney and William Paterson spoke openly for a small standing army. Randolph had argued the point at the beginning. Washington and Hamilton had been committed to a national military since 1783. When the "raise armies" clause came under consideration in August, the convention decided immediately to change the wording to "raise and support" in order to make the authority for peacetime forces unmistakable.[16] Fully a third of the 55 delegates had participated in the wild debates over the constitutionality of a military establishment in the early 1780s, and wanted no more dispute over the issue. In one way or another, as soldiers (one-third as veterans of the Continental Army), as congressmen, or as state officials, all the framers had experienced the war and its problems directly. "Those, who, during the Revolutionary storm, had confidential acquaintance with the conduct of affairs," remembered Gouverneur Morris, who as chairman of the committee of style actually wrote the final version, "knew well that to rely on militia was to lean on a broken reed."[17]

The convention never seriously debated allowing Congress a permanent army. As he had before, Elbridge Gerry protested vociferously: "The people were jealous on this head," he declared, "and great opposition . . . would spring" from failing to "check . . . standing armies in time of peace."[18] Virtually unsupported, Gerry tried to introduce a 2,000 or 3,000 limit to peacetime troops. Charles Cotesworth Pinckney and Jonathan Dayton of New Jersey invoked the argument about preparing for war before actual hostilities; "Mr. [John] Langdon [New Hampshire] saw no room for Mr. Gerry's distrust of the Representatives of the people."[19] Then the subject was dropped without a vote. Again in September, when the committee of eleven, reporting changes accepted in the draft Con-

stitution, endorsed George Mason's proposal to limit all army appropriations to two years, Gerry repeated his objections. The two-year rule, like
the annual mutiny act in Britain, provided for ongoing, active agreement
by the legislative branch to the existence of an army so that forces could
not continue because of bureaucratic momentum or parliamentary
maneuvering. Gerry insisted on more substantial checks, either in the
form of numbers or duration, and for the forces, not just the funding.
Only a tiny handful of delegates ever expressed similar reservations, and
their suggestions consisted chiefly of rhetorical gestures against standing
armies, statements reaffirming civilian supremacy or prohibiting standing
armies unless by consent of the legislature, in order to appease public
prejudice and thereby enhance the Constitution's popularity. Even then
the rest of the convention overrode all negative provisos, afraid that any
such statement would harm the exercise of the power by making Congress appear to violate the spirit of its own charter.[20] The Founding
Fathers were determined to provide for national security even if they
viewed armies as dangerous or jeopardized the chances for ratification by
the people. "[I]f they [armies] be necessary," Madison stated flatly, "the
calamity must be submitted to."[21]

Nationalists had achieved their most important military aim—
empowering the government to create a national army—with spectacular
ease. The reasons were many: the nationalist cast in the membership of
the convention; Shays's Rebellion and the belief in force to back up
government; the belief in regulars over militia; the need for effective
protection on the frontier; the acceptance of preparedness philosophy in
defense policy; and the clear necessity to give the government incontrovertible authority—absent in the Articles—to maintain a military establishment if conditions demanded. But on the second part of the nationalist military program, reforming the militia, the convention balked.
Nationalists had stressed the need for reform repeatedly in 1783, then
again in 1786 when Henry Knox published an extensive scheme for
reorganization. Reform had never gotten off the ground because the
Confederation possessed absolutely no authority over what had always
been exclusively state institutions. Nationalists planned to use the convention specifically to remove that stumbling block.[22] On August 18, in
an uncharacteristically nationalist move, Virginian George Mason
moved to allow Congress "to regulate the militia," a power included
earlier in the plans of Hamilton, Charles Pinckney, and the committee of
detail. Mason "hoped there would be no standing army . . . , unless it
might be for a few garrisons. The Militia ought therefore to be the more
effectually prepared for the public defence. Thirteen States will never
concur in any one system."[23] Almost unanimously, the delegates
accepted the need for strengthening the militia as a military force, for
imposing uniformity and tighter discipline. But total national control
struck many as politically and constitutionally dangerous. "[S]ubmitting

the militia to the Gen[era]l Government . . . might be necessary," agreed Oliver Ellsworth of Connecticut, but the states "would pine away to nothing after such a sacrifice of power;" it would be "vain" to expect them to give it up. Ellsworth preferred wording which enabled Congress to establish uniformity of "arms" and "exercise," but which left actual control, in normal times, in the hands of the states.[24] Convinced by the argument, Mason withdrew his motion in favor of one restricting congressional power to a select corps of militia, "one tenth part in any one year."[25] Extreme nationalists like Charles Cotesworth Pinckney and Madison objected. Even Ellsworth ridiculed the idea because it would lead to the neglect and eventual collapse of the other nine-tenths. The debate was heated and the deadlock obvious. Control of the militia touched the most fundamental issue before the convention: the division of power between states and central government. Disarming the states made Elbridge Gerry tremble. "[T]his [was] the last point remaining to be surrendered," he cried. "If it be agreed to . . . , the plan will have as black a mark as was set on Cain."[26]

Dividing authority over the militia, and leaving the states concurrent power similar to allowing the states concurrent taxing power, quickly appeared as the logical compromise. Mason and others grasped at the alternative in spite of John Langdon's apocryphal warning, borne out for the next century in congressional struggles to implement the provision with legislation, about confusing "distinct authorities" on the subject.[27] With tempers boiling the convention sent the problem to a committee of eleven for rewording. On August 21 the committee recommended a clause allowing Congress "[t]o make laws for organizing, arming, and disciplining the militia, and for governing such part of them as may be employed in the service of the United States, reserving to the States . . . the appointment of the Officers, and . . . training . . . according to the discipline prescribed" by the central government.[28] Again a bitter fight erupted over the extent of national control. "To make laws for organizing, arming, and disciplining" granted too much power for Ellsworth, Jonathan Dayton, Roger Sherman, and antinationalists Gerry and Luther Martin (Maryland). Rufus King tried to allay their fears by offering the committee's definitions: "organizing" meant specifying the size and composition of the units and proportioning the officers and men; "arming" meant specifying the type, size, and caliber of weapons; and "disciplining" was "prescribing the manual[,] exercise[,] evolutions[,] etc."[29] Gerry saw through such a narrow interpretation of the wording immediately. "[A] system of Despotism," he charged, "making the States drill-sergeants."[30] Yet Gerry and the other opponents could not devise a substitute motion that could satisfy either ardent nationalists, who demanded uniformity and reform, or southerners who wished their militias strengthened for future use on their open frontiers. The provision reported out by the committee of eleven passed with dissenting votes from Connecticut and Maryland only. At that point, Madison tried to restrict the states to the appointment of officers below the rank of general. "[A]bsolutely inadmissable," snapped Roger Sherman.[31] Added Gerry, mixing anger with sarcasm: "Let us at once destroy the State Gov[ernmen]ts[,] have an Executive for life or hereditary, and a proper Senate, and then there would be some consistency in giving full powers to the Gen[era]l Gov[ernmen]t."[32] The convention rejected Madison's resolution, heeding Gerry's warning "ag[ain]st pushing the experiment too far."[33] But Madison's effort indicated how strongly nationalists wanted control of the militia shifted to the central government.

Although the militia power ended up vague and to a great extent contradictory, it could not detract from the near total nationalist victory. The final version of the Constitution reported by the committee of style in September 1787 gave the new government sharp military teeth. Congress could establish any national military institutions it saw fit, provide rules for their governance, and "exercise exclusive legislation" over land for forts, arsenals, dockyards, and other "needful buildings." It could impose uniformity and national standards on the militia. Under several provisions the government could use troops, including militia, to enforce its will or to crush violence and rebellion. Congress was responsible for declaring war, but the President, who as Commander-in-Chief of the army, the navy, and the militia when in national service, was to wage war, to conduct all military operations in any way he desired.[34] Clearly the new government was empowered to establish, and to use, a standing army. The framers wanted a government able both to protect the nation from foreign countries and to protect a minority from popular despotism, from the majority, and from the licentiousness of the people. They rejected that basic tenet of English radical thought which separated the rulers and the ruled, power and liberty, into naturally warring camps. Most of them believed that popular prejudice, the existence of militia, and the nation's geographic separation from Europe made the classic standing army unnecessary. But the government must be able to keep up regular troops; the only other alternative was to rely exclusively on militia. Since the people and the government were one and the same, investing it with this power preserved, rather than threatened, liberty.

Certainly risks were involved; armies still represented the ultimate in power. They grew large and their influence bloated, mostly in wartime; therefore the decision to enter into war was given to the legislature, the power to conduct it to the executive. Both would have to agree before an army awakened from its peacetime somnolence to become a potent influence on society. The Constitution also prevented any use of the army for internal subversion. Since the President commanded it, his use of the military to overthrow the government would constitute a coup against himself. Should he lose control of the army or threaten the people or the other branches, those branches, especially Congress, could hamstring the army through the appropriation power, the power to confirm appointments, or by legislation to disband the troops. Theoretically there was—and is—no way the military can take over the government without destroying the ability of that government to function. The government cannot be taken over, only replaced, and all legitimate instruments of authority rendered inoperative. As long as the Constitution exists, and is accepted, and any of the institutions through which it works—Congress, the courts, and the executive—function normally, no army can take over the United States.

It was just such an absence of normal conditions that worried Elbridge Gerry and the Antifederalists after the convention. Once an army came into existence, it might attempt to displace the government, or end up terrorizing the people in some unsuccessful adventure, throwing the nation into chaos and setting in motion the processes which led to tyranny. Acting in concert, the branches of the government might use the army to abrogate the Constitution or otherwise alter the system. And what if conditions changed, if a huge military establishment became necessary, if the people lost their vigilance, could not the military infiltrate the process by which public policy was made, or, as almost happened at Newburgh, openly negotiate its willingness to protect the nation? For these and other questions, neither the Constitution nor its authors provided adequate answers.

Almost from the moment the Constitution was published in October 1787, it provoked a storm of controversy. For ten months, in newspapers, pamphlets, private letters, and in public speeches from pulpits and before state ratifying conventions, the new frame of government was subjected to intense analysis and scathing criticism. To Antifederalists, the old antinationalists, the proponents of state sovereignty, those concerned about individual freedom and frightened by the new plan of union—the Constitution allowed, even encouraged, standing armies in peacetime, a symbol of the dangerous powers the new government would possess. Shortened to a single emotional phrase, easily italicized for public use, "standing army" called to mind a perfect set of images with which to smear the Constitution and inflame popular passion. Armies were "dangerous," "the nursery of vice," "engines of despotism," the "grand machine of power," the "grand engine of oppression," and "*restringent* to the *rights* and *liberties* of mankind." Because of their "pernicious influence" ("vice and dissipation" included), "seven-eighths of the once free nations of the globe" had fallen into "bondage." Standing armies were the "bane of freedom," the "rock on which" American "liberties would suffer shipwreck"; eventually they would "subvert the forms of the government, under whose authority, they [were] raised."[35] In the army provision,

Antifederalists saw the worst of Federalist motives revealed. Federalists were "avowedly in favour of standing armies," asserted Robert Yates. "It is a language common to them, that no people can be kept in order unless the government have an army to awe them into obedience."[36]

Antifederalists rarely gave the army provision any extended analysis ("laboured argument" was "useless" to prove an "axiom").[37] Instead, they cited almost in shorthand the same evidence used for a century to show the threat of the standing army: historical examples (Caesar and Cromwell were favorites); political theorists ("Even Mr. Hume, an *aristocratical* Writer, candidly confessed, that *an army is a moral distemper in a government*"); and of course the prerevolutionary tradition—"the fatal evening of the 5th of March, 1770" as "sufficient warning."[38] Yet in spite of the rhetoric, many had profound doubts about the Constitution, and the standing army issue became part of a greater suspicion that such a government would lead to aristocracy, monarchy, or tyranny. Benjamin Gale of Connecticut, one of the few men in America to deduce the inner workings of the Newburgh plot, viewed the entire Constitution as the culmination of a conspiracy, first hatched in 1783, to insure commutation for army officers and to enrich financial manipulators.[39] One of Thomas Jefferson's few doubts in an otherwise favorable reaction was the lack of sufficient checks against permanent forces.[40]

Not only might an army overthrow the government, but the government itself might turn despotic and use its irresistible military power. Patrick Henry repeatedly honed in on the army: troops would "execute the execrable commands of tyranny," he told the Virginia ratifying convention, "and how are you to punish them? Will you order them to be punished? Who shall obey these orders? Will your mace-bearer be a match for a disciplined regiment?"[41] Antifederalists believed that republican government was impossible in a nation as large as the United States. With a central government so distant, so removed from the population, its interests, or any notion of preserving liberty, only soldiers could enforce the government's will.[42] Antifederalists depicted lurid scenes of tax collectors making rounds with soldiers, "the purgings of European prisons," "low ruffians bred among ourselves who do not love to work."[43] Henry even raised the specter of an army of slaves lording over Virginia planters and yeomen. Antifederalists scorned the two-year appropriations check universally. In England, appropriations ran for one year; no restraint pertained to executive control over the force. "If your American chief be a man of ambition and abilities," warned Henry, "how easy is it for him to render himself absolute! The army is in his hands, and if he be a man of address, it will be attached to him, and it will be the subject of long meditation with him to seize the first auspicious moment to accomplish his design."[44]

Fearing power and believing its abuse certain, Antifederalists argued persistently that national security could be safely entrusted to militia.

"Was it a standing army that gained the battles of Lexington and Bunker's Hill, and took the ill fated Burgoyne," asked one. "Is not a well regulated *militia* sufficient for every purpose of internal defence?"[45] Militia posed none of the grasping dangers of regulars; as Richard Henry Lee put it, "A militia, when properly formed, are in fact the people themselves."[46] Yet at the same time Antifederalists attacked the militia sections of the Constitution vehemently. Most of them saw no valid need for national control. Uniformity might in fact ruin the militia, weakening frontier units designed for Indian fighting, southern forces used for slave patrol, or northern units organized to repel seaborne invasion by European armies. Despite Madison's repeated denials, Patrick Henry argued in the Virginia convention that this provision robbed the states of security rather than protecting them. When its forces were in national service, a state would be left naked against insurrection or some other threat. Concurrent power was impossible. "The militia . . . is our ultimate safety," declared Henry. "We can have no security without it."[47]

Furthermore Antifederalists interpreted the militia provision as an attack on state power, an attempt to undercut the states by lodging the basis of sovereignty, the purse and the sword, in the national government. Ultimately national control of the militias posed a serious threat to liberty. "[U]nder colour of regulating," reasoned George Mason, Congress could destroy the militia, "the more easily to govern by a standing Army; or they may harrass the Militia, by such rigid Regulations and intollerable Burdens, as to make the People themselves desire its Abolition."[48] Since virtually every male served, the government might attack the citizenry under the guise of militia command: by levying excessive fines for malfeasance, by using martial law to punish dissent, or by redefining military obligation to discriminate against specific classes or groups. Pennsylvanians worried specifically about threats to religious liberty: Congress might, in defining conscientious objection, deny Quakers exemption from military service. The government might harass the people by marching them all over the union. All these fears stemmed directly from a common theme in Antifederalist thought, in Mason's words, "the natural propensity of rulers to oppress the people."[49] The Constitution might guarantee national security, but at a prohibitive cost to the very liberty it was meant to defend. Patrick Henry, despite frequent oratorical excesses, spoke for many: "It is a government of force, and the genius of despotism expressly."[50]

Painstakingly, patiently, categorically, Federalists denied all such accusations and fears. Never, although they used every conceivable defense of the military provisions in the Constitution, did Federalists ever endorse the classic standing army. Such institutions were "dangerous,"

they agreed, possibly "fatal," "the scourge of the old world," "an object of laudable circumspection and precaution."[51] However Antifederalists were poisoning the atmosphere with "improbabilities and absurdities," "mere insinuations unsupported by reasoning or fact," and indeed had raised such a "senseless clamor," a "sublimity of *nonsense* and *alarm*" in "every shape of *metaphoric terror*," that the army clause had "become a political bugbear."[52] Privately, of course, Federalists were not surprised. When the convention disbanded, Gerry had refused to sign the Constitution because, among other things, the new Congress could "raise armies and money without limit."[53] Edmund Randolph and George Mason had also withheld their signatures, and after their return to Virginia, Washington warned several friends that their "reasons will be clothed in [the] most terrific array for the purpose of alarming; some things are already addressed to the fears of the people and will no doubt have their effect."[54]

The major Federalist defense of the army power consisted of Hamilton's preparedness argument first advanced in 1783: the nation must be ready to fight in peacetime, first as a deterrent, then so that security would not be compromised by waiting until the actual outbreak of hostilities to raise an army, prepare supplies, and build defenses. Without forces on foot, an invading foe might penetrate into the bowels of the country before opposition could form. Shays's Rebellion also illustrated the consequences of unpreparedness; had troops been available, the rebellion might have been stamped out before the disorder spread or before bloodshed became a possibility. Federalists believed that requisitions on the states, the old system, had never worked effectively even when British troops were on American soil. They wanted the defense of the nation lodged in the central government to prevent, they said, 13 authorities from squabbling over strategy and leadership. Only this government could provide unified, economical direction, muster the resources, and orchestrate the effort required in war. "That a power to raise and equip troops at pleasure, may be abused, is certain," admitted one Federalist, "but that the public safety cannot be established without that power, is equally certain."[55]

Federalists always maintained that the power of the sword, along with that of the purse, was inherent in government. "All governments have possessed these powers," Hamilton told the New York convention. "[T]hey would be monsters without them, and incapable of exertion."[56] "The new government consists much less in the addition of NEW POWERS to the Union, than in the invigoration of its ORIGINAL POWERS"; according to Federalists, the Confederation had always possessed the power to raise armies, Harmar's regiment being "just as much a standing army as seventy thousand."[57] The Constitution safeguarded abuse by giving the President a veto and command of the military, and by requiring agreement between the Senate and the House of Representatives for the existence of an army. The two-year appropriation limitation, straightforward and inescapable, was far superior to the unwritten rules by which Parliament controlled its forces. Every legislature in America, Federalists pointed out, could raise and support armies, the limitations in state constitutions being either meaningless stipulations of civil supremacy or provisions against standing armies without legislative consent. In any case, the safest restraint by far was popular control over the government through elections. The authority to create military institutions emanated from the people themselves. Without the bond of trust and coincidence of interest between rulers and ruled, all government inevitably degenerated into tyranny. Politicians dared not adopt policies that endangered the citizenry or the government, or perilled their own re-election. Besides, Federalists contended, Congress would find large bodies of troops unnecessary. The militia would bear the burden of overall security since the possibility of sudden invasion on a grand scale was precluded by America's distance from Europe.[58]

In a clever twist of logic, Federalists maintained that the very danger of standing armies made national power over the militia necessary. Reform would make forces stronger, and if conditions came to the extremity, allow the people to resist any attempt at oppression with standing forces. Madison insisted that government must possess military power to keep order, and using militia to suppress rebellion would entail less abuse than the use of regulars. Most important, Federalists justified national control with the need for uniform arms, training, and organization. The state militias were useless in their present form, argued Federalists. Henry Lee mentioned the battle at Guilford Court House in North Carolina in 1780 to prove the point. "What did the militia do," he asked the Virginia convention. "The greatest number of them fled."[59] Again Federalists pointed out the safeguard inherent in the trust between rulers and ruled. Any Congress so stupid as to badger the population with unwarranted marches, fines, or punishments would surely be thrown out of office. Congressional authority, despite Antifederalist claims to the contrary, extended only when militia were called up into federal service. The states retained general control for their own security, and the population would be subjected to martial law only on those rare occasions when the militia were called out.[60]

The extent to which these arguments affected the ratification of the Constitution can never be known. The frequency of Antifederalist objections and the labored Federalist refutations indicated, however, not only the public apprehension about standing armies and attempts to change the status of the militia, but also the importance both sides attached to the issues. Nearly every state's ratifying convention proposed amendments to the Constitution that either warned against standing armies, limited Congress's power to raise forces, or banned quartering of regulars in private homes. Several conventions suggested restrictions on calling up the militia, marching it out of state, or subjecting militiamen to martial law in peacetime. Many wanted explicit guarantees that the states retained their authority over these forces.[61] The Bill of Rights, passed two years later, ended up including a prohibition on Congress from destroying the militia by disarming the population, and restricted the quartering of regulars in private homes. As heirs to the seventeenth-century English anti-army ideology, and their own conflicts with the British Army in America, the framers too understood the abuse of military power. But the entire military debate was so submerged in the larger struggle over accepting or rejecting the Constitution that most issues of national security were distorted beyond recognition.

Yet behind all the rhetoric lay a single, fundamental question: what role military forces could play in a republic, whether a republic could survive the threat inherent in a permanent military establishment. Paradoxically, Americans were at the same time unsure whether the nation could remain secure without such an establishment. What emerged in the 1780s were two different solutions to the dilemma, the broad and sometimes inchoate outlines of two clashing theories of national security that would divide military planners and color discussions of military policy until the advent of modern war. Significantly, in the struggle over the Constitution, these two opposing positions gained their first widespread public airing, and unfortunately became attached to emerging political factions.

Federalist theory, rooted deeply in the Continental Army experience and nationalist political philosophy, was already clearly developed by 1788: first, preparedness—maintain a basic working capacity in peacetime; second, centralize and to whatever extent possible, professionalize all defense policy and preparations. For expansion into the West, as a nucleus for a wartime regular army, and as a model for the militia, keep on foot a small regular army. Support that army and the nation's warmaking capacity with a military academy, stores of supplies, and facilities for manufacturing munitions. In order to provide the manpower and forces needed in wartime (and because the country might balk at a regular army), beef up the militia by bringing it under the national government. Security also implied internal order and safety from rebellion; the national army and restructured militia would suffice, if, of course, machinery existed for the national government to use these forces at the appropriate time.

No clear alternative policies were ever articulated in the 1780s, mostly because the nationalist opposition, in Congress and even in the battle over the Constitution, never coalesced as a unified group able to advance a coherent position on military issues. Even in the 1790s, the Republican party, in part because it never captured the executive and thus the responsiblity for meeting military crises, failed to define lucid alternatives. But hidden in Antifederalist speeches and writings lay the kernel of a theory which placed the entire burden of national defense on militia. Chiefly for political reasons, the nation must trust defense to citizen-soldiers, not regulars. Basically secure in the Western Hemisphere and isolated from the European state system of alliance and conflict, America need not waste its resources or endanger its liberties. The people were armed and organized militarily, and while tiny garrisons might be necessary on a fulltime basis, perhaps even a storehouse or two for extra arms, any threat, even on the frontier, could be met by overwhelming numbers of embattled citizens organized locally or regionally, acting in their own defense. If a major conflict erupted, as it had in 1775, time enough then, with wide ocean barriers, to create the necessary institutions and settle on the leadership. As for domestic tranquility, Antifederalists implied that any government dependent on the military to enforce its will was despotic and would not endure. The states as then constituted could maintain order through the legal process or through their militias.

For the next 12 years, both positions would continue to evolve, to be modified to fit each military crisis, and to be wedded ever more closely to the party conflict. One Antifederalist accusation would also continue (and survive in historical writing to the present): the framers of the Constitution were militarists, that is, men who wished to engraft onto the United States in peacetime the classical standing army, and to base government on the use of force.* Admittedly they drew up a Constitution that was in one sense unprecedented. Unlike the state constitutions and the Declaration of Independence, the Constitution contained no condemnation of standing armies or outright stipulation about the supremacy of civilian authority over the military. Unlike the Articles of Confederation, which maintained a studied, ambiguous silence, the Constitution invited the creation of regular peacetime forces. And yet the authors of the Constitution (which they had spent four arduous months in 1787 fabricating) most assuredly did not wish to create a monster capable of consuming the very government it was designed to protect. Some of them believed "a small standing army," as William Paterson put it, inevitable, and that ultimately government rested on coercion. To

---

*"Militarism" is a term that defies accurate definitions; most historical literature discusses it in the German context, but provides no hard-and-fast definition. Two good general works are Alfred Vagts, A *History of Militarism: Civilian and Military* (rev. ed., London, 1959), and Gerhard Ritter, *The Sword and the Scepter: The Problem of Militarism in Germany* (Coral Gables, Fla., 1964), trans. Heinz Norden, volume I. Vagts (p. 41) calls the "standing army in peacetime" the "greatest of all militaristic institutions," and I have used support for the classical standing army in peacetime as my benchmark for judging Federalist militarism. Certainly that was the definition used by contemporaries on both sides in late eighteenth-century America. Obviously in the twentieth century the definition would have to be much broader. Also see my discussion in Chapter 14 below.

James Madison, a weak government meant disunion, the Balkanization of America, and standing armies in the states. Almost to a man they believed in regulars and distrusted militia. They understood that the nation would not accept a large peacetime military establishment (and many thought it unneeded). They knew the militia could not be abolished or totally jettisoned in any crisis, although some doubted that it could ever be effectively reconstituted. Years later Gouverneur Morris claimed that the framers purposely destroyed the militia so that the nation would not rely "on that weak and inefficient force," and to protect the nation in the absence of a politically unacceptable national army, they expected a navy to be created.[62] Yet no one will ever be certain about the framers' intent because few men in America, no matter what their private, innermost thoughts on the subject, dared advocate a permanent, exclusive reliance on a standing army for defense. The riddles, the confusions of their own private and political motives, their disagreements over the requirements of security, the certain need to create a frame of government capable of being ratified, all make any definitive statement impossible.

The overriding barrier, to the framers and to nearly every American who thought about the problem at the time, was an inability to define clearly what "standing army" meant. Like the leaders of the Continental Army in 1783, the framers were groping for an institutional alternative to the classic standing army of European history, officer aristocrats and an alienated, disenfranchised, lower-class rank and file, on the one hand, and the militia on the other. The framers' solution was a small national establishment backed by a standardized, federalized militia (almost an army reserve). Because it lay beyond their experience and their understanding, they could not distinguish between a fulltime professional army and the traditional standing army. In their uncertainty, a few of the more thoughtful were moving toward an understanding of the difference, although none could spell it out clearly. Of all the men writing in this era, only "Baron" Steuben, a Prussian professional, a transatlantic figure who could reflect comparatively on the nature of military institutions and their social foundations from personal experience, realized that the classic standing army was probably impossible in the America of the late eighteenth century. All armies, he wrote, mirrored "the local situation of the country, the spirit of government, the character of the nation, and in many instances the Character of the Prince." Steuben advocated a small, highly disciplined corps of long-service professionals, and he even called it a standing army. But this army would be "composed of your brothers and your sons," he said. "Shall it be supposed [that] a cockade and feather, the *Vox et pretera nihil* [the voice and beyond that nothing], of the military character can alienate either their affections or their interest?"[63] The answer, obviously, was no.

PART TWO

★ ☆ ★ ☆ ★ ☆ ★ ☆ ★

Reign of the Federalists: Dilemmas of Power [1789-1797]

★

*in which
the Federalists, through control of the
Executive branch and the Congress, use
a series of military crises to create a
national military establishment, but in
the process furnish perfect popular issues
to the emerging opposition party, and
thereby sow the seeds for their own
downfall.*

★ ☆ ★ ☆ ★ ☆ ★ ☆ ★

6

★ ☆ ★ ☆ ★ ☆ ★ ☆ ★

Indian War:
Birth of the Legion
[1789-1792]

★

[Judge John Cleves] Symmes showed [the Indian chiefs] the coat-of-arms of the United States, which he carefully explained. "Well," said a Shawano captain, "let me give *my* interpretation. . . . If the United States were such lovers of peace as you describe them to be, they would have chosen . . . something more appropriate as an expression of it. There are, for instance, many agreeable and harmless birds. There is the dove, which would not harm the smallest creature—But what is the eagle? He is the largest of all birds! He is the enemy of all birds! He is proud, because he is conscious of his size and strength! On a tree, as well as in flight, he shows his pride, and looks down in scorn upon all the birds. His head, his eyes, his beak and his long crooked talons declare his strength and hostility. . . . You have not only put one of the instruments of war, a bundle of arrows, into one of his hands (claws), and rods in the other, but have painted him in the most fearful guise, . . . in posture of attack upon his prey."

Rev. John Heckewelder, a conversation near Cincinnati, 1789.[a]

Early afternoon, April 30, 1789: some clouds, but generally sunshine slanting down onto the half-enclosed portico of Federal Hall, overlooking Wall and Broad Streets, New York City, and onto the huge crowd—citizens, militia, dignitaries. George Washington rose from a chair, placed his right hand on a Bible, swore to preserve, protect, and defend the Constitution, and became the first President of the United States. The crowd's mood was optimistic, and at the inauguration almost reverential, but the country faced a variety of problems—in foreign relations, finance, economic affairs, and certainly on the frontier. The new Senate and House of Representatives had already begun the serious business of discussing institutions and policies to set the government in motion. But the situation was novel, totally without precedent or tradition. The nation was waiting expectantly to learn what tone and direction the new government would take. Seemingly the President had a free hand, but as he was soon to learn, with the Indians in the Northwest Territory the fledgling government was rapidly losing its freedom of action.[1]

Barely visible to the crowd during the ceremony on the portico stood the two officials most directly responsible for affairs in the West, Henry Knox and Arthur St. Clair. Scotch-born, St. Clair was 53 years old in 1789, a fleshy, pompous, experienced politician and soldier. In his twenties as a junior officer in the British Army, he had married a wealthy Boston girl and then migrated to western Pennsylvania, where he became prominent in politics, military affairs, and local society. During the war, after service with Washington at Trenton and Princeton, St. Clair rose to major general in the Continental Army. He was never an outstanding leader; in 1778 he was court martialed and exonerated for the loss of Fort Ticonderoga, supposedly an impregnable fortress. Afterwards he returned to Pennsylvania politics, entered Congress, gained election as President, and in 1787 became the first Governor of the Northwest Territory. In 1789 St. Clair had just returned from the Ohio region with two new Indian treaties. Ominously, however, the Governor had been directed a few months earlier by Secretary Knox that should "an Indian War . . . be inevitable," "many reasons would concur to render your presence necessary at the Seat of Government."[2] In truth both men knew the two treaties were worthless.

Almost imperceptibly, from 1786 onward, Indian relations along the entire northern length of the Ohio River watershed had worsened. The tribes on the Wabash River (present-day northern and western Indiana) and the Indians inhabiting the Maumee River Valley (northwestern Ohio) had never agreed to peace with the United States.[3]* Nor had the

---

*The tribes arrayed against the United States in the late 1780s and early 1790s were principally small groups along the Wabash River and its tributaries (the Wea, Kickapoo, Potawatomi, and Piankashaw), the Miami in present-day northern Indiana and northwestern Ohio, and the small tribes and fragments of tribes driven out of the Ohio Valley in the late 1770s and 1780s into the Maumee and Sandusky River areas (the Wyandot, Shawnee, Mingo, and Delaware). The Ottawa and Chippewa in present-day southern Michigan also participated, as did individuals from still other tribes. Pinpointing the location, size, and participation of the individual tribes is extremely difficult since they moved during this period, hunted and camped over sizable areas, and their population changed. A crude estimate (reports vary widely) of the number of warriors at any one time fighting the whites would be about 1,500, although at peak fighting strength, with all tribes united, they might have been able to field 2,000 to 2,500 warriors. According to contemporary estimates, about 4,200 whites lived within the boundaries of the entire Northwest Territory in 1790, with another 1,820 on the Spanish side of the Mississippi River above its confluence with the Ohio River. Kentucky contained 61,133 whites. See the maps on pages 66 and 105. Sources for these figures and for the maps are in note 3 of this chapter.

treaties signed by the Confederation in 1784, 1785, and 1786 with the arc of tribes extending from western New York into central Ohio satisfied the Indians. Watching unhappily as settlers flooded down the Ohio River, the tribes reacted angrily to American claims of territorial sovereignty by virtue of the "right of conquest" principle, stemming from victory over the Indians' ally, Great Britain. At Mohawk leader Joseph Brant's urging, and under British aegis, the Indians established a loose, volatile confederacy. Late in 1786 they asked Congress for another treaty session to settle on a boundary between whites and Indians, and to deal with the question of land ownership.[4]

Meanwhile the warfare—still isolated, still spasmodic—grew slowly more intense. Increasingly the government and settlers argued over which tribes were involved, and whether whites or Indians were responsible for the fighting. Westerners continually pressed their state governments and Congress for help, but they sensed reluctance, even hostility to their pleas. Easterners in fact blamed much of the conflict on the whites, who engulfed Indian land, who murdered and tortured as savagely as their foe, and who in spite of treaties assaulted Indian villages, often indiscriminately. (An expedition from Kentucky in 1786 commanded by Benjamin Logan wiped out several Shawnee towns and turned that tribe into an inveterate enemy.) On their part westerners viewed governmental authorities as "eastern," as uninterested in or biased against frontier needs. The federal army appeared too weak and too scattered to afford protection; militia laws usually prevented offensives unless authorized by state executives. And westerners believed in taking the offensive. It was a "Notorious truth," declared George Rogers Clark, that "fear would cause [Indians] to be peaceable when presents Make them believe we Are Afraid of them, . . . an Incouragement for them to Make War."[5] Guarding white settlements, either with horse rangers traversing assigned areas or with scouts concealed along the common avenues of approach, was ineffectual; only large expeditions to destroy Indian villages, and the establishment of a fort in the heart of Indian territory, could provide enduring safety. To the settlers treaties also were useless, especially the bungling attempts of the Confederation ("galling and Tyrannical" to the Indians, according to Harry Innes), negotiated by outsiders or prejudiced westerners like Richard Butler.[6] In sum, western settlers boiled with resentment, denied the protection they believed they were owed as American citizens.

Out of this different perception and interest there grew two basic views of how to deal with the Indians: one military; the other diplomatic. In 1783, when asked for recommendations that eventually became the basis of Confederation policy in the 1780s, George Washington unhesitatingly endorsed negotiations. Agree mutually on a boundary with the tribes, he reasoned, to separate settlers and Indians (Washington viewed the whites and Indians as equally guilty in causing friction). Treat generously, fairly, and in good faith, taking care not "to yield nor to grasp at too much." At all costs avoid war. It was "like driving the Wild Beasts of the forest which will return [as] soon as the pursuit is at an end," Washington warned. "In a word there is nothing to be obtained by an Indian War but the soil they live on and this can be had by purchase at less expense."[7] The Confederation followed the general's advice throughout the decade. In 1787, fearing the cost and the oppobrium of a bloodletting, unsure that whites would be justified in using force or that anything short of a truly genocidal war would bring peace, Congress authorized Governor St. Clair to hold the new talks requested by the Indians. But pessimism about the results and pressure from land speculators not to concede the north bank of the Ohio pushed Congress into forbidding St. Clair to alter either the terms or the boundary lines of previous treaties. And one instruction to the Governor belied all intentions of a negotiated settlement: "defeat all confederacies and combinations among the tribes."[8]

For over a year, St. Clair tried to gather the tribes together, all the while growing more pessimistic about the benefit of a treaty. In St. Clair's mind, eastern and western prejudices merged. At first, distrusting frontiersmen as "generally the agressors," he wanted his instructions modified to allow necessary concessions to the Indians.[9] But in the course of a year on the Ohio, observing conditions, exposed to the white viewpoint, subjected to firsthand reports of murder and pillage, he changed. In 1788 the army itself began regularly to suffer casualties. To St. Clair, the Wabash and Maumee tribes, under baneful British influence, aware of the relentless expansion of white settlement, and far removed from white power, would never treat. From midsummer to early winter, as information about Indian intentions streamed in, St. Clair hardened in his view that war was inevitable. More and more the instruction to sow confusion and discord amongst the tribes became paramount. On the eve of the conference, having already discussed military strategy with Knox, the Governor went so far as to order the Pennsylvania and Virginia militia readied for action in the belief that so many warriors gathered together might attack immediately if the talks failed.[10] In December 1788 the conference began, without Joseph Brant or representatives from the Wabash, Maumee, or Shawnee tribes. "Idle business," snorted Lieutenant Ebenezer Denny. "One half will . . . sign articles and receive presents, while the others are killing, scalping, and doing us every possible damage."[11] In truth the frontier was in harness for war, the army champing at the bit, and the official most responsible, Henry Knox, was viewing the negotiations as a device to isolate the Wabash and Miami tribes for attack, without provoking a general Indian war or inflaming American public opinion. "I am persuaded everything will be done on your part that can be with propriety to avoid a war," Knox told St. Clair, "and if that event should be inevitable, that the evils of it may be justly charged to the Indians."[12] It was not surprising that St. Clair negotiated with belligerence and arrogance, that the two treaties merely reaffirmed earlier agreements, and that the process confirmed Indian suspicion that the United States planned their extermination and the seizure of their lands. St. Clair did divide the tribes; at his urging, the Wyandot chiefs did agree to inform the Wabash tribes of the government's peaceful intentions and its demand that the raiding cease. But the prospects for peace were bleak. St. Clair reported the unvarnished facts to the President a few days after the inauguration.[13]

In later years, after the Washington administration's western policy had gone sour, it would be charged in the shrill language of the party struggle that the administration purposely sought an Indian war in order to encumber the government with debts and to introduce a standing army.[14] Nothing could be further from the truth. George Washington believed firmly in negotiating peace with Indians. His overriding interest, and that of the government, in the early 1790s was to avoid war. The British, helping the Indians with supplies and advice, held the most strategic posts which lay astride the Great Lakes supply route, making any American expedition into western Ohio dependent on the difficult and circuitous Ohio River for communication and transportation. And yet the administration slid inexorably into a war, against its will, unknowingly, unwittingly, all the time groping for peace and believing its policies were achieving it. In the end, of course, once confronted with reality, the administration demanded a large regular army. Federalists throughout the 1790s responded to military crises with orthodox Federalist military ideas: regulars instead of militia, national direction of all defense, and preparedness. In fact Federalists used every crisis expressly to implement the 1783 plans for a national military establishment. But in 1789 all that lay in the future. The crisis with the Indians was unwanted. How the Washington administration came to violate the President's own strictures on Indian relations, stated a half decade before, provides a case study in how America has often gone to war.

Avoiding War: Harmar's Campaign [1789–1790]

The proposed expedition is intended to exhibit to the Wabash Indians our power to punish them for their positive depredations, for their conniving at the depredations of others, and for their refusing to treat with the United States when invited thereto.

Secretary of War Knox, 1790.[b]

As he sat down to analyze the situation for the President in mid-June 1789, Henry Knox guessed that only a few tribes were causing the trouble, probably the Wabash group that had refused to treat with St. Clair. But if the warfare continued, especially raids by Kentuckians across the Ohio, even tribes nominally at peace would soon be hostile. The government had two choices: "raising an army, and extirpating the refractory tribes entirely"; or signing new treaties again, acknowledging as "prior occupants" the Indians' "right of the soil" to all lands not purchased by the government. An army would have to number 2,500 men at least, at a cost for a six-month campaign of $200,000, "a sum far exceeding the ability of the United States to advance, consistently with a due regard to other indispensable objects." But more important, given the "present confused state of injuries," the United States would appear the aggressor, a great and powerful civilization attacking restless, "ignorant" savages without visible provocation. Such a course of action, Knox argued, would "stain the character of the nation" at the outset of the new government. On the other hand, for about $16,000 in expenses, bribes, and presents, every tribe north of the Ohio River could be kept at peace. "[C]oercion and oppression," Knox complained, "would be beyond all pecuniary calculation."[15]

Knox's advice made good sense. An infant government, unorganized, without coherent administrative apparatus or sources of revenue, striving for the approval of its citizens, could not afford a war. Its army, which had never been organized for an offensive, remained weak, underequipped, and scattered over hundreds of miles of wilderness. As for munitions, Knox knew that some magazines needed rebuilding and regular maintenance to preserve deteriorating stocks of arms and cannon.[16] Furthermore a more serious Indian threat existed in Georgia and North Carolina. Hostilities already had flared up between Georgia and the powerful Creek Indians, who could throw 5,000 warriors into battle under the excellent leadership of a shrewd, well educated half-blood named Alexander McGillivray. In the summer of 1789, the administration began arrangements to head off such a disaster. Meanwhile it waited for Congress to establish the War Department and legalize the military establishment under the new Constitution. The transition of government was bound to be slow, but until accomplished, the administration could make no serious military or diplomatic moves in the Northwest.[17]

Between June and September 1789, the administration was subjected to a continual stream of pleas to protect the Ohio Valley frontier. Most of it came from Kentucky and from the new settlement in southwestern Ohio where former congressman John Cleves Symmes had put together a syndicate of New Jerseyans to purchase over a million acres of land. Both groups, and a third—the Ohio Company, centered around the settlement at Marietta—had politically potent conduits directly into the War Department, including congressmen who spoke frequently with Henry Knox. The cries for help, the complaints, and the accusation of insensitivity to the lives and property of citizens on the frontier came through loud and clear.[18]

The administration listened sympathetically, promising protection but at the same time pointing to the lack of money and the problems of transition in the government. To placate Symmes and the Kentuckians, Harmar was ordered to shift the bulk of the army and his headquarters westward to Fort Washington (present-day Cincinnati), Vincennes, and Louisville. Harmar might then be able to "awe the savages from collecting in large bodies" and "intercept their parties" on the way into Kentucky.[19] But the troop movement and Knox's verbal assurances did nothing to assuage western fears. For one thing Knox ordered the troops moved "silently and without any great notoriety," one company at a time, so that the Ohio Company inhabitants at Marietta would not be alarmed, or the Indians provoked.[20] Furthermore, in assuming the burden of defense, the administration ordered Kentucky to discharge all militia scouts and rangers, and to report all incidents to the army. Kentuckians were not fooled by the additional troops, whom they knew were stationed as much to stop Kentucky filibusters as to combat the Indians. The administration itself realized that the army, less than 600 strong and scattered from the Allegheny River in Pennsylvania to Vincennes, was now spread too thin; the troop disposition left the Ohio Company settlements in southeastern Ohio nearly naked. After a summer of sporadic Indian attacks, the requests for aid were still coming in, public appeals directly to the President. Simply enough, the army was too small.[21]

As a result, the administration moved in a direction which at the time seemed prudent, but which in retrospect became the first step down a long, inexorable path to war. On September 16, 1789, the President sent to Congress a letter from Governor St. Clair which outlined the deteriorating situation and the lack of troops, and which predicted war if the Kentuckians were not restrained ("They are in the habit of retaliation . . . without attending precisely to the nations from which injuries are received").[22] St. Clair asked for new authorization to call out the frontier militia, as a way of conciliating whites and of dealing with the Indians from strength. The letter was submitted quietly, a request for temporary authorization put before Congress in the midst of House deliberations on a bill "to recognize and adapt" the military establishment to the Constitution. The Senate attached the authorization to the House bill, and the House after first balking accepted it even though the Senate version specified no limit to the number of militia or the states from which they could be drawn. The House objected, some Federalists included, because the wording gave the President unconstitutional power to start a war. "This set the geese of the capital a cackling," sneered Fisher Ames. "Gerry figured as usual."[23] But the combination of administration maneuvering and reassurances, the press of other legislative concerns, and most of all the President's personal prestige—"a more than common knowledge of Western and Indian affairs," as Madison explained it—served to stifle congressional objections.[24] Only later, after Washington cited the amendment as authorization for Harmar's campaign, did Congress understand fully that it had given the President permission to wage war on his own authority.[25]

The administration of course had no such intention in September 1789. Gaining militia authority seemed a cautious, compromise measure which would pacify the frontiersmen, suggest determination to the Indians, and free the administration to punish recalcitrant tribes. On October 6, the President ordered Governor St. Clair to send feelers to the "Wabash and Illinois" Indians to ascertain if those tribes wished peace or war. The government wanted peace; "I would have it observed forcibly that . . . war . . . ought to be avoided by all means consistently with . . . security . . . and the national dignity." But if the tribes "should continue their hostilities, or meditate any incursions," St. Clair could mobilize 1,500 Virginia and Pennsylvania militia to undertake any "operations, offensive or defensive" he and Harmar "judge[d] necessary."[26]

It was a two-headed, inconsistent, contradictory policy from the beginning, reflecting the President's own uncertainty and the pressures which pulled the administration in opposite directions. Wanting peace, the government was making preparations which made war all the more likely. Over the next three months, Knox reported on the state of munitions, and made every effort to gain topographical information about the Northwest, even to the point of sending out an army patrol dressed as Indians and carrying no identification which might reveal a government connection.[27] Time and again over the next four years the administration would repeat these mistakes. Wanting peace it would undertake negotiations, then totally negate its diplomacy by breathing fire at the enemy and by escalating militarily. The trouble stemmed from two sources. First, the administration had little faith in negotiations or treaties; it underestimated the Indians' military resiliency and misread their mentality. Knox and Washington believed that the government could use force to punish the Indians into making peace, not realizing that what was to the government a punishing expedition was to the Indians total war. Second, its diplomatic overtures were meant to justify force as much as to gain peace. "If the Indians should refuse to attend the invitation to a treaty," Knox advised the President, "the United States would be exonerated from all imputations of injustice in taking proper measures for compelling the Indians to a peace, or to extirpate them."[28] Here also the administration was destined to fail, mainly because it never adequately publicized its peace overtures. In late 1789 the administration was tooling up to use force, but in its own mind avoiding war. Not until 1793 would the President understand fully the delicate moves necessary either to prevent hostilities or to use force. And not until 1794, in the Whiskey Rebellion against its own citizenry, would the administration apply these lessons cleanly and successfully.

For the next nine months, with its attention riveted on more pressing matters like Hamilton's financial program and the location of the national capital, the administration delayed, waiting for negotiations and building up its military strength on the frontier. All the while pressure to use force continued to intensify, until finally it overrode all the reservations which had been restraining the President. From Kentucky, from western Virginia, and from Ohio came a steady stream of pathetic appeals, of descriptions of murder and mayhem, of blunt demands for aid, or authority to retaliate on their own. From Harmar and from St. Clair came the same pictures, interlaced with warnings about western anger, Indian recalcitrance, and the necessity—indeed inevitability—of using force.[29] Naturally the invitation to treat failed, since it contained such arrogant challenges as "I do now make you the offer of peace; accept it or reject it, as you please."[30] The conclusion was inescapable: as Symmes told his friend, congressman Elias Boudinot, "nothing short of a formidable campaign carried into the heart of [Indian] country will ever give us peace."[31]

The administration made no irrevocable decision until June 1790, but as early as January the President knew he was going to have to act. Kentucky was alive with resentment at the government—because of the Indian business, because of fears that the East would oppose free navigation of the Mississippi past Spanish New Orleans, and because many in the district wanted statehood. The President had known for years about agitation to gain Kentucky independence, including a conspiracy by James Wilkinson and other leading Kentuckians to detach the region from the United States, perhaps as an independent nation under Spanish aegis. Spain wished nothing more than to protect her Louisiana colony by damming up American expansion or by siphoning off American settlers into the vast Louisiana wilderness. If "it is not the desire of the New Government to lose *all* its friends in that quarter," Washington confided to his diary, "a change must be made in this business."[32] The President knew also that westerners viewed federal military policy as a means of preventing offensives against the Indians as much as Indian attacks on whites. In 1789 and 1790 bands of frontiersmen crossed the Ohio to chase Indian raiders. Washington realized not only that Kentucky filibusters would continue "until the Government takes up the matter effectually," but that unless such unauthorized, indiscriminate retaliation ceased, every tribe in the Northwest would end up at war with the United States.[33]

Besides worries about Kentucky's loyalty and the outbreak of a general Indian war, two other factors intruded into the administration's calculations during the first five months of 1790. One lay in the background, never admitted or discussed by Washington or anyone else, at least openly: land speculation. Three companies had engrossed large areas of Ohio: the Symmes associates, the Scioto syndicate, and the Ohio Company. The list of shareholders in each read like the business (and political) register of New Jersey, Connecticut, Massachusetts, and New York, and included Assistant Secretary of the Treasury William Duer, a Scioto promoter who had to resign his office in part because of the conflict of interest. Almost every army officer owned shares in the Ohio Company, including Josiah Harmar; St. Clair owned over 1,000 Ohio Company acres; and many who were not shareholders in various ventures, like Senator Richard Henry Lee, wished to become so.* The President himself held tracts near Pittsburgh and on the Kanawha River in present-day West Virginia. Washington's doubts were outweighed by political reality; as Hamilton put it, "[t]here is a Western Country. It *will* be settled."[34] And as the administration knew, the settlements along the north bank of the Ohio had to be protected. Second, and much related, the government had to consider its own prestige. Could a new government, born against widespread opposition, struggling to establish itself, to win the loyalty of a diverse population, and to gain the respect of the nations of the world, stand idly by while its citizens were murdered and robbed by bandit savages? Phrased in those terms, the answer was self-evident.[35]

Between January and August 1790, the administration slipped gradually toward the final decision to use force. On January 12, in requesting Congress to set up a system to regulate Indian trade and relations, Washington asked for another regiment of regular infantry. The President cited the possibility of war with the Creeks (necessitating a 5,000-man army costing over $1,000,000 per annum—enough to scare any congressman) and the need for a chain of forts along the entire western frontier. This time the House readily assented, but critics in the Senate exploded. William Maclay of Pennsylvania saw through "all the art and address of ministerial management"—the documents solicited from officials, the "New phantoms," the "frightful pictures" of "dangers and distress [in] Georgia" (Georgia Senator James Gunn "contradicts all this"), "a dangerous and dreadful conspiracy" in Kentucky making it unwise "to put arms into the hands of the frontier people for their

---

*In what may have been the first explicit evidence of conflict of interest under the Constitution (or a "military-business complex"), Rev. Solomon Drown praised stockholder Harmar publicly at Marietta: "But to whom is this settlement more indebted than to the generous Chieftain, and other worthy Officers of yonder fortress, distinguished by the name of *Harmar!* With what cheerfulness and cordiality have ye entered into every measure promotive of the Company's interest." *An Oration delivered At Marietta, April 7, 1789, In Commemoration of the SETTLEMENT formed by the OHIO COMPANY* (Worcester, Mass., 1789), 9.

defense, lest they should use them against the United States."[36] Maclay mobilized others, who together battled furiously ("Give Knox his army, and he will soon have a war on hand," Maclay raged in his diary). But critics succeeded only in cutting the request in half, to a new battalion, about 400 extra men.[37] Ironically, doubting senators fought the bill because they smelled a plot to establish a standing army, or because of the expense, or out of their own bias for militia, not because they seriously feared a war. Like the administration most congressmen assumed that the placement of garrisons on the frontier as police would damp down hostilities and prevent war.*

In the midst of congressional deliberations, the administration took another small step: authorizing up to eight militia scouts for the defense of each frontier county at federal expense. Again the motives were pure: spring was approaching, prudence dictated local preparations, and the authorization would show the government's concern—peace, or at least that was what was explained to John Brown, the congressman from the Kentucky district of Virginia. The President (according to Brown) wanted a general system "to quiet the Hostile Indians"—treaties, army garrisons, and trade—in order to "establish peace upon the foundation of Interest and friendly intercourse."[38] But Congress was delaying too long on the request for a law, on money for negotiations, and on the regiment of troops. The administration made the decision hastily, revealing just how jumpy and nervous the President and the Secretary of War had become.

As the administration surely understood, none of this would prevent the conflict along and across the Ohio River. By spring 1790 the advice from every quarter was to use force. Richard Butler, as knowledgeable and experienced in Indian affairs as any westerner, claimed that "[t]here will be but little quiet . . . till [the Indians] are chastised, and that vile nest at Detroit removed. . . . I am perfectly satisfied [that with] posts . . . after a stroke made at the towns of the Miamis . . . , peace would follow."[39] Indeed much of the administration's hesitation after January had been tactical—uncertainty about which tribes to assault, concern about army communications and logistics, lack of adequate maps, worries about the expense, and most of all fears about damaging the government's image of justice and humanity. But in late May, with the campaigning season at hand, the administration could no longer contain the impulse to act. In a short memorandum for the President, Knox reviewed the reports of Indian pillage. "The result of the whole information shows the inefficacy of defensive operations." For as little as $13,000, and without provoking

---

*"*The mountain labored and a Mouse was born,*" sneered *The New-Jersey Journal and Political Intelligencer* in Elizabeth on May 26, 1790. "Five times the galleries shut; two or three Committees chosen to consider the subject; and public expectation set on tip-toe, and all for *Five Companies* of men, and an additional *Major!!!*"

friendly tribes or undermining St. Clair's peace overtures, 400 mounted troops could "strike a terror in the minds of the Indians hostilely disposed." Knox guessed that only 200 or so Indians were at fault: renegade Shawnee, Cherokee, and war parties from the Wabash tribes. One hundred regulars and 300 "picked militia" could ride quickly into enemy territory, each carrying 30-days' supplies, and wipe out the bandits. Such an expedition "would be highly satisfactory to the people of the frontiers."[40] The President agreed; on June 7, after several more blunt letters from the West arrived in Philadelphia, Knox ordered St. Clair and Harmar to organize the expedition.[41]

Looking back, the decision was the administration's Rubicon; Washington and Knox had committed themselves to the use of force, a commitment that led directly to war. In their minds it was only a punitive expedition designed to eliminate bandits and restore peace. "[T]he vengeance of the Union is to be pointed only against the perpetrators of the Mischief and not against the friendly nor even neutral tribes," Knox admonished St. Clair, "nor" should "the measures proposed . . . interfere with your plans for a general accommodation with the regular tribes."[42] Again, a month later, Knox warned St. Clair to distinguish between renegades and Indians acting under tribal authority, and Knox ordered the Governor to offer the Wabash tribes peace when the troops arrived at their villages, before the attack.[43] To Knox and the President, the expedition was a compromise, contingent measure. Unknown to them, at that very moment the administration was being committed to force by Governor St. Clair using "the alternative contained in my instructions [of October 6, 1789] from the President: that of punishing [the Wabash and Miami tribes]."[44] Worse still, the Governor and commanding general Josiah Harmar, for years chafing at the government's restrictions, had very different ideas about how force should be applied.

In early June, as the Governor was returning from the Illinois country where he had been extending the authority of his territorial government to the French settlements, he received notification from Major Hamtramck that the peace overture to the Wabash and Miami tribes had failed. St. Clair immediately left for Fort Washington, the newly constructed army headquarters at Cincinnati. With Harmar and contractor Robert Elliott, St. Clair in mid-July drew up plans for an expedition. Then, under his 1789 instructions, he called on Kentucky authorities for 1,000 militia, on Pennsylvania officials for 500, worked out schedules for rendezvous and supply, and left for New York to consult with the President and Knox. Unlike many westerners, St. Clair and Harmar never put much faith in retaliatory raids, except as a temporary expedient. In this case, far more than 200 bandits were involved; the whole Miami tribe, plus other tribes on the Maumee and upper Wabash Rivers, plus the Shawnee—altogether enough to field at least 1,100 warriors, had rejected peace. St. Clair and Harmar wanted a full-scale, two-pronged attack on the Wabash and Miami towns by 2,000 troops, a strategy they had worked out two years earlier. Marching from Fort Washington under Harmar, 300 regulars and 1,200 militia would strike the Miami villages on the Maumee; 300 militia and the Fort Knox garrison under Hamtramck would march up the Wabash from Vincennes, pinning down the Wabash tribes and devastating their villages. A single attack by one large army might be more efficient, but St. Clair thought it impossible to assemble enough militia at one time in one place; two invasions would be mutually supporting and prevent the tribes from massing for attack. Finally, with the tribes defeated and their villages destroyed, the army would establish a permanent garrison on the Maumee, deterring the tribes and cutting them off from the British at Detroit.[45]

In late August in New York, St. Clair argued his case forcefully before Knox and the President. Given the Governor's firsthand knowledge, his estimate of Indian strength and intentions, and General Harmar's approval, the administration accepted the new military strategy. Knox's proposal for a 400-man raid had contained several flaws anyway: the Secretary had identified the wrong Indians; the army possessed no cavalry, and unless regulars were used, the government would not command—or control—the expedition; and 400 horsemen would be hard pressed to carry 30-days' rations, ride that distance, or distinguish in a rapid advance "good" from "bad" Indians. Besides, St. Clair already had mobilized 1,500 militia, committing the government to their use unless the administration was willing on the one hand to send them home unpaid and enraged, or on the other to pay them without putting them into service and risking congressional ire. Furthermore any change at that late date would prevent a campaign that year. So unhappily, in spite of reports of bad feeling between the militia and the army, Knox and the President approved the St. Clair-Harmar plan. But the administration neither accepted nor approved the assumptions behind it. Knox still wanted the army's movements to "be so rapid and decisive as to astonish your enemy," even though he knew the expedition was infantry.[46] After St. Clair left New York, Knox and Washington discussed, and rejected unequivocally, the establishment of a post on the Maumee. Properly armed, supplied, and supported by forts north from Cincinnati, a Maumee fortress would require "considerable time and a great apparatus" to build, twice the existing military establishment to maintain, expose the army unnecessarily to attack, and provoke a confrontation with the British in Detroit. "The proposed expedition is intended to exhibit to the Wabash Indians our power to punish them for their positive depredations, for their conniving at the depredations of others, and for their refusing to treat with the United States when invited thereto."[47]

In its final form, Harmar's campaign was a slow, methodical infantry invasion over 150 miles into enemy territory, predicated on a policy which called for a fast-cavalry punitive raid. What no one realized at the time was that military strategy now controlled the Indian policy which it was supposed to serve. A 2,000-man, two-pronged expedition fully committed the military, political, and moral prestige of the United States government when no such commitment was intended or desired. Just why the administration blundered will probably never be known for certain. Perhaps, feeling as it did all during the summer of 1790 that war between England and Spain was imminent, and fearing that the two European antagonists would strike at each other's colonies (Canada and Louisiana) across American soil, the administration wanted to mobilize its full military potential on the frontier as a way of deterring Britain and Spain. For the most part, however, the administration kept the Indian expedition completely divorced from other foreign policy, even from the efforts then underway to negotiate the British out of the Great Lakes forts despite the fact that those posts were linked intimately to the Indian problem. But whatever the other goals of the campaign, the administration's assumptions about the use of force were fallacious, its knowledge of the western situation imprecise, and the internal pressures on it—from westerners, from politicians, and from its own understanding of governmental responsibility—intense. It made the decision in small, imperceptible steps, during a year in which the President and Knox were diverted by far more important questions—Hamilton's financial program, the fierce bargaining over the location of the national capital, and the threatened war between England and Spain to name only a few. St. Clair presented his plan for final decision in New York during a week when the government was in chaos, offices being dismantled and records being packed up for the removal of the capital from New York to Philadelphia, the President personally supervising the transportation of his household goods.[48] On the one hand the administration felt it had to act in Ohio— and to use Harmar's army lest the "raggamuffins of militia officers," as St. Clair called them in 1788, command the expedition, bringing on either defeat, a general Indian war, or some conflict with the British; on the other hand, the administration did not view its decision as particularly momentous.[49] The President and the Secretary of War wanted peace with the Indians, so they decided to force them into it. Both men saw clearly the dangers and disadvantages of inaction but not the dangers of going forward. In short, while Harmar might fail to bring an end to the conflict, it never occurred to the administration that he could be defeated in battle.

When St. Clair reached Fort Washington on September 22, preparations for the campaign were nearly complete. At mid-month, most of the Kentuckians had arrived and by the 31st, with the contingents from

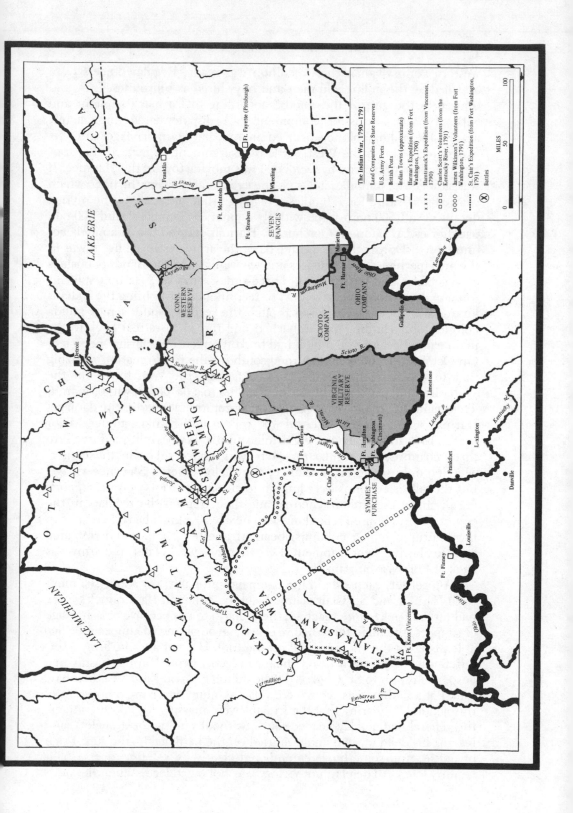

The Indian War, 1790-1791

Land Companies or State Reserves
U.S. Army Forts
British Posts
Indian Towns (approximate)
Harmar's Expedition (from Fort Washington, 1790)
Hamtramck's Expedition (from Vincennes, 1790)
Charles Scott's Volunteers (from the Kentucky River, 1791)
James Wilkinson's Volunteers (from Fort Washington, 1791)
St. Clair's Expedition (from Fort Washington, 1791)
Battles

MILES
0   50   100

western Pennsylvania, the expedition was ready. Regular officers were appalled by the militia: old men and boys hired as substitutes, "raw and unused to the gun or the woods" according to Harmar's adjutant and without proper arms or equipment.[50] A dispute flared immediately among the militia colonels over command, but Harmar, eager after six frustrating years in the West, settled the argument, organized the frontiersmen into units, and by October 1 was moving toward the Maumee. It was slow going, ten miles a day on the average, following the trace which weaved northward for 170 miles, dragging artillery, seeing to the myriad details of a 1,500-man force with its equipment, supplies, and 600-odd packhorses. At noon on October 17, Harmar entered the Miami villages unopposed. During the next three days, the army destroyed five towns in the area (perhaps 250 log houses and wigwams), and thousands of bushels of vegetables and buried corn. Three times, however, Harmar split his force to detach probing missions, to reconnoiter, or to bring the Indians lurking nearby to battle. Even though the second, under senior militia colonel John Hardin, was ambushed and forced to retreat back to the main camp because the militia had broken under fire, Harmar persisted. On October 21, the general turned south for the return march, realizing that to continue the campaign by attacking the Wea towns on the Wabash would expose his thinly clad militia to a desperate winter march. That night, hoping to surprise the enemy returning to assess the damage, Harmar sent a picked force of 400 militia and regulars under Major Wyllys back to the villages, eight miles north. Wyllys split *his* force into three columns, the militia on each wing and regulars in the center. Meeting only scattered resistance, the major entered Shawnee village. But the militia columns were lured into chasing warriors beyond supporting distance; the Indians then sprang their trap on the regulars in the center. Wyllys himself fell, along with nearly 50 men. The rest escaped to the returning militia columns, beat off another charge, and retreated back to Harmar's encampment. Less than two weeks later, the army was back at Fort Washington.[51]

Altogether, each side in the campaign probably lost about 200 men. Both Harmar and St. Clair claimed victory; although Hamtramck's force had turned back before reaching the Wabash towns because of a shortage of supplies, the main force had wreaked havoc on the Maumee and killed at least 100 of the enemy.[52] But on the trail, Harmar and the army knew differently. "Our loss is heavy, heavy indeed," wrote Harmar hastily in a desperate report to St. Clair. "All [the militia's] Great Kanhawa their blue Lick Battles, Bouquets &c &c &c was a damned farce in comparison of this action."[53] Fearing that the Indians were massing for another attack, the general had quickly headed south, without waiting for stragglers, and leaving his dead unseen and unburied on the battlefield—the surest sign of defeat, and something remembered clearly by veterans over a half-century later.[54] The claim of victory was hollow indeed. When the news reached the capital, now in Philadelphia, the President, Knox, Congress, and the American people recognized that fact immediately.

Campaigning for Peace: St. Clair's Defeat [1790–1792]

> The great object of the campaign will be, to convince the Indians of the futility of resistance, and of the absolute necessity of submitting to the justice and mercy of the United States.
>
> Henry Knox, 1791.[c]

> But, we are involved in actual war!
>
> George Washington, 1792.[d]

On December 14, 1790, Lieutenant Ebenezer Denny rode into Philadelphia with official dispatches describing the campaign. The President waited calmly, for more than a month "prepared for the worst" by rumors that Harmar "was a *drunkard*" and talk that there had been "disputes with *him* about command."[55] With unofficial reports in hand, Washington had opened the third session of Congress on December 8 with an apologia for his policy, attributing the campaign to the inefficacy of a defensive strategy, and citing authorization under the 1789 military establishment act. As justification, the President sent Congress dozens of documents including official correspondence and letters from the West.[56] The news in Denny's dispatch pouch touched off a wave of disgust and uncertainty in Congress which soon spread throughout the country. No one understood the policy, why Harmar had been defeated (there existed no doubt here—"two for One—Infamous Idea—and for Savages too," sneered one Rhode Islander), or even what had actually transpired during the march.[57] "I think the information that has been communicated to Congress . . . the most absurd that ever appeared," growled Maryland congressman William Smith.[58] For a month the administration kept silent, allowing the growing criticism to fall solely on Harmar, the natural scapegoat. During and after the expedition, the general had quarreled viciously with the militia; once back at Fort Washington, militia officers counterattacked by spreading stories that the general had been drunk the whole time. Although untrue, the accusation flew east like wildfire, gained wide acceptance in the absence of any other logical explanation for the defeat, and in the end saved the administration from an embarrassing public debate over its policy.[59]

Until Denny's arrival, Washington and Knox believed the story. But when they sat down to analyze the campaign and work out another strategy, a very different picture emerged. Denny attributed all the trouble to the militia. Composed of substitutes, poorly armed, badly equipped, and officered by inexperienced men instead of prominent

Indian fighters like Isaac Shelby or Benjamin Logan, the militia had been uncontrollable, disobedient, and at crucial times openly mutinous. They would follow some of their officers, but not others. Each battle had been lost because the militia had run, exposing the regulars to attack and decimation. After the October 22 defeat, many militia refused to return to the Indian villages. In camp and on the march, they flagrantly violated orders, firing off their muskets (one "almost in Colonel Hardin's face"), intimidating officers who tried to intervene.[60] Near the end Harmar had even threatened to arrest the militia leaders and send them home in disgrace.

In the light of later charges that the administration fabricated the Indian war in order to establish a standing army, this point is crucial: Washington and Knox used militia in 1790 because militia were politically acceptable and cheap compared to long-service regulars, and in fact the only force available. But Denny's account reinforced longstanding prejudices against militia held by Knox and the President. On January 5, Captain John Armstrong arrived in Philadelphia and corroborated Denny on every point. (In the second skirmish, the militia under Hardin fled, Leaving Armstrong alone with some thirty regulars; the captain escaped by hiding all night in a swamp, up to his chin in water, while Indians danced nearby in exultation over the bodies of his men.) Even western leaders agreed that the militia had performed miserably. Never again would a Federalist administration willingly use militia against Indians, indeed for any military crisis.[61]

And the administration knew it faced a crisis. Instead of being deterred or convinced to sue for peace, the savages would "consider themselves as victorious," intensify their raids, and perhaps gain allies from neighboring tribes.[62] Force was now mandatory. Without a backward glance, Knox and the President both assumed that another military expedition was necessary, unaware that their lack of alternatives stemmed directly from the original decision to use force six months earlier. Government losses must be recouped, respect for American arms reestablished. The primary goal remained, of course "the restoration of peace, and the effectual protection of the frontier inhabitants," but now more than ever, even should diplomacy succeed, the administration felt the need to impress "the minds of the indians . . . with the power of the United States, as the ground work of that system of justice and mercy, which it will be the glory of the general government to administer, to all the indians, within its limits."[63] In late January, the administration unveiled its new two-stage strategy for peace in the Northwest.

★ ☆ ★

In order to provide temporary defense for the exposed white settlements along the Ohio River, and to keep the Indians off balance, the administration asked authorization and appropriations for mounted forays by frontiersmen into Indian territory. This was what westerners most wanted, Kentuckians in particular. In December they had appealed for permission to attack Indian strongholds under their own officers.[64] To Knox, mounted volunteer rangers were superior to militia, certainly to draft or substitute militiamen, and, when not on the attack, rangers would provide area defense by patrolling the avenues of approach to their settlements. Knox had serious reservations, however, about the expense of such raids, whether they would interfere with regular army operations, and he knew they promised no permanent solution; but on balance he approved the concept. Mounted assaults were "highly acceptable to the Kentucky district," he told the President; "Kentucky leaders . . . will be answerable both for their being well ordered, and for their effect," and "they will probably produce the main effect intended—*That is, by carrying the war into the enemy's country, prevent in a great degree their invading the frontiers.*"[65]

The administration placed its real hopes, however, on a new expedition. This would be no punishing raid, but a full-scale, 3,000-man military invasion north from Cincinnati, so large and so powerful an army that it could overpower any combination of Indians even if organized or assisted by "certain malignant whites" (the British), whom the administration believed were supplying and encouraging the tribes.[66] At Miami village, the army would plant a "strong post and garrison," the head of a line of "subordinate posts" for supply and communication with Fort Washington (the strategy rejected in 1790).[67] Knox called a Maumee fort "little inferior to . . . Detroit," better in location to protect the Ohio Valley "than . . . a post at any other place whatever," and critical "to curb and overawe not only the Wabash Indians, but . . . all others who might be wavering, and disposed to . . . war."[68]* For manpower the administration submitted two requests: first, another regiment of permanent regulars, about 1,000 men, to man the additional garrisons planned to stretch from the Great Lakes to Georgia. For added argument, Knox recited the explosive tensions along the Southwest frontier, where Spanish intrigue and aggressive whites threatened to upset delicate relations with powerful Southern tribes. With a regular army numbering over 2,000 men, over 1,200 would be available to invade the Maumee along with the regiment of volunteer cavalry. The remainder of the expeditionary forces would be "levies": volunteers enlisted by the government for the duration of the campaign, perhaps four months. Levies were the administration's trump,

---

*Washington told Thomas Jefferson later that the post was "the primary object of the campaign, after the accomplishment of which, every thing else would be easy" (December 25, 1791, John C. Fitzpatrick, ed., *The Writings of George Washington* . . . [Washington, 1931-1944], XXXI, 449). The military theory was that a post containing a sizeable garrison in the heart of Indian territory would be able at all times to watch over the tribes and deter any mischief by its ability to send forth a large battle force quickly.

a new force to be raised, officered, and controlled by the national government, under regular army discipline and thus "more efficacious" and "more economical" than drafted militia, but as volunteers serving short enlistments, far cheaper than regulars and free of the odium of standing army. Like the short-term provincial regulars used late in the colonial period, levies constituted a political and military compromise between regulars and militia, in miniature what the French would call later the *levée en masse*, a method of using citizen-soldiers without having to use state militia. Levies were the embryo of the federal volunteer system which was destined to become the backbone of America's wartime armies in the nineteenth century, and with selective service, the basis for the mass armies in the age of total war and cold war.[69] Unfortunately, for a campaign against Indians in 1791, levies revealed the administration's political timidity, its underestimation of the enemy, and its arrogance and overconfidence. Militarily, the levies turned out to be a disaster.

Congress received the administration's proposals with a mixture of skepticism and discomfort. While some doubted the necessity for war, almost all disliked the extra quarter million of expense, which would require either new loans or new taxes. But three days after Knox presented his new plan, the administration gave Congress a long letter from Rufus Putnam, the leader of the Ohio Company settlements near Marietta. Putnam described in desperate tones the butchering of twelve men, a woman, and two children at supper in their blockhouse at Big Bottom, forty miles up the Muskingum River from Fort Harmar. The massacre constituted the first organized attack in Putnam's area since the 1780s, and given the distance from the Maumee, signaled an ominous extension of hostilities. Undermanned, with less than two dozen regulars in the vicinity, Putnam called his "situation . . . truly critical," the Ohio Company "in the utmost danger of being swallowed up."[70] Putnam begged for troops without which the settlers would face the unhappy choice of evacuation or death.

Doubt and uncertainty about Knox's proposals immediately evaporated in Congress. Representatives from New England, who for sectional reasons distrusted the administration's Indian policy, knew Putnam personally. Fisher Ames, the astute and often clinically objective Federalist from Massachusetts, wrote Putnam an emotional letter promising "to nurse the weak and to console the suffering remote settlements."[71] Rhode Island's two Senators guessed that over 70,000 New Englanders had moved to the frontiers since 1786, and the Ohio Company settlements were known to be backed financially by Yankees.[72] "Congress must either give up the idea of settling that Country, or forthwith send an armed force sufficient to extirpate the Indian Tribes," concluded another Bay State representative.[73] As a result of Putnam's letter, the administration's military program sailed through Congress easily: another regiment of regular infantry, up to 2,000 levies, and the establishment of whatever new posts the President wanted. To speed the organization of the army and the commencement of operations, Congress appropriated the money in the same bill, authorized the President to appoint levy officers without consent of the Senate, and the upper chamber promptly confirmed Washington's appointments in the regular regiments.[74] The administration won its blank check scarcely aware of the depth of opposition, in Congress and outside, to war in the Northwest.

The moment Congress finished in early March, the War Department became a hive of activity. Haste was imperative. The men would have to be recruited, the army organized, the supplies gathered, and the invasion launched before the fall—a huge task in an eighteenth-century country without a bureaucracy or a permanent military establishment experienced in such undertakings. Already Knox had outlined for the President in 35 pages exactly the steps to be taken, down to the details of strategy and orders to various commanders, militia and regular army. On March 9, instructions went to Brigadier General Charles Scott, as commander of the corps of mounted Kentucky rangers, to initiate "surprise and sudden attacks" on the Wabash Indian towns.[75] Scott and four other prominent Kentuckians, including the federal judge and the congressman from the district, were to select the men and organize the expedition. "Secrecy in forming, despatch in obtaining the men, and celerity in the movement, are indispensable."[76] The next day Knox authorized local militia officials in western Pennsylvania and Virginia (the other exposed frontier counties) to mobilize, at their own discretion, men to patrol each county against Indian incursion.[77] Next, Knox organized the levies and laid out plans to recruit the men.[78] Then on March 21, the Secretary handed Major General Arthur St. Clair, the new commanding general, his instructions for the campaign. Knox described the ranger expedition and empowered St. Clair to order additional mounted forays if necessary. St. Clair himself was to march carefully north from Fort Washington, into the Maumee Valley, building a chain of forts, bringing the Indians to battle, and finally establishing a permanent post at the Miami villages. Unlike the offhand, almost casual instructions given to St. Clair and Harmar the year before, Knox now spelled out everything in detail.[79] Knox had discussed all the arrangements at length with St. Clair and his new second in command, Richard Butler, in person, but the instructions had to be formalized, in writing, so that objectives, authority, and responsibility would be clearcut. Knox also arranged for weekly communication between Fort Washington and Philadelphia, expressly ordering St. Clair to keep the government regularly informed. The government of the United States, through the Secretary of War and the War Department, was finally assuming control over its army and all military operations, an elementary procedural change that was crucial in the creation of the American military establishment. In this case, the Washington administration had learned from its mistakes.

At the same time it readied the army for combat, the administration implemented a new, two-stage diplomatic offensive. The first, an invitation to the Miami tribes to negotiate peace, was pure politics—an attempt to avert accusations of aggression or genocide. "The great mass of the people of the United States," Knox admitted to St. Clair, wished to avoid an Indian war "under any circumstances" because the "sacrifices of blood and treasure" far exceeded "any advantage which can possibly be reaped."[80] If negotiations succeeded, the government would save money and win public approval; if not, there would be no doubt about the government's humanity. St. Clair and Scott were both ordered to delay operations until mid-May (convenient since preparations could not be completed any quicker), when the results of the peace mission would be known.

On March 11, Knox dispatched Thomas Proctor with assurances of friendship for the Senecas, Wyandots, and Delawares—all at peace with the United States—and with messages from St. Clair and Knox for the Miami and Wabash tribes. The mission was doomed from the beginning. Two months left Proctor without sufficient time: first, to convince the Seneca headmen to accompany him and serve as intermediaries; then, to complete the journey and report to St. Clair at Fort Washington. Knox made no provision for talks, which would delay the campaign until fall when the enlistments of the levies would expire. But the administration's language to the tribes foreclosed that possibility anyway. War, thundered Knox in his message to the tribes, "would be absolute destruction to you, your women, and your children." "Reflect that this is the last offer that can be made; that, if you do not embrace it now, your doom must be sealed for ever." To treat, the Indians would have to travel to army headquarters on the Ohio, where under American guns they could hear St. Clair "dictate" terms of "justice, moderation, and humanity."[81] Proctor's report of failure in May hardly ruffled the capital, where preparations for war were going forward under Knox's frenzied direction.*

The other branch of the administration's peace offensive began a few weeks later and stemmed from a desire to prevent an alliance between the Six Nations in New York and the hostile tribes further west, a confederacy long the dream of Mohawk leader Joseph Brant. In early March 1791, a small group of Virginia militia, patrolling the woods southeast of

---

*Actually the administration did not want negotiations. "In the present state of things," Knox advised the President privately, "the minds of the indians must be impressed with the power of the United States, as the ground work of that system of justice and mercy, which it will be the glory of the general government to administer to all indians, within its limits." See " . . . the report . . . upon the operations to be adopted . . . ," February 22, 1791, Northwest Territory Collection, Indiana Historical Society, Indianapolis, Ind.

Pittsburgh, tried to ambush an enemy raiding party. But the Indians, wary of a trap, escaped. When the pursuing whites lost the trail, one group headed for the trading post at the mouth of Big Beaver Creek in Pennsylvania, where Indians were known to gather. The scouts reached Big Beaver after a trek along the north bank of the Ohio, spied what they thought were enemies, attacked, and murdered three men and a woman. Unfortunately, the murdered Indians were Delawares, who had been trading peacefully. Immediately Indians in the Pittsburgh area retaliated, and suddenly western Pennsylvania was embroiled in war. In the confusion, angry whites tried to waylay Cornplanter, a chief of the friendly Seneca tribe who was passing through town on his return from Philadelphia. A few days later, Pennsylvania militia plundered a contractor's boat manned by friendly Indians, carrying among other things the gifts given to Cornplanter. "One act of violence of the lawless inhabitants of the frontiers," Knox exploded, "seems to succeed another . . . until all the tribes will be constrained, from principles of self defense, to unite against us."[82]

Frantically Knox tried to contain the spreading hostilities. He ordered investigations and assured Cornplanter that the Big Beaver massacre was a tragic mistake. But after conferring with the cabinet (the President was away on a tour of the South), Knox decided to assemble the Six Nations in conference and cement their friendship with the United States. The emissary was to be Timothy Pickering. After failing in business and farming after the war, Pickering, now a resident of northern Pennsylvania, had reentered politics and was seeking a federal post. In 1790 he had smoothed over relations with the Senecas, the first in a series of successes that would make him the administration's premier Indian envoy and which would provide him the springboard to a string of high government positions in the 1790s. In 1791, the government wanted Pickering to keep the Six Nations neutral at least, perhaps to commit themselves by sending fifty or sixty of their younger warriors to fight with St. Clair's army. The chiefs refused to send warriors, but Pickering did hold the tribes neutral. By early August, the administration was confident that Pickering's delicate mission, combined with a new Cherokee treaty negotiated by Governor of the Southwestern Territory William Blount, had isolated the Maumee and Wabash tribes, destroying the possibility of a hostile Indian confederacy enveloping the entire western frontier.[83]

Meanwhile the administration pushed forward with military preparations as rapidly as possible. In June and again in August, mounted rangers from Kentucky successfully raided Indian towns, destroying crops, killing

Indians, and returning with prisoners. The administration was encouraged by the unsettling effect on the enemy, the resulting calm along the frontier, and of course by the favorable public reaction in Kentucky.[84] In the main army, however, success eluded the administration. Recruiting lagged throughout the spring. Low pay and bounties, combined with the war's unpopularity, kept New Englanders (supposedly the section to provide the new regiment of regulars) away from enlisting. Even though recruiting went well in other areas, especially for the levies, Knox was compelled to delay the scheduled rendezvous at Fort Washington, partly because the Ohio was unusually shallow that year, preventing travel down river. As late as August, St. Clair's force at headquarters still numbered less than 600.[85] That month Knox and the general began seriously to consider using militia. Both hated the thought, but unless the army could begin its march in time to attack in good weather, operations would have to be cancelled until the next year. To the administration, counting on a quick victory to retrieve its prestige and to prevent criticism of its Indian policy, delay would be ruinous. Recruiting, clothing, paying, and transporting the levies only to lose them when their enlistments expired would be an enormous waste. The administration predicated its policy on a victory in 1791. After learning of diplomatic success with the Cherokees and the Six Nations, Knox began pressing St. Clair to hurry his preparations.[86]

Ultimately, the administration's haste killed St. Clair's army, if the motley collection of regulars, militia, and levies ever qualified as a real "army." The levies, sitting in Pittsburgh much of the summer, were rent by dissension, the officers hating the commander, Richard Butler, and threatening to resign, the strength of the battalions draining away through discharge, smallpox, accidents, and desertion. Although they had never been adequately trained, St. Clair claimed the levies were the strongest part of his force.[87] The militia, procured after August because of delays in transporting troops down the river, turned out to be much worse. All through the campaign they chafed under the discipline and at the crucial point in battle, they broke without firing a shot, exposing the rest of the army. After sixty militiamen deserted in a group, threatening to plunder the army's supply convoys, St. Clair had to detach a whole regiment of regulars to protect the supplies from his own troops.[88] Even the regulars were disappointing: "chiefly recruits unaccustomed with the use of fire arms, or the yells of Savages," lamented Captain John Armstrong worriedly on the campaign trail.[89] To Armstrong, who had served under the American flag since 1776, St. Clair's force was composed of "the worst and most dissatisfied troops I ever served with."[90]

All through the buildup and campaign, the logistical system was in chaos. In June many companies lacked sufficient arms for training. Quartermaster Samuel Hodgdon did not reach Fort Washington until

September 10, less than a month before the army sallied forth. "I am doing all in my power to systemize the business here," he wrote one week later; "every thing was in the utmost confusion."[91] Hodgdon failed. Several times on the march the army halted to allow supplies to catch up and sometimes the men marched on short rations. Powder was defective, the cavalry horses worn down and exhausted before the march began. The army headed north so late in the year that frost killed much of the forage along the trace, forcing St. Clair to detach parties to search for edible grass. Years later, Adjutant General Winthrop Sargent remembered an army "badly clothed, badly paid and badly fed."[92]

St. Clair himself deserved much of the blame for the disaster that followed. Several times during the summer, without a second in command or a quartermaster present, the general journeyed into Kentucky to plan mounted raids, arrange supplies, or collect militia. By October, with the army moving forward, he was exhausted, in agony from illness and recurring attacks of gout. Benjamin Van Cleve, then an eighteen-year old pack horseman, recalled the general being carried north to battle on a litter.[93] Pressed by his superiors to hurry, without aid from subordinates, bedeviled by an inadequate logistical system and a patchwork army of three different kinds of troops, St. Clair became testy and unreasonable. In July, after conflict between townsmen and officers, he placed Cincinnati under martial law, which threw promoter John Cleves Symmes into a rage. Earlier Symmes volunteered to accompany the army; St. Clair shot back, "I am willing you should go, Sir, but by G— you do not go as a Dutch deputy." Symmes did not understand the term, and when the general explained that the Dutch appointed "Burgers to attend the General . . . [to] advise him when to fight and when to decline it," Symmes realized that St. Clair would "consider . . . him . . . a spy."[94]

As the army crawled north in October, sometimes as little as five miles a day when it did move, St. Clair imposed regular army discipline, which further alienated the militia and levies. He held courts martial for officers who violated minor administrative rules, one for bad language to a superior. On October 22 discipline was so poor that St. Clair stopped to build a gallows. Midway through the campaign, the enlistments of the levies began expiring and the men demanded discharge. Instead of turning back, St. Clair pushed deeper into enemy territory, gambling that the levies would be afraid to leave the safety of the main army. "I Pray God that . . . the Enemy may not be disposed to give us battle," Armstrong wrote.[95]

The climax came on November 4. Halfway to the Miami village, after a march of five weeks, St. Clair's army of over 1,400 was annihilated by some 1,000 Indians. The enemy had been waiting. As Symmes later charged, "the moment that the troops crossed the Miami at Fort Hamilton, every old squaw must have known that the views of the main army were offensive and against what towns their designs were."[96] From American deserters and their own scouts, the Indians knew the strength and organization of the army down to the last detail. St. Clair knew nothing of the enemy. Half the night of November 3 the men lay under arms. Just before sunrise, after the tired soldiers had stood down, the Indians sprung their trap. The militia broke immediately and the enemy were nearly inside the camp before a defensive line could be organized. Crowded into less than two acres, the army fought well for three hours, caught in a murderous crossfire from an enemy obscured by the smoke of battle. More than 600 died, including Richard Butler, and 300 suffered wounds. Over 50 women camp followers with the army died also, according to Lieutenant Michael McDonough, "some of them cut in two, their bubbies cut off, and burning." "I saw a Capt. Smith just after he was scalped," McDonough related, "setting on his backside, his head smoking like a chimney."[97] Finally at the last possible moment, a remnant broke through and headed pell mell south toward the Ohio.

The President was with guests at dinner when the dispatches arrived in Philadelphia. Family lore had it that Washington excused himself, read the messages, and returned to the table without any visible sign of emotion. But after his company left at 10 o'clock, the President exploded in frustration and despair, pacing the upstairs of the mansion in front of longtime secretary Tobias Lear, alternately wringing his hands and clenching his fists, the huge body shaking with rage as he recounted his warnings to St. Clair: to be prepared, to fortify his army every night, and above all to beware of surprise attack.[98] For George Washington, who himself had led soldiers in the wilderness and 35 years before had watched as Edward Braddock's army was massacred in the forest east of Fort Duquesne, St. Clair's defeat was a nightmare come true. The gloom and shock which Washington felt reverberated through the stunned capital all during December 1791 and well into the new year. No one doubted the magnitude of the disaster. "Worse than a Braddock's defeat," lamented one westerner; "the most complete Victory ever known in this Country obtained by Indians," concluded congressman William Barry Grove.[99] But once the "great sensation," as Jefferson termed it, wore off, there began a hungry search for answers and explanation.[100] From all accounts St. Clair had performed credibly, so public scorn did not focus on the army's command, as it had in 1790.* (Washington and his advisers never

---

*"All accounts of the late action . . . reflect honour on the conduct of General St. Clair and his gallant troops," claimed *Dunlap's American Daily Advertiser*, a Federalist newspaper in Philadelphia (January 2, 1792). In February and March a violent controversy did break out over St. Clair's leadership, sparked by an anonymous letter from levy Colonel William Darke: "A general, enrapped ten-fold in flannel robes, unable to walk, placed on his

blamed St. Clair since to do so would have been to admit the error of selecting two incompetent generals in succession; in fact Washington publicly exonerated the general early in 1792.)[101] Instead there burst suddenly into public view the violent and searching debate which the administration had heretofore avoided—over its own military policy, the purpose of the war, and the future direction of Indian relations in the Northwest.

All along the eastern seaboard, especially in New England where the war had never been popular, people questioned the war's utility, particularly the expense involved in a campaign of doubtful necessity. "[E]verybody asks what business had we there," reported Bostonian William Eustis, twenty years later the Secretary of War during Madison's Presidency.[102] To a public uninformed of the administration's peace overtures and for the most part unconscious of the raids and murders in the West, the government appeared the aggressor. Newspapers teemed with attacks. Opponents of the war depicted the Indians as pure, innocent savages who wished only to live peacefully on traditional hunting grounds. They attacked only in retaliation for encroachments by lawless, barbaric frontiersmen. Some even saw a comparison with the Revolution: virtuous Indians defending land and liberty against assault by a distant, tyrannical, repressive regime bent on seizing land and exterminating the rightful inhabitants.[103]

More often critics questioned the government's wisdom, and even friends complained bitterly about the expense involved. A trackless wilderness could not possibly be worth the bankruptcy of the country or the blood of American soldiers when enough unsettled land remained for generations of settlers to come. Better to buy Indian friendship. Secretary of State Jefferson, who by early 1792 was thoroughly disenchanted with the drift of administration economic policy—the excise tax, assumption of state debts, a national bank, in short the Hamiltonian financial program—had long argued for changing "our tomahawk in[to] a golden chain of friendship"; "the most economical as well as most human conduct towards [Indians]" he argued during the buildup for the campaign, "is to bribe them into peace, and to retain them in peace by eternal bribes."[104] In early 1792, some of the administration's staunchest supporters said the same thing. New York Federalists, according to Vice-President Adams's son Charles, viewed the war "as a measure ruinous to our Credit, as a squander of blood and treasure, which might be saved by a comparatively small tribute."[105] In Congress, talk of new taxes to support another campaign produced much discomfort. Suddenly other political considerations and motives became entangled in Indian policy. Representatives

car, bolstered on all sides with pillows and medicines, and thus moving to attack the most active enemy in the world, was . . . tragi-comical . . . indeed." St. Clair's defenders immediately answered, which touched off a debate about the general's competence and his tactics. See *ibid.*, February 10, 15, March 6, 7, 1792.

from the southern backcountry and western Pennsylvania, for example, realized immediately that another campaign would prevent repeal of the whiskey tax, an administration measure hated by their constituents.[106]

Neither the justice of the war nor its expense were doubted in the least by westerners, but they had abhorred the government's Indian policy, especially the use of a regular army, for years. To them negotiations were absurd: "suing the Indians for peace . . . convinces them that we are beat and Cowed, and of course will cause nations not yet at war to join the confederacy," sneered George Rogers Clark, an expert at Indian warfare.[107] Westerners hated the regulars and the War Department: for the frictions, such as arrests, martial law, or destruction of property by soldiers without compensation; for government restrictions on the use of scouts, the off-again, on-again authorization for militia, and the War Department's obsession with musters and accounts in several copies; and for delays in pay and compensation.[108] In early 1791, for example, a mixup with the army contractors stirred up wrath in Kentucky. The firm of Elliott and Williams withheld money for the horses lost in Harmar's campaign supposedly because the government had not advanced enough cash. Actually the contractors had never specified whether Kentuckians would be compensated for the value of horses killed or merely the rental charge, and rather than pay both if an animal died, the firm refused to pay any damages until the dispute was settled. Some Kentuckians had to sue to get the money and at least two cases dragged on until 1794.[109]

For years, westerners had suspected that government policy masked a basic indifference to the lives and property of frontier whites, and that the regular army was designed to keep them from settling the Indian problem themselves. St. Clair's defeat vindicated their charges of federal ineptitude, their dislike of serving with regulars, and their arguments for the use of frontiersmen to fight the war. In a long critique of the campaign, land promoter John Cleves Symmes blasted the delays in assembling the army and the supply system, but he reserved his bitterest attack for the character of the troops. "These men who are to be purchased from the prisons, wheelbarrows, and brothels of the nation at two dollars per month," he told Elias Boudinot, "will never answer our purposes for fighting of Indians."[110] Use regulars for garrison duty; for combat, send skilled frontiersmen who understood the Indian and his methods. "Sure I am," concluded the Judge, "that one hundred Marlboroughs could not fight fifty Indians in the woods with success."[111] Among westerners, and to a growing, influential segment of opinion in the East, Symmes's analysis was unassailable. Jefferson accepted it; so did Senator James Monroe and Representative James Madison.[112] In the light of St. Clair's campaign, anything seemed better than regulars. Using "Hardy woodsmen acquainted with rifles . . . is *now* seen by every body," muttered Pickering sarcastically, "for *after* an event, every body is wonderfully wise."[113] By January 1792, barely a month after the news became public, opposition to the war was reaching a crescendo, one strain of opinion denigrating the war as unjust and clamoring for a negotiated settlement, another claiming the war had been mismanaged and pressing for a different kind of army. All agreed the war was unpopular, in the opinion of a British observer, so much so "that the people" would "compel" the administration "to make peace and to delegate powers to St. Clair to conclude it soon."[114]

For a month the administration suffered the criticism in silence. Then in late January 1792 it published a long public rebuttal by Henry Knox "to manifest that due pains have been taken . . . to avoid the evil."[115] Knox's summation of government policy had power and eloquence, citing the statistics of whites killed and property devastated, analyzing the origins of the war as "a remnant of the late general war" continued by "bandit savages," and recounting every single effort by the government to negotiate a peace.[116] But it failed completely to stem the mounting outcry. "Never was abuse more profusely and more unjustly ascribed to a government," sympathized one of Knox's friends, "than has been imputed to the executive . . . in this indian war."[117]

But beyond the attempt to answer its critics, the administration's real dilemma was to construct a new policy for victory on the frontier and guide that policy through a balky, hostile Congress. Washington and Knox now realized they they faced a full-scale war, and that political considerations could no longer be allowed to compromise military policy. For the year following the disaster, the administration received all sorts of advice, from the suggestions of experienced soldiers like Henry Lee and Frederick Steuben to crackpot proposals like building a 1,500-mile wall between whites and Indians along the frontier (one former Indian trader even offered to become the President's personal spy at Detroit).[118] The administration rejected almost all of it, and stuck to its original policy of negotiation and military escalation. Only this time there would be no halfway measures. The diplomacy would consist of well-orchestrated, loudly publicised, and truly serious efforts to negotiate a peace. And military policy would consist of forging a large, battle-ready regular army under competent, prudent leadership.

On December 19, St. Clair's aide Ebenezer Denny arrived in Philadelphia. As the first officer to reach the capital, Denny was grilled first by Knox and then over breakfast the next day by the President and Knox together. From Denny, and afterward from other observers, the administration learned just how badly the levies, "the short enlistment of part of the force" as Washington put it later, had prevented adequate training and forced the army into battle on a schedule completely unrelated to tactical or strategic considerations.[119] Knox and Washington also knew that St. Clair's generalship had been poor, especially his intelligence about the enemy's disposition and his failure to deploy the army behind cover in the Indian style of warfare. Yet using levies and the army's top command could both be changed. Neither Washington nor any other member of the cabinet questioned the need now for attacking the tribes or establishing a fort on the Maumee. Only force would establish a permanent peace. Unlike critics who viewed the campaign as proof of the futility of using regulars, Knox and Washington concluded that the performance of the militia and levies in 1790 and 1791 showed the necessity of regular troops, and (in cabinet meetings at least), Secretary of State Jefferson never spoke up in opposition.[120]

On January 11, the President sent Congress a review of his peace efforts, a flood of documents illustrating the military and diplomatic activity preceding the expedition, and the War Department's proposal for another campaign. Knox wanted four regiments of regular infantry, one of riflemen, and a battalion each of artillery and cavalry, a total in excess of 5,000 rank and file costing perhaps over $1,000,000 a year—triple the expense of the existing establishment. He justified the plan with a long analysis of conditions in the West: a government duty-bound to protect its citizens, opposed by a swelling coalition of hostile tribes, likely dispatching "emissaries" to the southern Indians "with tales of prowess and glory." Although the government would try once more to arrange a settlement, only by "superior force" could the Indians "be brought to listen to the dictates of peace, which have been sincerely and repeatedly offered to them." Neither defensive strategies nor militia would work; Knox argued forcefully for regulars, who if "*disciplined according to the nature of the service*," possessed of "obedience," "patience," "promptness," and "a proper pride of reputation," could meet "the greatest probable combination of the Indian enemy."[121]

The galleries were cleared in the House of Representatives to receive the administration's plan, and for several days Congress debated in secret. By all accounts the fight was fierce. In the three years since the new government had come into existence, there had grown up in Congress a determined, vocal opposition to the Federalists and to the Washington administration, composed of the remnant of Antifederalists, of senators and representatives concerned about the growing power of the national government, of ideologues who feared the onset of aristocracy in America, and of southerners and westerners who opposed the Hamiltonian financial and taxation programs. In early 1792 the opposition was just solidifying into an enduring legislative faction, and beginning its transformation into a popular political party with allies in state political groups, a partisan press, and a party structure to contest elections for local and national office.[122] Indeed a significant element in the opposition to the war was partisanship. For the emerging Republican party, the calamitous western policy provided a perfect popular issue to flay the administration for incompetence, and to accuse the Federalists of plotting the introduction of a standing army and introducing policies to strengthen Hamilton's financial edifice with added federal debts.

And yet St. Clair's defeat divided the capital along sectional lines which diffused and softened partisan thrusts. Western Republicans like William Findley and Albert Gallatin of Pennyslvania, while they wanted to use militia, while they hated standing armies, and while they wanted to repeal the whiskey excise, could not oppose protection for their home areas, nor, evidently, could James Madison, now becoming the administration's chief antagonist, from a state with an exposed frontier. Colleague James Monroe, however, did vote against the administration. Federalists were likewise split, torn on the one hand by the bitter dissent of New Englanders against the war and on the other by their general support for a national army and their desire to help the administration in crisis. North Carolinians Benjamin Hawkins and John Steele, however, both Federalists experienced in Indian affairs, from a state with an Indian frontier, stolidly refused to accept the Knox strategy for dealing with the tribes. Whatever the divisions (Kentucky's Arthur Campbell claimed it was a Quaker and mercantile interest in Congress which wanted to buy a "truly humiliating and unsafe peace"), the best estimates gave administration critics a solid majority.[123] Knox himself sensed it, enough to visit his old friend, congressman Elbridge Gerry, to plead with Gerry to introduce the administration's plan and act as a kind of floor leader in the House. Gerry was an independent who had at the critical moment switched from opposing to supporting the Constitution in the Massachusetts ratifying convention, but who, in Congress in 1789 and after, jealously fought expanding executive power. Gerry related to his wife the meeting with Knox: "my determination is now as it was then [in 1789] to support the executive in the due discharge of his duty . . . because I seriously think we never shall have so good a president as after this; altho I do not admit him to be infallible."[124] Gerry did not shepherd Knox's plan through the House, but on the crucial vote, either because of illness or out of sympathy for the President's plight, the old antimilitary standard-bearer was absent.

For two weeks, the House proceeded in secret, debating and finally voting on the administration's military program. On January 25, a select committee chaired by Madison reported out a bill and the next day, apparently in response to the heated public controversy, the House staged a public discussion. All the arguments then raging in the press were summarized on the floor. Some critics focused on the war itself: caused by whites; unjust; unwinnable with the British sitting in Detroit; and easily disposed of by negotiation. Others castigated administration policy, predicting another disaster if, instead of fighting with mounted volunteers, the government insisted on a slow, methodical assault by regulars (scum who hardly knew "whether the Indian and his horse are not the same animal") encumbered with baggage and artillery. And the expense—the waste—was scandalous. Two Virginians from districts bordering on the Ohio answered for the administration, using all of Knox's arguments about the peace overtures and the "savage barbarity" of the enemy. They argued most tellingly that the origins of the war had been rendered irrelevant; the real issue was whether the government would withdraw from the West. National dignity and honor demanded another campaign. The costs were disheartening, but inconsequential "when put in competition with the lives of our friends and brethren." Instead of dribbling away the money year after year, the government should now create a sizeable force, occupy posts in enemy areas, and settle the matter permanently. Some might prefer militia, but regulars properly trained would certainly not flee at some "very trifling disaster" or out of "some slight cause of discontent."[125]

The division in the debate was extremely revealing; the administration was defended by two Virginians from frontier districts, while every single opposing speaker was a Federalist, including stalwarts like Benjamin Goodhue, Elias Boudinot, and newly elected Georgia congressman Anthony Wayne. Yet on February 2, the Five Regiment Bill passed by the same margin it had in secret, a surprisingly comfortable 29–19. Cynical Charles Nisbet, the Scotch-born president of Dickinson College in Carlisle, Pennsylvania, thought the whole issue tainted by political hypocrisy. "Our Leaders flatter the People by declaiming against standing Armies, and pretending to believe that the Militia is the best Security of a Nation," he told an English friend, "but they are not in earnest, and their own Experience may convince them of the futility of this Notion."[126] The real division, however, was clearly sectional. Federalist New England opposed the war and voted that way, except for such partisans as Ames and Theodore Sedgwick. The Middle states and the South voted almost to a man for the administration despite deep misgivings. Albert Gallatin, who followed the debate closely from the Pennsylvania legislature, put the dilemma this way: the "friends" of "expeditions of the kind similar to those of [Charles] Scott and [James] Wilkinson" were "obliged to join those who have proposed the President's plan in order to oppose those who wish to forsake us altogether."[127]

In the normally pro-administration Senate, the Knox plan met more determined opposition. After three days of debate, the crucial provision to increase the size of the army lost by a single vote. The next day, North Carolina Federalist Benjamin Hawkins explained to the President that he voted no because he knew "of no efforts made by the executive to enduce indians to come to an accom[m]odation . . . except . . . a feeble one." Hawkins, who for thirty years after 1785 served the cause of Indian-white peace as negotiator and Indian agent in the South, disagreed about the origins of the war, on the military strategy pursued, and on the use of regulars. He had asked Secretary Knox if the President would give his opinions directly to a Senate committee. Knox thought not. "I have great respect for the War officer but he appears . . . to be anxiously desirous of having considerable standing military force," Hawkins related. "He is not alone in that opinion. We have some in the Senate who say that such an establishment is necessary, very more, and indispensible to the preservation of liberty. To a disposition of this sort, I attribute the feeble efforts made to purchase a peace."[128] Privately the President exploded; Hawkins (who well symbolized the administration's critics) completely misunderstood the origins of the war, the government's responsibilities, what was needed militarily, and how he, the President, viewed relations between the Senate and the Executive.[129] How Washington actually replied to Hawkins and the Senate is not clear. According to congressman William Findley, the Senate dallied on the frontier bill by appointing a committee to consider the Knox plan after rejecting its key provision because it intended to force the President to replace St. Clair. Indeed a bargain may well have been struck, whereby the administration agreed to a new commanding general (which it wanted anyway) and to undertake serious negotiations with the tribes. In 1792 St. Clair was replaced and the administration began a two-year effort to interest the tribes in a negotiated settlement, although mainly for political reasons. In any event, on February 17, Hawkins switched his vote and the two New York senators who had been absent before, Aaron Burr and Rufus King, added their votes to pass the bill by 15-12. In March, after further amendment and a Senate-House conference, the legislation finally went to the President for signature into law.[130]

Under the "Act for making further and more effectual provision for the protection of the Frontiers," Congress authorized five 960-man regiments for three-year enlistments to be organized in any fashion the President judged "expedient." To attract better people, officers and men would receive higher pay. The President could now employ volunteer cavalry and friendly Indians. The one concession to the opposition was a provision requiring the discharge of the new regiments whenever peace should be established in the West. And two months later, after another bitter fight, Congress revised the tariff schedule and authorized new loans to finance the increased establishment.[131] The administration had won a victory in Congress, over fierce opposition and in spite of widespread public disillusionment with its policies. The costs were substantial. Using the public outcry, Republicans instituted an elaborate congressional investigation of the defeat, and on the last day of the session, a committee published a report exonerating St. Clair but lambasting the War Department, and by implication Secretary Knox and the President, for inept management of supplies, contracts, disbursements, and army administration generally.[132] Already the Indian war had wounded the Washington administration deeply—by embarrassment, by widening the disagreements which split the cabinet and gave birth to the Republican party, and by wasting money and blood. Congress and the public gave the administration the army it wanted, in order to restore the peace to the frontier which many felt the administration had bungled away. The message was crystal clear: end the war, either by negotiation or by military victory.

In the aftermath of St. Clair's defeat and the battle over expanding the regular army, the Washington administration took two more steps to create a military establishment capable of winning the Indian war. First it reorganized the army and the administration of military affairs in Philadelphia. With Congress's blessing, the administration changed the supply, accounting, and contract system in the War Department, creating an Accountant to the War Department to countersign all monetary authorizations for salary, subsistence, recruiting, and contingent expenses. The Accountant would report to the Secretary of the Treasury, and the Treasury would issue all funds for War Department use, let all contracts, and handle all purchases of supplies and provisions. In addition, a paymaster would oversee the disbursement of pay and subsistence from the Treasurer to regimental and company paymasters, transmitting reports and warrants to the Accountant for review by the Treasury Department. The changeover introduced for the first time a formal system of accountability in the War Department, a double-check system on virtually all activities, a rationalization of administration, and as an illustration of administration sensitivity to the political heat generated by the Indian war, the new procedures transferred considerable power from the War Department to Secretary of the Treasury Alexander Hamilton.[133]

At about the same time, the President and Knox decided to abandon the regimental organization of the army in favor of a legionary structure. Steuben had suggested such a change in order to facilitate campaigning in the wilderness. Instead of being organized by combat function— infantry, cavalry, and artillery—the army was divided into four sublegions, in effect four little armies of about 1,200 men, each with its own integral cavalry and artillery, under a single command, and thus a self-contained force able to act independently with mobility, flexibility, and hitting power. Furthermore the command of a sublegion justified a brigadier general instead of a colonel, the traditional regimental commander. The administration hoped not only to enhance the offensive punch and combat efficiency of the army, but to attract the better veterans of the Revolution, some of whom had been generals and would not accept a lesser rank.[134]

The second major change ordered by the President in the spring of 1792 was a thorough overhaul of the army's leadership—starting at the top. Washington and Knox first discussed the appointment of a new commanding general in January, but they kept the discussion secret lest it "excite Jealousy" and jeopardize the administration's proposals in Congress.[135] In early March, with the 5,000-man army safely passed, the President prepared a list of veterans from the Revolution and the cabinet discussed each one's qualifications. Unfortunately, each was in some way flawed. Some were unknown, others "past the vigor of life" like Benjamin Lincoln, and still others like Jedidiah Huntington had "never discover'd much enterprise."[136] Washington judged Anthony Wayne "Open to flattery; vain; easily imposed upon; liable to be drawn into scrapes" and likely "addicted to the bottle."[137] The cabinet agreed: "brave and nothing else," Jefferson recorded in his notes, the kind of man who might "run his head ag[ains]t a wall where success was both impossible and useless."[138] The best prospect was Governor Henry Lee of Virginia, the brilliant cavalry leader of the Revolution, liked and respected by the President, but the cabinet reasoned that as a mere colonel in the Revolution Lee would "lose benefit of good seniors who w[oul]d not serve under him."[139] That point worried the administration most of all. The new commander needed enough rank in the Revolution so that the good officers, like former Brigadier General Daniel Morgan, could accept appointment without the dishonor of taking orders from a man whom he outranked ten years earlier.

Politics complicated the choice immeasurably. By the time the cabinet began its discussions, the maneuvering for different candidates had already become intense. The Virginians backed Henry Lee. Another possibility was Rufus Putnam, pushed forward by the Reverend Manasseh Cutler, a founder of the Ohio Company and one of the era's most potent lobbyists who happened to be in Philadelphia in March 1792 on company business. Other candidates also had their backers.[140] To the President, who wanted the appointment to damp down opposition and build up public confidence in the war effort, the dilemma was fast becoming intolerable. He would not appoint anyone "in whom he could foresee any material opposition," he told Jefferson, who was checking reaction in Virginia to Wayne.[141] Yet as Washington lamented to Lee, "to attempt to please every body is the sure way to please nobody."[142]

Finally in April, the President reluctantly picked Anthony Wayne—"Mad Anthony," the salty combat leader who had seized the British bastion at Stony Point in 1781 in a night assault by bayonet alone, Wayne the Pennsylvanian who failed after the war as a southern planter and then gained election to Congress in 1790 only to be unseated because of irregularities in his election. Wayne wanted the command badly. In 1789 he began soliciting the administration for a job, peppering friends and acquaintances with advice about the Indian situation. Because of debts,

Wayne could not enter his native Pennsylvania without fear of arrest, and the only way to visit his family safely seemed to be as a congressman or federal officer. Once in Congress, he openly criticized the administration's handling of the war in the Northwest, but then voted in favor of the 5,000-man army, perhaps influenced directly by his old friend, Knox, or by the old Continental Army connection, or even by hopes or promises of the new command.[143] In any event the reaction to Wayne's appointment was at best mixed: surprise generally, "extreme disgust" in Virginia, and in the Senate, according to Madison, the appointment "went through . . . rather against the bristles."[144] Washington had narrowed the possibilities down to Lee, James Wilkinson, Charles Cotesworth Pinckney, Morgan, and Wayne. Only the latter two, however, had been permanent generals during the Revolution (rather than brevet, or temporary, general officers). While known for "eclat," Morgan was illiterate, possibly an alcoholic, and under suspicion of bilking his own soldiers out of their land certificates after the war ("no head, health gone, speculator," noted Jefferson tersely at the cabinet meeting).[145] With all his warts, Wayne had the mind and the experience for a major independent command. Washington and Knox knew Anthony Wayne—his politics, his personality, his military strengths and weaknesses, and his opinion of how to deal with Indians, which matched that of the administration almost exactly. Chosen as the least of the possible evils, Wayne turned out to be among the most brilliant appointments in the Federalist era. In April his was the first name sent to the Senate, at the top of a long list of new officers, including men to fill the critical administrative posts of Quartermaster General, Paymaster, and Accountant to the War Department.[146] The army was now to be the Legion of the United States: a new organization, different generals, fresh officers, a revamped administration, new spirit—and victory.

The first four months of 1792 marked a major watershed in the creation of a national military establishment in the United States. Taken together, the decision by the administration to fight the Indian war wholly with regulars, the endorsement of that policy by Congress in approving an army of over 5,000 men, the internal reorganization of the army into a legion, the overhaul of military administration in Philadelphia, and the installation of new leadership—all began the transformation of the military establishment into the efficient military machine that eventually smashed the Indian confederacy in the Northwest. The 1792 reformation was another major step, like the establishment of the 1st Regiment in 1784 and the giving of clearcut military powers to the federal government in the Constitution of 1787, in the creation of the military establishment that Hamilton and Washington first proposed in 1783.

Like many reforms in military institutions or in businesses or in fact in any complex organization, the changes in 1792 were spawned by disaster and by necessity. To ideologue Republicans at the time and to many historians since, unaware of the Washington administration's blunders, the Indian war and the creation of Wayne's Legion seemed part of a grand Federalist design to graft a standing army onto American society. It is true that the administration attempted only halfheartedly to negotiate with the tribes, that it leaned naturally toward the use of force, and that it always preferred regulars to militia. Its posture in public and in Congress on Indian policy and on increasing the size of the army was indeed self-serving and purposely misrepresented to quiet congressional apprehension and public criticism. Unfortunately the administration moved brazenly on the frontier, but by stealth and indirection before the American people.

Yet the administration tried very hard, at times desperately, to avoid a war. From the beginning in 1789, Washington and Knox understood the political and financial disadvantages of an Indian war. Throughout they attempted in their own way to stop hostilities and yet at the same time to deter the Indians, weaken British influence in the area, prevent an Indian confederacy, maintain the prestige of the infant government, and satisfy the incessant demands of frontiersmen and land speculators— all with the least expenditure of blood, treasure, and political goodwill. The administration failed—because of its arrogance and its ignorance, because it miscalculated Indian motives, mismanaged the army, and misunderstood the implications of using force in the first place. Until 1792, the administration treated the Northwest situation casually, as a problem secondary to solidifying the new government in financial and foreign affairs. The administration invariably took the short-term, expedient course in Indian and military policy, allowing politics and finance to override military necessity. "The truth is," Pickering told his wife after learning of St. Clair's defeat, "the army as it was proposed to be constituted . . . was thought . . . so formidable that the Indians would not dare to stand in its way."[147] In the end, the administration was as bewildered and dismayed as the bitterest of its critics. As Knox reported to the President, in resignation and disgust, "an Indian war, of considerable extent, has been excited, not only contrary to the interest and intention of the General Government, but by means altogether without its control."[148]

7

★ ☆ ★ ☆ ★ ☆ ★ ☆ ★

The Murder of
the Militia System
[1792]

★

Some time ago there passed a milk-and-water law in Congress, with hardly a New England vote to it, and since that time there have been no hopes of a good militia. . . . Some people pretend to be jealous of the New England members, as attached to a standing army. The reason why they are so is, that they despair of ever seeing a militia, that will be worth one farthing. . . . He [Jeremiah Wadsworth] thanked God that the Government of the country was not left entirely to the House of Representatives, for he believed that they would make most wretched work of it.

Congressman Jeremiah Wadsworth, 1795.[a]

In the spring of 1792, the United States took another important step in creating a military establishment, when Congress passed the first national militia law in American history. For nearly a decade Federalists had pressed for reform of the state forces. To them, a uniform, strengthened militia resolved the dilemma of how to defend a nation which rejected standing forces but could not rely on weak, inefficient, state armies. The Constitution gave Congress power over the militia, but legislation lay buried for nearly three years, delayed and damaged by a confusing welter of partisan and local disagreements. Only St. Clair's defeat, which destroyed the regular army and left the frontiers naked, forced a reluctant and divided Congress into approving legislation. And in the end, the Uniform Militia Act of 1792 contained so many weaknesses and omissions that it failed utterly to reverse the process of decline suffered by the militia for nearly a century. Thus 1792 became a turning point. Congress fulfilled its duty "To provide for organizing, arming, and disciplining" the state forces and never again arrived at the agreement needed to confront the issue squarely. After 1792 the creation of some kind of national military establishment became inevitable. As the President put it that winter, "if Congress will not Enact a *proper* . . . law (not such a milk and water thin[g] as I expect to see if I ever see any) Defence and the Garrisons will always require some Troops."[1]

Washington first began pressing Congress to reorganize the militia in 1789, when he asked for special authority to call out units on the frontier. Indeed throughout the decade attempts at militia reform always followed after some military crisis, either on the frontier, a foreign war scare, or suppressing domestic turmoil. In 1789 Congress responded by appointing a committee to study legislation.[2] But other business quickly intervened, forcing adjournment before a bill could be drafted. When the second session convened in January 1790, the President decided to propose his own system of reform in order to speed congressional action. Using descriptions of various European militias, Baron Steuben's 1784 recommendations for a national system, Washington took the plan Secretary Knox had published in 1786 and added to it his own recommendations. Knox then worked Washington's ideas into a revision of the 1786 plan and submitted the result, with Washington's approval, to Congress in late January 1790.[3]

The administration's 1790 plan was the culmination of Federalist thinking about the militia, the direct progeny in refined and revised form of the ideas that nationalist officers first presented at the close of the war. The objectives were twofold: to remake the state forces in "powerful," "energetic," and "well constituted" armies, and second, in order to force such reforms, to bring the militia under national control. Strengthening clearly meant more training and education for the citizenry than state systems at the time provided. Yet Knox knew that every man could not be liable for the necessary training, and that such training for the older men would not necessarily produce good soldiers. Therefore he recommended dividing each state organization into three classes: an "advanced corps" of all men aged 18 to 20; a "main corps" of those 21 to 45; and a "reserved corps" of those 46 to 60. Classing was not novel. Washington, Steuben, Hamilton, and several of the officers had proposed it in 1783 as a means of getting better trained forces without wasting money and energy on units which because of age could not campaign effectively. Knox felt that with the country's aversion to a standing army, the only alternative to classing was using substitutes, inevitably "the most idle and worthless part of the community," a system which could only bring contempt on the militia.

Knox described the advanced corps not only as the flower of the militia force, a small army of perhaps 30,000 ready for immediate mobilization in crisis, but also as a school for young Americans to "imbibe a love of their country; reverence and obedience to its laws; courage and elevation of mind; openness and liberality of character;" and a "robustness" "greatly conducive" to defense and to producing a "glorious national spirit." For 30 days every year as 18- and 19-year-olds, and for 10 days at age 20, young men would attend "camps of discipline" where in spartan isolation ("remote from cities . . . to avoid the vices of populous places"), without any "amusements" save "those which correspond with war—the swimming of men and horses, running, wrestling, and such other exercises . . ."—the men would learn soldiering. After that, at 21, an individual would pass into the main corps, the "principal defence of the country," the large manpower pool from which the United States would draw its armies to oppose an invasion or fight a prolonged war. Although these men would muster only four days every year, the "constant accession" of the youth would make the main corps adequate for battle. Then at 46, an individual passed into the "reserved corps," a kind of home defense guard, liable for muster only twice a year and to be called out only when their state was repelling an actual invasion.

Clearly the administration's proposal would thoroughly nationalize all the militias. The federal government specified the organization of the units, provided the bulk of training, and assumed nearly every responsibility except specifying exemptions from service and the appointment of officers. Knox's plan included all sorts of details, like administration, musters, pay and subsistence, and mobilization procedures. Furthermore the federal government provided all arms, equipment, and clothing for the men. Officers would receive federal pay while training the advanced corps, and the government could mobilize forces on its own authority. While the states each appointed an inspector, a quartermaster, and an adjutant general, these officers would report partially to federal authorities. Knox made no provision for fines, the traditional method by which to enforce attendance at training or registration in the system or the possession of arms. Instead Knox planned to furnish all the necessary equipment from national stockpiles and to force young men to attend the yearly camps by making a certificate of graduation from the advanced corps "an indispensable qualification for exercising any of the rights of a free citizen" up to a specified age. Thus to vote, hold office, or exercise legal rights, an American youth would have to undergo military training—enough of it so that the "main corps," revitalized every year by a group from the training camps, could field effective forces without compelling attendance at quarterly musters. And to assure mobilization in an emergency, Knox wanted every company divided into twelve-man sections, so that federal authorities could draft individuals—for service up to three years—if enough did not volunteer.[4]

Congress and the public greeted the administration's system with shock and disbelief—"so palpably absurd and impolitic," snapped DeWitt

Clinton, "that I take it for granted it will meet with no success."[5] Certainly the plan was overly ambitious. The administration believed sincerely that the nation must prepare to defend itself, so it presented Congress and the country with a difficult dilemma: either create a standing army, a large, powerful national force of long-service professionals (distinguished from the frontier constabulary proposed by the nationalists in 1783), or revise the militia system. And quite likely, the administration purposely phrased its recommendations in exaggerated form in hopes that after the inevitable debates and compromises in Congress, the final legislation would ret.in those provisions necessary to transform the militia into a viable military institution. But the expense—over $400,000 annually for the advanced corps alone—shocked most congressmen and senators. "I believe Knox to be the most extravagant man almost living," complained Massachusetts representative Benjamin Goodhue.[6] Specific provisions of the plan seemed just as troubling. Classing was extremely unpopular, especially in New England and along the seaboard where young apprentices would be absent from their trades for a month every year. Many thought the annual training could militarize the nation. If young people "establish and fix their morals" between eighteen and twenty-one, argued "A Mechanic" in the Philadelphia *Freeman's Journal*, military camp was no place to learn "virtuous principles."[7] As one Pennsylvania congressman agreed, youth would learn only "Idleness & extravagance etc. etc."[8] The citizenship qualification and the possibility of a draft for three-years' service also provoked adverse comment. In areas with significant Quaker populations, Knox's position on conscientious objection seemed scandalous. The Secretary had been willing to relax the principle of universal obligation for officials, ministers, and "perhaps some religious sects." "But it ought to be remembered," he had added, "that measures of national importance never should be frustrated for the accommodation of individuals."[9] William Ellery refused to send the plan to a printer lest it so alarm Rhode Island Quakers that they abandon the Federalist party.[10] All told the reaction was almost universally negative. "There are a number of opinions," Knox learned from a Massachusetts friend, "all tend[ing] to damn it."[11]

For months, while debate raged over Hamilton's financial program and congressmen maneuvered fiercely over the location of a permanent and temporary national capital, the militia question languished in committee. Finally in late April, an expanded committee on national defense in the House began drafting legislation.[12] With the reaction to the Knox plan so strong, the committee purposely softened the administration's recommendations. Instead of classing younger men into a separate corps, the new bill put 18- to 24-year-olds into special light infantry or rifle companies attached to regular battalions and regiments. As schools "to promote military knowledge" and furnish "the means of immediate defense in case of invasion or insurrection," the companies would muster alone four times yearly, then with their parent unit twice more. All other companies would train only four times annually. Under the congressional plan, each militiaman would provide himself with a musket, ammunition, and accoutrements—knapsack, flints, bayonet, and cartridge pouch—instead of being armed at federal expense as the administration wished. Absence from muster or failure to own the proper equipment could cost a militiaman up to one dollar, depending on the offense. The committees made liberal provision for exemptions from service, but most groups excused (Quakers included) would pay a yearly tax of two dollars. The strongest sections of the bill, designed to insure trained, effective forces without Knox's military encampments, created new administrative officers. State adjutant generals would coordinate the various units, execute orders of state commanders-in-chief, and oversee everything "which relates to the general advancement of good order and discipline." Likewise state commissaries of military stores would superintend storage and issuing of all ordnance and equipment belonging to a state. Most important, the President would appoint a federal inspector to attend regimental musters at least once yearly, inspect arms and equipment, direct training, and in general "introduce a system of military discipline . . . agreeably to law and such orders" as received from the state commander.[13] This was as much reform as the committee was willing to recommend. In July 1790, at the end of the session, the bill was introduced, read, and printed for distribution so that public reaction could be tested before Congress debated so sensitive an issue. "I do not look upon it [as] a very perfect system," admitted Massachusetts representative George Thacher, a member of the committee. "[E]very time I run it over, I think I can point out imperfections."[14]

In truth the militia problem made most congressmen exceedingly uncomfortable. Few doubted the need for improving the institution, or for making it uniform throughout the country so that forces could better muster together in a national emergency. Yet while reform benefitted the nation as a whole, it also tread severely on local interests and raised several potentially explosive issues. As Rhode Island's senators explained, any law would touch the "Interest" and "Feelings of every Individual."[15] Every voter would feel the effect of more training or stiff fines, or view the schedule of exemptions with jealousy. Any national law would be bound to impinge on the local variations in each state system. In towns, classing worked a burden by increasing the obligation of apprentices. In the South, a uniform tactical structure might make heavier reliance on cavalry units for slave patrol impossible. Quakers, at times a potent lobby, feared a national law might not allow exemptions from service for reason of conscience. In addition, many representatives served in the militia themselves, and thus held pet theories as to how the institution should be organized for military effectiveness and to benefit or least inconvenience their constituents. The expense of a national system also endangered reform. And lurking behind every provision lay the threatening issue of national versus state power, of how much authority the national government could legitimately assume without rendering the states either powerless over their forces or the militia itself useless for local needs.

When the House began debating the bill in December 1790, under Washington's prodding and the pressure of Harmar's defeat, every provision was subjected to microscopic analysis. Some Federalists pushed for strengthening the bill, especially by arming the militia at federal expense. Others disagreed. The "squabble," reported Jonathan Trumbull, was "only in words—not in Blood," but the differences of opinion on everything, from the age of service to the number and purpose of muster days, to the number, rank, and pay of inspectors, made debate exasperating.[16] Most of the time discussion appeared soft, formless, almost without principle or importance ("puerile," snapped Trumbull; "too much into the minutiae of the business," remarked Timothy Bloodworth more charitably).[17] But agreement was impossible on any provision which increased the burden on individual citizens or provided for a specific national standard. Gradually, inexorably, the bill was stripped of its strongest provisions in order to satisfy the chorus of conflicting views. Erased was classing, opposed even by some staunch Federalists because it discriminated against "manufacturers and mechanics" and because the young men might live too scattered to muster together conveniently.[18] Federal inspectors were transferred to state control, partly to relieve the government of the expense of their salaries and partly because under the Constitution the states seemed to possess exclusive power to make militia appointments. After ten days the bill was in Trumbull's words "so mutilated, maimed, & murdered" that the House appointed a new committee to prepare another version.[19] But the bill reported in January 1791 solved nothing. The Quakers, who flooded Congress with petitions in favor of exemption on religious grounds without payment of a penalty tax, were upset because the new bill did not leave exemptions up to individual states. Friends in Philadelphia, the residence of Congress until 1800, continued to buttonhole individual congressmen and their Rhode Island brethren even organized a letter-writing campaign to pressure their representatives.[20] In the end, because agreement on specifics was impossible, because as one of Madison's friends put it, "There is great diversity of opinion both in and out of Congress on [the militia] and it is of a nature to excite much jealousy," the First Congress disbanded without further action.[21]

When the Second Congress met in October 1791, nothing had changed. "[T]here appears a general sense . . . of the pressing importance of a uniform regulation," reported George Thacher, but the Massachusetts representative doubted "whether any thing will be done this session."[22] Then in December St. Clair's defeat rocked the capital. With the regular army destroyed and the frontiers defenseless, the need for federal legislation suddenly became critical. The President possessed no power to mobilize frontier units (such authorization had lapsed) nor even formal authority to reimburse militiamen if called out by state officials.[23] Again the administration pressed for action and this time Congress obliged. The pressure was now intense with the 5,000-man army bill up for consideration. It would be the third law in three years swelling the size of the regulars, and at no time was the tradeoff between a regular army and militia reform more clearcut. "Anything is preferable to nothing," observed Republican James Monroe, "as it takes away one of the arguments for a standing army."[24]

In February, discussion began on the weakened revision of the 1790 congressional bill. Elias Boudinot, the New Jersey Federalist, former President of the Continental Congress, and chairman of the committee of national defense that had drafted the first congressional plan, begged his colleagues to stop haggling over every detail. "[A] plan of conciliation alone would ever procure . . . a militia bill," Boudinot reasoned. "[T]he law . . . must be very simple in its construction, and refer to as few objects as possible."[25] Boudinot understood the mood in Congress perfectly, but to other Federalists he was digging the grave for real reform. Wadsworth of Connecticut objected that "the subject had been managed . . . as to pare the bill . . . down to such an inadequate, defective system, that he did not feel much interested in its fate."[26] Yet he and others had to beat back strong efforts by some Republicans who denied any power in the federal government to regulate what seemed to them wholly state institutions. At one point a motion was introduced to remove the provision requiring uniform caliber muskets, basic to establishing a common militia system, on grounds that money would be wasted for new weapons. Unlike a year earlier, the entire 1792 debate hinged on the extent of national jurisdiction over the militia, an increasingly prominent bone of contention between the parties emerging in Congress. The result was an even weaker bill. By the time the House finished, the militia act was so lacking in strong measures for reform—classing, fines, an administrative structure to assure training and compliance with national standards— that the Senate could accept it without major disagreements. The most significant Senate modification—giving the President authority to call out militia to execute laws, suppress insurrections, or repel invasions— was promptly rejected by the House on the grounds that making this power exclusive to the executive would constitute a dangerous grant. (The two houses compromised by passing a separate law defining the procedures and conditions under which the President could call militia into federal service.) Finally, after a Senate-House conference and the added pressure of impending adjournment, Congress formally approved "an Act more effectually to provide for the National Defence, by establishing an Uniform Militia." Eleven days later, at the last possible moment (probably to register his disgust with such a weak measure), the President signed it into law.[27]

The Uniform Militia Act of 1792 put all "free able-bodied white male citizen[s]" from the ages of 18 through 45 in the militia and obligated them to arm themselves with a musket or rifle, ammunition, and basic accoutrements within six months. After five years muskets were to be of standard bore. Officers of the United States, the postal service, ferrymen on post roads, pilots, mariners, "and all persons" excused by state law were exempt from service. State legislatures were to arrange the men into units and if "convenient," into the tactical organization described in the law. Each state was to train its men according to the manual Baron Steuben had developed during the war unless "unavoidable circumstances" dictated otherwise. State adjutant generals were to oversee and administer local forces and each brigade would include an inspector to "superintend" the "exercise and maneuvers" and "introduce the system of military discipline." Nothing in the law, however, guaranteed training or even uniformity of structure and equipment. The law contained no provision for classing or any procedure for enforcing national guidelines. The government imposed no fines for malfeasance, against the states or individual militia, nor did the law establish any special officers to report on militia affairs to the President or Congress. If a state defied the national system, the federal government was impotent to intercede.[28]

Never again during the Federalist period did Congress act on militia reform, and in fact not until another century passed did the national government finally pass a law which imposed effective national regulations on the states. Only under the combined pressure of St. Clair's defeat, and the need for a statute implementing the provision in the Constitution on organizing the militia, did Congress summon the resolve to untangle such a thorny issue. Opportunities arose during the decade of the 1790s to amend and strengthen the law, especially in 1794 when war with England beckoned and 15,000 militiamen from four states marched into western Pennsylvania to crush the Whiskey Rebellion. Secretary Knox glumly related to Congress in December of that year all the discrepancies in state militia laws, especially the varying penalties for "non-equipment and armament." The War Department had been forced to provide nearly two-thirds of the men mobilized with weapons, and by Knox's estimate less than one quarter of some half-million militiamen in the nation possessed arms as required under the 1792 law. Once again

Knox asked Congress to establish a select corps and provide effective penalties to insure discipline and proper equipment.[29] Many congressmen backed him, including Republican Samuel Smith, who blasted the quality of the troops, recounting one incident when he had ordered his Maryland contingent to load their muskets and fifty had "put down the ball before the charge of powder." "The Government must either have a good militia or a standing army," added another representative, "and a militia [is] more agreeable to Republican principles." If a select corps "be struck out," Federalist Jeremiah Wadsworth admonished, "we give over every hope of mending our militia law; and we must remain as we are, in a loose, deranged, uncertain situation."[30]

The debate proved fruitless. Attempts were made to change the law in virtually every session for the next three decades, but Congress never acted.[31] Nearly everyone agreed that the 1792 law was a failure. Federalist Senator Charles Carroll of Carrollton, for example, called it initially "harmless," but after the Maryland legislature wrestled with legislation to implement the national statute, Carroll concluded that "Never in [his] judgment did a body of wise men pass so mischievous an act."[32] State legislation passed to implement the law contained tremendous variations on every subject, from unit structure to fines and number of musters.[33] "[I]t was generally allowed," announced one congressman in 1797 when the country teetered on the brink of war with France, "that the present militia laws were not only very expensive . . . , but very inadequate in their effects."[34] Yet a strong national militia might have cost hundreds of thousands of dollars annually. A revised system would have forced changes many states did not want, worked hardships on special groups, and certainly increased the burden on voters. No one could agree on fines, on exemptions, whether the states could administer training or if federal inspectors were needed, whether training camps would school youth to defend the country or debauch their morals, or indeed if a national system would revitalize the institution or destroy it. Worst of all, as the party struggle intensified, Congress agreed less and less on how far federal authority extended, given the ambiguity in the Constitution's language. Federalist military thinkers might desire classing, but party stalwarts from seaboard constituencies saw hardships worked on their townsmen, and some no doubt realized that a weak militia enhanced the need for a strong national military establishment. (William Maclay accused Knox of proposing an extreme plan for reform in 1790 in the knowledge that it would never pass, forcing Congress to assent to a standing army.)[35] Republicans might want a viable militia to fight the Indians and avert a national army, but too many party members believed in reducing federal budgets and minimizing the power of the central government over the states.

When the first session of the Second Congress adjourned in early summer 1792, the United States had crossed a watershed in the development of its military institutions. Congress had created the first effective peacetime army and, in the Uniform Militia Act, had dealt a crushing blow to an already dying militia system. The militias had been degenerating steadily for nearly a century. Designed as local defense forces to protect against Indian raids, foreign invasion, and domestic disorder, they had by mid-century with the movement of the frontier westward, the receding of the Indian threat, and the willingness of Britain to use its army in America, begun to lose their relevance. Embroiled increasingly in the European wars of empire against militarily advanced foes, Americans began increasingly to rely on British forces and volunteers serving in regularly constituted units. As an independent republic after 1783, the United States needed a military capable of opposing European armies and moving offensively to break Indian power in the West where states possessed no jurisdiction. War in America promised to be a sophisticated undertaking, not isolated, embattled communities warding off sporadic attack. Even if Americans fought defensive wars, the strategy and tactics needed to defeat an enemy would undoubtedly require offensive campaigns for which the state militias were unsuited and often, because of legal prohibitions against service out of state, unable legally to mount. By the 1790s, the old colonial militia had become an obsolete institution.

The calls for reform which began in 1783 and culminated in the act of 1792 revealed that many Americans sensed the inability of state institutions, poorly coordinated, badly disciplined, and casually armed, to meet the needs of the new republic. Perhaps, had Congress been able to implement the Constitution with a law which provided effective reform, the concept of the citizen-soldier and universal obligation might have been preserved within the institutional framework of the old colonial militia. Instead Americans almost unconsciously sought new alternatives. The 1792 law did not, as most historians have argued or implied, become the foundation for American military policy until the twentieth century. The act looked backward to colonial times, to a simpler military environment, to localism in defense when citizens could provide security by defending themselves, hastily organizing amateur campaigns, or calling in the British army and navy as a last resort. Only in the War of 1812, would militia once more be thrown into battle without reorganization, an experience that proved disastrous. In the 1790s Americans discovered a new method by which to mobilize the military potential of its citizenry: federal volunteers, the administration's political compromise in 1791, the levies who were enlisted, armed, trained, paid, and commanded in battle by the national government.[36] Volunteers enlisted for a limited term furnished an institutional alternative to the politically unpopular standing army and the militarily unreliable state militia, preserving the tradition of universal obligation and the citizen-soldier but within the new institutional context of volunteer forces fighting under the command and control of the national government. Because Americans in the eighteenth century did not discern this alternative of federal volunteers, because professional military thinkers into the twentieth century distrusted the citizen-soldier, because of the political power of the national guard and the need for state military forces, and above all because of the rhetoric of embattled farmers enshrined in Revolutionary mythology and dramatized down through history from Andrew Jackson to Alvin York, the militia has survived to the present. But as early as 1801 the weakness of the militia made this rhetoric hollow, a fact understood by some of the militia's most vocal admirers. On March 4, 1801, with the election won and charges of militarism receding into the background, Thomas Jefferson all but endorsed Federalist military theory. Defining what he considered "the essential principles of our Government," those "which ought to shape its Administration," the leader of the party which had always fought against the creation of a substantial national army and championed the cause of the militia, proclaimed "a well-disciplined militia, our best reliance in peace and for the first moments of war, *till regulars may relieve them*."[37]*

*Emphasis added.

8

Two Uses of Force

★

[F]orce displayed in due season, and with energy and promptness, will often put an end of opposition, and preclude the necessity of rigour. When you are known to be strong you may pardon; if thought to be weak you are compelled to punish. When therefore an insurrection was excited . . . , a force so great as to preclude all hope of successful resistance was called out to suppress it. . . . It was likewise a leading principal of [Federalist] policy to employ a strong regular force, for repressing the hostile spirit of the savages and protect[ing] the frontiers. . . .

Robert Goodloe Harper, March 5, 1801.[a]

In the space of a few short months in the summer and fall of 1794, the Federalists successfully applied military force in two separate but interrelated situations. First, the Washington administration defeated the Wabash and Miami Indians and their allies in battle, breaking the back of Indian resistance and British influence in the old Northwest. The purpose in Federalist minds after 1790 had always been the restoration of peace in the area, the punishment of an enemy, and the reestablishment of respect for the power of the government among Indians and white frontiersmen. Thus force created a governmental presence which would deter future hostility, stabilize a potentially explosive zone of conflict, and defeat an enemy. Above all, the use of military power forced an adversary to do the government's bidding.

Second, in the fall of 1794 the Washington administration mobilized 15,000 militiamen and crushed the Whiskey Rebellion in western Pennsylvania virtually without firing a shot. Again force restored the *status quo ante*; again it inspired respect, even fear, and to Federalists established a deterrent atmosphere which could last for years, making another such costly exercise unneeded. Most important, force maintained the orderly functioning of government and society after the coercion of law failed. In Federalist minds the purpose of using military action was similar in both episodes, although one was ostensibly to defeat a "foreign" enemy and the other was to suppress domestic turmoil. Federalists believed that force provided the ultimate tool to control or crush an enemy; its use established and demonstrated strength; and its proper application could save lives and prevent confrontations in the future.

The use of force by the government in 1794 was by no means the simple process most historians have pictured. It took the Washington administration nearly three years after St. Clair's defeat to bring the Indians to their knees, a slow, tortuous three years in which the Indian war became firmly politicized as a partisan issue and the administration absorbed some of the most vicious attacks in its eight-year reign. Victory was delayed not because of military considerations, although an entire campaign season was consumed in rebuilding the regular army, but because the government was forced into attempting negotiations in order to blunt public criticism of its goals and methods of prosecuting the war. Five years of dealing with the northwestern tribes taught the Washington administration valuable lessons about the use of force, lessons that were applied after initial hesitation with skill and determination against the Whiskey rebels: that force was a delicate business, a political act which required careful preparation beyond the mere mobilization of men and resources for a military expedition, and one in which an adversary must not only be respected, but met with force in overwhelming proportions.

Nor was the decision to send troops against the Whiskey rebels the easy one that historians have always assumed. Beset with foreign and domestic crises and under unrelenting assault by the Republican opposition, the Washington administration divided over how to respond to the rebellion. The President first rejected the advice of Alexander Hamilton and delayed the march of the militia, hoping to unite public opinion behind the government and assure that the militia would turn out. Then he partially jettisoned that tactic when the peace commission sent to negotiate with the rebels reported the situation hopeless. In the end, of course, the government suppressed the rebellion successfully, without bloodshed, with the near universal praise of political leaders and the public. Indeed, to most Federalists, the use of force was an unqualified and unquestioned victory; they learned little which failed to reinforce their assumptions about the positive advantages to be gained, as Hamilton put it, in appearing "like a *Hercules*, and inspir[ing] respect by the display of strength."[1] The militarism in the party was nurtured and encouraged. To those in the party whose predilection was rule by force, the events at mid-decade clearly proved the political and institutional benefits to be gained by coercing foreign or domestic opponents. To others, however, the experiences of the Indian war and the Whiskey Rebellion taught that force contained great dangers, perhaps even greater disadvantages than benefits. Philosophically and in practical political terms in the mid-1790s, there existed hidden beneath a surface unanimity profound differences of opinion among Federalist leaders over the advantages to be gained in the use of force, and how and under what circumstances force should be used. In slightly altered form, these differences were destined ultimately to destroy the Federalist party.

Winning Peace: The Politics of Victory in the Northwest
[1792–1794]

General Wayne and the Western Army. May their victories be the means of introducing Peace, Civilization and Happiness among our Savage Enemies.

Toast at a testimonial dinner for Alexander Hamilton and Henry Knox, 1795.[b]

As he stood above the headwaters of the Ohio River in the hamlet of Pittsburgh in mid-June 1792, Anthony Wayne must have realized the enormity of the undertaking. "I really feel awkwardly situated," he told Secretary Knox, "a General without troops is somewhat similar to a fish out of Water."[2] Before Wayne lay hundreds of miles of open frontier, unguarded except for militia and scattered handfuls of troops left from St. Clair's shattered army. So few were the men and so vast the distances that Wayne's deputy, Brigadier General James Wilkinson, questioned whether the army could maintain communications and protect its own forts, much less defend settlers in Kentucky and north of the river.[3] Nonetheless the new commanding general set to work, writing to Wilkinson at Fort Washington for intelligence of enemy movements and intentions and checking the progress of supplies heading downriver from Pittsburgh. Wayne then asked the War Department to send the new recruits quickly west and to forward "explicit" instructions from the President as to whether the army should remain at Pittsburgh for training or head for Cincinnati immediately.[4] The job was formidable and the responsibility for lives and the military reputation of the republic disquieting, but as events would show, Anthony Wayne was equal to the challenge.

In contrast to the frenzied preparations then beginning on the frontier, the War Department was moving with great caution during the spring of 1792. This time, the American army would not fall victim to haste or to the political temptation for a quick victory. Washington and Knox dared not risk another defeat which would hearten the Indians further, stiffen British resistance to surrendering the key forts along the

Great Lakes (perhaps even tempt British intervention), or disgrace the administration's military policy, particularly the reliance on regulars. Most important, another setback might destroy public confidence in the government altogether. In early 1792, Federalists were growing ever more sensitive to the divisive effects of partisan warfare in the Congress and the cabinet. "I fear . . . the national government has seen its best days," moaned Theodore Sedgwick in despair. "[T]he rancorous jealousy that began with the infancy of the government, and grows with its growth . . . produce in my mind serious doubts whether the machine will not soon have some of its wheels so disordered as to be incapable of regular process."[5] With some justification, the administration interpreted the opposition to its military proposals as partisan and ideological (Jefferson, after all, used the editorial "we" that spring in describing the effort to block the 5,000-man army).[6] The bitter attacks on the regular army, on administration plans for financing new campaigns, the "persecution" of the Secretary of War, and disagreements over the militia were all to Knox "a partial aversion to the government," and in Hamilton's view quite likely, given other southern assaults on administration programs, "a serious design to subvert the government [itself]."[7] Actually the scorn heaped on administration western policy was only in part motivated by party politics, but it stung the administration deeply, making it wary and unwilling to risk either a military reversal or anything that could spark renewed public censure.

Part of the government's caution stemmed strictly from military considerations. The army was nowhere near ready for battle and the administration knew it. Washington and Knox wanted the best men possible inducted into the army, and the War Department instructed recruiters to enlist only "brave, robust, faithful soldiers" ("vagabonds . . . unwarily and unworthily" shanghaied into the ranks served "grudgingly," deserted, and "set bad examples to others," warned the recruiting instructions).[8] Such instructions were not novel, but this time the government was serious, warning recruiting officers of their own personal liability for financial losses resulting from desertions from recruiting stations. The result was extremely slow recruiting—only 130 men by May 1 and a mere 1,083 moving to Pittsburgh by late June.[9] Another reason for delay was the extensive overhaul of army logistics, both in Philadelphia and on the frontier. The Treasury now supervised supplies and contracts, but it did not take full charge until mid-May and as late as August, Hamilton was still tinkering with new procedures.[10] In addition, Knox revamped the army's own supply system. In April he appointed James O'Hara, a veteran officer and Pittsburgh merchant, as Quartermaster General. During the summer and fall of 1792 O'Hara established a whole new logistical network, with deputies in Philadelphia, Pittsburgh, and Fort Washington, all designed to speed material to the army and free Wayne from the nagging responsibility for supply.[11] But it all took time; by June Knox suspected that an army could not be ready before late August, then learned from Wilkinson that the old units along the Ohio were in such disarray that another campaign might well require changes in the Articles of War, the promotion system, and training procedures—in short a thorough-going reform of the army internally.[12] In August, the Secretary informed General Wayne that "an active campaign this year" looks very doubtful.[13] Both the President and Knox wanted Wayne to bide his time, organize his forces carefully at Pittsburgh, and train them thoroughly for the fighting ahead.

Wayne also realized by late summer that a campaign in 1792 was impossible, but the eager general knew that the condition of the army was not the most important reason. Wayne understood the war's unpopularity and the political considerations that drove the administration almost desperately to seek negotiations with the tribes. All through the summer, the general watched unhappily, chafing at the government's faintheartedness, as a parade of agents sallied forth to persuade the Indians to talk peace. There was "but little expectation of an Honorable and lasting peace, with a victorious, haughty, and insidious enemy—stimulated by British emissaries," he sneered in a letter to Wilkinson. "But such was the prevailing disposition . . . in Congress, that government was compelled to adopt the measure of attempting every possible means of procuring peace."[14] Wayne was perfectly correct. For the next two years, while he slowly built the army into a powerful striking force, the administration took the utmost pains to restore public support for its western policy before the inevitable campaign that would reestablish its military reputation with the Indian tribes and the world.

With public doubt and criticism of the war reaching a crescendo, and with the need to keep the enemy off balance while its military forces were rebuilt, the Washington administration in January 1792 almost by instinct decided to dispatch new feelers to the Indian tribes to initiate negotiations leading to a peaceful settlement. As in years past, the government doubted that the missions of Captains Peter Pond and William Steedman authorized in January, and others ordered through the army commander at Fort Knox the next month, would bring any peaceful results. Pond and Steedman were to travel to Forts Niagara and Detroit, "Mix with the Miami and Wabash Indians," "Find their views and intentions," if they were disposed to peace "ripen their judgment" and "persuade some of the most influential chiefs" to visit Philadelphia, and in general to "Insinuate, upon all favorable occasions, the humane disposition of the United States."[15] Both men, however, carried arrogant messages which while admitting that "our forces have been defeated," warned the tribes that "the numbers . . . were . . . small, compared with the numbers we are about to send" and called on the Indians to "ask a peace of us."[16] Furthermore Knox ordered the two to travel incognito as traders, to ascertain Indian strength, losses in battle, sources of supply, and future military plans—in effect to spy on the enemy as well as act as diplomats. These were cosmetic missions, but the administration was desperate. Even after Pond and Steedman reported that the British would not permit supplies to pass along the Great Lakes to a negotiating site, the cabinet decided unanimously to continue the peace offensive, agreeing that a settlement might well be worth conceding some of the territory north of the Ohio granted to investors and state governments.[17]

A few weeks later, the administration learned to its surprise that a peaceful settlement might indeed be possible, and it seized the opportunity gratefully. Immediately after St. Clair's defeat, the government had renewed an invitation to the Six Nations to visit Philadelphia, hoping to keep those strategically located tribes neutral in the war and perhaps gain their help as intermediaries with their hostile cousins to the west. In mid-March, warriors and chiefs (minus Mohawk Joseph Brant, the most important leader, who had received a special invitation from Knox), arrived in the capital for six weeks of discussions and entertainment. The result was a treaty reaffirming mutual friendship and continued peace. In the course of the visit, however, Knox and Washington learned to their astonishment that the Six Nations interpreted the whites as fighting for territorial gains. (Timothy Pickering, who handled relations with the tribes, was not at all surprised; as he told Washington, "Indians have been so often deceived by White people, that *White Man* is, among many of them, but another name for *Liar*.")[18] Knox and the President realized immediately that the Miami and Wabash probably labored under the same misconception, thus providing a real opening for some sort of negotiation. The government approached several of the Six Nations chiefs to act as emissaries, and one, a Stockbridge named Hendrick Aupaumut, agreed.[19]

To get its message across unequivocally, the administration decided to send several messengers: Aupaumut to the council of Indians soon to assemble at Auglaize near the Maumee ("inform the said Indians of the desire of the United States for Peace and that they claim no Indian lands but those purchased at a fair treaty"); Captain Alexander Trueman, to carry a speech and wampum from the government to the Maumee villages; and another agent from Wilkinson and Major Hamtramck "to intimate" the government's "desire for peace."[20] (Hamtramck had already signed an agreement with the Wea and Eel River Miamis, encouraging Knox even more.) The chief emissary was Rufus Putnam, the leader of the Ohio Company settlements at Marietta and recently commissioned brigadier general. Putnam would contact the hostile tribes, "convince" them of the government's "humane dispositions," "make a truce," and persuade their chieftains to journey to Philadelphia for formal negotiations. *"You will make it clearly understood,"* Knox instructed, *"that we want not a foot of their land, and that it is theirs, and theirs only; that they have the right to sell, and . . . to refuse to sell, and that the United States will guaranty to them their said just right."* At Fort Jefferson, the northernmost post on the line from Fort Washington, Putnam would meet Indian representatives. As a gesture of goodwill, he could release all Indians imprisoned at army headquarters. He could offer adjusted compensation for lands ceded at the 1789 Fort Harmar treaty, permanent allowances of money and supplies, and promise from the United States the "blessings of civilization" and "the expense of teaching them to read and write, to plough, and to sow" as "the white people do." Fundamentally, Putnam's mission was to allay Indian suspicion and induce them to negotiate ("all we require . . . is a peacable demeanor; that they neither plunder the frontiers . . . or murder the inhabitants").[21]

For the first time in months, the administration began to believe peace might be possible. Knox ordered Wayne positively to block any Kentucky forays against the tribes, and especially an attack planned against the Indian council, "until the effects of the pacific overtures be known."[22] Wayne himself was under orders not to make any provocative military movements. In late May, British minister George Hammond told Hamilton "that the present was a moment peculiarly favorable not only to the immediate restoration of peace, but to the future establishment of tranquility . . . on a permanent basis."[23] Not even the murder of the two officers Wilkinson had sent in late winter could discourage Knox. When Joseph Brant arrived in Philadelphia for talks (itself a positive sign), he explained that the two officers had asked so many questions about the Indians and local geography after being taken prisoner that their captors concluded they were spies and executed them on the spot. The chiefs in council, according to the Mohawk leader, were extremely unhappy about the incident. Because the meetings with Brant were so amicable and apparently productive (Brant consented to lend his good auspices to the government at the September Indian council), Knox accepted the explanation and emerged from the talks even more optimistic.[24]

In the end, the administration's hopes proved unfounded. Alexander Trueman and John Hardin, a militia colonel carrying a peace message from army headquarters, were both murdered, bringing to four the total number of American agents killed under flags of truce. Reports reached Philadelphia that British Indian agent Alexander McKee boasted of five slain, and that the Indians had no wish for peace until the United States dismantled its forts and retired south of the Ohio River. Rufus Putnam himself barely escaped an apparent assassination attempt, and had to shift his diplomatic mission in mid-summer from the Maumee to Indiana where Wabash tribes might possibly be detached from the Indian alliance. The killings frightened Putnam, but enraged Wayne and Wilkinson because Trueman and some of the others had been military officers, sacrificed (in Wayne's words "martyrs") to a politically motivated (and useless) policy of peace and appeasement.[25] Knox, however, refused to give up hope until the Auglaize council listened to the Six Nations chiefs sent by the government. Although by fall the administration did begin to lose hope, in early November just as Congress reconvened, news reached Philadelphia of a treaty signed by Putnam and the Illinois and Wabash tribes. Also, the Six Nations reported that the council at Auglaize would agree to negotiations, and other information indicated that the powerful Creek tribe in the South would under no circumstances join the hostile confederation. By mid-November, the administration was elated again, believing its patience had paid off.[26]

Actually, peace was an impossibility in 1792. Egged on by McKee and other British agents, the Indians wanted a boundary with the whites along the Ohio River. The administration never understood Indian mentality— the pride, the defiance, and the deep suspicion with which the redmen viewed whites. As one chief declared at the Auglaize council, citing documents captured from St. Clair's army, the United States aimed to erect forts on Indian land, "drive all the Indians out of the Country," and after peace returned, "give them Hoe's . . . to plant Corn" for the whites, "and make them labour, like Beasts"—American "Oxen" and "Pack Horses."[27] Instructions to American emissaries invariably assumed a patronizing tone, as if a munificent government, fresh from a resounding victory, could afford to be magnanimous. Knox emphasized the insignificance of the defeat and the residual military strength of the United States; the administration set an immediate truce as a precondition to negotiations, implying that the Indians were the aggressors. Offers to treat always mentioned the Fort Harmar treaty as the basis for settlement, a treaty the administration considered fair but one which the Indians viewed as a *casus belli*.[28] Ironically, with peace so distant, the mood of optimism that swept Philadelphia in November 1792 was destined to backfire badly on the administration.

When Congress reconvened in November 1792, opponents of the Indian war and the strengthened Republican party were determined to attack the war and the military establishment. The President tried to justify his policies once again with a flood of documents illustrating his most recent diplomatic forays, but the hope of a peace settlement only incited new efforts to slash the regular regiments. The first clash came over the right of the Secretaries of War and the Treasury to testify in person about the report of the committee investigating St. Clair's defeat. Federalists wanted the administration defense read into the record with the prestige of a personal appearance; Republicans argued an infringement of legislative independence—and won, after two days of vitriolic argument, a continued investigation with testimony from executive departments in writing.[29] Then the administration's enemies rammed a motion through the House demanding that the War Department submit a detailed estimate for its 1793 contingency funds, unusual because the fund was normally estimated by the government and voted by Congress as a lump sum.[30] Finally on December 20, North Carolina congressman John Steele moved to reduce the army to two regiments. His motives were twofold, Steele explained to the House: to switch from regulars to militia, so that the frontiers could at last be effectively defended; and to save money, reducing the federal debt and making new taxes unnecessary.[31]

Pointing to the "immense and fruitless expenses," the "disgrace of military character," the "folly and ambition" and "ignorance" of administration policy, the North Carolina Federalist emphasized that the military now consumed two-thirds of the national budget. Militia expeditions brought results, Steele declared, while regulars, as he showed with historical examples as far back as Braddock's defeat, invariably failed. Although a Federalist and eventually a member of the administration (after 1796 Comptroller of the Treasury), Steele represented the western district of North Carolina and was convinced that administration policy was misguided. Several southerners and Republicans rose to support him. Then, early in January 1793, the Federalists answered. Jeremiah Wadsworth of Connecticut attacked the call for militia, disputed Steele's figures on budgets and expenditures, and argued that reducing the army would destroy the American position at the bargaining table with the Indians. Wadsworth, too, reviewed the history of frontier warfare, pointing to the "military disgraces," the poor discipline and lack of training of Harmar's and St. Clair's "regulars," and the inability of militia on the defensive ever to prevent Indian assaults. Other Federalists recounted examples when regulars successfully defeated Indians, and pleaded with the House not to demobilize American forces just when peace negotiations were beginning. The President planned and proposed the present system; Congress should defer to his judgment. Steele replied with increasingly bitter charges of militarism and administration treason to the principles of '76, rejecting standing armies in peacetime. For three days the debate raged, but as James Hillhouse sarcastically noted, no new information or ideas were offered beyond those mentioned a year earlier when the House approved the 5,000-man army. On January 5, Steele's motion lost by 16 votes, almost exactly the same division as a year earlier. This time, however, the vote was partisan, even though some New England Federalists voted against the war and Republicans from Georgia, Virginia, and Pennsylvania, the areas most threatened by the Indians, voted in favor of regulars.[32]

The debate over reducing the military establishment had a wider significance that Federalists readily perceived. For the first time James Madison spoke openly against the use of regulars, and although he abstained from the final vote, Madison's position revealed a hardened, more rigid party element in the debate which had never before been so pronounced. Fisher Ames for one viewed Madison as a "desperate party leader," commanding a "solid column" of Virginians disciplined like "Prussians."[33] Although he certainly overstated the case, Ames and other administration stalwarts were reacting to the heightened criticism of the war in the press and in Congress, criticism that even the most sustained peace effort and a full summer of military inactivity had not been able to blunt.[34] The debate between regulars and militia had always possessed the potential for party identification, partly because of the ideological dimension of standing army versus "the people" as militia, partly because the issue fit perfectly into the contest between national and state power. Each time the issue had surfaced—in the discussion over national security in the 1780s and in the struggle over the Constitution—factions had grasped the opposing positions. Now, in early 1793, as it was beginning its metamorphosis from a legislative faction into a developed political party organized on the local level to contest elections and to seize power, the Republican party embraced the military issue almost as a matter of course. Opposition to regulars was a popular issue, part of Revolutionary tradition, congruent with Republican philosophy of states rights and their democratic rhetoric, and above all perfect for attacking the Washington administration's incompetence, underhandedness, and discriminatory financial policies. In addition many Republicans believed that Indian policy had been disastrous, that Militia promised more success and could safeguard the nation generally, and that the expenses of the war and regulars were dangerous Hamiltonian expedients. Most importantly, a year later in 1794 after the war crisis with Great Britain and the suppression of the Whiskey Rebellion, many Republicans would conclude sincerely that the Federalists aimed at a classic standing army. For the remainder of the decade, the creation of a national military establishment would be unmistakeably partisan, fully integrated into the wider framework of national politics.

In the wake of the savage attacks by Steele and the Republicans, the Washington administration became more firmly attached than ever to a negotiated settlement. For one thing, neither Knox nor the President yet had full confidence in the army. Both worried constantly whether Wayne was devoting sufficient time to training, to supplies, and to constructing an efficient intelligence network, and whether the quantity and quality of his recruits would permit an offensive in 1793. "I am told," growled the President, "notwithstanding pointed instructions . . . on this head, that *boys* in *many instances*, and the worst miscreants in others are received."[35] Recruiting in autumn 1792 had been so poor that the army was still 30 percent understrength; experienced veterans Nicholas Fish and Winthrop Sargent both rejected the adjutant generalship; flints, rifles, powder, and medical supplies were missing (the new supply system was just getting organized—deputy quartermaster John Belli at Fort Washington slept only four hours a day for three months running). Stores at advanced posts were dangerously low because the trip from Fort Washington to Fort Jefferson took ten days, each animal in a convoy depositing only a bushel and a half of grain after feeding the convoy and escort en route. By December even Wayne admitted to "great difficulties."[36] With the army in disarray and dissent at a peak, the only answer was negotiations. "The public voice demands it," Knox lamented. "Citizens of no Country could more explicitly . . . express decided disapprobation of this War."[37]

Until January 1793, the administration evidently hoped sincerely to negotiate a peaceful termination of the war, especially after learning from the British that the Auglaize Indian council was willing to listen to American negotiators in the spring of 1793 at Sandusky.[38] In January, however, Wayne informed the President of the Indian demand for an Ohio River boundary, and three weeks later, Cornplanter and other Six Nations' chiefs confirmed the fact in person.[39] Publicly the administration still exuded optimism, but Washington and the others knew the chances for peace were now non-existent.[40] Negotiations would go forward purely to convince the public of the government's good intentions and to give Wayne time to ready the army—"merely to gratify public opinion," Jefferson recorded in his notes at the cabinet meeting in late February, "not from an expectation of success." Jefferson argued strongly that military preparations proceed "without the least relaxation," and that a date should be set for settlement beyond which negotiations could not be "protracted" in order to prevent the launching of an offensive. "The President took up the thing instantly," Jefferson remembered, "and declared that he was so much in the opinion that the treaty would end in nothing that he then, in the presence of us all, gave orders to General Knox, not to slacken the preparation for the campaign in the least, but to exert every nerve."[41] The administration knew full well that the British would not cooperate by allowing American supplies to move up the Great Lakes to a treaty site and, from spies and the Six Nations, clearly the Indians would settle for nothing short of expulsion of all whites from the area north of the Ohio River.[42] The British, through agents like Matthew Elliott and Alexander McKee, had been supplying the tribes with arms and food for a decade, manipulating intertribal politics and relations with the United States, attempting to preserve British influence over the tribes, and by the early 1790s, hoping to establish an exclusively Indian barrier state to block American expansion into the old Northwest. On their side, Washington and his advisers were perfectly willing to negotiate an end to the war, although they undoubtedly felt some ambivalence because they wanted also to reestablish respect for the government's power with a military victory. But once they realized a compromise peace was impossible, the entire diplomatic effort became a sham, contrived to "prove to all our citizens," as Jefferson explained later, "that peace was unattainable on terms which any one of them would admit."[43] It was all done in secret, of course, although the President intimated the plan to his old friend Henry Lee and, to knowledgeable observers, the administration's strategy was obvious. George Beckwith, the British military agent in Philadelphia at the time, guessed it a month before the cabinet made its final decisions. "They cannot mask 10,000 men," he charged, "nor are 8,000 stands of arms" sent to Pittsburgh "to be lodged in idleness." "In a Government scarcely formed," with "its origin built on opinion, it was found impossible to draw the strength of the country into action at once." Therefore, "the most artful mearsures have been pursued in order to . . . lead the people into this business."[44]

The one problem with such a policy was how to maintain a peaceful demeanor and at the same time prepare the army for battle. Although some predicted that negotiations would consume the whole summer, preventing any military offensive, the administration had no such intentions.[45] On March 5, Knox explained the mechanics of the negotiations to General Wayne and ordered him to accelerate training, gather his supplies, inspect his men and equipment, and move the army downriver to Fort Washington in mid-April.[46] The general was not, however, to provoke the Indians in any manner. Wayne and the Governors of Virginia and Kentucky all had the negotiating effort carefully outlined to them, and all three were asked to issue proclamations forbidding any "irruptions into the Indian Country" until explicit authorization came from Philadelphia.[47] Twice Knox specifically warned Wayne against "any demonstrations of Stores or Magazines . . . at the head of your line and particularly . . . any considerable accumulation of troops at your advanced posts."[48] If army movements torpedoed the conference, the peace commissioners would probably be murdered and the administration would fall victim to charges of bad faith, inspiring the opposition to new heights of invective and destroying the purpose of negotiations in the first place. But at the same time Knox arranged a code for Wayne and the peace envoys so that they could inform the army immediately if they failed to sign a treaty. The message was to be sent by no fewer than six separate messengers. Also, Knox continually discussed strategy in his correspondence with the general, explicitly ordering the army to be prepared for immediate combat in August.[49] At army headquarters, the conflict between keeping the truce and building up supplies and men was readily apparent. Army commanders were placed in an impossible dilemma. "The conduct of the General Government is inexplicable," muttered James Wilkinson, who saw Wayne's March 5 orders through a "private channel."[50] Once Wilkinson finally understood the policy, he exploded in anger. "[T]he Army will not move until Aug[us]t," he railed, "our Hands are tied."[51]

Eventually, the administration's dual policy of negotiation and escalation caused the first crisis in civil-military relations between the new army and its civilian superiors in American history. In late April 1793, the negotiators left Philadelphia for the West. Washington had appointed the most prestigious, experienced men he could find for the mission: Timothy Pickering, Benjamin Lincoln, and former Virginia Governor Beverley Randolph. (So desperate was the President that he approached Charles Thomson, the former secretary of the Confederation Congress who had been forced out in 1789, but who was greatly trusted by the Delawares; Washington also considered appointing John Steele as a means of defusing the opposition.)[52] Armed with silver gifts, $20,000 to proffer bribes, and accompanied by a bevy of Quakers, missionaries, interpreters, and retainers, the three were to persuade the tribes to reconfirm the boundaries drawn in 1789 at Fort Harmar. If served an ultimatum, the government would relinquish lands south of the boundary, but in no case any areas already sold, reserved, or settled. As bait the commissioners could guarantee the Indian "right of soil," relinquish most of the reservations on the Indian land granted to the government in the 1789 agreement, and promise to dismantle all military posts in the Ohio region. In addition, they could promise another $150,000 settlement and an annual stipend of $10,000. To the administration, these were generous terms. The tenor of the instructions was more conciliatory than any similar diplomatic instructions since the Federalists had come to power.[53]

During June and part of July, the Americans waited at Fort Niagara for a following wind on Lake Erie and for word from the Indian council at Sandusky. In truth, the tribes were suspicious from the beginning. In January they had wondered over a mixup in the meeting place; they had specified lower Sandusky and Knox in his first speech had mentioned Maumee rapids. Then Wayne's sudden movement down the Ohio to Cincinnati had aroused more suspicion. "The extreme jealousy of the

Indians will naturally prompt them to magnify every thing wearing a hostile appearance," the peace commission warned Knox.[54] The Indians intended to scout around the army, and attack if new troops marched to Fort Jefferson. In late June the commission wrote Knox again, noting that every escort accompanying provisions north from Fort Washington could upset the delicate negotiation. The warnings came too late. On July 5, a party of Indians disembarked at Niagara, angrily demanding an explanation of Wayne's movements. No invitation to treat had come, said Joseph Brant, because the council wanted to know whether the United States still wanted talks. Pickering desperately reassured the warriors, not only of the commission's authority, but of the government's sincerity, and after exchanging speeches and wampum, Brant agreed to conduct the American mission to Sandusky. On July 10, the commissioners angrily informed Knox about Indian charges of Wayne building a road past Fort Jefferson, stockpiling food and munitions at the post, and collecting large numbers of horses, cattle, and soldiers at the forward locations for an offensive. The commissioners demanded that the army withdraw all supplies, animals, and men in excess of what was needed for Fort Jefferson's security.[55]

Knox first notified the army of the commissioners' worry on June 7, but Wayne did not receive the letter until after he had ordered the contractors to deposit 60 days' flour for the entire army at Fort Jefferson (which involved sending hundreds of horses in convoys north). Wayne responded to this warning unwillingly, telling Knox that no troops or supplies would be moved north except those "indispensably necessary" for the coming campaign.[56] Acidly the general quoted back Knox's orders, underlining the inconsistency of postponing supplies and men while preparing to attack in August. Then on July 20, having received the accusations about Wayne's conduct from the peace envoys, Knox rebuked the general "in the name of the President" to "instantly withdraw" the extra men at the head of the line. "The army is to remain," Knox warned ominously, "in the vicinity of Fort Washington until the event of the treaty be known."[57] Wayne reacted to this order with anger and defiance. In a long letter he disputed Indian charges: no road had been built *beyond* Jefferson; provisions in the line of forts, neglected by the contractors, had fallen dangerously low; the troops in garrison were the minimum necessary to guard cattle and horses and less than 200 extra were in the posts, merely *"preparatory arrangements"* fully explained in earlier dispatches. Wayne recounted incident after incident of Indian sniping and soldiers slain. He complained bitterly that "as Commander in Chief of the Legion of the United States, some *confidence* ought to have been placed in my *honor* as well *as Conduct*." Bluntly he asked Knox "to inform the *Commissioners* that I have never yet forfeited either my *word or honor*, to living man," and also, Knox should phrase every future order as explicitly as the one of July 20.[58]

The general had been placed in exactly the dilemma which every limited war imposes on military commanders. As commander-in-chief of the army, charged with the security of his own forces and the responsibility for gaining military victory, Anthony Wayne objected to limits placed on his military activity for diplomatic or political purposes. If Wayne left the forts north of Cincinnati bereft of the supplies necessary to launch an offensive, if he failed to improve the road and to reinforce those posts with advance parties, he would not be prepared to invade the Indian country before the end of the campaign season as the government wished. Perhaps even better than military commanders in the twentieth century, Wayne understood the political and diplomatic calculations which limited and sometimes hamstrung his military options. Like many of his successors, Wayne concluded that such restraints gave advantages to a savage and uncompromising foe, that the promise of negotiations was an illusion and in fact designed to forestall his own offensive, and that the government exhibited dangerous weakness, surrendering unnecessarily to internal political pressure, misleading and encouraging the enemy. All the elements for a civil-military blowup existed in the summer of 1793: a contradictory governmental policy; confusing, conflicting orders from the War Department to the army commander; and a general who disagreed with his government's policy and chafed under its restrictions. Only Knox's direct order ("a very peremptory mandate from the President," according to James Wilkinson), plus Wayne's loyalty and his ability to curb his anger and frustration, kept the situation under control.[59] The same day he wrote Knox, Wayne ordered all the extra men, stores, and animals returned from Fort Jefferson to the main army encampment on the Ohio.[60]

Confident that the negotiations would proceed, the three American envoys left Niagara in mid-July and within a week arrived at British Indian agent Matthew Elliott's house south of Detroit. There they remained for a month, prohibited from entering Detroit by the British and prevented from meeting the Indians by a combination of British manipulation and internal Indian disagreement. Brant had misled the commissioners. Actually, the tribes were hopelessly divided: a few for peace on any terms, others for war, and Brant and the Six Nations for negotiating a new, compromise boundary. The most hostile wanted nothing less than the expulsion of the Americans from north of the Ohio River, and given Indian success in battle, a message which arrived at the council from the Creeks promising aid, and Wayne's menacing activity above Cincinnati, the peace element among the tribes never had a chance. Publication in a Philadelphia newspaper of a request for bids on supply contracts for American forts to be built on the Maumee and at Detroit also damaged American protestations of peaceful intent. After several exchanges of messages, the Indians informed the commission that they would treat on no other terms than an Ohio boundary. Knowing that the government could never submit to a cession of such magnitude, the peace commissioners refused the council's ultimatum, and within 24 hours set sail for Presque Isle, Pennsylvania.[61]

Upon landing, the envoys hurried messengers to the army with the signal that negotiations had failed. Wayne had been waiting eagerly. Since early spring he had been planning strategy and perfecting his forces, neither of which had been easy tasks. Twice the administration had vetoed his strategy of a two-pronged advance on the Maumee, one from Cincinnati, the other from Pittsburgh to Presque Isle and along the southern edge of Lake Erie. The government stuck doggedly to its conservative plan of a line of forts spaced every twenty miles from Fort Washington to the Maumee.[62] Even more trouble for the general were his relations with Kentucky. During June, Wayne had asked the state Board of War to ready 1,500 mounted volunteers to accompany the army on the campaign. The Board pressed for volunteer officers to equal regulars in rank, and to fight in separate units. Wayne detected a connection between Kentucky arguments and "those sported on the floor of Congress the last session in Opposition" to regulars. And he also suspected the jealousy of James Wilkinson, who had hoped for command of the army in 1792, had always argued the superiority of mounted volunteers, and throughout the summer had carried on his private correspondence with Kentucky leaders, filling them with doubts about Wayne's leadership and administration policy. No Kentuckians would be permitted to steal "a March . . . from the Army," Wayne insisted to Knox, "in order to burn a few Wigwams," then return *tryumphantly and safe . . .* —leaving the Legion to contend with the combined force of the Savages and exposed to every difficulty and danger."[63] Eventually Wayne smoothed over the difficulty, and when the news arrived from the peace envoys in mid-September, the general alerted the army for action and ordered Kentucky Major General Charles Scott to appear at Fort Jefferson on October 1 with 1,500 mounted troops.[64]

For weeks Wayne had worried that the limits on his preparations and the lateness of the season would prevent a full scale offensive. "[H]owever we must do the best we can, to protect the Fronteers," he declared to Knox.[65] Once the order to march went out, however, Kentucky failed to provide the auxiliaries and Wayne had to demand a draft of state militia. Then disease struck. On October 5, nearly a month after ordering the advance, the army still lay on the Ohio, racked with influenza and reinforced by less than 400 frontiersmen. Wayne was losing hope. "[U]nless more powerfully supported . . . , I will content myself by taking a strong position advanced of Jefferson, and by exerting every power . . . , endeavour to protect the Fronteers and to secure the Posts and Army during the Winter."[66] On reaching Jefferson, the general discovered the post nearly empty of provisions and the contractors unable to furnish more because of insufficient transport. At the end of the month, advanced a mere six miles further, Wayne convened a council of war. Given the army's instructions, intelligence of the enemy, the strength and logistical problems of the Legion, and Kentucky Governor Isaac Shelby's request to have the volunteers raid the Auglaize village alone, Wayne polled his generals on whether the army should advance, how far, and whether the Kentuckians should be allowed to mount an independent assault. Unanimously, both volunteer and regular generals opposed a raid as risky and recommended that the army stay put—because of cold weather, low supplies, lack of forage and clothing, because the army was still understrength, and because if the army did advance, any retrograde movement would "reflect great Discredit on the Arms of the United States."[67] Reluctantly Wayne accepted the advice, erected Fort Greenville, and settled down for the winter. The campaign of 1793 was over.

With the failure of the peace commission and Wayne's abortive offensive, the administration abandoned the policy of negotiation it had pursued since 1792. Even though the war continued, the administration in its own mind had overcome the greatest hurdle to restoring peace to the frontier: public charges that the government itself was to blame for hostilities and criticism that the use of regulars prolonged the conflict. Actually, more than the administration's policies, events themselves conspired to alter public opinion in favor of using force in the Northwest. In 1793 war broke out between France and Britain, and for most of the summer the administration struggled frantically to keep the country neutral. Through astute diplomacy and manipulation of public opinion, French ambassador Edmond Genet's attempts to pull the United States into the European conflagration were blocked, but the administration still worried about the forces Genet had organized in the Southwest to invade Spanish possessions in Louisiana and Florida, raising the possibility of war with Spain. At the same time, relations between the state of Georgia and the Creeks had worsened, threatening a full-scale Indian war in the South and also a Spanish conflict. But the most important factor affecting the Indian war was the worsening state of Anglo-American relations. Britain in 1793 began seizing American ships and impressing American seamen in an effort to build up her forces and cut off neutral trade with France. Then in December 1793, the nation gained final proof of what everyone had suspected for years: Britain not only supplied the Indians, but actually encouraged them in war against the United States. When Joseph Brant left the Indian council, he accused British agent Alexander McKee publicly of persuading the western tribes to choose war unless the Americans agreed to an Ohio boundary. Corroboration came from Wayne's spy at the council, who related how McKee huddled with the chiefs nightly, counselling them to take a hard line and promising money and supplies for the next campaign. The three American peace emissaries, who returned to Philadelphia in October 1793, also blamed the British directly for the treaty's failure. [68]

Taken together, the international situation and the war crisis with Britain altered the public perception of the frontier situation. The elaborate charade of negotiations shifted the onus for hostilities onto the Indians and their British allies, making the Indian war a part of the struggle against Britain. Furthermore the opposition party flayed the administration, as it had throughout the neutrality crisis in mid-1793, to take strong action against England. In January 1794, James Madison introduced resolutions for commercial retaliation against Britain. In late March, after more news of attacks on American shipping, a speech by Canadian governor Lord Dorchester predicting war between the two countries and promising aid to the Indians, including British troops, whipped Congress and the public into a frenzy. Reports from London indicated the British would in no case surrender the posts on American territory, and the administration considered Dorchester's statement to the Indians a virtual declaration of war. In May the cabinet authorized Wayne, who now had standing orders to go on the offensive, to use 2,000 frontiersmen as auxiliaries because the Legion remained understrength. The administration wanted the war terminated, if nothing else to relieve the pressure on a country facing military encirclement—war with Britain, with the Indians on both frontiers, and possibly with Spain in the Southwest. In June the administration learned of a new British fort on American soil at the rapids of the Maumee. It was indeed the last straw. Determinedly Knox authorized Wayne to "dislodge" the British garrison if necessary, if "it shall promise complete success." [69]

During the winter of 1793–1794 Wayne had prepared carefully to move north, building Fort Recovery on the site of St. Clair's defeat and organizing the army for a rapid spring advance. In January, because of a false peace feeler from the Delaware tribe, Wayne slowed. In June, the garrison at Fort Recovery repulsed two days of assaults from several hundred Indians, breaking the back of Indian military power although Wayne did not know it. Then on July 28, at 8:00 A.M., 2,000 regulars supported by over 1,500 Kentucky volunteers broke camp at Greenville and headed north on the attack. Within two weeks the army occupied the Indian villages at the confluence of the Auglaize and Maumee Rivers, where Wayne constructed Fort Defiance. "[W]e have gained possession," boasted the general, "of the grand emporium of the hostile Indians of the West, without loss of blood." [70] Once again Wayne called on the enemy to surrender. On August 15 he began the march northeast along the Maumee toward the rapids and the British fort. Stopping nightly in well fortified encampments, Wayne advanced cautiously. At 6:30 on the morning of August 20, the lead elements broke camp and began scouting through the forest toward Fort Miami, feeling for the enemy. After the army advanced about three miles into a thickly wooded glen of trees, undergrowth and felled logs, over 1,000 Indians and a company of Canadian militia opened fire. Wayne's advance units fell back, but the main army came up fast, returned the musketry, and then charged with the bayonet. For nearly an hour the Legionnaires pursued the enemy, out of the woods and onto the meadow along the river. Finally the Indians broke and, on seeing the gates of the British fort closed tightly, melted into the forest.

That night Wayne camped a half mile below the British guns. At dawn the major in command of the fort, upholding the honor of King and Army despite the possibility of annihilation, warned the Americans to stay out of range. Flushed with victory, Wayne replied sarcastically and led his light infantry within pistol shot of the stockade, reconnoitering the works. But the British avoided overt provocation. For three days, American forces burned and pillaged the Indian towns, British storehouses, and crops around the post. Then Wayne marched back to Auglaize, leaving a swath of destruction for miles on both sides of the Maumee. By late November, at a cost of less than 200 casualties, the army was back in Greenville.[71]

Four years after sending Harmar's expedition into the Indian country, the Washington administration had finally broken the Indian hold on the old Northwest and destroyed British influence over the tribes. Force, as the Treaty of Greenville would prove a year later restored peace, recouped the reputation of American arms, and regained for the government the respect of its citizens in the West. Successfully employed it did that and more. It justified American policy, the use of regulars, and the creation of a military establishment. After four years, with all the changes in American politics, the emergence of political parties, the new issues, the altered international scene, few Americans looked backward. Wayne's victory wiped out the miscalculations, the expenditures, the bitter arguments over the army and western policy. Only the critics after 1794, and one man—the Secretary of War who had administered the policy and applied the force—dared ask publicly what might have been.

Maintaining Order: The Washington Administration's Decision to Crush the Whiskey Rebellion [1794]

> Government supposes controul—It is that power by which individuals in society are kept from doing injury to each other and are brought to co-operate to a common end. The instruments by which it must act are either the *authority* of the laws or *force*. . . . Those . . . who preach

doctrines, or set examples, which undermine or subvert the authority of
the laws . . . incapacitate us for a *government* of *laws*, and consequently
prepare the way for one of *force*, for mankind *must have government of
one sort or another.*

Alexander Hamilton, 1794.[c]

One of the fundamental questions raised in the era of the American
Revolution, especially during debates over state and national constitutions, was on what foundation the ultimate authority of government
rested. Most Americans agreed, as did men as opposed over the Constitution of 1789 as James Madison and Richard Henry Lee, that government
was based either on law or on force, and that ultimately law was the only
firm basis on which to build a healthy republican society. They also
agreed that once the law failed, either through individual disobedience or
riot and rebellion, force would be necessary to restore order and compel
citizens to fulfill their social obligations.[72]

The Whiskey Rebellion, which erupted in July 1794 in western Pennsylvania, presented the Washington administration with just such a clearcut case of the failure of law and the necessity for coercion. After learning
of the attack on whiskey tax collector John Neville's estate, the administration set in motion the machinery for the use of force without a hint of
internal disagreement. Within ten days, however, the policy was
reversed. Suddenly it became unclear to the President and his advisers
whether it was possible to use force, and if it was feasible, whether a
military expedition would restore order and respect for the law or provoke
civil war and deeper disdain for the whiskey excise and the federal
government's authority generally. When the cabinet split in its recommendations, Washington decided to delay the militia expedition (Wayne
was on the march, leaving no regulars available), and suddenly the
process by which the government responded to the rebellion degenerated
into a patchwork series of disjointed and incongruous decisions. In the
light of the initial reaction, the administration's decision to crush the
rebellion is a fascinating case study in the process of suppressing disorder, and raises intriguing questions about the use of force which
are still relevant today.

To understand the administration's response, the rebellion must be
viewed in the wider context in which Federalists themselves placed it.
Federalists reacted not simply to the violence and intimidation of excise
officials in western Pennsylvania, although this had been mounting steadily since the tax took effect in 1791. Equally important was the growing
Federalist distrust of the motives of the Republicans, and the bitterness

that had come to characterize national politics. In public and in private Federalists universally explained the rebellion as the product of dissent ("those damnable disorganizing opinions wh[ich] many weak & honest men utter to exercise the *Liberty of speech!*"), or the outgrowth of faction ("a set of *leading partizans*" who "had always maintained a systematic opposition" to the government).[73] Ever since the Republicans emerged as an organized force, Federalists began to see them as successors to Antifederalism, as men bent, in Hamilton's description of Madison and Jefferson in 1792, on "measures, which . . . would subvert the Government."[74] Thereafter, every political battle, large or small, led Federalists to a more conspiratorial and seditious interpretation of the opposition. The spiral of suspicion became reciprocal; by late 1793, Jefferson was repeating thirdhand stories of Federalist conversations about the necessity of a "President for life, and an hereditary Senate."[75]* Politics itself was now a poisonous process, filled with hate and suspicion, and characterized by wild and vicious charges that many on both sides believed instinctively. In such an atmosphere, many Federalists could readily accept Attorney General William Bradford's interpretation of the rebellion as part of "a formed and regular plan for weakening and perhaps overthrowing the General Government."[76]

A second element which explains the administration's initial determination to use the militia was the episode in 1792 when resistance to the excise in western Pennsylvania led Hamilton to recommend immediate government intervention with force. The excise tax on spirits had passed Congress in 1791 as an integral part of Hamilton's financial program. It had sparked immediate resentment in the backcountry as discriminatory against westerners who shipped their grain east in the form of whiskey, and it became an explosive issue for political leaders who opposed other administration policies, especially around Pittsburgh where local office

---

*The incident was a minor one in 1793, but later was blown out of proportion and gained political significance. Vice-President Adams made the remark one day in a conversation with Senators John Langdon (N.H.) and John Taylor (Va.), both Republicans, after the Senate had adjourned. According to Adams twenty years later, he had been angered and egged into the statement by Taylor's "Insolence" and "Sophistry" in a discussion of political theory and the French Revolution. And the remark was meant to show Adams's contempt for Taylor. (John Adams to John Langdon, February 27, 1812, *Letters by Washington, Adams, Jefferson, and Others . . . to John Langdon* [Philadelphia, 1880], 17–19.) But Republicans immediately spread the word about this new evidence for Adams's monarchism. Federalist Tench Coxe, for one, was influenced to work against Adams in the 1796 election because of the story, which led to Coxe's loss of his government position as Commissioner of the Revenue, and eventually to his switch to the Republican party. (Tench Coxe to John Taylor, January 10, 1798, Tench Coxe Papers, Historical Society of Pennsylvania, Philadelphia, Pa.) The general course of party politics in the 1790s, and especially the Federalists' view of the opposition party, will be covered in detail in Chapter 10.

seekers stirred up popular opposition to gain support in their own interne-cine struggles.⁷⁷ In August 1792, resistance to the law hardened when local leaders resolved to "persist" in "legal" measures "that may obstruct the operation of the Law."⁷⁸ Subsequent resolutions called for more rallies, the creation of county committees of correspondence and the intimidation of anyone who favored or obeyed the law. John Neville, the excise inspector responsible for collecting the tax, immediately informed his superior in Philadelphia that the law was now unenforceable and that he could not enter Washington County, the seat of the most determined resistance, without risking his life. The day after Neville sent the report, a mob shot up one of his inspection stations and threatened to murder the owner for allowing his house to be used for registering stills.⁷⁹

Hamilton had been waiting for such an incident. Earlier, when he heard of riots against the excise in North Carolina, he told the Virginia Supervisor of Revenue that "the thing must be brought to an issue," and the Secretary asked if Virginia's militia was reliable.⁸⁰ The situation in Pennsylvania, he told Chief Justice John Jay, marked "a crisis in the affairs of the Country."⁸¹ Hamilton's first active move was to send Penn-sylvania supervisor George Clymer to Pittsburgh—a "preparatory step."⁸² Then Hamilton asked Attorney General Edmund Randolph for a legal opinion about the opposition to the law and the government's options. To the President, Hamilton was more blunt: "Moderation enough has been shewn," he argued, "'tis time to assume a different tone." First the government should "exert the full force of the Law against the Offenders." Then if court action proved impossible, "as is rather to be expected," the President could mobilize troops.⁸³

Hamilton's eagerness to use force, however, was not matched by Randolph, Jay, or Rufus King, to whom Hamilton wrote for advice. Jay and King cautioned him to wait until Congress convened so that "all the Branches of Gov[ernmen]t [can] move together" backed solidly by public opinion.⁸⁴ Randolph also emphasized the dangers of overreaction. The mere resolutions of a meeting could not justify legal prosecution, he told Hamilton, and "improper interference" by the President might "inlist against him even those who execrate the spirit of the Pittsburgh proceedings." Randolph was willing to support a presidential proclama-tion, but he edited Hamilton's draft to remove what he considered provocative language—words like "criminality" and any mention whatso-ever of the military.⁸⁵

Washington accepted the idea of a proclamation. He would enforce the law, he confided to Hamilton, to the point of using force if necessary. But if the regular army was used, "there would be the cry at once, 'The cat is let out; We now see for what purpose an Army was raised.'" Force could only be the "dernier resort."⁸⁶

The debate over how to respond in 1792 matched almost exactly the one that would develop in 1794. Hamilton already leaned toward military suppression. Randolph (who moved from Attorney General to Secretary of State after Jefferson retired) was inclined to be more lenient, more concerned with public opinion and the government's image. Washington stood in the middle. He accepted Hamilton's premises about the necessity for strict enforcement lest the laws and government itself be undermined, but he sensed that force would not only need public support but also have political overtones beyond the simple enforcement of the law. Most important, the whole episode in 1792 strengthened the tendency to react more harshly in 1794. The government was lenient in 1792, almost circumspect. Yet the violence continued. In early 1794 it began to mount in tempo and frequency as the tax came to symbolize western grievances against the national government and finally culminated in an armed attack on Neville. Given the continual incidents in western Pennsylvania, the view that political opposition was actually a conspiracy to subvert governmental institutions, and the obvious failure of lenience in 1792, neither the President nor any member of his cabinet had any reason to doubt their informants in Pittsburgh who described the assault on Neville as the beginning of a "civil War."[87] Hamilton spoke for all when he told representatives of the Pennsylvania government that "the crisis was arrived when it must be determined whether the Government can maintain itself."[88]

What forced the administration to pause in 1794—in fact what changed the whole nature of the crisis, led to the split in the cabinet, and caused a delay of nearly two months in sending troops to Pittsburgh—was a flood of obstacles that forced the President to waver and to realize the dangers in a policy of immediate military suppression. First news of the attack on John Neville's estate reached Philadelphia on July 25. After sending the information to state authorities, Washington met with the cabinet and decided to lay the facts before Supreme Court Justice James Wilson. (The 1792 act on mobilizing militia required a federal judge to certify that the judicial process had collapsed before the executive could call up troops.) Wilson was a longtime ally and a good Federalist, and the administration was eager to act quickly. But when Wilson did not reply immediately, wanting the papers authenticated, Washington and his advisers grew anxious; suddenly they realized that only correspondence supported the existence of actual rebellion, and it was by no means certain what kind of evidence Wilson would require.[89]

The other alternative was to ask the state of Pennsylvania to call up its militia. Here the problems were immense. Similar situations in the past had caused confusion, discord, and crippling delays. In 1783, when army recruits had surrounded Congress and the government of Pennsylvania, waving their muskets and demanding back pay, the state had refused to act. During Shays's Rebellion coordination between national and state governments had been extremely difficult despite agreement on both sides that force was mandatory. But the most potent obstacles were political: Pennsylvania's administration was solidly Republican. Governor Thomas Mifflin had been suspect in Washington's mind ever since his service on the Board of War and his involvement in the so-called Conway Cabal, and Mifflin's chief adviser, Secretary of State Alexander Dallas, was also a leading member of the opposition. Their only response to the rebellion had been to instruct judges and county officials to round up the rioters for trial.[90] Moreover, formal relations between the federal government and the state were already sour. In May, Washington had forced Pennsylvania to suspend a project to lay out the town of Presque Isle so as not to provoke the Six Nations into joining the hostile tribes facing Wayne in the Northwest. Mifflin had exploded at this interference in state affairs, and after an angry exchange of letters, Washington and Secretary of War Henry Knox began to doubt the Governor's willingness to honor national obligations.[91]

In spite of these difficulties, by August 1 the administration felt it had no choice. Even if Wilson freed them to mobilize militia, Washington and the cabinet would need the help of the Pennsylvanians to use state forces. Therefore, on August 2, at its own request the administration met with Mifflin, Dallas, state Chief Justice Thomas McKean, and state Attorney General Jared Ingersoll. Most historians have used this conference only to gauge the mood of the administration; in reality, it marked a major turning point in policy. The state officials were so uncooperative that the President realized an immediate resort to force could backfire, heaping criticism on the government for overreaction and unnecessary repression, and shifting the issue publicly from defiance of the law to the use of force itself. And as the President soon found out, in order to gain cooperation from the state of Pennsylvania, the administration would have to delay a military expedition.

Washington began the conference by declaring that events around Pittsburgh struck "at the root of all law and order." "[T]he most spirited and firm measures were necessary . . . for if such proceedings were tolerated there was an end to our Constitution and laws." In evidence he cited correspondence, depositions, and newspaper extracts showing that the insurgents had robbed the mail and were planning another meeting to organize military resistance. He then asked for help from the Pennsylvanians. Randolph followed with a direct request to call out troops under a 1783 state militia law. The state officials were silent. Finally Ingersoll replied that this law had been repealed and McKean, evidently presenting the official Pennsylvania position, claimed that "the judiciary power" was still "equal to the task," that "the employment of a military force, at this period, would be as bad as anything that the Rioters had done—equally unconstitutional and illegal."

Then Hamilton spoke. "[C]o-operating sources of opposition to the Constitution and laws," he maintained, had produced a "crisis" over "whether the Government can maintain itself." "[A]n immediate resort to Military force" was necessary simply to compel "obedience to the laws." But the Pennsylvanians refused to budge and the two sides began quarreling over Judge Alexander Addison's opinion that the courts could restore order and that force would only unite the rioters and swell their numbers.[92]

What then passed has been lost. Undoubtedly it was bitter because Mifflin adamantly refused to call out his forces immediately, and he argued heatedly that out of hatred for the excise, unwillingness to march on fellow citizens, or desire to avoid a long expedition, large numbers of the militia might ignore his orders.[93] The administration believed it.[94] Certainly without the Governor's aid, the Pennsylvania militia would be useless. To gain his help, the administration struck a bargain: in return for Mifflin's cooperation in mobilization, the President agreed that he would initiate any call for troops, justify the measure publicly, and then give Mifflin time to convene the legislature and open negotiations with the rebels. The terms were deliberately vague, probably to avoid irrevocable commitments, but the administration had agreed informally to suspend military suppression for several weeks.[95]

Clearly Mifflin's intransigence and the fear that the militia might not turn out forced Washington for the first time to question whether he had the public backing to justify force. An immediate call to arms might reveal the government's military weakness and stimulate a divisive public debate over government reaction, especially if Mifflin, a leading Republican, publicly declared that force was unnecessary. The recommendations from the cabinet to the President reflected this dilemma. Hamilton and Knox stuck to a military solution: raise 12,000 men immediately, a "super abundant" force, to disabuse the insurgents of success and to demonstrate "at home and abroad" the "power of the Government to execute the laws."[96] But Bradford, Randolph, and Mifflin, the latter in a long and probably unsolicited letter justifying his earlier opposition, advised delay.[97] And it was Randolph's eloquent recitation of the dangers that finally persuaded the President to reverse the government's earlier intention to use force immediately.

"Unnecessarily harsh action" without any "spirit of reconciliation," wrote the Secretary, would only broaden the opposition to the government, perhaps even unite the whole West in civil war. The militias were unstable, the expense would be huge, and party politics already had produced bitter national division. Better to negotiate with the rebels, as had been discussed at the August 2 meeting and as the President was then considering. But if the administration offered "reconciliation . . . with one hand" while brandishing "terror . . . in the other," it would be "considered delusive by the insurgents and the rest of the world," a trick "only to gloss over hostility; to endeavour to divide; to sound out the strength of the insurgents; and to discover the most culpable persons" for punishment. It would fail, Randolph implied, just as every negotiating effort with the Indians up to 1793 had failed to convince the public of the government's sincerity. Issue a proclamation against the rebels and send a peace commission, Randolph urged. If it failed, prosecute them. If the courts failed, *then* call out the militia.[98]

On August 4, Wilson finally certified the situation beyond the "ordinary course of judicial proceedings," and by the end of the cabinet meeting on August 6, the President had decided on a course of action, one far closer to Randolph's rather than Hamilton's recommendations.[99] The key was a federal commission to negotiate with the rebels, partly to divide the rebels and gain intelligence, but mostly to blunt any possible public criticism and to gain the time to prepare the public should force prove ultimately necessary.[100] At the same time, Washington decided to issue a preliminary call to the militia—to test their loyalty, to convince the rebels of his determination, and to gain the time needed to organize an expedition. The entire package was a compromise designed to keep all options open and to anticipate the widest possible range of reactions from the public, the militia, and the rebels. Above all, Washington predicated his policy on public opinion, exactly as he had done in the Indian war the year before. "[T]he Pres[iden]t means to convince [the rebels] and the world . . . of the *moderation* and *the firmness* of the Gov[ernment]," Bradford explained to his father-in-law. If after the negotiations the rebels refused to submit to the law, "the weight of the public opinion will give energy to the *dernier* resort."[101] On August 7, the government issued a proclamation ordering the rebels to disperse and stating the government's intention to ready the militia; simultaneously Knox wrote the governors of four states to alert their troops, and Bradford hurriedly left for Pittsburgh to meet with the insurgents.[102]

Publicly the government was now committed to a peaceful solution of the rebellion. It was a shaky committment at best, mostly tactical, and indicative more of the President's uncertainty and fear of public opinion than a belief that force could be avoided. Perhaps it was sincere. Between August 7 and August 24, the administration made no serious military preparations for an expedition. The peace commission received very flexible instructions and the authority to grant a blanket amnesty for all unlawful acts as well as absolution from previously uncollected excise taxes.[103] But the administration was also applying the very same tactics it had used to reassure the public during the Indian war; Washington recognized that open military preparations at the same time that peace was offered to the insurgents would make the negotiations appear fake. Not until August 24, when the first definitive reports from the peace commission arrived, did the administration decide purposely to use the negotiations, in Randolph's words, as a sham "to gloss over hostility."

Bradford left the moment his instructions were approved, before either Pennsylvania Supreme Court Justice Jasper Yeates or Senator James Ross, a trusted confidant of the President and a resident of the most rebellious county, could be informed of their membership on the federal commission. At Lancaster, Bradford was joined by Yeates (Ross was near Pittsburgh) and the two rode up to forty miles a day in order to arrive in time for a meeting of the insurgents scheduled for August 14 at Parkinson's ferry on the Monongahela. As the two sped westward they became convinced that it would be impossible to restore order. Among the first people Bradford met on the journey were Neville and the federal marshal for the state, both of whom had narrowly escaped from Pittsburgh. They all but advised Bradford to turn back. By the time Bradford and Yeates reached Bedford, they learned that there were new riots, that a proclamation by Governor Mifflin was ridiculed by the rebels, and that the impending meeting would be stacked against more moderate westerners.[104]

Exhausted by a week's travel, already prejudiced about the situation and skeptical of their chances for success, Bradford and Yeates reached Parkinson's ferry on August 15. There they met Ross who had attended the meeting and who biased them further. Actually moderates had been able to manipulate the proceedings into rejecting any further violence and negotiating with the federal commissioners. Yet to Ross, circulating among the spectators and delegates, listening to rumors and plans, this outcome only masked what he felt to be the basic intransigence of the populace, or at least a sizable and uncontrollable minority.[105]

Still tired and evidently a bit jittery about their personal safety, Bradford, Yeates, and Ross went on to Pittsburgh where they spent all day on August 17 conferring with leading residents of the town. They were told that moderates were forced to play along with the fireaters or jeopardize their own safety and that of the town itself and that through intimidation and continual violence the extremists held the upper hand.[106] This testimony only reinforced what Bradford and Yeates had heard for a week on the road, and what Ross had deduced from observations on the scene. That night the commissioners decided to inform the government of their feelings even though they were not scheduled to meet the negotiating committee from the Parkinson's ferry meeting for another three days.

The faction at the meeting advocating civil war, they reported, was very small. But a second group, "numerous and violent," would resist the excise "at all hazards." These radicals were forcing the moderates— a majority—"to turn Hypocrites, and even to appear as Leaders of these *Enragées*" out of fear of reprisal and doubts about legal protection. While they dominated the negotiating committee, the moderates were so "over- awed" that they would not "express . . . real opinions," much less press the insurgents to accept the government's terms. "We see not any Pros- pect of inforcing . . . the Laws," concluded the commissioners, "but by the Physical strength of the Nation."[107] In a private letter Bradford used harsher language: the insurgents were really delaying until cold weather made military operations impossible. This would provide "time to strengthen themselves—to circulate the manifesto they are preparing— to tamper with . . . Kentucky—to procure Ammunition and . . . seduce the well-affected." As for negotiations, "any man who would openly recommend obedience . . . would be in danger of assassination."[108] Thus, barely two days after arriving, before meeting any of the rebels, and without consulting the state commission, the federal envoys recom- mended immediate mobilization.

When these reports reached Philadelphia on August 23, Washington called an emergency cabinet meeting and within 24 hours decided on a policy of force.[109] It was not just the information from the commission- ers. Bradford's dismal letters on the road undoubtedly contributed to the doubts about suspending military preparations. Articles in the opposition press calling for lenience and evidence that widespread hatred of the excise was giving the rebels sympathy also made the administration apprehensive.[110] But most dangerous of all, the administration feared that the sending of commissioners was misleading the rebels by giving the appearance of a weak and uncertain government. Sometime after August 15, Commissioner of the Revenue Tench Coxe—a Pennsylvanian— received a long letter from Hugh Brackenridge in Pittsburgh, pleading for delay and negotiations, but arguing that support for the rebels existed in nearby areas of Virginia and that the eastern militia might have to fight its way all across a hostile Pennsylvania in order to suppress the insurrec- tion. According to Brackenridge, the excise was part of a "funding system detested and abhorred" by most of the nation. "There is a growling, lurking discontent at this system that is ready to burst and discover itself everywhere." Brackenridge argued that the question was not an expedi- tion to Pittsburgh, but an aroused yeomanry, swelling as it progressed, marching on Philadelphia; and in an ominous tone, Brackenridge spoke specifically of an "application to the British" for aid—a possibility verified by British minister George Hammond, who had been approached by two men each claiming to represent the rebels, and both proposing some kind of alliance with the Crown.[111] Coming on the heels of Brackenridge's letter (which the administration interpreted as a bold threat of revolution generally), the reports of the peace commission convinced the administration that it must show the government's power by crushing the rebellion with military force.

Solemnly, for eight hours on August 24, Washington reviewed the situation with Hamilton and Randolph (Knox was in New England on private business). First the President asked whether the militia should be assembled at once. The two Secretaries, apparently now in agreement, recommended mobilizing Virginia's since Governor Henry Lee was an old friend of the President who had recently pledged his help unequivocally.[112] Washington then asked if additional forces were necessary and the two cabinet officers agreed that the total should be raised to 15,000, partly to include riflemen which the insurgents feared especially. The three then decided where and when the units would assemble and where their supplies would be stockpiled. As soon as the meeting broke up, Hamilton, acting for the absent Secretary of War, began ordering the arms and supplies. Although the decision was not irrevocable, the administration was committed to force prior to any word that negotiations had started. But public opinion was still a crucial consideration. Governor Lee was to keep his orders secret until September 1, to allow negotiations to proceed and to honor the informal agreement with Mifflin made in early August. And the peace commission was specifically ordered to continue the talks. The administration wanted to be certain that it could not be charged with insincerity or bad faith.[113]

Meanwhile in Pittsburgh, the rebel negotiators unexpectedly agreed to recommend the government's terms to the committee of sixty, an executive group of township representatives, and to call the committee into session on August 28. Suddenly the commissioners were hopeful. They wrote Randolph that to insure that the populace would submit to the law, they were requiring each citizen to declare his loyalty at his local polling place. Moderates, they added, were beginning to surface and the situation had improved to the point where they felt they could agree to withhold an expedition until the oath-signing took place on September 14. Bradford, Yeates, and Ross fully expected the committee of sixty to accept the terms, authorize local meetings, and—together with other moderates—silence the extremists, convincing the majority to abide by the law.[114]

These hopes proved short-lived. When the rebel negotiators recommended submission to the committee of sixty, the reaction was hostile. Fireaters immediately accused the negotiators of accepting government bribes and so great was the intimidation that the moderates on the committee demanded a secret ballot taken in such a way that their votes would not be disclosed by their handwriting. When the votes were tallied, approval of the government's terms—amnesty and future excise prosecutions in state courts in return for the oaths—won by only 34 to 23. Bradford and the other government representatives were stunned. If 23 leaders refused to obey the law, enforcement would be impossible. In their reports to Philadelphia, the three pointed this out and described the hostile mood. Military resistance had been openly advocated; nearly 1,000 packhorses were seen on the way to Maryland to procure military supplies. If the vote had been public, submission would have lost and the commissioners viewed the actual tally as an accurate reflection of mass opinion. Their recommendation was "Military coercion."[115]

With all hope of reconciliation gone, the commissioners decided to return to one of the original purposes of their mission—as they put it, leaving "the Government free from any reasonable grounds of censure."[116] They informed the rebels that the militia would undoubtedly march and that those who resisted further would be punished. On September 11, the people must assemble at their local polling places to sign explicit oaths of loyalty. Under this pressure the rebels caved in. On September 2, the two groups of negotiators and the representatives of the state government agreed to the terms. The next day Bradford and Yeates left for Philadelphia; Ross remained to monitor the oath-taking and report the results.[117]

From Bedford, Pennsylvania, Bradford and Yeates explained their actions to the administration. The Redstone meeting had posed a dilemma: to the "violent party" and most westerners, the fiery speeches and closeness of the vote had really represented a rejection of the government's offer. But to people "at a distance," it appeared to be a decision for submission. The rebels were willing to have the citizenry vote by ballot, for or against submitting, so that a large percentage of yes votes would make a military expedition seem unwarranted. To counter this stratagem, the commissioners "determined to address [themselves] to fears" and demand individual affirmations to abide by the excise. But force was still mandatory because the moderates had been promised "prompt and effectual" protection and because the rebels still believed that the militia would not turn out. Bradford and Yeates expected the voting to be meaningless. "Measures will still be taken," they predicted, "to procure . . . an expression" of submission from the people, but it "will not be such a one as Government can rely on."[118]

The administration received the report on September 8.[119] Again the commission precipitated action—this time a final decision to send in the militia. No one in the administration had believed the commissioners' earlier optimism. Increasingly the administration had come to feel that the rebels' belief in their own invulnerability, either because of public sympathy or the instability of the militia, called into question the whole fabric of governmental authority. Riots elsewhere in Pennsylvania and in Maryland indicated that the rebellion was spreading and that there was general disrespect for the excise. On September 9, the President ordered all militia units to march to their rendezvous.[120]

The one decision left, if military suppression were to proceed, was to order the troops over the mountains from their rendezvous in Carlisle and Cumberland, Maryland. Once more the President delayed, again for the same reason: the government's public image. Morally the government had to wait for the results of the oath-taking, and not until the week after September 9 was the administration absolutely certain that public opinion unequivocally supported a military expedition. The tide turned with the publication of the description of the close vote at the Redstone meeting. Actually the administration had been publicizing the violence and preparing the public for action since mid-August. But on September 10, the Philadelphia militia responded enthusiastically to Mifflin's exhortations to march. The next day the Republican party newspaper came out with a strong endorsement of military suppression, and by September 15 Federalists were crowing about the numbers of people volunteering for the expedition. "A federal and military spirit has at length awakened in this city," wrote Bradford gleefully, "and it carries every thing before it."[121] Even Randolph admitted that "the spirit, which the States manifested, is astonishing." "All these circumstances," he added in an acknowledgment that the administration's patience had paid off, "furnish a conviction that the energy of the Government is and will be greatly increased."[122]

By September 18, the administration had received early returns of the oath-signing in western Pennsylvania. It was "just in the situation we expected," Bradford informed Yeates; "great divisions and some tumults."[123] In a later report Ross described "great diversity of opinion" in one county, and he enclosed letters describing intimidations and disorder at the polls and a plan to "waylay" him and steal the oaths.[124] The administration's hands were now free. While most westerners were "disposed to pursue the path of Duty," Hamilton told Mifflin, "there is a large and violent Party, which can only be controuled by the application of Force."[125] On September 25, with units from New Jersey, Maryland, and Virginia converging on Carlisle and Cumberland, Washington issued a long proclamation justifying "this resort to military coercion."[126] Within another five days, he and Hamilton were on the road to join the army.

Two months later the rebellion had ended and Henry Lee, whom the President appointed commander of the militia army, was withdrawing all his forces except for a detachment which remained near Pittsburgh until mid-1795. Considering the fervor surrounding the rebellion, the army was surprisingly light-handed. Washington and Hamilton tried very hard to prevent wanton violence or destruction of private property—the kind of thing expected from armies in the eighteenth century—and when two deaths occurred in Carlisle, Hamilton apologized profusely to the Pennsylvania governor. On leaving the army, Washington again cautioned Lee to maintain discipline.[127] The march of the militia had been almost anticlimactic. At the head of the troops rode a galaxy of the nation's leaders—Washington, Hamilton, Mifflin, Dallas, Lee—and in their wake came a bevy of judicial officers and the exiled excise officials. They encountered only a cowering populace, terrified by the approach of a crusading army, and a void left by the escape of most of the rebel leaders. Once in the insurgent counties, the army arrested several men, but scarcely a handful were paraded back to Philadelphia for trial. Of these, only two were convicted of treason, and both received pardons from the President.[128] The rebellion has long been interpreted as a milestone in the creation of federal authority, and in most respects that is its chief significance. Certainly to the Federalists, who had long been striving for a strong national government, it was a major test: the new government successfully crushed organized and violent resistance to the laws. As Alexander Hamilton put it, speaking for many in the party, "the insurrection will do us a great deal of good and add to the solidity of every thing in this country."[129]

"A lesson to Governments and People"

The strength of a government is the affection of the people, and while that is maintained, every invader, every insurgent, will as certainly count upon the fear of its strength, as if it had with one army of Citizens [mowed] down another.

Edmund Randolph, 1794.[d]

In early 1795, with the Indian war in Ohio and the insurrection in western Pennsylvania over, Alexander Hamilton and Henry Knox retired from the cabinet. Six weeks earlier, Knox had sent the President a final report on Indian affairs. The principal cause of Indian war, Knox wrote, was the chronic encroachment of frontier whites "by force or fraud" onto Indian lands. In "unguarded moments" Indians retaliated, then whites sought revenge, and soon the West was embroiled in conflict. To prevent future wars, Knox recommended a chain of forts manned by regulars and the punishment of any white infraction of the law by military courts martial. To maintain friendly relations with the tribes, the government must also establish a system of resident agents and trading posts administered by federal authorities. But the main thrust of Knox's statement was that war solved little on the frontier. "The United States can get nothing by an Indian war," he noted sadly, "but [we] risk men, money and reputation." Americans had been "more destructive to the Indian natives than . . . the conquerors of Mexico and Peru." The United States, "More powerful and more enlightened" than its Indian neighbors, owed a "responsibility of national character" to act with justice and humanity. [130]

Knox only repeated statements he had made earlier—in 1789 and throughout the war. Yet in another sense, this valedictory from the man who had executed the nation's military policy for nearly ten years was a rejection of the very policy he had managed. In Knox's analysis, Wayne's victory became the sucessful conclusion of a senseless war, the culmination of a policy based on waging war to gain peace. Knox and Washington had learned a costly lesson beyond the tactics of how to apply force in a society based on the consent of the governed, a lesson gained at the expense of much blood, treasure, and public censure. Simply enough they learned that on the frontier, force gained very little. Knox also recognized that the use of force, particularly against Indians, involved a certain moral bankruptcy. To him, making war on simple, uncivilized redmen somehow degraded the American people and the government.

Alexander Hamilton never accepted this view. To him force was a positive tool. The display of military power in the Whiskey Rebellion made the government a grander machine, more impressive and more permanent. Force did not simply restore order or pacify Indians; it spoke a language of its own, imparting confidence to friends and threatening punishment to enemies, endowing its wielders with prestige and with respect. The threat of force could be used, as he had used it in 1783, to frighten men into agreeing to specific policies. As early as 1792 he had pushed for a military solution to enforce the excise. In 1794 when rebellion broke out, Hamilton was the chief spokesman for immediate application of military power, opposing a peace commission until troops were actually poised at the mountains in a show of governmental power. [131] In his eagerness to crush the rebellion Hamilton agreed to organize the whole expedition while Knox was out of town, and it is even possible that Hamilton encouraged Knox to leave so that he, Hamilton, could be certain the operation was managed correctly. [132] For Alexander Hamilton, force gave the government power and stature. "[G]overment can never said to be established," he argued in early August when the administration wavered between delay and immediate action, "until some signal display, has manifested its power of military coercion." [133]

Hamilton's views predominated among Federalists in 1794, but in reality his position contained the seeds of a militarism which in the end very few Federalists were willing to follow. Some in the party in 1794 refused to see the Whiskey Rebellion in such simple terms. They realized that the government response constituted a crisis as great as the maintenance of the law. Carried to their logical conclusion, said Randolph, Hamilton's ideas "would heap curses upon the government. The strength of a government is the affection of the people."[134] Washington agreed with Randolph. Once the confrontation with Mifflin forced him to reassess the situation, the President followed a policy based primarily on public opinion, on making the government appear moderate, just, and humane—saddened and distressed by the need to coerce its citizens.[135] What he realized in the midst of the crisis was that regardless of the excise or even the maintenance of the law, force itself was a controversial act. Randolph argued and the President accepted a theory that the manner and conditions surrounding the use of force can divide as well as unite the community and undermine a government or institution under attack as well as protect them. Washington and other Federalists undoubtedly sympathized with Hamilton's position and even his statement a few weeks later, when under attack for accompanying the militia to Pittsburgh, Hamilton declared that he had "long since . . . learnt to hold popular opinion of no value."[136] But the President at least knew he could not govern on such principles. He sensed that he could defuse the crisis and prevent bloodshed by sending a peace commission, and he was correct. "The Heads of the Hydra," boasted James Ross, "were cut off by the Commissioners."[137] Because the cabinet sessions remained hidden and because the expedition was organized under the guise of rhetoric about peace and the necessity for prudent preparations, the government escaped from the rebellion with its image untarnished. The commissioners, as Randolph explained, "amply prepared the public mind" for force.[138] George Washington understood that force applied clumsily, too quickly, or without clear-cut justification, smacked of tyranny and repression. But used with skill, it could, as Justice James Iredell told a grand jury in Richmond the next year, bring "Success beyond the most sanguine expectations" and be "a lesson to Governments and People."[139]

Most Federalists in the early and mid-1790s never discerned the essential conflict between the advantages and dangers of using force, internally or internationally. Henry Knox, for example, wavered, just as he wavered between joining the nationalist conspirators or staying with Washington during the Newburgh conspiracy. He could point out the necessity for morality in government and at the same time with Hamilton recommend immediate military suppression of the Whiskey Rebellion. He could publicly oppose all through his career a standing army in peacetime, yet he could work, sometimes deviously, for a national military establishment, and in an unguarded moment admit he disliked a

Paul Revere's engraving of the Boston Massacre, perhaps the most widely circulated and the most profoundly antimilitary piece of propaganda in American history. The actual scene, of course, looked very different. (Courtesy Prints and Photographs Division, Library of Congress)

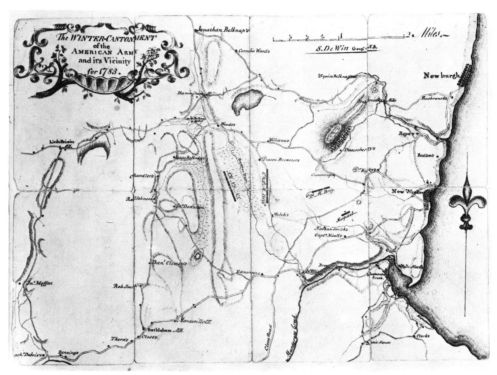

The Newburgh Cantonment. The map of the camp at Newburgh, above, was drawn in early 1783 by Simeon De Witt, an Assistant Geographer with the Continental Army. The New Building, top right, depicted in a sketch by historian Benson Lossing from later descriptions, was located according to Lossing about a quarter mile south of Deacon Brewster's (center of the map). No doubt the camp looked in 1783 about the same as it did in the early nineteenth-century painting, bottom right, reproduced by Lossing— minus the huts and destruction wreaked by a large army in residence for well over a year. (Courtesy The New-York Historical Society, New York City; Benson J. Lossing, *Pictorial Field Book of the Revolution* . . . [New York, 1859])

Above, Gouverneur Morris and Robert Morris in the Office of Finance, 1783, by Charles Willson Peale. (Courtesy The Pennsylvania Academy of the Fine Arts)

Right, Colonel Alexander Hamilton in 1781, as depicted by John Trumbull in his "Surrender of Lord Cornwallis." (Courtesy Yale University Art Gallery)

George Washington in 1783, as painted by Joseph Wright. According to some, Wright's was the most literal depiction of the general done on paper or canvas. (Courtesy The Historical Society of Pennsylvania)

Above, Major General Henry Knox in 1783, by Charles Willson Peale. (Courtesy Independence National Historical Park Collection, Philadelphia)

Right, Elbridge Gerry in 1789, by John Ramage. (Courtesy of Elbridge Thomas Gerry, Old Westbury, New York, great, great grandson of Gerry)

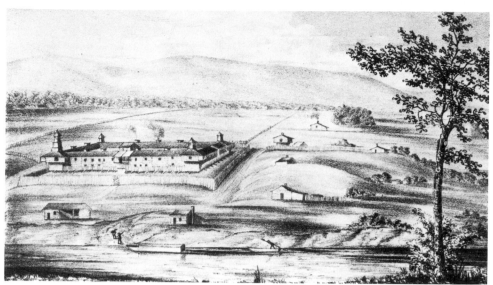

Confluence of the Muskingum and Ohio Rivers about 1790. On the left bank of the Muskingum lay the Ohio Company settlement around Campus Martius, a fortified town and seedling for present-day Marietta. Above, the view is probably from Fort Harmar on the right bank of the Muskingum, seen below in the 1790 drawing by army surgeon Joseph Gilman. Below, in the Fort Harmar view, the river in the background is the Ohio. (S. P. Hildreth, *Pioneer History* . . . [Cincinnati, 1848])

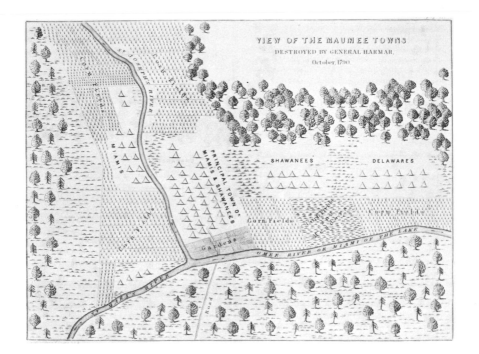

Above, the Indian villages at the headwaters of the Maumee River, sketched here by Harmar's aide and adjutant, Ebenezer Denny. Major Wyllys and his three columns forded the Maumee to the right (off the drawing), below the villages, and fought on the north bank. (William Denny, ed., "The Military Journal of Major Ebenezer Denny," *Memoirs of the Historical Society of Pennsylvania*, VII [1860])

Top left, the inauguration of President Washington, from a nineteenth-century photo-lithograph. (Courtesy The New-York Historical Society, New York City) Bottom left, Fort Washington, the headquarters of the American army from 1789 to 1792, as sketched by an officer at the time. (Charles Cist, *Sketches and Statistics of Cincinnati in 1851* [Cincinnati, 1851])

Protagonists in the Indian War. Miami chief Little Turtle, facing page top, leader of the confederated forces against Harmar and St. Clair, by an unknown artist; General Josiah Harmar, facing page bottom, by Raphael Peale, probably done in the mid or late 1790s; Shawnee chief Black Hoof, above right, who began fighting the whites at Braddock's defeat in 1755, and who led the Shawnee in the 1790s along with the more famous Blue Jacket; and General Arthur St. Clair, above left, about 1782–1783, painted by Charles Willson Peale. (Courtesy Indiana Historical Society Library; Lent to the Diplomatic Reception Rooms of the Department of State by Mrs. Robert Newbegin; Thomas L. McKenney and James Hall, *History of the Indian Tribes of North America* . . . [Philadelphia, 1858]; Courtesy Independence National Historical Park Collection, Philadelphia)

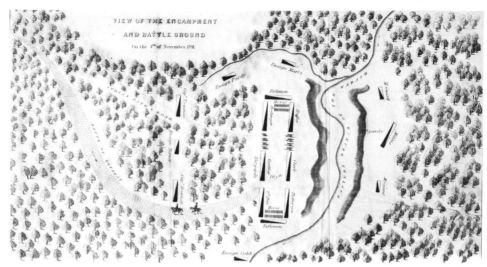

At St. Clair's battle, the first clash occurred at the right between the Indians and the militia, who then retreated back into the main encampment. (William Denny, ed., "The Military Journal of Major Ebenezer Denny,"*Memoirs of the Historical Society of Pennsylvania*, VII [1860])

A contemporary view of Detroit in 1794, near the end of its influence as the center of British control over the Indians in the Northwest. (Courtesy The New York Public Library, Astor, Lenox and Tilden Foundations, I. N. Phelps Stokes Collection, Prints Division)

Pittsburgh in 1790, from a contemporary sketch and the later drawing by
Seth Eastman. The view is from the south side of the Monongahela River.
(Courtesy Carnegie Library of Pittsburgh)

Joseph Brant and the Indians confront the American peace commissioners
in "Meeting at Buffalo Creek, 1793" by the nineteenth-century Canadian
artist Cornelius Krieghoff, who copied a sketch of the scene done by a
British officer present at the time of the meeting. (Courtesy the Canada
Steamship Lines, Limited Collection)

Left, Major General Anthony Wayne in the 1790s, by Edward Savage. (Courtesy The New-York Historical Society, New York City)

The Battle of Fallen Timbers. Wayne's victory sketched by historian Benson Lossing, right, and painted by Alonzo Chappel, below, both in the mid-nineteenth century. (Benson J. Lossing, *The Pictorial Field-Book of the War of 1812 . . .* [New York, 1868]; Henry B. Dawson, *Battles of the United States by Sea and Land . . .* [New York, 1858])

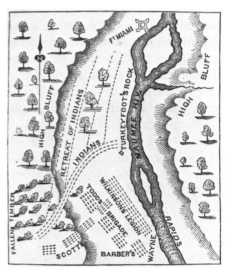

Alexander Hamilton in 1792, by John Trumbull. Discussing the eulogy he was to give the next day in 1804, after Hamilton's death, close friend Gouverneur Morris confided to his diary: "indiscreet, vain, and opinioned. . . . He was in principle opposed to republican and attached to monarchical government, and then his opinions were generally known. . . ." (Courtesy Yale University Art Gallery; Anne Cary Morris, ed., *The Diary and Letters of Gouverneur Morris* . . . [New York, 1888], II, 456)

President Washington reviewing the Whiskey Army, according to the contemporary artist Frederic Kemmelmeyer. (Courtesy The Henry Francis du Pont Winterthur Museum)

Wayne became virtually untouchable in the public mind after his victory, portrayed at the time in heroic terms by Frederic Kemmelmeyer. (Courtesy The Henry Francis du Pont Winterthur Museum)

standing army "unless I commanded it."[140] John Adams felt no such ambivalence. Throughout his career, the New England lawyer, revolutionary leader, and diplomat distrusted the military. In 1776 when Hamilton was just a young captain of provincial volunteers, Adams in Congress warned General Horatio Gates that "we [in Congress] don't choose to trust you generals, with too much power, for too long [a] time."[141] During the war crisis with Britain in early 1794, Adams then in his second term as Vice-President predicted to Jefferson that "Another War would add two or three hundred Millions of Dollars to our Debt, raise Up a many headed and many bellied Monster of an Army to tyrannize over us, totally dissadjust our present Government, and accelerate the Advent of Monarchy and Aristocracy by at least fifty Years."[142] In microcosm, Washington, Hamilton, Knox, and Adams embodied Federalist thinking on the military and the use of force. Four years after Knox and Hamilton left the cabinet, these disagreements over force exploded into public view in a conflict over command of the army in the Quasi-war with France, a conflict that provoked the first open break between President Adams and his cabinet, divided the Federalist party irreparably, and lost its control of the national government forever.

9

★ ☆ ★ ☆ ★ ☆ ★ ☆ ★

Creating the Peace Establishment
[1794-1798]

★

[W]e live in a country in which we cannot say it is either war or peace. There was a sort of intermediate state; and until that unhappy race of men who live in an uncivilized state, in our country, be extinguished, that will always be the case; a state which requires vigilance, even an armed vigilance, to guard against depredation.

Congressman William Vans Murray, 1797.[a]

In the course of winning the Indian war after 1792, the Washington administration created the first effective military establishment in the United States since the Revolution. Much of the credit belonged to Anthony Wayne, who by revising the training, by reorganization, by instilling discipline, and by infusing new spirit into officers and men, almost by sheer force of will built the Legion into a battle-ready striking force. Wayne inspired new attitudes. He refused to follow St. Clair's old road north to the Maumee; he defied the British in front of Fort Miami; he erased the stain of defeat and gave the fledgling army a pride and self-respect on which to build a permanent tradition and identity. Yet almost everything that Wayne and his superiors in the War Department built was justified to Congress and to the public on the grounds of military necessity. So too was the military program Federalists pushed through Congress to protect the nation against Britain in 1794: coast and harbor forts, a corps of engineers and artillerists to man them, naval vessels, and new arsenals and armories to manufacture and store arms and equipment.[1] Like Wayne's army, these were the seedlings for the components of the nineteenth-century constabulary. The American military came into existence piecemeal. The Federalist leadership sold it to a suspicious public over Republican objections, one element at a time, always as a temporary defensive expedient. The one question which remained unanswered was whether the men, forts, supply networks, equipment, administrative agencies—all the myriad institutions which together made up the military establishment—would survive once the threat of hostilities faded. Indeed after 1794, the coast forts lapsed into disrepair, the navy was slashed, and intense pressure reappeared to reduce or even abolish regular forces. Federalists resisted stubbornly, however. In a series of fierce struggles in the hiatus between the war scare with Britain and the Quasi-war with France which began in 1798, they saved the key element in the military establishment—the regular army. After 1794, Republicans no longer contested the existence of a frontier army, but they did argue strongly, believing that the Federalists wished to convert Wayne's Legion into the classic standing army for internal use, that the forces must be kept at the bare minimum. In the course of these battles, Congress reduced the size of the force, reorganized it, and together with new rules and regulations promulgated by the War Department, transformed it into the constabulary that lasted through the nineteenth century.

Until 1794 much of the resistance to an army was phrased in terms of opposition to using regulars against the Indians, an argument which papered over the fundamental issue of whether to maintain a permanent force in peacetime, and submerged it in disputes over the justice and necessity of the northwestern war. A few antimilitary politicians understood this fact, and after Wayne's victory in August 1794, they prepared to renew the battle over reducing the army. Republicans at the opening of the Third Congress in November were in the mood to attack the military establishment anyway. Four years of stealthy increases in its size, repeated attempts to raise a sizable regular force during the crisis with Britain, and even the government's response to the Whiskey Rebellion seemed convincing evidence of Federalist intentions to create a standing army and militarize the country—"the old trick of turning every contingency into a resource for accumulating force in the government," as Madison explained to Jefferson at the height of the war fever.[2] Republicans realized, however, that such accusations were not nearly as persuasive as finance. Swollen by the naval and coast artillery programs, by Wayne's Legion, and by the costs of Indian affairs, the War Department's budget reached $2,700,000 in 1794, more than double any previous year and nearly 40 percent of total government expenses.[3] Such figures made good antimilitary argument, and with partisanship, anti-standing army ideology, and Wayne's victory (which would trigger a reduction in forces automatically), contributed to the growing pressure to shrink the regulars.

Knowing the danger, the administration tried to avoid a confrontation; unfortunately, the Legion bill of 1792 and with it the enlistments of half of Wayne's force were due to expire in 1795 soon after the session ended, and unless Congress acted, the army would simply melt away. Wayne reminded the War Department as early as September 1794 that without reenlistments he could not follow up the victory at Fallen Timbers, and through the winter he grew increasingly insistent.[4] Therefore in November 1794 at the beginning of the session, the President informed Congress of the problem and asked for some new "inducements" to insure that recruits could be found, since legislation to attract more recruits had lost a year earlier in a disagreement between the Senate and House.[5] Congress responded by appointing a committee of three Republicans, including two from frontier districts, John Smilie of Pennsylvania and Henry Dearborn of Maine, to revamp recruiting procedures and to review the entire legislative basis of the army. Dearborn, an experienced combat veteran of the Continental Army, the Republicans' most prominent military expert, and later Jefferson's Secretary of War, returned with a report recommending that the Legion be cut back to two regiments: "the western war will hereafter be chiefly defensive," and Fallen Timbers proved that "even for an offensive war" (Wayne's army had never exceeded 3,300 regulars), the Legion's authorized strength of 4,800 was unnecessary.[6]

Henry Knox had been waiting for such an attack and immediately sent the House a long letter by Wayne written specifically to keep the Legion intact. Without a full army, contended the general, he could not occupy all his forts, safeguard convoys of supplies, or check Indian forays. Unquestionably the British were "tampering with hostile chiefs" to stop a peace treaty, and His Majesty's agents knew the Legion's strength and when enlistments would expire. Unless his army was expanded to full strength, with higher pay, bounties, and more rations as inducements, the victory might prove fruitless, and war against "a fierce and savage enemy whose tender mercies are cruelty" would surely continue.[7] Regulars furnished the best protection, Wayne insisted, and as proof he enclosed a detailed estimate showing them to be cheaper than mounted volunteers. Then as added argument against the Dearborn report, the President introduced Knox's valedictory on the entire problem of Indian affairs, that sensible, almost despairing document which admitted the Indian war had been a mistake and which tied future peaceful relations to a system of Indian trading houses, agents, and a line of fortified posts all along the frontier.[8] In effect, the administration was arguing that the size and composition of the army must await a general discussion of frontier security and Indian relations. All it wished in December 1794 was permission to keep the Legion together until a peace treaty ended the northwestern war. There would be ample time later to consider a long-range policy.

Republicans never accepted the administration's position. In a short but heated debate over the Dearborn report, Federalists diverted Republican calls for reduction on the grounds of expense only by passing a resolution asking the President to submit a general estimate of the troops needed for frontier security. This time newly installed Secretary of War Timothy Pickering presented the administration case. It was "extremely embarrassing" to recommend continuing the Legion, Pickering admitted in January 1795, because "our situation" contained "no definite object [for] military operations." But he pointed out that the long string of posts on each side of the Ohio required many men for garrisons and supply convoys. Furthermore the seacoast forts "now erecting" must be manned as long as relations with Britain remained uncertain. "[W]hile negotiations with the foreign nations who possess adjoining territories are depending," Pickering argued; "while a restoration of peace with the Western Indians is uncertain; and while an extension of open war with other and more powerful tribes [the Creeks and Cherokees] is impending; it would seem highly inexpedient and unsafe to depend on a permanent force, short of our present military establishment, especially when it is considered that sickness and other contingencies will forever make large deductions from its efficient numbers."[9]

Eventually the administration got its way. Federalists in Congress repeated all the points raised by Pickering and Wayne, emphasizing the "unsettled state of affairs" and hammering on the theme that reduction in early 1795 might mislead the northwestern tribes and leave the Creek and Cherokee frontiers naked to attack.[10] In spite of whispers that Wayne was a tyrant and had botched the campaign, Jeffersonians found it difficult to question a victorious general's requests or the assumptions behind them. Their only realistic argument was economy, which Federalists quickly countered by citing Wayne's estimate that regulars proved the cheapest and most effective forces. Furthermore the uncertainty over relations with Great Britain made Republicans hesitant to argue for military reductions. Through the winter of 1793–1794, relations between Britain and the United States had steadily worsened, because of the western forts and British support for the Indians, naval conflicts, and the festering sores of pre-revolutionary debts, commercial discrimination, and other unresolved questions from the Revolution. In 1794 in order to avert war, the administration dispatched Chief Justice John Jay to London to negotiate a general settlement, and both parties in Congress were conscious that any military legislation might affect the talks. In addition western Republicans like William Findley did not want to tamper with the army until peace on the frontier was a certainty. "Madison and about a dozen more only were left in a hollow minority," gloated Theodore Sedgwick after the first day's debate.[11] Madison stimulated some heat by moving to limit the Legion to frontier operations, claiming that it might otherwise become the standing army to execute the laws that Federalists were obviously plotting. But Federalists brushed aside the accusation with ease. Madison's crowd "must have time to exhaust their spleen . . . and then we shall have the question," purred Sedgwick. "I am always mighty tranquil when sure of victory."[12]

On March 3, 1795, Congress repealed all previous army legislation (except for the engineers and artillery) and authorized a complete Legion for another three years. It was an important victory, because no longer was the existence of the army tied to the Indian war. Pay for privates was cut, but rations, bounties, and other benefits were increased and the President gained broad authority to revamp army organization or discharge unneeded men as he saw fit.[13] The law pleased most Federalists, not only by the result but by the huge margins by which Republican amendments failed. Yet the 1795 debate was only the first round in a battle that would continue for another two years. Blinded by the ease of their victory, Federalists overlooked the possibility that once Jay negotiated peace with Britain and an Indian treaty was signed, their most telling arguments for retaining a substantial regular army would evaporate. By the time Madison left Congress after that session, he had become thoroughly alarmed by, in his words, the "growing apathy to the evil and danger of standing armies," and for the rest of the decade, his influence would linger in regular Republican assaults and charges against the Federalists for favoring a "standing army."[14] And by the opening of the Fourth Congress in December 1795, a new and crucial issue would emerge to affect the army's future: James Wilkinson's campaign to discredit Anthony Wayne and take over the army. The alliance between the Republicans and Wilkinson would undermine another Federalist defense of the military: the credibility and character of Wayne and the victory at Fallen Timbers.

Wilkinson had entered the service as a lieutenant colonel in the fall of 1791, shortly before St. Clair's defeat. For the large, outwardly jovial Kentuckian the commission represented a new beginning after failures in business and in a plot to detach Kentucky from the United States and merge it into Spanish Louisiana. The administration knew of the conspiracy and of Wilkinson's relentless ambitions, but Washington's policy in those days had been to smother talk of secession by attaching leading Kentuckians to the national government.[15] That summer Wilkinson had led one of the successful raids by frontiersmen into the Indian country, so he was a natural choice for leader of an army smarting from defeat and long unpopular in Kentucky. In March 1792, after St. Clair and Harmar had resigned, Wilkinson became a brigadier and the only general officer in service. From Ohio he waited while the administration decided on a new commanding general, expecting he would be named.[16]

If Wilkinson was bitterly disappointed, he kept it to himself. Through 1792, as the army was rebuilding, he remained on the frontier, while Wayne near Pittsburgh organized the new recruits and began the painful process of molding them into a combat army. Outwardly, relations were friendly, but almost immediately Wilkinson tried to erode Wayne's authority. As the ranking officer on the frontier, Wilkinson corresponded independently with the War Department, ostensibly to give Knox a direct and speedy channel of communication for coordinating frontier defenses and supervising the peace feelers then going to the Indian tribes. Wilkinson used this correspondence, however, to bombard the Secretary with complaints, proposals, and questions about all the myriad details of army organization. Wayne caught on quickly. Wilkinson's letters to him, while polite, were arrogant and overbearing, and on several occasions Wilkinson used Wayne's distance to question or modify specific orders. In November, Wilkinson sent the general a 27-page letter describing the forts near Cincinnati as a separate district and requesting additional prerogatives for himself. Wayne decided to go directly to Knox to confirm Wilkinson's subordinate position.[17]

Besides attempting to carve out an independent command, Wilkinson used other ploys to undermine Wayne. He carefully maintained cordial relations with important politicians, especially his old Kentucky friends, feeding them confidential information about the government's plans and openly criticizing military strategy.[18] But his most serious attempt to embarrass Wayne involved splitting the officer corps and compromising the loyalty of the officers under his immediate control in Ohio. From the beginning Wilkinson spoke disparagingly of Wayne to other officers. With grace and charm the Kentuckian soon gathered a small coterie of close friends and confidants. Some who resisted his overtures or refused to compromise their loyalty to the commander-in-chief suffered severe consequences. In early 1793, Wilkinson literally forced Captain John Armstrong out of service, evidently because he had served with Wayne during the Revolution and refused to become Wilkinson's ally.[19]

In the spring of 1793, when Wayne moved the bulk of his forces from Pittsburgh down the Ohio to Cincinnati, the dissension increased. Wilkinson "remove[d] myself" to Fort Jefferson, he told Harry Innes sarcastically, to avoid "daily and hourly scenes, which however ridiculous are extremely disgusting."[20] Wilkinson became even more popular, a magnet for all the officers who disliked Wayne or had suffered the general's most formidable wrath. The effect on the army was disastrous. Through the winter of 1793–1794, the officer corps was in turmoil, and according to one officer, split into "two distinct parties."[21] Wilkinson's group openly criticized Wayne, one even writing to a congressman, accusing the commander of being "ignorant, jealous, Partial, Rude, Ungentlemanly, and Unjust."[22] Others, in open revolt, demanded furloughs, and when

Wayne refused, submitted their resignations. The general summarily rejected them and threatened to jail any officer who left camp. The result was hostility so deep that halfway through a march into the Indian country, American officers were killing each other in duels.[23] Tempers cooled with the onset of spring in 1794 and the prospect of a hard campaign. The split was irrevocable, however, and left lasting scars on the army. Two years later officers still quarreled and were identified— almost every one—as partisans of one general or the other.[24]

Wayne was partly to blame for this situation; some of the charges were true. Quick to jump to conclusions, stubborn, temperamental, secretive about his reasoning and his motives, Wayne rarely confided in anyone during his first two years in command. He punished shirkers relentlessly, and even in cases where the guilt was unclear, he was abrasive and dictatorial. As one veteran put it, "when he speaks, Heaven shrieks, and all stands in Awe."[25] From his own standpoint, Wayne had inherited a defeated, dispirited army which had to be rebuilt with leadership, toughness, and discipline. There was too much to be done to worry about wounded feelings, and as commanding general he owed explanations to no one except his superiors in Philadelphia. Whatever the justification. Wayne's personality and methods played directly into Wilkinson's hands. Long before the army left Pittsburgh for Fort Washington, where Wilkinson was stationed, the old camaraderie in the peacetime officer corps had disintegrated into grumbling and mistrust.

Of all the officers in the army, Wilkinson had the least grounds for complaint. Wayne pampered him from the start, asking his advice, allowing him extra command responsibilities, even the chance to choose his own duties and headquarters. Perhaps Wayne sensed his subordinate's disappointment at not getting the command, for never once did he respond harshly to Wilkinson's pompous, sometimes patronizing, letters. But perhaps inevitably, Wayne began to view his subordinate differently, apparently during the summer of 1793. The first suspicions may well have come with John Armstrong's court martial and resignation. As the summer wore on, Wayne increasingly saw the discontent in the officer corps as a conspiracy against himself and the government. At the start of the advance into the Indian country in October 1793, he suddenly found his logistical system in chaos, with supplies and transport utterly lacking for an extended foray into enemy territory. To the eager general, it smacked of sabotage, undoubtedly related to the rebelliousness among his officers.[26] Since no evidence existed to implicate Wilkinson, relations between the two remained outwardly friendly, though growing more formal and distant. The open break did not occur for another six months.

In the spring of 1794, knowing a campaign was imminent, Wilkinson came out into the open. Realizing that his only hope for command lay in ruining Wayne's reputation before a military victory made him invulnerable to criticism, Wilkinson began a whispering campaign in Cincinnati that Congress had lost confidence in Wayne's leadership. Then in his most striking move, Wilkinson published an anonymous newspaper attack on the general, blaming him for the dissension in the army and charging him with stupidity, waste, incompetence, favoritism, and every other form of malfeasance possible for a general officer. Wayne was charged with purposely disregarding a peace feeler from the Indians so that he could gain the glory of a smashing victory. Wayne had allegedly suppressed and overturned the findings of courts martial, arrested officers on pretenses, and confined them for months without trial, all the while shielding "his pimps and parasites from justice."[27] The accusations were widely reprinted and Wayne soon learned their ultimate source.[28] But Wilkinson went even further. Making the same charges privately to the War Department, he demanded that Wayne hold a court of inquiry to put down rumors that he, Wilkinson, had attempted to undermine the supply system or injure the service.[29] It was his first mistake.

Since Wilkinson had not pressed formal charges, the Secretary of War could assume that the letter was private and thus delay any action, pleading that an investigation would disrupt the army on the eve of battle.[30] Besides, the administration knew the accusations were motivated by a plot to ruin Wayne. After publishing a reply to the attack in the Federalist party newspaper, the administration let the matter rest.[31]

Less than two months later, Wayne defeated the Indians at Fallen Timbers, rendering his methods, the discontent—indeed, all the charges—irrelevant. But Wilkinson was prepared. He or one of his men kept a detailed diary during the campaign of all of Wayne's activities, describing the tactics of the battle, the orders given, and the intelligence from spies and prisoners about the effects of the defeat.[32] Starting a week afterwards, in long letters to political intimates and to several congressmen, Wilkinson derided the entire conduct of the campaign. Wayne, he claimed, had directed none of the fighting. Furthermore, the battle itself was a "puny victory" which would not crush Indian power in the Northwest because Wayne had not followed elementary tactics or pursued the enemy. "The whole operation," Wilkinson insisted, "presents us a tissue of improvidence, disarray, precipitancy, Error and Ignorance, of thoughtless temerity, unseasonable cautions, and shameful omissions."[33]

Wilkinson's new charges in the fall of 1794 finally forced the administration to act, for until he was silenced, the whole military establishment might be in jeopardy. Knowing that the army was slated to expire before next session of Congress ended, and that a full-fledged investigation of the campaign would exacerbate disagreements over the army, perhaps undermine Wayne's credibility, and furnish additional ammunition to the Republicans, the administration tried to settle the dispute between the two generals privately. In December, just as the session began, Knox asked both generals to compromise their differences and work together. Knox wrote formally to Wilkinson, telling him to forget his charges unless he could produce specific facts warranting an official investigation.[34] Wayne responded angrily to Knox's request, explaining that he had indulged "the Brigadier" for over a year, that the charges were false, and that the whole dispute stemmed from Wilkinson's character ("this vile assassin") and from a deep-laid conspiracy by anarchists to ruin the army and subvert the government.[35] Wilkinson quieted down. Guessing from the tenor of Knox's letters that the administration would protect Wayne, he abandoned executive channels and did not press the matter further. Instead he consolidated the group of officers around him and began to work through Congress.

For the next year, nothing happened. The army settled down to garrison life in the forts north of Cincinnati while Wayne patiently negotiated a final settlement with the Indians. Most officers kept their differences in check, although the dispute flared occasionally between embittered partisans of one or the other. The generals themselves avoided contact, but Wilkinson, while spending his time on routine matters and private business (which still included secret machinations with Spanish officials in Louisiana), was far from idle. Somehow, either through his own political connections or through those of the officers who supported him, he constructed a working relationship with the Republicans in Congress.[36] Certainly the elements for an alliance were present. Wilkinson needed Wayne out of the service; the Jeffersonians wanted to attack the administration and cut back both the size of the army and the amount of money it consumed. Wilkinson charged that the campaign had been mishandled, that Wayne was a wretched (though lucky) general, and claimed that as a Kentucky soldier, a Revolutionary war veteran, and an experienced peacetime officer, he could with mounted frontiersmen have defeated the Indians more quickly and more cheaply. His arguments fitted perfectly with the Republican strategy. By boosting James Wilkinson, they could embarrass the administration and undermine the Federalist argument that Fallen Timbers proved the ultimate worth of a regular army.

In 1795 the entire context of military policy changed. Treaties with Britain (Jay's Treaty) and with the Indians in Ohio (Treaty of Greenville), as well as improved conditions in the Southwest, erased all threat of war or hostilities for the first time in years. Yet the President was sufficiently concerned about relations with the Indians, British intentions to evacuate the Great Lakes forts, and the troops needed for garrisoning the posts on the frontier to view reducing the army as unwise. He intimated as much to Congress when it met in December 1795, and through Secretary of War Pickering, submitted a comprehensive status report on military programs voted in 1794. While the statement seemed neutral enough, the cold facts were unmistakeable: in the first year of peace in half a decade, the elements for a permanent military establishment either existed or would soon be complete, and the administration wished no change.[37]

The Fourth Congress is usually remembered for the fight over Jay's Treaty, but it also produced the most crucial debate in the history of the creation of the United States military establishment. In 1796, Congress ratified the basic dimensions of military policy for the next century, not as wartime expedients, but as the permanent foundations for American security in peacetime. It was a particularly heated and partisan session. Years later Albert Gallatin recalled the Fourth Congress as the high tide of his party's strength in opposition.[38] Republicans could not effectively attack the programs for arsenals, stores, or the navy, even though they reduced the number of frigates from six to three after news arrived of a treaty with the Algerine pirates, for it was easy to argue, as supporters of government projects always have, that it would be wasteful to abandon programs already begun.[39] As a result, the biggest battle developed over the size of the army, its composition, and whether Anthony Wayne or James Wilkinson would be its commander-in-chief.

From the beginning Republicans pointed to the lack of a military threat, suggesting that revenue saved by a reduced military establishment would decrease the public debt and finance other projects, arguments which weakened Federalist ranks and convinced western Republicans in fear of Indians to change their votes.[40] In late January 1796, a Republican-dominated committee appointed by the House to study alterations in the army began its investigation by consulting Pickering, and through him, soliciting the President's views. The administration still wanted the Legion; Pickering claimed that to deter the Indians, protect their lands from whites, and provide a "model" establishment for future war, the country needed a sizable army. Over forty posts lay scattered along the western frontier alone; Pickering thought the legionary organization would lend itself to a divisional arrangement, enabling sublegion and battalion officers to "inspect and regulate" smaller posts while the commanding general saw to overall inspection, apportioning of the forces, and advising the President. If the army were to garrison all its forts, occupy those to be evacuated by Britain under the Jay Treaty and by Spain under Pinckney's Treaty, police Indian relations, and man the seacoast batteries, no cuts could be made. At the very least the committee should "suspend its report" until it could hear Wayne's views, until the new posts were occupied, and until relations with the Creeks—suddenly uncertain again—stabilized.[41]

It was substantially the same administration argument from the year before—potential threats and present "circumstances"—and it was beginning to sound hollow. Over the next few weeks, the committee listened to Wayne, who came to Philadelphia to defend his reputation against Wilkinson, and to James McHenry, the new Secretary of War pressed into service when Pickering moved to the State Department.[42] Both Wayne and McHenry understandably opposed cutbacks, McHenry adding that the army must look to the threat of British forces in Canada and Spanish troops in Louisiana. "[T]he safest course" would be "to leave the establishment as it stands for the present."[43] The committee was thoroughly unsympathetic. On March 25 it recommended to the House a 60 percent reduction in the Legion's authorized strength, to 2,000 men, reorganized into four regiments of eight companies each—together with the thousand man corps of engineers and artillerists, an adequate force in the committee's view, since with about the same number of men, the Legion had disposed of the Indians. And in a parting shot at the administration, designed to embarrass Wayne and provoke his resignation, the committee stated that a brigadier, without any staff, would be sufficient to command the new army.[44]

Debate began in mid-April 1796 at the height of the battle in the House over providing funds to implement Jay's 1795 treaty with Britain. Theodore Sedgwick questioned immediately whether such a shrunken army could provide the troops to fill British and Spanish forts on American territory. Henry Dearborn, who had done much of the spade work for the committee, replied that new posts would be manned by closing smaller, obsolete forts nearby. Because the Legion had never functioned at full strength, the committee's proposals would "consolidate" rather than reduce the army. And with small units scattered in many garrisons, there would be no need for large staffs or for cavalry, riflemen, and light infantry. The new army would constitute a peacetime frontier constabulary organized tactically for garrision, with more companies in a battalion to allow units to be scattered without losing tactical integrity, and to provide a larger proportion of officers to oversee Indian relations and the administration of a detached post. Ideologues on both sides, however, insisted on their day. Wayne's close friend Thomas Hartley of Pennsylvania conjured up all sorts of military bugaboos, from imminent wars to British duplicity on the forts. Republican William Branch Giles tagged any force larger than the proposed constabulary a standing army to intimidate the populace; "Government would be better without any army, as it was always better for Governments to rest upon the affections of the people than to be supported by terror." Moderates were in control, however; opponents of the army had the votes. Gallatin allowed calmly that the Legion had come into existence for a war, and won it, and while the refashioned army might not "altogether prevent Indian depredations, a Peace Establishment was now sufficient." Even such Federalist stal-

warts as James Hillhouse and Robert Goodloe Harper could not object.[45]
By a lopsided margin, the House accepted the report, in spite of the
omission of the major generalcy which, as Chauncey Goodrich splut-
tered, was no more than a plot "to get rid of Gen[era]l Wayne and place
the army in the hands of a Jacobin and what is worse a western incendi-
ary."[46] The only major change was the addition of a troop of dragoons for
patrol in the Southwest.

The House bill was a major triumph for the Republicans, and certainly a victory for James Wilkinson. Everyone understood, however, that
in the Senate, the administration and Wayne were much stronger. Wilkinson and his coterie, watching the legislation nervously (as army officers
always have), worried over cuts that might force officers out of the
service, could not believe that the Senate would agree to axe Wayne.[47] In
May it happened: while accepting a reduction, the Senate categorically
refused to make Wilkinson commander-in-chief or to cut the dragoons.[48]
Republicans were irate. Wilkinson's friends published a blast in the party
newspaper, loudly accusing the administration of covering up the charges
against Wayne.[49] But neither side would budge. Finally after a week of
deadlock, in order to release the legislation and prevent a continuance of
the Legion at wartime strength, the Jeffersonians relented. Under a joint
conference compromise, the Senate accepted a much smaller complement of dragoons and a reduction in force level while the House agreed
to keep Wayne, although that section of the law would remain in effect a
mere nine months, forcing the next session to reopen the question of
command.[50]

For the first time since 1789, Republicans succeeded in paring down
the army's authorized strength, and by mandating regiments with small
companies, reorganizing it into a truly peacetime institution. The reasons
for success were many. Federalists lacked their usual majority in the
House, and with the battle over Jay's Treaty and a new Secretary of War
installed during the legislative process, the administration could not
manage its partisans with its usual skill. The Wilkinson dispute undoubtedly hurt Wayne's credibility, diverted some Federalists who had supported the Kentuckian, and provided a bargaining point by which the
Republican House forced the Senate into agreeing to reductions. Most
important, the absence of military danger and the large budgetary
demands of the army gave opponents powerful, persuasive arguments.
Also, in that session Gallatin succeeded not only in reducing military
appropriations by 20 percent, but in preparing Congress to accept future
military appropriations on an item by item basis.[51] Yet in one of those
peculiar ironies that characterized the Federalists throughout their history, in defeat they achieved an objective for which they had long been
striving: a peacetime regular army. Despite its legislative reduction the
army actually survived at approximately its actual strength. After five

years of nearly continuous Indian conflict, Republicans accepted the concept of frontier garrisons as a means of Indian control, intelligence, and security—an old if not always successful mode of stabilizing Indian borders and preventing conflict. Their objection had never been to regular garrisons, only to using regulars to fight Indians and after 1794 (when they became convinced that Federalists aimed at the classic standing army) to allowing the frontier army to grow into a force capable of internal use. Furthermore within ten days of passage of the military establishment bill, Congress enacted a Federalist plan that would guide Indian relations until the 1830s. The army became responsible for patrolling Indian boundaries, keeping the races apart, capturing and prosecuting whites who violated the borders, overseeing generally relations with the tribes. The act, culminating nearly a decade of searching for peace in the West, irrevocably committed the nation to a peacetime military establishment.[52]

In institutional terms the act of 1796 became the foundation of American military policy for the next century, establishing a small, almost skeletal army grouped in small units to man isolated frontier posts, a corps of artillery and engineers to garrison coastal forts and train incoming officers in the mystery of the science of war, and a tiny cavalry for patrol and communications. In outline the army would not change for a hundred years, although it would grow larger and change its tactics, for example, by adding more cavalry for the broader stretches of the trans-Mississippi West. But because its mission of garrison, police, and deterrence—and the strategy of chains of forts controlling the river and overland transportation routes—would not change, neither would the army's basic profile. In the next session of Congress another long debate ensued over reducing the army and abolishing the cavalry, but with the aid of a Presidential veto and some intense politicking neither became law.[53] Every war would inspire army expansion or reorganization, but afterwards it invariably returned to its 1796 outline. Born in a partisan attack on the military, opposed by an administration obsessed with the security needs of the moment, and shaped by the intense personal struggle between two sensitive generals and the peculiar international and domestic situation of the Washington administration's last year in office, the "Act to ascertain and fix the Military Establishment" of 1796 marked the true beginning of America's peacetime army.

In the next two years, the pieces fell into place and the army adjusted to its future. The question of command was resolved within six months. Realizing that the administration would never replace Wayne "after his victories and his treaties," Wilkinson decided to end the matter by making legal accusations to force the administration into a formal court of inquiry.[54] "I am truly sick of the service," he explained to an army confidant; "I would not give five guineas for the choice."[55] The administration procrastinated until the military establishment bill passed Congress; then the President asked for an opinion from the cabinet, noting the peculiarity of the situation. The Articles of War contained no provision for trying a commanding general since only he possessed the power to convene military courts. Furthermore any officer who sat in judgement would be subordinate, thereby jeopardizing his career if he decided his superior was guilty. Faced with this legal tangle, the administration again procrastinated.[56] But Wilkinson refused to be put off. With all his stratagems exhausted and his position as Wayne's subordinate increasingly untenable, he decided to travel in person to the capital, as much "to support many allegations," he explained, "as to defend my own fame against a vanity of foul and infamous imputations."[57] Once in Philadelphia, Wilkinson forced the administration into action by threatening to take the matter directly to Congress for public investigation.[58] As a result, in a tortured review of the Constitution and the Articles of War, the Attorney General ruled that Wayne could be tried, if President Washington—as Commander-in-Chief—so ordered.[59] But the next month the feud ended with an abruptness no one foresaw. On his way to establish winter quarters at Pittsburgh, Wayne suffered another of his recurring attacks of gout—followed by fever and intestinal pains—and died. The administration had no grounds for removing Wilkinson, and because the rank of major general was to expire in less than three months, the President could hardly appoint a replacement for Wayne. To renew the rank of major general in order to justify a replacement would only rekindle the controversy, and possibly reward Wilkinson. A few diehard Federalists adopted Wilkinson's own tactic by pushing to eliminate the rank of general altogether, but since these same men had previously argued the necessity for a major general, the House hardly listened.[60] After five years of bitterness and recrimination, James Wilkinson had won.

For the War Department, the first task under the 1796 law was to restructure the army. At the end of the summer, McHenry changed the four sublegions into regiments, and reassigned the officers to their new units.[61] The process of reorganization and rationalization went much deeper, however. In 1796, McHenry worked out regulations for the recruiting service, for the commandants of posts, and for the distribution of fuel and straw. There had been regulations before, but these were more formal and more systematic, reflecting the War Department's effort to make the army a permanent, more mature, and more ordered institution.[62] The same process occurred administratively in Philadelphia as McHenry attempted to regularize the flow of paper and the activities of the Superintendent of Military Stores, the storekeepers, and the Indian agents.[63] Near the end of the year in a classic bureaucratic struggle, McHenry subordinated the accountant's office, made the Secretary's position supreme under the President in military matters, and completed the process of administrative rationalization.[64]

The army confronted the future in other important ways. In March 1797, after Britain relinquished her American forts, Wilkinson was ordered to close all unnecessary posts and transfer the bulk of his forces to the Great Lakes and the southwestern frontier, thus beginning a process that would recur throughout the nineteenth century as settlement expanded westward.[65] At the same time the War Department reorganized the supply system by classifying posts according to districts and letting contracts on a regional basis.[66]

In 1798, with help from Wilkinson and Colonel John Hamtramck, the highest ranking officer remaining from the original enlistment in the 1780s, McHenry completed a long set of Army Regulations, outlining rules and routine procedures for command, household activities, and other everyday details of army life.[67] One of McHenry's motives probably was to limit Wilkinson's authority and prevent him from making the army into a personal fiefdom. In 1797 evidence came to light that Wilkinson had renewed his secret contact with the Spanish (or possibly the French or English or all three), evidence so damning that the general had to plead his case directly with the President.[68] And the next year McHenry and Wilkinson battled over the chain of command—whether all orders from the War Department had to be transmitted through the commanding general.[69] But whatever the reason, the regulations were long overdue and constituted a milestone in the institutionalization of the military establishment. The army might still reflect the personality of its commanding general, but no longer would it respond to whim, especially in routine matters of policy or administration. Henceforth its internal life would be determined by government policy and the impersonal authority of rank and office.

In certain respects the establishment remained incomplete. Arsenals, frigates, and harbor batteries were unfinished, and Federalists still tried doggedly to change the small informal school for the corps of engineers and artillerists at West Point into a full-fledged military academy.[70] Not until the Quasi-war with France in 1798 and 1799 did the nation become committed to a navy and a coast defense system, and not until 1802 was the United States Military Academy created, ironically by the very Jeffersonians who had always opposed professional forces. The first and in most respects the key element in institutionalization, however, was the army. By 1798, while other components of the military were still fragile and unsettled, it had become permanent, and if not as mature as other institutions in other countries at the time, at least it had developed into a functioning organization with defined mission, ordered internal life, and clearly outlined structure. In the form it assumed in 1796, the army would continue for another century, the operational arm of a military establishment which guided the nation's march across the continent.[71]

PART THREE

★ ☆ ★ ☆ ★ ☆ ★ ☆ ★

Frenzy and Collapse
[1797-1801]

★

*in which
the Federalists, haunted by the fear of
opposition conspiracy, pass a militaristic
defense program to deal with the Quasi-
war with France—and in the process,
shatter their own party, unleash a bitter
internecine feud between President John
Adams and Alexander Hamilton, and
lose the Presidential election to the
Republicans in 1800.*

★ ☆ ★ ☆ ★ ☆ ★ ☆ ★

10

★ ☆ ★ ☆ ★ ☆ ★ ☆ ★

Federalist Motives in 1798:
A Reinterpretation

★

|T|here existed a domestic—what . . . shall I call it?—a conspiracy, a
faction leagued with a foreign Power to effect a revolution or a subjuga-
tion of this country, by the arms of that foreign Power.

Congressman Robert Goodloe Harper, 1798.ª

In 1813, a short time after their friendship had been renewed, the two
old Revolutionary warhorses Thomas Jefferson and John Adams very
nearly lost the thread over the publication of a letter Jefferson had written
years before, during the heat of the party struggle. In it Jefferson had
denounced the Federalists, and in the process accused Adams of a
disbelief in scientific progress. The wizened New Englander wanted an
explanation. Jefferson replied that the letter was "political," a "confidential communication . . . never meant to trouble the public mind." But he
defended the letter's description of the mood of the late 1790s, a time
when party warfare had reached unparalleled bitterness and a Federalist
congress had passed the Alien and Sedition Acts, new taxes, and the
largest military program since independence. To Jefferson, "the character of the times" was "terrorism," pure and simple: "None can conceive
who did not witness them, and they were felt by one party only."[1]

In response Adams exploded, citing all the "Terrorism" that Federalists had suffered in those years: "Chaises Rebellion;" "Gallatins [Whiskey]
Insurrection;" the "Terrorism of Fries's" Rebellion in 1799; the Genet
crisis, which Adams felt would have produced either a revolution or war
with England had not the yellow fever epidemic intervened in the fall of
1793; and most of all, the frenzy and war fever in the spring of 1798 during
the XYZ crisis at the beginning of the Quasi-war with France, when
10,000 men paraded in Philadelphia, "When even Governor Mifflin

193

himself, thought it his Duty to order a Patrol of Horse and Foot to preserve the peace; when Markett Street was as full as Men could stand by one another . . . ; when some of my Domesticks in Phrenzy, determined to sacrifice their Lives in my defence; . . . when I myself judged it prudent and necessary to order Chests of Arms from the War Office to be brought through bye Lanes and back Doors . . . to defend my House. . . ." Adams blamed Republican editors for the crisis and he could not help chiding the sage of Monticello, "What think you of Terrorism, Mr. Jefferson?"[2]

The two aging giants of the Revolution soon forgot this disagreement, but historians have for the most part accepted Jefferson's interpretation of the Federalists during the war crisis of the later 1790s. The Alien and Sedition Acts and the huge military program which were passed at the beginning of the Quasi-war have left an indelible stain on the Federalist party. Echoing Jefferson's belief that only *his* supporters experienced the terrors of the age, most historians have viewed the legislation as a coldly partisan adventure in militarism and repression designed to destroy the Republican party. In the traditional interpretation, the laws allowing the President to arrest or deport dangerous aliens or citizens of an enemy power, and making criticism of the government a crime, were the "logical culmination" of repressive and authoritarian Federalist political philosophy. Adams's feelings of "terrorism" were unjustified and, in the case of some Federalists, deliberately fabricated to induce national hysteria; Federalists "took advantage of the foreign crisis to strike at their domestic political opponents," using the acts "as a means of retaining political power."[3] The military program—mobilization of the militia, expanded coast defenses, a navy, and the addition of a provisional army and a new regular army—had similarly partisan purposes: the militarization of the country and the suppression of the opposition by force.[4]

Part of this interpretation is no doubt valid. Federalist political theory was elitist and anti-democratic, and a few in the party (who would later back Alexander Hamilton when the party divided in 1799) did attempt to use the French crisis to perpetuate their hold on the national government, especially by prosecuting newspaper editors under the Sedition law and by attempting to establish a permanent standing army. A few even intended the army to suppress political opposition, although not by the direct application of force as historians have thought.* Certainly by 1798, fears about the motives and loyalty of the Jeffersonians was robbing some leaders of their political judgment. Yet as a body, the Federalists were

---

*My reasoning and evidence about the specific motives of the High Federalists, or Hamiltonians, for an army is treated at length in Chapters 11 and 12 below, especially pages 225–229, 243–246, and 249–255. In this chapter, my analysis applies to the motives of the Federalists generally, and to specific groups or individuals in the party only in greater or lesser degree.

neither paranoid about the opposition (since paranoia implies *unjustified* fear) nor conspirators moving desperately to eradicate their antagonists.[5] Many of them (including Hamilton's friends) had honestly concluded, after five years of increasing tension and violent political strife, that the Republicans were dedicated agents of the French, bent on overturning the Constitution, and furthermore Federalists had good cause for these fears—not proof, but enough evidence for honest, balanced men logically to reach such conclusions. Their attempt to silence dissent with the Sedition law, and to arm the country, was not an attempt to destroy liberty but to prove to France that the nation was united, and should war come, to keep ranks closed for what all agreed would be a monumental struggle. (Even the Hamiltonians' militaristic bid to establish a permanent, classical standing army, which was overwhelmingly rejected by the rest of the party, was less a partisan ploy than a dream of American empire, personal ambitions, and the sincerely held belief that the only way to shore up the vulnerable institutions of a republic and save the United States was to add an army to the machinery of government.) The Federalists as a group had decided by 1798 that the greatest danger was dissent and disunion, which made the Republicans the chief enemy, and that the greatest military menace was internal revolt timed to coincide with an invasion by a French expeditionary force.

Apart from rational Federalist motives, the legislation can also be traced to what Adams and Jefferson labeled "terrorism." The Federalist program became law in an atmosphere charged with raw emotion—after a year of extreme tension in Congress, in the midst of an unprecedented national hysteria. The Alien and Sedition Acts, the troop buildup and provisional armies, and the additional taxes were miscalulations that cost the Federalists control of the government and ultimately their existence as an organized political party. But their blunder and the militarism that finally split the party stemmed not from some self-induced paranoia or out of some anti-libertarian design to reverse the Revolution, but from the fact that on the verge of their own special Armageddon, under the acute stress of possible disunion and war with a nightmarish enemy, in a country racked with suspicion and a city shaken by fear and rumor, the Federalists saw no other way to preserve their civilization or protect American independence.

To understand the Federalist legislation in 1798, it is necessary to go back to the beginning of the 1790s when the national government was just beginning, and trace forward the Federalist perception of events and of the nature of the opposition party. The decade of the 1790s was one of progressively more vicious party warfare, in which the Federalists slowly came to the conclusion that their opponents were agents of the French attempting to overthrow the national government. The image had roots extending back before the Republicans existed as a political party and even before the Constitution went into effect. One element was the Federalist fear that opposition to a strong central government had not died with the ratification of the Constitution, and ironically it was James Madison who spread the alarm and sensitized Federalists to the danger. On the day that Virginia ratified the Constitution in June 1788, Madison predicted that the Antifederalists would continue their struggle. "I suspect the plan will be to engage ⅔ of the Legislatures in the task of undoing the work," he wrote Washington, "or to get a Congress appointed . . . that will commit suicide on their own authority."[6] Through the summer and fall, Madison and other leaders grew increasingly alarmed about the movement for a second constitutional convention and the pressure for structural amendments that would eviscerate the new government's power.[7] For a time their fears were justified, but in the elections for the new Congress, Federalists won smashing victories and the effort to convene another convention eventually collapsed.[8]

Yet in the spring of 1789, when the First Congress began its deliberations in New York, Federalists were still divided on the residual strength of Antifederal sentiment. Many were surprised by the harmony in the first session. "Our debates," reported South Carolinian William Loughton Smith, "are conducted with a moderation and ability extremely unusual in so large a body."[9] Realizing the danger, Madison maneuvered the Bill of Rights through the First Congress precisely to head off many of the more dangerous structural amendments that Antifederalists hoped would reverse the Federalist victory in 1788.[10] It worked beautifully; Madison's plot administered the *coup de grace* to an Antifederalism already dying as an organized political force.

For the next two years Federalists focused their attention chiefly on the legislative faction that arose in Congress to fight Hamilton's financial program, and they detected no significant connection to Antifederalism. For one thing the loose coalition seemed to lack a popular base either in the states or in the electorate. It was led, too, by Madison, a man of impeccable Federalist credentials, and by Jefferson, a member of the administration who had publicly supported the Constitution. Nor could Federalists uncover any lucid general philosophy that could be tied to Antifederalism.[11] Only John Quincy Adams, of all the Federalist observers in 1790, recognized any real similarity between the two, and even in 1791, after all the controversy in Congress, the dispute between Jefferson and the Adamses over Thomas Paine's *Rights of Man*, and the establishment of an anti-administration newspaper in the capital, few Federalists saw any clear relationship between their opponents in the 1790s and those who had opposed the Constitution in 1788.[12]

The change came in 1792, after another year of heated debate over Federalist programs and wild accusations in the newspapers. Suspicions were aroused in the spring of 1791 when Jefferson and Madison, on a botanical expedition to New York and New England, stopped off in New York City to meet leaders of the old Clintonian party, some of the most prominent former Antifederalists and leaders of the second convention movement.[13] By the next winter, with the cabinet quarreling publicly, men like Fisher Ames and Hamilton began to note the similarity between Republicans and Antifederalists. "We hear, incessantly, from the old foes of the Constitution, 'this is unconstitutional, and that is,'" grumbled Ames. "If the Constitution is what they affect to think it, their former opposition to such a nonentity was improper."[14] That fall, after Federalists faced their first serious opposition in several congressional elections and a bid by the opposition to install George Clinton as Vice-President, other Federalists began openly to label the opposition Antifederal. "No party of importance can be so foolish," argued Senator Ralph Izard of South Carolina, but others, like Charles Adams, the Vice-President's son, and Marylander Charles Carroll, were not so certain.[15] Izard himself admitted that the old party labels were now commonly used to identify opposing sides.

For the rest of the decade it was an article of Federalist faith that Republican roots lay in Antifederalism and that their spirit and principles stemmed from the same antipathy to strong central government. Historians have generally dismissed this refrain as a clever attempt to discredit the emerging Jeffersonian party, or as intemperate suspicion. The prevailing interpretation is that parties in the 1790s bore little or no relationship to those of the 1780s.[16] But recent evidence suggests that the Federalists may indeed have been correct. From the very beginning, the handful of Antifederalists in the first session of Congress fought the administration over interpreting the Constitution, and quickly joined Madison in the sectional faction opposing Hamilton.[17] In Pennsylvania and New York, the two states which contained developed political parties during the 1780s, in Maryland, and probably in other states as well, the Antifederalists became the Republican nucleus, and nationwide almost every Antifederalist of note became a Republican.[18] Switching of parties was invariably away from Federalism, which in 1789 was probably at the zenith of its appeal.[19] Also, many of the issues in the two decades were strikingly similar. Hamilton's program, for example, had been fully developed ten years earlier by Robert Morris, and the Republicans opposed a national military establishment in the same terms as had their predecessors in the 1780s. In fact, certain basic tenets of both movements—the rhetoric against aristocracy, the distrust of national power, of commercialism, and the incipient democratic ideals—coincided closely.[20]

The implications of all this were enormous. It suggested that the opposition was more inveterate, more resilient, and more dangerous than Federalists had ever dreamed. It meant that the opposition planned to overturn the Constitution and with it all that Federalists valued: a firm union, national credit, national institutions, and by implication the entire social order. Obviously it revealed a "party formed to abolish this government," a "serious design to subvert the government," a "general overthrow of our establishment."[21] In late 1792 Federalists began to call their antagonists "Jacobins," to speak of secret designs, and to view themselves, in John Adams's words, as "the Friends of the Constitution, order and good government."[22] And the very fact of opposition in organized form seemed cause for alarm. Dire, apocryphal predictions of disunion and of a government incapable of functioning began to creep into Federalist correspondence. "I see how much power this government needs," lamented Ames, "and yet how little is given; how much is done and contrived against it; how much it ought to do, and yet how little it does, or is disposed, or capable to do; how few, how sleepy, how obnoxious its friends are, and how alert its foes."[23]

Like the awareness of an Antifederal connection, the apocryphal warnings of doom and the interpretation of the opposition as a conspiracy were just beginning in 1792 and not surprisingly they originated with the men most under attack: Hamilton, John Adams, and the leaders in Congress. And even these men retained a modicum of balance. Jefferson and Madison were seen not as traitors, but as greedy, unprincipled politicians grasping for power, men whose politics were probably less dangerous because they sprang more from ambition than from belief.[24] But by the end of the year a peculiar psychological process had begun. The venomous political style of the 1790s, the secretiveness of both sides in their attacks and machinations, the eighteenth-century predilection for conspiratorial interpretations especially when dealing with parties which both groups misunderstood and mistrusted, all combined to set in motion an irreversible spiral of suspicion. Hamilton guessed it that summer, although within another five years he, too, would succumb to its compelling power. "One side appears to believe that there is a serious plot to overturn the state Governments and substitute monarchy. . . . The other side firmly believes that there is a serious plot to overturn the General Government and elevate the separate power of the states upon its ruins. Both sides may be equally wrong and their mutual jealousies may be materially causes of the appearances which mutually disturb them, and sharpen them against each other."[25]

The gulf of suspicion widened dramatically in 1793 and 1794, when the French Revolution and the war between France and England began to crowd domestic issues out of national politics. In rapid succession came the wild celebrations of the French Revolution; the virulent attacks on the administration's neutrality policy; French minister Edmond Genet's efforts to use the United States as a base to attack British shipping and European colonies along American borders; the appearance of the Democratic-Republican Societies; the war crises with Spain and Britain; and finally the Whiskey Rebellion. Everywhere, in public and offstage, Federalists saw the guiding hand of the Republicans—conniving with Genet, goading the public to oppose its own government, embarrassing the administration on every issue possible, and embracing France so completely as to call into question the party's loyalty to the American government.

Federalists suspected Madison and Jefferson of French sympathies as early as 1789. Before foreign policy became an important bone of contention, Hamilton detected in both "*a womanish attachment to France and a womanish resentment against Great Britain.*"[26] And at the beginning of the Genet crisis, Hamilton concluded immediately who was behind all of the popular fervor: "with *very few exceptions*, . . . the same men who have been uniformly the enemies and disturbers of the Government."[27] Through the summer and fall of 1793, as the controversy swirled in the newspapers, as Republicans stepped up their accusations about the administration's monarchical pretensions and pro-British sympathies, as Genet maneuvered to send privateers from American ports, through the popular meetings, the cabinet battles, and the diplomatic crises, Federalists became more and more angered by Republican complicity with the French. "Notwithstanding the conduct of Genet towards this country," complained William Loughton Smith, after Genet had been discredited by flouting the President publicly and by losing the support of the French government at home, "a party still adheres to him, among whom are men, called by some, virtuous, respectable, and the best friends of the people: Mufflin, Dallas, Madison, Giles, Taylor, Munroe, &ca. [who all] associate with him or dine at his house and thus countenance him in his measures."[28] Even more discouraging, despite their own efforts to mobilize support, was Republican success in arousing popular protest through mass meetings and scurrilous newspaper attacks on the administration's policy of neutrality.[29]

Two ominous developments coincided with the Genet crisis in 1793. Soon after the young minister's arrival, a Democratic Society was founded in Philadelphia. Within another year and a half, thirty-odd more appeared all over the country, just as the Jacobin Club of Paris had spawned affiliates all over France. The analogy was not lost on Federalists nor was the similarity between this nationwide network of political organizations, led by Republicans and allied to them ideologically, and the Sons of Liberty and the Committees of Correspondence before 1776. The sudden emergence of the clubs had all the trappings of the first stage of revolution. Federalists tried desperately, through economic pressure, press attacks, and counter organizations, to stamp the societies out, but to no avail.[30]

The second development was diplomatic. In the wake of Genet's arrival, the United States nearly became embroiled in war, first with Spain and then with England. The French minister succeeded in recruiting Americans for a series of attacks on Spanish possessions in Florida and Louisiana, and only with the greatest difficulty was the administration able to head off these assaults and prevent war with Spain.[31] From the beginning, Federalists felt that Genet's tactics were designed to push the United States into the European war on France's side, and that Madison, Jefferson, and the rest of the opposition fully supported such involvement. To Federalists, who were coming to see the convulsion in Europe as a grand struggle for their own philosophy and social values, war against Britain would be disastrous. In early 1794, caught on the verge of war with Britain, their fears were confirmed first by Madison's commercial resolutions, then by the fierce Republican opposition to military preparations and to the Jay mission.[32] By spring, the nation was flush with war fever, with Britain as the enemy.

The foreign policy tangle in 1793 and 1794 affected the thinking of Federalists in two ways. First it deepened immeasurably their doubts about the future of the government. The Genet crisis and its aftermath expanded public participation in politics, widening both the base and the appeal of the opposition. As both parties strained for public approval, the atmosphere in Philadelphia grew more poisonous. One congressman received a murder threat from "15 Republicans and boys of Liberty to exterpate Torys" who claimed they had "form[ed] a conspiracy" to "mangle [his] body."[33] Another, a newcomer to the Congress, was shocked by the intensity of the hatred. "He who would envy a Member of Congress," Thomas Blount informed his brother, "would envy the Damned in Hell."[34] This situation convinced Federalists that by vilification and misrepresentation, the people were being tricked, their loyalty to the government purposely undermined.[35] "No free government," growled George Cabot, "however perfect its form and virtuous its administration, can withstand the continued assaults of unrefuted calumny."[36]

As their gloom deepened, so too did Federalists' suspicion about the motives of the opposition. Secrecy bothered them immensely. Much of Genet's activity was of course carried on behind the scenes; so too was that of the Democratic Societies. Genet's explosive scheme to launch attacks by American volunteers on Florida and Louisiana was implemented as quietly as possible, given the need to recruit large numbers of men. It thus took no stretch of the imagination to see in all the secrecy, the staging of mass meetings, the hidden manipulations, in the apparently orchestrated newspaper campaign, some grander design. Federalists spoke more frequently of a "malignant," "diabolical" opposition, of "artifice," of "well fabricated" plans and of "dexterous management."[37] Just what was implied by Republican desires for war with Britain and "draw[ing] America into the views of France," as Henry Lee called it, Federalists were not prepared to say.[38] At this point they made no explicit accusations of actual disloyalty to the United States, but the tone of their remarks was heavy with the implication. Nor did they draw a direct connection between the goal of rendering the national government impotent and the political ideology of the French Revolution, despite a propensity to call their opponents, in shorthand, jacobins and anarchists. Yet seeds were being sown in 1793 and 1794 that would bear bitter fruit within a mere half decade.

When the Whiskey Rebellion erupted in the summer of 1794, some of the worst Federalist fears were confirmed. Even with months and in some cases years of warning, close observers of conditions in western Pennsylvania (like officials in the Treasury Department) could legitimately wonder why at that particular juncture the agitation had suddenly changed into revolt. For the administration, beset for over a year by unremitting crisis, the answer was clearly conspiracy, probably by opposition leaders, to bring down the government.[39] During and after the rebellion all sorts of wild rumors circulated in Philadelphia. One letter printed in the *Aurora* reported the discovery, in an insurgent's house, of proof that the rebellion had "been in agitation these three years and was no less than to overthrow the whole government . . . [and join] Great Britain."[40] Yet even for more moderate Federalists, who had difficulty swallowing a conspiracy interpretation, the rebellion unhappily vindicated all the warnings about the corrosive effect of party strife. Few believed that the excise had been anything other than a pretext around which to rally discontent. Faction was the standard Federalist explanation: "a set of *leading partisans*," as the chief party newspaper charged, "have always maintained a systematic opposition to the measures of the government."[41] According to Federalist newspapers, "gross falsehoods" perpetrated by Republican sheets and "speeches, votes, and lying letters" disseminated by opposition congressmen, stirred up the people and raised up "the resentments, the ambition, and the hopes" of western Pennsylvanians.[42] Once the kindling had been laid, the Democratic Societies ignited the fire. Other evidence also pointed to the Republican party's complicity, like the activities of Albert Gallatin, William Findley, and John Smilie, party stalwarts from the Pittsburgh area who had been involved with the rebels. Comptroller of the Treasury Oliver Wolcott, Jr., was scandalized that these three, by cleverly renouncing the rebellion at the last possible moment, could escape punishment.[43] All these interpretations, fulfilling year-old predictions, were spread by Hamilton and endorsed by the President in a speech to Congress in November 1794, thereby becoming Federalist dogma. Ominously, the President's speech touched off a five-day debate in the House of Representatives over freedom of the press, sedition, and criticism of the government which anticipated almost exactly the Alien and Sedition Act debates in 1798.[44]

Because of the thrust of Federalist thinking and the drama of violence and military reaction, the rebellion seemed all at once to reveal an underlying meaning, a unifying pattern, behind the events of the past few years. Afterward it became possible to link Antifederal origins, attacks on the administration, vilification of Federalists and their programs, and French sympathy into an explanation of the opposition far more elaborate and far more sinister than ever before. The existence of a hostile conspiracy rooted in hatred of the Constitution, playing upon the structural weakness of republican institutions, using propaganda to loosen loyalty to the federal government, and somehow connected to France was not yet provable to any but a tiny minority, like Hamilton and transplanted Englishman William Cobbett.[45] But after 1794, such an interpretation became the context in which Federalist leaders and newspapers explained events. Each new crisis or fact became warped to fit, creating a circle of tautology whereby Federalist assumptions molded events into the very evidence to prove their assumptions, transforming suspicion into fact and fear into conspiracy.

For the moment, the administration's success in crushing the insurrection left Federalists hopeful. One congressman called it "the happiest event that ever happened," since it would "give the Government . . . a tone, an energy, and dignity, which will defy all efforts of Anarchy and Jacobinism."[46] But this illusion was quickly shattered, and for the next two years, every political episode deepened Federalist despondency. A month after the troops returned from Pittsburgh, Hamilton and Knox retired from the cabinet, throwing the government into a desperate search for able officers that lasted over a year. "In fact the government does not seem to grow better, as to its agents," lamented William Vans Murray. "Instead of growing more mellow—it seems more crude and green."[47] Important Federalists rebuffed Presidential overtures, mostly to avoid the slander and hatred of public life or because of the low salaries, but this in no way lessened the effect. "Time," moaned Ames, the barometer of Federalist despair, "I begin to think, is against us."[48] In 1795 an intercepted French dispatch led to Edmund Randolph's resignation from the cabinet amid charges of treason, revealing that the government could be infiltrated at the very highest levels, and that even longtime friends and supporters were subject to the corruptions of party and French ideas. The struggle over the Jay Treaty proved to be the worst evidence of national weakness and Republican designs. Late in 1794, the Chief Justice had succeeded in resolving American differences with Britain, but in return for British withdrawal from the northwestern posts (promised for 1796) and American entry into the West Indies trade, Jay was forced into several concessions that angered the country and led even the President to consider rejecting the agreement. As in the case of the rebellion, Federalists could not believe the protests to be spontaneous or that the populace was so ignorant of the nation's interest in closer ties to Great Britain. Party leaders searched assiduously for signs that the uproar had been staged, and found the evidence in the leadership of the meetings, the timing of the protests, and the coordination of the newspaper campaign. The very success of the opposition, along with the revelation that the traitor Edmund Randolph had counseled the President to delay approving the treaty (to give protests the time to develop), proved that a devious plot lay behind it, and this in turn suggested a far more dangerous malignancy than mere hostility to a treaty. When the Republicans almost scuttled the agreement in the House of Representatives, which, according to Federalists, had no business meddling in foreign policy, the flaws in the nature of the government became all the more evident.[49]

All these events contributed to the mounting evidence of Republican attachment to France. The scraps were large and small: the foreign birth of several Republican leaders; James Monroe's seemingly partisan performance as ambassador in Paris; indications that Gallatin and others were conniving with French spy Victor Collot; and the continual, almost daily, articles in Republican newspapers defending France and assailing the Federalists and the administration for pro-British prejudice. The press was probably the most convincing factor of all; pieces like the one comparing Federalists with the decimated French nobility (not softened by the observation that "The public opinion of this country tho abhorrent to the shedding of blood is no less decisive against aristocracy in every shape") heightened Federalist apprehension immeasurably.[50] At the end of 1796 came French minister Pierre Adet's open intervention on Jefferson's side in the climactic Presidential election. Federalists were appalled and outraged, and for the first time the theme of threatened American independence, which was to pervade their thinking for the next two years, appeared prominently in their correspondence.[51] Adet's interference meant that France had now openly, in the President's words, sought "to sway the government, and control its measures," and Republicans either unwittingly or by design were aiding a foreign power.[52] While Federalists did not yet conclude that their opponents were receiving orders from Paris, Adet's action furnished one more piece of evidence to weaken the idea, still current as late as 1796, that the party's pro-French stance was merely a tactic in its campaign for power.[53]

In spite of all their claims that the people were being deceived and that reason, right, and justice were on their side, Federalists were shaken profoundly by the Jay Treaty fight and the battles in 1795 and 1796, all of which sapped them of their last hopes that the government could withstand such onslaughts. They knew, as Washington put it, that the opposition was "always working, like bees, to distill their poison," and as Federalist morale plummeted, their rhetoric grew more severe.[54] The government became a ship beset by storms, a frail wooden shell awash in a hostile sea. Society in their minds became a human body stricken with morbid tumors eating away its vital organs.[55] As the months passed, a sense of dread, of depression, of hopelessness came more and more to dominate their understanding of politics. George Washington's retirement was symptomatic. For years Federalists had depended on his personal standing; as Jefferson noted, "They see that nothing can support them but the Colossus of the President's merits with the people."[56] Even Adams's victory could not dispel their foreboding. In February 1797, Philadelphia Federalists marked Washington's 65th birthday with a huge celebration unparalleled in scope and emotion. For a whole day the city was on holiday, the President subjected to parades, visitations, the ringing of bells, and the firing of cannon. In the evening, over a thousand persons supped and danced with him in an outdoor amphitheatre, then cheered beneath his window until long after midnight. The expression of sentiment left the President at a loss for words, his wife in tears. Yet in its size and pomp, the birthday party became a spectacle, almost as if a city and a nation were venting all of their apprehensions in celebration of the one man who could still inspire respect and trust. Ten days later in a simple ceremony stark by contrast, John Adams assumed the Presidency.[57]

There comes a time, especially in periods of tension and uncertainty, when people start to assemble and assign meaning to the rumors, speculations, and observations that have disturbed them. Federalist leaders had been searching for an underlying pattern to events ever since 1792, and certainly by 1797 enough had occurred to convince them of the malevolence of the opposition. Federalists of all persuasions could agree with the newspaper writer who summed it up: "That there has existed in this country, ever since the arrival of Genet, a set of men hostile to its peace and happiness, is a truth supported by ten thousand proofs."[58] Yet it would be a mistake to mix a jumble of Federalist conclusions together into some coherent interpretation of the opposition or the direction of political events. While they were certain that conspiracies existed, that the Republicans engaged in them, that the government was frail and growing weaker all the time, and that France and the opposition were determined to transform America, their understanding of the nature of the opposition and its motives was still vague. Despite all the accusations and the pessimism, even the most extreme, suspicious Federalists were not yet certain that the opposition party was engaged in a single, over-arching plot with France to revolutionize the country. It would take another year of crisis and stress, to change their minds.

One riddle that Federalists had never been able to unravel was the exact relationship between France and her American adherents. Certainly Republican leaders mingled often with the large French refugee community in the eastern cities. That the Republican party was "French" and its leaders the tools of French policy seemed incontrovertible, but the nature of the connection and what each side hoped to gain was still obscure. As the two nations edged closer to war in late 1796 and early 1797 over the Jay Treaty, America's unwillingness to honor certain sections of the 1778 treaty of alliance, and French interference with American trade, Federalists began to search for an answer in French policy itself. Unfortunately, however, information about the Directory's intentions was hard to obtain. For nearly three years the ambassador to France had been James Monroe, a partisan Republican who to Federalists had become so untrustworthy that the administration had recalled him. In his place went Charles Cotesworth Pinckney, a solid, respectable South Carolinian whom the Directory refused to accept, a fact which the Adams administration learned a few days after the inauguration. As a result, official information about French affairs came from John Quincy Adams, the new President's oldest son who was minister to the Netherlands, a country which had recently become a French satellite.[59]

Isolated in Europe and dependent on newspapers and correspondence from Federalist friends, Adams's information about the opposition party in America was secondhand and thus from the start distorted by suspicion and partisanship. Much sooner than his fellow Federalists, Adams postulated a working relationship between the Directory and Republicans which colored his diplomatic reports. In 1796, at the height of the Jay Treaty struggle, Adams wrote his father that France's principal goal was to cripple England, and to aid in their own machinations; Republicans had convinced the Directory that the treaty would firmly cement the two English-speaking countries in alliance against France. Both the Republicans and the French wanted war between England and the United States in order to kill the treaty and to oust the Federalists from power, which would eventually bring about the "triumph of French party, French principles, and French influence" in America. Adams even believed, without "the shadow of a doubt," that there existed some plan to introduce "into the American Constitution a Directory instead of a President."[60]

Yet at the same time, young Adams could be perceptive and level headed. He accurately predicted Adet's intervention in the Presidential election but refused to be frightened by the possibility of a Jefferson victory. "If, instead of Jefferson, the ex-Vicomte de Barras himself were President . . . he could not stagger the system," Adams concluded.[61] But the Massachusetts diplomat did dread French hostility to America, the product he thought of her need to ruin British commerce and of her "fear and jealousy towards the United States themselves. . . ."[62] In February 1797, Adams saw no change in French motives. While the treaty and his father's election forced France to abandon her plan to change the American government internally ("a train which they had so long been concerting and laying"), they still felt "assured that by persevering and bearing harder upon us, they shall compel the American government to submit, or succeed in overturning it." Over and over again Adams warned of the danger of internal division. "It cannot be too strenuously repeated, because the final event depends altogether upon this single point of fact," he told his father. "The French government has been led to believe, that the *people* of the United States have but a feeble attachment to their government, and will not support them in a contest with that of France. It is upon the idea of this internal weakness and division alone, that the French have hitherto ventured upon their late measures, and . . . it is impossible to ascertain how far it will lead them." If the people united for war, however, France knew she could do little damage to America. Because of this, and because of recent shipping losses in an attempted invasion of Ireland, France had no intentions of sending an army to North America.[63] But within two months, Adams reversed himself completely, and in another long letter to his father, revealed the most "pernicious" plot of all. War was now France's policy. Knowing that the "eastern states" were beyond her "influence," she planned to invade the South, and with active support from that section and the West, dismantle the union and establish a vassal republic. This would weaken "a rising power which they behold with suspicion and jealousy" and establish a territory on which to house a portion of the French army, "the return of which into France they already dread." The plan, guessed Adams, "must have been formed as early as the time of Genet's instructions." Thomas Paine no doubt knew it since he was preparing to leave France for America to "promote the design." And he was sailing with James Monroe. "Where can the imagination stop in reflecting upon these things? Can Monroe? Can—"[64]

Adams's reports profoundly influenced both the Federalists' understanding of the Franco-American crisis in 1797 and their view of the opposition party. Many of them had long postulated inveterate French hatred for the United States and some had even guessed the French design for disunion in the West.[65] But Adams's dispatches gave these ideas authenticity, the stamp of firsthand observation by an official of the government. The President showed his son's analyses to other party leaders; John Quincy's most explosive revelation—the plan to establish a satellite republic in the South and West—was even printed in the newspapers.[66] Other American diplomats abroad echoed the danger of internal dissension, and Federalists at home immediately picked it up, deploring the lack of unity in American politics both because it misled the French and because it undermined loyalty to the government, preventing the administration from meeting French pressure with any authority.[67]

Everywhere Federalists looked in 1797 they found evidence to corroborate Adams's interpretation of the crisis, and his suspicion, long implicit in nearly every interpretation of the opposition, that the Republican connection with France was treasonous. In May the New York *Minerva* reprinted from a Paris newspaper a letter from Jefferson to Philip Mazzei in which Jefferson had described Federalists as "an Anglican monarchical, & aristocratical party" quite divorced from "the main body of our citizens" who "remain[ed] true to their republican principles."[68] Here was perfect proof, in "traiterous correspondence," of misleading information fed to the French "in order to effect a change of men and measures in this country."[69] Even Adams's fears of conspiracy rang true that summer. For over a year, the government had been receiving information about French efforts to detach the West, particularly French General Victor Collot's reconnaissance of western geography and defenses, and apparent sentiment toward secession.[70] At the same time new intelligence reports reached Philadelphia of secret maneuvers between James Wilkinson and agents of the Spanish administration in Louisiana, reviving old worries about the Spanish conspiracy to detach the West from the union and suggesting that Wilkinson and Collot were somehow linked together.[71]

Although Collot had returned to the East by mid-1797, the government was still plainly worried about his plans and about Wilkinson, who had by now become the subject of a continuing stream of damaging information. McHenry and Pickering used every source possible to monitor the conspiracies: army officers, officials in the territories, even a double agent—a former French officer who acted as Collot's quartermaster and who in return for money from McHenry to support his amours in Philadelphia, spied on the general's activities.[72] Then in July, William Blount was dramatically expelled from the Senate for conspiring to attack Louisiana and Florida with British help. Federalists were aghast. "How shocking the idea is," raged Wolcott, "that in the bosom of our country, even in our *Senate*, native citizens are found, who treasonably conspire to plunge us in War!!!"[73] In the wake of Blount's exposure, the *Minerva* recalled another intended plot by leading Vermonters to incite a French-style revolution in Canada.[74] Added to this, the government knew of Spanish attempts to stir up the Indians in the Southwest (Secretary McHenry ordered security tightened at all army installations), and Pickering heard rumors of another plot, this one to enlist volunteers on southern frontiers either to invade and occupy Indian lands or neighboring foreign colonies.[75]

All these schemes concerned the West, involved leading Republicans, and pointed exactly toward the kind of treason that John Quincy Adams had predicted. In an atmosphere laden with sedition and conspiracy, Federalists could not refrain either from linking the plots together or from suspecting the involvement of the opposition party. Wolcott was certain in 1796 that Albert Gallatin had helped plan Collot's mission, and that Gallatin and William Findley had furnished the Frenchman with letters of introduction.[76] Wilkinson and all his Kentucky lieutenants, including such notables as Senator John Brown and Federal Judge Harry Innes, were Republicans, as were the Vermonters supposedly planning the revolt in Canada. Blount, too, was a conspicuous party chieftain, and when ambassador Rufus King in London interrogated John Chisolm, one of the leading conspirators, King pressed hard to learn if other Republicans were involved. Chisolm did recall going to Blount's residence in response to a summons from the Senator, and to his surprise finding Jefferson and Wilkinson present, but fearing some kind of doublecross, Chisolm left quickly. He could not say whether the Vice-President and the General knew of the plan.[77] But some connection with Republican designs was an unavoidable conclusion for Federalists. "We are not without fears," wrote Elias Boudinot, "that this may be a scheme of the Demo's and frenchified Americans to ruin England in the American opinion. . . ."[78] For Federalists, the implications of John Quincy Adams's line of reasoning was becoming all too clear in 1797. French tactics were to divide, subvert, and overthrow governments. Thus the state of half war that America was approaching was more dangerous than open hostilities, and infinitely more frustrating because the real enemy could not be confronted directly. As Wolcott put it, "*War* may be compared to an acute but not mortal disorder, while *foreign influence* is to popular governments sometimes a slow, but always a corrosive and fatal poison."[79]

For the moment, however, the government's major problem was not the opposition as much as France herself. For this reason, the new President called a special session of Congress. Understanding the need to restore unity, both to convince France of American resolve and to assure full public support for the administration in the event of open hostilities, several party leaders advocated new negotiations. "I would accumulate the proof of French violence and demonstrate to all our citizens that nothing possible has been omitted," explained Hamilton to William Loughton Smith. "The idea is a plausible one that as we sent an Envoy Extraordinary to Britain so ought we to send one to France. And plausible ideas are always enough for the multitude."[80] At Hamilton's urging the cabinet unanimously pressed on the President a new effort to negotiate. Adams accepted the idea, proposed it to Congress, and Elbridge Gerry, John Marshall, and Charles Cotesworth Pinckney were confirmed as envoys to attempt to resolve the two nations' differences. But the session itself was by no means tranquil. After the presidential election the opposition had paused in its attacks, waiting to see the tone of the new administration, especially how Adams would handle the war crisis. When he advocated military preparations along with negotiations, however, Republicans interpreted his policy as the prelude to war, and party warfare returned with all its old venom. The House of Representatives spent nearly three weeks debating a reply to Adams's address; in both houses Republicans fought vociferously against naval and military measures; and in the press, opposition editors resumed their assault on the Federalists—not only the President, but also Hamilton, who finally suffered public exposure of his affair with the wife of the assistant cashier of the Bank of the United States. Monroe's return in June fueled the flames. Republicans staged a huge public dinner for him and the returning diplomat immediately became embroiled in a public quarrel with Secretary of State Pickering over the recall. Finally, in a mood of bitterness and recrimination, Congress adjourned on July 8. Adams and the lawmakers left Philadelphia for home, John Marshall and Elbridge Gerry sailed for France to join Pinckney, and the country settled down to await the result.[81]

By all accounts the long hiatus that followed did no one any good. By December 1797, a few days after Congress reconvened, there still was no news of the mission and both parties were getting jittery.[82]* In January, numerous reports arrived that the envoys had not been received, but

---

*About this time, Vice-President Jefferson recorded the following story in his notes: "Mr. [Abraham] Baldwin tells me, that in a conversation yesterday with [Federalist Senator Benjamin] Goodhue, on the state of our affairs, Goodhue said, 'I'll tell you what, I have made up my mind on this subject; I would rather the old ship should go down than not;' (meaning the Union of the States.) Mr. Hillhouse [Federalist Senator from Connecticut] coming up, 'Well,' says Mr. Baldwin, 'I'll tell my old friend Hillhouse what you say;' and he told him. 'Well,' says Goodhue, 'I repeat that I would rather the old ship should go down, if we are to be always kept pumping so.'" Entry for Feb. 6, 1798, Franklin B. Sawvel, ed., *The Complete Anas of Thomas Jefferson* (New York, 1903), 189.

these were unofficial and only increased the anxiety in Philadelphia.[83] At the end of the month, the tension and hatred finally boiled over. During a conversation in the House chamber, Federalist congressman Roger Griswold insulted one of his colleagues, Matthew Lyon of Vermont, whereupon Lyon, a sensitive, hot-tempered Irishman, turned in anger and spat in Griswold's face. Federalists were outraged, and the next two weeks were lost in fruitless debate over whether to expel the Vermonter. Two weeks later, Griswold took his revenge. Stealing silently up behind Lyon, who sat reading before the House came to order, Griswold hit his adversary over the head with a club. Under repeated blows, Lyon retreated toward a fireplace, grabbed the tongs, and got in a single blow before the two grappled and fell to the floor scuffling. Federalists watched in glee, but soon the two were separated. Then a few minutes later, Lyon began the right all over again with a cane, and for a moment, the two dueled, cane against hickory club, until stopped by their colleagues.[84]

When the government learned three weeks later that the mission to France had failed, the news came almost as a relief. Through agents (Messieurs X, Y, and Z as later described), the French government had asked the American envoys for a bribe before any negotiations could take place, and given their rather cold reception in Paris as well as the insulting request for money, the Americans broke off the talks and demanded their passports. When the news reached the United States and became public, war seemed certain. Now the months of tension and uncertainty which had spawned such hatred as the Lyon-Griswold affair was over. The effects, however, were lasting. For nearly a year Federalists had been waiting, as Abigail Adams said, "with consumate patience," "restraining their indignation," repressing their desire to silence criticism, unify the country, rekindle partriotism, and confront the enemies of the Republic.[85] As the months passed and their frustration grew, they brooded on the nature of the crisis, the opposition, and the events of the past half decade. Their resolve hardened; their views grew more extreme. To Sedgwick, Republicans were the "most detestable faction that ever disgraced a community," "positively devoted to a foreign country."[86] Massachusetts congressman Dwight Foster was just as determined. "We need more Energy," he told his wife in exasperation. "Our Government has not the Nerve sufficient to stem the Torrents which press and resist the Assaults which are continually made by its foreign and domestic Enemies."[87] The strain of that thinking and brooding and waiting created tremendous pressure to act once the restraints were lifted. As the President's nephew saw it, "a sullen stillness seems to reign throughout the U.S. which only portends the Gathering Storm." "We are ready to rally round the standard of our Government," he continued, "and we shall be able to crush the faction into Dust. The Spirit of the People only wants to be rouzed."[88]

When the dispatches from the three envoys were released to the public, there began a three-month period of turbulence and emotion in Philadelphia and across the country that very nearly became national hysteria. Federalists were amazed and gratified. The tales of duplicity and bribery revealed in the dispatches immediately produced a storm of vocal, patriotic anger. "The real Jacobins are for the present struck dumb," exulted Abigail Adams. "It has been like an electrical shock, as far as it has yet extended."[89] In the capital, one party leader after another happily related the change in public feeling, the unity, the burning resentment towards France.[90] The evidence was overwhelming. In Boston, Federalist candidates won landslide victories in gubernatorial and legislative elections.[91] French cockades suddenly disappeared from the streets of Philadelphia; at the New Theater on Chestnut Street, audiences booed old French favorites and called repeatedly for songs like the *President's March* and *Yankee Doodle*, cheering wildly at each refrain and at one performance pelting the band with fruit until it satisfied the demands for patriotic songs.[92] Petitions and memorials attacking France and pledging support for the government, and for staunch defense measures, began to roll into Philadelphia. They came from all corners of the country, from towns and counties, from Masons in Massachusetts, militia companies in Virginia, from grand juries and town meetings, college students and merchants. By May it was a veritable flood, sometimes as many as five a day reaching Congress and five in ten days to the President from Philadelphia alone, one bearing five thousand signatures. Adams labored hours every day answering them and often the addresses and his replies were published in the newspapers, whipping up more fervor.[93]

Unquestionably the massive outpouring of sentiment put pressure on Congress to act. The "authority" of the government, in George Cabot's estimation, was "now at its zenith," assuring that any legislation which struck at France and prepared the country for war would have the full backing of the public.[94] But pressure also came from party leaders who immediately began the chant that Congress was lagging behind public opinion. Secretary of State Pickering, knowing of the divisions in Congress, purposely rushed publication of the dispatches. "The indignant voice of the people," he told Rufus King, "must irresistibly urge the adoption of efficient measures of defence by sea as well as by land."[95] As evidence of popular feeling piled up, however, and Congress continued to move slowly, passing laws mainly on naval matters, a few Federalists began explicitly to point out the danger of caution.[96] (Members of the cabinet solicited letters from Federalists to pressure wavering congressmen.) Massachusetts Federalists warned friends in the capital that at heart the country was for peace, and all the old dissension—stimulated by an opposition desperate to prevent war—would reappear, encouraging France and weakening the United States. Congress must act while it had the support and could sustain it. For this reason, many Federalists wanted a declaration of war, not only to rally the public, but to meet directly all the "Seditions, conspiracies, seductions and all the Arts which the french use to fraternise and overturn nations."[97] For this reason, too, Federalists poured forth their venom on Elbridge Gerry for remaining in France after negotiations had broken off. Gerry's presence held out a hope of peace, deluding the people, providing ammunition for insidious Republican pleas against arming, sapping American resolve. From Europe, John Quincy Adams and Rufus King added to the clamor. King felt the French were holding Gerry in Paris precisely to divide the American public, and on the subject of Congress he was no less explicit. "If [the Government] temporizes, if it wastes itself in words, if it stops short . . . ," he admonished Hamilton, "the next Election will convulse the Country, and may, as the Directory intend and expect it shall, give the Government to those who will deliver it to the same ruin that continues to dessolate Europe."[98]

While these pressures were building, two things happened that pushed Federalists over the brink. Within a few days after the shock of seeing the XYZ papers, the opposition presses revived and the Republican leadership in Congress, while weakened by key absences, again began contesting Federalist proposals.[99] Had the Republicans toned down their attacks or moderated their invective, more extreme measures like the Sedition bill might have been avoided. As it was, however, their recalcitrance provoked Federalists and furnished the final proof of Republican loyalty to France. Again and again Federalist leaders repeated that France won her battles by allying with parties in enemy nations, by dividing, by overturning governments.[100] "The Good sense of the American people in general directs them Right . . . ," observed Abigail Adams, "but in distant and remote parts of the union, this continued abuse, deception, and falshood is productive of great mischief."[101] The "Jacobins" published all sorts of slander, she told a relative; "we cannot have safety, or security whilst these things are permitted unchecked."[102] Other leaders reacted more extremely. Judge Alexander Addison labeled the opposition "vipers in our bosom, vultures preying on our bowels," and Hamilton told Washington that he was certain that "the powerful faction" was bent on revolution and determined "to make this Country a province of France."[103] Congressional leaders were no less extreme. "The Jacobinic party is more bitter and more Hell hardened . . . than ever," growled Senator Uriah Tracy. "They fight every inch of ground, and I am fully convinced they never will yield till violence is introduced; we must have a partial civil War . . . ; and the bayonet must convince some, who are beyond reach of other arguments."[104]

Simultaneous with the Republican revival, a wave of panic and hysteria swept the nation. Rumors of conspiracies abounded. In New

England the clergy unleashed a wave of fear by uncovering the plot by a tiny Bavarian religious sect to destroy government, religion, and all order throughout the civilized world. Closer to the capital, William Cobbett spread word of a plan by the United Irishmen to aid France in overthrowing the government of the United States. In Virginia rumors flew of secret and treasonous correspondence between opposition congressmen and the Directory.[105] And in Philadelphia, which had become the focus of all the pressures for action and of all the patriotic fervor, the hysteria reached its peak. Members of Congress exchanged reports that France intended to invade North America and was counting on help in the West and South for subversive projects.[106] In April, a young girl discovered a letter in the gutter behind the President's house which told of a plot by emigré Frenchmen and American accomplices to burn down the city and massacre all the inhabitants. The President dismissed the thing as a fake, but when another warning was slipped under congressman Harrison Gray Otis's door ten days later, Adams and local officials became so frightened that they readied military forces to block the conspirators.[107] The *Aurora* ridiculed these precautions as "HUMBUG" and "*silly business*" calculated merely to "*strengthen the hands of government*," but in fact between mid-April and the end of June four serious fires broke out in the city, two of which smacked strongly of arson and contributed to the growing frenzy.[108] For three days in early May cavalry patrolled the streets to prevent rioting between groups of young men sporting black or tricolor cockades, and to guard against threatened attacks on the Mint and military storehouses. Editor Benjamin Bache was assaulted and his house attacked by mobs, and it was at this point, as Adams remembered to Jefferson 15 years later, that the President had arms quietly brought into his residence.[109] By this time, the streets of the city were alive to the sound of patriotic young men drilling in preparation for war. "Every appearance of revolution is dayly manifested," lamented Senator Tazewell, who was convinced that the hysteria was being used by Federalist extremists.[110] At last in June, with the session nearing its end and the tumult and emotion beginning to rise toward its 4th of July climax, Federalists uncovered what many of them thought was the final and irrefutable proof of Republican treason. On June 13, a leading Republican and known French sympathizer, Dr. George Logan, left Philadelphia on a personal mission of peace. Logan kept his motives hidden, but Federalist newspapers predicted the worst. Then on June 16, Bache published a confidential letter from Talleyrand to the American envoys, a bare two days after the President received it from France and two days before Adams revealed its existence to Congress. At the same time, word leaked out of letters addressed to Bache bearing the seal of the French Office of Foreign Affairs. The outcry was immediate—and vicious. (Bache, it turned out, was innocent of any treason and insisted he received the Talleyrand letter from a man in Philadelphia, but in the confusion of the ensuing newspaper and pamphlet battle, Federalist charges of treason on the floor of Congress and in the public prints had spectacular impact.)[111] Now it all seemed so simple—all the musing and suspicion and nightmares that had been building for years. To Cobbett, Bache's treason fit a pattern. Jefferson was seen entering Bache's house the day the dispatch arrived; Bache had been seen recently with Collot, with Spanish officials, with Logan, with the head of the United Irishmen, and with Republican senators. A vast and insidious plot was in train: to have Congress delay, to make the people opposed to war, to keep the country divided and disarmed. Then even a small French invasion— 10,000 men—in the South "would see swarms of villains flying to their standard from every quarter; their army would augment in its progress like a ball of snow rolled down a hill. . . ." "If ever people on earth were dancing on the edge of a precipice," Cobbett cried, "we are at this moment."[112]

In the wake of these sensational disclosures and then the boisterous reception for returning diplomat John Marshall, Federalists introduced a new, harsher, and more repressive Sedition bill. On July 3, legislation passed quadrupling the regular army. On July 4, in "a scene of uproar and confusion," with a deafening military parade in the streets drowning out debate, the Senate passed the Sedition measure on a strict party vote.[113] Within another two weeks, the House assented, Adams signed the measure into law, and the President approved the last, and most critical, element in the military program: the twelve new regiments of regular troops.

It would be easy, especially since historians have for so long emphasized other factors, to write off most of this legislation to the combined passions of the moment: frustration, anxiety, pressures from public opinion and party extremists, hysteria, fright. All indeed played a part. Yet it would be a mistake to view the Federalist program, even the most repressive legislation, within the context of emotion alone. Behind the wild events in the spring of 1798 lay a constellation of assumption and belief that prepared Federalists to react as they did. For half a decade events had led them to question, with increasing frequency and sincerity, Republican attachment to the Constitution. Beginning in the Revolution, many future Federalists began to doubt the vitality of American institutions; since the early 1790s, they had viewed politics not as a legitimate process of conflict over America's future direction, but as a connected series of hidden manipulations and conspiracies. France was the purveyor of revolution and her strategy was internal subversion. When the crisis arrived, all the events of the past decade seemed to fall into place. The Alien and Sedition Acts and the military program were designed in part to suppress the Republican party because Federalists were certain first, that internal opposition itself was the greatest danger in any conflict with France, and second, that France could not be defeated without unity at home. Very little of this was justification for perpetuating themselves in power. Federalist understanding of the state of the nation, of politics, of French relations, and of the nature of the opposition had pointed toward these conclusions for years; they voiced their worries in private as much as in public, and so often and with such force that the web of correspondence itself reinforced their beliefs. By the spring of 1798, the idea that the Republican party constituted a huge and monstrous conspiracy to revolutionize American society in line with French foreign policy had compelling power. To many Federalists Bache's "treason" was hardly surprising. "Persons intimately acquainted with the state of Parties in this Country," explained Roger Griswold, "have for a long time ceased to doubt the existence of a French faction . . . ; this circumstance therefore will like proof from the holy writ open the eyes of the blind."[114]*

The last question which must be asked is whether the Federalists were justified in their perception of the Republican opposition. In one respect the question cannot be answered definitively; there is no modern investigation, based on systematic research in the sources, of whether the Republicans, or even some of them, were actually conspiring with France or planning to overthrow the Constitution. Studies of the top Republican leadership, of the nature of the party and its operations, and of French sources provide no evidence at all for such an interpretation. And yet the Federalists supposed otherwise for reasons that were justified and supported strongly by good evidence.

To begin with, many of their accusations and suspicions were quite correct. Republicans and Antifederalists were very much related, not only by ideology but by personnel as well. A few of the Democratic Societies were more than harmless political clubs; the Mingo Creek Society was closely involved in the Whiskey Rebellion and the Kentucky Society furnished ammunition and encouragement to George Rogers

---

*One of the President's sons, Thomas Boylston Adams, in Europe in August 1798 with his brother John Quincy, agreed: "The remarks of Mr. Thatcher & the reference of Mr. Harper respecting a conspiracy against the Government, will I hope result in some discovery of consequence—a false alarm would be very hurtful in business of this nature. As the existence of a treacherous correspondence with the french I have no doubt, nor have had for three years past, and I have thought the Government culpable for not using *all* the means in its power to detect & expose it. If a few of our *honest scruples* are not got over, the enemies of our Country & Government may organize insurrection & rebellion in perfect security—fearless of discovery & in defiance of punishment." To Joseph Pitcairn, Aug. 10, 1798, "Letters of Thomas Boylston Adams," *Quarterly Publication of the Historical and Philosophical Society of Ohio*, XII (1917), 18.

Clark for his projected attack on Louisiana.[114] The evidence for Republican attachment to France was overwhelming, as obvious to Federalists as the incessant newspaper pieces and as obscure as the marriage of Edmond Genet into the Clinton family in New York. While France did not as a matter of policy overturn governments by internal subversion, beginning in 1795 government after government in Europe succumbed to republican coups, sometimes with French assistance and nearly always with French approval. A tide of revolutionary fervor was sweeping Europe and America in this era, and the Federalists were right to view the threat in international terms.[115] French refugees lived in the seaboard cities in the United States, especially Philadelphia, where a large, politically active community frequently mingled with members of the opposition. French Foreign Minister Talleyrand himself had lived in exile in America in the 1790s.[116] Last, Americans did engage in activities that came very close to treason, or at least a loose definition of the term. The whole matter of loyalty was as confused then as it has been in the twentieth century. In the spring of 1798, no less a personage than Virginia lawyer St. George Tucker claimed that 100,000 Americans might join an invading French army, and that he might also. When asked— incredulously—whether he could join the French against his own country, Tucker replied that he would join the French in favor of his own country.[117] At the time, George Rogers Clark still held his commission as a general in the French Army, and considered himself loyal more to France than to the United States government. When Clark travelled to Philadelphia in June, the height of the frenzy, the administration gave him the option of resigning his French commission or leaving the country. The old Kentucky warrior promised nothing on either score; later that summer, an army detachment sent to arrest him at home was attacked and disarmed by Clark's men.[118]

None of this, of course, proved that the Republican party was itself a conspiracy. Yet conspiracies *were* afoot in the 1790s, and for sheer number and range of seditious plots this decade was perhaps unique in American history. Several Federalist leaders had themselves engaged in a conspiracy in 1783 and there was no reason to suppose their enemies could not or would not do the same. Furthermore, the differences between conspiracy, sedition, treason, and normal political activity were hopelessly confused in eighteenth-century political theory. Neither side in the party struggle conceived of "parties" as legitimate. For Federalists, as for nearly every group that held the reins of government in England and America in this century, it was impossible to distinguish between opposition to men and policies and a plot to upset the established order. Party and faction were nearly synonymous, and faction was understood to operate normally in the conspiratorial mode.[119] Federalists were by no means unusual in finding designs in small scraps of evidence, in imparting malicious possibilities to seemingly unrelated events, or in interpreting a lack of evidence as proof itself that a plot was more villainous and sinister.

Like others of their age, Federalists were alive to these dangers because of their reading of history and of republican theory. Republics were fragile political constructs, dependent on the virtue of their populations and particularly vulnerable not only to external threats but to internal degeneration as well. Few had survived in recorded history, and Federalists like most of the Revolutionary generation knew it. History was a cyclical process in which societies rose and declined with an inevitability that individual human action could barely affect. As a result every indication of the progressive weakening of the government, no matter how small, struck Federalists with tremendous force. They were also sensitized by a peculiar apocryphal psychology, particularly those in New England where the Puritan jeremiad and themes of doom, corruption, and imminent disaster were old traditions. Like the rest of their generation, Federalists had what one historian called a "sense of historic grandeur," a tendency to see their own as a particularly historic epoch and to ascribe to their every act momentous historical importance.[120] The result was a specific cast of mind far more potent than the simple sum of political ideology, historical understanding, and apocryphal psychology, a cast of mind that prepared the Federalists and in fact drove them toward a pessimistic and malevolent interpretation both of events and of the character of the opposition party.

From the distance of two centuries it is easy to dismiss the Federalists' perception of events, no matter how understandable, and to discount any justification for the huge armies they proposed in 1798 and after. None of their dire predictions were borne out. The Jeffersonians acceded to power and on balance left the Federalist governmental edifice and American society relatively undisturbed; the Constitution and the national government continued, grew stronger, and even survived the fiery test of civil war and the massive social, economic, and international upheavals of the twentieth century. Yet looking ahead in 1798 none of this seemed foreordained. The generation of the Federalists had witnessed too much fundamental political change: a colonial revolution; two experiences in constitution-making at the national level and many more within the states; two rebellions in large, important states; and finally the convulsion of the French Revolution which shook the political and social fabric of the western world to its very foundations. To doubt in 1798 the viability of their own institutions and the independence of the nation was only realistic.

Finally, to view the Alien and Sedition Acts and the military program in 1798 more as a partisan effort to crush an opposing political party than as an attempt to silence dissent and protect the nation in a wartime crisis is to misread completely the mood of the Federalists and of the country in the spring of 1798. No doubt some in the party cynically used the crisis for party purposes, and unquestionably the Hamiltonians wanted to change the very nature of the national government by making an army permanent. Yet the elimination of the Republicans was at the same time a defensive blow against France, and the conjunction in some Federalist minds was so complete that the two motives became indistinguishable. The country was at war or virtually at war; a formal declaration was chiefly a procedural issue and of more importance in rallying the public and dealing with aliens, spies, and traitors, than internationally, where it would only constitute a ratification of the existing situation. Viewed as a response to war, the Alien and Sedition Acts were merely the first in a long, unfortunate string of attacks on civil liberties in wartime, akin to the legislation and executive action in the Civil War, World Wars I and II, and the Cold War. Expansion of military forces in wartime has always been traditional and prudent. Perhaps in the last analysis, most Federalists who agreed in 1798 to support armies, taxes, and the Alien and Sedition Acts were only responding to the age-old question of how to defend liberty without destroying it.

11

★ ☆ ★ ☆ ★ ☆ ★ ☆ ★

Forging the Sword of Federalism:
The New and Provisional Armies
[1798]

★

I can see no conclusion for us other than one of these; either to receive
constitutions, armies and fraternity, at the usual price and submit like
the rest to the will of *France*; or at least to engraft a military spirit upon
our national character and become a *warlike people*. This result is in
either case not pleasant in prospect, but can we help it?

John Quincy Adams, 1798.[a]

The military response of Alexander Hamilton and the Federalist
leadership in Congress to the nightmare of conspiracy, invasion, and
internal revolution was to create a series of armies that would intimidate
the political opposition, check rebellion, protect the nation from French
invasion, and ultimately, introduce the classic standing army in the
United States. But the military program adopted in 1798 also had deep
roots in Federalist military philosophy. For a decade after the Revolution,
Federalists consistently argued that the only way to avoid war was
through military strength, and that no nation could afford to remain
defenseless while an opponent prepared for battle. Alexander Hamilton
and others had argued these principles all through the 1780s and in the
debate over the Constitution in 1788, they gained wide acceptance
among Federalists.

In 1794, on the verge of war with Great Britain, Federalists for the
first time worked out a practical defense program to fit the theories of
deterrence, preparedness, and defense. Their first instinct was to protect
the nation from overseas attack. "We mean to act just as you would do
yourself, if your house was beset by a band of Robbers," congressman

219

William Barry Grove told a friend, "fly to your arms and defend your property."[1] Most important, Federalists wanted to prevent a war. In their minds, military preparation could avert a conflict by exhibiting American resolve and forcing Britain to reconsider the advantages to be gained by hostilities; if war ensued anyway, the nation would be ready for the fighting.[2] Several Federalist proposals in 1794—to fortify harbors, coastal points, and to procure the necessary arms, supplies, and men for the new posts—stimulated only token opposition. But on the other hand the small navy (passed as much to counter the Mediterranean pirates, whom the English spurred on to attack American commerce), provoked tremendous heat. Yet to Federalists, who had advocated coast defenses and a navy for years, both were small, passive programs, of minor consequence because of the time needed for construction and deployment. The only certain way to show American determination and defend the country should war come was land power. On March 10, the same day that the House passed the naval bill, Theodore Sedgwick served notice that he would introduce some important resolutions. "[I]t ought no longer to remain uncertain," he announced, "whether the property and best interests of our citizens were . . . to be insulted and injured with impunity."[3]

Two days later, speaking for the administration and for the Federalist leadership in Congress, Theodore Sedgwick proposed raising fifteen regiments of "auxiliary or provisional troops."[4] Men would be enlisted, armed, and equipped for two years, and officers appointed, but unless war broke out, they would serve on active duty only 24 days at a maximum per year for training. It was a shadow, paper army, what four years later would be called the Provisional Army. It possessed, as Sedgwick admitted, all the advantages of regulars: the troops would enlist for a stated term, gain training and discipline, and serve under national authority. But they would not constitute a threat to liberty or a drain on federal revenue because the force would never be embodied except for training or in case of war. A shrewd compromise similar to the levies enlisted for St. Clair's campaign in 1791, the Provisional Army was a regular forced organized in such a way as to minimize the political dangers of cost and similarity to the classic standing army. But Republicans saw through it immediately, and realized that such a force posed great dangers. Senator James Monroe visualized it as a permanent fixture—"the commencement of a military establishment," with "one common chief . . . as generalissimo," most certainly Alexander Hamilton. "The influence of such an institution upon the measures of the government in the patronage it gives etc.," Monroe continued to Jefferson, "you will readily conceive—nor can it be doubted that if it sh[oul]d be so disposed as its leaders will be, it may even remodel and form itself by the English standard."[5]

In the end, even after modification and repeated parliamentary maneuvers to reintroduce the measure or substitute full-time regulars, the Provisional Army lost. To defeat it, Republicans in the House advocated authorizing the President to create a select corps of militia, armed by the federal government and held in readiness to act as minutemen for the duration of the crisis. A special committee on defense proposed a select corps, set the figure at 80,000, and recommended that independent volunteer companies be accepted along with regular militia units. Federalists agreed, since a partial mobilization of militia would also serve as a warning to Britain. But once adopted, the militia plan helped to convince many in the party that enough preparation had been made, and that an army would require so much additional revenue that new taxes would be needed. On the final vote, the Provisional Army failed, 50 to 32. Madison reported with pleasure that even reduced to a 10,000-man force, it "was strangled more easily . . . than I had expected."[6]

The debate over defense in 1794 was a rehearsal for 1798, as were discussions of a land tax and a Sedition Act. Coast protection, a navy, and a land army were the proper, orthodox, eighteenth-century military tools with which a nation with a long coast line and commercial interests prepared for overseas attack. By 1795, having won the Indian war, crushed the Whiskey Rebellion, and settled the conflict with Britain peacefully, Federalists found nothing to question the effectiveness of military power either as a deterrent to war or a positive tool of statecraft. Nor did Federalists find anything to shake their long-standing belief in the primacy of regulars, especially after the failure to reform the militia in 1792 and reports of inadequate arms and lax discipline after the return of the Whiskey expedition in 1794. No evidence survives to indicate that Federalists proposed the Provisional Army in 1794 for any reason other than their belief in the military inferiority of militia and their determination to deter the British. As Sedgwick explained privately, "the real object . . . is the preservation of peace—G. B. will be very slow to go to war should she find us prepared for her."[7] Few Federalists in 1794 questioned the loyalty of the opposition party, particularly if the United States fought Britain, the traditional foe in the popular mind, despoiler of American commerce, instigator behind the Indian war, and the *bête noire* of the Republican party. Three years later, however, when the enemy was France, the purpose of the army would no longer be purely external.

From the beginning of the French crisis in late winter 1797, leading Federalists called for strong military preparations, again as a deterrent and to prepare the nation for war. ("My plan is to combine *energy* with *moderation*," wrote Hamilton.)[8] Through the cabinet, which became the willing conduit to the President and to Congress for his ideas, Hamilton argued for orthodox Federalist fare: further fortification of seaports; naval armaments including arming of merchant vessels, convoys, privateering, and the purchase of more vessels for the navy; an increase in cavalry and artillery; limited shipping embargoes; new internal taxes; and a provisional army of 25,000 men. To Pickering, who specifically solicited the New Yorker's views, Hamilton explained that he wanted "a *permanent army in case of invasion*," a "*stable* force" that could "oppose . . . the first torrent." "Mere militia," he felt, "would involve incalculable dangers and calamities." A provisional army, "as a substitute for a standing army," could be engaged more quickly and "be a solid resource in case of need."[9] These considerations aside, Hamilton and other Federalists who favored an army in 1797 invariably mentioned a new and critically important factor: the danger of internal revolt. Some talked of slave insurrection, but their language indicated more fear of whites than blacks.[10] As Hamilton asked McHenry, "who can guarantee us that France may not sport in this country a preseliting army?"[11]

In 1797, before the XYZ sensation and before another year of tension and emotion erased so much Federalist caution, Hamilton and his friends were far ahead of the rest of the party on the need for an army and its uses internally. Most Federalists were very sensitive to the antipathy to standing armies, wary of supporting a large force until war appeared imminent. Eventually leaders like Pickering, Harper, and Sedgwick brought over the rest of the party with fears of sedition and disloyalty, and with the argument about preparations before hostilities preventing actual war. Although the extremists—those who sided with Hamilton when the party later divided—would win the bulk of their program, support within the party generally always remained fragile, and moderates in Congress invariably insisted on limiting the measures proposed by the congressional leadership. When John Adams opened the special session of Congress which appointed the XYZ negotiators in 1797, he devoted the bulk of his remarks on preparedness to naval matters, paying scant attention to the Provisional Army that had been recommended unanimously by the cabinet.[12] Congress agreed to consider all of his recommendations; the Senate appointed select committees and in the House, William Loughton Smith of South Carolina introduced ten resolutions repeating in outline the Hamilton plan sent from the Secretary of War.[13]

But both chambers squirmed at the cost—by McHenry's estimate at least $1,500,000 every year minimum—especially before negotiations were attempted. Even the Senate, where Federalists enjoyed a two to one majority, balked at many proposals and defeated the Provisional Army by a huge margin.[14] In the House, where Republicans again offered the 80,000 militia mobilization as an alternative, the Provisional Army never had a chance. By the time Congress adjourned, the most substantial portion of Hamilton's plan had gone down to defeat.[15]

According to Sedgwick, Jefferson (now Vice-President), and others, the Federalists had been thwarted by "the events of Europe coming to us in astonishing and rapid success, to wit, the public bankruptcy of England," French military victories, "the Austrian peace, mutiny of the British fleet, Irish insurrection . . . and, above all, the warning voice . . . of Mr. King [American ambassador to Britain], to abandon all thought of connection with Great Britain, that she is going down irrecoverably, and will sink us also, if we do not clear ourselves." This "brought over several to the pacific party."[16] Yet both sides left Philadelphia in July 1797 in an ugly mood: the Federalist leadership angry and humiliated by the spinelessness of their own moderates, Republicans pessimistic because of the passion exhibited and the depth of support for war preparations.

Underneath Congress's inaction lay fundamental disagreements about the nature of military power that were never resolved. Most moderate Federalists accepted the assumptions behind the Hamiltonian military program. (Jefferson noted how consistent were both party positions in 1794 and 1797.) Connecticut Senator Uriah Tracy, an extremist who wrote the Provisional Army bill in the Senate and along with Sedgwick pressed for its adoption, revealed in his correspondence the key thought. "May we not yield so much . . . as to invite rather than repel attack?" he asked. "Can a Country expect to repel invasion and interruption by declaring they not only never will fight; but never will prepare either by Land or water, any effectual defence?"[17] Added Sedgwick, "if a negotiation had any chance of success, it would be from the dignified and defensible attitude which we should assume."[18]

One of Sedgwick's and Tracy's most consistent antagonists in the Senate was Henry Tazewell of Virginia. Tazewell accepted John Quincy Adams's reasoning and predicted that the chance of war was very good. "It is a settled determination with France to secure a territory in America bordering on us," Tazewell wrote. "Her numerous army accustomed to victory" needed to be "out of the way," and the result would be "a strong force favourable to France near us, . . . one of the most serious events that can happen." But to Tazewell, a firm Republican, the answer was negotiation. Every act that prepared the nation for war provoked France rather than deterred her, thus undermining any hope of accommodation. "The measures which have been proposed, and talked of out of doors," he continued, "irritating and provoking" measures, "all lead to war." They proved to France with "scarcely a doubt," the insincerity of the effort to negotiate.[19] In essence, the three senators expressed the heart of the partisan disagreement over preparedness. Both positions had developed slowly over five years and sprang from more profound differences of military and political philosophy. (Because of their belief in militia, at least to block an invasion initially, Republicans could logically view armies as unnecessary—and indeed dangerous because of the possibility of repression, because of the patronage opportunity it gave Federalists, and because of the centralizing power it added in draining federal revenue and creating new public debt.) But by 1797, neither side was listening to the debate. A year later, in slightly altered form, the whole controversy reoccurred, over exactly the same military program. That time, however, the extremists within the Federalist party triumphed.

In that wild spring of 1798, as talk of conspiracy raced through Philadelphia and the nation teetered on the verge of war, pressures for the Federalist military program, particularly some kind of regular army, became irresistible. Realizing this, Republican leaders caucused immediately after the President notified Congress that negotiations with France had been broken off and agreed to go along with passive defenses.[20] Within a few short weeks, new laws to prohibit arms exports, expand the coast defense system, and purchase cannon and other arms or establish foundries to manufacture them rolled through Congress with hardly any debate.[21] Nor did Republicans object violently to another regiment of artillerists and engineers to support the expanded harbor battery system, although they did fight hard to defeat the proviso for five-year enlistments, an obvious ploy to attach the new regiment onto the permanent regular military establishment.[22] Yet to Federalists, these were relatively minor successes. On April 9, McHenry asked Congress for three new regiments and a Provisional Army of 20,000 men, which with more naval vessels represented the Hamiltonian program modified only slightly by President Adams. "To forbear . . . from taking naval and military measures, to secure our trade, defend our territory in case of invasion, and prevent or suppress domestic insurrection, would be to offer up the United States a certain prey to France," McHenry assured Congress, "and exhibit to the world a sad spectacle of national degradation and imbecility."[23] Within two weeks, a provisional army bill was presented to the Senate and accepted.[24]

The House exploded in anger and vituperation. The moment the bill was introduced, before first reading—an extraordinary break in procedure—John Nicholas of Virginia jumped up to object. "It was not necessary to pass a bill of this sort under any possible modification," he declared heatedly, and thus began a vicious month-long battle, the lengthiest and most all-encompassing debate on national defense since the Revolution.[25] Republicans found the Provisional Army scheme fraught with constitutional and political dangers. First of all, "provisional" forces were illegal. The Senate bill gave the President authority "to cause to be inlisted" a 20,000-man force "whenever he shall judge the public safety requires the measure," but the Constitution empowered Congress to raise armies and nowhere in that document was there any mention of "provisional" forces.[26] Second, no army was needed because the nation faced no danger. France had little interest in a country which carried no weight in European politics; she knew her strength consisted of men, not ships or money, and that she therefore could not engage in overseas adventures. The threat of invasion, snapped Richard Brent of Virginia, was "mere bugbear."[27] Third, if danger threatened, the militia provided far better protection than the "refuse of society" that would enlist in a provisional army.[28] A regular army of 200,000 could not defend 1,300 miles of southern coastline, Brent reasoned, but militia were everywhere and the President since 1797 had authority to mobilize 80,000. Republicans rehashed all the old arguments about the superiority of citizen-soldiers. At one point Thomas Sumter, the "Gamecock of the Revolution," the aged hero of countless guerrilla battles in the South, presented a long dissertation on militia prowess, detailing incidents and anecdotes of regiments and long forgotten crossroads where his partisans had stood against the British.

Unconstitutional, unnecessary, and inferior, the Provisional Army to Republicans could only represent a bold attempt to militarize the country. Obviously it was the standing army for which Federalists had always panted—in Joseph McDowell's words, a "system of terror."[29] The proof lay in section three which allowed the President to accept any companies that volunteered as units with their own arms and equipment. The volunteer corps would be rich, zealous Federalists in unlimited numbers under Presidential command—a praetorian guard siphoning off the best young men from the militia, creating jealousy, and destroying discipline and organizational integrity. And for what purpose? For internal control, answered Gallatin. Like similar forces in England and Ireland, this mongrel corps (neither militia nor regular) was being raised for "fictitious conspiracies, pop-gun plots, and every other party artifice."[30] Obsessed with revolution, with "perturbators and disorganizers," Federalists were "arming one part of the people to guard against the other," to take over America.[31] "Certain gentlemen are determined to take every means which leads to expense and patronage," growled Nathaniel Macon, "and others are as determined in opposing that expense and that patronage."[32] Privately and in the press Republicans were just as agitated. "Such is the intolerance of J[ohn] A[dams] and his party," charged Virginia Senator Stevens T. Mason, "and so favorable to their views do they consider the present state of things, that there is no calculating how far they will go to attain their favorite object of crushing . . . Republicanism."[33]

Republicans had finally guessed the true motives of their antagonists. On the floor of Congress, Federalists used every conceivable justification they could muster: the proximity of French forces in the West Indies and the danger of invasion; the need for a deterrent posture and the inexpensiveness of provisional forces; the weakness of the militia, particularly in the South. They repeated all their old attacks on state forces, replete with long recollections of battles during the Revolution. Stubbornly they defended the volunteer corps as temporary and cheap, a corps of the most zealous and upstanding with the "strongest and dearest bond . . . with the community."[34] Wealth itself posed no dangers; true the volunteers would be formidable, but to whom, asked Jonathan Dayton? "To the invaders of our country—to the turbulent and seditious—to insurgents—to daring infractors of the laws."[35] Dayton and the others rarely admitted what Federalists in private asserted repeatedly: the need for an army to "save us from internal opposition."[36] Federalists worried constantly about invasion, insurrection, and they distrusted the militia. Their greatest fear, however, was attack "by a powerful army of veterans" who in Pickering's estimation "would hold out their lures" and "entice multitudes" to "join their standard, as has happened in every republic in Europe which they [the French] have fraternized."[37] In simple terms, Federalists wished to revive "the spirit of 1776," to overawe the seditious multitudes infesting the country, "to keep in check these people," to "put arms into the hands of all our friends," and to cement to the government the "great body of feeble, deluded, or calculating Neuters who in all Societies join those at last whom they think strongest."[38] Many knew also, as Senator James Ross put it, that the Provisional Army would have "an effect upon political opinions and perhaps insure some of our Elections."[39] And some probably had more malicious designs. In Baltimore later that summer one Federalist lambasted his friends for indiscretion. "They seemed to imagine, that nothing was left to be done, but to exterminate everyone who had been of the *Democratic* side."[40] But for most members of the party, the Provisional Army was an act to contain disloyalty in the population and an assertion of military orthodoxy— deterrence and preparedness.

The debate in Congress was the last time before the Republicans seized power that the issues surrounding national security were argued in detail by men like Sumter, Daniel Morgan, William Shepard (who had commanded the militia at Springfield during Shays's Rebellion), and other veterans of the Revolution. Under blistering attack by the opposition, Federalist majorities wavered and then broke; the final Provisional Army act emerged from Congress weakened and stripped of the provisions Federalist leaders wanted most. Under the law the President could activate the army only if war were declared, the country invaded, or in "imminent danger" of invasion—and then only 10,000 men, if Congress was not sitting. Pickering argued persuasively that the volunteer corps would remain empty since the men might be subjected to service anywhere in the union and were not exempt from normal militia duty.[41] And the President had no authority to organize the anticipated companies into larger military units, or in fact to take any preliminary steps, like appointing officers, to ready the Provisional Army for mobilization.[42]

Hamilton, the cabinet, and party chieftains in Congress wanted an army raised immediately—not provisionally and not just for invasion. Their reasons were not entirely military. A Provisional Army with volunteer units provided new patronage and established a vigilante corps along with a subterranean Federalist military network to intimidate citizens from joining the French standard. But an army actually enlisted and embodied possessed other advantages. First, there was the possibility of resurrecting the name and political magic of George Washington. The final Provisional Army statute provided for a new and unprecedented rank, that of lieutenant general.[43] Hamilton had suggested to the aged general a political trip through the South, and while Washington had refused, he had indicated a willingness to leave retirement if military necessity demanded it. Quickly Hamilton and Pickering began preparing Washington for the possibility.[44] Second, Federalist leaders in Philadelphia, approaching a political crossroads of monumental proportions and distrustful of John Adams, desperately wanted Hamilton back in the government. "I wish you were in a situation not only 'to see all the cards,' but to play them," urged Pickering. "With all my soul I would give you my *hand*, and engage in any other *game* in which I might best co-operate, on the same side, *to win the stakes*."[45] For Hamilton, ready and waiting in New York, and for a few others in the top leadership, there existed one last motive for the army, a tentative and uncertain motive, perhaps, and one they never admitted openly even in private correspondence. Nevertheless they had evidently become so disturbed by the Republican connection to France and the possibility of internal revolution, so pessimistic about the ability of the government and Constitution to survive, that they wished to install a classic, European standing army as a permanent fixture in America, changing the structure of government through legislation in a kind of constitutional coup. The evidence is circumstantial to be sure. But these men worked feverishly to establish and perfect an army long past the time when invasion seemed possible or internal revolution probable, long past the time when they might hope that John Adams would allow an army to be used in any foreign adventure. In 1798, as Sedgwick admitted in an offhand remark later, they tried to make the army permanent by allowing for the enlistment of soldiers for a five-year term rather than the duration of hostilities with France.[46] The Hamiltonians, the so-called High Federalists, wanted a standing army in 1798. The only question at issue was how to impose it on an unwilling nation, the Federalist party, and the President.

In early June, Robert Goodloe Harper attempted to strengthen the volunteer corps and allow the President to appoint and commission all Provisional Army officers. In spite of stubborn Republican resistance, Harper's resolutions carried.[47] Then in early July, Harper introduced the complete Hamiltonian program: expansion of the Provisional Army to 50,000 with complete mobilization of 12,500; the appointment of all its officers; and Presidential authority to activate all its non-commissioned officers and to obtain ten frigates or ships of the line.[48] With diplomatic information pointing toward war, with the frenzy, the rumors of conspiracy, and the tumult in Philadelphia streets reaching their peak, the Federalist leadership was beginning its final push toward an open break with France. "Step by step Congress have been led on to warlike measures," cried Senator Tazewell bitterly, "when a majority were in truth against a Declaration of War."[49] On Sunday evening July 1, Federalists caucused at Senator William Bingham's house. To the leadership's horror, moderates refused to support an open declaration, fearing they would be branded war mongers in the next elections. Still convinced that public opinion was far ahead of Congress, Sedgwick and the others resolved to press ahead with the wartime program anyway. Fisher Ames, retired from Congress but watching closely from his home in Dedham, settled on the same strategy. "I should imagine a number, who would flinch from a *declaration of war*," he told Pickering, "would urge the enacting, one by one, [of] the effects of a state of war." "Several votes could be gained for strong measures, from the dread of being urged to adopt still stronger." Ames saw several advantages in forbearing a formal declaration, but the basic policy would not differ in any respect. As he put it, "Wage war, and call it self-defence."[50] In Congress, Harper, Sedgwick, and the others had no other alternative.

In the end, the strategy was only partly successful. Perhaps moderate Federalists could not bring themselves to swallow such a swollen military program or perhaps they felt that with the other naval and military preparations, with the land tax and the Alien and Sedition Acts, the political dangers were too intense. Moderates absolutely refused to go along with a permanent standing army; "The Army could not have been carried," Sedgwick remembered bitterly in 1799, "on any other terms" than enlistment for the duration of hostilities.[51] Immediately after Harper introduced his resolutions, moderate Republican Samuel Smith proposed as a compromise, evidently to wean away moderate Federalists, an addition of eight regiments of infantry and six troops of dragoons to the regular army. Jeffersonians had steadfastly maintained during the struggle over the Provisional Army that they would support a regular force if war looked likely; some also feared a slave revolt if French troops landed, or even an invasion by a black army under Haitian revolutionary Toussaint L'Ouverture, an ally of France. Federalist leaders succeeded in upping the number of regiments to twelve, but only with the tie-breaking vote of Speaker Jonathan Dayton. Harper continued to press for enlargement of the Provisional Army and the navy, but it was too late. On July 9, the House approved the twelve regiments and dragoons—soon known as the New Army—by the lopsided margin of 60 to 11. Except for approving three more ships, Congress never debated the rest of Harper's motions.[52]

Here at last was the army for which Hamilton and his congressional allies had so long yearned. Suddenly the Provisional Army—only 10,000 strong and to be activated only under strictly limited circumstances if the President ordered—seemed distinctly secondary.* True the Provisional Army provided patronage in the form of several hundred new appointments, and the volunteer companies—already signing up in federal service—provided a noisy band of partisans drilling and parading in the cities, no mean political and psychological advantage. But the New Army—twelve spanking new regiments of regulars, over 12,000 men, mandated by law without the need for an invasion or Presidential approval—overshadowed the others. Here was the army to check sedition, block invasion, stiffen the populace, and bring Alexander Hamilton back into a position of formal power and influence, and perhaps, if war ensued, of preeminence. The absence of a declaration of war and the size of the army annoyed and frustrated Hamiltonian leaders. But on balance they emerged from the second session of the Fifth Congress pleased that public opinion had united against France and behind their program, most of which Congress had approved. Furthermore John Adams had responded with strength and determination during the war fever; Federalists felt certain that his normal volatility was now circumscribed by the political and diplomatic situation. To a degree they were correct. But unknown to Hamilton and his adherents, High Federalism had already reached its pinnacle in the summer of 1798. Already the Federalist party was divided by the army issue; warning signals existed, notably the refusal of moderates to support Hamilton's huge land force. Warning signals existed, too, in the behavior of the man who occupied the one powerful office Alexander Hamilton could not control.

*Most historians have misnamed the army in 1798 the "Provisional Army." Actually during the Quasi-war five separate and distinct "armies" existed, at least legally. First was the four regiments on the frontier created in 1796 out of Wayne's Legion, which with the artillerists and engineers was called the "old" or "western" army. The second was the "New Army," consisting of 12 regiments of infantry and 6 troops of dragoons voted by Congress in July 1798. These two constituted the regular army and existed as an organized force, the "old" army as regiments 1 through 4 and the "New Army" as regiments 5 through 16. Third was the volunteer corps, independent volunteer companies in existence at the time or raised specifically for the crisis, which were taken into federal service under the May 1798 Provisional Army law. The fourth was the 10,000-man "Provisional Army" authorized in the same statute. The last was the "Eventual Army," over 28 regiments authorized by a March 1799 law also provisionally, meaning that the President for about a year had the authority to appoint officers but not to mobilize them or enlist troops unless war ensued or the country was in danger of invasion. The most important of the five was the New Army, the only one to enlist soldiers specifically for the crisis. Although some officers were appointed, neither the Provisional Army or the Eventual Army were ever organized, and the War Department devoted little attention to them, or to the volunteer companies. The names of the different forces are those used by contemporaries. The clearest delineation of the various armies at the time is in Jefferson to Madison, February 5, 1799, Paul Leicester Ford, ed., *The Works of Thomas Jefferson* (New York, 1892-1899), IX, 32.

Through the spring of 1798, John Adams played along with the High Federalists. Beneath the surface, however, lay a profound and thinly-veiled suspicion. Adams knew that Hamilton and other party stalwarts had schemed to throw the Presidential election to Thomas Pinckney in 1796.[53] Within three months of taking office, Adams learned also that Hamilton was influencing the cabinet and attempting to run the government from New York City.[54] Adams was a vain, extraordinarily sensitive man, attuned to precedent, to his own dignity, and to the prerogatives of his office. He was incensed by the birthday ball for Washington in 1798 which Adams believed degraded his office and lengthened the shadow of comparison under which he labored as President. Nor was it the only social snub the Adamses suffered at the hands of society in the Federalist capital.[55]

Adams respected Hamilton's ability, but disliked and distrusted him. "A proud, spirited, conceited, aspiring Mortal," Adams confided to his wife; "As great a Hypocrite as any in the U.S." "I shall take no notice of his Puppy head but retain the same opinion . . . and maintain the same conduct towards him I always did, that is to keep him at a distance."[56] Adams never agreed with the need for a huge land army, the heart of Hamilton's platform. Certainly the President did not fear France. "[W]here is it possible for her to get ships to send thirty thousand Men here," he asked Elbridge Gerry. "We are double the number we were in 1775. We have four times the military skill, and we have eight times the Munitions of War. What would 30,000 men do here?"[57] Adams was just as susceptible to fears of internal subversion as others in the party, but the old Massachusetts revolutionary, the lawyer who had defended the British soldiers on trial for their part in the Boston Massacre, was far more sensitive to the political costs. Years later he remembered his reaction to Hamilton's proposal for a provisional army. "The army of fifty thousand men . . . appeared to me to be one of the wildest extravagances of a knight-errant." "Such an army without an enemy to combat, would have raised a rebellion in every State in the Union. The very idea of the expense of it would have turned President, Senate, and House out of doors."[58]

All through 1797 and 1798 Adams watched while his cabinet, with loud approval from certain party leaders, recommended armies to him and to the Congress. Adams was too shrewd a politician not to have realized what was happening. In April 1798 Harper approached him obliquely about replacing McHenry with Hamilton. Wisely Adams led Harper to believe that such an "arrangement" would be acceptable.[59] The President's motives, with Harper and indeed throughout the first year and a half in office, were to unify the country, maintaining at least a semblance of harmony in the Federalist party. Adams's chief problem was France. He willingly accepted and in fact urged on Congress military preparedness in 1797 as a way of negotiating tacitly with the French government. When the crisis exploded in 1798, preparedness made sense not only militarily, but to strengthen the nation's position with France. "I therefore animated [the United States] to war," he explained later.[60] To disavow any of the Hamiltonian program or to risk a public fight by refusing to allow the cabinet to recommend an army, would have undermined Adams diplomatically. Therefore he took the only other recourse available. In messages to Congress on Franco-American relations, Adams neglected the army in favor of naval and maritime preparation, which were far more to his military and political inclination anyway. John Adams did not wish to be saddled with a large army or with Alexander Hamilton. But the President could not fully control events. As he put it later to Benjamin Rush, "[Hamilton's] friends . . . in [the] Senate and House embarrassed me with . . . more troops than I wanted."[61]

Once it became apparent that new forces would be raised, Adams faced the same problem every wartime American President has faced: to whom to entrust the army's leadership. The first priority was to neutralize Hamilton, for whom he knew the army had been designed. Federalists spoke openly of their expectation and on three different occasions Pickering boldly suggested Hamilton as commander-in-chief to the President.[62] Adams seriously considered appointing all the surviving generals of the Revolution at their wartime rank, letting each one decline if he wished. (Hamilton's highest rank had been colonel.) The other alternative was to appoint George Washington, whose name was on everyone's lips. Hamilton's supporters could not object openly; the political benefits would be great; and the old general was not expected to accept an active role in any case. Adams knew the appointment would further unify the nation and have tremendous impact abroad, specifically on the French. "We must have your name, if you will, in any case permit us to use it," the President told Washington. "There will be more efficacy in it than in many an army."[63] On June 2, the day after the Federalist war caucus met and without consulting his cabinet or anyone else, Adams hastily submitted the name to the Senate. "I think no appointment could have been made which would have stifled the Envy and Ambition, the thirst of power and command which was rising in a mass throughout the United States," remarked the President's wife. "Those who expected to have filled this place, dare not publickly avow this disappointment."[64]*

---

*Some were asserting every power and faculty for Col H—n," Abigail told her son-in-law on July 7. "The president decided without communication, and sent in the nomination of the old General without the least intimation what his own mind will be. . . . you can hardly conceive what a powerful interest is made for H—n. I am surprizd at the want of knowledge of Human Nature—that man would in my mind become a second Buonaparty if he was possessed of equal power. . . ." Abigail Adams to William Smith, July 7, 1798, Smith-Carter Collection, Massachusetts Historical Society, Boston, Mass.

Unhappily for Adams, the choice turned sour almost immediately. Washington was happy in retirement, unconvinced that invasion was likely, and uncertain how the public would view his return at age 66 after so long in high office. Adams did not secure the general's consent beforehand and the letter to Mount Vernon sounding him out contained no direct offer. Many in Philadelphia, including the Senate, were uncertain whether Washington would accept.[65] In his reply to the President, before learning of formal appointment, and also in two private letters to the Secretary of War, Washington clearly laid out conditions for accepting command. Most important, he must be allowed to name his ranking subordinates. Washington explained that he could not simply accept old generals from the Revolution, or choose his staff on the basis of wartime rank. He did not intend to leave Mount Vernon unless "the emergency *becomes evident*," so he counted on the best officers to organize and train the army with only broad direction from Virginia.[66] There is little doubt that Washington was thinking of Hamilton, since in an earlier exchange of letters, the ex-President had inquired about possible service under his command and Hamilton had expressed a desire to be Inspector General with a command in the line.[67]

Simultaneously in Philadelphia, Hamilton and the cabinet began maneuvering to make certain that the New Yorker would gain effective control of the army. In a long letter on July 6, the day before Hamilton arrived in the capital, Pickering pleaded with Washington to name Hamilton "the *Second* to you—and the *Chief in your absence*." Pickering related that in conversation, the President had shown reluctance, so Pickering had pressed home the argument that "The choice of principal officers" must satisfy the new "Commander in Chief." Therefore "To ensure [Hamilton's] appointment," Pickering concluded, "I apprehend the weight of your opinion may be necessary."[68] On July 8, after discussions with Hamilton, Pickering, and the President, McHenry left for Mount Vernon to deliver Washington's commission, to convince the general to accept, and then to discuss the organization of the army, particularly the chief officers to be appointed. McHenry spent two and a half days in Virginia; during the first, Washington accepted and showed the Secretary the letters sent explaining the conditions of his service. Then the two conferred about prospective officers. After arriving at a list of generals and staff, the most difficult problem became Hamilton. Washington readily agreed to place Hamilton over Henry Knox, but Charles Cotesworth Pinckney presented a different problem. Pinckney appeared indispensable because of his important connections in the South, where any invasion and campaign would occur, and Washington was uncertain whether the former major general would serve under a former colonel.[69] McHenry undoubtedly used every argument available: Hamilton's talent, his military experience, the long years of association and confidence between Washington and his ex-aide, and most telling, the expectation by party leaders and the public that Hamilton would be second in command. To the end, Washington remained annoyed and undecided. McHenry left Mount Vernon on July 14 with the impression of victory and a list of generals which began with Hamilton, Pinckney, and then Knox. To Knox, Washington explained that Hamilton was second in command; to Hamilton, however, the general was vague. "After all," he concluded, "it rests with the President to use his pleasure."[70]

Adams was at breakfast with his wife on July 17 when McHenry returned with Washington's acceptance and the list of general officers. If Adams had not realized it earlier, the list proved that he was losing the battle to keep the army away from Hamilton. Immediately the President challenged McHenry to justify placing Hamilton first, and putting Pinckney over Knox. McHenry replied that the order was Washington's and for proof he produced Washington's private letter to Hamilton which spelled out the general's wishes. McHenry thought this satisfied the President, but Adams said nothing as he wrote out the message for the Senate with the list in Washington's order. While the two conferred Pickering brought word that the Senate had adjourned for the day; the three then discussed the rest of the top appointments, some of which Washington had left open. Pickering objected strongly to naming William S. Smith, the President's son-in-law, a brigadier and Adjutant General, but Smith was on Washington's list and this time Adams was adamant.[71]

That night the President changed his mind. In the morning he told McHenry that Hamilton could not be elevated over Knox, who was entitled to rank second to Washington. Adams refused to be mollified and McHenry finally extracted the promise to submit the list to the Senate with Hamilton's name first on condition that any officer dissatisfied with his relative rank could appeal to Washington or a board of officers. That day, July 18, Adams sent 14 names to the Senate to fill positions in the New and Provisional Armies, among them John Brooks, Speaker Jonathan Dayton, William R. Davie of North Carolina, and William S. Smith of New York, brigadier general and Adjutant General.[72]

Pickering and McHenry both opposed Smith's nomination and tried hard once again to dissuade the President. Pickering was determined not to jeopardize the purity of the army; Smith's reputation in New York was notorious for some disreputable land speculations in which he had gambled away other people's money, and after John Quincy Adams's appointment as Minister to Prussia a few months earlier, another officeholder from the Presidential family smacked of nepotism. When Adams stood fast, Pickering followed the nomination over to Congress, called several senators out of the deliberations, and persuaded them to reject Smith. That evening a Senate delegation asked Adams to withdraw the nomination, but the President declared his son-in-law a brave and talented veteran who deserved to be a general and whose business dealings were no more questionable than others up for office. The next morning, the Senate rejected Smith by an overwhelming majority; Adams immediately nominated William North, who was not Washington's or the cabinet's choice and who did not want the job, and the Senate approved. The rest of the list passed without trouble. Hamilton's friends were jubilant. Nearly everyone interpreted the order of names, in nomination and confirmation, as indicating relative rank, and Alexander Hamilton topped the roll, "Inspector General of the Army, with the rank of Major General."[73]

Once again Adams had been thwarted. Knox was the ranking officer from the war, an old Massachusetts associate of the President, a man who could be trusted and who in very personal terms had offered his services to Adams.[74] With Knox the army would be safe. The same was true of William S. Smith. Appointing his son-in-law was for Adams far more than sentiment or kindness to a relative. In eighteenth-century armies the adjutant general was the executive agent of the commander, the officer who wrote out orders and handled the correspondence. The adjutant general would know about every major plan, policy, troop movement, and appointment in the army. Smith would have been an Adams spy in an otherwise purely Hamiltonian force. Pickering understood this fact as well as he understood Smith's financial dealings. Adams knew it too. In addition, Smith's rejection was a personal affront which embarrassed and rankled the President. On July 25 Adams and his family departed abruptly for the family home in Quincy, embittered, resentful, angry over the problem of the army—and determined either to keep Hamilton away from the command or to destroy the New Army altogether.

What followed that summer has been often described by historians: the cabinet intrigue, the incredible web of correspondence that flowed between Philadelphia, Massachusetts, Mount Vernon, and New York, all designed to insure Hamilton's position. Many historians have pictured the affair as a misunderstanding between the President, the cabinet, Hamilton, and Washington.[75] It was far from that. All parties knew that Washington intended to be a figurehead for the New Army, and that whoever emerged as ranking subordinate would be the actual commander. The confusion resulted from Adams's determination to reverse what the cabinet, Hamilton, and most Federalists considered a closed question. How the cabinet outmaneuvered its own President is one of the most bizarre episodes in the history of the Presidency.

Adams left Philadelphia without informing the cabinet or signing any of the generals' commissions, undoubtedly on purpose. Although Pickering quickly dispatched them after Adams, the President allowed them to remain on his desk untouched. No one in the cabinet thought very much about it. In late July, after McHenry informed the generals of their appointments, Hamilton journeyed to Philadelphia and together the two plunged into the work of organizing the army. Hamilton was aghast at McHenry's work habits. For months rumor had circulated in the capital that the easygoing Secretary could not handle the great tasks of war minister and Hamilton's experience seemed ample proof. Candidly Hamilton told McHenry that, "plunged in a vast mass of details," he needed to delegate some of his authority.[76] To speed the work, Hamilton suggested that he and Knox be called immediately into active service. McHenry, glad for the aid and suffering poor health, gladly accepted and on August 4 asked the President to activate Washington and the two major generals (Pinckney, the third, was in transit from France).[77]

Adams was waiting for just such an opening. In Quincy, in the bosom of his family and away from all the pressures at the capital, Adams replied curtly that he considered Washington already in service. The major generals could not be activated until relative rank was settled, and Knox, by virtue of previous service was "legally entitled" to precedence. "Any other plan will occasion long delay and much confusion," threatened the President.[78] McHenry was astounded. Immediately he fired back a long, pleading letter citing Washington's list, the general's conditions for service, the order of Senate nomination and confirmation, and the "disagreeable consequences" of such an "alteration."[79] Adams could not be swayed. "You know, Sir, that no rank has ever been settled by me." "The power and authority are in the President," he snapped. "There has been too much intrigue in this business. . . ; if I shall ultimately be the dupe of it, I am much mistaken in myself."[80]

Adams's decision caught the cabinet totally by surprise and threw it into a frenzy. Desperate letters flew back and forth among Hamilton in New York, Washington, and leading Federalists, especially in New England. The entire affair of rank was reviewed from the beginning, motives analyzed, public opinion considered, strategies propounded and discarded. Pickering dissected the President's letter for every nuance, and very quickly thought he discovered an opening: a statement by the President that Washington would surely approve the ranking that he, the President, desired. From this emerged the cabinet's strategy. First, to mollify Adams, McHenry agreed to follow orders and date the commissions separately with Knox first. But it was only a tactic to gain time for Hamilton, Pickering, and McHenry to work on Washington; actually McHenry in consultation with his fellow department heads decided to delay sending the commissions to the generals. Meantime the cabinet bombarded Washington with delicate, cunning letters, describing how

valuable and talented Hamilton was, and how ridiculous, indeed pernicious, would be a policy of allowing wartime rank to determine precedence twenty years afterward. The public, the Senate, and the general
himself expected Hamilton to be named. In letters filled with gossip,
Pickering accused the President of capriciously reversing the rank out of
meanness and hatred for Hamilton. Only Washington could undo the
mischief.[81]

The second element in cabinet strategy involved a direct confrontation with the President. Together the department heads decided that
Secretary of the Treasury Wolcott should make the appeal because he
had been away in Connecticut in July when Washington had been
nominated and the generals selected; Wolcott could not be accused of
plotting behind the President's back. The letter was stiff, legalistic—
almost insubordinate. Wolcott reminded Adams that Washington had
been appointed without prior notification and had agreed expecting "that
the principal arrangements should be made in concert." Washington
"after *mature deliberation* settled the rank." In a new army, wartime
service should not override *"comparative qualification."* No one expected
Knox to rank first, not even in New England. If necessary, let Washington decide the question, Wolcott concluded. But "whatever may have
been the opinion of the President respecting the . . . order of appointment, the opinion of General Washington and the expectation of the
public is, that General Hamilton will be confirmed in a rank second only
to the Commander in Chief."[82] Along with Wolcott's letter came the
commissions, undated. The cabinet could do no more. As Wolcott
instructed Hamilton, *"say nothing* and *do nothing* until you have heard
from me."[83]

By the time Wolcott's letter reached Quincy, the cabinet's machinations had begun to take effect. Hamilton had declared positively that he
would resign rather than serve under Knox, which influenced Washington greatly.[84] Convinced by the cabinet that the President was about to
commit a grave error, that his own dignity was under assault, and finally
that Hamilton's resolve would hamstring the creation of an army, Washington began to consider resigning himself.[85] He intimated as much to
McHenry, then ten days later, annoyed by the intrigue, Washington
decided to confront the President directly. Adams had already begun to
weaken. For several weeks his wife had lain critically ill and apparently
near death, affecting the President as he himself admitted, with depression, "Agitation and Anxiety."[86] Wolcott's letter, and one from George
Cabot also championing Hamilton, so enraged the President that he
could not bear to draft a suitable reply. Afterwards a letter arrived from
McHenry quoting Washington's threat to resign. Adams started to waver.
Without comment he returned the commissions dated all on the same
day, a concession which could be interpreted either way. Then on

October 8, Washington's letter reached Quincy. In no uncertain terms the general demanded an explanation for the change in relative rank of the major generals, for Adams's appointment of William North as Adjutant General, and for Adams's plan to name another man if North refused—all "without the least intimation to me." Washington explained the difficult situation in which he had been placed by being appointed before his wishes were known, emphasizing that as a result he had made his stipulations privately so as not to appear to denigrate the power of the Presidency or sully his own appointment. Implicitly threatening to resign, Washington demanded to know if Adams intended "to reverse the order of the three Major Generals . . . and . . . to appoint another Adjutant General without my concurrence."[87]

Finally the President caved in. If, as seemed likely, Washington quit in a huff and every general followed, Adams would be castigated by the Federalist party and the nation, ruining his position of strength with the French and thus killing any chance of negotiating an end to hostilities. Badgered on one side by Knox and on the other by Hamilton's Massachusetts clique, deeply affected by Abigail's sickness, boxed in at last by the plotting, by political considerations, and by international realities, Adams had no alternative but to capitulate. But in defeat he served notice on the Hamiltonians that the struggle had only begun. He, the President of the United States, washed his hands of their precious army—of recruiting, of supplies, even of the appointments to the officer corps. "Regiments are costly articles every where, and more so in this country than any other under the sun," Adams admonished McHenry. Keeping up an army "without an enemy to fight" would backfire on the government, and "At present there is no more prospect of seeing a French army here, than there is in Heaven."[88]

It was a mark of the High Federalists' obsession with the army that they would risk a public explosion and an open break with the President over command. By cramming Hamilton down the President's throat, they succeeded in uniting Adams with the Republicans on the army issue. The fight over rank merged in the President's mind with the near fatal illness of his wife and the personal insult suffered in William S. Smith's rejection for the adjutancy. In one single stroke the Hamiltonians alienated the President personally and politically, reawakened the old suspicion of Adams in Federalist minds, of the Federalists in Adams's mind, and united within him the motives of personal revenge, political advantage, and international statesmanship. By the end of the struggle over Hamilton's position, Adams if for no other reason than to protect himself and the nation from Hamilton, was determined to seek an accord with France and destroy the army at its roots. At the same time he decided to cut it off at the top by not lifting a finger to aid in its formation or its operations. If necessary, too, he could use his authority to block any military adventures. Adams was President of the United States, the head of the executive branch, maker of foreign policy, first citizen of the country, and under the Constitution "Commander in Chief of the Army and Navy . . . and of the Militia . . . when called into the actual Service of the United States." Unlike his antagonist in 1798, a mere major general, John Adams had no illusions. "What benefit can war be to him?" asked Abigail about her husband just as the crisis unfolded. "He has no ambition for military Glory."[89]

12

★ ☆ ★ ☆ ★ ☆ ★ ☆ ★

Major General Hamilton,
Mr. Secretary McHenry, and the
Halting History of the New Army
[1798-1800]

★

[T]he militia never did any good to this country except in the single affair of Bunker's Hill . . . ; we must have a standing army of 50,000 men, which being stationed in different parts of the continent might serve as rallying points for the militia, and so render them of some service.

Timothy Pickering, 1798.[a]

From the very beginning, Federalist leaders in Congress and the cabinet conceived of the New Army as a bulwark against rebellion, as the nucleus for the military force that might eventually have to face a French army in battle, and as the seedling for a permanent American standing army. Except as a vehicle for patronage and as a paper force to impress the Republicans and France, the Provisional Army never again figured importantly in Federalist plans. Instead, McHenry and the army high command devoted almost all their time and energy for the next two years to the regulars, the 16 regiments of the old frontier army and the New Army. Because of the danger of insurrection, the army had to be politically pure; and at the same time, it had to be transformed organizationally from a sleepy western constabulary into a force capable of victory over a French army that by 1798, through innovations in tactics and organization, had become the scourge of Europe. Both tasks, especially finding politically reliable men from the mass of names put forward for the officer corps, demanded herculean efforts. Yet Federalists agreed that the army must be raised immediately, since neither France nor domestic opponents were likely to act at the government's convenience. Troops had to be enlisted while patriotic fervor was at a peak and before cold weather would hamper recruiting, training, or preparations for winter quarters. The story of the attempt to build a competent army, including Federalist frustration and failure, revealed the depth of their obsession with a standing army and their motives for the military program of 1798.

James McHenry returned to Philadelphia in late July 1798 eager to meet the challenge. Two weeks had already been lost by the trip to Mount Vernon and precious little had been accomplished beyond attempts to purchase arms and construction on coast fortifications.[1] The Secretary's first major decision on the New Army was to apportion the regiments regionally, four each to New England, the Middle states including Maryland, and the South and West. After that, he speeded up production of arms at Springfield and began the construction of another arsenal. To prepare for enlisting soldiers, McHenry wrote out detailed recruiting instructions, then began the process of procuring clothing, tents, and camp equipment for the recruiting stations. By late September 1798, the War Department was ready to advertise publicly for contractors.[2]

By far the most critical factor was appointing the officers. Without them to staff individual recruiting posts, to collect and distribute supplies to the enlistees, to assemble companies, and to begin training, no army could exist. Twelve regiments called for nearly 400 officers and McHenry, afraid that unsolicited recommendations often stemmed from friendship or attempts to reform young men with a stint in service, decided to divide the job of selection. In New England, the President, Knox, and John Brooks could narrow the choices from the mass of prospects; Hamilton and Jonathan Dayton could handle the Middle states and Washington the South. To each general McHenry sent lists of men recommended and a list of all officers in each region surviving from the Revolution, asking the generals to gather information about individual qualifications and possible rank. Names of the best prospects were to be returned as quickly as possible to Philadelphia for collation and forwarding to Adams for a final decision. By late August, McHenry judged progress to be excellent. "I can give almost instant life and activity to the recruiting service from one end of the Union to the other," he boasted.[3]

Inside of six weeks, the Secretary's claim turned to ashes. Part of the problem was that McHenry suffered continual distractions from the primary goal of organizing the new regiments, sometimes major ones like the squabble over Hamilton's rank, others like the preparation of rules for accepting volunteer companies into the Provisional Army, a task which could not be delayed without losing good volunteers.[4] Occasionally the distractions could be downright annoying, like the request by Martha Washington's granddaughter for the color staff from the general's first company, suitably reconditioned with her favorite motto and a new eagle crest for presentation to her own special volunteer company.[5] Others who approached the Secretary had grander political goals. McHenry was bombarded with requests for commissions from Federalist politicians bent on exploiting a new patronage opportunity. While most were content to push for friends, some, like Senator Tracy, interfered with the selection process for partisan purposes in his home state.[6] All of it drained the Secretary's time, energy, and patience.

As he delved deeper into the work, more and more serious obstacles appeared. The rank controversy prevented the establishment of a chain of command through which McHenry could act, but more important it so alienated the President that he never approved McHenry's plan to organize the twelve regiments regionally or cooperated in selecting the officers. Washington also disrupted War Department plans by pleading ignorance of officers in the South outside Virginia, and since Charles Cotesworth Pinckney had not yet returned from Europe, McHenry was forced to open a separate correspondence with Brigadier General William R. Davie in North Carolina.[7] On the subject of supplies, as necessary for recruiting as appointing officers, McHenry was asked by Wolcott in the Treasury to work out a detailed monthly schedule of War Department monetary needs only to find that the Treasury was unable to fund supply contracts and arms purchases at the same time.[8] In the midst of all these troubles, yellow fever struck Philadelphia, forcing McHenry and his assistants to scatter to temporary offices in Trenton, Germantown, and other nearby communities.[9]

Overshadowing all else, however, and a problem destined to dog McHenry throughout his tenure, was communication. The Secretary worked in or near Philadelphia, and except for a brief month in November–December 1798, the men with whom he had to consult resided elsewhere. The President, in no cooperative mood, stayed in Massachusetts except when Congress was in session. General Washington, at one point ill and on another occasion incommunicato while on personal business in the new federal city, remained in Virginia. Hamilton lived in New York. McHenry asked the Inspector General to move to the capital, but Hamilton, pointing to the speed of the New York–Philadelphia mails and his ability to make the trip on short notice, refused for financial reasons to leave his law practice in the city.[10] The result was confusion and delay. McHenry had to propose everything to Hamilton and Washington first, wait for their ideas, and then submit recommendations to the President for approval. If any of the parties wished modifications, the whole process could be repeated. Thus simple decisions took weeks to implement. Furthermore, by September 1798 McHenry could not bypass either the generals or the President. Adams already had accused McHenry of plotting and Washington was complaining bitterly of being denied information about the military establishment and War Department activities.[11]

Unfortunately James McHenry was not a cold, determined administrator like Pickering, nor did he have the military experience or reputation that Knox had possessed to give added weight to the authority of the office. Unlike his predecessors, McHenry was caught between an uncooperative President and two domineering generals, both of whom far outranked the Secretary in military knowledge and prestige and both of whom, while refusing to abandon their homes or other pursuits, pestered him constantly for information. In addition, Washington and Hamilton expected McHenry to follow their advice to the letter; the easygoing McHenry, eager to oblige, ended up deferring to both. The wonder is that McHenry completed so much of the preparations for raising the New Army. Like most of the Secretaries of War for the next century thrown suddenly into the chaos of wartime expansion, McHenry presided over a War Department designed to administer a small, peacetime establishment and to handle constabulary functions, an organization unprepared for emergency. Reorganization and adjustment were necessary and as Secretaries of War in similar situations even in the twentieth century would discover, a few months were needed for the transition to wartime procedures.[12]

None of the generals or leading Federalists understood the problem. To most, hoping and expecting the army would spring forth instantly, the explanation for delay was McHenry's personal inadequacy. Well before the summer of 1798, rumors circulated about replacing McHenry.[13] At the end of July after a trip to Philadelphia, Hamilton, out of impatience, concern for his own reputation, and eagerness to be called into active service, began spreading stories that McHenry was overloaded.[14] Washington, also concerned about his own reputation and annoyed because of the failure to be informed about everything transpiring in Philadelphia, agreed. So did the cabinet, aware firsthand of the War Department's troubles. Very quickly the feeling grew in Federalist circles, and although McHenry defended himself privately as best he could, the criticism began to tell.[15] Finally in mid-October, frustrated by the obstacles, angered by prodding from critical friends, and tired out by the uncertainty of dealing with the President and his generals at a distance, McHenry decided to assemble Washington and the major generals in Philadelphia. Together they could prepare a list of officers for appointment and settle definitely on policies for recruiting, supply, and organization.[16]

McHenry's decision to defer to Washington, Hamilton, and Charles Cotesworth Pinckney (who had returned from France) meant that the

Secretary had surrendered control over the broader policies that would shape the New Army. Thereafter he became a middleman and on matters of high policy, a subordinate of Alexander Hamilton. Yet McHenry in no way lost responsibility for raising and administering the army. Through-out the rest of his term (and by historians ever since), McHenry was judged incompetent. By early 1799 the clamor reached such a pitch that party leaders felt compelled to see Adams. Later Presidents would usually manage to sacrifice a Secretary of War who became identified with the chaos of transition to a wartime establishment. But John Adams, content to see the War Department sink into a morass of confusion in order to abort Hamiltonian militarism, let McHenry continue.[17] In public, for political and diplomatic reasons, Adams went so far as to push for action, to support larger forces, and even to try to appoint the officers for the huge Eventual Army voted by Congress in 1799. To McHenry, however, the President remained aloof and unhelpful. "All the declamations, as well as demonstrations, of Trenchard and Gordon, Bolingbroke, Barnard and Walpole, Hume, Burgh and Burke, rush upon my memory and frighten me out of my wits," the President declared.[18] If asked to choose between the army and the navy, "I should be at no loss."[19] Months before a single soldier enlisted, the New Army was doomed to failure.

In mid-November 1798, a month after the settlement of Hamilton's rank and fully three months after Congress voted the regiments, Washington, Hamilton, and Charles Cotesworth Pinckney assembled in Philadelphia to organize the New Army. (Knox refused to serve because the other two major generals outranked him.) Although convened by McHenry, the generals believed their real purpose was to rectify the Secretary's mistakes, provide him with a detailed set of plans and policies for the military establishment, and begin the recruiting immediately. To Federalists everywhere, the greatest obstacle was McHenry himself. "Depend upon it," Wolcott had warned Hamilton, "the arrangements of the War Department are all defective, and . . . nothing will succeed without a thorough reform."[20] But in spite of the best efforts of Hamilton and Washington, the problems continued to multiply. The true flaws in the New Army were just beginning to appear.

From the start, the chief snag was appointing officers. Preoccupied with rebellion, Federalists insisted on choosing only the most politically trustworthy men. "The Brawlers against Governmental measures . . . are very desirous of obtaining Commissions," Washington warned McHenry in September. "The motives ascribed to them are, that in such a situation they would endeavour to divide, and contaminate the Army, by artful and seditious discourses, and perhaps at a critical moment bring on confusion."[21] In common with all the leaders of the party, the three generals approached every candidate with suspicion. For five hours a day they meticulously reviewed applications and recommendations, searching for talented men with suitable political leanings, attempting to assign to each the appropriate rank. It was backbreaking labor, made all the more difficult by the decision to apportion regiments to the states by population and by the scarcity of information. To avoid the appearance of partisanship, and because the experience might "inspire a zeal for the service and the cause in which the incumbents are employed," Hamilton suggested appointing some Republicans in "inferior grades."[22] But the others overruled him, and when Adams proposed Aaron Burr and Frederick Augustus Muhlenberg of Pennsylvania as brigadiers to widen the administration's popularity in two key states, Hamilton joined in a categorical refusal.[23]

When at last after a month of toil the generals produced their final list, the process was only half over. Adams ordered the names submitted to each cabinet member, then to party leaders in Congress. By the time all interested parties (including Senator Tracy who insisted on naming the Connecticut officers personally) weeded out unacceptables, it was mid-January. McHenry then notified the officers of their appointment. For the Carolinas, Georgia, Kentucky, and Tennessee, however, McHenry submitted no candidates to the Senate. Federalists in those states were so difficult to find, and information so spotty, that the high command postponed any selections until Pinckney himself could travel south and consult with Davie and Brigadier General William Washington in Charleston. And of course none of the new officers could receive commissions because Adams thought it unfair to assign relative rank in each grade until the final roster of officers was complete. McHenry could not produce such a tally until late spring. Thus by basing appointment on political qualifications, the Federalists delayed the formation of the New Army by at least three months.[24]

Another conflict, again entailing great delay and much confusion, was to insist upon a complete review of all policy within the military establishment, from the table of organization of the regiments and the supply system down to the size of the ration and the cut of the uniforms. McHenry, Hamilton, and other Federalist leaders had two goals in mind, both of which might require reform and reorganization. First, the New Army was to be the beginning of a standing army, distinguishable in purpose and probably structure from the frontier constabulary already on foot; second, it must be capable tactically and strategically of waging the new warfare then sweeping Europe. When Washington arrived in Philadelphia, McHenry posed a long series of questions about the new regiments: how to apportion officers among the states; whether to recruit all 12 regiments, appoint officers immediately, and where to station forces;

whether to reinforce or redeploy the western army; how to reform the supply system and the type of supplies to be purchased; and where to build magazines. All during the month spent selecting officers, the three generals considered these questions, studying all aspects of each problem. Sometimes they conferred with other members of the cabinet, particularly Oliver Wolcott about the ability of the Treasury to finance the preparations and the recruiting service. On December 13, Washington sent McHenry a detailed set of answers drafted by Hamilton, arguing that the officers should be appointed immediately and the whole force raised as quickly as possible. Washington added detailed comments about the artillery, disposition of forces, methods for supplying rations, and the addition of two more magazines.[25]

Hamilton wanted to go much further. Appended to the answers went a long dissertation on the need for thorough-going military reform. First Hamilton wanted to increase the number of privates in each infantry regiment in order to enlarge each command (to attract the best officers) and to provide platoon units in each company for maneuvering the columns. With more privates, each company would possess more weight in the attack. In addition, Hamilton wanted the dragoon and artillery regiments increased. He also asked for a variety of minor changes. Not even the size of the daily ration or the style of uniform and insignia ("The Cockade of the non-commissioned officers, musicians, and privates to be of leather with eagles of Tin") escaped the Inspector General, much less important reforms like making riflemen a part of every regiment and establishing a Quartermaster General to oversee the distribution of supplies.[26] Clearly Alexander Hamilton was taking over the military establishment and attempting to perfect it in every detail as a model for the future. In all matters of substantive policy in Philadelphia that November and December, Hamilton generated the ideas and worked out the details. Washington acted as the conduit through which the Inspector General pressed his wishes on the War Department, but his function was mostly as figurehead.[27] McHenry presented all these changes verbatim to Congress, and the chairmen of the Senate and House committees on defense, James Gunn and Harrison Gray Otis, corresponded directly with Hamilton. As Gunn told the New Yorker, "The President has no talent for war, and McHenry is an infant in *detail*; and, if I am correct, General Washington is not to take the field, but in the event of the provisional army being called into service."[28] Hamilton drafted the legislation, advised both committee chairmen, and plotted congressional strategy. In the end, Congress approved virtually all of Hamilton's plans, including a reorganization law which laid the basis for transforming the regiments into a complete field army.[29]

Most of the revisions were justified, despite the time they cost McHenry and Hamilton in the critical early months of 1799 when recruiting should have taken precedence. No Secretary of War had ever worked out systematic policies for the functioning of the establishment. Regulations and the structure had evolved piecemeal in response to congressional fiat, military crisis, and the whim of a Secretary or a commanding general who tinkered with one procedure or another. Between 1796 and early 1798, McHenry rationalized the army, but his goal was to fashion an efficient, economical constabulary for service in small frontier garrisons. Hamilton, Washington, and to a great extent McHenry himself understood the need to separate the "old" or "western" army from the New Army, which had to be prepared to defend the United States against the most powerful, innovative army in the western world. But equally important, Hamilton and the other generals simply mistrusted McHenry; they arrived in Philadelphia prejudiced against his earlier preparations and determined to create a perfect military institution, not only as "an eligible standard for the augmentations with which particular emergencies may compel a resort," but in Hamilton's case to build a lasting standing army bearing his own personal stamp.[30] This fact, as much as any other, caused the confusion and discord that marked the New Army throughout its history.

During the first six months of 1799, the burden of raising the New Army fell on Hamilton in New York. In an effort to free McHenry from the details of everyday administration (and to circumvent his suspected incompetence), Hamilton and Washington insisted on a command structure whereby all of the army north of Virginia, including Wilkinson's western army, reported to Hamilton, while Pinckney commanded all forces further south. In addition Hamilton supervised the recruiting service nationwide.[31] While Hamilton busied himself with details—writing to Wilkinson, notifying officers, distributing forces, revising recruiting instructions, arranging the states into districts for recruiting—McHenry worked to provide the means to begin enlisting. By late March, the Secretary finally compiled a list of all officers in the service for the Inspector General's use. For food and supplies, McHenry ordered the new War Department agents in each state to let contracts for articles not scheduled to come from Philadelphia. To assure proper pay for the troops, he also ordered paymaster Caleb Swan to the capital from the western army. In April and May, enlisting finally began and to everyone's surprise, given the delays and predictions that spring planting would interfere with volunteering, the regiments began to fill up fast. "I permit myself to hope that in the summer and fall the army will be at its complement," Hamilton informed Washington.[32]

Yet the work was frustrating in the extreme and for the rest of the year the New Army was beset by trouble. Administratively, the army was in chaos. The President, still suspicious and through 1799 increasingly unhappy with the military program with which his administration was saddled, did everything in his power to hamper progress. He provided no direction and no aid to the War Department, but at the same time all appointments for vacancies in the officer corps and all matters of high policy had to be cleared in Quincy. Sometimes his replies were oblique, noncommittal, or the problem was returned to Philadelphia for further consultation. In June 1799 Adams purposely tried to overload the War Department by ordering the appointment of officers for the Eventual Army, a provisional force of over 25 regiments voted by Congress in March 1799 to be raised if war were declared or invasion threatened, either unlikely by that date. Theodore Sedgwick was incredulous at the order, but McHenry avoided becoming bogged down in the task by asking senators to provide most of the references.[33] Adding to the tangle, Hamilton tried to run the War Department from New York, constantly interfering in every detail of business, but never explaining to McHenry exactly what needed to be done, and when, lest McHenry be confronted directly with the dimunition of his authority. Hamilton attempted reform of the military establishment and creation of the New Army simultaneously, a diffusion of effort that time after time added delay and confusion.

Throughout 1799, the administrative situation hampered recruiting, produced defective supplies, and caused discontent in the officer corps. Since General Pinckney had to travel south to find politically reliable men, officers for the 5th regiment in South Carolina and Georgia were not appointed until June. Mixups in shipments the next month provided the 5th with clothing for recruits, but no bounty money. The 6th in North Carolina had money but no clothing.[34] The payroll system never functioned adequately. Due to failure in procedure and McHenry's delay both in ordering the Paymaster General to Philadelphia and transmitting proper pay and muster forms to Hamilton, a mutiny nearly engulfed the 12th and 13th regiments. In New England and Deep South units, soldiers spent six months in service before receiving any cash.[35] The supply system broke down immediately and remained in chronic disarray until the end. At first the problem was getting adequate clothing to recruiting stations. The clothing contract signed in 1798 never produced a decent supply because of a scarcity of white kersey, and cloth supplies appeared to be so low for 1799 that McHenry could not find a bidder. As a result, Purveyor of Public Supplies Tench Francis, responsible for all articles not furnished by contract, purchased cloth and other materials, hired tailors, and manufactured the uniforms himself. Once sewn, the clothing began dribbling out in small packages to recruiting points in early spring. But then the distribution, supervised by Commissary of Military Stores Samuel Hodgdon, also collapsed. Parts of uniforms arrived at their destinations piecemeal: "*Coats* without a corresponding number of *vests*, Car-

touche boxes without belts etc. etc. nothing intire—nothing systematic,"
exploded Hamilton. "Tis the scene of the worst periods of our revolution
. . . over again . . . with caricature."[36] Reports of deficient clothing,
camp equipment, ramrods, muskets, and tents streamed in through the
summer and fall. "The shoes which have been dealt out," reported
congressmen John Allen from Connecticut, "are of the very worst leather
and worst manufacture. A march of 20 miles would totally ruin the
greater part of them—and the *heels* of many of them drop off immediately on handling."[37] Inferior supplies and lack of money drove off
potential soldiers, stimulated desertion from enlisting stations, and generally contributed to poor morale and discipline. In September Hamilton
warned regimental commanders to stop officers' complaints lest the
criticism "foster discontent in the minds of the Soldiery."[38]

By the time the New Army disbanded in May 1800, few of these
problems had been solved and the 12 regiments never became a dependable fighting force. Less than half the authorized number of men ever
enlisted, so each regiment limped along, companies of unequal size,
perpetually understrength. During the summer of 1799 the army lay
scattered in its recruiting stations, and after assembling in three-regiment
groups to ease supply difficulties, spent the fall constructing encampments for the cold weather to come. Serious training did not begin in
most units until early winter, about the time debate began in Congress
over demobilization. No regiment ever had enough equipment, and most
of what each received was worthless. The Union Brigade, the 11th, 12th,
and 13th regiments under the command of William S. Smith—given a
lieutenant colonelcy by the high command in an attempt to placate
Adams—was typical. Huddled together for the winter at Scotch Plains,
New Jersey, the brigade had by spring consumed all its wood and was
drinking polluted water. The 11th possessed one flint for every four men;
the 12th had three spades for all its 358 rank and file; the 13th had no
colors, slings, bayonets, belts, scabbards, or cartridges, and some of the
musket barrels were so poorly made that the weapons could not be fired
safely. Adjutant General William North, who inspected the camp in early
spring, thought military knowledge was improving and the discipline
about "as good as can be expected from the inexperience of the majority
of the Officers."[39] But many lay sick, leading North to predict widespread
death unless the brigade moved. The New Army ended its existence in
1800 in despair, a shabby joke on the great hopes Federalists had entertained two years earlier. Fittingly, smallpox broke out in Scotch Plains
just before the brigade dissolved.[40]

James McHenry, certainly unequal to the task, was only one element
in a continuing administrative nightmare. By its very nature the New
Army never had a chance. If fears of rebellion and distrust of the
opposition created a wholly political army—the only one in American

history—politics ruined it. Six months were consumed in settling Hamilton's rank and finding Federalist officers, months when the army's procedures could have been reformed, supplies procured, and most important of all, able recruits enlisted. "Had the Organization of the Augmented Corps . . . tread as close on the passage of the Law, as the nature of the case would have permitted, a finer army of the size . . . the World had never seen," lamented Washington in March 1799; "but the golden opportunity is passed and probably will never occur again." "The zeal, enthusiasm, and indeed resentments . . . is now no more; they are evaporated, and a listlessness has supplied its place."[41]

Washington understood that the most significant and damaging factor, one which sapped the vitality of the New Army and crippled it in embryo, was the prospect of peace. True to his resolve, at the very first diplomatic opportunity, John Adams pulled the rug out from under his Hamiltonian enemies by moving to end hostilities. A month earlier, in February 1799, hardly four months after losing the battle over Hamilton's rank, the President nominated William Vans Murray to reopen negotiations with France. In one single stroke, Adams destroyed the sense of mission within the army and the most potent public justification for its existence. Through the rest of 1799, as Hamilton and the War Department struggled frantically to organize the regiments, military ardor steadily diminished, and the New Army slowly changed from the symbol of American determination into a political liability that eventually helped destroy the Federalist party.

Nearly every account of the army in the Quasi-war has stressed its political nature, implying, however vaguely, that Federalist leaders planned to use the army against the Republicans, perhaps even in the election of 1800. Yet no Republican at the time ever spelled out exactly how the troops were to be used, and there exists no indication in all the mass of correspondence concerning the military that Federalists contemplated any such thing—no contingency plans, no troop dispositions, no evidence of discussions for interfering with elections, nothing. In fact the army's leaders exercised extreme caution in all civil-military matters. Instead of stationing them in the South, which everyone assumed to be the target of French invasion and possible rebellion, McHenry with the concurrence of the high command decided at the outset to recruit and distribute the regiments in proportion to the national population, in spite of the knowledge that qualified Federalist officers would be difficult to find below the Potomac. Hamilton and the War Department assembled the regiments into brigades purely for military reasons, for training, for convenience of supply, and to gain lower prices for rations. Locations were selected partly for the security of major cities, but mostly because sites like Harpers Ferry and Scotch Plains were thought to be good in terms of available land, wood, water, and other necessities.[42] Sensitivity to civilian feelings permeated down to company level. Lieutenant Colonel Thomas Parker, commandant of the 8th in Virginia, warned his recruiting officers that "opposers of Federal measures will have a watchful eye on every part of your Conduct." "Treat the Citizens of every class," he added, "Indiscriminately with decency and respect and be attentive to [the men's] own moral as well as military character."[43] On at least one occasion when soldiers stole or destroyed civilian property near Harpers Ferry, Parker forbade any enlisted man from leaving camp without a written pass.[44] Hamilton and other High Federalists knew full well that John Adams exercised ultimate control over the army, and after the battle over rank in 1798, it would have been utterly quixotic for them to believe that the army could be used operationally for partisan purposes.

The only evidence for the political use of the force rests on some pointed private references by the most extreme Federalists about crushing the opposition. Most were expressions of hatred and disgust, more in the nature of hopes than of plans, more emotion than rational analysis of practical alternatives. "We are strong now, from our recent success against France," wrote Tracy in January 1799, "and should malecontents now dare to oppose, I think we should successfully attack them, and save much future trouble, probably bloodshed: and establish the Gov[ernmen]t with more advantage, than if no opposition had ever occurred."[45] The more explicit, damning statement came from Hamilton. In early 1799 he told Sedgwick and Dayton, two leaders in Congress, that despite the favorable results of congressional elections in some states, the opposition had hardly diminished. And "some parts of the Union which, in time past, have been the soundest, have of late exhibited signs of a gangrene begun and progressive."[46] To Dayton, Hamilton sent a bold plan for shifting the balance of political power radically toward the central government: new canals and roads, extension of the power of the federal judiciary, direct taxes, broader laws against sedition and inflammatory politics, and a standing army, including a skeletal force of twelve regiments, volunteer companies, and the Eventual Army with an officer corps appointed (but not in service) permanently. In his letter to Sedgwick, Hamilton pointed to the growing militancy of the opposition in Virginia. "When a clever force has been collected, let them be drawn toward Virginia, for which there is an obvious pretext, then let measures be taken to act upon the laws and put Virginia to the test of resistance."[47]

Yet none of their correspondence indicates that Federalists intended to eradicate the Republican party with force. Every extremist statement about crushing the opposition came at times when Federalists were most afraid of rebellion: in the spring and early summer of 1798 when the war hysteria was at its height and rumors of revolt abounded; and during the first few months of 1799 after the Virginia and Kentucky legislatures declared the Alien and Sedition Acts unconstitutional, argued that states had the right to obstruct their operation, and called on other state legislatures to join in opposition.[48] To many Federalists, the Kentucky and Virginia resolutions smacked of the revolution they had always predicted. "They are certainly meant as the tocsin of insurrection," asserted John Quincy Adams, no extremist.[49] Between January and April 1799, rumors swept Federalist ranks that Virginia was preparing for civil war, and in fact the legislature voted to raise taxes, reorganize the militia, purchase additional arms, and construct an armory in Richmond.[50] Jefferson was also uneasy. "Several parts of this state [Pennsylvania] are so violent that we fear an insurrection," he wrote in February. "This is not the kind of opposition the American people will permit." "[K]eep away all show of force, and they will bear down the evil propensities of government, by the constitutional means of election and petition." Rebellion, Jefferson concluded, "is the only thing we have to fear."[51] Within another month opposition to the tax program enacted in 1798 erupted in northeastern Pennsylvania. Led by German farmers and tradesmen, tax assessors were driven out of towns, threatened, and the federal marshall forced at gunpoint to release several prisoners who had helped keep the tax law from being enforced. In March 1799 Adams proclaimed three counties in rebellion and sent several companies of the New Army, along with Pennsylvania volunteer companies, to suppress the disorder. While all in the government agreed that the uprising was minor, and it was easily suppressed without real opposition, the whole affair gave credence to Federalist worries.[52] Hamilton, like the other Federalists who spoke of dealing with their antagonists militarily, was responding to specific threats. To both Sedgwick and Dayton, Hamilton placed his proposals explicitly within the context of the Virginia and Kentucky resolutions and Virginia's martial preparations. Hamilton wished to move troops toward Virginia not to jail or overturn the Republicans in that state, but to threaten the opposition, parade the government's power, and to nip a civil war in the bud as the Washington administration had done in western Pennsylvania in 1794. "This plan will give time for the fervor of the moment to subside," he concluded, "for reason to resume the reins, and, by dividing its enemies, will enable the government to triumph with ease."[53] Even the most extreme Federalists sensed by 1799 that the army was a mastodon, so crude a political instrument that to use it in any except a conventional military situation or without visible provocation was impossible. Federalists understood the difference between having an army and using it. Much as he wanted to make Republicans "feel the bayonet," Tracy admitted that they somehow had to "bring us to it."[54]

Yet as Federalists well knew, the army did possess very real political advantages. All standing armies in the eighteenth century were understood to have a direct influence on politics by the threat of their use, an intimidating presence that not only deterred active sedition but intruded into legitimate political discourse. Unmistakably many Federalists viewed the 1798 military program in this context, especially the top leaders who could no longer distinguish between dissent and treason. Some, like Pickering, openly called the 12 regiments a "standing army."[55] In 1798 Sedgwick tried to include making enlistments in the New Army run for five years instead of the duration of hostilities, implying a permanent army not tied to war with France. Hamilton pressed constantly for the same provision.[56] The program Hamilton suggested to Dayton in early 1799 clearly sought to make the New Army permanent, and Hamilton's insistence on perfection in organization all through 1798 and 1799 revealed a determination to make the regiments the beginnings of an enduring army.

Federalists added the 30,000-man Eventual Army in the 1799 session of Congress precisely to frighten the Republicans. The statute allowed the President to substitute volunteer companies for militia to suppress disorder or execute the laws. "No Act of Congress has ever struck the Jacobins with more horror," beamed Sedgwick.[57] For extreme Federalists, the New Army along with the rest of the military forces authorized during the Quasi-war were designed to intimidate, to create behind the Alien and Sedition Acts a force capable of enforcing the laws, checking or preventing rebellion, and inhibiting partisan attacks on the government. As Tracy put it, "the only principle by which Democrats can be governed . . . is fear."[58]

At the same time there existed another element in the Federalist affinity for the army in the late 1790s. As institutions, armies had always caricatured Federalist social and political values, and military experience had been a central element in the origins of the party. As these values and the party came under massive assault during the French Revolution by domestic opposition, and as the Federalists turned in upon themselves with the self-image of beleaguered patriots, their emotional attachment to the military grew stronger. By 1798 the army quite clearly had emerged as the symbol of a powerful, ordered, stable, nationalist, patriotic institution unfettered by dissent or by uncertainty, and above all else it was dependable. A few Federalist leaders had come to believe that the government could not survive unless it possessed a permanent standing army. When Adams deflated the war fever with his nomination of William Vans Murray as envoy to France, the sense of isolation for extreme Federalists sharpened. Through 1799, in response to revitalized Republican opposition, extremists clung ever more closely to the army as the refuge for their values and their power within the government, while Adams tried to disassociate himself from a Hamiltonian cancer that might consume his administration.

Alexander Hamilton never revealed his motives to friends in those years, and even his actions as Inspector General leave doubts as to his ultimate purposes. Without question from the beginning of the French crisis, Hamilton aimed at control of the army. He peremptorily rejected suggestions that he take over the War Department or fill a recently vacated Senate seat from New York.[59] On the other hand, military command had gripped his imagination ever since the latter years of the Revolution when he had chafed in a staff position. After dinner one evening in the capital in 1791, Hamilton told Jefferson and Adams (according to Jefferson) that "The greatest man that ever lived was Julius Caesar."[60] During the Whiskey Rebellion Hamilton had hounded the President for permission to accompany the troops into western Pennsylvania. When Washington approached him in the spring of 1798 about leaving private life, Hamilton replied that if offered *"a station in which the service I may render may be proportionate to the sacrifice I am to make*—I shall be willing to go into the army."[61] Hamilton wanted the Inspector Generalship, an office from which he could form and discipline the new regiments, molding them to his own specifications. At the same time he angled for an active troop command, knowing that Washington would head the army in name only. When Adams balked over naming him second in command, Hamilton encouraged his friends in the cabinet to override the President in spite of the risk of unhinging the administration. After that victory, Hamilton set out to undermine confidence in McHenry, the last bar to ultimate supremacy over the military establishment.

Hamilton's plans for the army may never have been certain even in his own mind. Several times he spoke enthusiastically of invading Spanish or French possessions in the western hemisphere, including South America, and especially of seizing the Floridas and Louisiana.[62] That he consistently advocated a 50,000-man military establishment implied strongly that Hamilton thought in terms of offensive operations. For many in Europe and America, the immense, wealthy, corrupt, and weakened Spanish empire made an inviting target. Like many of his contemporaries, Hamilton was infected with dreams of lasting historical fame, and in the eighteenth century military command or founding an empire were thought to be one of the best avenues to immortal renown. "What a pity that so many Suvoroffs and Buonapartes in embryo," opined congressman Harper only half in jest, "should be chilled into mere Lawyers, Planters, and merchants by the cold breath of Peace!"[63] Hamilton never considered using the army for a coup, although Abigail Adams and Jefferson both voiced suspicion.[64] More than anyone else, Hamilton knew the New Army was weak, that Washington would never permit a move on the government, and that any attempt would plunge the country immediately into chaos and civil war. The most logical explanation of Hamilton's plans is that the New Yorker hoped in 1798 to become the permanent chief of a lasting American standing army. Such a position appealed to his sense of grandeur, to his image of himself as a dashing and romantic soldier. The general who commanded the United States Army did not have to be elected, nor, because of the nature of military rank, did he have to worry about periodic reappointment or even the wishes of the President. From such a secure position, Hamilton could continue to pull the strings of power, influencing key Federalists, plotting strategy with the congressional leadership, manipulating the cabinet—without the slightest personal worry about public opinion or about the President, as long as the general had enough support in Congress to keep his office from being abolished, as had almost happened to Anthony Wayne in 1796. That is one reason why Hamilton pressed Dayton in early 1799 to make the New Army perpetual, and why as late as 1800, when the army was clearly unpopular and about to drag the Federalists down to defeat, Hamilton still wanted the swollen establishment to remain.[65] Finally, if Hamilton harbored ambitions for the Presidency (as Adams believed), no other road except military triumph lay open to a man so feared and hated by major sections of the electorate.[66*]

Adams's nomination of the Murray mission to France in February 1799 ruined all these plans. Until Murray's negotiations ended in success, of course, the army could not be demobilized. "Our operations and preparations by sea and land are not to be relaxed in the smallest degree," the President insisted. "On the contrary, I wish them to be animated with fresh energy."[67] Hamilton must have realized immediately, however, that under no circumstances would Adams allow offensives into the Floridas or Louisiana. And within a short while Hamilton must also have realized that the army was destined to grow more and more unpopular as the threat of war waned. But he was trapped. Chief of an impotent little army, hamstrung by a hostile President and a mediocre Secretary of War, and tied to an army hated by the public, Hamilton still could not resign because to abandon a half-formed army in the midst of the hostilities would damage his reputation, to say nothing of his self-respect.

With no other alternative, Hamilton labored on, pushing the recruiting service, seeing to supplies, managing the mass of details required for putting the army on a sound footing. But increasingly he turned to

---

*Wrote John Quincy Adams late in life: "The army was the creature of Colonel Hamilton and was, together with a French war, the basis of his views of personal ambition. His influence over General Washington and over the whole Federal Party was very great. His services to that cause had been eminent, his career as Secretary of the Treasury brilliant and rivalizing with that of Mr. Jefferson as Secretary of State. His talents were of the highest order, his ambition transcendent, and his disposition to intrigue irrepressible." John Quincy Adams, *Parties in the United States*, ed. Charles True Adams (New York, 1941), 25-26.

reforming the military establishment. During the first winter (1798–1799) he worked out innumerable changes, both to speed the creation of the force and to remodel it into a complete fighting field army. Now, a year later, his plans were more basic and more substantial, almost as if he was trying to dispel his frustration and restore his injured dignity by perfecting the military establishment for all time. Hamilton spent days early in the fall of 1799 conferring with Wilkinson over the redeployment of the western army, analyzing the best locations for the forts and the proper distribution of units. In November and December Hamilton worked on tactical manuals, on a plan for a military academy, and on designs for a new uniform, as well as the distribution of supplies, the proper transmission of musters and reports, the duties and authority of various officials in the War Department and staff officers in regiments.

Denied fame as a great general in battle, Hamilton wanted to leave the military establishment as a personal memorial to his military genius. But the effort was useless. By early 1800, it was obvious that the army could not survive the pressure of public opinion in an election year; the New Army would be disbanded and its generals released from service. As an added insult (although Hamilton always denied any wounded feelings), Adams refused to promote the New Yorker to Lieutenant General and Commander-in-Chief after Washington's death in December 1799. By January 1800, Hamilton was sunk in depression, restless, his mood a strange mixture of anger, resignation, and embarrassment.[69] Increasingly he turned his energy to the coming presidential election, to his festering hatred for the man who had shattered the dream of power and glory, and to a revenge that could heal Hamilton's injured pride, even if the party and the principles for which he had so long labored were destroyed in the process.

13

★ ☆ ★ ☆ ★ ☆ ★ ☆ ★

Adams and Hamilton:
The Politics of
Demobilization and Defeat
[1799-1801]

★

> That army was as unpopular, as if it had been a ferocious wild beast let
> loose upon the nation to devour it. In newspapers, in pamphlets, and in
> common conversation they [the soldiers] were called cannibals. A thou-
> sand anecdotes, true or false, of their licentiousness, were propagated
> and believed.
>
> John Adams, 1815.[a]

While Hamilton and McHenry toiled vainly to establish the New
Army in 1799, the rift between the President and the Federalist leadership
exploded suddenly into public view. Without the slightest consultation
with the cabinet or party elders in Congress, Adams on February 18 asked
the Senate to confirm William Vans Murray as minister to resume talks
with France. The nation was stunned and the Hamiltonians mortified. "It
is solely the President's act, and we were all thunderstruck when we heard
of it," raged Pickering. "Confidence in the President is lost—the federal
citizens thought the thing incredible: the Jacobins alone are pleased."[1]
"There is not a Sound mind from Maine to Georgia that has not been
shocked at it," lamented another Hamiltonian stalwart.[2] At first the
Senate wanted to reject the nomination summarily, but when the wonder
wore off, party leaders decided to refer the matter to a committee, so that
in Pickering's words, "the measure may be rendered less mischievous."[3] A
few days later the committee met with the President, and in an angry
confrontation which included a threat by Adams to resign and turn the

government over to Vice-President Jefferson, the President agreed to nominate two more envoys to join Murray in Europe, and to delay their departure until France gave explicit assurances that the three would be honorably received. As a compromise, however, the meeting failed. Adams had thrown down the gauntlet. Within the party, battle lines were drawn immediately; as one partisan observed, "There certainly will be serious difficulties in supporting Mr. Adams at the next election."[4] For the rest of the year, the Federalist party slowly but inexorably disintegrated. Finally, after two years in office, John Adams had declared his independence.

Adams made the decision with none of the haste or passion his enemies thought. His aim had always been peace and by early 1799, information from abroad showed unmistakably that France wished some accommodation. To continue the hostilities, Adams knew, was to risk allowing events to drive one side or the other into declaring war. "For what end or object should the war have been continued," he asked years later. "*Cui Bono?* What Profit? What Loss? Losses enough. Taxes enough."[5] Bankruptcy was one possibility; an alliance of necessity with Britain another. Adams's worst fear was civil war, and the evidence seemed to point in that direction: the animosity between the parties; the hatred for Britain; and the sentiment in Kentucky, Virginia, and Pennsylvania for peace with France or perhaps for rebellion if the government insisted on war.[6]

Above all, Adams recognized that he was losing control of the government. Since taking office, the proud New Englander had moved in the shadow of his predecessor, circumscribed by Washington's cabinet ("I knew it would turn the world upside down if I removed them"), working uneasily with the party leadership in Congress, trying at all times to avoid the suffocating embrace of Alexander Hamilton.[7] Adams struggled as best he could, using his patronage power to gain control of the party and following his instincts when possible on major issues of policy.[8] But by the fall of 1798, the battles over the army convinced him once and for all that the Hamiltonians were bent on stripping the Presidency of its authority. "It was impossible not to perceive a profound and artful plot hatching in England, France, Spain, South and North America to draw me into a decided instead of a *quasi* war," he recalled, "and a perpetual alliance . . . with Great Britain."[9] Conscious of being President by only three electoral votes, Adams proposed to Washington on two occasions the appointment of Republicans Frederick Muhlenberg and Aaron Burr as generals. On both the President was rebuffed. The Hamiltonians also vetoed Adams's son-in-law for a generalcy and Adjutant General. "With all my ministers against me, a great majority of the Senate and of the House of Representatives, I was no more at liberty than a man in prison, chained to the floor and bound hand and foot."[10] Adams was too proud and egotistical a man to suffer such indignity, and too sensitive to the political implications of such a coup against the Presidency. Undoubtedly Adams saw the trend in early December 1798 when he delivered his opening address to the third session of Congress with Generals Washington, Hamilton, and Pinckney sitting behind him up on the Speaker's platform. A few weeks later, Adams asked Senator Sedgwick if the army reorganization bill would give new powers to the commander-in-chief. No, replied Sedgwick (relating the conversation), only the new title of General. "'What,' said he [Adams], 'are you going to appoint him general over the President?' 'I have not been so blind [as not to see the] effort among those who call themselves the friends of government to annihilate the essential powers given to the president. This sir (raising his voice) my understanding has perceived and my heart felt.'"[11] After being forced by Federalist senators to compromise on the terms of the Murray mission, Adams threatened to resign the office to Jefferson: "If combinations of senators, generals, and heads of department shall be formed, such as I cannot resist, and measures demanded of me that I cannot adopt, my remedy is plain and certain."[12]* Adams first broached the possibility of a new mission to France just a few days after losing the struggle to keep command of the army away from Hamilton. "A war with France, an alliance with England, and Alexander Hamilton the father of their speculating systems at the head of our Army and the State, were their [the Hamiltonians] hobby-horse, their vision of sovereign felicity," claimed Adams years later. "No wonder they hate the author of their defeat."[13]

Adams also sensed currents running deep in the electorate that other Federalists missed entirely. Returns from the congressional elections in the fall and winter of 1798–1799 were mixed in spite of the war fever, which tended to discredit Republicans on the basis of their pro-French record. During the summer, Federalists predicted smashing victories and party leaders, especially Pickering, who mailed hundreds of copies of the XYZ papers in pamphlet form all over the country, worked hard for Federalist candidates.[14] Yet in several states, Republicans gained re-election and in New Jersey Federalists lost three of five House seats, the first time that the opposition had ever won a congressional contest in that state. Federalists made small gains in New England, but lost ground in the Middle states and only in the South did the results match earlier

---

*Adams added: "I will try my own strength at resistance first, however." Near the end of his life, Adams remembered the issue just as clearly. He told Harrison Gray Otis: "I must confess I was very sore on the subject of my mission to France. I was running the gauntlett between the two [French and British partisans] all the way fighting both and the Senate behaving as if possessed of the Devil in their nocturnal caucuses at Binghams and sending to me committees after committees to insult me to my face by snapping and snubbing at me as if I had been their servant boy." March 16, 1823, Adams Family Papers, Massachusetts Historical Society, Boston, Mass.

optimism. While many Federalists focused on the triumphs and explained away the losses—strong Federalists refused to run, or local issues, conditions, or personalities distorted the outcome—Adams realized that much of the Federalist program was unpopular.[15] In the elections, the opposition had rebounded strongly, attacking the administration's foreign policy, the Alien and Sedition Acts, the tax program, and the standing army. Republicans also detected the shift in public sentiment. "The X.Y.Z. delusion is wearing off," Jefferson announced.[16] During the first two months of 1799, Congress received petitions complaining about the burden of government expenditures and standing armies.[17] As usual Federalists attributed the outcry to hidden Republican manipulation, the same kind that produced the Virginia and Kentucky resolutions, but Adams understood the fundamental danger of taxes and armies as political issues. He told Sedgwick just a few days before nominating Murray that "it is weakness to apprehend anything from [the Virginians], but if you [Sedgwick] must have an Army I will give it to you, but remember it will make the government more unpopular than all the other acts. They have submitted with more patience than any people ever did to the burden of taxes which has been liberally laid on, but their patience will not last always."[18] Many years into retirement, Adams recalled his diplomatic moves in 1799 as "the most disinterested and meritorious actions of my life."[19] But in reality the decision to reopen negotiations neatly fulfilled all of the President's personal and political goals: to avoid a brutally divisive war; to save American independence from a British alliance; to undermine the army and strike back at Hamilton, thereby preserving the President's authority and personal dignity; and to disassociate himself from a program which might doom his chance for re-election. "The Reasons which determined me are too long to be written," Adams noted at the time in a letter to his wife.[20] Abigail replied knowingly; one "inducement," she guessed immediately, was "the Army arrangement . . . , I mean the intrigues which the organization of it naturally created; for rank, for power, for Authority etc."[21]

Through 1799, the split in the party widened steadily. In October, over the objections of part of the cabinet and Hamilton, who happened suspiciously to be in the temporary capital of Trenton at the time, Adams ordered Chief Justice Oliver Ellsworth and newly-elected North Carolina Governor William R. Davie, the other two negotiators, to sail for France and join Murray, thus assuring fierce Hamiltonian opposition in the upcoming Presidential contest. All the while the New Army and the land tax which financed it grew ever more unpopular. Republican newspapers publicized dramatically every instance of conflict between the military and citizens who happened in their path. In June marines and cartmen fought a pitched battle on the Albany docks over a horse stabbed by a sergeant.[22] In August two drunken privates knifed a tavern owner who refused to allow them to gamble in his establishment— "convincing proof," trumpeted the *Aurora*, "that the *privates* who exchange the price of honest industry, for the *humiliating duties* of soldiers, are 'villians more desperate, and cut-throats equally bloody minded, with the soldiery of the British monarchy.'"[23] The next month near Bristol, Pennsylvania, a local law enforcement officer was "kicked and maltreated" by soldiers when he attempted to arrest a thief who had escaped by enlisting in the army.[24] During the 1799 gubernatorial election in Pennsylvania, Republicans published a temporary newspaper called the "Cannibal's Progress" specifically to list army excesses.[25] The order to Ellsworth and Davie to sail for Europe ended all justification for the army in the public mind and by the time the Sixth Congress convened in December 1799, even confirmed Hamiltonians admitted that the army had become the object of hatred and ridicule.

The mood among Federalists in Philadelphia that December oscillated between anger and despair. In spite of large majorities in the House and Senate, the party had come unstuck, with Adams openly at war with his cabinet and Hamilton, with the Federalists in Congress leaderless, suspicious of friends as well as enemies, and divided over the peace mission and what role Congress should assume. Before formal business began dissension spilled over into a confusing battle between southern and northern Federalists over the speakership in the party caucus, a struggle which very nearly enabled the Republicans to elect their own Nathaniel Macon. Then came the news of the death of George Washington. For days the eulogies, the black clothing, the somber processionals, and most of all the knowledge that the great anchor of the party was gone, deepened Federalist gloom. "[H]is name was really the Talisman, which enchained sedition; it was the bond of Union, and the center of energy," cried Roger Griswold. "[W]e scarcely thought it important to look for any other means of defence."[26] Overshadowing everything was the election, and both sides knew the army would be a major issue.

On New Year's Day 1800, the Republicans opened the assault anticipated by Hamiltonian leaders: Virginia representative John Nicholas moved to repeal the laws authorizing the twelve regiments of regulars, the dragoons, and all the new general officers.[27] Republicans phrased most of their arguments in practical terms, specifically the dismal financial picture. Nicholas justified his resolution with estimates for the 1800 budget: $14,000,000 needed, of which half would be gobbled up by the army and navy, against estimated revenues of approximately $9,000,000. The difference could only be met by loans at exorbitant interest—and for what? Mostly for a useless army, emphasized Republicans. France no longer had reason or inclination to invade or attack the United States, and if she did, the tiny force would provide no real defense compared to the militia. Federalists responded with all sorts of suppositions: disarmament would exhibit weakness and undermine negotiations in Paris; the militias were unstable and ineffective; the risks of upsetting the integrated system of defense set up in 1798 were not outweighed by the savings, especially considering the fact that favorable news from Paris was expected in a few short months. Money was minor, they contended, compared to American independence or blood, compared to Britain's sacrifices, compared to American resources. The army was "evidence of our spirit rather than of our strength," insisted Harrison Gray Otis, chairman of the committee on defense, "a pledge of our union and further exertions."[28] Gallatin, Nicholas, and Macon responded with more analysis of the diplomatic situation and the improbability of French invasion. Again they emphasized the budget deficit. France knew from the Revolution of the large, warlike population in the United States, reasoned Gallatin. "But our moneyed resources are limited, and the only source of danger to us is our consuming those resources for useless objects and exhausting ourselves for the fear of imaginary dangers."[29]

The debate consumed an entire week—a long, involved, tiresome charade dragging on to "a later hour every afternoon," Otis complained, until the participants, sunk in fatigue, eagerly sought to escape "the polluted atmosphere of the Hall."[30] The only fireworks occurred outside, when congressman John Randolph, after calling the army a "handful of ragamuffins" and "loungers who live off the public" in his maiden speech, sat down at theatre in front of two marine officers who promptly jostled the freshman legislator and plucked at his coat, muttering "ragamuffin" under their breath.[31] Although friends intervened to prevent any challenge that evening, Randolph in a letter to the President arrogantly claimed an insult to the House and demanded punishment of the officers. Adams told the House to protect its own dignity; the parties then clashed over who was to blame for the incident and whether Randolph deserved censure.[32]

The Randolph affair was, as British ambassador Robert Liston reported, an "absurd interlude," but in a sense it was an important symbol of the battle over disbanding the New Army.[33] Neither side publicly admitted its true motives. High Federalists knew that with peace almost certain, the army could not be justified to the public. Yet most of them could not bear to see it disbanded and according to Wolcott, many—"the Generals, and . . . the officers, with their connections," as well as the "wisest and best" Federalists—wished it "preserved as a permanent establishment."[34] Ames and Hamilton, unable or unwilling to differentiate electioneering from incipient revolution, still talked about Virginia plans for overthrowing the government by force. For others, the fears remained vague and indistinct, fears of "turbulent ambition" or of France or of national humiliation with disarming before a peace settlement.[35] Nonetheless, the dilemma was real. "Nothing . . . is more certain than that the army is unpopular," Wolcott maintained. But "Nobody has thought it prudent to say that the army is kept on foot to suppress or prevent rebellions."[36]

Republicans also hid their real feelings. Certainly they wished to dramatize the army as an election issue, but many of their fears were indeed sincere. With no prospect of invasion and every indication of a negotiated peace, they saw no purpose in the force other than political intimidation, possible use of troops to interfere with the election, or a coup by Hamilton and his friends. "Can such an army under Hamilton be disbanded," Jefferson wondered in the spring of 1799, "Even if a H[ouse] of Repr[esentatives] can be got willing and wishing to disband them?"[37] One Virginian worried openly about "the soldiers quartered" in Richmond "and the probability of their being quartered at the Court-houses where elections are to be held."[38] Some of these fears were evidently shared by moderates in both parties. In March 1800, the House (where Federalists held a three to two majority) passed a bill prohibiting military forces from appearing "armed" or "embodied" at polling places, or as close as a mile if the "officer presiding over or conducting" the election "signified in writing" that the "vicinity of such troops will incommode, or . . . overawe the voters."[39] But on a strange and ominous note, the Hamiltonian-dominated Senate without comment refused to concur, and the legislation died.

The leadership of both sides concealed their motives in order to appeal to moderate Federalists, the same kind of group which had been critically important in the evenly split Fifth Congress and which now, swelled by victories in the 1798–1799 elections, comprised the balance in the House. Mostly from the South, new to national politics ("not pledged by any act to support the system of the last Congress," noted Wolcott), and extremely sensitive to public opinion in home districts which normally sent Republicans to Philadelphia, the moderates tended to look for leadership to John Marshall.[40] Marshall, himself newly elected but an experienced diplomat and political leader, was not as yet identified with any Federalist faction, but he was on record as opposed to the Alien and Sedition Acts because of their unpopularity in the South. In December, counting noses and realizing the power that public opinion and financial arguments would have on the moderates, Sedgwick and his friends worked out a compromise to save the army even before the Republican onslaught: suspend all new enlistments to save money, but retain the force until news from Paris was more definite. Marshall accepted the compromise readily and spoke for it, as did the conservative Republican from Baltimore, Samuel Smith, the original sponsor of the New Army statute. Late on the afternoon of January 10, the vote was taken. Party lines held and the Nicholas resolution disbanding the New Army lost decisively, 60 to 39.[41]

Most Hamiltonians disliked the plan intensely because it meant surrendering to public sentiment, spelling the eventual demise of the army just as soon as news of peace arrived. "Whatever may be the obstacles to an army," George Cabot retorted when informed of the situation in Congress, "they ought to be overcome; the whole world is becoming military, and if we are wholly otherwise, we shall be as sheep among wolves."[42] Yet as Sedgwick explained, there existed no other prospect of saving the army. If Congress adjourned before news of peace arrived, then the army would continue until the next session, through the summer and fall of the critical Presidential election. Federalists had indeed gauged the mood of the southern moderates accurately. On January 13, Otis introduced the compromise resolution to retain the 4,000 some-odd men on hand. Without serious debate or opposition, the House concurred and in February, as the Secretary of War predicted, the Senate also caved in. "It is the apprehension of expence that paralyses, that appalls," McHenry noted sadly.[43]

John Adams kept silent all through the struggle in Congress, no doubt happy to remain in the background while his enemies in the party agonized over the assault on their army. In New York, Hamilton watched the proceedings glumly, his anger and frustration growing steadily. "When will Congress probably adjourn?" he growled impatiently to Sedgwick. "Will any thing be settled as to a certain *election?*" "Will my presence be requested as to this or any other purpose, and when?"[44] In Congress and the War Department, the future of the 12 regiments hung suspended from February through April, awaiting definite word from Paris. The contest for the Presidency, however, was already well underway. A year earlier Jefferson had outlined a platform on which to stand and in several states Republicans established new newspapers to attack the administration. Jockeying in the states for selection of electors had also begun and Federalists were alive to the danger.[45] At the end of January 1800, the Massachusetts congressional delegation released a circular letter warning of the Republican plan "to democratize the character of the State Legislatures . . . to affect the choice of electors . . . so as to secure an antifederal President."[46] For the moment, however, the party split hung in limbo as both Federalist factions waited for the outcome of voting for the state assembly in New York. Adams hoped to avoid open war with his party antagonists until the contest in Hamilton's home state was over. Hamilton and his friends, although already determined to keep Adams from re-election, had no wish to disavow him openly and thereby disturb the voters in the normally Federalist stronghold of New York City. By the time voting began on April 29, the tension back in Philadelphia had become excruciating.

In the ten days that followed, Adams suffered a crucial defeat at the polls and the Federalist party burst apart. In the aftermath, the New Army, along with whatever plans the Hamiltonians ever had for it, were irrevocably consigned to oblivion. At mid-morning on May 3, Philadelphia learned of the stunning upset of the Federalist ticket in New York City. New York was pivotal, the first to begin the process of choosing Presidential electors, a closely divided, swing state that usually went Federalist by virtue of the margin in the city. Federalists in the capital were shocked by the loss. It "will doubtless turn the scale of the Union," groaned Pickering; the "only chance of a federal President will be by General C. C. Pinckney."[47] That night Federalists caucused. With little opposition, Sedgwick and the party leadership unveiled and then imposed the plan Hamilton had secretly tried in 1796 and which Federalists had been discussing for weeks: support Adams and Pinckney (the latter for Vice-President) equally in public and work for Pinckney electoral votes in the South, particularly in his home state of South Carolina. Since each elector cast two votes without formal distinction between President and Vice-President, the general would end up with a majority. "Even though the consequence should be the election of *Jefferson*," Hamilton declared, "my mind is made up." "If we must have an *enemy* at the head of the Government, let it be one whom we can oppose, and for whom we are not responsible, who will not involve our party in the disgrace of his foolish and bad measures."[48]

The result in New York likewise shook John Adams. But is also freed the President to move openly without fear of undermining his election chances in Hamilton's home state. In fact, the defeat made it imperative that the President disassociate himself publicly from Hamiltonian policy; the voters had obviously repudiated the party and its record equally as much as its Presidential candidate. In addition, Adams knew full well of the plotting underway to deny him re-election. In mid-March he had received two anonymous letters outlining completely the electoral strategy for putting someone else in the Presidency while appearing to support Adams. "Hamilton's command gives him the means of working against you most powerfully," Adams read.[49] Since military and revenue officers were being organized into a huge political octopus for this purpose, Adams was urged to disband the regiments and reassert his authority over the federal bureaucracy. The Federalist caucus on May 3 confirmed these warnings, and galvanized the President into action.

On Monday evening May 5, Adams summoned James McHenry away from a dinner party on the pretext of discussing a new appointment in the War Department. Passionately the President confronted McHenry with all the backstage maneuvering of the past several months, in the cabinet and in party politics, demanding an explanation. "You are subservient to Hamilton, who ruled Washington, and would still rule if he could," thundered Adams. "Hamilton is an intriguant—the greatest intriguant in the World—a man devoid of every moral principle—a Bastard, and as much a foreigner as Gallatin." McHenry replied as best he could, explaining, justifying, trying to conciliate his angry superior. But Adams would not relent. Mercilessly he berated the Secretary, not only with his suspicions, but with every error ascribed to McHenry's administration of the War Department since mid-1798. Finally the Secretary, deeply wounded and probably near tears, offered to resign. Adams accepted immediately, and in an abrupt change of tone, tried to smooth over his accusations of ineptitude and dishonesty. Both men were uncomfortable. After a brief discussion of the details of McHenry's retirement, the interview ended. Five days later, without any warning or personal meeting, the President fired Timothy Pickering.[50]

High Federalists reacted with horror and rage. "Every tormenting passion rankles in the bosom of that weak and frantic old man," cried Sedgwick; the same "course of madness or treachery which began with the last mission to France," muttered another.[51] For weeks there had circulated rumors and predictions of a change in the cabinet, some even published in the *Aurora*, but many Hamiltonians felt that Adams did not dare such action in the midst of an election battle.[52] Afterwards, however, a different interpretation emerged. It all stemmed from Adams's paranoia and personal resentment, according to Pickering, beginning in 1798 with the rejection of son-in-law William S. Smith for the adjutancy (Adams "was by somebody immediately informed of my exertions in this case; and he has never forgiven me"), and it deepened with the controversy over Hamilton's rank in the New Army.[53] McHenry thought the disagreements over diplomacy in 1799 and the Federalist caucus in 1800 were more important, but both Secretaries agreed that the root cause was the President's emotional instability, his feelings of persecution and his hatred for certain individuals. Pickering in addition spread stories of a deal between Adams and Jefferson, whereby Adams, knowing his chances for re-election had been crippled, would step into the Vice Presidency in a new Republican administration.[54] Hamiltonians believed it all, especially the deal with Jefferson which as gossip ran wild in May and June, intensifying their anger.[55] By the summer, they were determined to elect Pinckney. "If they cannot carry General Pinckney," McHenry concluded, "of the two evils" (Adams and Jefferson), they "prefer Mr. Jefferson."[56]

The Hamiltonian assessment of Adams's motives was partially correct, but the wily old New Englander acted for far more complex reasons.

In reality he fired his ministers to divorce himself dramatically and publicly from taxes and armies. A month later in a similar move, against the advice of the truncated cabinet, Adams pardoned John Fries and the other rebels from the northeastern Pennsylvania uprising in 1799.[57] Like most Presidents in such situations, Adams disclaimed any electioneering. He did tell Pickering and other Federalists in early May that he expected Jefferson to win the Presidency and he consistently, openly exhibited unbridled suspicion about the Hamiltonians during that two-week stretch. Yet there is no denying that John Adams ran and ran hard for re-election, that he considered the election in February 1799 when he initiated another mission to France, and that he worked hard before and after May 1800 to win a second term, including some of the first public campaigning in American history.[58]

But even more than his own re-election, Adams wished in May 1800 to prevent Alexander Hamilton from seizing the government. For years the President had blocked Hamilton's bid for power through the army and in 1800 the old revolutionary leader believed he had to stop Hamilton from placing a puppet in the Presidency through the vehicle of the electoral college. If the result was a victory for Thomas Jefferson, so be it. After slandering Hamilton in the interview with McHenry, Adams declared flatly: "Mr. Jefferson is an infinitely better man [than Hamilton]; a wiser one, . . . and, if President, will act wisely. I know it and would rather be Vice President under [Jefferson], or even Minister Resident at the Hague, than indebted to such a being as Hamilton for the Presidency."[59] By his action in the spring of 1800, Adams not only gained public approval, but drove his Federalist opponents out into the open, goaded them into wild attacks, and forced the secondary leaders of the party and officials in the federal bureaucracy, both of whom would manage the elections in the states, to choose openly between himself and the Hamiltonians. In Adams's mind, however, the need to repay the insults to himself and to his office were secondary to the necessity of preventing a band of extremists from reversing the Revolution.[60]

If part of Adams's strategy in early May was to destroy the New Army as his anonymous informant had urged two months earlier, it worked perfectly. Although the diplomatic situation had not changed dramatically, reports trickling into Philadelphia in March and April provided increasing proof that the American envoys would reach Paris and gain a cordial reception from the new French government under Napoleon Bonaparte.[61] Hamiltonians sensed that the army was doomed; the New York election returns suggested the danger in flouting public apprehension blatantly. So to deny the Republicans credit for disbanding the troops, Robert Goodloe Harper moved on May 7 to give the President that authority when relations with France warranted, and without even a formal roll call, the House quickly agreed. Adams announced that he would dismantle the army immediately on the same day that he demanded Pickering's resignation. Outraged, the Hamiltonians in the Senate removed the President's authority from the House bill and ordered the New Army demobilized on or before June 15. John Adams was not to gain the satisfaction or the political advantage from Hamilton's return to private life and the end of the army. On May 14 the President signed the bill and the next day, as Congress adjourned, he ordered McHenry to begin demobilization.[62] Speaking for the Hamiltonians, Harper boasted in a campaign letter to his constituents that new diplomatic and military conditions in Europe convinced Federalists "that the measure might be safely adopted. . . . They therefore brought it forward themselves, and passed it into a law."[63] But Senator Stevens Mason of Virginia, although surprised like most Republicans who were not privy to the byzantine maneuvering which had produced the act, came closer to the mark: "the [military] system would have been still pursued had [Federalists] not quarreled among themselves about the management of these mischiefs."[64]

In New York the news came as no surprise to Hamilton, and he accepted it calmly. For weeks the army had been of little interest compared to the election in the city and to party strategy in the conflict with Adams. Stiffly Hamilton attended to the details of demobilization: informing his subordinates; removing equipment and supplies from the brigade camps to permanent storehouses; arranging the pay and accounts of the men; easing the transition generally back to an army of frontier garrisons. Hamilton cared now only about destroying John Adams. The general spent the last week of May with the Union Brigade at Scotch Plains and part of June in New England, but his real purpose was politics and even in front of the troops, Hamilton laced his goodbyes with pointed references to the election and exhortations to work for General Pinckney's candidacy. Once back in New York, long political reports to allies took precedence over notice to the War Department that "military operations [have] ceased."[65] In mid-June, in what must have been a bittersweet moment, Adams could savor the formal demise of the New Army. Colonel William S. Smith informed his father-in-law that the Union Brigade was disbanded: "retirement from the field has been without confusion, disturbance or riot, and meets with the applause of the adjacent Country."[66]

The first and only completely political army in American history was no more. As an issue in Congress and between the parties, in the highest councils of the Adams administration, and in the diplomacy and politics of Adams's entire Presidency, its influence had already been monumental. By mid-summer 1800, the outlines of the Presidential contest had clearly emerged. What appeared to the voters as a battle between Federalists and Republicans was actually a contest between Hamiltonians and Adams, and between Adams and the Republican party, united for assault on the President, the Hamiltonians, and all the Federalist policies of the past decade. Once again the New Army worked its poison. As one of several issues used by Republicans in the campaign it helped to elevate Thomas Jefferson into the Presidency; and as a festering sore at the heart of the animosity between Adams and Hamilton, it crippled the Federalist party and contributed to its destruction as a force in national politics.

Republicans used the New Army and military issues in several ways. Speeches, handbills, and virtually every declaration of party principle included, and often began with, a denunciation of Federalist plans to threaten civil liberty and impose tyranny. Republicans cited the army and militarism along with taxes, the war policy, and a British alliance, as evidence of a longstanding plot to introduce monarchy and the way in which Federalist commercialism sapped the resources of American farmers. The military became a motif for ridicule and character assassination; Hamilton became Alexander I and on one occasion the *Aurora* parodied Adams, McHenry, and Pickering as officers of the ship "*Administration*" sailing on an "ocean for a league round . . . covered with regimentals."[67] The most repeated charge, however, was that the Federalists had aimed to establish the classic standing army, and party spokesmen, sometimes obliquely and sometimes directly, drummed on that theme over and over again from 1798 onwards. "The Alien and the Sedition laws have . . . had some effect . . . , but the project of raising a *large Standing Army*, and the *measures of enormous Expense* . . . are involving the Country," reported one Pennsylvanian at the beginning. "[T]here is a very numberous class of people . . . who will be more readily convinced . . . *by the applications of the Tax gatherer*, than by the soundest Logic or the best political Arithmetic. There is, as Mr. Gallatin has observed, '*Great Sensibility in the Breeches* pocket.'"[68] Of all the issues in the long and vengeful election, none was used with more versatility or heat than the army.

Adams's enemies within the party mentioned the army too—the William S. Smith affair, the firing of Pickering, Adams's hatred for Hamilton—but as an issue it was used mostly to illustrate the President's vanity and madness. For Hamilton, however, the army had become a personal affront that ate at him like a cancer and finally near the end of the campaign drove him into a bitter assault on the President which has tarnished Hamilton's reputation for nearly two centuries. During his trip to New England in June, Hamilton attacked Adams brutally in public speeches and private conversations. But after sounding Federalists in the states, party leaders informed Hamilton and his lieutenants that the

Brigadier General James Wilkinson, about 1797, by Charles Willson Peale. (Courtesy Independence National Historical Park Collection, Philadelphia)

Timothy Pickering in the early 1790s, age about fifty, by Charles Willson Peale. (Courtesy Independence National Historical Park Collection, Philadelphia)

"The Treaty of Greenville, 1795," believed to have been painted at the time by an officer on General Wayne's staff. The officers at center are the general, his aide William Henry Harrison, and scout William Wells, acting as interpreter. Little Turtle is one of the Indian chiefs. (Courtesy Chicago Historical Society)

View of several Public Buildings, in Philadelphia

State House Yard in Philadelphia, the seat of the government in the 1790s, according to an engraving published in 1790. The building with the steeple in the center was Independence Hall. Congress met in Congress Hall, the next building on the left. (Courtesy The Historical Society of Pennsylvania)

The Lyon-Griswold fight as seen by contemporaries. (Courtesy The New-York Historical Society, New York City)

T. Clarke Sculp.ᵗ Philad.ᵃ

FRIGATE UNITED STATES

Preparation for **WAR** to defend Commerce.

The Swedish Church Southwark with the building of the **FRIGATE PHILADELPHIA.**

The Other Dimensions of the Military Establishment. The frigate *United States*, top left, from a 1797 magazine engraving; bottom left, Fort Mifflin constructed at the confluence of the Schuykill and Delaware Rivers to guard Philadelphia, as it appeared in the late 1790s, but painted in the nineteenth century; and, above, the construction of the frigate *Philadelphia*, from an 1800 engraving published in that city. (Courtesy Prints and Photographs Division, Library of Congress; Courtesy The New-York Historical Society, New York City)

TO ALL BRAVE, HEALTHY, ABLE BODIED, AND WELL
DISPOSED YOUNG MEN,

IN THIS NEIGHBOURHOOD, WHO HAVE ANY INCLINATION TO JOIN THE TROOPS,
NOW RAISING UNDER

GENERAL WASHINGTON,

FOR THE DEFENCE OF THE

LIBERTIES AND INDEPENDENCE
OF THE UNITED STATES,

Against the hostile designs of foreign enemies,

TAKE NOTICE,

THAT *tuesday, wednsday, thursday, friday and saturday at Spotswood in* ..... county, attendance will be given by ..... *Lieutenant* ..... *Recruiting* ..... with his music and recruiting party of ..... company in ..... *Battalion* of the 11th regiment of infantry, commanded by Lieutenant Colonel Aaron Ogden, for the purpose of receiving the enrollment of such youth of SPIRIT, as may be willing to enter into this HONOURABLE service.

The ENCOURAGEMENT at this time, to enlist, is truly liberal and generous, namely, a bounty of TWELVE dollars, an annual and fully sufficient supply of good and handsome clothing, a daily allowance of a large and ample ration of provisions, together with SIXTY dollars a year in GOLD and SILVER money on account of pay, the whole of which the soldier may lay up for himself and friends, as all articles proper for his subsistance and comfort are provided by law, without any expence to him.

Those who may favour this recruiting party with their attendance as above, will have an opportunity of hearing and seeing in a more particular manner, the great advantages which these brave men will have, who shall embrace this opportunity of spending a few happy years in viewing the different parts of this beautiful continent, in the honourable and truly respectable character of a soldier, after which, he may, if he pleases return home to his friends, with his pockets FULL of money and his head COVERED with laurels.

GOD SAVE THE UNITED STATES.

Recruiting during the Quasi-war. Left, the newly created Marine Corps begins its recruiting, as depicted probably by a twentieth-century artist. Above, the army recruiting poster, often reproduced as an example of Revolutionary War recruiting, was for Lieutenant Colonel Aaron Ogden's 11th Regiment in the New Army, 1799. (Marine Corps Photograph in the National Archives; U.S. Signal Corps Photograph in the National Archives)

"THE TIMES; a POLITICAL PORTRAIT," a Federalist view of the army in 1798 or early 1799. General Washington on the chariot, with the volunteers hidden in the background, leads American forces against the French, who are landing at left ("The Cannibals are landing"). Jefferson, Gallatin, and company try to hold back the chariot ("Stop de wheels of de gouvernement"). Note the caption, the Republican party newspaper in the foreground, and the dog. (Courtesy The New-York Historical Society, New York City)

President John Adams in 1800, by Charles B. J. F. de Saint-Memin. (Courtesy The Metropolitan Museum of Art, Gift of William H. Huntington, 1883)

Abigail Adams in 1800, by Gilbert Stuart. (Courtesy Massachusetts Historical Society)

46 4 8

Secretary of War James McHenry in the late 1790s, by Charles B. J. F.
de Saint-Memin. (Courtesy Frick Art Reference Library, New York City)

The Rise of West Point. Although continuously occupied by American troops after the Revolution, West Point was used mostly as a recruiting station and storehouse, as depicted above in the early 1790s by an unknown artist, probably Sir Archibald Robertson. The troops are likely recruits for Wayne's Legion. Even after becoming headquarters for the Corps of Artillerists and Engineers, West Point was still the sleepy, bucolic post shown in 1800, top right, from across the Hudson River. However by the time the Jeffersonians were finished with it, West Point in George Catlin's famous 1828 view, bottom right, was a bustling military school. (From the collection of the late Lieutenant General Raymond A. Wheeler, USA, courtesy Mrs. Virginia M. Wheeler, Washington, D.C.; Courtesy West Point Museum Collections, United States Military Academy; Courtesy Anne S. K. Brown Military Collection, Brown University Library)

The peacetime atmosphere on Chestnut Street, Philadelphia, as one might approach the War Department offices in the 1790s. This view looks east. From 1792 through 1796, the War Department was on the southeast corner of 5th and Chestnut, in the center just past the building with the cupola (part of the State House). From 1797 on, the offices were across Chestnut in the third building distinguishable on the left side of the street. (Courtesy The Historical Society of Pennsylvania)

A nineteenth-century militia muster, as lampooned in a contemporary engraving. (Courtesy Anne S. K. Brown Military Collection, Brown University Library)

THE NATIONS BULWARK.

President must not be opposed openly. "We must not be even suspected of having any thing further in view than the running of Mr. A. or Mr. P.," reported former New Jersey Senator Richard Stockton. "A public avowal . . . to drop . . . the first gentleman, would cause the loss of any ticket [of electors] supposed to be actuated by these principles." Secondary leaders backed Adams believing he had acted wisely in foreign policy and within his rights in reshuffling the cabinet. "You have seen and know the description of Men we have in these stations." "These men have for four years been holding up Mr. A. as one of the wisest and firmest men in the United States. What reason could be given for so sudden a change," Stockton concluded; "nothing but private anecdotes not proper to be mentioned."[69]

But Hamilton's anger could be contained no longer. Since May he had been considering some kind of formal attack on the President.[70] That summer when Adams publicly called the Hamiltonians militarists, a British faction, and a secret cabal aiming to rob him of the Presidency, Hamilton was goaded to fury. "We fight *Adams* on very unequal grounds—because we do not declare the motives of our dislike."[71] Most serious of all, Hamilton's electoral strategy seemed to be failing. Mc-Henry reported in late July that Maryland's Federalists were confused for it had been publicly declared that the congressional caucus wanted Adams to win. "If no contrary impression by prominent characters is publicly divulged from any quarter, what can be done here to obtain a superiority, or even an equal number of votes for General Pinckney," asked the former Secretary.[72] New England was the shakiest of all. Since Adams's open blasts and the emergence of his design to forge a third party attached to his own candidacy, hopes of carrying equal electoral votes for Pinckney had slipped. Should Federalist electors in Massachusetts throw away Pinckney votes, then surely southern Federalists would retaliate by throwing away Adams votes, allowing Jefferson to win easily. Worse yet, Adams acted as if Jefferson were no evil, and "if Mr. A. sh[oul]d be only Vice it w[oul]d be revenge if not victory," groaned Fisher Ames.[73] "What is to be done in Massachusetts?—what in other States?"[74] "Federalists" must "remain attached to the principles of their cause," replied Wolcott, who remained in the cabinet and acted as a clearinghouse for political information from Hamiltonians. "If these are not abandoned we shall remain a party, and in a short time regain our influence." "The unjust accusations of [Adams's] personal friends . . . ought . . . to be answered in a high and fearless tone . . . and if the gauntlet of controversy is offered by the Adamites, it ought to be instantly accepted."[75]

Wolcott blanched when Hamilton suggested circulating an attack on Adams "in the shape of a *defence of myself*." Hamilton admitted he was "in a very belligerent humor." He had written Adams for an explanation of the President's charges without result. Hamilton had then pressed

McHenry for inside information so he could circulate it as a "letter to a friend, with my signature."[76] Wolcott, and especially the two Hamiltonian leaders in Massachusetts, Ames and Cabot, tried to stop Hamilton. All three emphasized that the letter "must be done with infinite care and circumspection" lest "anger" or "*jealousy* . . . be excited."[77] Under no circumstances should Hamilton admit his authorship. All three looked beyond the election. The decision of the caucus must be fairly honored. Jefferson would win and a public vendetta between Adams and Hamilton would destroy the party forever. "The question is not, I fear, how we shall fight," warned Ames, "but how we and all Federalists shall fall, that we may fall, like Antis, the stronger for our fall."[78]

Hamilton could not be deterred. As the election approached its climax, he wanted to destroy Adams and the justification became the "promoting of Mr. Pinckney's election and the vindication of ourselves."[79] The letter Hamilton drafted in September glossed over his true motives: he disclaimed anger over not receiving promotion to lieutenant general after Washington's death; there was of course no mention of making the New Army perpetual or waging offensive war in Latin America; and Hamilton admitted that his interpretation of Adams's political motives for firing Pickering and McHenry was "mere conjecture."[80] Yet the attack on Adams's foreign policy and behavior in office became in the end both personal and vindictive. And Hamilton always planned it for "general circulation," as he told Wolcott in late September. "Anonymous publications can effect nothing."[81] When informed in Albany that his letter against Adams had been published widely by the Republicans, Hamilton appeared "pleased," according to his close friend Robert Troup who was there, and "replied that he had well considered it and had no doubt it would be productive of good."[82]

Federalists were amazed and disgusted by Hamilton's performance. Friends viewed it with sadness; Adams's partisans rushed into print quickly to defend the President and attack Hamilton, and one, Noah Webster, squarely attributed Hamilton's rage to his disappointments over the army. The result was confusion and further demoralization within party ranks.[83] Adams viewed the publication, indeed all of Hamilton's activity since early 1800, as convincing proof of all the President's earlier interpretations of the man and his motives. In July, Adams learned of Hamilton's intemperate speeches in New England. "Hamilton said, that it was little consequence who was president," related Abigail Adams; "for his part, he did not expect his Head to remain four years later upon his Shoulders, unless it was at the Head of a victorious Army."[84] Adams's campaign that summer and fall was shrewdly conceived and as one historian has pointed out, strangely modern. Below New York the President ran on the record of his administration and on his career, emphasizing peace and prosperity, recalling long forgotten visits, people, and events in which he had played a role as far back as the 1770s. Once back in New England, where Jefferson presented no threat, Adams's adversary became the Hamiltonians, and the President attacked boldly to upset their electoral schemes. Above all, Hamilton could not be allowed to win. "The last mission to France, and the consequent dismission of the twelve regiments, although an essential branch of my system of policy, has been to those who have been intriguing and laboring for an army of fifty thousand men, an unpardonable fault," Adams wrote near the end. "If by their folly they have thrown themselves on their backs, and jacobins should walk over their bellies, as military gentlemen [describe] promotions over their heads, whom should they blame but themselves?"[85]

As an indicator of the schisms in the Federalist party, Hamilton's public attack was devastating. In pamphlet form it came too late to affect the voting. Adams ran stronger in 1800 than he had in 1796 and lost by the surprisingly thin electoral margin of 73 to 65. Any of a dozen factors were responsible for the defeat, but unquestionably the New Army affected the result and quite possibly lay at the root of the President's defeat. Certainly the army and tax issues swayed voters, but how deeply and whether the electorate voted on the issues at all in 1800 is impossible to tell. It is likely that the military was so merged in the public mind with other issues that it could not be separated out. The most explicit effect of the New Army was the split in the party, which molded Adams's policy and his campaign, and which prevented him from capitalizing on the strength Federalists had achieved in the South in the congressional elections of 1798–1799. South of Delaware Adams ran as poorly as he had in 1796. But if the President lost the election anywhere, it was in New York, a state he had carried four years earlier but where his election depended on the one man for whom the split over the army was overriding. Adams never stood a chance of gaining the state's 12 electoral votes. Hamilton slated for the Assembly men whom he could control, and it is debatable whether Hamiltonian electors would ever have allowed Adams to win re-election. As Adams was told nearly two months before the polls opened, "Hamilton says that you will not have a vote in N[ew] York *in any event*."[86]

As they prepared to leave national life, Adams and his wife had no doubt what caused the defeat. "It would require a volume instead of a single letter to unfold to you, all the machinations which have combined to produce this Change in the Administration," Mrs. Adams explained to her eldest son. "Honest Men have been cheated, and duped, ambitious men have seen themselves and their plots discovered, and counteracted, by a watchfulness which they could not elude; and were therefore determined to get rid of, at any hazard."[87] To his dying day John Adams held to that interpretation. Hamilton and his British faction were responsible. They had passed the program that furnished Jefferson with the ammunition for victory. They had pushed for a war that divided the nation and well might have thrown the United States into the grasp of Britain, provoked a civil war, and shattered the union. They had dreamed of expeditions to South America. "Let me repeat . . . once more, . . . the faction was dizzy," insisted Adams in 1815. "Their brains turned round. They knew not, they saw not the precipice on which they stood."[88]

To save himself and the nation from such a dangerous course, Adams had exploded Hamilton's dreams. Whether Adams correctly guessed the Hamiltonians' true designs about an American empire and a British alliance will probably never be known for certain. But the President's analysis of their militarism and of the possible consequences of their military program in 1799 and 1800 was absolutely correct. Adams understood, as did many Federalists, that government in America rested ultimately on consent. Edmund Randolph had expressed it perfectly in 1794: "The strength of a government is the affection of the people."[89] In 1798, the overwhelming majority of the party believed an army necessary—but only temporarily. As late as 1801, John Quincy Adams claimed that the "only strong and real argument [Hamiltonians] had" for "an army at hand" was "to check projects of disunion and rebellion," although John Quincy found the justification "no longer formidable" by that date and he "doubted whether Hamilton himself would have the courage to confess it." Even if the thought sometimes repulsed them, John Adams and his supporters recognized the transforming fact of the Revolution, that the people were ultimately sovereign. No group, no party, no government could rule by force without bringing on revolt and revolution. "No," concluded Adams's son, rejecting rule by force which would destroy the country. "If the attachment of the people must desert us, let it at least be altogether in their own wrong."[90]

Beyond the Hamiltonian bid for power and glory, beyond the personal or political differences with Adams, there lay concealed a fundamental disagreement about the nature of government that has existed throughout history. Hamilton and his adherents also succumbed to the hysteria of the 1790s, but they believed the government could rule, that they could preserve their values and their world, if necessary by force alone. In 1787 some members of the Constitutional Convention urged that all governments needed an army for "weight," as a final arbiter to preserve society, but that only a government based on law could endure. Ten years of suspicion, of change, revolution, and opposition, persuaded some that the threat of coercion must become constant, visible, perhaps active in the political process—that a standing army must be added to the American state. "I see no prospect for the support of the government but in those strongholds the army and navy," said Sedgwick's son in 1800.[91] Perhaps a few had always accepted the need for force. Alexander Hamilton never rejected a standing army except when an open disavowal was mandatory; in practice he felt that force or the threat of its use was an effective tool of statecraft which need not tear society asunder even if the people no longer gave their consent. Indeed Hamilton and a few Federalists had from the beginning of their careers been drawn magnetically to armies, to the order armies represented, to the society and the virtue they symbolized, and to the political benefits they promised. Most Federalists could unite in favor of a small national military establishment for the West and for a program of preparedness at times when war threatened. Adams himself always supported the frontier constabulary—presiding over McHenry's reorganizations in 1797–1798, another rationalization effort in 1800, encouraging the development of the arsenals so that the United States would be self-sufficient in munitions, and backing the Hamiltonian plan for a military academy in the midst of fierce Republican attacks on the New Army.[92] But most of the party, like Adams, understood the danger of the classic European standing army. When Hamilton and his coterie constructed an American version and bid to perpetuate it, Adams responded and the party disintegrated. Despite the passions of forty years in politics, the anger of governing in the shadow of Washington, and the disappointment of losing his bid for re-election, John Adams never wavered in his belief that he had pursued the right course. "I desire no other inscription over my gravestone," he wrote after a decade and a half of reflection, "than: 'Here lies John Adams, who took upon himself the responsibility of the peace with France in the year 1800.'"[93]

PART FOUR

★ ☆ ★ ☆ ★ ☆ ★ ☆ ★

Eagle and Sword

★

*how
the American military establishment
was born, and whether its chief
supporters were militarists; or, how the
Eagle gained its Sword, and what that
process represented in the creation of
the United States.*

★ ☆ ★ ☆ ★ ☆ ★ ☆ ★

14

★ ☆ ★ ☆ ★ ☆ ★ ☆ ★

Politics, Militarism,
and Institution-Forming
in the New Nation
[1783-1802]

★

Can any body of men to be raised in this country tread down the
substantial yeomanry? This is quite an Utopian dread. It is infinitely
cheaper to raise and embody an Army at leisure, when the storm is seen
to be approaching, than all at once, when twenty things must be done at
the same time.

Fisher Ames, 1794.[a]

. . . you understand the game behind the curtain too well not to perceive
the old trick of turning every contingency into a resource for accumulating force in the government.

James Madison, 1794.[b]

From the beginning of their rise to power, even before the Revolution ended, the Federalists and the policies they advocated provoked
vehement opposition. Some had fought the nationalists in the 1780s only
to become Federalists themselves in the 1790s. In fact during the twenty
years after independence, the structure of government in the states and
nation changed radically; men switched sides; parties surfaced, faded,
reformed, and finally solidified; but always, inevitably, the fundmental
issues remained, issues such as how to defend the republic, and when and
how to use force against foreign and domestic foes. As Americans of that
era struggled to outgrow the dominant Whig ideology that permeated
their thinking and adapt military institutions to the new condition of

independence, the rhetoric always remained the same. Harrison Gray Otis expressed it perfectly during the long, exasperating debate over demobilization in 1800: "This alarm relative to standing armies has been at least rung a thousand times a year since the first British army was landed in this country."[1]

The accusation of Federalist militarism was a common theme all through the 1790s and in much of the historiography ever since. The interpretation, never worked out completely by Republican pamphleteers or in its entirety by historians studying the period of Federalist rise and reign, emerged piecemeal beginning in the late eighteenth century. A short rendition, combining contemporary charges and historical interpretations, purposely overstated in order to highlight the overall conception, would read something like this: in 1783 the nationalists, frustrated in their efforts to make the central government supreme with the Impost, plotted a coup to replace the Articles of Confederation with a military government or nationalist directorate. Failing in the Newburgh conspiracy, they returned to legitimate political activity. But rule by force was never far from mind. In 1787, they constructed a government with authority to raise a standing army. In 1794, Alexander Hamilton provoked the Whiskey Rebellion by unnecessarily prosecuting delinquent distillers in federal courts in order to brandish the government's military power and chill political opposition. Finally in 1798, Federalists imposed a standing army on the nation and made ready with force either to forestall a Republican victory at the polls, or to prevent the Jefferson administration from taking power.

The real test of Federalist militarism, however, not only for the Republicans in the eighteenth century but for historians since, was support for an American standing army in peacetime. Aristocratic in intent, anti-democratic in political philosphy, obsessed with the mob and with revolution, and aggressive in foreign policy, the Federalists were attracted to an army both on abstract political or philosophical grounds and as a positive tool of statecraft. Again and again Federalists tried to influence politics with force. As nationalists they had supported half-pay for Continental Army officers in order to establish a military lobby in each state. Nationalist officers founded the Society of the Cincinnati as the beginning of a hereditary aristocracy, and to perpetuate the officer corps as a force in politics. Then in 1783 nationalists proposed a standing army in the guise of a small military establishment to police the frontier and safeguard American security. When that lost in 1783, and again in 1784 and 1785, they inserted in the Constitution the authority to provide for an army, fully intending to implement the power at the earliest opportunity, which came in 1790. "Instead of fighting the Indians by a Land Office, and . . . mounted riflemen . . . , an occasion for the gradual introduction of that which sundry laws carefully denominate 'the military establishment,' has been greedily seized."[2] According to James Callender, Hamilton's purpose "was to spin out the war, to create the necessity, or at least the pretence for a standing army, to squander the public money, and to multiply jobs."[3]

At the same time, it has been alleged that the Federalists worked to destroy the militia, either directly or by bringing it under federal authority, in order to rob the states and the people of the only countervailing power to a standing army. Nationalists proposed classing in 1783 to disarm the bulk of the citizenry, Hamilton even suggesting a tiny, truncated militia limited to urban areas. In 1787 the framers attempted to absorb state forces into the federal government as a way of eradicating them (hence the Second Amendment, guaranteeing the existence of state militia). In 1790, Henry Knox purposely submitted an absurdly extreme plan of militia reform in hopes of heading off real improvements. Federalists never supported realistic plans for an effective militia unless the federal government gained absolute control, clearly a prerequisite and most likely the first step in their plot to eliminate the militia altogether.

The militia alternative dispelled by the weak 1792 law, Federalists pushed ahead for the rest of the decade with their plans for a standing army. In 1794 they put forth the "provisional" army as a thinly veiled substitute. ("[L]ess subtlety has prevailed in this than in some other instances," remarked Madison.)[4] Later that same year Federalists stimulated the Whiskey affair to weaken public resistance to armies. In 1795 and 1796, even though Indian power had been crushed to the Northwest, Federalists attempted to retain the swollen military establishment and convert it into a classic standing army for internal use. "I am extremely sorry to remark a growing apathy of the evil and danger," Madison noted glumly.[5] Finally in 1798 and 1799, the Federalist plot burst spectacularly into public view: a standing army to be permanent, Alexander Hamilton at its head, an army to widen the patronage base of the party, to crush dissent, to overthrow the Constitution, to steal the election, and to perpetuate Federalist tyranny.[6]

Like so many historical interpretations first advanced in the heat of political battle, the Jeffersonian picture of the Federalists as militarists contains enough fact and valid review of the evidence to make the entire interpretation plausible. But on episode after episode, Jeffersonians and historians distorted facts to fit a comprehensive interpretation. There exists little evidence that nationalists planned or supported half-pay during the Revolution, or the Society of the Cincinnati afterwards, to embed a permanent military faction within the body politic, although they did in the 1780s enlist veteran officers to lobby for the impost. In 1783, nationalist leaders conspired not to seize the government by military coup, but to remold the Articles of Confederation by threatening Congress with an army mutiny, and indirectly, with the possibility of a coup by dissident officers.

No persuasive evidence has been found that Alexander Hamilton knowingly provoked the Whiskey Rebellion. Indeed the weight of knowledge about Hamilton and conditions in 1794 point strongly in the opposite direction. Much of the backcountry was in uproar against the Whiskey tax, but 1794 was not the year for a rebellion. Relations with Britain hung suspended between peace and war; Pennsylvania was controlled by the opposition party and already was at odds with the government over opening up the Presque Isle area for settlement; Pittsburgh lay astride the chief supply route to Wayne's army, then in the midst of its climactic campaign against the Indians; as a result of the Indian war, the federal government lay completely at the mercy of the states for militia help. Hamilton certainly knew that the government was unprepared militarily and politically for insurrection, and he could have predicted on the basis of the 1792 experience that the administration would divide over how to restore order in western Pennsylvania. To have provoked a rebellion under these circumstances would have been desperate and foolhardy. Alexander Hamilton had no reason for such recklessness.[7]

Jefferson's party and later historians came closest to the truth in their assessment of Federalist motives during the Quasi-war with France. Hamilton and his supporters did attempt to establish a permanent standing army in the United States, partly to suppress dissent and block a Republican victory at the polls. They had no plans, however, for a direct coup, to use the army operationally against the opposition (unless rebellion erupted), or to block Jefferson's accession to power with force. High Federalists acted not to perpetuate an unconstitutional tyranny, but to block revolt, internal subversion, revolution, and to preserve both American independence and their own social values, which they understood to be under massive assault by a combination of French subversion and Republican political activity.

The centerpiece in the argument for Federalist militarism has always been the Federalist insistence, beginning in 1783, on a standing army under the cloak of military necessity, both on the frontier and to meet foreign threats. There also the Jeffersonian interpretation has been in error. First of all, Federalists could never agree completely on questions of defense, and were in fact so divided on military as well as other issues that the terms "Federalism" or "the Federalists" are nearly as meaningless as "the friends of government" or "the friends of order," definitions used by the Federalists themselves. In 1783 some nationalists balked at the leadership's proposal for a national army. During the Constitutional

Convention, Federalists allowed for an army unanimously, but for ideological as well as political reasons, reluctantly. Some in the party voted against an army in the early 1790s to register disapproval of the Indian war. The administration never sought the conflict and indeed authorized Harmar's and St. Clair's expeditions expecting to avert a full-fledged war. As Fisher Ames so aptly wrote in 1793, "even folly could not have chosen . . . ["This most unwelcome Indian war"] as a good thing *per se*."[8] Federalists always quarreled among themselves over militia reform, whether it was wise and what shape it would take. Federalist Dwight Foster explained in 1795 that "this is a subject which affects the various Interests of Individuals in every part of the United States and consequently many great and various are the Sentiments and opinions which are formed by different persons on Questions of this Nature."[9]* In 1796, many Federalists voted with the Jeffersonians to reduce and reorganize the western army into a small frontier constabulary. The Provisional Army lost in the Federalist-controlled House of Representatives in 1794 and 1797. In 1798, Federalist moderates refused to approve five-year enlistments in the regular army, the one provision designed to assure the permanence of a sizable military establishment. John Adams, Alexander Hamilton, and their respective supporters together destroyed the party over the issue of a standing army.

Until 1798, the Federalist leadership exercised extreme care—even timidity—on the army issue. Washington and Knox waged offensive war in the West without regulars and waited until disaster struck before summoning up the courage to ask Congress for a 5,000-man army. In 1792, the President refused to use troops to enforce the Whiskey tax in part out of fears of being misinterpreted. "[T]here would be the cry at once, 'The cat is let out; We now see for what purpose an Army was raised.'"[10] In every foreign crisis —1794, 1797, and 1798—Federalist leaders advocated "provisional" armies to circumvent public resistance to standing forces, and not until 1796 did a Federalist administration risk asking Congress formally for a military academy. Such caution was well-founded. Time after time, on issues involving the military, the party fractured. At the end when the issue clearly involved a permanent standing army in peacetime, the rank and file inside Congress and out,

*There exists no hard evidence that the Federalists in Congress or the Washington administration advanced a politically unacceptable plan of militia reform in order to force the establishment of a regular army. Federalist military thinkers wanted both; both fit their political plans for strengthening the national government. At the same time there existed a military danger: reform of the militia which would be ineffective militarily but which would ease pressure for a regular army, leaving the nation militarily weak. Thus from 1789 through 1792, the administration and Federalists in Congress who eventually voted against the 1792 act wanted the militia transformed into an effective military force, or no militia reform at all, so that a regular army would have to be established. To them, either eventuality gave the national government control over the nation's military forces and military power.

whether out of fear of public reaction or sincerely held belief, took its stand with Adams against militarism. "The army was the first decisive symptom of a schism in the Federal Party," remembered John Quincy Adams, "which accomplished its [the party's] final overthrow and that of the administration."[11]

And yet if the Jeffersonian interpretation is invalid in its entirety, and the Federalists as a group were not militarists, there nonetheless existed within the party a militaristic streak that ran from the party's roots all the way to the top of its leadership. Its benchmark, as Jeffersonians sensed, was support for the classical standing army. Militarism is an elusive concept today, difficult to define precisely even for historians using the model of Prussia and Germany.[12] Today militarism would be defined more as a system of thought, a combination of the belief in the positive virtues of war, violence, and the use of force, the advantages in the martial life, and the so-called "martial virtues," or mores, of extremist professional soldiers. But Americans in the eighteenth century, although they rarely if ever used the term, had no doubt as to what militarism meant. It was not necessarily an aggressive, opportunistic, militarily-based foreign policy as surfaced one hundred years later in the United States, although that, too, was included when in the end Federalist militarism revealed itself in 1798. Americans during and after the Revolution understood militarism as military control of government, as rule by a military clique or by a tyrant who gained power by force of arms and maintained his position by using force against the populace. Because of their political heritage, because they viewed a standing army as the one uncontrollable institution in society, because they believed it must inevitably undermine civilian authority, debauch the virtue of a population, and become the tool by which a tyrant would rise and hold power, Americans defined militarism and the standing army as one and the same. The existence of such a force inevitably destroyed liberty, producing a military dictatorship and leading to the imposition of military values and practices on society. Arbitrary government, observed one commentator in 1791, "is always supported by purchasing one part of the people, to overawe the other; or in other words, by keeping up standing armies to hold the people in captivity."[13] Furthermore, militarism included a propensity—even desire—to use force internally against the people as an instrument of policy. Americans debated and disagreed over the proper response to disorder, riot, and rebellion, the kind and amount of military force necessary to preserve order and the normal functioning of society. But some came to the conclusion that a permanent standing army was necessary in order to coerce the people, and silence them into obedience to authority. The great majority of Federalists categorically rejected standing armies in peacetime. There was a military element in Federalist social and philosophical thought, but it grew from the conjunction of the military and the aristocracy in eighteenth-century society, in a time of deference when the military was not "professional" in the sense of being a vocation or a constellation of beliefs distinct from those of ruling elites. (In England, for example, the military and naval officers corps stemmed directly out of the upper classes and nobility, many officers serving in Parliament while holding commissions or exercising commands.) If there was a single position on which Federalists could agree, beyond the shadings of opinion and disagreements over the peripheral questions which were invariably involved, it was support for the creation of a national military establishment distinguishable in size, shape, and function from the classical European standing army. For all his battles against Hamiltonian militarism and his support for a navy throughout his career, John Adams always encouraged McHenry and the War Department to improve the permanent military establishment, and Adams in early 1800, at the very time that the New Army was being demobilized, asked Congress to establish a permanent and comprehensive military academy.[14]

Federalists believed in the superiority of regulars over militia, that the central government in order to be supreme must possess the power of the sword, that in order to safeguard American security the government must rule and control in all matters of defense, and that the only sure way to protect the nation was to prepare for war in peacetime. They felt that the militia could protect the nation in wartime only if reformed and brought under national control. Federalists believed so strongly in national supremacy and in regulars that they were willing to destroy the militia as it existed rather than allow such unreliable forces to mislead Americans into believing that the United States was secure. "The danger we meant chiefly to provide against," remarked Gouverneur Morris in 1815, remembering the debates over the militia in the Constitutional Convention, "was, the hazarding of the national safety by a reliance on that expensive and inefficient force."[15]

Immediately after independence, Federalists no better than other Americans discerned the difference between a national, regular, professional army and the institution which was the scourge of European history. During the 1790s, many began to understand that an Indian-fighting constabulary or a small national establishment which included coast forts, a navy, and a military academy posed no political threat to American institutions. Steuben had first presented the essential distinction in 1784 in suggesting a small but completely national militia: "yes Fellow Citizens I admit it—it is a Standing Army, but composed of your brothers and your sons. Can you require or conceive a better security. Are they not your natural guardians?"[16] In 1790 Knox differentiated a frontier army from the classic standing army.[17] Four years later, Fisher Ames asked whether "any body of men to be raised in this country [could] tread down the substantial yeomanry? This is quite an Utopian dread."[18] In 1798 Robert Goodloe Harper called "A regular force and a standing army . . . quite different things," claiming the latter impossible because the two-year appropriation clause in the Constitution made any army subject to Congress.[19] Significantly, the Republican leadership, despite its use of the standing army accusation in partisan propaganda, had come by the end of the decade to recognize and to accept a frontier constabulary, a small national establishment, and reliance on regulars in wartime, as distinct from a classical standing army.* The distinguishing factor clearly was permanence and the internal threat to liberty posed by large, regular, permanent, peacetime forces.

Militarism lay buried deep in the Federalist party, surfacing only in moments of acute stress or crisis. And it was probably consistent only in the tiniest handful of individuals, if at all, before the late 1790s. When it finally burst forth full-blown during the Quasi-war to sweep, fracture, and finally drag the party down to defeat, it was limited to a faction led by Alexander Hamilton, which had become consumed with fears of conspiracy, of Republican complicity with France, and of the government's vulnerability to internal subversion masquerading as normal political activity. Unlike other Federalists who shared such fears, the Hamiltonians turned to the standing army as the solution, as the one institution capable of preserving American independence, deferential social and political forms, and in some cases their own personal power. Hamiltonians wanted the army precisely for the reasons most Americans rejected it: its ability to suppress dissent and intimidate the population. Especially in New England, Federalism appealed to an insecure elite unable to migrate, unable to transfer its wealth or influence to the new areas of the nation, an elite which rested on talent but experienced difficulty after the Revolution maintaining its traditional status or its ability to distinguish itself from the multitude in the seaboard centers of Federalist power.[20] To many of these Federalists, the army was timeless, ordered, hierarchical. In an army, what mattered was position—rank—not personality. The army represented tradition and stability in a world staggering through a wave of democratic revolution.

There is little proof that even these Federalists believed consistently in the classic standing army before 1798. Those who pressed for a national military establishment in the 1780s did so for understandable political and military reasons: the need to build up the Confederation, to open the West, and to avoid dependence on the militia. After Shays's Rebellion in 1786, knowing the frequency and revolutionary possibilities of mob action in the eighteenth century, the framers of the Constitution could hardly refrain from debating the ultimate source of governmental

*For an explanation of the Republican position, see below, pages 300–303.

authority, and some from concluding that government rested on coercion. To advocate regulars for the Indian war, preparedness in 1794 and 1798, and a larger army on the frontier between 1794 and 1797, was legitimate on military grounds alone. Only a tiny handful of men believed consistently throughout the two decades of the 1780s and 1790s that force was a positive instrument within society. Even for Alexander Hamilton, force was but one part in a larger political vision, not an end in itself.

And yet when militarism emerged in 1798, it did not spring forth out of a void, or entirely from the anxieties engendered by the politics of the 1790s. The men who stood with Hamilton at the end probably emerged from the Revolution without the fear of standing armies, many because as officers they saw armies firsthand, others perhaps because they discerned the weakness of the Confederation or sensed already a conflict between liberty and order. If they began with conventional views of the danger, they gradually in the 1780s grew less convinced, then ambivalent in the early 1790s, and finally in favor of standing armies by the Quasi-war. For most of them it was undoubtedly a strange, disconcerting odyssey; standing armies were always entangled with other, more pressing issues like preparedness or the Indian war. But the journey paralleled their progressively weakening confidence in the virtue of the people and the viability of republican government, until finally order and deference decisively outweighed traditional conceptions of civil liberty. A tiny handful of this group had toyed obliquely with militarism before, using the army to break the political deadlock in 1783, arguing tentatively for standing armies in 1787 and after, or seizing the first opportunity available to brandish military power internally at the population to enforce the laws.* Some may even have sought a standing army, as Republicans argued, under the guise of a frontier constabulary or "provisional" forces for preparedness. But when the crisis arrived against dreaded France, after five years of unremitting talk of conspiracy and assaults by the opposition, they embraced militarism completely: the standing army was in their minds the last anchor for Constitution and government, for their values, for patronage, for political intimidation, to neutralize an unreliable President, and to wage an offensive foreign war in order to affect internal politics, establish an American empire, and enhance their own personal power.

---

*It is virtually impossible to pinpoint belief in the standing army. Such a position was so politically damning that no one could commit himself in print. (Knox in 1791 wrote to a good friend that he opposed a standing army "unless I commanded it," then crossed out the latter phrase heavily. To Benjamin Lincoln, Jan. 31, 1790, Henry Knox Papers, MHS.) But evidently some Federalists talked guardedly of the need for a standing army internally. See Benjamin Hawkins to Washington, Feb. 10, 1792, Elizabeth G. McPherson, ed., "Unpublished Letters from North Carolinians to Washington," *North Carolina Historical Review*, XII (1935), 164.

Without question the leader of this group was Alexander Hamilton. Hamilton did not fear armies like others of his countrymen. He loved them, lusted for military command, and never spoke out against the standing army in peacetime unless such a statement became politically obligatory. Throughout his career he exploited armies or force for political gain, stimulating a mutiny and using the threat of a coup in 1783, eagerly using force in the early 1790s to enforce the law and build up the federal government, and finally using the army as a vehicle to advance his own power and dream of greatness. For all his talent, his brilliance, and his contributions to the birth of the nation, Alexander Hamilton was the personification of American militarism. Yet at the same time Hamilton created the American military establishment, as its chief spokesman in Congress in 1783 and its chief public defender during the struggle to ratify the Constitution in 1788. From 1792 to 1794, he helped put the War Department on a sound administrative footing. In 1799 and 1800, he presided over further reorganization, generating ideas on virtually every military subject while exercising operational control of the New Army in a most difficult period. No man save perhaps Henry Knox contributed more to the birth of a peacetime military establishment than Alexander Hamilton, and no one posed a greater danger to the nation's emerging military traditions.

Beyond their internal divisions and their folly over the military, the Federalists must be remembered as the creators of the military establishment that has survived until today. Above all else, the Federalists were nation builders. In a young republic devoid of national institutions, they created a binding union, a strong central government, and breathed life into that government through institutions and policies that gave it permanence and durability. In 1783 they put forth a complete outline of the military establishment necessary for national defense, an outline which attempted to overcome or circumvent the powerful local impulses which reappeared after the Revolution, the intense hatred of standing armies, and the propensity of Americans to equate security with geography and militia. Four years later they established a government capable of implementing their program, and then for 12 years afterward, they used every military crisis to build piecemeal the elements in their original plan of defense. Their success was astonishing. Twenty years after the winning of independence, even though the Jeffersonians had acceded to power, the United States possessed almost exactly the establishment nationalists advocated in 1783: a chain of forts along the northern and western frontier manned by an army of 2,500-odd officers and men; frigates, navy yards, and a marine corps; arsenals at Springfield, Massachusetts, and

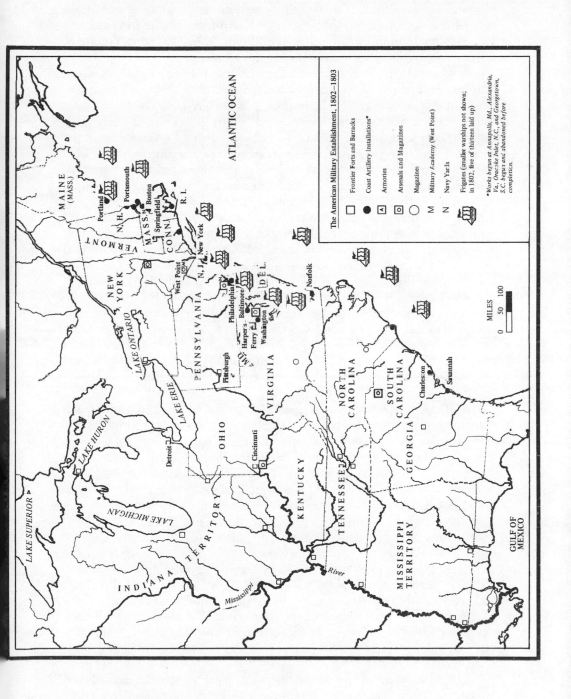

The American Military Establishment, 1802–1803

Frontier Forts and Barracks □
Coast Artillery Installations* ●
Armories ◁
Arsenals and Magazines ◉
Magazine M
Military Academy (West Point) N
Navy Yards
Frigates (smaller warships not shown; in 1802, five of thirteen laid up)

*Works begun at Annapolis, Md., Alexandria, Va., Oracoke Inlet, N.C., and Georgetown, S.C. begun and abandoned before completion.

ATLANTIC OCEAN

MAINE (MASS.)
N.H.
Portland
Portsmouth
Boston
Springfield
MASS.
CONN.
R.I.
VERMONT
NEW YORK
New York
West Point
N.J.
PENNSYLVANIA
DEL.
Philadelphia
Baltimore
Harper's Ferry
Washington
Norfolk
Pittsburgh
VIRGINIA
OHIO
Cincinnati
Detroit
NORTH CAROLINA
SOUTH CAROLINA
Charleston
Savannah
GEORGIA
KENTUCKY
TENNESSEE
INDIANA TERRITORY
MISSISSIPPI TERRITORY
Mississippi River
GULF OF MEXICO

LAKE SUPERIOR
LAKE MICHIGAN
LAKE HURON
LAKE ERIE
LAKE ONTARIO

MILES
0 50 100

Harpers Ferry, Virginia, as well as storehouses for supplies at various other locations; coast forts along the seaboard from Maine to Georgia; a newly-formed military academy at West Point, New York; and a group of agencies in Washington to administer the whole.[21]

Although Federalists provided the dynamic force and guiding vision behind the birth of a military establishment, they did not act alone. Without the *need* for such institutions, especially in a country so profoundly suspicious of regular armies, all their efforts would likely have failed. The nation did indeed face security problems. No longer could the former colonials depend on the British army, navy, or ministry, which for over a century had provided an umbrella of defense and taken responsibility for American security. At its birth, the United States was a large, rich nation with great military potential, but also, with its long coastline, seaborne commerce, vast frontier, and hostile European-held territory nearby, a nation immensely vulnerable to surprise attack and invasion. Poised to the north, in control of the Great Lakes and the most important forts in the Northwest, with access to the Lake Champlain-Hudson River corridor, lay the British. To the west lay the Spanish. Both possessed great influence on Indian tribes which held the key to the fur trade, to frontier security, and in fact to the ability of the new nation to occupy over half its newly-won territory. So pressing was the need for a constabulary—to awe the tribes, negotiate treaties, police the area, and safeguard the strategic waterways—that it was antinationalists who proposed and then voted for the first unit of troops around which the military establishment was eventually built.

If the frontier problem gave birth to the army, the Indian war transformed it into a functioning military establishment. Most institutions are defined by their goals, and Harmar's regiment in the 1780s was never capable of performing the missions for which it was created. Answering both to the Confederation and to the states, hamstrung by too few men, too little money, and mediocre leadership, the First Regiment could not halt the slow slide toward war along the Ohio or provide the policing necessary to open up the West. As an institution, it was truncated, imperfect, partially-formed, immature. Like so many nascent organizations, the army could not become fully institutionalized until it met the crucial test of organizational effectiveness: fulfilling its mission, which in the army's case in the 1780s meant deterring war, or failing that, victory in combat with the enemy. The imperfections and flaws were fully exposed only after disaster struck—an incident like Major Wyllys's summary execution of deserters (leading to reform of the Articles of War), Harmar's defeat, and finally the army's virtual annihilation under St. Clair in November 1791.

The magnitude of the defeat led to a nearly complete institutional transformation of the military establishment. First, it increased the size of

the army and opened up a huge inflow of resources (Congress appropriated $155,500 for the War Department in 1790; in 1793, the Department
spent $1,130,000).[23] Congress in 1792 committed the government to a
force of 5,000 regulars, voted the money to support them, and never
again in the decade prevented the army from performing its duties by
inadequate funding. In addition, the 1792 law upped the pay and benefits
(bounties, rations, and the like) for both officers and enlisted men in
order to make the service more attractive. More important still, defeat
provided new leadership and victory to give the army a sense of identity,
solidarity, and tradition on which to build a permanent future. Wayne's
was a new regime. The army was revamped tactically into a legion. The
general immediately began weeding out incompetent officers, and instilling pride and discipline into the ranks. In effect Wayne forced the army
to confront its organizational mission. During the first winter, he asked
Knox for flags and standards, promising, *"They shall not be lost."*[24] Where
St. Clair has used names or places for the daily challenge and password,
Wayne experimented with phrases that would improve army morale
("Soldierly—Appearance") and promote aggressiveness ("Always—
Ready").[25] The Legion stormed into the Maumee Valley in 1794 with
tremendous morale and fighting spirit, and when it returned, having
smashed the Indians and insulted a British garrison, the officers and men
had gained the pride, the confidence, and the legends with which to
relate spiritually to Washington's vaunted Continentals and to victorious
armies of ages past. Armies are built to some extent on pride and
tradition, to give the men the energy and courage to suffer through
fatigue and face death in battle. "Mad" Anthony erased the stain of
defeat, gave the army victory, and with his methods and personality, the
esteem to sustain it far into the future. Even his worst troubles added
solidity to the institution. The bitter battle with James Wilkinson split the
officer corps into warring camps, but it also tightened the sense of
community and identification in the core group that would see the army
through the lean years of peace ahead.

The most significant outcome of the Indian war, however, was the
enlargement and increasing complexity of the administrative apparatus.
Size required specialization of function, leading quickly to new offices in
the army and the War Department. Until 1791, the army lacked any
separate staff or logistical officers except for William North, who served as
adjutant and inspector until he resigned in 1787. Harmar used regimental
officers for these duties, and Knox hired men—Francis Mentges as
inspector, for example—on an *ad hoc* basis. But in 1790 Congress authorized two inspectors. The next year, St. Clair had a separate, specially
appointed Quartermaster General and an Adjutant General. In Wayne's
army, Quartermaster James O'Hara appointed deputies for the key posts
in the logistical network, and the 1792 Legion bill called for a separate

Paymaster. The real change, however, occurred in Philadelphia. Until 1791, the War Department consisted only of the Secretary, an assistant Secretary (to 1786) or chief clerk (after 1789), two or three clerks, and an office keeper-door keeper-messenger (until his death in 1792, a free black named Caesar Lloyd Cummings who had served in the office since the beginning of the Board of War in 1777). The Indian war clearly created burdens that the Department could not handle. From 1790 through 1795, the Secretary corresponded with county lieutenants and paid militia for service against the Indians. A larger army meant more and larger contracts, adding to the accounting tasks and the complexity of keeping track of public money. For years, in addition, the Department had supervised Revolutionary War claims and pensions and administered Indian affairs, first through superintendents for the Northern and Southern Departments, and then after 1789 through the territorial governors. Beginning in 1790, however, special negotiations with various tribes increased markedly; then in 1792, four Indian agents were appointed temporarily (but eventually permanently) to four groups of tribes—as always, more men who needed orders, supplies, answers to their letters and reports, and accounts serviced. Nor had the appointment of inspectors, a quartermaster, or an adjutant in the army eased the Department's ability to manage routine business and a campaign at the same time. After a long investigation of St. Clair's defeat, Congress authorized an accountant for the War Department, a paymaster for the army, and switched nearly the entire supply system to the Treasury. Adding to the increasing complexity of the bureaucracy, all accounts were to be checked by the Auditor and Comptroller in the Treasury. Yet even without responsibility for logistics, the department was growing. By 1793, the Secretary supervised six clerks, including Chief Clerk John Stagg, Accountant Joseph Howell with five clerks of his own, and a separate ordnance department with nine storekeepers maintaining stocks of supplies as far separated as Massachusetts and South Carolina.[26]

The process of bureaucratization accelerated dramatically in 1794, when a succession of new programs—for coast forts, corps of engineers and artillerists, new arsenals, ships for a navy—overloaded the War Department once again. Also that year, the government organized and supported a 15,000-man militia force to crush the Whiskey Rebellion. Each new system, especially the forts and ships, required the purchase of huge amounts of supplies in bewildering varieties, and the spending of gigantic sums of money. Each site for an arsenal had to be selected, the land purchased, the buildings designed and erected. Harbor forts or batteries required engineers for design, for supervision of construction, and each site needed a purchasing agent for materials. For the ships, naval agents, architects, and battalions of craftsmen and laborers had to be hired—more men, more orders, extra accounts. To deal with the flood of new paperwork and the decisions, Congress created the office of Superintendent of Military Stores to collect and distribute all the material bought (the War Department had been administering storehouses all over the country ever since the war). Internally, Knox organized the War Department into separate departments—quartermaster, hospital, and the like—in order to divide the flow of supplies by function and assure proper accounting, and the Treasury standardized forms for keeping track of various articles. In 1795, Hamilton succeeded in centralizing all government purchasing in a new office, the Purveyor of Public Supplies. The War Department in this instance lost authority, but the bureaucracy in the capital was growing, increasing in complexity, beginning to feed on itself, gaining system and permanence.[27]

The completion of the process occurred between 1796 and 1798 when Secretary James McHenry rationalized the different agencies and brought them under a system of impersonal regulations. At some point, probably in 1795, the military establishment as a whole contained enough of a hierarchical structure, enough separate offices with different functions, a sufficiently clear definition of the institution's mission and the interrelationships between each element in the bureaucracy, to enable the organization to take on an internal life of its own distinguishable from the actions of the Congress, the President, or the cabinet officer in charge. The major determinant was size. By that year, the Department supervised officers and installations all over the country: an arsenal in Springfield; a storehouse at West Point; an Indian agent at Canandaigua, New York; a frigate under construction in Norfolk; harbor batteries beginning in Charleston; forts in Ohio; purchasing agents, express riders, recruiting captains, clerks, contractors. The sheer size of the organization, the range of activity, and the complexity of vertical and horizontal interrelationships was beyond the direction of a single individual, causing a proliferation of offices and inevitably the decentralization of authority. (The logistical system by itself involved the Treasury [Purveyor, Auditor, Comptroller], War Department [Superintendent of Military Stores and storekeepers, Accountant], army [Quartermaster and deputies, regimental quartermasters], and civilians [contractors, purchasing agents].)[28] The flow of paper—invoices, inventories, musters, reports, warrants, accounts, not to speak of correspondence—was nearly uncontrollable. Because of size, complexity, distance, and the difficulty of communication, formal rules became a necessity to keep the institution functioning rationally and efficiently (and to keep track of public money), especially in a military establishment which included separate institutions like the army and a disparate collection of officials engaging in such varied activities.

A few months after taking office, McHenry began working out rules and regulations for every facet of army life, and to systemize the activities of the Indian agents and department of military stores.[29] The next year, McHenry won a classic bureaucratic struggle for power with Accountant William Simmons over the Accountant's office powers, establishing the Secretary as the dominant, and sole, fount of authority.[30] In total, of course, the whole military establishment was relatively modest even by eighteenth-century standards, nor was it run with the driving efficiency that the paperwork or the variety of activity implied. A French officer who had fought in the Revolution was appalled, visiting the War Department in 1796, to find no door keeper on duty at 11 in the morning, only two clerks working, and the Secretary absent at the barber getting a shave.[31] But as an institution, it was nearly complete. By 1801, the military establishment, scattered from New Hampshire to Georgia to the Mississippi and now shorn of its naval responsibilities, still maintained an administrative apparatus at the capital and in the field of over eighty civilian employees.[32]

What happened between 1790 and 1798 was a process known as institutionalization: the creation of a complex organization with an internal life of its own, with different offices layered on a hierarchical basis, each having a mission related to the goal of the institution, each with duties defined by law or by internal organizational rules, each interacting with the others, and each performing its duties on a day-to-day basis without specific orders or at the personal direction of the highest authorities. The growth of a national bureaucracy was a natural, almost inevitable process, one that flowed directly out of independence from Britain and then out of the decision in 1788 for a strong central government. Much of public policy, along with the bureaus to make that policy and implement it, had been forged in London. After 1783, the same problems—the economy, taxes, order, justice, foreign relations, defense—had to be decided on the western side of the Atlantic. In institutional terms, what took decades of development and evolution in London happened virtually overnight in Philadelphia. Most new nations undergo such a process when power is transferred from the center of empire to a former colony. In the United States, however, the old colonial administration had existed only at the provincial level; an American central government, the "native" bureaucracy, had to develop from nothing after independence. In the United States, the bureaucracy developed first out of the war, and then from the policies hammered out to deal with the country's problems. Decisions of policy invariably added duties to each executive department; for example, nearly every law relating to Indian-white relations between 1790 and 1802—and beyond—added authority and responsibility to the War Department.[33] Opponents of the military establishment (remembering like many knowledgeable Americans the imperial bureaucracy before the war) very clearly understood the forces at work, although their analysis had the process working in reverse.

"Whenever an office was established, something was found for it to do," complained one congressman in the debate over setting up a separate navy department. "Soon after the War Department was established, we had an Indian war; and after that . . . ceased, another establishment was made under the name of the Accountant's Office."[34]

The Indian war won and the process of rationalization nearly complete, the army settled down to a permanent future. As long as the nation needed troops or perceived a threat to American security, the military establishment would continue. The Quasi-war also led to reorganization, added solidity to the coast artillery system, and split off the navy from the War Department. Like all military institutions, the American establishment in future generations would experience cycles of growth and contraction, and remain vulnerable to political attack or to crippling from lack of money. But the Quasi-war had a very positive effect on the army's future, and in the end went far toward erasing the great ideological stumbling block to a national military establishment: the fear of standing armies. The Hamiltonian military program was militarism, as some Republicans recognized as early as 1794 when Sedgwick proposed the first Provisional Army; a small constabulary, exiled in frontier garrisons and carefully limited in size and function, was not an institution which posed any internal political threat. For many Republicans, Federalists, and for the American people, the New and Provisional Armies clearly and dramatically exposed the difference between a classical standing army and the frontier military establishment.

After the mid-1790s, the establishment was shaped more by technological change, by geography, and by the nature of the military threat, all constants in western armies and indeed factors which had molded the American army from its beginning. The size and location of the western posts, for example, had depended on the waterway systems in the West and British control of Lakes Erie, Ontario, and Forts Detroit, Niagara, and Oswego. The only penetration the United States could support logistically was along the Ohio River, then north and south from secure river forts to outflank the tribes in Ohio and the Southwest. Significantly, once the Miami and Wabash confederacy was broken and the British and Spanish ejected from American territory, the army shifted its western perimeter to a north-south axis running along the Mississippi, then turning east to skirt the Great Lakes. Likewise the creation of harbor forts was an act of military orthodoxy for the eighteenth century, directly the result of geography, ordnance, and naval technology.

The most important change in the peacetime army in the century after the Federalists left office, and the one element in their 1783 plans they failed to implement, was the establishment of a system of military education and the development of a professional officer corps. The officers who served under Harmar and his successors, with the possible exception of some who volunteered for the Indian war exclusively, did not see themselves as uniquely devoted to the service of the state or to a higher calling. Nor did they possess a special body of expertise which grew out of broad education or long experience.[35] There were no professional journals, associations, or schools for officers, no prescribed training to prepare individuals for life in the institution or recognized procedures for socialization once a man was admitted into the corps. Commissions at all levels, as in England, could be bought—not with money necessarily, but with political influence. Senator Ralph Izard sent his son, George, all over Europe for schooling that could groom him for high command in the peacetime army, then wangled a command for the young man at Fort Pinckney.[36] Very few of the officers were willing to commit themselves to a lifetime in the service. Many seemed to be adventurers seeking the main chance; money was always on their minds and most had no understanding of conflict of interest. Most of Harmar's group owned shares in the Ohio Company. John Armstrong, Jr., was an inveterate speculator and gambler in western lands, lotteries, and securities.[37] John Hamtramck also dabbled in land, and in 1799 while commandant at Detroit, Hamtramck formed a partnership for a whiskey business (whiskey was part of the ration, a major item in army contracts, and a constant source of trouble in controlling enlisted men).[38] James O'Hara spent four years as Quartermaster General of the army, then became on resignation a major civilian contractor for the next six.[39] Many officers were arrogant, and contemptuous of civilians. The line between civilian and military authority in officers' minds, certainly a prerequisite to professionalism, was never clearly drawn. At least twice, early in the 1790s in Cincinnati and again later after the army occupied Detroit, disputes between the military and civilian officials exploded and had to be settled at the capital.[40] How much fighting, how many petty disputes boiled beneath the surface or flared up locally around posts, recruiting parties, or whenever civilians and officers met, is impossible to tell. But judging by the hatred and jealousy on both sides, the mutual dependence, the efforts of the War Department to economize and prevent war and the desire of many frontiersmen to obtain army contracts, to exploit the soldiers, or to bilk the Indians—and given the type of men involved— the friction was certainly substantial. "There is in this State at this Time the whole of the 4th and 3 companies of the 3d. Reg[imen]t of the standing army, held more generally in Contempt by the Citizens than ever I saw any other Description of People at any other Time or place," reported William Blount from Knoxville in 1797, "and were they to extract one drip of Citizens' blood by Military authority as is said to have been the case at Detroit under the eye of the Commander in Chief it is highly probable it would produce a Sluce that would require what in governmental language would be called a Constitutional or Patriotic army to stop it."[41]

And yet there did develop over the two decades after the Revolution a sense of solidarity and community in the officer corps which was central to the birth of an enduring military establishment. Much of it developed at first in the 1780s out of the isolation, the comradeship at wilderness posts, and the shared hardships of defeat in 1790 and 1791. When nearly all of these men left the army in 1792 and 1793, either forced out by the new leadership, or bad health, or simple fatigue with army life, Wayne and others sensed it, and spoke of the "old officers" as a definable body.[42] For many of Wayne's officers, solidarity came additionally from the pride of victory, from the bitter internecine feud between the two generals, and from the struggle in the middle of the decade to retain a peacetime army of substance. In the winter of 1794–1795, the officers in Ohio had several formal meetings to petition the government for bounty lands, and Congress did indeed recognize the officer corps as a group owed peculiar consideration when it passed a law to compensate widows of those slain in service.[43]

Certainly the development of a corporate self-identity was natural in a uniformed group, penned up in small garrisons on the frontier, men in an institution known to the western world as special, even unique, and looked on by Americans with distaste and suspicion. But the sense of community was also critical in the institutionalization process. The development of a nucleus of men who would choose to make their career and bind their identity to the institution gave the army stability and continuity. Like the process of administrative bureaucratization, it would sustain the American military establishment through the many years of dull routine that lay ahead. And evidently the sense of membership in an unusual body went beyond the simple bond of friendship. After a stint back east, Major Jacob Kingsbury (in 1800 a veteran of over twenty years' service in the Revolution and in peacetime) longed to return to his regiment. As he told a fellow officer in strangely modern tones, "I have never Heard a Syllable of the Army News since I have been at home."[44] By the late 1790s, the corps in fact exhibited characteristics it would retain to the present day: worries over advancement and assignment, fear and disgust at the Congress especially when reductions or reorganizations were under consideration, and political maneuvers for high promotion.[45] In early 1801, former inspector (1783–1787) and adjutant (1798–1800) William North, a good soldier and solid Federalist, reminded John Hamtramck of the well-worn path to high command in the American army. First, cultivate "Gen. W[ilkinson]" who "it has been said, *entre nous*, was friendly to the Politics of the now reigning Party" and who is "very capable of acting generously by those to whom he is friendly." Then, of course, "be well with the Com[an]d[e]r in Ch[ie]f [the President]; his friendship or vanity frequently decides the lot of those who look for promotion." "[D]o your duty," North added, and "if I should [be] a friend of influence in the New Government, I will speak . . . of your services and merits." North was not sanguine, however. "I think, as . . . the party which have been bellowing and howling against the army, navy and all sorts of expense which the federalists thought necessary for our security, are now in power, there will be little hopes of your getting the rank and pay of a Brig." As for himself, North was glad to be "out of the great world, teach my four children to fear God and as far as possible to Do good to their rascally fellow creatures, cultivate my farm, and avoid the follies of my contemporaries as much as possible."[46]

In the final analysis, the struggle over the military establishment possessed a significance far greater than the militarism of one wing of the Federalist party, or even the formation of national institutions after the Revolution. Only one set of issues (and rarely the primary ones before Congress or the public), the debates over the military nonetheless lay at the very heart of American political life during this era. Like most every important problem facing the new nation—economic policy, foreign relations, the opening of the West, the relationship of the people to government—national defense was in a very real sense new to Americans, and not susceptible to resolution within the context of their political heritage or their experience as provincials in the British empire. Like most of the other issues, defense became submerged and entangled in the contest over the supremacy of national or state government. Like the others, it suffered distortion in the play of sectional self-interest and emerging partisanship. And like all the others, national defense came rapidly to represent a fundamental division within the post-revolutionary political leadership over the shape and future direction of the United States, not only as a society but also as an enduring national entity.

One of the most important results of the American Revolution, too often neglected by historians, was the stripping away of the central authority which for over a century had been the final arbiter of the most fundamental issues facing American society. By leaving the British empire, Americans were forced to confront problems with which they had dealt before only in the most peripheral manner. Nearly every major difficulty the new nation faced after 1783 flowed directly out of independence. Before 1775, Americans had never been allowed to determine for themselves the method of their defense, just as they could not control their economy, determine their relationship with foreign countries, oversee the opening of the West, develop their own tradition in law, or decide the nature of their own government. The heart of their political tradition was opposition politics, the radical Whig ideology in which the prejudice against standing armies and the identification of militia with virtue and liberty was so central. Undoubtedly radical Whig philosophy had appealed to Americans in part because of their powerlessness within the empire, because they were ruled chiefly by executive power over which they had limited influence. Independence changed all that. What had before been decided in Whitehall, in the drawing rooms of London, or in the well of Parliament now had to be determined on the western side of the Atlantic, and politics in America after the Revolution was for the most part a struggle to resolve dilemmas which had previously been beyond American control.

What made the resolution of the issues so difficult was that the opposition ideology, with its intense suspicion of power, its distrust of faction, and its assumption of conspiracy in the political process, was not easily adapted to the exercise of self-government. In this ideology, any powerful government by its very nature threatened liberty. American experience with such issues as defense, too, had been at the provincial level where options were usually circumscribed by Crown policy and where in American minds, local interests and needs tended to be paramount. Furthermore, before the Revolution, Americans possessed no usable heritage of national political life; their experience with intercolonial forums, often for the purpose of military cooperation, promised very little. Thus in a very real sense, the issues were new, the philosophy of government unsuited to strong policies, and the political process and arena in which to resolve national problems nearly nonexistent. Americans also knew, as events in the twenty years before 1775 so dramatically illustrated, that a central government which possessed the power of the purse and the power of the sword had the ability to touch the lives of its citizens very directly. Therefore one possibility after 1783, quite naturally, was to charge the states with such responsibilities as defense, an alternative which lay behind much of the early opposition to a national military establishment and which conceivably could have been adopted after the Revolution. The United States could have relied on militia to garrison western and seacoast forts, to overawe or fight the Indians, to guard state magazines and maintain state arsenals. Instead of a navy of capital ships, the United States could have substituted coastal gunboats, floating batteries commissioned and commanded by the states, or privateers. It was by no means certain, in 1783 or after, that the United States would establish any national institutions for defense.

And yet in the eighteenth-century world, the management of defense, of trade, of foreign policy and colonial affairs (the West in America), belonged to central governments. The power of the purse and of the sword defined government; allowing the states to decide such matters had enormous implications for the nation as a whole. To leave such powers in the hands of the states as they were constituted in the 1770s and 1780s would have meant added instability, a more democratic polity generally, a weak or nonexistent foreign policy in political and commercial terms, and a difficult, uncertain business environment since so much of American economic life—cities with economic hinterlands, commercial agriculture, waterborne trade of all sorts—cut across state boundaries. Total reliance on the states militarily would have made a coordinated Indian policy, frontier security, and preparation for war extremely difficult. With its own military forces, a state could defy the national will, leave itself vulnerable to foreign invasion or conquest, or become so powerful as to threaten its neighbors. The implications, clearly, were anarchy and dissolution of the union, perhaps even the overthrow of republican government or the loss of independence.

One of the first groups to conclude that the Confederation might not wholly avert these dangers were the conservative delegates who entered the Congress at the low point of the war. Even before the Articles were ratified, these spokesmen for the mercantile community and their allies began to advocate policies to assure the winning of independence and the strengthening of the union. By the end of the war, as the nationalist faction under Robert Morris's leadership, they had worked out the outlines of programs that in economic and military affairs at least were destined to become the fundamental testaments of the Federalist party.[47] Historians who have viewed politics before and after 1789 as separate have missed the essential unity in the period, a unity that came first from the issues and second from the existence of the nationalist group. For nearly twenty years after the Revolution, the nationalists provided the dynamic element in American politics, establishing a stronger central government and initiating the programs that became national policy. Until the early 1790s, party development was a process of the nationalists accumulating allies, building a coalition in the various states in favor of a strong government; then after 1789 in classic eighteenth-century fashion, organizing a party by means of "interest," by using executive patronage and advocating foreign and domestic policies which appealed to crucial social and economic groups. The dilemma for the nationalists, once in power and controlling the Federalist party, was that almost every significant program or action alienated important national leaders and eventually whole constituencies, setting in motion a chain reaction of defection to the residual Antifederalist groups, until finally, under Hamilton's sway, what was left of the old nationalist faction shattered the Federalist party in an effort to eradicate some of the very same forces which they had tried to circumvent twenty years earlier.

But beyond the kaleidoscope of shifting personal loyalties and factional alignments, the issues in national politics after the Revolution remained essentially the same. The debate over defense, despite the distortion of charges about standing armies and the other questions to which the army was always attached—ratification of the Constitution, the Indian war, and preparedness in 1794 and 1798—began with a nationalist plan in 1783 and continued for a decade and a half over whether to create a national military establishment. By the late 1780s, nationalist opponents responded with the ancient alternative of English standing army debates, the militia, and with it an alternative theory of national security. And yet this debate, at heart regulars versus militia, represented a much more fundamental division in the political life of the era. In formulating answers to the problems raised by independence, nationalists slowly drew together a broader picture of the kind of society that should develop in the United States. Their vision emerged haltingly, piecemeal, and it was never quite fully or explicitly articulated. But in outline, the nationalists and their Federalist successors advocated a traditional, deferential society, ordered, urban in orientation, cosmopolitan, and congenial to mercantile capitalism. Certainly the division over the military reflected such a view. The national military establishment proposed by nationalists implied diversity, division of labor, complexity, hierarchy, specialization, and professionalization in society—a stable nation which could protect its interests in the Atlantic world of trade and empire, and if necessary project military power offensively. Conversely, to champion the militia meant to support localism, a more isolationist and defensive foreign policy, a less diverse and more egalitarian society in which independent yeomen subsisting on their own labor relied on themselves and their local institutions for military defense.

It was almost inevitable that divisions of such profound importance would spawn parties, and that the party struggle would lead to the bitter, ideological strife that characterized politics in the 1790s. One monumental result of the Revolution was the transferrence of sovereignty, of ultimate control over government, to the people. Parties came into existence in part to educate the public and to mobilize public support for the leadership on the various questions which together would likely shape the nation's future. Durable parties did not appear earlier in part because of the novelty of the issues. Americans turned inward after the war, to local concerns, and after the nationalists left Congress in 1783 to consolidate support in the states for a new government, there were no burning national issues. Most important, there existed before 1789 no viable national forum in which lasting parties could develop. Rotation in office and frequent elections for the legislatures which sent delegates produced too much turbulence in Congress, and because of its structure and weak formal authority, Congress could rarely sponsor a policy capable of stimulating extended national debate. Significantly, however, in state after state during the 1780s, essentially local issues produced localist-cosmopolitan divisions very similar to what developed later in Philadelphia, and when an issue of great national import arose in Congress, as near the end of the war, factions materialized.[48]

The bitterness which came to dominate the party struggle after 1790 was also understandable, a natural outgrowth of the colonial political heritage. For a hundred years the issues of defense had been imbued with

deeper political and social meanings. Because so much of the nationalists'
and Federalists' program was tainted with old categories from English
politics, the opposition could legitimately suspect Federalists of a design
to replace republicanism with monarchy or aristocracy, just as advocacy
of policies that smacked of European currency finance or a political and
commercial connection to England could evoke the same fears. Conspiracy was assumed in the old radical Whig ideology and reinforced by the
perception of the British ministry before 1775 as engaged in a plot to
eradicate American freedom; power attacked and corrupted liberty, but
never openly, never avowedly. In a young nation where loyalties and
institutions were new, where the difference between political action and
conspiracy were not readily distinguishable, and in an age swept by
democratic revolution in which the forces of democracy battled monarchy, it was all too easy for each party in America to identify and
characterize the other as attached to the forces struggling in Europe,
especially after the United States became embroiled diplomatically and
each party adopted a posture which appeared to favor one side or the
other.

The tragedy was that in the mid-1790s, just when the hatred and
suspicion intensified and party lines hardened, a consensus of sorts began
to take form on the question of a national army. In rapid succession
starting in 1794 came the administration's Provisional Army scheme, the
massive use of force during the Whiskey crisis, and the renewal of the
regular army without the normal proviso limiting the use of troops to the
frontier. ("The debate brought out an avowal that the Executive ought to
be free to use the regular troops, as well as the Militia, in support of the
laws against our own Citizens," reported Madison worriedly.)[49] All
together, events finally convinced Republicans that the administration
and its supporters wanted an army for internal use. In response, the
Republican party initiated a strident, partisan, and in an unprecedented
way, unified attack on the Federalists for plans to introduce the classical
standing army.[50] But at the same time, the incidents which led to the new
Republican perception allowed many in the party to discern clearly for
the first time the difference between a frontier constabulary and its
militaristic cousin, and to accept the former as a necessary appendage of
the federal government. Federalist arguments about western defense had
always made sense militarily. As early as 1784, Arthur Lee, John Francis
Mercer, and even Elbridge Gerry had been willing to support a few
permanent posts, a small federal presence on the frontier. Most western
Republicans and a few in the party leadership had never really publicly
opposed regulars for fighting the Indians, nor had they ever disputed the
need for posts and regular garrisons. By 1795, with the failure of militia
reform, with Wayne's victory and the clear need to stabilize Indian
relations (especially given foreign colonies nearby), the urgency of posts
and troops in the West seemed incontrovertible. For the rest of the

decade, their attention riveted on the specter of a standing army, Republicans made no serious effort to abolish the frontier army, only to reduce its size and limit its function in order to hold down federal spending and assure that the constabulary could not be converted into the tool for Federalist tyranny.

Similarly, many Republicans through the mid-1790s began swinging over to the belief that some defensive preparations were necessary if war threatened. Despite the fear that armaments provoked war as much as deterring it, some in the party felt compelled, either by public opinion or by their own reading of the military possibilities, to accept seacoast forts and a corps of engineers and artillerists to build and man them. Unlike a navy, forts were entirely defensive and could be left dormant in peacetime, avoiding a permanent naval officer corps and relieving the government of the large appropriations to maintain ships and dockyards. And from the acceptance of a coast artillery and a frontier army, a system of arsenals and magazines flowed naturally. Even without the obvious need to support the permanent establishment, arms should be stockpiled for a war emergency and to allow the United States a source of munitions and supplies independent of foreign powers.

The most striking change in Republican thinking, however, came in the last half of the decade over the relative merits of regulars and militia. For public consumption, the party continued its attack on Federalist military doctrine. But well-informed Republicans understood the transformation in warfare taking place in Europe during the wars of the French Revolution. As the French in battle after battle decimated the armies of the *ancien régime*, it was becoming clear that the limited, linear warfare of the eighteenth century was dying. The astounding success of French armies using the new tactics—greater use of artillery, the switch to lighter infantry and greater dependence on skirmishers, attack in column and swift maneuvering in different formations—drove home not only the superiority of large masses of regulars, but the need for skilled and experienced officers at all levels of command.[51] "This country" should abandon any "idea of depending on Militia for prosecuting a war," admitted Henry Dearborn, Jefferson's future Secretary of War, in 1798. "[T]hey may be useful on sudden emergencies, but without better discipline than I ever expect to see . . . , it is hardly possible with almost any numbers, to oppose with success, a well appointed regular Army of only fifteen or twenty thousand men." The "moment when war with France is considered as inevitable," the United States must raise "at least one hundred Regiments." Dearborn concluded: "More is to be feared from the want of information and discipline in the officers of the Militia Generally, than from want of discipline in the privates."[52] Leading Republicans seemed to understand by the late 1790s that citizen-soldiers enlisted, trained, and led by the federal government were far superior to militia, and posed but a minor political threat in wartime. During periods of peace, however, such a force was neither necessary nor logical. Thomas Jefferson echoed Dearborn's sentiments. "I am for relying, for internal defence, on our militia solely," Jefferson told Elbridge Gerry in a long "profession of my political faith" early in 1799, "and not for a standing army in time of peace, which may overawe the public senti- ment." But Jefferson would entrust the nation's security to state forces only "till actual invasion," when, as he elaborated in his inaugural message two years later, "regulars may relieve them."[53]

Thus by 1800, in spite of the deeper social and political implications of regulars and militia, the disagreement over the birth of an American military establishment had all but ceased. Republicans continued to proclaim their faith in militia, and most no doubt believed it as strongly as ever, but in reality much of their rhetoric after 1795 was more political than military, partisans jousting with their fear of a Federalist plot to use legitimate military arguments and foreign crisis to militarize the nation. Based in the South, Republicans no doubt sincerely feared a standing army. Unlike in New England, where the fear of the standing army was political and doctrinaire, the South had suffered the ravages of the British army during the Revolution and had beaten that army in a savage struggle of terrorism and guerrilla action very akin to what today is called "people's war." Southerners could logically believe in the people as an effective military force. But the acceptance by the Republican leadership of the distinction between the classical standing army and a frontier constabulary assured the future of the military establishment. A change in political regime did not in 1800 promise the abolition of a national army on the frontiers. And except for an initial cutback in the size of the army, Jefferson's adminstration left the Federalist military edifice essen- tially untouched.

The final irony occurred within a year after Jefferson acceded to power. Federalists had always wanted a military academy because they believed that military leadership required education and expertise, and because officers in their minds would have to stay abreast of military science if the small peacetime army were to become the nucleus of larger wartime forces. Many of the Continental Army officers who advised Washington and Hamilton had recommended an academy in 1783, as had the general himself. Washington thought of recommending it to Congress in 1793 just as the neutrality crisis was heating up (Jefferson opposed it as unconstitutional), but feared the issue was too divisive and waited three more years to the eve of his retirement before proposing it formally.[54] In the meantime a training program had begun in the corps of artillerists and engineers, and in fact one of the chief impulses behind the effort for formal officer education was the need for technically competent people in those branches.* But the school never amounted to much even after strengthening in 1798 and efforts by the Adams adminis- tration to find instructors and begin a corps of cadets. What Federalists really desired was in Oliver Wolcott's words, a "University of Mars," which would include instruction in infantry, cavalry, and the navy as well as strictly technical areas of artillery and engineering.[55] John Adams agreed, but in the antimilitary atmosphere of spring 1800, Congress balked by a large margin.[56]

One of Jefferson's first acts in office was to order Secretary of War Dearborn to install a new inspector of fortifications at West Point and appoint a superintendent for a military academy. The new President's motives have never been convincingly explained. Perhaps he wished to found a national university which would avoid the traditional emphasis on classics and become the model for education in science, foreign languages, and other subjects of practical use. He may even have thought of it as a training ground for instructors to revitalize the militia. Certainly a school for engineers would free the country from dependence on foreign officers in critical military specialties, something that had bothered Adams tremendously during the Quasi-war, since most of the army's engineers were French by birth.† Yet Jefferson must surely have understood after a decade of debate the larger meaning of a military academy, that the Federalists desired it in part to make a military establishment self-perpetuating, that it could develop an elite officer corps for some future standing army, and that it would add to the permanence of the military by making the army a separate, self-sustaining group, possibly with an ethic all its own. In any event, in March 1802, Jefferson signed into law a bill which, while reducing and reforming the army, made the Corps of Engineers separate from the artillery and established a military academy.[57] Ironically, Thomas Jefferson completed the nationalist military program of 1783. The man who had risen to power on the ashes of a Federalist party consumed by militarism created the institution destined in the twentieth century to become the heart and soul of the very kind of military establishment so long feared by his party and his countrymen.

---

*The Duke de la Rochefoucault-Liancourt, in his *Travels Through the United States of North America* (London, 1799), II, 625, described the problem: "Those [coast artillery fortifications] which the Union erects and keeps up are few, and almost all incomplete. Good engineers being scarce, the Americans are obliged to employ such as they can get, who are generally foreigners who do not half understand their business, and who are generally more attentive to their own interest than that of the United States. Great plans are drawn; the works are begun at great expence; there is a want of money the following year; and the fortifications are either entirely relinquished, or reduced to so small a scale, that they are either good for nothing or at least defective, so that the money spent the preceding year may be said to be thrown away."

†The first Superintendent, Jonathan Williams, guessed that Jefferson's chief reason for beginning the Academy was the need for trained engineers in order to support the coast artillery system. But even Williams indicated that he was uncertain about the President's motives. See Williams's report, Dec. 14, 1802, Jonathan Williams Papers, United States Military Academy Library, West Point, N.Y.

Notes

Chapter 1

HEADNOTES

a. Jonathan Rawson, *Compendium of Military Duty . . . for the Militia of the United States* (Dover, N.H., 1793), vii.
b. To Joseph Warren, Jan. 7, 1776, *Warren–Adams Letters . . .* [Massachusetts Historical Society, *Collections*, LXXII-LXXIII] (Boston, 1917-1925), I, 197-198.
c. Boston Massacre Oration, Mar. 5, 1774, in Peter Edes, ed., *Orations . . . to Commemorate the [Boston Massacre] . . .* (Boston, 1785), 51.
d. To Gouverneur Morris, Feb. 21, 1783, Henry Knox Papers, MHS.

SOURCE NOTES

1. For a sample of American feeling about standing armies, see the *New York Journal and Weekly Register*, Nov. 15, 1787, Jan. 10, 17, 24, 28, 1788; *Pennsylvania Packet* (Philadelphia), Oct. 3, 1787; *Freeman's Journals* (Philadelphia), Oct. 24, Dec. 12, 1787, Jan. 16, 1788; Josiah Quincy, *Observations on . . . the Boston Port-Bill . . .* (Boston, 1774), 33-36; John Dickinson, *Letters from a Farmer in Pennsylvania . . .* (Philadelphia, 1768), 60-62; Edes, ed., *Massacre Orations, passim*.
2. The warfare system is covered by Walter Millis, *Arms and Men: A Study of American Military History* (New York, 1956), 12-18 and Theodore Ropp, *War in the Modern World* (rev. ed., New York, 1962), ch. 1. For the armies, see Walter L. Dorn, *Competition for Empire, 1740-1763* (New York, 1940), 81-83; Hans Speier, *Social Order and the Risks of War; Papers in Political Sociology* (New York, 1952), 234-259; and J. R. Western, "War on a New Scale: Professionalism in Armies, Navies, and Diplomacy," Alfred Cobban, *The Eighteenth Century: Europe in the Age of Enlightenment* (New York, 1969), 182-216. For tactics, see Peter Paret, *Yorck and the Era of Prussian*

Reform, 1807–1815 (Princeton, 1966), ch. 1; Liddell Hart, *The Ghost of Napoleon* (New Haven, n.d.), 15–69; J. F. C. Fuller, *British Light Infantry in the Eighteenth Century* (London, 1925), ch. 3–7; Robert S. Quimby, *The Background of Napoleonic Warfare: The Theory of Military Tactics in Eighteenth-Century France* (New York, 1957); David Syrett, "The Methodology of British Amphibious Operations during the Seven Years' and American Wars," *Mariners Mirror*, LVIII (1972), 269–280.

3. For the issue in English politics, see Lois G. Schwoerer, "*No Standing Armies!*": *The Antiarmy Ideology in Seventeenth-Century England* (Baltimore, 1974); J. R. Western, *The English Militia in the Eighteenth Century: The Story of a Political Issue, 1660–1802* (London and Toronto, 1965), 5–16, 27–29, 46–48, 77–84; J. G. A. Pocock, "Machiavelli, Harrington, and English Political Ideologies in the Eighteenth Century," *WMQ*, XXII (1965), 560–567; J. S. Omond, *Parliament and the Army, 1642–1904* (Cambridge, England, 1933), 4–14, 21–23, 26–37, 39–41; J. W. Fortescue, *A History of the British Army* (London, 1899–1930), I, 384–389, II, 15–26; Charles M. Clode, *The Military Forces of the Crown; Their Administration and Government* (London, 1867), I, 80–81, 85–86, 125, 127, 128, 499–501. For the standing army debates and literature, see John Trenchard, *An Argument Shewing, that a Standing Army is Inconsistent with a Free Government . . .* (London, 1697) and *A Short History of Standing Armies in England* (London, 1698); Lois Green Schwoerer, The Standing Army Controversy in England, 1697–1700 (unpub. Ph.D. thesis, Bryn Mawr College, 1956), particularly 13, 15, 19–22, 64–121, 134. More convenient is Schwoerer's "The Literature of the Standing Army Controversy, 1697–1699," *Huntington Library Quarterly*, XXVIII (1965), 187–212 and E. Arnold Miller, "Some Arguments Used by English Pamphleteers, 1697–1700, Concerning a Standing Army," *Journal of Modern History*, XVIII (1946), 306–313.

4. For Americans' use of history see H. Trevor Colbourn, *The Lamp of Experience: Whig History and the Intellectual Origins of the American Revolution* (Chapel Hill, 1965), especially 21, 23–24; Douglass G. Adair, "'Experience Must be Our Only Guide:' History, Democratic Theory and the United States Constitution," in Ray Allen Billington, ed., *The Reinterpretation of Early American History* (San Marino, Cal., 1966), 129–144. Radical Whig theory and its transmission to America is covered in Caroline Robbins, *The Eighteenth-Century Commonwealthman* (Cambridge, 1959); Bernard Bailyn, *Ideological Origins of the American Revolution* (Cambridge, 1967), especially 34–54, 112–116; Oscar and Mary Handlin, "James Burgh and American Revolutionary Theory," Massachusetts Historical Society, *Proceedings*, LXXIII (1961), 38–57; Caroline Robbins, "The Strenuous Whig, Thomas Hollis of Lincoln's Inn," *WMQ*, VII (1950), 406–453. Relevant passages of the writings are [John Trenchard and Thomas Gordon], *Cato's Letters* (London, 1724), III, 232–242, IV, 122–154; James Burgh, *Political Disquisitions . . .* (Philadelphia, 1775), II, 341 ff. See also Schwoerer, "*No Standing Armies!*", 195–197.

5. Quoted in David Richard Millar, The Militia, the Army and Independency in Colonial Massachusetts (unpub. Ph.D. thesis, Cornell Univ., 1967), 81.

See also T. H. Breen, "Might and Polity in Seventeenth-Century Massachusetts: A Reappraisal of the Puritan Militia," paper delivered at the American Historical Association Convention, Dec. 1970.

6. F. W. Hamilton, *The Origin and History of the First or Grenadier Guards* (London, 1874), I, 91, 99, 101, 148–150, 197–198, 279–281; Stephen Saunders Webb, Officers and Governors: The Role of the British Army in Imperial Politics and the Administration of the American Colonies, 1689–1722 (unpub. Ph.D. thesis, Univ. of Wisconsin, 1965), especially 43–48, 128; Stephen Saunders Webb, "'Brave Men and Servants to His Royal Highness': The Household of James Stuart in the Evolution of English Imperialism," *Perspectives in American History*, VIII (1974), 55–80.

7. Quoted in Richard Henry Marcus, The Militia of Colonial Connecticut, 1639–1775: An Institutional Study (unpub. Ph.D. thesis, Univ. of Colorado, 1965), 329. For the contact both before and during the Seven Years' War, see Douglas Edward Leach, "British Regular Forces and the Growth of Anglo-American Tensions before 1760," paper delivered at the American Historical Association Convention, Dec. 1970; Stanley McCrory Pargellis, *Lord Loudoun in North American* (New Haven, 1933), ch. 3–4, 7; Alan Rogers, *Empire and Liberty: American Resistance to British Authority, 1755–1763* (Berkeley, 1974), ch. IV–IX.

8. John Shy, *Toward Lexington: The Role of the British Army in the Coming of the American Revolution* (Princeton, 1965), 393–398.

9. *Ibid.*, 20–83, 140–231; Irving Mark, *Agrarian Conflicts in Colonial New York, 1711–1775* (New York, 1940), 131–163; Staughton Lynd, *Anti-Federalism in Dutchess County, New York: A Study of Democracy and Class Conflict in the Revolutionary Era* (Chicago, 1962), 37–54.

10. To Jedidiah Morse, Jan. 5, 1816, WJA, X, 202–203.

11. Orations by Joseph Warren (1772) and John Hancock (1774) in Edes, ed., *Massacre Orations*, 23, 77. Accounts of the massacre and its aftermath are Shy, *Toward Lexington*, 303–320, and Hiller B. Zobel, *The Boston Massacre* (New York, 1970). For the way in which the army was played up in the press, see Oliver M. Dickerson, ed., *Boston under Military Rule, 1768–1769, as revealed in a Journal of the Times* (Boston, 1936). The Boston incident was not an isolated instance of civil-military friction. See Lee R. Boyer, "Lobster Backs, Liberty Boys, and Laborers in the Streets: New York's Golden Hill and Nassau Street Riots," *New-York Historical Society Quarterly*, LVII (1973), 281–308.

12. "Antidespot," *No Standing Army in the British Colonies . . .* (New York, 1775), 5. For the impact of the army before the Revolution, see Bailyn, *Ideological Origins*, 112–117, 119; Shy, *Toward Lexington*, 379, 380–385, 397; Arthur A. Ekirch, *The Civilian and the Military* (New York, 1956), 7–13.

13. An excellent description of the colonial warfare system in its cultural setting is Daniel J. Boorstin, *The Americans: The Colonial Experience* (New York, 1958), 345–362.

14. For surveys of the militia system, see Louis Morton, "The Origins of American Military Policy," *Military Affairs*, XXI (1958), 75–82; Jack S. Radabaugh, "The Militia of Colonial Massachusetts," *ibid.*, XVIII (1954),

1-18; and dissertations cited below. For the operation of the system in the seventeenth century and the adaptation process, see Douglas E. Leach, "The Military System of Plymouth Colony," *New England Quarterly*, XXIV (1951), 342-364; Philip Alexander Bruce, *Institutional History of Virginia in the Seventeenth Century* (New York, 1910), II, 3-70; Breen, "Reappraisal of Puritan Militia"; Marcus, Militia of Connecticut, ch. 1; Millar, Militia, Army and Independency in Massachusetts, 7-18, 25; Frederick Stokes Aldridge, Organization and Administration of the Militia System of Colonial Virginia (unpub. Ph.D. thesis, American Univ., 1964), 30-40.

15. Shy, *Toward Lexington*, 6-14, 17-19; David William Cole, The Organization and Administration of the South Carolina Militia System, 1670-1703 (unpub. Ph.D. thesis, Univ. of South Carolina, 1950), iii-iv, 34, 59, 64-68, 140; Millar, Militia, Army and Independency in Massachusetts, 30, 48, 51; Marcus, Militia of Connecticut, 49-54, 66, 76-77, 234, 253, 257, 318-335, 368-369; Archibald Hanna, Jr., New England Military Institutions, 1693-1750 (unpub. Ph.D. thesis, Yale Univ., 1950), 18, 48, 53; Edwin P. Tanner, *The Province of New Jersey 1664-1738* (New York, 1908), ch. 25; Aldridge, Militia of Virginia, 130-132, 135-137, 220, 241, 244-246; Philip Karl Lundeberg, A History of the North Carolina Militia, 1784-1848 (unpub. M.A. thesis, Duke Univ., 1947), 18-19; Richard L. Morton, *Colonial Virginia* (Chapel Hill, 1960), II, 643, 679, 680-681, 709-710; H. J. Eckenrode, *The Revolution in Virginia* (Boston, 1916), 109-110.

16. To Peter Collinson, Dec. 19, 1756, quoted in Marcus, Militia of Connecticut, 326. For militia development along these lines see Morrison Sharp, "Leadership and Democracy in the Early New England System of Defense," *American Historical Review*, L (1945), 244-245; Jack P. Greene, *The Quest for Power: The Lower Houses of Assembly in the Southern Royal Colonies, 1684-1776* (Chapel Hill, 1963), 299; Cole, South Carolina Militia, 64-68, 140; Hanna, New England Military, 18, 57-95, 112-123, 303-304; Alden T. Vaughan, *New England Frontier: Puritans and Indians, 1620-1675* (Boston, 1965), 122-154; Douglas Edward Leach, *Flintlock and Tomahawk: New England in King Philip's War* (New York, 1958), 13, 45-46, 91-93, 103-104, 123-124, 182-187; John W. Shy, "A New Look at Colonial Militia," *WMQ*, XX (1963), 181-185; Jack Sheldon Radabaugh, The Military System of Colonial Massachusetts (unpub. Ph.D. thesis, Univ. of Southern California, 1965), 581; Millar, Militia, Army and Independency in Massachusetts, 154, 168-169, 176; Hugh Jameson, The Organization of the Militia of the Middle States During the War for Independence, 1775-1781 (unpub. Ph.D. thesis, Univ. of Michigan, 1936), 83-84.

17. See, for example, Millar, Militia, Army and Independency in Massachusetts, 142; E. Milton Wheeler, "Development and Organization of the North Carolina Militia," *North Carolina Historical Review*, XLI (1964), 307-323; Aldridge, Militia of Virginia, 115-122.

18. Diary, July 21, 1786, L. H. Butterfield, ed., *Diary and Autobiography of John Adams* (Cambridge, 1961), III, 195.

19. Trenchard, *Argument*, 22. See also *ibid.*, 18-25; [John Trenchard], A *Letter . . . to the Author of the Balancing Letter* (London, 1697), 8-11;

[Trenchard and Gordon], *Cato's Letters*, II, 106 ff.; James Lovell, Mar. 5, 1771, John Hancock, Mar. 5, 1774, and Thomas Welsh, Mar. 5, 1783, in Edes, *Massacre Orations*, 8, 51, 172; Western, *English Militia*, 5–8, 11–16, 46–48, 77–84, 89–103.

20. To the President of Congress, Dec. 20, 1776, WGW, VI, 403.

21. To Hamilton, Sept. 1, 1796, *ibid.*, XXXV, 199–200.

22. To William Knox, July 20, 1781, Francis S. Drake, *Life and Correspondence of Henry Knox* . . . (Boston, 1873), 66.

23. To Gouverneur Morris, Feb. 21, 1783, Knox Papers, MHS. Knox's wartime service is covered in North Callahan, *Henry Knox: General Washington's General* (New York and Toronto, 1958), ch. 2–12.

24. For Pickering's experience, see Octavius Pickering and Charles Upham, *The Life of Timothy Pickering* (Boston, 1863–1867), I, 69–405; Edward Hake Phillips, The Public Career of Timothy Pickering, Federalist, 1745–1802 (unpub. Ph.D. thesis, Harvard Univ., 1950), ch. I–II.

25. Aug. 11, 1782, Bernard C. Steiner, *The Life and Correspondence of James McHenry* . . . (Cleveland, 1907), 45.

26. To Tobias Lear, Jan. 2, 1800, *WAH*, X, 357.

27. To James Duane, Sept. 3, 1780, *PAH*, II, 401.

28. Hamilton to Duane, Sept. 3, 1780, *ibid.*, 407. For Hamilton's wartime career, see John C. Miller, *Alexander Hamilton: Portrait in Paradox* (New York, 1959), 17–79; Broadus Mitchell, *Alexander Hamilton: The Revolutionary Years* (New York, 1970).

29. Excellent discussions of Federalist ideology are David Hackett Fischer, *The Revolution of American Conservatism: The Federalist Party in the Era of Jeffersonian Democracy* (New York, 1965), ch. 1; James M. Banner, Jr., *To the Hartford Convention: The Federalists and the Origins of Party Politics in Massachusetts, 1789–1815* (New York, 1970), 22, 26–31, 53–83; Linda K. Kerber, *Federalists in Dissent: Imagery and Ideology in Jeffersonian America* (Ithaca and London, 1970), ch. 6.

30. William A. Benton, "Pennsylvania Revolutionary Officers and the Federal Constitution," *Pennsylvania History*, XXXI (1964), 419–435; Edwin G. Burrows, "Military Experience and the Origins of Federalism and Antifederalism," in Jacob Judd and Irwin H. Polishook, eds., *Aspects of Early New York Society and Politics* (Tarrytown, N.Y., 1974), 83–92; Jackson Turner Main, *Political Parties before the Constitution* (Chapel Hill, 1973), 363, 385–387. My own crude attempts to show such a correlation for Federalists and Republicans in the 1790s did not work, at least statistically. Slightly less than one-third of the Federalists in the Fourth, Fifth, and Sixth Congresses were veterans of the Continental Army officer corps, almost exactly the same percentage as the Jeffersonian representatives. For party identification, I used Manning J. Dauer, *The Adams Federalists* (Baltimore, 1953), 288–326, and Rudolph M. Bell, *Party and Faction in American Politics: The House of Representatives, 1789–1801* (Westport, Conn., 1973), 252–259. Military service can be found in Billie Bob Lightfoot, The State Delegations in Congress, 1789–1801 (unpub. Ph.D. thesis, Univ. of Texas, 1958), and Francis B. Heitman, *Historical Register of Officers of the Continental Army* . . . (rev. ed., Washington, 1914). Similarly, 35 percent of the

elite civil appointees during Adam's administration were officer veterans (see Sidney Aronson, *Status and Kinship in the Higher Civil Service . . .* [Cambridge, 1964], 205–207). Carl Prince kindly made available statistics on the civil service in the states during the 1790s. For the civil service as a whole, about 18 percent of the 2,000-odd appointees were officer veterans. The figure jumps to 31 percent if only higher civil appointees are counted, that is, men who were visible in their communities and possessed patronage power themselves (customs collectors, naval officers, surveyors of customs, inspectors of internal revenue, supervisors of internal revenue, commissioners of loans, naval agents, assistant storekeepers in the War Department, federal judges, federal attorneys, and federal marshalls). In spite of these low percentages, and the apparent lack of statistical difference between Federalists and Republicans, I still believe a correlation exists between service in the Continental Army and Federalism. The ideological link is clearcut; Washington's cabinet contained a very definite Continental Army tone; and significantly, a subjective list of Federalist leaders (Fischer's "Federalists of the old school," in *Revolution of American Conservatism*) showed 44 percent as officer veterans. A definitive answer must await a study of the later political affiliations of the whole Continental Army officer corps.

31. For the Cincinnati, see Callahan, *Henry Knox*, ch. 12; Wallace Evan Davies, *Patriotism on Parade: The Story of Veterans and Hereditary Organizations in America, 1783–1900* (Cambridge, 1955), 3–5, 12; Edgar Erskine Hume, "Early Opposition to the Cincinnati," *Americana*, XXX (1936), 597–638; Sidney Kaplan, "Veterans Officers and Politics in Massachusetts, 1783–1787," WMQ, IX (1952), 29–57. For an example of the link between half-pay and a standing army, see William Thayer to David Howell, Aug. 26, 1782, Brown Papers, John Carter Brown Library, Brown Univ., Providence, R.I.

Chapter 2

HEADNOTES

a. To Alexander Hamilton, Apr. 4, 1783, *PAH*, III, 315–316.

SOURCE NOTES

1. "John Montgars" [John Armstrong, Jr.] to Pickering, Jan. 20, 1820, Timothy Pickering Papers, MHS.
2. Armstrong used the pseudonym, he told Pickering, to avoid being "gazetted" as a writer of history, and to insure that Pickering's reply would not be prejudiced by knowing his correspondent. Armstrong to Pickering, Oct. 6, 1825, *ibid*. Although Edmund C. Burnett questions Armstrong's authorship of the addresses (*The Continental Congress* [New York, 1941], 567), most historians disagree. Armstrong himself admitted writing them. See

Armstrong to Horatio Gates, Apr. 29, 1783, *LMCC*, VII, 155n; Gates to Armstrong, June 22, 1783, in George Bancroft, *History of the Formation of the Constitution of the United States of America* (2d ed., New York, 1882), I, 318. See also Armstrong's long review of William Johnson's *Sketches of the Life and Correspondence of Nathanael Greene . . .* (Charleston, 1822) in the *United States Magazine*, new ser., I (1823), 1–44; John Armstrong, Jr., *Letters Addressed to the Army . . . in* 1783 (Kingston, N.Y., 1803).

3. Major accounts are Bancroft, *History of the Constitution*, I, 76–101; Louis Clinton Hatch, *The Administration of the American Revolutionary Army* (New York, 1904), 142–178; John Corbin, *Two Frontiers of Freedom* (New York, 1940), 50–68; Carl Ferdinand Johnson, The Army and Politics, 1783–1784 (unpub. M.A. thesis, Univ. of Wisconsin, 1949); Merrill Jensen, *The New Nation: A History of the United States During the Confederation, 1781–1789* (New York, 1950), 67–84; E. James Ferguson, *The Power of the Purse: A History of Public Finance, 1776–1790* (Chapel Hill, 1961), 155–168; Forrest McDonald, *E. Pluribus Unum: The Formation of the American Republic, 1776–1790* (Boston, 1965), 22–29; James Thomas Flexner, *George Washington* (Boston, 1965–1972), II, 467–508; Don Higginbotham, *The War of American Independence: Military Attitudes, Policies, and Practice, 1763–1789* (New York, 1971), 405–412.

4. As anything approaching a coup d'etat, however, the Newburgh conspiracy never got off the ground. A few days after the addresses were circulated, Washington faced down the officer corps in a tense meeting. Three months later the Revolutionary Army dissolved. Analyzing the affair as a coup, then, becomes an analysis of an event that never happened, using evidence that probably never existed, or was immediately destroyed because of its seditious implications. Yet if the events of the first months of 1783 did constitute an embryonic coup, a narrative—even one based on circumstantial evidence—can indicate the intentions of the leading participants.

5. Henry Knox *et al.*, "The address and petition of the officers of the Army of the United States," Dec. 1782, in *JCC*, XXIV, 291–293.

6. Jensen, *New Nation*, 33–36; *LMCC*, VI, 397–399, 405–408, 494, 514, 516, 518, 528. Rufus Putnam felt that if the committee was not given satisfaction by Massachusetts, the army should not be trusted with arms. Putnam to Samuel Adams, Oct. 18, 1782, Samuel Adams Papers, NYPL. See also Henry Ten Eyck to Henry Glen, Nov. 24, 1782, Henry Glen Papers, NYPL.

7. Knox to Lincoln, Nov. 25, 1782, Lincoln to Knox, Dec. 3, 20, 1782, Henry Knox Papers, MHS. See Knox's draft of the petition, *ibid.*, 171, 172.

8. Dec. 1782, William Henry Smith, ed., *The St. Clair Papers . . .* (Cincinnati, 1882), I, 575. The formal instructions from the army were much more moderate. See "Instructions from the Committee of the Army . . . ," Dec. 7, 1782, Alexander McDougall Papers, NYHS.

9. Ebenezer Huntington to Andrew Huntington, Dec. 9, 1782, G. W. F. Blanchfield, ed., *Letters Written by Ebenezer Huntington during the American Revolution* (New York, 1914), 102. For the background in the army, see Hatch, *Revolutionary Army*, 142–149; Johnson, Army in Politics, 6–13; Ferguson, *Power of the Purse*, 155–156; Sidney Kaplan, "Pay, Pension and Power: Economic Grievances of the Massachusetts Officers of the Revolu-

tion," *Boston Public Library Bulletin*, III (1951), 15–34, 127–142; Samuel Shaw to John Eliot, Apr. 1783, Josiah Quincy, *The Journals of Major Samuel Shaw* . . . (Boston, 1847), 101–102.

10. James Madison, "Notes on Debates," Dec. 24, 1782, *PJM*, V, 442. Interesting accounts of Rhode Island's action are Ferguson, *Power of the Purse*, 152–153 and McDonald, *E. Pluribus Unum*, 20–22.

11. Jonathan Arnold to the Governor of R.I., Jan. 8, 1783, *LMCC*, VII, 7.

12. To James Duane, Sept. 3, 1780, *PAH*, II, 404. Background on the nationalists and their financial program is in Jensen, *New Nation*, 54–67; Ferguson, *Power of the Purse*, 109–155; McDonald, *E. Pluribus Unum*, 1–6; Clarence L. Ver Steeg, *Robert Morris: Revolutionary Financier* (Philadelphia, 1954).

13. To Edmund Randolph, Dec. 30, 1782, *PJM*, V, 473.

14. To Washington, Apr. 8, 1783, *PAH*, III, 318–319.

15. To John Jay, Jan. 1, 1783, Jared Sparks, *The Life of Gouverneur Morris* . . . (Boston, 1832), I, 249. Hamilton said essentially the same thing, but with less optimism, to George Clinton, Jan. 12, 1783, *PAH*, III, 240.

16. Diary entry, Dec. 30, 1783, Robert Morris Papers, LC.

17. McDougall to Knox, Jan. 9, 1783, McDougall and Ogden to Knox, Feb. 8, 1783, *LMCC*, VII, 14n, 35n.

18. Jan. 9, 1783, *ibid.*, 14n.

19. The evidence against the three is circumstantial but damning. See the reasoning in Richard H. Kohn, "The Inside History of the Newburgh Conspiracy: America and the Coup d'Etat," *WMQ*, XXVII (1970), 193n.

20. See the note to his "Notes on Debates," Feb. 21, 1783, *PJM*, VI, 272. Madison's correspondence and notes (*PJM*, and the James Madison Papers, LC and NYPL) indicate that he had no inside knowledge of nationalist intrigue. He did, however, deduce the broad outline of events.

21. Madison, "Notes on Debates," Jan. 6, 7, 1783, *PJM*, VI, 16, 18.

22. Madison, "Notes on Debates," Jan. 9–10, 13, 1783, *ibid.*, 26, 31–34.

23. *Ibid.*; Madison and Joseph Jones to the Governor of Virginia, Jan. 14, 1783, Abner Nash to James Iredell, Jan. 18, 1783, *LMCC*, VII, 16, 19.

24. Diary entries, Jan. 15, 30, 31, 1783, Robert Morris Papers, LC, show Morris trying to torpedo Congress's attempts to put a valuation of lands taxing system into effect. For his action on foreign loans, see Madison, "Notes on Debates," Jan. 17, 1783, *PJM*, VI, 51. For an indication of his motives, see Hamilton to Washington, Apr. 8, 1783, *PAH*, III, 319.

25. To the President of Congress, Jan. 24, 1783, Francis Wharton, ed., *The Revolutionary Diplomatic Correspondence of the United States* (Washington, 1889), VI, 228–229. For the reaction in Congress, see Madison, "Notes on Debates," Jan. 24, 1783, *PJM*, VI, 120–121. An indication of Morris's strategy is in Hamilton to Washington, Apr. 8, 1783, *PAH*, III, 319.

26. *JCC*, XXIV, 94–95.

27. *Ibid.*, 93–95, 97–98; Madison, "Notes on Debates," Jan. 25, 27, 28, Feb. 4, 25, 1783, *PJM*, VI, 129–130, 134–137, 141–149, 187–188, 282–283; Rhode Island delegates to the Governor of R.I., Feb. 11, 1783, *LMCC*, VII, 29.

28. Jan. 29, 1783, *LMCC*, VII, 28.

29. "Notes on Debates," Jan. 28, 1783, *PJM*, VI, 143n.

30. Nationalist thinking can be gleaned from G. Morris to Knox, Feb. 7, 1783,

McDougall and Ogden to Knox, Feb. 8, 1783, *LMCC*, VII, 34n–36n; Hamilton to Washington, Feb. 13, Apr. 8, 1783, *PAH*, III, 253–255, 317–321; G. Morris to Greene, Feb. 15, 1783, Sparks, *Gouverneur Morris*, I, 250–251.

31. See, for example, R. Morris to Washington, Oct. 16, 1782, Robert Morris Collection, Henry E. Huntington Library, San Marino, Cal.; McDougall to Knox, Feb. 19, 1783, *LMCC*, VII, 50n.

32. Feb. 8, 1783, *LMCC*, VII, 35n–36n. This was sent to the different state units. See the entry for Feb. 15, 1783, in a long series of documents which appears to be an official record of army proceedings for redress, in the Knox Papers, LIII, MHS.

33. Feb. 7, 1783, *LMCC*, VII, 34n. Since the two letters are dated so closely, and because Morris's was so incriminating, it is likely that Brooks carried both.

34. "Brutus" to Knox, Feb. 12, 1783, Knox Papers, MHS. I am indebted to Dr. Mary-Jo Kline for identifying "Brutus." She pointed out that while McDougall partially masked his handwriting in the letter, he did not do so for the address. Compare the handwriting of the addresses in the two "Brutus" letters (*ibid.*, XI, 120, 165) with that of the McDougall letter of Feb. 19, 1783 (*ibid.*). Also, Knox never mentioned "our friend B—" except in two letters to McDougall (Mar. 3, 12, 1783, McDougall Papers, NYHS).

35. To Washington, Mar. 25, 1783, *PAH*, III, 306.

36. John Brooks's role and activities are the least understood of any individual's in the whole incident—and they are crucial. I have reconstructed it from obscure circumstantial evidence. His role in the meeting with the grand committee (above, p. 22) implies that he was working solidly with the nationalists. That he was entrusted with the first direct meeting between the people in Philadelphia and those at Newburgh implies this also. He arrived on February 13 (entry for Feb. 13, 1783, Newburgh records, Knox Papers, LIII, MHS), but he drops out of all surviving evidence until the March 15 meeting, when he was solidly behind Washington as Knox's helper in drawing up the resolutions reaffirming the army's loyalty to Congress. It is possible that Knox convinced him not to play the nationalists' game. Pickering suspected this (to Gates, May 28, 1783, Pickering Papers, MHS). It is also possible that Brooks tipped off Washington as Armstrong later told Gates (Apr. 29, 1783, *LMCC*, VII, 155n) and as Pickering agreed (to Gates, May 28, 1783, Pickering Papers, MHS). But it is likely that if he did, he was *instructed* to do so, since Hamilton himself tipped off Washington less than a week after Brooks left Philadelphia (below, p. 27). Certainly Brooks remained in the good graces of Washington and the nationalists judging by the offices he was offered in the 1790s (see Samuel Eliot Morison, "John Brooks," Allen Johnson and Dumas Malone, eds., *Dictionary of American Biography* [New York, 1928–1936], III, 80).

37. A good indication of nationalist thinking at this time is "Brutus" [McDougall] to Knox, Feb. 12, 1783, Knox Papers, MHS. Hamilton spelled out the general nationalist design in two letters to Washington, Mar. 25, 1783, Apr. 8, 1783, *PAH*, III, 305–306, 317–321.

38. An indication of this hotheadedness is Armstrong to Gates, Apr. 22, 29, May 9, 30, June 26, 1783, *LMCC*, VII, 150n, 155n, 160n, 175n, 199n.

39. Only three members of this group can be identified for certain: Armstrong, Christopher Richmond, and William Barber—all involved in the writing and circulation of the addresses (Gates to Armstrong, June 22, 1783, Bancroft, *History of the Constitution*, I, 318). Two other *very likely* suspects are William Eustis (see *ibid.*) and Pickering (see Pickering to Gates, May 28, 1783, Pickering Papers, MHS). Armstrong was 24, Eustis 29 years old. Richmond's and Barber's ages are unknown. Most officers who served as aides, secretaries, and staff assistants were under 30.

40. For the existence of a Gates group see the reasoning in Kohn, "Newburgh Conspiracy," *WMQ*, XXVII, 200n; Paul David Nelson, "Horatio Gates at Newburgh, 1783: A Misunderstood Role," with my rebuttal, *ibid.*, XXIX (1972), 143–158; C. Edward Skeen, "The Newburgh Conspiracy Reconsidered," with my rebuttal, *ibid.*, XXXI (1974), 273–298.

41. Duer told King that the conspirators approached Morris ("Notes on a conversation with William Duer," Oct. 12, 1788, *LCRK*, I, 621–622). January is a guess. It is unlikely the date would be in 1782, before Gates and the young officers knew if the army would petition Congress for redress, or the course the agitation in Newburgh would take. It was certainly before February 4, since Armstrong implied that Brooks could have been the agent to inform them of Morris's help (Armstrong to Gates, Apr. 29, 1783, *LMCC*, VII, 155n). I have found no evidence other than some routine letters that the nationalists and Gates people were in direct contact. The oblique reference to the financier and the army crisis in Gates's letter to Richard Peters (Feb. 20, 1783, Sol Feinstone Collection, American Philosophical Society, Philadelphia, Pa.) suggests strongly that no direct correspondence took place.

42. This is speculation. It figures, however, since Morris needed contacts in the army in January. And afterwards, Armstrong's story to Duer implied that the Gates group was encouraged by Morris.

43. Two years earlier, Hamilton considered Gates his "enemy personally" (to James Duane, Sept. 6, 1780, *PAH*, II, 420). See also Broadus Mitchell, *Alexander Hamilton* (New York, 1957–1962), I, 146–152; Jonathan Gregory Rossie, The Politics of Command: The Continental Congress and Its Generals (unpub. Ph.D. thesis, Univ. of Wisconsin, 1966), ch. VIII–XI, XIII–XIV; John C. Miller, *Triumph of Freedom, 1775–1783* (Boston, 1948), 253–261.

44. Elias Boudinot to Greene, Feb. 13, 1783, *LMCC*, VII, 42–43. See also diary entry, Feb. 13, 1783, Robert Morris Papers, LC. There had been rumors of a preliminary treaty for several days. See James Craig to Isaac Craig, Feb. 11, 1783, *Monthly Bulletin of the Carnegie Library of Pittsburgh*, XVI (1911), 196–197. Not everyone, however, thought peace was certain. An indication of the ambiguity is in Charles Pettit to Greene, Feb. 26, 1783, Nathanael Greene Papers, WLCL.

45. There is no direct evidence of a plan. My reconstruction is based on the timing of Hamilton's letter (see next paragraph), the fact that Washington was tipped off, and later events. Ogden told Armstrong later than the plan had gone awry because Brooks tipped off Washington (Armstrong to Gates, Apr. 29, 1783, *LMCC*, VII, 155n). Duer had the same information ("Notes on conversation," Oct. 12, 1788, *LCRK*, I, 622) in slightly garbled form. Given Hamilton's direct tip-off, I think Ogden's story about Brooks was a

nationalist fake, planted in order to cover themselves and explain to the Gates group why the scheme had not worked and why Washington was so obviously prepared.

46. Feb. 13, 1783, *PAH*, III, 253–255. In a postscript, Hamilton said: "General Knox has the confidence of the Army and is a man of sense. I think he may be safely made use of." Jensen (*New Nation*, 71) interprets this letter as sounding out Washington either to lead or join the mutiny and coup. I disagree, and interpret the letter as a simple tip-off of a possible explosion— Hamilton "coaching" Washington, as Ferguson (*Power of the Purse*, 159– 160) puts it. Certainly it was a tip-off; Knox knew what was happening, and the postscript was obviously insurance should Washington not get the point. Second, it is inconceivable to me that Hamilton or any nationalist could possibly think Washington, after his record since 1775, would countenance, much less join, direct military interference in politics. Hamilton knew him too well.

47. For Brooks's mission, see the reasoning in n. 36 and 45.

48. Entry for Feb. 13, 1783, Newburgh records, Knox Papers, LIII, MHS; Knox to McDougall, Mar. 3, 1783, McDougall Papers, NYHS.

49. Knox Papers, MHS.

50. Knox to G. Morris, Feb. 21, 1783, *ibid.*

51. Knox to McDougall, Feb. 21, 1783, *ibid.*, 148. There is circumstantial evidence that Knox wavered. Brooks arrived on February 13, but Knox did not write these letters until February 21. And on March 11, after the first address appeared, Washington wrote Knox immediately to come from West Point and help. But Knox claimed ice in the river prevented a quick trip (Knox to Washington, Mar. 11, 1783, *ibid.*). Knox may have been waiting to see which side to join.

52. My guess is that the letters arrived February 25. The trip from Newburgh to Philadelphia took three to six days, depending on the weather. Since the nationalists acted on February 26, the letters probably arrived on the 25th or 26th. The nationalists' lack of hesitation is indicated by the speed of McDougall's letter to Knox (Feb. 26) and Robert Morris's quick request to make his resignation public (see p. 28).

53. Madison, "Notes on Debates," Feb. 18–20, 1783, *PJM*, VI, 249–251, 258– 266.

54. Madison, "Notes on Debates," Feb. 25–28, 1783, *ibid.*, 282–283, 289–290, 297–299, 300–301; *JCC*, XXIV, 145–151, 154–156.

55. For the rumors, see Madison to Randolph, Feb. 13, 25, 1783, "Notes on Debates," Feb. 20, 1783, *PJM*, 232–233, 266, 286; Joseph Jones to Washington, Feb. 27, 1783, *LMCC*, VII, 61.

56. "Brutus" [McDougall] to Knox, Feb. 27, 1783, Knox Papers, MHS. This does not imply that the nationalists were still using Knox. McDougall may not have known of the decision to use Gates. Second, Knox was still a firm contact, and such an obviously fabricated rumor would have to be spread very secretly, under a pseudonym.

57. Madison, "Notes on Debates," Feb. 27, 1783, *PJM*, VI, 297; *JCC*, XXIV, 151. Morris's request (to the President of Congress, Feb. 26, 1783) is in Wharton, ed., *Revolutionary Diplomatic Correspondence*, VI, 266. The

original letter of resignation was published in the *Freeman's Journal* (Phila.), Mar. 5, 1783.

58. Gates called Stewart "a kind of agent from our friends in congress and in the administration" (Gates to Armstrong, June 22, 1783, Bancroft, *History of the Constitution*, I, 318). Armstrong remembered later than Stewart was very nationalist in his financial views (Armstrong to Jared Sparks, May 19, 1833, John Armstrong, Jr. Photostats, NYHS) and McDonald tabs Stewart (McDonald, *E. Pluribus Unum*, 27) as a holder of a large amount of public securities.

59. See Washington to Baron Steuben, Feb. 18, 1783, *WGW*, XXVI, 143.

60. See the map of the cantonment by Simeon DeWitt, 1783, NYHS.

61. King, "Notes on conversation," Oct. 12, 1788, *LCRK*, I, 622. See also Armstrong to Sparks, May 19, 1833, Armstrong Photostats, NYHS.

62. There is no record of Stewart's meeting with Gates. But judging by the rumors that began circulating (see next paragraph) and by what Armstrong told Duer (King, "Notes on conversation," Oct. 12, 1788, *LCRK*, I, 622), Stewart undoubtedly pledged Morris's help. The story of Brooks's treachery (see n. 45 above), accepted by Gates and Pickering (Pickering to Gates, May 28, 1783, Pickering Papers, MHS) suggests that the Gates group was unaware of the tip-off sent to Washington. Stewart definitely told the Gates group to act. See Gates to Armstrong, June 22, 1783, Bancroft, *History of the Constitution*, I, 318; Washington to Hamilton, Mar. 12, 1783, *PAH*, III, 286.

63. Washington to Hamilton, Mar. 12, 1783, *PAH*, III, 286.

64. Armstrong to Sparks, May 5, 1835, Armstrong Photostats, NYHS; Gates to Armstrong, June 22, 1783, Bancroft, *History of the Constitution*, I, 318; Armstrong, *Letters . . . to the Army*, 3, and 3n.

65. *JCC*, XXIV, 295–297.

66. To Hamilton, Mar. 12, 1783, *PAH*, III, 287.

67. To Hamilton, Mar. 4, 1783, *ibid.*, 278.

68. To Washington, Feb. 27, 1783, *LMCC*, VII, 61.

69. Washington to Hamilton, Mar. 4, 1783, *PAH*, III, 278.

70. *Ibid.*

71. General orders, Mar. 11, 1783, *WGW*, XXVI, 208.

72. This, evidently, was Washington's strategy. See Washington to Hamilton, Mar. 12, 1783, *PAH*, III, 287. Washington's other preparations are less clear. He called for Knox immediately, but the latter was delayed (Knox to Washington, Mar. 11, 1783, Knox Papers, MHS). Washington also published Congress's resolve of January 25 promising action on pay (general orders, Mar. 13, 1783, *WGW*, XXVI, 221–222). He also did a little personal persuading to win over important officers. See William Gordon, *The History of the . . . Establishment of the . . . United States . . .* (London, 1788), IV, 356; Charles Brooks, *History of the Town of Medford . . .* (Boston, 1855), 138.

73. The second address is also in *JCC*, XXIV, 298–299.

74. Benjamin Walker to Steuben, Jan. 23, 1783, F. W. A. Steuben Papers, NYHS. For descriptions of the building, see E. M. Ruttenber and L. H. Clark *et al.*, comps., *History of Orange County, New York . . .* (Philadel-

phia, 1881), 226; John J. Nutt, comp., *Newburgh: Her Institutions, Industries and Leading Citizens* . . . (Newburgh, 1891), 36–37. The building has been reconstructed outside New Windsor, N.Y.

75. The speech is in *JCC*, XXIV, 306–310.

76. Although some officers later denied a letter had been read, others remembered it. For the meeting and its impact, see James V. Armstrong to George Bancroft, Mar. 22, 1865, Edward Hand to William Irvine, Apr. 19, 1783, Bancroft Transcripts, NYPL; Pickering to Gates, May 28, 1783, David Cobb to Pickering, Nov. 9, 1825, Nicholas Fish to Pickering, Nov. 30, 1825, Pickering's notebooks [1827], Pickering Papers, MHS; Philip Schuyler to Stephen Van Rensselaer, Mar. 17, 1783, in Benson J. Lossing, *The Life and Times of Philip Schuyler* (New York, 1873), II, 427n; Bernardus Swartwout's journal, Mar. 15, 1783, Miscellaneous Papers, NYHS; Bancroft, *History of the Constitution*, I, 97–98. The best description of the scene is Samuel Shaw to John Eliot, Apr. 1783, Quincy, *Journals of Shaw*, 104.

77. *JCC*, XXIV, 310–311. I am convinced that the whole meeting was managed by Washington and his confidants. Knox's later career testifies to his fidelity to Washington. Putnam had drafted a speech deprecating the addresses (Knox Papers, XII, 22, MHS), perhaps as a draft for Washington, or to deliver himself at the meeting should it be necessary. Also, there is evidence that one of Washington's aides, David Humphreys, moved through the crowd during the general's speech (Pickering to Armstrong, July 15, 1825, Pickering Papers, MHS), perhaps gauging the speech's impact on the officers so that others—Knox, Putnam, Brooks—could take appropriate action.

78. Pickering to Samuel Hodgdon, Mar. 16, 1783, Pickering Papers, MHS. Pickering left doubts as to whether he objected openly. See Pickering to Gates, May 28, 1783, Pickering's notebooks [1827], *ibid*.; Pickering to his wife, Mar. 16, 18, 1783, Timothy Pickering Papers, EI. Gordon states that no one objected (Gordon, *History of U.S.*, IV, 357–358), while Duer claimed Pickering spoke (King, "Notes on conversation," Oct. 12, 1788, *LCRK*, I, 622). General Hand stated: "Some grumbling from Old Pa., but the vote nem. con." (to Irvine, Apr. 19, 1783, Bancroft Transcripts, NYPL). In any case, Pickering evidently did not side openly with the Gates group.

79. "Notes on Debates," Mar. 17, 1783, *PJM*, VI, 348.

80. *Ibid*.

81. *JCC*, XXIV, 176, 178–179; William Floyd to George Clinton, Mar. 12, 1783, McDougall to Knox, Mar. 15, 1783, *LMCC*, VII, 72, 72n. For Dyer's consistency on the question, see Larry R. Gerlach, "Connecticut and Commutation, 1778–1784," *Connecticut Historical Society Bulletin*, XXXIII (1968), 53–55.

82. Dyer to Governor Trumbull, Mar. 18, 1783, Jonathan Trumbull, Jr. Papers, CHS. Dyer's bravado belies the mood of the letter. John Adams characterized Dyer as "long winded and roundabout—obscure and cloudy. Very talkative and very tedious, yet an honest, worthy Man, means and judges well." Diary, Sept. 15, 1775, L. H. Butterfield *et al.*, eds., *Diary and Autobiography of John Adams* (Cambridge, 1961), II, 173.

83. To Trumbull, Apr. 12, 1783, Trumbull, Jr. Papers, CHS.

84. "Notes on Debates," Mar. 20, 1783, *PJM*, VI, 370. See also David Howell to

Nicholas Brown, July 30, 1783, Brown Papers, John Carter Brown Library, Brown Univ., Providence, R. I.

85. Madison, "Notes on Debates," Mar. 22, 1783, *PTJ*, VI, 375; *JCC*, XXIV, 202–203, 207–210.

86. *JCC*, XXIV, 188–192, 256–261; Stephen Higginson to Theophilus Parsons, Sr., Apr. [7], 1783, *LMCC*, VII, 123; Madison to Thomas Jefferson, Apr. 22, 1783, *PTJ*, VI, 262–263; Ferguson, *Power of the Purse*, 164–167.

87. Madison, "Notes on Debates," Mar. 22, 1783, *PJM*, VI, 375; *JCC*, XXIV, 210n.

88. To Lincoln, Mar. 16, 1783, Knox Papers, MHS.

89. To Lincoln, Mar. 19, 1783, in Frank Landon Humphreys, *Life and Times of David Humphreys* (New York, 1917), I, 270.

90. *Boston Gazette*, Apr. 21, 28, 1783; *Connecticut Courant* (Hartford), Apr. 15, 1783; *Connecticut Gazette* (New London), Apr. 25, 1783; *Freeman's Journal* (Philadelphia), Apr. 2, 1783; *Virginia Gazette* (Richmond), July 12, 19, 26, 1783; *Gazette of the State of Georgia* (Savannah), June 5, 12, 19, July 10, 1783.

91. Huntington to Andrew Huntington, Mar. 18, 1783, Connecticut Historical Society, *Collections*, XX (Hartford, 1923), 460. For a sampling of reactions to the event, see North Carolina delegates to the Governor of N.C., Mar. 24, 1783, Boudinot to the Marquis de Lafayette, Apr. 12, 1783, *LMCC*, VII, 100, 136; Jefferson to Washington, Apr. 16, 1784, *PTJ*, VII, 106–107; John Murray, *Jerubbaal, or Tyranny's Grave Destroyed . . .* (Newburyport, Mass., 1784), 44, "Brutus" [Robert Yates], *New York Journal and Weekly Register*, Jan. 24, 1788. Benjamin Gale was a particularly perceptive private citizen, but his sources of information are unknown. See the *Connecticut Courant* (Hartford), Sept. 2, Oct. 7, 1783; Phillip D. Jordan, Jr., "Connecticut Anti-Federalism on the Eve of the Constitutional Convention, A Letter from Benjamin Gale to Erastus Wolcott, February 10, 1787," *Conn. Hist. Soc. Bull.*, XXVIII (1963), 14–21; Gale's address to the Killingworth Town Meeting, Nov. 12, 1787, Benjamin Gale Papers, Yale Univ. Library, New Haven, Conn. Most of these suspicions came from antinationalists. And they came closest to the truth. See, for example, Mercy Warren, *History of the . . . American Revolution* (Boston, 1805), III, 271–272; Arthur Lee to St. George Tucker, July 21, 1783, Tucker-Coleman Papers, College of William and Mary Library, Williamsburg, Va.

92. Hamilton to Washington, Mar. 17, 25, Apr. 8, 1783, Washington to Hamilton, Mar. 12, 31, Apr. 4, 16, 1783, *PAH*, III, 290–293, 305–306, 317–321, 286–288, 309–311, 315–316, 329–330. Hamilton understood Washington's reputation and political future, and he wanted to stay in Washington's good graces. To deny the accusation of plotting would have been dangerous in the extreme since Hamilton had no idea how much information Washington had, or from what source. But Hamilton of course claimed that he and his friends had been working through Washington and had not been neglecting the army's interest. To admit otherwise, and especially to admit working with Gates, would have killed Hamilton forever in Washington's eyes.

93. See the *Address and Recommendations to the States by . . . Congress . . .* (Philadelphia, 1783), 83. This pamphlet was drawn up by a committee of

Hamilton, Madison, and Oliver Ellsworth to sell the impost, but Madison was the sole author. See *JCC*, XXIV, 277; Madison, "Notes on Debates," Apr. 26, 1783, *PJM*, VI, 498. In a circular letter to the state governors, Washington also used the army claims to buttress the impost request (June 8, 1783, WGW, XXVI, 488–489, 491–492).

94. For reactions to commutation, see John Chester to Ebenezer Huntington, Sept. 21, 1783, Worthington C. Ford, ed., *Correspondence and Journals of Samuel Blachley Webb* (New York, 1893–1894), III, 247; William Williams to the President of Congress, Nov. 1, 1783, Papers of the Continental Congress, item 66, RG 360, NA. Madison told Randolph (Sept. 8, 1783, *PJM*, VII, 308) that the agitation "has increased to such a degree as to produce almost a general anarchy." See also Jackson Turner Main, *The Antifederalists: Critics of the Constitution, 1781–1788* (Chapel Hill, 1961), 84–102, 106–109; William H. Glasson, *Federal Military Pensions in the United States* (New York, 1918), 43–49.

95. To Pickering, Sept. 6, 1823, Pickering Papers, MHS.

96. For the composition of the Continental Army, see John Sellers, "The Common Soldier of the Revolution," paper read at the Sixth Military History Symposium, October 1974, USAF Academy, Colorado Springs, Colo.; Edward C. Papenfuse and Gregory A. Stiverson, "General Smallwood's Recruits: The Peacetime Career of the Revolutionary War Private," WMQ, XXX (1973), 117–132; and especially Mark Edward Lender, The Enlisted Line: The Continental Soldiers of New Jersey (unpub. Ph.D. thesis, Rutgers University, 1975). For the conditions of military intervention, see Edward Shils, "The Military in the Political Development of the New States," John J. Johnson, ed., *The Role of the Military in Underdeveloped Countries* (Princeton, 1962), 7–67; Morris Janowitz, *The Military in the Political Development of New Nations: An Essay in Comparative Analysis* (Chicago, 1964); Samuel P. Huntington, *Political Order in Changing Societies* (New Haven and London, 1968), ch. 4; and especially S. E. Finer, *The Man on Horseback: The Role of the Military in Politics* (London, 1962); S. E. Finer, "The Man on Horseback—1974," *Armed Forces and Society*, I (1974), 5–27. I do not believe the United States possessed the same kind of internal problems or divisions that twentieth-century new nations have faced, despite some superficial similarities. See, for example, Paul Goodman, "The First American Party System" and Richard P. McCormick, "Political Development and the Second Party System," William Nisbet Chambers and Walter Dean Burnham, eds., *The American Party Systems: Stages of Political Development* (New York, 1967), 58–59, 62–63, 114–115. For a differing view, see Seymour Martin Lipset, *The First New Nation: The United States in Historical and Comparative Perspective* (New York, 1963), Part I.

97. England at this time probably conformed most closely to Janowitz's "aristocratic" model of civil-military relations. See his "Military Elites and the Study of War," *Journal of Conflict Resolution*, I (1957), 9–18. For examples of the interchange between the British Army and the government, see Stephen Saunders Webb, Soldiers and Governors: The Role of the British Army in Imperial Government and the Administration of the American Colonies, 1689–1722 (unpub. Ph.D. thesis, Univ. of Wisconsin, 1965).

Good discussions of civil-military relations are Samuel P. Huntington, *The Soldier and the State: The Theory and Politics of Civil-Military Relations* (Cambridge, 1957), especially ch. IV; Louis Smith, *American Democracy and Military Power: A Study of Civil Control of the Military Power in the United States* (Chicago, 1951), especially ch. I.

98. The categories are described excellently in Finer, *Man on Horseback*, ch. VII-XI. Also see Samuel P. Huntington, ed., *The Changing Patterns of Military Politics* [*International Yearbook of Political Behavior Research*, III] (Glencoe, Ill., 1962), especially the introduction and the essays by Harold Lasswell, David Rapoport, and Martha Derthick.

99. In their excellent novel, *Seven Days in May* (Bantam ed., New York, 1963), Fletcher Knebel and Charles W. Bailey II make this point explicitly. After blocking the attempted coup by General James M. Scott, President Jordan Lyman goes to elaborate lengths to cover up the affair. He explains away the resignations of the conspirators—even at the risk of further unpopularity—and rewards several characters to insure their silence. Lyman knew instinctively, the authors imply, that any knowledge that a coup had been attempted would make a future attempt possible simply because it had been tried previously. Also, it would destroy the trust between the American people and the military. See pp. 85, 140, 141, 301, 371-372.

100. To Washington, Apr. 16, 1784, *PTJ*, VII, 106-107. The letter generally concerns the problem of the Cincinnati.

Chapter 3

HEADNOTE

a. To Samuel Adams, May 20, 1783, *LMCC*, VII, 167.

SOURCE NOTES

1. To Washington, Mar. 25, 1783, *PAH*, III, 307. See also Robert Morris diary, Apr. 24, May 1, 3, 27, 1783, committee report, May 23, 1783, *ibid.*, 341n, 343n, 365n, 363-364; *JCC*, XXIV, 283-284, 359.

2. To Hamilton, Apr. 22, 1783, *PAH*, III, 336. See also the letters in *LMCC*, VII, 149-175.

3. See Knox to the President of Congress, Jan. 3, 1784, Papers of the Continental Congress, item 38, *RG* 360, NA. Several congressional committees considered demobilization. One, consisting of Hamilton, Bland, Peters, Samuel Osgood, and Oliver Wolcott, Sr. (later replaced by Thomas Fitzsimons), was appointed March 22 to consider Washington's letter of March 18 asking for a settlement of army accounts. It reported on April 1. Another, consisting of Hamilton, Peters, and Gorham was appointed April 4 "to consider means of reducing expenditures in the military department." It reported April 7. The same three men were appointed on May 9 as a committee "to consider and report the means of reducing expenditures in all other Departments as well as the military." It reported May 23. For these

and other actions on demobilization, see *PAH*, III, 308n, 313n, 317n, 356n; Madison, "Notes on Debates," May 20, 23, 1783, *PJM*, VII, 54, 66–67; letters in *LMCC*, VII, 149–175, 188, 189, 348; *JCC*, XXIV, 230, 265n, 269–270, 337–339, 358–361, 363–365, 390, 426, 496, XXV, 606, 703; conference with Sir Guy Carleton, May 6, 1783, Washington to Pickering, Nov. 3, 1783, to Charles Armand-Tuffin, Nov. 3, 1783, to Knox, Dec. 3, 4, 1783, to the President of Congress, Dec. 21, 1783, *WGW*, XXVI, 402–406, XXVII, 229, 256–258, 278–280; Merrill Jensen, *The New Nation: A History of the United States During the Confederation, 1781–1789* (New York, 1950), 77–82; E. James Ferguson, *The Power of the Purse: A History of American Public Finance, 1776–1790* (Chapel Hill, 1961), 168–171; Dixon Wector, *When Johnny Comes Marching Home* (Cambridge, 1944), part I.

4. To Elias Boudinot, July 9, 1788, L. H. Butterfield, ed., *Letters of Benjamin Rush* (Princeton, 1951), I, 473.

5. To Gouverneur Morris, Sept. 24, 1783, Henry P. Johnston, ed., *The Correspondence and Public Papers of John Jay* (New York, 1890–1893), III, 84. For the Pennsylvania and New York requests, see Madison, "Notes on Debates," Apr. 4, 1783, *PJM*, VI, 432–433, 434n; George Clinton to Hamilton and Floyd, Apr. 1, 1783, resolutions of the N.Y. Senate and Assembly, Mar. 27, 1783, Hamilton to Clinton, June 1, Oct. 3, 1783, *PAH*, III, 311–313, 372, 465–468; *JCC*, XXIV, 264n–265n; Clinton to Washington, Apr. 13, 1783; *Public Papers of George Clinton* (New York, 1899–1914), VIII, 136–137. For foreign policy assumptions in this era, see Felix Gilbert, *The Beginnings of American Foreign Policy: To the Farewell Address* (Harper ed., New York, 1965), especially ch. IV; the interesting (but overstated) Frederick W. Marks III, *Independence on Trial: Foreign Affairs and the Making of the Constitution* (Baton Rouge, 1973); R. W. Van Alstyne, *The Rising American Empire* (Oxford and New York, 1960), ch. I–IV; and Richard W. Van Alstyne, *Genesis of American Nationalism* (Waltham, Mass., 1970).

6. Madison, "Notes on Debates," Apr. 4, 1783, *PJM*, VI, 433.

7. Apr. 9, 1783, *PAH*, III, 322.

8. The following discussion is based on John Paterson to Washington, Apr. 16, 1783, George Washington Papers, LC; Jedidiah Huntington to Washington, Apr. 16, 1783, Jared Sparks, ed., *Correspondence of the American Revolution . . . Letters . . . to George Washington* (Boston, 1853), IV, 27–28; Knox to Washington, Apr. 17, 1783, Henry Knox Papers, MHS; William Heath to Washington, Apr. 17, 1783, *The Heath Papers* [Massachusetts Historical Society, *Collections*, 7th ser., IV–V] (Boston, 1904–1905), I, 386–388; Pickering to Washington, Apr. 22, 1783, Octavius Pickering and Charles Upham, *The Life of Timothy Pickering* (Boston, 1863–1867), IV, 431–443; Rufus Putnam to Washington, 1783, Rowena Buell, ed., *The Memoirs of Rufus Putnam . . .* (Boston, 1903), 198–215; Clinton to Washington, Apr. 1783, *Clinton Papers*, VIII, 144–147; Edward Hand, "On a Peace Establishment," 1783, Edward Hand Papers, Peter Force Transcripts, LC; Benjamin Lincoln, report to Congress, Mar. 3, 1783, to Hamilton *et al.*, May 1783, Papers of the Cont. Cong., item 38, *RG* 360, NA. For Steuben's ideas see his two reports dated 1783 in the F.W.A. Steuben Papers, NYHS; plan for a peace establishment enclosed in Steuben to Washington, Apr. 21, 1783, Washing-

ton Papers, LC; *A Letter on the Subject of an Established Militia, and Military Establishments . . .* (New York, 1784).

9. Sparks, ed., *Letters to Washington*, IV, 28.
10. Steuben Papers, NYHS.
11. *Ibid.*
12. Lincoln to Hamilton, May 1783, Papers of the Cont. Cong., item 38, *RG* 360, NA. See also Lincoln to Robert Morris, July 18, 1783, to the President of Congress, June 14, July 28, Aug. 8, 1783, *ibid.*, item 149.
13. *Clinton Papers*, VIII, 146–147.
14. Pickering and Upham, *Pickering*, IV, 432.
15. See John McAuley Palmer, *Washington, Lincoln, Wilson: Three War Statesmen* (Garden City, N.Y., 1930), 10–27, 55–71; Arthur A. Ekirch, Jr., *The Civilian and the Military* (New York, 1956), 20–21; C. Joseph Bernardo and Eugene H. Bacon, *American Military Policy: Its Development Since 1775* (2d ed., Harrisburg, 1961), 48–53; Walter Millis, *Arms and Men: A Study of American Military History* (New York, 1956), 42–46. Russell F. Weigley (*Towards an American Army: Military Thought from Washington to Marshall* [New York, 1962], 10–14) has revised this interpretation substantially.
16. To Washington, Apr. 8, 1783, *PAH*, III, 321.
17. "Sentiments . . . ," enclosed in Washington to Hamilton, May 2, 1783, *WGW*, XXVI, 375.
18. To Steuben, Mar. 15, 1784, *ibid.*, XXVII, 360.
19. *Ibid.*
20. The entire report is in *ibid.*, XXVI, 374–398.
21. Lincoln sent his report directly to the committee (Lincoln to Hamilton, May 1783, Papers of the Cont. Cong., item 38, *RG* 360, NA). Steuben's ideas were forwarded through congressman Richard Peters (Peters to Steuben, Apr. 23, May 6, 1783, *LMCC*, VII, 150, 156). In late May or early June the committee also received a report by Chief Engineer Louis Du Portail (*PAH*, III, 382, 390 and n). For Hamilton's other committee work, see *ibid.*, 344–378.
22. Hamilton's "Report on a Military Peace Establishment," May–June 1783, is in *PAH*, III, 378–397. For my dating of this document see note 26 below.
23. *Ibid.*, 379–382.
24. To Samuel Adams, May 20, 1783, *LMCC*, VII, 167.
25. To Edmund Randolph, June 17, 1783, *PJM*, VII, 159.
26. *JCC*, XXV, 774n and *PAH*, III, 378n–379n date the report's delivery as June 18. However an endorsement on a draft (Papers of the Cont. Cong., item 38, fol. 344, *RG* 360, NA) says it was read June 17. And Washington ("Observations on an Intended Report . . . ," Sept. 8, 1783, *WGW*, XXVII, 140) mentions the 17th as the date of reading.
27. To ———, May 1783, *LMCC*, VII, 156.
28. "Notes on Debates," June 21, 1783, *PJM*, VII, 177.
29. To Nathaniel Gorham, Aug. 5, 1783, *LMCC*, VII, 252. The richest sources for the mutiny are *JCC*, *LMCC*, the Papers of the Cont. Cong., item 38, *RG* 360, NA, and the Elias Boudinot Papers, HSP. See also Varnum L. Collins, *The Continental Congress at Princeton* (Princeton, 1908), ch. 1.
30. Washington to the President of Congress, July 16, 1783, *WGW*, XXVII, 70.

Also see Samuel Holten to John Hancock, Aug. 28, 1783, Autograph Collection, Independence National Historical Park, Philadelphia, Pa.; McHenry to Washington, July 31, 1783, *LMCC*, VII, 244–245; *JCC*, XXIV, 482.

31. To Lincoln, Aug. 17, 1783, Papers of the Cont. Cong., item 148, *RG* 360, NA. For other information see Schuyler to the President of Congress, July 29, 1783, Ephraim Douglas to Lincoln, Aug. 18, 1783, items 153, 149, *ibid.*; *JCC*, XXIV, 501n; "Instructions to Baron Steuben," July 12, 1783, *WGW*, XXVII, 482; Walter H. Mohr, *Federal Indian Relations, 1774–1788* (Philadelphia, 1933), 94–100. The importance of the British-held posts in American thinking can be seen in Hamilton, "The Defence No. VII," Aug. 12, 1795, *PAH*, XIX, 116–118.

32. Washington to James Duane, Sept. 7, 1783, "Observations on an Intended Report of a Committee of Congress on a Peace Establishment," Sept. 8, 1783, *WGW*, XXVII, 133–140, 140–144.

33. *JCC*, XXV, 548–551; Washington to Hamilton, Oct. 18, 1783, *PAH*, III, 470; Washington to Clinton, Sept. 11, 1783, to Knox, Oct. 23, 1783, *WGW*, XXVII, 147–148, 203; Samuel Shaw to Knox, Oct. 11, 1783, Knox Papers, MHS.

34. Steuben to Washington, Aug. 22, 1783, Steuben Papers, NYHS; Washington to Clinton, Aug. 29, 1783, *WGW*, XXVII, 120–121; Boudinot to the Commissioners at Paris, Oct. 27, 1783, *LMCC*, VII, 357.

35. To Thomas C. Hazard, Aug. 26, 1783, *LMCC*, VIII, 842. Madison admitted (to Jefferson, Sept. 20, 1783, *PJM*, VII, 353) that the proposal for a military establishment "is supported and quickened by the prescence of the Commander in Chief, but without any prospect of a hasty issue."

36. *JCC*, XXIV, 524–526.

37. *Ibid.*, 806–807.

38. To Thomas C. Hazard, Aug. 26, 1783, *LMCC*, VIII, 842.

39. Ellery and Howell to William Greene, Sept. 8, 1783, William Read Staples, *Rhode Island in the Continental Congress* (Providence, 1870), 445.

40. Dyer to Washington, Aug. 18, 1789, Washington Papers, LC. For the Massachusetts action, see Madison to Edmund Randolph, July 21, 1783, *PJM*, VII, 242; Samuel Adams to Gerry, Sept. 9, 1783, Samuel Adams Papers, NYPL; Samuel Holten to James Sullivan, Aug. 21, 1783, Autograph Collection, Independence National Hist. Park.

41. Nov. 23, 1783, Elbridge Gerry Papers, LC.

42. For background on congressional affairs generally and the nationalist movement, see Joseph L. Davis, Sections, Factions, and Political Centralism in the Confederation Period: 1774–1787 (unpub. Ph.D. thesis, Univ. of Wisconsin, 1972), ch. III–V, VIII.

Chapter 4

HEADNOTE

a. To James Monroe, Jan. 5, 1784, James C. Ballagh, ed., *The Letters of Richard Henry Lee* (New York, 1911–1914), II, 288.

SOURCE NOTES

1. To William Greene, Dec. 24, 1783, *LMCC*, VII, 398.
2. Samuel Osgood to John Adams, Jan. 14, 1784, *ibid.*, 415. For opinion that congressmen received, see Tristam Dalton to Gerry, Dec. 1, 1783, Elbridge Gerry Papers, LC; Edmund Pendleton to James Madison, Oct. 6, 1783, *PJM*, VII, 372; Richard Henry Lee to James Monroe, Ballagh, ed., *Letters of Richard Henry Lee*, II, 287–289.
3. Howell to Jonathan Arnold, Feb. 21, 1784, Gerry to Samuel Holten, Apr. 21, 1784, *LMCC*, VII, 451, 498.
4. Merrill Jensen, "The Creation of the National Domain, 1781–1784," *Mississippi Valley Historical Review*, XXVI (1939), 323–342; John Beatty to William Livingston, Feb. 25, 1784, William Livingston Papers, MHS; Hugh Williamson to Alexander Martin, Mar. 19, 1784, *LMCC*, VII, 475–476. For Howell's position, see his letters to Paul Allen and Nicholas Brown, July 30, Sept. 18, 1783, Brown Papers, John Carter Brown Library, Brown Univ., Providence, R.I.
5. To the President of Congress, Dec. 16, 1783, Papers of the Continental Congress, item 153, *RG* 360, NA.
6. Samuel Osgood to John Adams, Jan. 14, 1784, *LMCC*, VII, 415. See also the New York delegates to the Governor of N.Y., Oct. 16, 1783, Massachusetts delegates to the Mass. Assembly, Oct. 23, 1783, *ibid.*, 340, 349; Dalton to Gerry, Dec. 1, 1783, Gerry Papers, LC. For the pressure on the New York delegates see Clinton to Hamilton and William Floyd, with enclosure, Apr. 1, 1783, James Duane and Ezra L'Hommedieu to Hamilton and Floyd, Sept. 1, 1783, Hamilton to Duane, Sept. 26, 1783, Hamilton to Clinton, Oct. 3, 1783, *PAH*, III, 311–313, 135–136, 158, 161–169.
7. Jan. 30, 1784, Edward Hand Papers, LC.
8. For New York's action, see *Journal of the Senate of the State of New York*, 7th Assembly, 1st meeting, 1784 (New York, 1784), 6; *New York Journal* (extract), Jan. 28, 1784, Papers of the Cont. Cong., item 38, *RG* 360, NA; Clinton to Frederick Haldimand, Mar. 19, 1784, Haldimand to Clinton, May 10, 1784, Charles Thomson Papers, LC; Benjamin Walker to Steuben, Feb. 14, 1784, James Fairlie to Steuben, Mar. 23, 1784, F.W.A. Steuben Papers, NYHS; William Hull to [Henry?] Jackson, Mar. 25, 1784, Stauffer Collection, NYPL.
9. William Ellery to Jabez Bowen, Apr. 10. 1784, *LMCC*, VII, 489. Burnett in *ibid.*, lxxi, lxxii dates the arrival of Paine and DeWitt. The latter conferred with Clinton the day before leaving for Congress (DeWitt to Clinton, Mar. 9, 1784, Emmet Collection, NYPL). Howell's motion is in the *JCC*, XXVI, 163. I have reconstructed the motives of the four men on the basis of the timing of the motion and on their statements and actions during and after the floor fight on troops described below.
10. The report is in the *JCC*, XXVI, 201–207.
11. This and the following analysis are based on the roll-call votes in *ibid.*, XXVII, 428–437, 466–467, 487–488, 499–502, 512–524, 530–540; Paine to Clinton, Apr. 29, 1784, to Livingston, May 24, 1784, Massachusetts delegates to the Mass. Assembly, June 4, 1784, Williamson to Duane, June 8, 1784, Monroe to the Governor of Virginia, June 11, 1784, Williamson to the

Governor of North Carolina, Sept. 30, 1784, Gerry to the Mass. Assembly, Oct. 25, 1784, Thomas Stone to Monroe, Dec. 15, 1784, *LMCC*, VII, 504, 534, 542–543, 546–547, 551, 594, 604–605, 629; Monroe to Jefferson, May 14, 25, June 1, 1784, Gerry to Jefferson, Aug. 24, 1784, *PTJ*, VII, 252, 291, 300, 412–413.

12. To Robert R. Livingston, May 24, 1784, *LMCC*, VII, 535. See also the New York delegates to Clinton, Apr. 4, 1784, *ibid.*, 487; *JCC*, XXVI, 201.

13. To Livingston, May 24, 1784, *LMCC*, VII, 535.

14. *Ibid.*, 534.

15. *JCC*, XXVII, 428. Although the Howell-Monroe motion did not mention using Knox's regiment, I believe the small number of men proposed (the report called for 896) implied using the unit to occupy the British posts.

16. To Alexander Martin, Sept. 30, 1784, *LMCC*, VII, 594.

17. *Ibid.*, 594–595.

18. See the Hardy-Mercer motion, *JCC*, XXVII, 435–436; Monroe to Jefferson, June 1, 1784, *PTJ*, VII, 300; Massachusetts delegates to the Mass. Assembly, June 4, 1784, *LMCC*, VII, 542–543.

19. The final resolutions are in the *JCC*, XXVII, 524, 538–540, 551–553.

20. Williamson to Duane, June 8, 1784, Monroe to Benjamin Harrison, June 11, 1784, *LMCC*, VII, 546–547, 551–552.

21. To Monroe, Dec. 15, 1784, *ibid.*, 629.

22. Massachusetts delegates to the Mass. Assembly, June 4, 1784, *ibid.*, 543.

23. To the Mass. Assembly, Oct. 25, 1784, *ibid.*, 604–605. For the reaction to the delegates' June letter, see committee report, Mass. Legislature, July 9, 1784, Samuel Adams Papers, NYPL.

24. Committee of the House and Senate, Nov. 1, 1784, *Journal of the House of Representatives, Massachusetts* (Boston, 1784), 2d session, 174.

25. For the 1785 resolution and the thinking behind it, see the *JCC*, XXVIII, 28–29, 88–89, 223–224, 240–241, 247–248, 352–353, 390–391; Richard Dobbs Spaight to James Iredell, Mar. 10, 1785, King to Gerry, Apr. 11, 1785, Monroe to Madison, May 8, 1785, R. H. Lee to Madison, May 30, 1785, New Hampshire delegates to the Governor of N.H., May 29, 1785, Spaight to the Governor of North Carolina, June 5, 1785, R. H. Lee to Lafayette, June 11, 1785, Massachusetts delegates to the Governor of Mass., Aug. 23, 1785, *LMCC*, VIII, 64, 87, 115–116, 130, 132, 135–136, 138, 163, 197; Monroe to Jefferson, Apr. 12, 1785, *PTJ*, VIII, 77; Patrick Henry to the Virginia delegates, Apr. 16, 1785, to Joseph Martin, Apr. 16, 1785, William Wirt Henry, *Patrick Henry: Life, Correspondence, and Speeches* (New York, 1891), III, 292, 294–296; Mercer to Madison, Nov. 12, 1784, *PJM*, VIII, 134–135.

26. *JCC*, XXVII, 672, XXVIII, 5, 16–18, 21–24, 101–102, 129, 185, 195, 348, 369–370. My view of Knox differs from that presented by Harry M. Ward, *The Department of War, 1781–1795* (Pittsburgh, 1962), *passim*.

27. Matthew Griswold to Lt.-Governor Huntington, July 21, 1784, Emmet Collection, NYPL; Arthur Lee to Gerry, Aug. 8, 1784, Phillip and Elsie Sang Collection, Southern Illinois Univ. Library, Carbondale, Ill.; Clinton to Richard Butler and Arthur Lee, Aug. 13, 1784, Henry O'Reilly Papers, NYHS; Joseph Carleton to the President of Cong., Nov. 1, 1784, Papers of

the Cont. Cong., item 60, *RG* 360, NA; Carleton to Josiah Harmar, Dec. 17, 1784, Josiah Harmar Papers, WLCL.

28. John Dickinson to Morris, Aug. 19, 1784, Morris to Dickinson, Aug. 19, 1784, Consul Wright Butterfield, ed., *Journal of Capt. Jonathan Heart . . .* (Albany, 1885), 33–34. See also "Conference with Messrs. Lee and Butler," [July 23, 1784], *Pennsylvania Archives, First Series* (Philadelphia, 1852–1854), X, 295.

29. William Denny, ed., "Military Journal of Major Ebenezer Denny," *Memoirs of the Historical Society of Pennsylvania*, VII (1860), 258.

30. Dickinson to Harmar, Aug. 14, 1784, Butterfield, ed., *Journal of Heart*, 27–28. Within two weeks, Harmar enlisted 100 men (to Dickinson, Aug. 28, 1784, *ibid.*, 36–37).

31. John Robert Shaw, *A Narrative of the Life & Travels of John Robert Shaw . . .* (Lexington, Ky., 1807), 116.

32. *Ibid.*, 119–120.

33. *Ibid.*, 121–131; James O'Hara to Harmar, Feb. 15, 1785, Mary Carson Darlington, comp., *Fort Pitt and Letters from the Frontier* (Pittsburgh, 1892), 210–211; Harmar to Dickinson, Dec. 5, 1784, Jan. 15, 1785, Butterfield, ed., *Journal of Heart*, 48, 53; Hallock F. Raup, ed., "Journal of Griffith Evans . . . , 1784–1785," *Pennsylvania Magazine of History and Biography*, LXV (1941), 227–228; JCC, XXVIII, 334; Erkuries Beatty diary, Oct. 7, 1784—Aug. 10, 1785, NYHS; Journal of Arthur Lee, Dec. 28, 1784, in Neville B. Craig, *The Olden Time* (Pittsburgh, 1846–1848), II, 342–343. Harmar's return of deserters (Dec. 5, 1784, *Pa. Archives*, X, 388–389) showed 60 of his 260-man detachment gone.

34. Hamtramck to Nicholas Fish, Aug. 31, 1785, Nicholas Fish Papers (typescript), LC. See also Fish to Harmar, July 13, 1785, Doughty to Fish, July 14, 18, 1785, Hamtramck to Fish, Sept. 9, 1785, *ibid.*

35. To Fish, Dec. 4, 1785, *ibid.* See also Doughty to Fish, Oct. 4, 1785, *ibid.*; Butterfield, ed., *Journal of Heart*, 3, 14–15, 18–19. Money and supplies for the march were furnished by the agents of contractor William Duer. See Knox to Fish, July 22, Oct. 3, 1785, Fish to Doughty, July 25, Aug. 29, 1785, to Hamtramck, Oct. 5, 1785, Fish Papers, LC.

36. John Armstrong, report to Harmar, Apr. 12, 1785, Archer Butler Hulbert, ed., *Ohio in the Time of the Confederation* [Marietta College Historical Publications, III] (Marietta, 1918), 106–109; Harmar to Knox, Oct. 23, 1785, Doughty to [Harmar?], Nov. 30, 1785, Harmar to R. H. Lee, May 1, 1785, Armstrong to Harmar, May 13, 1785, Papers of the Cont. Cong., item 150, 163, *RG* 360, NA; Harmar to Knox, June 1, 1785, Butterfield, ed., *Journal of Heart*, 72–73 and n; Hamtramck to Fish, Dec. 4, 1785, Fish Papers, LC; William Butler to Thomas Barton and George Bush, Mar. 10, 1785, Darlington Memorial Library, Univ. of Pittsburgh, Pittsburgh, Pa.

37. Doughty to [Harmar?], Nov. 30, 1785, Papers of the Cont. Cong., item 150, *RG* 360, NA.

38. Report, Feb. 6, 1787, item 151, *ibid.* See also Knox to David Ramsay, Apr. 6, 1786, Knox to Harmar (extract), May 12, 1786, Knox to William Grayson, July 12, 1787, item 150, *ibid.*; Knox report, Apr. 20, 1787, JCC, XXXII, 222.

39. To John Beatty, Dec. 22, 1785, Joseph M. Beatty, Jr., ed., "Letters of the Four Beatty Brothers of the Continental Army, 1774–1794," *Pa. Mag. Hist. Biog.*, XLIV (1920), 258.

40. Hutchins to Congress, Oct. 12, 1786, Hulbert, ed., *Ohio in the Confederation*, 161–171; Hutchins to the President of Congress, Nov. 24, 1785, Mar. 16, July 8, Aug. 13, Sept. 13, Dec. 2, 1786, Papers of the Cont. Cong., item 60, RG 360, NA; William North————, Aug. 7, 1786, Northwest Territory Collection, Indiana Historical Society, Indianapolis, Ind.

41. To Knox, July 1, 1785, Harmar Papers, WLCL. For other reports and opinion, see Knox to Ramsay, Feb. 13, 1786, Butler to Knox, Dec. 13, 1786, Papers of the Cont. Cong., item 150, RG 360, NA; David Humphreys to Jefferson, June 5, 1786, *PTJ*, IX, 609; Samuel Holden Parsons to Jonathan Heart, Dec. 20, 1785, *Pennsylvania Journal* (Phila.), Oct. 22, 1785, Draper Collection, 11J40, 32J107, State Historical Society of Wisconsin, Madison, Wis.; Parsons to William S. Johnson, Oct. 27, 1785, Charles S. Hall, *Life and Letters of Samuel Holden Parsons* (Binghamton, N.Y., 1905), 474–475; J. Q. Adams to John Adams, Aug. 3, 1785, Worthington Chauncey Ford, ed., *Writings of John Quincy Adams* (New York, 1913–1917), I, 17–18; John Jay to Lafayette, July 15, 1785, Henry P. Johnston, ed., *The Correspondence and Public Papers of John Jay* (New York, 1890–1893), III, 160–161. British policy is covered in A. L. Burt, *The United States, Great Britain, and British North America from the Revolution to . . . the War of 1812* (New Haven, 1940), 82–101; Charles R. Ritcheson, *Aftermath of Revolution: British Policy Toward the United States, 1783–1795* (Dallas, Tex., 1969), 75–87, 151, 164–170, 384–385.

42. Knox to Harmar (extract), May 12, 1786, Doughty to Knox (extract), July 22, 1787, Knox to the President of Congress, Sept. 3, 1787, Knox report, Oct. 2, 1787, Papers of the Cont. Cong., item 150, 151, RG 360, NA; John Armstrong to Harmar, May 1786, John Armstrong Papers, Ind. Hist. Soc. For the activities of the Kentuckians, see James Alton James, *The Life of George Rogers Clark* (Chicago, 1928), 333–357; L. C. Helderman, "The Northwest Expedition of George Rogers Clark, 1786–1787," *Miss. Vall. Hist. Rev.*, XXV (1938), 317–334; Charles Gano Talbert, *Benjamin Logan: Kentucky Frontiersman* (Lexington, 1962), 202–213; George Rogers Clark to Major John Wyllys, June 25, 1786, Harmar Papers, WLCL.

43. Benjamin Lincoln to the President of Cong., June 11, 14, July 28, Aug. 8, 1783, Lincoln to Morris, July 18, 1783, Papers of the Cont. Cong., item 149, RG 360, NA; Morris to the President of Congress, July 28, 1783, Francis Wharton, ed., *The Revolutionary Diplomatic Correspondence of the United States* (Washington, 1889), VI, 612–613.

44. Report of rough budget, Mar. 31, 1785, *JCC*, XXVIII, 214–215; ration estimate, [May 21, 1785?], Papers of the Cont. Cong., item 150, RG 360, NA; memorandum of clothing contract, 1785, Paul P. Hoffman and John L. Molyneaux, eds., Lee Family Papers (microfilm ed., Charlottesville, 1966), reel 7, exposure 548. The total budget estimate for 1785 was approximately $3,000,000, but over 80 percent was earmarked for interest payments. Figures in the text have been rounded off. The clothing for one man was slightly less than nine pounds New York currency. I used the conversion figure of $2.50/pound computed by Forrest McDonald, *We the People:*

The Economic Origins of the Constitution (Chicago, 1958), 385.

45. To Reading Beatty, Dec. 12, 1786, Beatty, ed., "Letters," *Pa. Mag. Hist. Biog.*, XLIV, 258–259. See also Beatty diary, Apr. 28–29, 1785, NYHS; "Diary of Major Erkuries Beatty . . . ," Oct. 27, 1786–Jan. 27, 1787, *Magazine of American History*, I (1877), 380–381; Knox to the President of Congress, Aug. 1, 1786, Papers of the Cont. Cong., item 150, RG 360, NA; Beatty to Harmar, Sept. 27, 1789, Knox to Harmar, Oct. 29, 1789, Harmar Papers, WLCL.

46. Estimate of clothing deficiency, May 21, 1785, Knox to the President of Cong., July 26, 1786, Papers of the Cont. Cong., item 150, RG 360, NA; King to Gerry, Apr. 30, 1786, *LMCC*, VIII, 346; Journal of Joseph Buell, Jan. 1, Feb., July 8, Aug. 27, 1786, S. P. Hildreth, *Pioneer History . . .* (Cincinnati, 1848), 141, 142, 144–147; Journal of Richard Butler, Nov. 15, 1785, Craig, *Olden Time*, II, 481.

47. Board of Treasury to Knox, June 14, 1786, Papers of the Cont. Cong., item 150, RG 360, NA. See also Knox to the Board, June 9, 1786, to the President of Cong., June 15, 1786, *ibid.*; King to Gerry, June 18, 1786, *LMCC*, VIII, 393.

48. Knox to the Board of Treasury, Dec. 20, 1787, Lee Family Papers, r. 7, exp. 648. For his orders to Harmar, see Knox to Harmar, May 12, 1786 (extract), Jan. 22, 1787 (extract), Papers of the Cont. Cong., item 150, RG 360, NA. Knox stressed the usefulness of the army continually. See the *JCC*, XXX, 155–158, 257, XXXII, 328, XXXIV, 140, 362–366.

49. To Knox, June 14, 1788, "Denny journal," (appendix), *Mem. Hist. Soc. Pa.*, VII, 432–433. For these problems, see also the *JCC*, XXX, 225–227; Knox to Thomson, Aug. 18, 1785, Papers of the Cont. Cong., item 150, RG 360, NA; Hamtramck to Fish, Sept. 4, 1785, Fish Papers, LC; Knox to Benjamin Franklin, Feb. 16, Apr. 15, 1788, Harmar to Peter Muhlenberg, June 30, 1788, *Pa. Archives*, XI, 240–241, 268–269, 325–326. For examples of state authority over the force, see the minutes of the Supreme Executive Council, Oct. 20, 1785, Oct. 23, 1787, Jan. 10, Apr. 18, June 18, 1788, *Colonial Records of Pennsylvania* (Philadelphia, 1852–1853), XIV, 559, XV, 301, 367–368, 437, 475. Seven of the 17 infantry officers who survived from the Confederation army into Anthony Wayne's tenure as commanding general resigned in 1792 or 1793. One other ensign, commissioned in 1790, was cashiered in 1793. (See the list of officers in service, 1790, in Josiah Harmar's Orderly Book, Pennsylvania Historical and Museum Commission, Harrisburg, Pa. The artillery officers, probably more competent because of the technical skill required, tended to remain in service.)

50. Feb. 13, 1786, quoted in Knox's report, Mar. 21, 1786, *JCC*, XXX, 120.

51. *Ibid.*, 119–121, 136–137. See also Fish to Wyllys, May 21, 1786, Fish Papers, LC; John Taylor to Leonard Gansevoort, Mar. 29, 1786, Leonard Gansevoort Papers, Rutgers Univ. Library, New Brunswick, N.J.

52. *JCC*, XXX, 433–435.

53. *Ibid.*, 316–322. Knox had recommended revising the Articles of War months earlier. See his report, Sept. 27, 1785, Papers of the Cont. Cong., item 151, RG 360, NA. See also *Rules and Articles for the Better Government of the Troops . . . of the United States . . .* (Philadelphia, 1791).

54. In May 1786, Knox requested $600 from Congress for Harmar "to employ

Agents, to discover the Designs of the Indians from time to time, and to discover the conduct of the British Officers" in the lake forts. *JCC*, XXX, 257.

55. "A Citizen," *Maryland Journal* (Baltimore), Jan. 30, 1787, Draper Collection, 11J133–137, State Hist. Soc. Wis. See also Walter Finney to Robert Patterson, July 3, 1786, *ibid.*, 11J74; Harry Innes to John Brown, Dec. 7, 1787, Innes File, Kentucky Historical Society, Frankfurt, Ky.; John Cleves Symmes to the President of Congress, May 3, 1787, Harmar to Knox, July 23, 1788, Papers of the Cont. Cong., item 56, 163, *RG* 360, NA; G. R. Clark to John Brown, Aug. 20, 1789, *The Commonwealth* (Frankfort, Ky.), July 25, 1838. A good account of the social life and operations of the army in this period is James Ripley Jacobs, *The Beginning of the U.S. Army, 1783–1812* (Princeton, 1947), 16–39. For a positive interpretation of the army's usefulness and activity, see Alan S. Brown, "The Role of the Army in Western Settlement, Josiah Harmar's Command, 1785–1790," *Pa. Mag. Hist. Biog.*, XLIII (1969), 161–178.

56. See Thomas Rodney, report of debates, May 3, 1786, George Bancroft, *History of the Formation of the Constitution of the United States of America* (2d ed., New York, 1882), I, 500.

Chapter 5

HEADNOTE

a. *An Inquiry into the Principles and Policy of the Government of the United States* (repr. New Haven, 1950), 175.

SOURCE NOTES

1. For the rebellion, I have relied on Robert J. Taylor, *Western Massachusetts in the Revolution* (Providence, 1954), 103–167; Van Beck Hall, *Politics Without Parties: Massachusetts, 1780–1791* (Pittsburgh, 1972), ch. 4–7.

2. Oct. 23, 1786, Henry Knox Papers, MHS. For his letters to friends and reports to Congress, and the result, see Knox to Jeremiah Wadsworth, Oct. 3, 1786, to John Jay, Oct. 3, 1786, to Robert Morris, Nov. 17, 1786, *ibid.*; *JCC*, XXXI, 675–676, 681, 698–700, 739–740, 751–753, 875, 886–888, 891–893. The Confederation's role is described excellently in Joseph P. Warren, "The Confederation and the Shays Rebellion," *American Historical Review*, XI (1905), 42–67.

3. Nov. 5, 1786, WGW, XXIX, 50–52. "I fear we may live to see another revolution," wrote John Marshall (to James Wilkinson, Jan. 1, 1787, Reuben Durrett Collection, Univ. of Chicago Library, Chicago, Ill.).

4. To the Governor of Virginia, Dec. 8, 1786, *LMCC*, VIII, 517. Robert A. Feer ("Shay's Rebellion and the Constitution: A Study in Causation," *New England Quarterly*, XLII [1969], 388–410) argues that the impact of the rebellion was minimal, but his analysis relies heavily on an "if" question:

whether the convening of the convention and the writing and ratification of the Constitution would have been different if the rebellion had never happened. Certainly on the question of maintaining order, the rebellion had direct impact. See William M. Wiecek, *The Guarantee Clause of the U.S. Constitution* (Ithaca and London, 1972), 28-42. For the question of mob action and reaction to it, see Gordon Wood, *The Creation of the American Republic* (Chapel Hill, 1969), 319-328, Part IV; Pauline Maier, "Popular Uprisings and Civil Authority in Eighteenth-Century America," *WMQ*, XXVII (1970), 3-35.

5. McHenry's notes, May 29, 1787, in Max Farrand, ed., *The Records of the Federal Convention of 1787* (rev. ed., New Haven, 1937), I, 25. Unless otherwise noted, all speeches are from James Madison's notes.

6. Yates's notes, May 29, 1787, *ibid.*, 24. For Randolph's plan, see *ibid.*, I, 20-22, III, 593-594.

7. For Pinckney's plan, see *ibid.*, III, 595-609.

8. Yates's notes, June 15, 1787, *ibid.*, I, 246. See also McHenry before the Maryland House of Delegates, Nov. 29, 1787, *ibid.*, III, 145; Ellsworth, John Lansing, and William R. Davie in Jonathan Elliot, ed., *The Debates in the Several State Conventions, on the Adoption of the Federal Constitution . . .* (Washington, 1854), II, 185, 217, IV, 17.

9. "Observations . . . ," Paul Leicester Ford, ed., *Pamphlets on the Constitution . . .* (Brooklyn, 1888), 263.

10. To St. George Tucker (extract), Sept. 28, 1787, *Georgia Gazette* (Savannah), Mar. 20, 1788.

11. Yates's and King's notes, June 20, 1787, Farrand, ed., *Records*, I, 346, 339.

12. June 18, 1787, *ibid.*, 284. See also Madison on May 31, 1787, Madison to Washington, Oct. 18, 1787, *ibid.*, I, 54, III, 131-132; Madison to Jefferson, Oct. 24, 1787, *PTJ*, XII, 274.

13. Speech in the New York ratifying convention, June 20, 1788, *PAH*, V, 19-20. See also his Federalist 16, Jacob E. Cooke, ed., *The Federalist* (Middletown, Conn., 1961), 99-105; Ellsworth in Elliot, ed., *Debates*, II, 197.

14. Elliot, ed., *Debates*, IV, 260-261. Madison told the Virginia convention that "public force must be used when resistance to the laws required it, otherwise society would be destroyed." *Ibid.*, III, 384.

15. Report of the committee of detail, Aug. 6, 1787, Farrand, ed., *Records*, II, 182, 185, 188. Documents used and drawn up by the committee are in *ibid.*, II, 129-175, IV, 37-51.

16. Aug. 18, 1787, *ibid.*, II, 329.

17. To Moss Kent, Jan. 2, 1815, *ibid.*, III, 421.

18. Aug. 18, 1787, *ibid.*, II, 329.

19. *Ibid.*, 330.

20. See Pinckney's suggestions, Aug. 20, 1787, and debate on Sept. 5, 14, 1787, *ibid.*, II, 341, III, 508-509, 616-617.

21. Elliot, ed., *Debates*, III, 309.

22. Madison to Washington, Apr. 16, 1787, *Documentary History of the Constitution of the United States, 1787-1870* (Washington, 1894-1905), IV, 118. Knox's plan was published under the title *A Plan for the General Arrangement of the Militia of the United States* (New York, 1786), and is

described in John McAuley Palmer, *Washington, Lincoln, Wilson: Three War Statesmen* (Garden City, N.Y., 1930), 86–94.

23. Farrand, ed., *Records*, II, 326. For earlier suggestions about putting the militia under national control, see *ibid.*, I, 293, II. 136.
24. Aug. 18, 1787, *ibid.*, II, 330–331.
25. *Ibid.*, 331.
26. *Ibid.*, 332.
27. *Ibid.*, 331.
28. Convention Journal, Aug. 21, 1787, *ibid.*, 352.
29. Aug. 23, 1787, *ibid.*, 384–385.
30. *Ibid.*
31. *Ibid.*, 388.
32. *Ibid.*
33. *Ibid.*
34. See the Constitution: Preamble; Article I, Section VIII, paragraphs 11–17, Section X, paragraph 3; Article II, Section II, paragraph 1; Article IV, Section IV. The best interpretative study of the convention is Merrill Jensen, *The Making of the American Constitution* (Princeton, 1964). For a day-by-day description, see Charles Warren, *The Making of the Constitution* (Boston, 1928). An interpretation of the army power different from my own is Bernard Donahoe and Marshall Smelser, "The Congressional Power to Raise Armies: The Constitutional and Ratifying Conventions, 1787–1788," *Review of Politics*, XXXII (1971), 202–204. Also for war powers, see the statements (some of which I disagree with) by Henry Steele Commager, Richard B. Morris, Alfred H. Kelly, Alpheus T. Mason, Irving Brant, Arthur J. Goldberg, William H. Rehnquist, and Joseph H. Crown and Hoch Reid, in U.S. Senate, 92C 1S, Committee on Foreign Relations, *War Powers Legislation* (Washington, 1972), 18–19, 79–81, 85–86, 252–255, 638–639, 770, 797–799, 827–828, 835–837; and the excellent article by Charles A. Lofgren, "War-Making Under the Constitution: The Original Understanding," *Yale Law Journal*, LXXXI (1972), 672–702. For an interpretation of the Founding Fathers' intentions with which I am in near total disagreement, see Samuel P. Huntington, *The Soldier and the State: The Theory and Politics of Civil-Military Relations* (Cambridge, 1957), ch. VII.
35. "Solon," *Independent Chronicle* (Boston), Oct. 18, 1787; "Brutus" [Robert Yates], *New York Journal*, Oct. 18, 1787, Jan. 24, 1788; "Son of Liberty," "Cincinnatus," *ibid.*, Nov. 8, 15, 1787; "Centinel" [Samuel Bryan], *Freeman's Journal* (Phila.), Oct. 24, 1787; Dissent of the Minority, *Pennsylvania Packet* (Phila.), Dec. 18, 1787; Mercy Warren, "Observations," Ford, ed., *Pamphlets*, 10; John Dawson in Elliot, ed., *Debates*, III, 611; Joseph Varnum in *Debates and Proceedings in the Convention of . . . Massachusetts . . . which finally ratified the Constitution* (Boston, 1856), 238. Many newspaper pseudonyms are identified by Cecelia M. Kenyon, *The Antifederalists* (Indianapolis, 1966).
36. "Brutus," *N.Y. Journal*, Jan. 28, 1788. For other statements about Federalist motives on the army provision, see Jeremiah Hill to George Thatcher, Jan. 1, 1788, William F. Goodwin, ed., "The Thatcher Papers," *Historical Magazine*, new ser., VI (1869), 260; Richard Henry Lee, "Letters of a

Federal Farmer," Ford, ed., *Pamphlets*, 304; "Cincinnatus," "Centinel" [Bryan], "Brutus" [Yates], *N.Y. Journal*, Nov. 22, 1787, Jan. 7, 28, 1788, "Agrippa" [James Winthrop], *Massachusetts Gazette* (Boston), Dec. 11, 1787; "Philadelphiensis" [Benjamin Workman], *Freeman's Journal* (Phila.), Dec. 12, 26, 1787; Dissent of the Minority, *Pa. Packet* (Phila.), Dec. 18, 1787; Luther Martin, *Genuine Information* . . . (Philadelphia, 1788), 51.

37. "Brutus" [Yates], *N.Y. Journal*, Jan. 10, 17, 1788.

38. "Democratical Federalist," *Pa. Packet* (Phila.), Oct. 3, 1787; Varnum in *Mass. Debates*, 239. See also anonymous, *N.Y. Journal* (daily), Jan. 26, 1788; Thompson in *Mass. Debates*, 180; "Cincinnatus," "Brutus" [Yates], *N.Y. Journal*, Nov. 15, 1787, Jan. 10, 17, 1788.

39. See his address to the Killingworth, Conn., town meeting, Nov. 12, 1787, Benjamin Gale Papers, Yale Univ. Library, New Haven, Conn.; Philip D. Jordan, Jr., "Connecticut Anti-Federalism on the Eve of the Constitutional Convention, A Letter from Benjamin Gale to Erastus Wolcott, February 10, 1787," *Connecticut Historical Society Bulletin*, XXVIII (1963), 14–21.

40. Jefferson to Madison, Dec. 20, 1787, to Alexander Donald, Feb. 7, 1788, *PTJ*, XII, 440, 571.

41. Elliot, ed., *Debates*, III, 51.

42. See "Philadelphiensis" [Workman], *Freeman's Journal* (Phila.), Dec. 26, 1787, "Agrippa" [Winthrop], *Mass. Gazette* (Boston), Dec. 11, 1787; Lee, "Letters," Ford, ed., *Pamphlets*, 293.

43. "Philadelphiensis" [Workman], *Freeman's Journal* (Phila.), Dec. 12, 1787.

44. Elliot, ed., *Debates*, III, 59. For a lack of checks, see *ibid.*, 51–52, 56, 60, 496, 590; "Cincinnatus," *N.Y. Journal*, Nov. 22, 1787; Martin, *Genuine Information*, 87–90; Lee, "Letters," Ford, ed., *Pamphlets*, 305 and *An Additional Number of Letters from the Federal Farmer* . . . (repr. Chicago, 1962), 168–172.

45. "Democratic Federalist," *Pa. Packet* (Phila.), Oct. 3, 1787. See also Thompson in *Mass. Debates*, 180; Henry in Elliot, ed., *Debates*, III, 314, 388; Petition of Franklin County Freemen, John Bach McMaster and Frederick D. Stone, eds., *Pennsylvania and the Federal Constitution, 1787–1788* (Lancaster, 1888), 502; "Cincinnatus," *N.Y. Journal*, Nov. 22, 1787.

46. *Additional Number of Letters*, 169.

47. Elliot, ed., *Debates*, III, 385. See also Mason, Henry, Grayson in *ibid.*, 378–381, 412, 415–420, 422–424; Luther Martin in Maryland House of Delegates, Nov. 29, 1787, Farrand, ed., *Records*, III, 157; Martin, "Letters," Paul Leicester Ford, ed., *Essays on the Constitution* . . . (Brooklyn, 1892), 358–359; Martin, *Genuine Information*, 53–54.

48. To Jefferson, May 26, 1788, *PTJ*, XIII, 205.

49. Elliot, ed., *Debates*, III, 381.

50. *Ibid.*, 412. See also *ibid.*, 378–396, 402, 415–420, 422–428; Martin, "Letters," Ford. ed., *Essays*, 358–359; "Centinel" [Bryan], *N.Y. Journal* (daily), Jan. 14, 1788; Dissent of Minority, *Pa. Packet* (Phila.), Dec. 18, 1787. For general descriptions of Antifederalist thought, see Kenyon, *Antifederalists*, xxi–cxvi; Jackson Turner Main, *The Antifederalists: Critics of the Constitution, 1781–1788* (Chapel Hill, 1961), 119–186.

51. Hamilton and Madison in Cooke, ed., *Federalist*, 46, 271.

52. Hamilton, *ibid.*, 152; Roger Sherman, "Countryman," Ford, ed., *Essays*, 218; Hanson, "*Remarks . . . ,*" Ford, ed., *Pamphlets*, 234; "Cassius," *Mass. Gazette* (Boston), Dec. 14, 1787; "Citizens of America," *New Haven Gazette*, Nov. 29, 1787; "Citizen," *Pa. Gazette* (Phila.), Nov. 7, 1787; *Mass. Centinel* (Boston), Oct. 31, 1787.

53. Sept. 15, 1787, Farrand, ed., *Records*, II, 633. For Gerry's position, see also Martin, "Letters," *ibid.*, III, 259; Gerry to John Adams, Sept. 20, 1787, Elbridge Gerry Papers, LC.

54. To Knox, Oct. 15, 1787, WGW, XXIX, 289. See also to Humphreys, Oct. 10, 1787, to Bushrod Washington, Nov. 10, 1787, to David Stuart, Nov. 30, 1787, *ibid.*, 287, 310, 323.

55. "Giles Hickory," *American Magazine* (Jan. 1788), 76. See also Gore and Phillips in *Mass. Debates*, 166–167; Henry Lee, Marshall, and Iredell in Elliot, ed., *Debates*, III, 180, 227, IV, 96; *Conn. Courant* (Hartford), Dec. 3, 1787; *Ga. Gazette* (Savannah), Nov. 22, 1787; "Pro-Constitution," *Mass. Centinel* (Boston), Oct. 24, 1787; Hamilton in Cooke, ed., *Federalist*, 147–148.

56. Remarks, June 27, 1788, *PAH*, V, 96.

57. Madison in Cooke, ed., *Federalist*, 314; James Wilson in the Pennsylvania Convention, McMaster and Stone, eds., *Pennsylvania and the Constitution*, 409. See also Madison in Cooke, ed., *Federalists*, 247, 314; R. R. Livingston in Elliot, ed., *Debates*, II, 279, 386; John Jay, "Address," Ford, ed., *Pamphlets*, 72; "Pro-Constitution," *Mass. Centinel* (Boston), Oct. 24, 1787; anonymous, [Apr. 1788?], Julian Parks Boyd, ed., "A North Carolina Citizen on the Federal Constitution, 1788," *North Carolina Historical Review*, XVI (1939), 42.

58. Noah Webster, "Examination," Cox, "Examination," Hanson, "Remarks," Ford, ed., *Pamphlets*, 51, 150–151, 234–235; Sherman, "Countryman," Ford, ed., *Essays*, 222–223; "Giles Hickory," *American Magazine* (Jan. 1788), 76; "Impartial," *American Museum*, 2d ed., II (Oct. 1787), 377; Sedgwick, Dawes in *Mass. Debates*, 197–199; "The Republican," "Citizen of New Haven," *Conn. Courant* (Hartford), Jan. 7, 1788; "Candidus," *Providence Gazette*, Dec. 22, 1787; "Marcus" [Iredell], Griffith J. McRee, *Life and Correspondence of James Iredell* (New York, 1858), II, 209 ff.; Hamilton and Madison in Cooke, ed., *Federalist*, 45–48, 273–274, 320–322; Timothy Pickering to Charles Tillinghast, Dec. 24, 1787; Octavius Pickering and Charles Upham, *The Life of Timothy Pickering* (Boston, 1863–1867), II, 365–366; Nicholas, Randolph, Madison, Marshall in Elliot, ed., *Debates*, III, 13, 117–118, 143–246, 413, 419–421; Roger Sherman to———, Dec. 8, 1787, Roger Sherman Papers, Yale Univ. Lib.

59. Elliot, ed., *Debates*, III, 178.

60. For these arguments, see Corbin, Randolph, Madison, Nicholas, Henry Lee, Pendleton, Johnson in *ibid.*, 113, 206, 378–382, 389–390, 406–407, 413–415, 440–441, 645; Hamilton's speech, July 19, 1788, *PAH*, V, 180; Webster, "Examination," Ford, ed., *Pamphlets*, 52; anonymous [Apr. 1788?], Boyd, ed., "North Carolinian," *N.C. Hist. Rev.*, XVI, 50; Hamilton in Cooke, ed., *Federalist*, 181–187.

61. A convenient compilation is in Edward Dumbauld, *The Bill of Rights and What it Means Today* (Norman, Okla., 1957), 173–205.
62. To Moss Kent, Jan. 12, 1815, Farrand, ed., *Records*, III, 420–421.
63. A *Letter on the Subject of an Established Militia, and Military Establishments* . . . (New York, 1784), 16. Richard Peters called Steuben's proposal "Wonderfully adapted to our circumstance and would make us formidable without endangering our civil Liberties of which some Declaimers affect to be so much afraid." To Horatio Gates, Feb. 23, 1784, Emmet Collection, NYPL.

Chapter 6

HEADNOTES

a. John Heckewelder diary, Aug. 18, 1792, Paul A. W. Wallace, ed., *Thirty Thousand Miles with John Heckewelder* (Pittsburgh, 1958), 275.
b. To Arthur St. Clair, Sept. 14, 1790, William Henry Smith, ed., *The St. Clair Papers* . . . (Cincinnati, 1882), II, 181.
c. "[R]eport to the President . . . upon the operations to be adopted for the ensuing year upon the frontiers," Feb. 22, 1791, Northwest Territory Collection, Indiana Historical Society, Indianapolis, Ind.
d. "Errors of Government Towards the Indians," Feb. 1792, WGW, XXXI, 491.

SOURCE NOTES

1. An excellent account of Washington's inauguration is in Douglas Southall Freeman's *George Washington* (New York, 1948–1954), VI, 188–193.
2. Dec. 8, 1788, Arthur St. Clair Papers, Peter Force Transcripts, LC. St. Clair's career is covered in Smith, ed., *St. Clair Papers*, I.
3. It is extremely difficult to identify all the tribes and tribal fragments in the Indiana-Ohio region for this period, to pinpoint their towns and settlements (most hunted and camped over a wide area), and to estimate their numbers. Tribes moved and lived mixed together, population changed, and different observers of varying reliability recorded names, locations, and numbers at different times. My figures are my own estimates. To locate the tribes and to make the maps on pages 66 and 105, I used the following secondary sources: Alexander Scott Withers, *Chronicles of Border Warfare* . . . (Cincinnati, 1895), ed. Reuben Gold Thwaites, 393n; Frederick Webb Hodge, *Handbook of American Indians North of Mexico* [*Smithsonian Bureau of American Ethnology Bulletin* 30] (Washington, 1912), especially I, 155, 419, 771, 852–854, II, 174, 240, 289–293; H. C. Shetrone, "The Indians in Ohio With a Map of the Ohio Country," *Ohio Archeological and Historical Quarterly*, XXVII (1918), 274–428; Evarts B. Greene and Virginia D. Harrington, *American Population before the Federal Census of 1790* (New York, 1932), 201–202; Randolph Chandler Downes, *Frontier*

Ohio, 1788-1803 [Ohio Historical Collections, III] (Columbus, 1935), ch. I; Frank N. Wilcox, *Ohio Indian Trails* (3d ed., Cleveland, 1934); Otho Winger, "The Indians Who Opposed Harmar," *Ohio Arch. Hist. Quar.*, L (1941), 55–59; Charles G. Talbert, "Kentucky Invades Ohio—1786," *Register Kentucky Historical Society*, LIV (1956), 203–213; George I. Quimby, *Indian Life on the Upper Great Lakes, 11,000 B.C. to A.D. 1800* (Chicago, 1960), ch. 11–16; Jack Jule Gifford, The Northwest Indian War, 1784–1795 (unpub. Ph.D. thesis Univ. of California—Los Angeles, 1964), ch. I; Herman R. Friis, A *Series of Population Maps of the Colonies and the United States, 1625–1790* (rev. ed., New York, 1968); Bert Anson, *The Miami Indians* (Norman, Okla., 1970), ch. 3–4; Paul Woehrmann, *At the Headwaters of the Maumee: A History of the Forts of Fort Wayne* (Indianapolis, 1971), ch. I-II; John D. Barnhart & Dorothy L. Riker, *Indiana to 1816: The Colonial Period* (Indianapolis, 1971), 65–67, 95–96, 139, 156–157, 172, 179, 285; R. David Edmunds, "Wea Participation in the Northwest Indian Wars, 1790–1795," *Filson Club History Quarterly*, XLVI (1972), 241–253; Barbara Graymont, *The Iroquois in the American Revolution* (Syracuse, 1972). Most helpful for locating the Indian towns are the following expert testimony reports filed with the Indian Claims Commission, most apparently done in the 1960s, but all listed here published in 1973 by Clearwater Publishing Company, New York: Erminie Wheeler-Voegelin, *Ethnohistorical report on Indian use and occupancy from 1640 to 1806 . . . by the "Wyandot, Ottawa, Chippewa, Munsee and Delaware, Shawanee and Pottawatamy nations"* . . . ; Erminie Wheeler-Voegelin, *Ethnohistorical report on Indian use and occupancy from . . . by the "Wyandot, Potawatomy, Ottawas and Chippeway"* . . . ; Helen Hornbeck Tanner, *The Greenville Treaty in Ohio, 1795*; Erminie Wheeler-Voegelin, *Ethnohistorical report on Indian use and occupancy . . . by "the Tribes of Indians, called the Wyandots, Delawares, Shawanoes, Ottawas, Chipewas, Putawatines, Miami, Eelriver, Weed's, Kickapoos, Piankashaws, and Kaskasias"* . . . ; Gay Ramabhushanam, *Ethnohistorical report on Indian use and occupation . . . of Ohio, south and east of the Greenville Treaty line of 1795*; Erminie Wheeler-Voegelin, *Ethnohistorical report on Indian use and occupancy . . . by the "Ottoway, Chippeway, Wyandotte and Pottawatamie nations"* . . . ; Helen Hornbeck Tanner, *Ethnohistorical report on the location of the Wyandot, Delaware and Shawnee Tribes* . . . ; Erminie Wheeler-Voegelin, *Anthropological report on the Indian occupancy . . . by the "Ottawa, Chippewa and Pottawatamie Nations"* . . . ; Donald J. Berthong, *Historical report on the Miami, Wea and Potawatomi use and occupancy* . . . ; Joseph Jablow, *Anthropological study of Illinois, Kickapoo and Potawatomi tribes* . . . ; David B. Stout, *Reports on the Kickapoo; Illinois and Potawatomi* . . . ; Erminie Wheeler-Voegelin, et al., *Anthropological report on Miami, Wea and Eel River* . . . ; and Donald H. Kent, *Historical report on Pennsylvania's purchases from the Six Nations, Wyandot and Delware*. . . . Interesting source materials on population and fighting strength are in the *PTJ*, XVIII, 217; John Hamtramck to Josiah Harmar, Aug. 7, 20, 1790, Gayle Thornbrough, ed., *Outpost on the Wabash, 1787-1791 . . . [Indiana Historical Society Publications*, XIX] (Indianapolis, 1957), 246–247; "Account of Indians . . . ," "Given to J[ames?] M[adison?] by Judge Turner," Dec. 20, 1791,

Miscellaneous Collection, Ohio Historical Society, Columbus, Ohio.

4. Background on Indian relations is in Walter H. Mohr, *Federal Indian Relations, 1774–1788* (Philadelphia, 1933), ch. III; Randolph Chandler Downes, *Council Fires on the Upper Ohio* . . . (Pittsburgh, 1940), ch. 12; Reginald Horsman, *Expansion and American Indian Policy, 1783–1812* (East Lansing, Mich., 1967), ch. II–III.

5. To Patrick Henry, [Apr. or May 1786], Benjamin Franklin Collection, Yale Univ. Library, New Haven, Conn.

6. To Arthur Campbell, Sept. 18, 1788, Draper Collection, 90D51, State Historical Society of Wisconsin, Madison, Wis. For other eastern opinion and western perception of it, as well as western thoughts see John Miller to Anthony Wayne, June 27, 1786, Anthony Wayne Papers, Burton Historical Collection, Detroit Public Library, Detroit, Mich.; Thomas Marshall *et al.* to Edmund Randolph, Dec. 22, 1786, Preston Davie Collection, Southern Historical Collection, Univ. of North Carolina Library, Chapel Hill, N.C.; John Cleves Symmes to the President of Congress, May 3, 1787, Papers of the Continental Congress, item 56, *RG* 360, NA; Harry Innes to John Brown, Dec. 7, 1787, Innes File, Kentucky Historical Society, Frankfurt, Ky.; William McMachen and Archibald Woods to James Wood, Dec. 15, 1787, Archibald Woods Papers, College of William and Mary Library, Williamsburg, Va.; Jonathan Dayton to Symmes, Sept. 12–13, 1788, John Cleves Symmes microfilm (Collection of John J. James), LC. Some Kentuckians tended to exaggerate the Indian menace as an argument for Kentucky statehood, statehood allowing them greater independence and speed in responding to attack. See Patricia Watlington, *The Partisan Spirit: Kentucky Politics, 1779–1792* (New York, 1972), 92–93.

7. To James Duane, Sept. 7, 1783, *WGW*, XXVII, 133–140.

8. Charles Thomson to St. Clair, Oct. 26, 1788, *ASP, IA,* I, 9. See also "Speech of the United Indian Nations . . . ," Dec. 18, 1786, Thomson to St. Clair, July 2, 1788, *ibid.*, 8–9. For an indication of the speculators' influence, see John Brown to James Breckinridge, Jan. 28, 1788, Letters to James Breckinridge, Univ. of Virginia Library, Charlottesville, Va.

9. To Knox, Jan. 27, 1788, St. Clair Papers (Force Transcripts), LC.

10. See St. Clair to Knox, Mar. 14, July 5, 16, Sept. 15 (two letters), Oct. 26, 1788, to Butler, Aug. 7, 1788, to the Governors of Va. and Pa., Sept. 1, 1788, Proceedings of the Va. Council, Aug. 25, Oct. 15, 1788, *ibid.*; St. Clair to Knox, Nov. 12, 1788, Arthur St. Clair Papers, Ohio State Library, Columbus, Ohio.

11. Journal, May 28, 1788, William Denny, ed., "The Military Journal of Major Ebenezer Denny," *Memoirs of the Historical Society of Pennsylvania*, VII (1860), 323. See also Symmes to Dayton, Aug. 21, 1788, Beverley W. Bond, Jr., ed., *The Correspondence of John Cleves Symmes* (New York, 1926), 41–42.

12. Jan. 5, 1789, St. Clair Papers (Force Transcripts), LC. See also Harmar to Charles Thomson, July 23, 1788, Papers of the Cont. Cong., item 163, *RG* 360, NA. See also Harmar to Hamtramck, Aug. 7, Oct. 13, 1788, Thornbrough, ed., *Outpost on the Wabash*, 100, 137; Knox to Harmar, Dec. 8, 1788, Josiah Harmar Papers, WLCL.

13. St. Clair to Knox, Jan. 18, 1789, Smith, ed., *St. Clair Papers*, II, 108–109;

St. Clair to Washington, May 2, 1789, *ASP, IA*, I, 10. Harmar was similarly pessimistic (to Hamtramck, Feb. 15, 1789, Thornbrough, ed., *Outpost on the Wabash*, 152). The treaty and its background is discussed in Downes, *Frontier Ohio*, 3-16; Horsman, *Expansion and American Indian Policy*, 42-49.

14. A Citizen [William Findley], *A Review of the Revenue System* . . . (Philadelphia, 1794), 63-71; [John Taylor], *A Definition of Parties* . . . (Philadelphia, 1794), 4; James T. Callender, *Sedgwick & Co. or A Key to the Six Per Cent Cabinet* (Philadelphia, 1798), 39-44, 47-48, 51-52; James T. Callender, *The Prospect Before Us* (Richmond, 1800-1801), II, part 2, 18-26.

15. To Washington, June 15, 1789, George Washington Papers, LC. See also St. Clair to Knox, June 14, 1789, *ibid*.

16. Knox to Washington, Sept. 1789, "Return of Troops . . . ," May 5, 1789, *ibid*.; "Statement of Troops . . . ," Aug. 8, 1789, *ASP, MA*, I, 5-6; Knox to Harmar, Mar. 30, Oct. 29, 1789, Harmar Papers, WLCL.

17. The administration considered a Creek war far more dangerous than a war in Ohio, since the Creeks were so strong, backed by the Spanish, and if pressed, could escape into the Spanish refuge of Florida. See Knox's report, July 6, 1789, *ASP, IA*, I, 15-16; Knox to Washington, Feb. 15, 1790, Jared Sparks, ed., *Correspondence of the American Revolution . . . Letters . . . to George Washington* . . . (Boston, 1853), IV, 315-320. Washington went to great lengths to arrange negotiations, even after initial failure. See Arthur P. Whitaker, "Alexander McGillivray, 1789-1793," *North Carolina Historical Review*, V (1928), 289-301; John Walton Caughey, *McGillivray of the Creeks* (Norman, Okla., 1938), 40-46. On policy in general, see Horsman, *Expansion and American Indian Policy*, 54-59, 66-71, 84-85. For the problems of transition, see John Brown to G. R. Clark, July 5, 1789, Draper Collection, 53J80, State Hist. Soc. Wis.

18. See [Arthur Campbell] to [John Brown or Andrew Moore], May 1789, Arthur Campbell Papers, The Filson Club, Louisville, Ky.; George Nicholas to James Madison, May 8, 1789, James Madison Papers, LC; Harmar to St. Clair, May 8, 1789, Peter Force Miscellany, LC; Symmes to Dayton, May 18-20, 22, 1789, Dayton to Symmes, Aug. 15, 1789, Bond, ed., *Correspondence of Symmes*, 78-80, 96-97, 228; Symmes to Dayton, May 27, July 17, 1789, Dayton to Symmes, May 16, 1789, Symmes microfilm (James Transcripts), LC; Samuel Holden Parsons to Oliver Ellsworth, May 20, 1789, Charles S. Hall, *Life and Letters of Samuel Holden Parsons* (Binghamton, N.Y., 1903), 558-559; John Brown to G. R. Clark, July 5, 1789, Draper Collection, 53J80, State Hist. Soc. Wis.

19. Knox to Harmar, June 10, 1789, Harmar Papers, WLCL.

20. *Ibid*.

21. [Kentucky] Convention to Washington, July 26, 1789, Robert Johnson to Washington, Aug. 22, 1789, *ASP, IA*, I, 84; Brown to Innes, Sept. 13, 1789, Emmet Collection, NYPL; Knox to Winthrop Sargent, Nov. 9, 1789, Frederick S. Allis Jr. and Roy Bartolomei, eds., The Winthrop Sargent Papers (microfilm ed., Boston, 1965), reel 3, exposure 114; Washington to Beverley Randolph, May 16, 1789, Randolph to a county lieutenant, June 1, 1789, in the *Kentucky Gazette* (Lexington), Aug. 1, 1789; Robert Lawson to St. Clair, Aug. 16, 1789, Force Miscellany, LC.

22. St. Clair to Washington, Sept. 14, 1789, Smith, ed., *St. Clair Papers*, II, 124. I believe St. Clair's letter was solicited by the administration. The Governor had been in New York much of this summer, no more privy to reports from the West than Knox or Washington. My evidence is the timing of the request in relation to the military bill, and St. Clair's departure a few days after writing the letter. See William Smith to O. H. Williams, Sept. 18, 21, 1789, Otho H. Williams Papers, Maryland Historical Society, Baltimore, Md.

23. To Theodore Sedgwick, Oct. 6, 1789, Theodore Sedgwick Papers, MHS.

24. To Anthony Wayne, July 31, 1789, Bancroft Transcripts, NYPL.

25. For congressional action, see AC, 1C 1S, 85, 89, 92, 93–94, 893–894, 911, 912, 927, 2199–2200; Linda Grant De Pauw *et al.*, eds., *Senate Legislative Journal* [*Documentary History of the First Federal Congress* . . . , I] (Baltimore, 1972), 185, 196, 200 and n, 205, 206, 207.

26. Oct. 6, 1789, WGW, XXX, 429–431.

27. *Ibid.*; Knox to Washington, Sept. 1789, Washington Papers, LC; Knox to the Governor of Va., Dec. 10, 1789, Sherwin McRae, ed., *Calendar of Virginia State Papers* . . . (Richmond, 1875–1893), V, 75; Knox to Harmar, Jan. 16, 1790, Harmar Papers, WLCL; Harmar to Armstrong, Feb. 2, 1790, John Armstrong Papers, Ind. Hist. Soc.

28. Notes submitted to the President, n.d. [Sept.–Oct. 1789], Washington Papers, 4th ser., CCXLV, 77, LC. Compare this statement to one similar in Washington to St. Clair, Oct. 6, 1789, WGW, XXX, 429–431. This and other internal evidence dates Knox's notes.

29. See Knox to St. Clair, Dec. 19, 1789, Clarence E. Carter *et al.*, eds., *Territorial Papers of the United States* (Washington, 1934–date), III, 224–225; John P. Duvall *et al.* to Washington, Dec. 12, 1789, George Clendinen to Washington, Dec. 27, 1789, Benjamin Wilson *et al.* to Washington, Feb. 2, 1790, county lieutenants to Knox, Harmar to Knox, Mar. 24, 1790, *ASP, IA*, I, 85–87, 91; Harmar to Hamtramck, Oct. 25, 1789, Knox to Harmar, Dec. 19, 1789, Thornbrough, ed., *Outpost on the Wabash*, 195, 210–212; Dayton to Symmes, Feb. 16, 1790, Bond, ed., *Correspondence of Symmes*, 241; Symmes to Dayton, Apr. 30, 1790, Symmes microfilm (James Transcripts), LC; Harmar to Knox, Jan. 14, 1790, "Denny Journal," *Mem. Hist. Soc. Pa.*, VII, 449; St. Clair to Knox, Jan. 26, May 1, 1790, Smith, ed., *St. Clair Papers*, II, 132, 136; Brown to Innes, Apr. 27, June 8, 1790, Innes Papers, LC; Rufus Putnam to Fisher Ames [Jan.? 1790], William Parker Cutler and Julia Perkins Cutler, *Life Journal and Correspondence of Rev. Manasseh Cutler, LL.D.* (Cincinnati, 1888), II, 373–383.

30. Journal of Antoine Gamelin, Apr. 11, 1790, *ASP, IA*, I, 93. The statement was in a speech by St. Clair and it was removed by Gamelin after he realized its effect. The tone of the speech was the same, however.

31. May 1, 1790, "Judge Symmes on Indian Hostilities," *Proceedings of the New Jersey Historical Society*, new ser., VII (1922), 293.

32. Jan. 25, 1790, John C. Fitzpatrick, ed., *The Diaries of George Washington, 1748–1789* (Boston, 1925), IV, 76–77. Washington noted a specific letter on the threat of secession, probably George Nicholas to James Madison, May 8, 1789, Madison Papers, LC. For knowledge of the Wilkinson plot, see

Thomas Marshall to Washington, Feb. 12, 1789, in T. M. Green, *The Spanish Conspiracy* (Cincinnati, 1891), 250n–253n; St. Clair to Major Dunn, Dec. 5, 1789, quoted in James Alton James, *Oliver Pollock: The Life and Times of an Unknown Patriot* (New York and London, 1937), 332; St. Clair to Washington, Jan. 24, 1790, St. Clair Papers, Ohio State Lib.; editorial note, *PTJ*, XIX, 436–442, 469–484.

33. Jan. 25, 1790, Fitzpatrick, ed., *Washington Diaries*, IV, 76–77. For the Kentucky raids, see Harmar to Hamtramck, Oct. 25, 1789, Thornbrough, ed., *Outpost on the Wabash*, 195; James Wilkinson to Harmar, Apr. 7, 1790, Harmar Papers, WLCL; *Ky. Gazette* (Lexington), Apr. 26, 1790.

34. To St. Clair, May 19, 1790 *PAH*, VI, 421. Land companies are covered in Shaw Livermore, *Early American Land Companies: Their Influence on Corporate Development* (New York and London, 1939), 134–144; Joseph Stancliffe Davis, *Essays on the Earlier History of American Corporations* (Cambridge, 1917), I, 130–150, 213–253; Charles Swain Hall, *Benjamin Tallmadge: Revolutionary Soldier and American Businessman* (New York, 1943), ch. XI. A list of Ohio Company stockholders is in Archer Butler Hulbert, ed., *The Records . . . of the Ohio Company* [*Marietta College Historical Collections*, I–II] (Marietta, 1917), 235–242. St. Clair's Ohio Company lands were listed by Rufus Putnam, Sept. 10, 1790, St. Clair Papers, Ohio State Lib. For William Duer's activities, see *PAH*, VI, 346–347 and notes; *PTJ*, XIX, 442–469; Trustees to Benjamin Walker, Sept. 11, 1790, Scioto and Ohio Land Company Papers, NYHS. For the Lee interest, see Dayton to Symmes, May 10, 1789, Symmes microfilm (James Transcripts), LC; Arthur Lee to M. De Barth, July 3, 1790, Paul P. Hoffman and John L. Molyneaux, eds., Lee Family Papers (microfilm ed., Charlottesville, 1966), r. 7, exp. 800. Washington's lands are mentioned in Freeman, *George Washington*, VI, 14, 18–19, 33, 297–298. Washington sold the bulk of his Ohio and Kanawha River lands after Harmar's defeat. See Washington to George Clendinen, Mar. 31, 1791, WGW, XXXI, 255–256.

35. Almost every administration pronouncement in the January–September 1790 period reveals that they viewed the prestige factor in these terms. A particularly interesting statement by an opponent agreed; see Stuart Gerry Brown, ed., *The Autobiography of James Monroe* (Syracuse, 1959), 52.

36. Apr. 16, 1790, Charles A. Beard, ed., *Journal of William Maclay . . .* (New York, 1927), 234–235.

37. Apr. 15, 1790, *ibid.*, 233. For the congressional proceedings, see *ibid.*, 233–239; First Annual Address to Congress, Jan. 8, 1790, WGW, XXX, 491–492; *ASP, IA*, I, 59–64; AC, 1C 2S, 935, 959–960, 962, 964, 965, 1058, 2222–2224; De Pauw *et al.*, eds., *Senate Legislative Journal*, 298–269, 270, 281, 285, 288 and n, 289–291, 293, 295, 300; William Few to Joseph Clay, Apr. 14, 1790, Emmet Collection, NYPL; Maclay to George Logan, Apr. 25, 1790, George Logan Papers, HSP.

38. To Innes, Apr. 27, 1790, Innes Papers, LC. For the administration's actions, see Knox to Innes, Apr. 13, July 29, 1790, *ibid.*; Knox to David Shepherd (circular), Apr. 13, 1790, Brown to G. R. Clark, Apr. 27, 1790, Draper Collection, 2SS163–166, 53J88, State Hist. Soc. Wis.; Knox to St. Clair or Harmar, Mar. 3, 1790, *ASP, IA*, I, 101. The broader dimension of Indian policy at this time is covered in Francis Paul Prucha, *American*

Indian Policy in the Formative Years: The Indian Trade and Intercourse Acts, 1790–1834 (Cambridge, 1962), ch. III.

39. To William Irvine, May 10, 1790, Draper Collection, 1AA465, State Hist. Soc. Wis.

40. "Summary Statement of the Situation of the Frontiers . . . ," May 27, 1790, Smith ed., *St. Clair Papers*, II, 146–147. The manuscript is in the Washington Papers, LC.

41. Knox to St. Clair, June 7, 1790, Smith, ed., *St. Clair Papers*, II, 147–148; Knox to Harmar, June 7, 1790, ASP, IA, I, 97–98; Knox to Beverley Randolph, June 10, 1790, McRae, ed., *Calendar Va. State Papers*, V, 167. Knox cited Judge Symmes's persuasive letter of May 1 (see n. 31 above) and had possibly received by this time St. Clair's letter of May 1 from Cahokia (Smith, ed., *St. Clair Papers*, II, 136–140). Dating the decision is almost impossible. But British secret agent George Beckwith, in conversation with leading administration officials (and especially Hamilton) at the time and naturally sensitive because of the British-held forts about any military activity, claimed as early as April 7 that a determination had been made for an expedition. See Samuel Flagg Bemis, *Jay's Treaty: A Study in Commerce and Diplomacy* (2d ed., New Haven and London, 1972), 78–79.

42. June 7, 1790, Smith, ed., *St. Clair Papers*, II, 148.

43. July 20, 1790, St. Clair Papers, Ohio State Lib. For other indications of administration policy, see Knox to Beverley Randolph, July 17, 1790, McRae, ed., *Calendar Va. State Papers*, V, 187–188; Knox to county lieutenants, July 17, 1790, St. Clair Papers, Ohio State Lib.; Knox to Innes, July 29, 1790, Knox to county lieutenants, July 29, 1790, Innes Papers, LC; Washington to Knox, Aug. 13, 1790, WGW, XXXI, 91–92.

44. To Knox, Aug. 23, 1790, Smith, ed., *St. Clair Papers*, II, 160.

45. For St. Clair's activities and the development of the St. Clair-Harmar proposal, see St. Clair to Knox, May 1, Aug. 23, 1790, to Butler, Aug. 16, 1790, Knox to St. Clair, Sept. 14, 1790, *ibid.*, 136–140, 155–162, 150–152, 181–183; St. Clair to Harmar, May 2, 1790, Harmar Papers, WLCL; journal, July 11, 1790, "Denny Journal," *Mem. Hist. Soc. Pa.*, VII, 457; St. Clair to county lieutenants, July 15, 1790, ASP, IA, I, 93–95. For St. Clair's earlier ideas on the Maumee post strategy, see St. Clair to Knox, Sept. 15, 1788 (2 letters), to John Wyllys, Nov. 28, 1788, to John Jay, Dec. 13, 1788, St. Clair Papers (Force Transcripts), LC.

46. To Harmar, Aug. 24, 1790, ASP, IA, I, 99.

47. Knox to St. Clair, Sept. 14, 1790, Smith, ed., *St. Clair Papers*, II, 181. No formal record of the discussions exists, but see St. Clair to Knox, Aug. 23, 1790, Knox to St. Clair, Aug. 23, 1790, *ibid.*, 155–163; St. Clair to Knox, Aug. 28, 1790, St. Clair Papers, Ohio State Lib.; Knox to Harmar, Aug. 24, 1790, to Beverley Randolph, Sept. 2, 1790, to Elliott and Williams, Sept. 3, 1790, ASP, IA, I, 99; Knox to Hamilton, Aug. 23, 1790, Hamilton's conversations with George Beckwith, Aug. 8–12, Oct. 15–20, 1790, PAH, VI, 563–564, 550–552, VII, 112–113.

48. Freeman, *George Washington*, VI, 276–278.

49. St. Clair to Knox (private), Sept. 15, 1788, St. Clair Papers (Force Transcripts) LC.

50. Sept. 18, 1790, "Denny Journal," *Mem. Hist. Soc. Pa.*, VII, 344.

51. For the preparations, march, and battles, see Sept. 18–25, Oct. 21, 1790, *ibid.*, 344, 351–353; journal of Capt. John Armstrong, Oct. 19–20, 1790, Charles Cist, ed., *The Cincinnati Miscellany . . .* (Cincinnati, 1845–1846), I, 196–197; Denny's report to Knox, Jan. 1, 1791, St. Clair Papers, Ohio State Lib.; Harmar to Knox, Nov. 23, 1790, Harmar Papers, WLCL; St. Clair to Knox, Oct. 9, 1790, Harmar to Knox, Nov. 4, 1790, general orders, Oct. 17, 18, 20–23, Nov. 4, 1790, "Return of Killed . . . ," Nov. 4, 1790, *ASP, IA,* I, 96, 104–106; Josiah Harmar Orderly Book, Pennsylvania Historical and Museum Commission, Harrisburg, Pa.; "Proceedings of a Court of Inquiry . . . ," Sept. 15–23, 1791, *AC,* 2C 1S, 1113–1150; Symmes to Dayton, Nov. 6, 1790, Symmes microfilm (James Transcripts), LC; Downes, *Frontier Ohio,* 23–26; H. S. Knapp, *History of the Maumee Valley . . .* (Toledo, 1877), 64–69; James Ripley Jacobs, *The Beginning of the U.S. Army, 1783–1812* (Princeton, 1947), 51–65; Howard Peckham, "Josiah Harmar and His Indian Expedition," *Ohio Arch. Hist. Quar.,* LV (1946), 227–241.
52. St. Clair to Knox, Nov. 6, 1790, Harmar to Knox, Nov. 4, 1790, *ASP, IA,* I, 104. For Hamtramck's activities, see his letter to Harmar, Nov. 2, 1790, Thornbrough, ed., *Outpost on the Wabash,* 259–262.
53. Oct. 24, 1790, Northwest Territory Collection, Ind. Hist. Soc.
54. Thomas Bourne interview, Oct. 31, 1844, Draper Collection, 4U1–2, State Hist. Soc. Wis. The best source for Harmar's thinking is Denny's report to Knox, Jan. 1, 1791, St. Clair Papers, Ohio State Lib.
55. To Knox, Nov. 19, 1790, WGW, XXXI, 156. Denny's arrival was noted in the *Gazette of the United States* (Phila.), Dec. 15, 1790.
56. Washington to George Clinton, Dec. 1, 1790, Second Annual Address to Congress, Dec. 8, 1790, WGW, XXXI, 160, 166; *ASP, IA,* I, 83–104; *Gazette of the U.S.* (Phila.), Dec. 8, 1790.
57. William Allen to Theodore Foster, Feb. 7, 1791, Theodore Foster Papers, Rhode Island Historical Society, Providence, R.I. See also Henry Van Schaack to Sedgwick, Jan. 4, 1791, Sedgwick Papers, MHS.
58. To O. H. Williams, Dec. 16, 1790, Williams Papers, Md. Hist. Soc.
59. For the question of Harmar's intoxication, see Symmes to Dayton, Nov. 4, 1791, Bond, ed., *Correspondence of Symmes,* 138; Patrick Henry to James Monroe, Jan. 24, 1791, William Wirt Henry, *Patrick Henry: Life, Correspondence, and Speeches* (New York, 1891), II, 461; John Armstrong to Harmar, Mar. 1, 1791, William Ferguson to Harmar, Mar. 28, 1791, Harmar Papers, WLCL; Harmar to Washington (transcript), Mar. 28, 1791, Washington Papers (Ephemera), LC; "Proceedings of a Court of Inquiry . . . ," Sept. 15–23, 1791, *AC,* 2C 1S, 1113–1150; *Ky. Gazette* (Lexington), Aug. 27, 1791 in *Gazette of the U.S.* (Phila.), Oct. 8, 1791. For a sampling of the general reaction see George Thacher to James Sullivan, Dec. 9, 1790, George Thacher Papers, MHS; Alexander White to Gates, Dec. 26, 1790, Horatio Gates Papers, NYHS; William Stuart to Griffith Evans, Dec. 21, 1790, Griffith Evans Papers, HSP; Knox to Harmar, Jan. 31, 1791, Harmar Papers, WLCL; Paine Wingate to Josiah Bartlett, Dec. 18, 1790, Jan. 26, 1791, Charles E. L. Wingate, *Life and Letters of Paine Wingate* (Medford, Mass., 1930), II, 544, 384; Joseph Stanton and Theodore Foster to the

Governor of R.I., Feb. 17, 1791, Arthur Fenner to Foster, Feb. 17, 1791, Governor's Correspondence, Rhode Island State Archives, Providence, R.I.; Sedgwick to Benjamin Bourne, Jan. 23, 1791, Personal Papers Miscellaneous, LC; *Gazette of the U.S.* (Phila.), Mar. 2, 9, 12, May 4, 7, Oct. 8, 1791; *Connecticut Courant* (Hartford), Dec. 27, 1790.

60. Report to Knox, Jan. 1, 1791, St. Clair Papers, Ohio State Lib.
61. *Federal Gazette and Philadelphia Daily Advertiser*, Jan. 7, 1791; Armstrong to Harmar, Mar. 1, 1791, Harmar Papers, WLCL; Armstrong journal, Oct. 19, 20, 1790, Cist, ed., *Cincinnati Miscellany*, I, 196–197; James Breckinridge to Brown, John Brown Papers, Yale Univ. Lib.; Brown to Robert Patterson, Jan. 5, 1791, Draper Collection, 3MM22, State Hist. Soc. Wis.
62. Knox, ". . . report to the President . . . , upon the operations to be adopted for the ensuing year upon the frontiers," Feb. 22, 1791, Northwest Territory Collection, Ind. Hist. Soc.
63. *Ibid.*
64. Memorial of the Kentucky counties enclosed in Charles Scott to Washington, Dec. 4, 1790, Washington Papers, LC; Va. Council, Dec. 29, 1790, Memorial to Governor of Va., n.d., *ASP, IA*, I, 109–111.
65. Knox, ". . . report . . . upon operations . . . ," Feb. 22, 1791, Northwest Territory Collection, Ind. Hist. Soc. See also Knox's reports to Washington, Jan. 5, 15, 22, 1791, and Knox's instructions to Charles Scott, Mar. 9, 1791, *ASP, IA*, I, 107, 108–109, 112–113, 129–130.
66. Knox report to Washington, Jan. 22, 1791, *ASP, IA*, I, 122. A good indication of administration views of British complicity was Madison's conversation with George Beckwith, Apr. 18, 1791, Madison Papers, LC.
67. Knox report to Washington, Jan. 22, 1791, *ASP, IA*, I, 112.
68. *Ibid.*
69. Administration thinking is revealed in Knox's reports to Washington, Jan. 5, 15, 22, 1791, Knox to Scott, Mar. 9, 1791, to St. Clair, Mar. 21, 1791, *ASP, IA*, I, 107, 108–109, 112–113, 129–130, 171–174; Knox, ". . . report . . . upon operations . . . ," Feb. 22, 1791, Northwest Territory Collection, Ind. Hist. Soc. General Emory Upton in *The Military Policy of the United States* [62C 2S, Senate Document no. 494l] (Washington, 1912), 79, was the first to identify correctly the "levies."
70. To Washington, Jan. 8, 1791, *ASP, IA*, I, 121–122. See also Putnam to Knox, Jan. 8, 1791, David Zeigler to St. Clair, Jan. 8, 1791, *ibid.*, 122; "Extract of a letter from Marietta, to a member of Congress, dated January 6, 1791," *Gazette of the U.S.* (Phila.), Jan. 29, 1791; Putnam to William Duer, Jan. 9, 1791, Scioto and Ohio Co. Land Papers, NYHS. The letter arrived January 26 (John Steele to William Blount, Jan. 27, 1791, William Blount Papers, LC).
71. Feb. 22, 1791, Buell, *Rufus Putnam*, 250.
72. Joseph Stanton and Theodore Foster to Arthur Fenner, Feb. 17, 1791, Governor's Correspondence, R.I. State Archives.
73. George Thacher to Benjamin Chadbourne, Jan. 30, 1791, Thacher Papers, MHS.
74. AC, 1C 3S, 1757, 1759, 1761, 1771, 1772, 1774, 1785–1786, 2350–2353; De Pauw, *et al.*, *Senate Legislative Journal*, 603–606, 607, 616, 619–620, 622–

625, 656–657, 659, 660, 667–668, 669, 675, 690, 698; committee report, Feb. 1, 1791, Records of Select Committees, 1C 1S to 4C 1S, Records of the United States House of Representatives, *RG* 233, NA. For further congressional comment and reaction, see the letters cited above, and Wingate to Bartlett, Jan. 27, 1791, Wingate, *Paine Wingate*, II, 385; Sedgwick to Ephraim Williams, Jan. 27, 1791, Sedgwick Papers, MHS; Abraham Baldwin to Joseph Clay, Jan. 30, 1791, Ferdinand J. Dreer Collection, HSP; Benjamin Goodhue to ———, n.d., Goodhue Papers, EI; Phineas Bond to the Duke of Leeds, Feb. 1, Mar. 14, 1791, J. Franklin Jameson, ed., "Letters of Phineas Bond, British Consul at Philadelphia . . . ," *Second Annual Report of the Historical Manuscripts Commission of the American Historical Association* (Washington, 1898), 473–474, 481.

75. Knox to Scott, Mar. 9, 1791, *ASP, IA,* I, 129–131.
76. *Ibid.* In formal terms Knox was replying to Scott's letter of December 4, 1790, asking for permission to send an expedition against the Indians. Knox set up the Kentucky Board of War to assure the enlistment of good men for the ranger regiment and not the kind that had accompanied Harmar. Knox undoubtedly created the Board and planned the expedition with John Brown, the Kentucky congressman. See George Nicholas to Brown, Dec. 31, 1790, Huntley Dupre, ed., "Three Letters of George Nicholas to John Brown," *Register Kentucky Historical Society,* XLI (1943), 508; Knox to the Governor of Va., Mar. 14, 1791, Northwest Territory Collection, Ind. Hist. Soc.; Charles Gano Talbert, *Benjamin Logan: Kentucky Frontiersmen* (Lexington, 1962), 250–252.
77. Knox to the county lieutenants, Mar. 10, 1791, Northwest Territory Collection, Ind. Hist. Soc. See also Knox to [David] Shepherd and James Marsh, Mar. 3, 1791, Knox to the Governor of Pa., to the Governor of Va., Mar. 14, 1791, *ibid.*
78. Knox to Washington, Mar. 14, 1791, with "Plan for the Corps of Levies," *ibid.*
79. Knox to St. Clair, Mar. 21, 1791, *ASP, IA,* I, 171–174.
80. *Ibid.*
81. Message to the Miami Indians, Mar. 11, 1791, *ibid.,* 147. See also Knox's instructions to Proctor, Mar. 11, 1791, Proctor's journal, Mar. 11–June 7, 1791, *ibid.,* 145–146, 149–162.
82. To St. Clair, Apr. 19, 1791, *ASP, IA,* I, 174. See Knox to Washington, Mar. 31, 1791, Washington Papers, LC; Knox to Washington, Apr. 10, 1791, Sparks, ed., *Letters to Washington,* IV, 366–368; Presley Neville to Thomas Mifflin, Mar. 25, 1791, *Pennsylvania Archives, Second Series* (Harrisburg, 1887–1896), IV, 651–652. For the Big Beaver incident, see Cornplanter *et al.* to Knox, Mar. 17, 1791, *ASP, IA,* I, 145; David Shepherd to Beverley Randolph, May 9, 1791, James Morrison to Richard Butler, May 30, 1791, McRae, ed., *Calendar Va. State Papers,* V, 301, 317; Isaac Craig to Knox, Mar. 16, 1791, John Wilkins, Jr. to Mifflin, Mar. 31, 1791, *Pa. Archives,* IV, 647–648, 655–656; Rev. Ralph Emmett Fall, "Captain Samuel Brady (1756–1795), Chief of the Rangers, And His Kin," *West Virginia History,* XXIX (1968), 218–221.
83. For administration thinking, see Knox to Pickering, May 2, 1791, to George

Clinton, Apr. 12, May 11, 1791, Clinton to Knox, Apr. 1791, Knox to Richard Butler, June 9, July 21, 1791, *ASP, IA,* I, 165–166, 167, 167–168, 188, 191; Rufus King to Hamilton (extract), 1791, Henry O'Reilly Papers, NYHS; Knox to Washington, Apr. 10, May 30, Aug. 17, 1791, Washington Papers, LC; Knox to Philip Schuyler, June 28, 1791, Philip Schuyler Papers, NYPL. For Knox's reaction to Big Beaver, see his letters to St. Clair, Mar. 28, Apr. 19, 1791, *ASP, IA,* I, 166, 174–175, and to Mifflin, Mar. 28, 1791, *Calendar Va. State Papers,* V, 317–318. For Pickering's missions, see Pickering to Samuel Hodgdon, Aug. 25, 1791, *Charles Hamilton Auction Number 15* (New York, 1966), 96; Edward Hake Phillips, "Timothy Pickering at His Best: Indian-Commissioner, 1790–1794," *Essex Institute Historical Collections,* CII (1966), 165–171.

84. John Brown to William Irvine, Apr. 28, 1791, William Irvine Papers, HSP; Knox to Washington, June 6, 16, 1791, Washington Papers, LC; Hamilton to King, July 8, 1791, *PAH,* VIII, 532; Arthur Campbell to——, July 16, 1791, Campbell Papers, Filson Club. For the raids, see the reports by Charles Scott and James Wilkinson, June 28, 1791, Aug. 24, 1791, *ASP, IA,* I, 131–135; Talbert, *Benjamin Logan,* 25–54.

85. Henry Jackson to Knox, May 16, 1791, John Williams to Knox, May 27, 1791, Henry Knox Papers, MHS; Knox to Washington, May 30, 1791, Washington Papers, LC; Brown to Irvine, Aug. 22, 1791, Newbold-Irvine Papers, HSP.

86. "Winthrop Sargent's Diary . . . [of] St. Clair's Expedition . . . ," *Ohio Arch. Hist. Quar.,* XXXIII (1924), 239; Knox to St. Clair, Aug. 1, 25, Sept. 1, 1791, Knox to Butler, July 21, Aug. 25, 1791, *ASP, IA,* I, 181–182, 192; Knox to Washington, Sept. 24, 1791, Washington Papers, LC.

87. William Darke to Washington, July 24, 1791, Miscellaneous Letters of the Department of State, General Records of the Department of State, *RG* 59, NA; St. Clair to Knox (private), Nov. 17, 1791, St. Clair Papers, Ohio State Lib.

88. James Wilkinson to St. Clair, Sept. 24, 1791, Northwest Territory Collection, Ind. Hist. Soc.; Sargent's diary, Oct. 10, 20–21, 1791, *Ohio Arch. Hist. Quar.,* XXXIII, 242, 246–247; journal, Oct. 22–30, Nov. 2, 1791, "Denny Journal," *Mem. Hist. Soc. Pa.,* VII; 363–365, 367; "Declaration of John Wade . . . ," Oct. 27, 1791, "Canadian Archives, Colonial Office Records," *Michigan Pioneer and Historical Society, Collections,* XXIV (1894), 328. For militia authorization see Knox to the Governor of Va., July 15, 1791, Northwest Territory Collection, Ind. Hist. Soc.; Knox to Washington, Sept. 24, 1791, Washington Papers, LC.

89. To Richard C. Anderson, Oct. 28, 1791, Armstrong Papers, Ind. Hist. Soc.

90. *Ibid.*

91. To Isaac Craig, Sept. 18, 1791, Isaac Craig Papers, Carnegie Library of Pittsburg, Pittsburg, Pa.

92. Sargent's diary, introduction by Sargent, *Ohio Arch. Hist. Quar.,* XXXIII, 242. See also Oct. 20–27, 1791, *ibid.,* 246–251; journal, Oct. 22–30, 1791, "Denny Journal," *Mem. Hist. Soc. Pa.,* VII, 362–365; Symmes to Boudinot, Jan. 12, 1792, Beverley W. Bond, Jr., ed., *The Intimate Letters of John Cleves Symmes and his Family* (Cincinnati, 1956), 115–118; St. Clair to

Knox, Oct. 6, Nov. 1, 1791, *ASP, IA,* I, 136–137; Fitzsimons committee report, May 8, 1792, *AC,* 2C 1S, 1106–1113; John Armstrong to Alexander Hamilton, Sept. 17, 1791, Armstrong Papers, Ind. Hist. Soc.; returns of arms needed for certain campaigns, June 3, 4, 6, 9, 11, 20, 1791, Craig Papers, Carnegie Lib. of Pittsburgh.

93. Beverley W. Bond, Jr., "Memoirs of Benjamin Van Cleve," *Quarterly Publication of the Historical and Philosophical Society of Ohio,* XVII (1922), 24.

94. Symmes to Dayton (transcript), Aug. 15, 1791, Symmes Papers (Miami Purchase), Cincinnati Hist. Soc.

95. To Richard C. Anderson, Oct. 28, 1791, Armstrong Papers, Ind. Hist. Soc. See also adjutant Crawford's orderly book, Oct. 16, 20, 22, 27, 1791, William D. Wilkins Papers, Burton Hist. Collection, Detroit Public Lib.; Zachariah Holliday interview, Oct. 1844, Draper Collection, 11J230, State Hist. Soc. Wis.; Sargent's diary, Oct. 20–21, 1791, *Ohio Arch. Hist. Quar.,* XXXIII, 246–51; journal, Oct. 2–6, 22–30, Nov. 2, 1791, "Denny Journal," *Mem. Hist. Soc. Pa.,* VII, 358, 362–365, 367; "Declaration of John Wade . . . ," Oct. 27, 1791, William Darke to Sarah Darke, Nov. 1, 1791, "Canadian Archives," *Mich. Pioneer Hist. Collections,* XXIV, 328, 331; St. Clair to Knox, Nov. 1, 1791, *ASP, IA,* I, 136–137.

96. To Boudinot, Jan. 12, 1792, Bond, ed., *Intimate Letters of Symmes,* 116–117.

97. To his brother, Nov. 10, 1791, St. Clair Papers (Force Transcripts), LC. See also "Remarkable Adventures of Jackson Johonnet . . . ," in Samuel L. Metcalf, *A Collection of . . . Narratives . . . of Indian Warfare . . .* (Lexington, 1821), 97; Simon Girty to Alexander McKee, Oct. 28, 1791, "Canadian Archives," *Mich. Pioneer Hist. Collections,* XXIV, 329–330; journal, Nov. 4, 1791, "Denny Journal," *Mem. Hist. Soc. Pa.,* VII, 368–375; Sargent's "Narrative . . . ," *Ohio Arch. Hist. Quar.,* XXXIII, 256–273. A useful compilation of shorter accounts of the battle is the appendix in Gordon L. Wilson, Arthur St. Clair and the Administration of the Old Northwest, 1788–1802 (unpub. Ph.D. thesis, Univ. of Southern California, 1957), 453–494. For St. Clair's explanation, see St. Clair to Knox, Nov. 9, 1791, *ASP, IA,* I, 137–138; [Arthur St. Clair], *A Narrative of . . . the Campaign against the Indians . . .* (Philadelphia, 1812). The Indians lost less than two dozen killed and about forty wounded. See McKee to Sir John Johnson, Dec. 5, 1791, "Canadian Archives," *Mich. Pioneer Hist. Collections,* XXIV, 336. According to one observer, over two hundred females accompanied the army, of whom fifty-six died ("St. Clair's Defeat," *American Historical Record,* I, [1872], 486–487n). For a list of equipment lost, see "Return . . . ," Sargent Papers, r.3, exp. 276. A good secondary account is Jacobs, *Beginning of U.S. Army,* 72–115.

98. Benson J. Lossing, ed., *Recollections and Private Memoirs of Washington, by . . . George Washington Parke Custis . . .* (New York, 1860), 416–419.

99. Dudley Woodbridge to Roger Griswold, Jan. 7, 1792, Wolcott-Griswold-Williams-Woodbridge-Rogers Family Papers, Univ. of Virginia Library, Charlottesville, Va.; Grove to Alexander Martin, Dec. 10, 1791, Governor's Papers, North Carolina Department of Archives and History, Raleigh, N.C.

100. Jefferson to Thomas Mann Randolph, Dec. 11, 1791, Edgehill-Randolph Collection, Univ. of Va. Lib. Other reaction is in Abigail Adams to Cotton Tufts, Dec. 19, 1791, Adams Family Papers, MHS; Elias Boudinot to Elisha Boudinot, Dec. 26, 1791, J. J. Boudinot, *The Life, Public Services, Addresses, and Letters of Elias Boudinot, LL.D.* (Boston and New York, 1896), II, 81; Fisher Ames to Thomas Dwight, Dec. 9, 1791, Seth Ames, ed., *Works of Fisher Ames . . .* (Boston, 1854), I, 107; Paine Wingate to Christopher Tappan, Dec. 8, 1791, Stan V. Henkels, *Collection of Autograph Letters . . .* [Catalogue 1974] (Philadelphia, 1912–1914), I, 70; Hammond to Grenville, Dec. 8, 1791, British State Papers, Ford Transcripts, NYPL; Pickering to his wife, Dec. 8, 1791, Pickering Transcripts, EI; Knox to Craig, Dec. 8, 1791, Craig Papers, Carnegie Lib. of Pittsburgh.

101. "As the President has given his public Testimony in favour of Genl. Sinclair, the Enquiry into his Conduct is knocked on the Head, and the Committee of Congress according to Orders, have found him not guilty," wrote transplanted Englishman and Dickinson College President Charles Nisbet (to Alexander Addison, May 10, 1792, Alexander Addison Papers, Univ. of Pittsburgh Lib.).

102. To Andrew Craigie, Dec. 18, 1791, Andrew Craigie Papers, American Antiquarian Society, Worcester, Mass. See also Christopher Gore to King, Dec. 25, 1791, *LCRK*, I, 403–404; Walter Livingston to his son, Jan. 7, 1792, Robert R. Livingston Papers, NYHS; George Partridge to Benjamin Goodhue, Jan. 8, 1792, Goodhue Family Papers, New York Society Library, New York, N.Y.

103. For a sampling of newspaper arguments, see the *National Gazette* (Phila.) Jan. 9, 12, 16, 21, 23, 26, Mar. 1, 1792; *General Advertiser* (Phila.), Jan. 4, Feb. 1, 11, 20, 21, 1792. An excellent catalogue of anti-administration arguments is Donald H. Stewart, *The Opposition Press of the Federalist Period* (Albany, 1969), 565–567.

104. To Charles Carroll, Apr. 15, 1791, Thomas Jefferson Papers, LC. See also Jefferson to Innes, Mar. 7, 1791, to Monroe, Apr. 17, 1791, to Washington, Apr. 17, 1791, *WTJ*, V, 295, 319, 321. For this generation's thinking generally about Indians, see Bernard W. Sheehan, *Seeds of Extinction: Jeffersonian Philanthropy and the American Indian* (Chapel Hill, 1973).

105. To Abigail Adams, Apr. 22, 1792, Adams Papers, MHS.

106. See John Steele to John Haywood, Dec. 5, 1791, Ernest Haywood Collection, Southern Hist. Collection, Univ. of N.C. Lib.; Steele to Joseph Winston, Jan. 15, 1792, H. M. Wagstaff, ed., *The Papers of John Steele* [Publications of the North Carolina Historical Commission] (Raleigh, 1924), I, 81–83. For other statements about the expense, see Ames to Dwight, Jan. 13, 1792, Ames, ed., *Fisher Ames*, I, 109–110; Wingate to Jeremy Belknap, Jan. 5, Feb. 2, 1792, Wingate, *Paine Wingate*, II, 398, 405; Brown to Innes, Jan. 20, 1792, Innes Papers, LC.

107. To Jonathan Clark, May 11, 1792, George Rogers Clark Papers, Virginia Historical Society, Richmond, Va.

108. For instances of civil-military friction in Kentucky and the Northwest Territory, see Symmes to Dayton, Aug. 15, 1791, Symmes to Dayton and Boudinot, Jan. 25, 1792, Bond, ed., *Correspondence of Symmes*, 146–150, 161; Henry Lee to John Bradford, Oct. 19, 1789, *Ky. Gazette* (Lexington),

Oct. 24, 1789; Thornbrough, ed., *Outpost on the Wabash*, 208–209n. Knox voiced concern to Capt. John Armstrong, Apr. 26, 1791, Cist, ed., *Cincinnati Miscellany*, I, 174. Examples of the War Department's paperwork mania are Knox's various letters to county lieutenants, Apr. 13, July 17, 1790, Mar. 10, 1791, Oct. 5, 1791, Northwest Territory Collection, Ind. Hist. Soc.; Knox to county lieutenants, July 29, 1790, Isaac Shelby Papers, Filson Club. For complaints about compensation, see Henry Lee to [representatives in Congress?], Jan. 9, 1792, Lee Family Papers, r.7, exp. 827; "Genuine Federalist" to Washington, Dec. 25, 1792, Washington Papers, LC; Christopher Greenup to Jefferson, Jan. 28, 1793, Miscellaneous Letters of Department of State, *RG* 59, NA.

109. For the fight over compensation for horses, see Elliott and Williams to Harmar, Jan. 5 [1791?], Harmar Papers, WLCL; *Ky. Gazette* (Lexington), Apr. 9, 1791; Samuel Smith to [O. H. Williams?], June 16, 1791, Williams to Smith, June 26, 1791, O. H. Williams Papers, Md. Hist. Soc.; Hamilton to Nicholas, Aug. 31, 1792, *PAH*, XII, 301–302; "Copy of a Writ," Kentucky District Court, Nov. 24, 1792, court decision, Mar. 22, 1794, Alexander Hamilton Papers, LC; cases of Philip Buckner, James Lambert, Moses Moore, George Caldwell, and Joshua Cantrill, Mar. 20, 1792, Dec. 17, 1793, Mar. 18, July 22, 1794, Records of the U.S. District Court [Kentucky], 1789–1800 (microfilm), Kentucky Historical Society, Frankfurt, Ky.

110. Jan. 12, 1792, Bond, ed., *Intimate Letters of Symmes*, 115–118.

111. *Ibid*.

112. See Jefferson to Thomas Mann Randolph, Dec. 11, 1791, Edgehill-Randolph Collection, Univ. of Va. Lib.; Jefferson to Archibald Stuart, Mar. 14, 1792, *WTJ*, V, 454–455; Monroe to St. George Tucker, Jan. 24, 1792, James Monroe Papers, Va. Hist. Soc., Monroe to Archibald Stuart, Mar. 14, 1792, James Monroe Papers, Univ. of Va. Lib., James Monroe Papers in Virginia Repositories [University of Virginia Library Microfilm Publication Number Seven] (Charlottesville, 1969); Madison to Hubbard Taylor, Oct. 11, 1791, Hubbard Taylor Papers, Univ. of Kentucky Library, Lexington, Ky.

113. To his wife, Jan. 7, 1792, Pickering Transcripts, EI.

114. Charles Stevenson to J. G. Simcoe, Jan. 7, 1792, Brig. General E. A. Cruikshank, ed., *The Correspondence of Lieut. Governor John Graves Simcoe . . .* (Toronto, 1923–1931), I, 100. Several observers called the war "unpopular." See Ames to Dwight, Jan. 13, 30, 1792, Ames, ed., *Fisher Ames*, I, 109–110, 111; Benjamin Goodhue to Stephen Goodhue, Jan. 24, 1792, Goodhue Papers, EI; Thacher to John Hancock, Jan. 26, 1792, Thacher Papers, MHS; Abigail Adams to Mary Cranch, Feb. 5, 1792, Stewart Mitchell, ed., *New Letters of Abigail Adams, 1788–1801* (Boston, 1947), 77; Thomas Adams to William Cranch, Jan. 28, 1792, William Cranch Papers, Cincinnati Hist. Soc.

115. Washington to Knox, Jan. 16, 1792, WGW, XXXI, 459. The administration's "white paper," entitled "The Causes of the existing Hostilities between the United States and certain Tribes of Indians, . . . stated and explained from official and authentic Documents, . . ." was prefaced by a letter from Washington which was written by Jefferson and edited by Hamilton, then back dated to make it appear as if the President, acting

alone, ordered the Secretary of War to explain administration policy. This procedure masked what was a carefully calculated effort to answer critics and rally the public behind the administration. See Washington to Knox, Jan. 16, 1792, *ibid.*, 459; Jefferson's draft, Jan. 25, 1792, *WTJ*, V, 430–431; and Hamilton to Washington, Jan. 25, 1792, *PAH*, X, 563. Knox's paper was published widely in the newspapers and as a broadside.

116. "The Causes of the existing Hostilities . . . ," Jan. 26, 1792, *AC*, 2C 1S, 1046–1052.

117. David McClure to Knox, Oct. 1, 1792, Knox Papers, MHS. See also Tobias Lear to Washington, July 21, 1792, Washington Papers, LC.

118. See Lee to Washington, Dec. 1791, B. Rutherford to Washington, Mar. 13, 1792, Washington Papers, LC; Steuben to Hamilton, Jan. 2, Feb. 5, 1792, O. H. Williams to Hamilton, Mar. 5, 1792, *PAH*, X, 499–501, XI, 16–17, 108; Samuel Galt to Washington, Dec. 13, 1791, "Proposition by Ezekiel Scott . . . ," Dec. 14, 1792, Miscellaneous Letters of Department of State, General Records of the Department of State, RG 59, NA; "A Citizen," *American Daily Advertiser* (Phila.), Feb. 10, 1792.

119. "Errors of Government Towards the Indians," Feb. 1792, *WGW*, XXXI, 492. This memorandum was apparently provoked by a long letter from Federalist Senator Benjamin Hawkins (Feb. 10, 1792, Elizabeth G. McPherson, ed., "Unpublished Letters from North Carolinians to Washington," *N.C. Hist. Rev.*, XII [1935], 162–165) in which Hawkins explained his reasons for opposing the administration's military program in the Senate. Denny's meetings were recounted in his journal, Dec. 19, 20, 1791, *Mem. Hist. Soc. Pa.*, VII, 380. The administration received a devastating critique of the campaign from army chaplain John Hurt, who gave it to Madison (Hurt to Washington, Jan. 1, 1792, Miscellaneous Letters of Department of State, RG 59, NA).

120. For administration thinking, see Washington to Knox, Dec. 26, 1791, "Errors . . . ," Feb. 1792, *WGW*, XXXI, 450–451, 491–494; Knox's plan, Dec. 26, 1791, *ASP, IA*, I, 197–202; cabinet notes, Mar. 9, 1792, Franklin B. Sawvel, ed., *The Complete Anas of Thomas Jefferson* (New York, 1903), 61.

121. Dec. 26, 1791, *ASP, IA*, I, 197–199.

122. The best discussions of the development of the national Republican party in 1792 and before are Kenneth Russell Bowling, Politics in the First Congress, 1789–1791 (unpub. Ph.D. thesis, Univ. of Wisconsin, 1968); Noble E. Cunningham, Jr., *The Jeffersonian Republicans: The Formation of Party Organization, 1789–1801* (Chapel Hill, 1957), ch. 1, 267–272. For the ideological dimension, all too often underplayed, see Richard Buel, Jr., *Securing the Revolution: Ideology in American Politics, 1789–1815* (Ithaca and London, 1972), part I.

123. To Isaac Shelby, Mar. 20, 1792, Draper Collection, 11DD23–24, State Hist. Soc. Wis. Albert Gallatin claimed critics had a majority in Congress (to Jean Badollet, Jan. 7, 1792, Albert Gallatin Papers, NYHS).

124. Jan. 16, 1792, Phillip and Elsie Sang Collection, Southern Illinois Univ. Library, Carbondale, Ill. For statements by and about congressmen on the war, see the documents in notes 106, 112, 119, 123, and in addition, Ames to Dwight, Jan. 13, 30, 1792, Ames, ed., *Fisher Ames*, I, 109–110, 111;

Benjamin Goodhue to Stephen Goodhue, Jan. 24, 1792, Goodhue Papers, EI; George Thacher to Hancock, Jan. 26, 1792, to Nathaniel Wells, Feb. 1, 1792, Thacher Papers, MHS; Steele to Winston [P. S. of Jan. 22, 1792], Wagstaff, ed., *Papers of Steele*, I, 82–83; Wingate to Belknap, Jan. 5, 30, Feb. 2, 1792, to Bartlett, Jan. 16, Feb. 13, 1792, Wingate, *Paine Wingate*, II, 398, 404–405, 400–401, 405–406; Madison to Pendleton, Jan. 21, 1792, Madison Papers, LC; Roger Sherman to Simeon Baldwin, Jan. 2, 1792, Roger Sherman Papers, Yale Univ. Lib.; Monroe to [John Breckinridge?], Apr. 6, 1792, Papers of the Breckinridge Family, LC; Aaron Burr to [Washington?], Mar. 13, 1792, Miscellaneous Letters of Department of State, RG 59, NA; William L. Smith to Edward Rutledge, Jan. 16, 1792, George C. Rogers, ed., "The Letters of William Loughton Smith . . . ," *South Carolina Historical Magazine*, LXIX (1968), 234–235; Findley to Addison, Feb. 10, 1792, Addison Papers, Univ. of Pittsburgh Lib.

125. AC, 2C 1S, 337–348. The speeches were summarized in the *Annals*, and speakers identified only by which side they supported. This was highly unusual; given earlier proceedings in secret, including a vote, the public debate smacks of being staged.

126. To the Earl of Buchan, Jan. 10, 1792, Founders Collection, Dickinson College Lib.

127. To Jean Badollet, Jan. 21, 1792, Gallatin Papers, NYHS. See the roll calls in AC, 2C 1S, 354–355.

128. Hawkins to Washington, Feb. 10, 1792, McPherson, ed., "Unpublished Letters," *N.C. Hist. Rev.*, XII, 164. Senator Burr said essentially the same thing on the subject of negotiations. See Burr to [Washington?], Mar. 13, 1792, Miscellaneous Letters of Department of State, RG 59, NA.

129. "Errors of Government Towards the Indians," Feb. 1792, WGW, XXXI, 491–494.

130. For the Senate's action, see AC, 2C 1S, 80, 83, 84, 88, 94, 428–430, 431–432; Findley to Addison, Feb. 10, 1792, Addison Papers, Univ. of Pittsburgh Lib.; Wingate to Bartlett, Feb. 13, 20, 1792, Wingate, *Paine Wingate*, II, 406, 408; Knox to Washington, Feb. 18, 1792, Washington Papers, LC; Monroe to Archibald Stuart, Mar. 14, 1792, James Monroe Papers (microfilm); Findley, *Review of Revenue System*, 69. For an indication of the Senate debate, held in secret as was all Senate debate, see Pierce Butler's notes [1792], Pierce Butler Papers, HSP.

131. For these laws, see AC, 2C 1S, 1343–1346, 1364–1370. The request for higher pay for officers originated in a petition from the officers. See "Report on memorial . . . ," Jan. 4, 1792, Records of Select Committees, 1C 1S to 4C 1S, House Records, RG 233, NA.

132. For the committee and its report, see AC, 2C 1S, 356, 490–494, 549, 601–602, 1106–1113; Hammond to Grenville, Apr. 5, 29, 1792, British State Papers, Ford Transcripts, NYPL.

133. AC, 2C 1S, 1383–1386; report on changing War and Treasury Departments, Feb. 29, 1792, Records of Select Committees, 1C 1S to 4C 1S, House Records, RG 233, NA; Monroe to Tench Coxe, [April?] 12, 1792, James Monroe Papers (microfilm); Coxe to Hamilton, May 6, 1792, Hamilton to Knox, May 28, 1792, Hamilton to Washington, July 22, Aug. 10,

1792, *PAH*, XI, 364–365, 450, XII, 77, 185–186; Leonard D. White, *The Federalists: A Study in Administrative History* (New York, 1948), 360–361.

134. There is no *direct* evidence of when the administration decided on a legionary structure, or why. Immediately after the five regiment bill passed, Washington asked Congress for special authority to appoint extra brigadiers (*AC*, 2C 1S, 110, 481–482, 483, 1350). On April 9, when he sent his list of appointments to the Senate, Washington spoke of a "Legionary" organization, the first specific designation of the army in those terms (*Journal of the Executive Proceedings of the Senate . . .* [Washington, 1828], I, 117). There is some evidence that Congress considered such a structure; the five regiment bill recommended that one regiment consist of two battalions of infantry and one squadron of dragoons (*AC*, 2C 1S, 1343–1344). The composition of a sublegion can be seen in Knox to the House, Dec. 27, 1792, *ASP*, *MA*, I, 40–41.

135. Washington to Knox, Jan. 22, 1792, *WGW*, XXXI, 463.

136. "Opinion of the General Officers," [Mar. 9, 1792], *ibid.*, 509–515.

137. *Ibid.*

138. Cabinet notes, Mar. 9, 1792, Sawvel, ed., *Anas of Jefferson*, 61–62.

139. *Ibid.*

140. See Parker and Cutler, *Manasseh Cutler*, 471–488; John Steele to Arthur Campbell, Jan. 29, 1792, Campbell Papers, Filson Club; Henry Lee to Madison, Jan. 17, 1792, Madison Papers, LC; Madison to Lee, Jan. 21, 1792, William C. Rives Papers, LC; Benjamin Hawkins to Washington, Mar. 16, 1792, MacPherson, ed., "Letters to Washington," *N.C. Hist. Rev.*, XII, 165; Richard Henry Lee to Henry Lee, Mar. 25, 1792, James C. Ballagh, ed., *The Letters of Richard Henry Lee* (New York, 1911–1914), II, 549; John Brown to Harry Innes, Apr. 13, 1792, Innes Papers, LC.

141. Jefferson to Monroe, Apr. 11, 1792, *WTJ*, V, 503.

142. June 30, 1792, *WGW*, XXXII, 78. Years later, Madison characterized Washington's approach to public opinion and appointments: "Although not idolizing public opinion, no man could be more attentive to the means of ascertaining it. In comparing the candidates for office, he was particularly inquisitive as to their standing with the public and the opinion entertained of them by men of public weight." Elizabeth Fleet, ed., "Madison's 'Detached Memorandum,'" *WMQ*, III (1946), 541.

143. For Wayne's activities in the 1780s and early 1790s, see Harry Emerson Wildes, *Anthony Wayne: Trouble Shooter of the American Revolution* (New York, 1941), 316–349. For his efforts to gain a federal post and his ideas about the Indian situation, see Wayne to Washington, Apr. 6, 1789, Bancroft Transcripts, NYPL; Madison to Wayne, July 31, 1789, Aedanus Burke to Wayne, Nov. 12, 1789, Anthony Wayne Papers, HSP; Pierce Butler and Ralph Izard to Wayne, Ralph Izard Papers, South Caroliniana Library, Univ. of South Carolina, Columbia, S.C.; Wayne to Butler and Izard, Sept. 1, 1789, to Isaac Wayne, Dec. 15, 1791, Anthony Wayne Papers, Burton Hist. Collection, Detroit Public Lib.; Wayne to Knox, May 12, 1790, to John Berrien, Dec. 5, 1791, Anthony Wayne Papers, WLCL.

144. The quotations are from Monroe to Jefferson, June 17, 1792, Stanislaus Murray Hamilton, ed., *The Writings of James Monroe* (New York, 1898–

1903), I, 232; Madison to Henry Lee, Apr. 15, 1792, Madison Papers, LC.
See also Brown to Innes, Apr. 13, 1792, Innes Papers, LC; Lee to Madison,
Apr. 18, 1792, Madison Papers, LC; William Darke to Lee, May 12, 1792,
Washington Papers, LC; Lee to Washington, June 15, 1792, WGW, XXXII,
75n.
145. "Opinion . . . ," [Mar. 9, 1792], WGW, XXXI, 511; cabinet notes, Mar. 9,
1792, Sawvel, ed., *Anas of Jefferson*, 62.
146. See the *Senate Executive Journal*, I, 117–119, 120, 121, 122, 123–124.
147. Jan. 7, 1792, Pickering Transcripts, EI.
148. Dec. 26, 1792, *ASP, IA*, I, 198.

Chapter 7

HEADNOTE

a. AC, 3C 2S, 1221.

SOURCE NOTES

1. "Errors of Government Towards the Indians," Feb. 1792, WGW, XXXI,
494.
2. To the Senate and House of Representatives, Aug. 7, 1789, *ibid.*, 372–373;
AC, 1C 1S, 688.
3. Entries for Dec. 18–21, 1789, John C. Fitzpatrick, ed., *The Diaries of
George Washington, 1748–1799* (Boston and New York, 1925), IV, 59–60;
Knox to Washington, Jan. 18, 1790, AC, 1C 2S, 2087–2088.
4. The complete plan is in AC, 1C 2S, 2088–2107.
5. To Charles Clinton, Feb. 8, 1790, Miscellaneous Collection, NYHS.
6. To Stephen Phillips, Jan. 25, 1790, Phillips Family Collection, MHS.
7. Mar. 17, 1790.
8. William Irvine to John Nicholson, Feb. 21, 1790, Simon Gratz Collection,
HSP.
9. AC, 1C 2S, 2099. For a survey of opinion on the exemption issue, see
Richard Wilson Renner, "Conscientious Objection and the Federal Government, 1787–1792," *Military Affairs*, XXXVIII (1974), 142–145.
10. See William Ellery to Benjamin Huntington, Feb. 2, Mar. 8, 1790, Benjamin Huntington Papers, Rhode Island State Archives, Providence, R.I.
11. Henry Jackson to Knox, Feb. 21, 1790, Henry Knox Papers, MHS. For
other reactions, besides the documents quoted above, see Henry Wynkoop
to Reading Beattie, Jan. 21, 1790, Joseph M. Beatty, Jr., ed., "The Letters of
Judge Henry Wynkoop . . . ," *Pennsylvania Magazine of History and
Biography*, XXXVIII (1914), 187; James Madison to Thomas Jefferson, Jan.
24, 1790, *PTJ*, XVI, 125; Knox to William Eustis, Jan. 31, 1790, Knox
Papers, MHS; Madison to ———, Feb. 2, 1790, Roberts Autograph Collection, Haverford College Library, Haverford, Pa.; J[oseph?] B. V[arnum?] to
[George Thacher?], Feb. 7, 1790, George Thacher Papers, Boston Public
Library, Boston, Mass.; Edward Carrington to Madison, Mar. 2, 1790,

James Madison Papers, NYPL; Paine Wingate to Timothy Pickering, Mar. 7, 1790, Charles E. L. Wingate, *Life and Letters of Paine Wingate* (Medford, Mass., 1930), II, 353; Henry Van Schaack to Theodore Sedgwick, Mar. 10, 1790, Theodore Sedgwick Papers, MHS; John Quincy Adams to John Adams, Apr. 5, 1790, Worthington Chauncey Ford, ed., *Writings of John Quincy Adams* (New York, 1913-1917), I, 54; entry for Apr. 16, 1790, Charles A. Beard, ed., *The Journal of William Maclay . . .* (New York, 1927), 235.

12. *AC*, 1C 2S, 1058, 1544, 1546.
13. For the bill, see *ibid.*, 1658, and the *Gazette of the United States* (Phila.), July 14, 17, 21, 1790.
14. To General Goodwin, July 8, 1790, Thacher Papers, MHS.
15. Joseph Stanton and Theodoré Foster to the Governor of R.I., Feb. 17, 1791, Governor's Correspondence, R.I. State Archives.
16. To [William Williams?], Jan. 1, 1791, Jonathan Trumbull, Jr. Papers, CHS.
17. Trumbull to William Williams, Dec. 25, 1790, Autograph Collection, Harvard Univ. Library, Cambridge, Mass.; *AC*, 1C 3S, 1817.
18. James Jackson in *AC*, 1C 3S, 1814.
19. To Williams, Dec. 25, 1790, Autograph Collection, Harvard Univ. Lib.
20. See Benjamin Bourn to Moses Brown, Dec. 25, 1790, Jan. 12, 1791, Moses Brown Papers, Rhode Island Historical Society, Providence, R.I.; James Pemberton to Moses Brown and Thomas Arnold, Jan. 19, 1791, Almy-Brown Papers, R.I. Hist. Soc.; various constituents to Theodore Foster, Jan. 1791, Theodore Foster Papers, R.I. Hist. Soc.
21. Edward Carrington to Madison, Feb. 2, 1791, James Madison Papers, LC. For the debate and congressional action, see *AC*, 1C 3S, 1804-1828, 1837, 1840.
22. To William Wedgeny, Nov. 11, 1791, Thacher Papers, MHS.
23. Under the act of March 3, 1791, the President could "engage a body to serve as cavalry" and, if a new regiment could not be recruited "in time to prosecute such military operations as exigencies" required, he could substitute an equal number of militia. The authorization in the bill was obviously meant to be temporary, and, except for cavalry, limited to less than a thousand militia (see *AC*, 1C 3S, 2351). Knox pointed out the lack of proper mobilization procedure when preparing temporary defense measures, telling Washington that the only alternative was to request the governors of exposed states to call out their militias. Jan. 1, 1792, George Washington Papers, LC.
24. To Archibald Stuart, Mar. 14, 1792, James Monroe Papers, Virginia Historical Society, Richmond, Va., in James Monroe Papers in Virginia Repositories [Univ. of Virginia Library Microfilm Publication Number Seven] (Charlottesville, 1969). See also William Barry Grove to Governor Alexander Martin, Mar. 7, 1792, Governor's Papers, North Carolina Department of Archives and History, Raleigh, N.C.
25. *AC*, 2C 1S, 419.
26. *Ibid.*, 420.
27. The debate in the House, Senate action, and the voting can be followed in *ibid.*, 103, 104, 111, 112, 113, 114, 115, 122-123, 128, 418-424, 432, 433, 435, 436, 552-553, 577, 578-579, 1392. The House vote was 31 to 27. It did

not follow any sectional or party pattern. Staunch Federalists like Ames, Sedgwick, and Boudinot voted for it, as did nearly all the anti-administration Virginians like Madison and Abraham Venable. Opponents included important Federalists like Wadsworth and Thacher as well as administration enemies William Findley, Nathaniel Macon, and Thomas Sumter. Several Federalists voted against it, undoubtedly because it was too weak, and several Republicans, with the exception of the Virginians who were faced with the Indian threat in the Kentucky district, voted against because it took too much power away from the states. The best account of the drafting of the law is Richard H. Fraser, The Foundations of American Military Policy, 1783–1800 (unpub. Ph.D. thesis, Univ. of Oklahoma, 1959), 259–284. See also Howard White, *Executive Influence in Determining Military Policy in the United States* [*University of Illinois Studies in the Social Sciences*, XII] (Urbana, 1924), 92–93; John K. Mahon, *The American Militia: Decade of Decision, 1789–1800* [*University of Florida Monographs, Social Sciences*, VI] (Gainesville, 1960), 17–18.

28. The law is in AC, 2C 1S, 1392–1395. With the exception of Jim Dan Hill (*The Minute Man in Peace and War: A History of the National Guard* [Harrisburg, 1964], 9–10), military analysts and historians have emphasized the weakness of the bill. See Brevet Major General Emory Upton, *The Military Policy of the United States* [62C 2S, Senate Document no. 494] (Washington, 1912), 85; John McAuley Palmer, *America in Arms; The Experience of the United States with Military Organization* (New Haven, 1941), 50–53; C. Joseph Bernardo and Eugene H. Bacon, *American Military Policy: Its Development Since 1775* (2d ed., Harrisburg, 1961), 77–82; Walter Millis, *Arms and Men: A Study in American Military History* (New York, 1956), 50–52; Arthur A. Ekirch, Jr., *The Civilian and the Military* (New York, 1956), 33–35; Frazer, Foundations of American Military Policy, 449–462; T. Harry Williams, *Americans at War: The Development of the American Military System* (Baton Rouge, La., 1960), 18–19; Mahon, *American Militia*, 18–21; Russell F. Weigley, *Towards an American Army: Military Thought from Washington to Marshall* (New York and London, 1962), 20–21 and *History of the United States Army* (New York and London, 1967), 93–94.

29. Knox to the Speaker of the House with enclosure, Dec. 10, 1794, AC, 3C 2S, 1396–1399.

30. The debate is in *ibid.*, 1067–1071, 1214–1221, 1233–1237. Washington recommended action in November 1794 (Sixth Annual Address to Congress, Nov. 18, 1794, WGW, XXXIV, 35). To trace action on the bill, see AC, 3C 2S, 1024, 1067–1071, 1162, 1214–1221, 1233–1237, 1396–1399; committee report, Dec. 29, 1794, ASP, MA, I, 107–108. The bill under discussion was printed as a broadside (see Charles Evans, *American Bibliography* [New York, 1941–1942], X, 228).

31. John A. Logan, *The Volunteer Soldier of America* . . . (Chicago and New York, 1887), 164–165. After the Whiskey Rebellion, Congress changed the procedures for calling out the militia and the scales of their pay while in national service. See AC, 3C 2S, 1490–1492, 1508–1510.

32. To John Henry, Dec, 3, 23, 1792, Kate Mason Rowland, *The Life of Charles Carroll* . . . (New York, 1898), II, 190, 193–194.

33. See Fraser, Foundations of American Military Policy, 299–330, 451–452.
34. Jonathan Williams in AC, 5C 2S, 642.
35. Apr. 16, 1790, Beard, ed., *Journal of Maclay*, 235.
36. General Emory Upton was the first to recognize the significance of the levies. See his *Military Policy of the U.S.*, 79.
37. First Inaugural Address, Mar. 4, 1801, James D. Richardson, ed., *A compilation of the Messages and Papers of the Presidents, 1789–1897* (Washington, 1896–1899), I, 323.

Chapter 8

HEADNOTES

a. "Letter . . . of principles and system of the Federalists," *Select Works of Robert Goodloe Harper* . . . (Baltimore, 1814), 338.
b. Given by the merchants of Philadelphia at City Tavern, Feb. 18, 1795, *Aurora* (Phila.), Feb. 23, 1795.
c. "Tully," *Gazette of the United States* (Phila.), Aug. 28, 1794.
d. To Washington, Aug. 5, 1794, George Washington Papers, LC.

SOURCE NOTES

1. To James McHenry, Mar. 18, 1799, John C. Hamilton, *History of the Republic . . . , as traced in the Writings of Alexander Hamilton* . . . (New York, 1850–1851), V, 235–236.
2. June 15, 1792, Anthony Wayne Papers, WLCL.
3. Wilkinson to Knox (extract), July 6, 1792, Anthony Wayne Papers, HSP; Wilkinson to Wayne, July 12, 1792, Wayne Papers, WLCL. A description of the western settlements about this time is in John Heckewelder's travel diary, Paul A. W. Wallace, *Thirty Thousand Miles with John Heckewelder* (Pittsburgh, 1958), 262, 266, 269–272, 282. The number of regulars on the frontier at this time totaled 28 officers and 790 rank and file, including officers' servants and sick unfit for duty (Wilkinson to Knox [extract], July 6, 1792, Wayne Papers, HSP). These troops had about three months supplies stockpiled. See E[lliott] and W[illiams] to Knox, May 9, 1792, Samuel Smith Papers, LC.
4. To Knox, June 15, 1792, Wayne Papers, WLCL.
5. To Theophilus Parsons, Jan. 16, 1792, Theophilus Parsons, *Memoir of Theophilus Parsons* (Boston, 1859), 467–468. See also Fisher Ames to George Richards Minot, Nov. 30, 1791, to Theodore Dwight, Jan. 23, 1792, to Minot, Mar. 8, 1792, Seth Ames, ed., *The Works of Fisher Ames* . . . (Boston, 1854), I, 105, 110–111, 114–115; Abigail Adams to Mary Cranch, Apr. 20, 1792, Stewart Mitchell, ed., *New Letters of Abigail Adams, 1788–1801* (Boston, 1947), 83.
6. To Archibald Stuart, Mar. 14, 1792, *WTJ*, VI, 407. See also Jefferson to Nicholas Lewis, Apr. 12, 1792, *ibid.*, 504–505.
7. Knox to Edward Carrington, July 24, 1792, Henry Knox Papers, Virginia

Historical Society, Richmond, Va.; Hamilton to John Adams, June 25, 1792, *PAH*, XI, 559. See also Hamilton to Carrington, May 26, 1792, Washington to Hamilton, July 29, 1792, Hamilton to Washington, with enclosures, Aug. 18, Sept. 9, 1792, *ibid.*, XI, 432–433, 441–444, XII, 129–134, 228–229, 249–252, 347–350.

8. Copies of the printed recruiting instructions, Apr. 7 and Apr. 12, 1792, are in the Torrence Collection, Cincinnati Historical Society, Cincinnati, Ohio and the Bezaleel Howe Papers, NYHS. See also Washington to Knox, Aug. 22, 1792, *WGW*, XXXII, 127; report on recruiting service, Apr. 23, 1792, Records of Committee Reports, 1C 1S to 4C 1S, Records of the United States House of Representatives, *RG* 233, NA.

9. Knox to Wayne, June 22, 29, July 13, Sept. 21, 1792, Wayne to Knox, Aug. 24, 1792, *WKPM*, 23, 24–25, 32, 101, 73–74; schedule of recruits marched, June 22, 1792, Wayne to Wilkinson, July 10, 1792, Wayne Papers, HSP.

10. Washington to Hamilton, May 7, 1792, Hamilton to Knox, May 13, 28, Aug. 6, 1792, Hamilton to Washington, July 22, 1792, *PAH*, XI, 371, 398, 450, XII, 168–169, 77.

11. Knox to O'Hara, Apr. 19, June 29, Aug. 6, 1792, Hodgdon to O'Hara, Aug. 8, Sept. 5, 1792, Letterbook, James O'Hara Papers, Indiana Historical Society, Indianapolis, Ind.

12. Knox to Wayne, June 22, 29, 1792, *WKPM*, 23, 24–25; Knox to Wilkinson, July 17, 1792, James Wilkinson Papers, Chicago Historical Society, Chicago, Ill.

13. Knox to Wayne, Aug. 10, 1792, Wayne Papers, WLCL. See also Washington to Knox, Aug. 5, 22, 1792, *WGW*, XXXII, 108, 127.

14. Aug. 5, 1792, Wayne Papers, HSP. See also Wayne to Sharp Delany, Aug. 24, 1792, Wayne Papers, WLCL; Wayne to Knox, Aug. 24, 1792, *WKPM*, 73–74.

15. Knox to Pond and Steedman, Jan. 9, 1792, *ASP, IA*, I, 227. For the other agents sent, see Knox to Wilkinson, Feb. 11, 1792, Wilkinson Papers, Chicago Hist. Soc.

16. Knox to Pond and Steedman, Jan. 9, 1792, *ASP, IA*, I, 227.

17. Cabinet opinion, Feb. 25, 1792, *WTJ*, VI, 191; cabinet notes, Mar. 9, 1792, Franklin B. Sawvel, ed., *The Complete Anas of Thomas Jefferson* (New York, 1903), 57–62.

18. Mar. 21, 1792, *PAH*, XI, 377.

19. For the background to the meeting, see *ibid.*, 372n; Knox to Brant, Feb. 25, 1792, *ASP, IA*, I, 228. For administration surprise about the Indians' views, see Pickering to Washington, Mar. 21, 1792, *PAH*, XI, 375–378; Knox to Wilkinson (extract), Apr. 27, 1792, General James Wilkinson, *Memoirs of My Own Times* (Philadelphia, 1816), II, appendix XIX; Knox to Putnam, May 22, 1792, *ASP, IA*, I, 234. A measure of how much the administration changed its policy after meeting the chiefs is the fact that the cabinet and the President had earlier decided not to use the Six Nations as emissaries (cabinet notes, Mar. 9, 1792, Sawvel, ed., *Anas of Jefferson*, 60–62). The visit of the Six Nations' chiefs and the mediation effort can be followed generally in Knox to Washington, Apr. 18, 1792, Washington Papers, LC; Knox to Israel Chapin, Apr. 23, 28, 1792, Washington's message to Five Nations delegation, Apr. 25, 1792, Knox to Aupaumut, May 8, 1792, *ASP,*

IA, I, 231, 232, 233; Joseph D. Ibbotson, "Samuel Kirkland, the Treaty of 1792, and the Indian Barrier State," *New York History*, XIX (1938), 380–391; Edward Hake Phillips, "Timothy Pickering at his Best: Indian-Commissioner, 1790–1794," *Essex Institute Historical Collections*, CII (1966), 177–180. An interesting. description of the entertainment and gift-giving involved in the meeting is Katherine C. Turner, *Red Men Calling on the Great White Father* (Norman, Okla., 1951), 8–15.

20. See Knox's instructions to the various agents, Apr. 3, May 8, 1792, *ASP, IA*, I, 229–230, 233.

21. "Instructions to . . . Putnam," May 22, 1792, *ibid.*, 234–236.

22. Knox to Wayne, June 15, 1792, *WKPM*, 19. Wayne was also ordered to write to the county lieutenants to this effect (Wayne to the lieutenant of Mason County, June 23, 1792, Draper Collection, 4U206, State Historical Society of Wisconsin, Madison, Wis.). John Heckewelder, a Moravian missionary, was convinced enough of the government's sincerity to accept an appointment as Putnam's assistant in May 1792. See his travel diary, Wallace, ed., *John Heckewelder*, 259–260.

23. "Conversation . . . ," May 28–29, 1792, *PAH*, XI, 446. See also Hammond to Lord Grenville, June 8, 1792, *ibid.*, 448n; Jefferson to Lafayette, June 16, 1792, *WTJ*, VI, 78.

24. Knox to Wayne, June 22, 29, 1792, *WKPM*, 22–23, 25; Knox to Brant, June 27, 1792, *ASP, IA*, I, 236; Knox to Wilkinson, July 17, 1792, Wilkinson Papers, Chicago Hist. Soc.; Turner, *Red Men*, 18–20.

25. Wayne to Wilkinson, Aug. 5, 1792, Wayne Papers, HSP. See also Wilkinson to Wayne, July 12, 1792, Wayne to Sharp Delany, Aug. 24, 1792, Wayne Papers, WLCL; Putnam to Knox, July 14, 1792, Wayne to Putnam, Aug. 6, 1792, Rowena Buell, ed., *The Memoirs of Rufus Putnam* . . . (Boston and New York, 1903), 296, 311–312; Wayne to Knox, Aug. 3, 1792, *WKPM*, 56–57. For the murders and the course of negotiating efforts during the summer, see Putnam to Knox, July 8, 11, 14, 1792, Putnam to Hamtramck, July 24, 1792, Knox to Putnam, Aug. 7, 1792, Buell, ed., *Rufus Putnam*, 280–283, 293, 305, 313–314; deposition of John May, Oct. 11, 1792, *ASP, IA*, I, 243; deposition of William Smellie [Smally], Oct. 11, 1792, John Jay Papers, NYHS.

26. See Knox to Washington, Sept. 15, 1792, Washington Papers, LC; Washington to Gouverneur Morris, Oct. 20, 1792, *WGW*, XXXII, 189; Knox to the Senate, Nov. 8, 1792, "A Treaty of peace and friendship . . . ," Sept. 27, 1792, *ASP, IA*, I, 319, 338; Knox to Wayne, Nov. 9, 1792, *WKPM*, 132. For expressions of hope, see Jonathan Trumbull, Jr. to [William?] Williams, Nov. 10, 1792, Jonathan Trumbull, Jr. Papers, CHS; Paine Wingate to Josiah Bartlett, Nov. 8, 1792, Charles E. L. Wingate, *Life and Letters of Paine Wingate* (Medford, Mass., 1930), II, 411; Roger Sherman to Governor Huntington, Dec. 10, 1792, Ferdinand Dreer Collection, HSP; Henry Van Schaack to Sedgwick, Dec. 29, 1792, Theodore Sedgwick Papers, MHS.

27. Speech of Messqualkinol, Sept. 30, 1792, "Canadian Archives, Colonial Office Records," *Michigan Pioneer and Historical Society, Collections*, XXIV (1894), 494.

28. See Knox's instructions to Pond and Steedman, Jan. 9, 1792, to Trueman,

Apr. 3, 1792, to Aupaumut, May 8, 1792, to Putnam, May 22, 1792, Knox to the Miami, Wabash, etc., Apr. 4, 1792, *ASP, IA*, I, 227, 229–230, 233, 234–236.

29. Knox to the Speaker of the House, Nov. 1792, *ASP, MA*, I, 39; *AC*, 2C 2S, 611–615, 672, 679–689; Washington to Knox, Sept. 3, 1792, *WGW*, XXXII, 140; Jefferson to Thomas Mann Randolph, Nov. 16, 1792, *WTJ*, VII, 134.

30. See Knox to the Speaker, with enclosures, Dec. 11, 1792, *ASP, MA*, I, 39–40; *AC*, 2C 2S, 672, 750. On November 14, Hamilton submitted his general estimate for 1793, which included nearly $1,100,000 for the military establishment (*PAH*, XIII, 118–147).

31. *AC*, 2C 2S, 750. For an indication of Steele's attitudes on this and Indian wars in general, see his motion in draft, Dec. 28, 1792, John Steele Papers, Southern Historical Collection, Univ. of North Carolina Library, Chapel Hill, N.C.; Steele to McDowell, Nov. 20, 1794, Kemp P. Battle, ed., *Letters of Nathaniel Macon, John Steele and William Barry Grove* [James Sprunt Historical Monograph, no. 3] (Chapel Hill, 1902), 18; After the Second Congress, Steele, although elected to the North Carolina legislature, applied for a job with the administration; eventually he became Comptroller of the Treasury.

32. The debate can be followed in *AC*, 2C 2S, 750, 762–768, 773–802. Knox described the opposition "from Maryland Eastward" as against "the principle of the War," while "Southern Citizens" opposed mostly "the manner of carrying it on." To Wayne, Jan. 5, 1793, *WKPM*, 165.

33. To Theodore Dwight, Jan. 1793, Ames, ed., *Fisher Ames*, I, 127. Thomas Hartley, a close friend of Wayne and a Pennsylvania Federalist, also attributed Steele's attack to party motives (to Wayne, Jan. 11, 1793, Wayne Papers, HSP). For Madison's position, see the *AC*, 2C 2S, 792, 801–802.

34. When Congress met, the newspaper war had begun afresh. See, for example, *Federal Gazette* (Phila.), Aug. 16, 18, 23, 25, 28, 31, Sept. 5, 8, 1792; *National Gazette* (Phila.), Nov. 21, 1792, Jan. 9, 19, 26, Feb. 9, May 8, 1793; *Kentucky Gazette* (Lexington), Dec. 1, 1792.

35. To Knox, Aug. 22, 1792, *WGW*, XXXII, 127. See also, Knox to Wayne, Aug. 7, 24, Sept. 28, Oct. 5, Nov. 24, 1792, *WKPM*, 61, 63, 73–74, 111, 112–113, 141; Knox to Wayne, Aug. 10, 1792, Wayne Papers, WLCL; Rufus King to G. Morris, Sept. 1, 1792, *LCRK*, I, 426.

36. To William Atlee, Dec. 12, 1792, Personal Papers Miscellaneous, LC. For army problems, see Wayne to Knox, Aug. 24, 1792, Knox to Wayne, Sept. 1, 1792, *WKPM*, 73–74, 82–83; Knox to Hamilton, Nov. 3, 1792, Wayne to Wilkinson, Nov. 7, 18, 1792, Wilkinson to Wayne, Nov. 13, 1792, Wayne Papers, HSP; Fourth Annual Address to Congress, Nov. 6, 1792, *WGW*, XXXII, 206; Knox, "Statement of Troops . . . ," Nov. 6, 1792, *ASP, IA*, I, 318; Knox to Nicholas Fish, Aug. 29, 1792, Fish to Knox, Sept. 7, 1792, Northwest Territory Papers, WLCL; John Belli to O'Hara, Dec. 16, 1792, Letterbook, O'Hara Papers, Ind. Hist. Soc.

37. Dec. 7, 1792, Jan. 5, 1793, *WKPM*, 148–149, 165.

38. Conversations with George Hammond, Nov. 22, Dec. 15–28, *PAH*, XIII, 213–215, 326–328; Hammond to Simcoe, Nov. 27, 1792, Brig. General E. A. Cruikshank, ed., *The Correspondence of Lieut. Governor John Graves Simcoe . . .* (Toronto, 1923–1931), I, 267–269.

39. Journal of the President, Jan. 5, 21, 25, Feb. 1, 11, 1793, Washington Papers, LC.

40. "Strong hopes of a General Peace prevail here," wrote Henry Lee from Philadelphia on February 15, after talking with Knox (to James Wood, Sherwin McRae, ed., *Calendar Virginia State Papers* [Richmond, 1875–1893], VI, 292).

41. Cabinet notes, Feb. 24, 1793, Sawvel, ed., *Anas of Jefferson*, 108–109. For the meeting, see also the Journal of the President, Feb. 24, 1793, cabinet to the President, Feb. 25, 1793, Washington Papers, LC; Jefferson to G. Morris, Mar. 12, 1793, *WTJ*, VII, 201.

42. See the Journal of the President, Feb. 16, 17, 24, 1793, Washington Papers, LC; Washington to the various cabinet officers, Feb. 17, 24, 1793, WGW, XXXII, 348–349, 356; William Hull to Hamilton, Feb. 6, 1793, Aupaumut to Pickering, received Feb. 24, 1793, Timothy Pickering Papers, MHS; Simcoe to Hammond, Feb. 3, 1793, "Canadian Archives," *Mich. Pioneer Hist. Collections*, XXIV, 529–530; Simcoe to Allured Clarke, Jan. 27, 1793, to Dorchester, Jan. 14, 1793, Cruikshank, ed., *Correspondence of Simcoe*, I, 280–282, 299.

43. To Thomas Pinckney, Nov. 27, 1793, Andrew A. Lipscomb and Albert E. Bergh, eds., *Writings of Thomas Jefferson* (Washington, 1903), IX, 258.

44. To Lord Dorchester, Jan. 14, 1793, Cruikshank, ed., *Correspondence of Simcoe*, I, 299. For administration statements and understanding of policy by outsiders, see Albert Gallatin to Thomas Clarke, Mar. 9, 1793, Albert Gallatin Papers, NYHS; Tobias Lear to David Humphreys, Apr. 8, 1793, Autograph Collection, Philip H. and A. S. W. Rosenbach Foundation, Philadelphia, Pa.; Washington to Henry Lee, May 6, 1793, WGW, XXXII, 449; Jefferson to Harry Innes, May 23, 1793, Harry Innes Papers, LC; John Brown to Isaac Shelby, July 14, 1793, Shelby Family Papers, LC; Thomas McKean to Edward Telfair, Aug. 2, 1793, Edward Telfair Papers, Duke Univ. Library, Durham, N.C.

45. See, for example, John Preston to Francis Preston, May 31, 1793, Preston Papers, College of William and Mary College Library, Williamsburg, Va.

46. *WKPM*, 198–200.

47. Knox to Wayne, Apr. 13, 1793, *ibid.*, 218; Knox to Henry Lee, Apr. 24, 1793, McRae, ed., *Calendar Va. State Papers*, VI, 350; Knox to Isaac Shelby, Apr. 24, 1793, Isaac Shelby Papers, The Filson Club, Louisville, Ky.

48. Knox to Wayne, Apr. 13, 1793, *WKPM*, 218.

49. Knox to Wayne, Apr. 13, 20, 1793, *ibid.*, 218–219, 221–223; Knox to peace commissioners, Apr. 29, 1793, Pickering Papers, MHS.

50. To Shelby, Apr. 11, 1793, Shelby Family Papers, LC.

51. To Innes, May 18, 1793, Innes Papers, LC.

52. See Washington to Thomson, Jan. 31, 1793, Charles Thomson Papers, LC. Benjamin Hawkins suggested naming Steele in a letter proposing negotiations "to endure a general acquiescence in the measures which must of necessity be pursued." See Hawkins to Washington, Feb. 20, 1793, Miscellaneous Letters of the Department of State, General Records of the Department of State, *RG* 59, NA.

53. "Instructions . . . ," Apr. 26, 1793, *ASP, IA*, I, 340–342. See also Journal of the President, Feb. 28, Mar. 25, 1793, Washington Papers, LC; Washing-

ton, circular to cabinet officers, Mar. 21, 1793, WGW, XXXII, 395–396. Knox estimated the expenses for the treaty at over $80,000 (to the Speaker of the House, Feb. 19, 1793, Reports of the Secretary of War, 1C 1S to 2C 2S, House Records, RG 233, NA).

54. May 27, 1793, *ASP, IA,* I, 345. For Indian suspicion, see Alexander McKee to Simcoe, Jan. 30, 1793, Cruikshank, ed., *Correspondence of Simcoe,* I, 282.

55. Commissioners to Knox, June 26, July 10, 1793, journal of the commissioners, July 5–9, 1793, *ASP, IA,* I, 348, 349–351; "Minutes of a council . . . ," July 7–9, 1793, "Canadian Archives," *Mich. Pioneer Hist. Collections,* XXIV, 560–568; Brant's speech, July 7, 1793, Pickering's speech, July 8, 1793, Cruikshank, ed., *Correspondence of Simcoe,* I, 378; Pickering to his wife, July 9, 1793, Pickering Transcripts, EI; diary, July 29, 1793, Wallace, ed., *John Heckewelder,* 315–316.

56. Wayne to Knox, July 2, 1793, *WKPM,* 250–252. The June 7 letter was not found, but see Knox to Wayne, June 28, July 2, 1793, *WKPM,* 248, 251–253; commissioners to [Knox] (extract), May 27, 1793, Wayne Papers, HSP; Wilkinson to Shelby, June 24, 1793, Shelby Family Papers, LC.

57. July 20, 1793, *WKPM,* 256–257. For Washington's mood at this time, see his letter to Henry Lee, July 21, 1793, WGW, XXXIII, 22.

58. Aug. 8, 1793, *WKPM,* 260–266. Knopf has mixed Wayne's Aug. 7 draft with the Aug. 8 letter actually sent, which was milder. See the manuscripts in the Wayne Papers, HSP.

59. To Shelby, Aug. 20, 1793, Shelby Family Papers, LC.

60. Wayne to Wilkinson, Aug. 8, 1793, Wayne Papers, HSP. For Wilkinson's feelings, see his letters to Shelby, June 24, 1793, Shelby Family Papers, LC, and to Innes, Aug. 20, 1793, Innes Papers, LC.

61. Journal of the commissioners, with speeches, July 14, 30, 31, Aug. 1, 12–14, 16, 1793, commissioners to Knox, Aug. 21, 1793, *ASP, IA,* I, 351, 352–354, 355, 356, 359; Jacob Lindley's travel account, June 10, July 29–Aug. 1, 1793, Joseph Moore's journal, June 28, July 25, 1793, Jacob Lindley *et al.,* "Expedition to Detroit, 1793," *Mich. Pioneer Hist. Collections,* XVII, 584–608, 618–620, 643, 653; Pickering to his wife, July 9, Aug. 12, 21, 1793, Pickering Transcripts, EI; Heckewelder, memorandum, June 17–23, 1793, Aupaumut to Pickering, Aug. 6, 1793, "Instructions to the Runner," Aug. [14?], 1793, Heckewelder to Pickering, Jan. 4, 1794, Pickering Papers, MHS; Simcoe to Butler and McKee, June 22, 1793, Brant to Simcoe, July 28, 1793, McKee to Simcoe, June 29, July 1, 28, Aug. 22, 1793, "Canadian Archives," *Mich. Pioneer Hist. Collections,* XXIV, 555, 571–573, 558, 559, 595; western Indians to Washington, n.d., to the commissioners, July 27, 1793, speech of commissioners, July 31, 1793, Joseph Chew to McKee, Aug. [?], 1793, Simcoe to Dorchester, Nov. 10, 1793, Cruikshank, ed., *Correspondence of Simcoe,* I, 283–284, 401–402, 405–409, II, 38, 101–104; travel diary, July 2–Aug. 20, 1793, Wallace, ed., *John Heckewelder,* 312–320; deposition of William Wells, Sept. 16, 1793, Dwight L. Smith, ed., "William Wells and the Indian Council of 1793," *Indiana Magazine of History,* LVI (1960), 219–226. For the negotiation from the British viewpoint, see Reginald Horsman, *Matthew Elliott, British Indian Agent* (Detroit, 1964), 72–91;

Reginald Horsman, "The British Indian Department and the Abortive Treaty of Lower Sandusky, 1793," *Ohio Historical Quarterly*, LXX (1961), 189–213; Fred Waldo Shipman, The Indian Council of 1793: A Clash of Policies (unpub. M.A. thesis, Clark University, 1933). For Pickering's view, see Phillips, "Timothy Pickering," *Essex Institute Hist. Collections*, CII, 182–193.

62. See Knox to Wayne, Apr. 20, Aug. 16, 1793, Wayne to Knox, Jan. 24, Apr. 27, 1793, *WKPM*, 176, 221–223, 269–270, 228–230; cabinet meeting, Aug. 1793 [noted Sept. 4, 1793], Sawvel, ed., *Anas of Jefferson*, 172–173.

63. The quotation is from Wayne to Knox, June 20, 1793, *WKPM*, 244–245. See also Knox to Wayne, May 17, 1793, Wayne to Knox, July 2, 1793, *ibid.*, 238–239, 253; minutes of Board of War, June 24, 1793, Wayne to county lieutenants, June 30, 1793, Wayne Papers, HSP; Wilkinson to Hand, Aug. 20, 1792, Emmet Collection, NYPL; Wilkinson to Shelby, Apr. 11, June 24, 1793, Shelby Family Papers, LC; Edmund Randolph to Washington, June 11, 1793, Washington Papers, LC.

64. Wayne to Knox, Sept. 17, 1793, *WKPM*, 272–273; general orders, Sept. 11, 1793, Wayne to Scott, Sept. 12, 1793, Wayne Papers, HSP; Scott to Shelby, Sept. 14, 1793, Draper Collection, 5U25, State Hist. Soc. Wis.

65. Sept. 17, 1793, *WKPM*, 273.

66. To Knox, Oct. 5, 1793, *ibid.*, 277. For the problems with the volunteers, see Isaac Shelby to Scott, Sept. 18, 1793, Northwest Territory Papers, WLCL; Wayne to Scott, Sept. 26, 1793, to Shelby, Sept. 26, 1793, James Young Love and Thomas Love Papers, Filson Club.

67. Thomas Posey to Wayne, Nov. 2, 1793, Wayne Papers, HSP. See also minutes of a council of war, Oct. 31, 1793, Scott to Wayne, Nov. 1, 1793, Thomas Barbee to Wayne, Nov. 1, 1793, Wilkinson and Posey to Wayne, Nov. 1, 1793, *ibid.*

68. For the council and the information about it in Philadelphia, see Jefferson to Enoch Edwards, Dec. 30, 1793, *WTJ*, VIII, 134; deposition of Wells, Sept. 16, 1793, *Ind. Magazine Hist.*, LVI, 219–226; Beverley Randolph to Pickering, Oct. 4, 1793, Pickering Papers, MHS; Charles Storer to Pickering, Oct. 4, 1793, Pickering to Washington, Oct. 15, 1793, Washington Papers, LC; journal [conversation with Pickering], Jan. 11, 1794, Dwight Foster Papers, American Antiquarian Society, Worcester, Mass.; Simcoe to Dorchester, Nov. 10, 1793, Cruikshank, ed., *Correspondence of Simcoe*, II, 101–104; Horsman, *Matthew Elliott*, 82–91. For the background internationally and internally see Samuel Flagg Bemis, *Jay's Treaty: A Study in Commerce and Diplomacy* (rev. ed., New Haven and London, 1962), 183–217; Alexander DeConde, *Entangling Alliance: Politics and Diplomacy under George Washington* (Durham, N.C., 1958), 87–91, 180–256, 269–303; Dumas Malone, *Jefferson and His Time* (Boston, 1948–date), III, 68–162; John Alexander Carroll and Mary Wells Ashworth, *George Washington: First in Peace* [completing the biography by Douglas Southall Freeman] (New York, 1957), 132–148; Alfred F. Young, *The Democratic Republicans of New York: The Origins, 1763–1797* (Chapel Hill, 1967), 349–365; Harry Ammon, *The Genet Mission* (New York, 1973); Arthur Preston Whitaker, *The Spanish-American Frontier: 1783–1795* . . . (Boston, 1927),

185–197; William H. Masterson, *William Blount* (Baton Rouge, 1954), 238–249, 251–258; James A. James, *The Life of George Rogers Clark* (Chicago, 1929), 410–411, 419–427; Frederick J. Turner, "The Origin of Genet's Projected Attack on Louisiana and the Floridas," *American Historical Review*, III (1898), 650–671; cabinet opinions, June 1, 4, Aug. 4, 31, 1793, Jefferson to Carmichael and Short, June 30, 1793, *WTJ*, VII, 275–277, 281, 424–435, 465, VIII, 10; cabinet opinions, June 1, 1793, Medad Mitchell to Hamilton, Aug. 27, 1793, *PAH*, XIV, 507–508, XV, 288–300; Washington to Knox, June 14, 1793, to Knox and Pickens, July 26, 1793, Fifth Annual Address to Congress, Dec. 3, 1793, *WGW*, XXXII, 502–503, XXXIII, 31–32, 167–168.

69. June 7, 1794, *WKPM*, 336–337. See also Knox to Wayne, Mar. 31, 1794, *ibid.*, 316–317; Knox to Wayne, July 11, 1794, Autograph Collection, Rosenbach Foundation; Washington to Knox, Apr. 4, May 1, 1794, *WGW*, XXXIII, 313–314, 349; Knox to Washington, May 12, 1794, cabinet memorandum, May 13, 1794, Washington Papers, LC; Sedgwick to Ephraim Williams, Feb. 26, 1794, Sedgwick Papers, MHS; Bemis, *Jay's Treaty*, 253–278; DeConde, *Entangling Alliance*, 92–100; Carroll and Ashworth, *George Washington*, 149–164.

70. To Knox, Aug. 14, 1793, *ASP, IA*, I, 490. For the January peace feeler, see Wayne to Knox, Jan. 8, 18, 25, Mar. 3, 20, 1794, *WKPM*, 297–313; Wayne to the Indians, Jan. 14, 1794, McKee to Chew, Feb. 1, 1794, Elliott to McKee, Feb. 11, 1794, Cruikshank, ed., *Correspondence of Simcoe*, II, 131–132, 139, 152; Dorchester to Dundas, Mar. 28, 1794, "Canadian Archives," *Mich. Pioneer Hist. Collections*, XXIV, 654.

71. For the campaign and battle, see Jacobs, *Beginning of U.S. Army*, 171–178; Thomas R. Case, "The Battle of Fallen Timbers," *Northwest Ohio Quarterly*, XXXV (1963), 54–68; Jack Jule Gifford, The Northwest Indian War, 1783–1795 (unpub. Ph.D. thesis, Univ. of California—Los Angeles, 1964) ch. X; Wayne to the Indians, Aug. 13, 1794, to Knox, Aug. 14, 1794, "Return of Killed, wounded, and missing . . . ," Aug. 20, 1794, William Campbell to Wayne, Aug. 21, 22, 1794, Wayne to Campbell, Aug. 21, 22, 1794, *ASP, IA*, I, 490, 492, 493–494; Wayne to Knox, Aug. 28, 1794, *WKPM*, 351–355; R. C. McGrane, ed., "William Clark's Journal of General Wayne's Campaign," *Mississippi Valley Historical Review*, I (1914), 418–444; John B. Linn, ed., "Captain John Cooke's Journal," *American Historical Record*, II (1873), 311–316, 339–345; Lieutenant Boyer, *A Journal of Wayne's Campaign* (Cincinnati, 1866); Frazer E. Wilson, ed., *Journal of Capt. Daniel Bradley* (Greenville, Ohio, 1935), 62–74; *Journal of Thomas Taylor Underwood* (Cincinnati, 1945); Dwight L. Smith, ed., *From Greene Ville to Fallen Timbers: A Journal of the Wayne Campaign . . .* (Indianapolis, 1952); Dwight L. Smith, ed., *With Captain Edward Miller in the Wayne Campaign of 1794* (Ann Arbor, 1965); diary of Nathaniel Hart, Aug. 20, 1794, reminiscences of General Brady, Aug. 13, 1842, Draper Collection 5U 100–101, 5U126–150, State Hist. Soc. Wis. For the British-Indian viewpoint, see diary of Alexander Harrow, Aug. 18–24, 1794, Harrow Family Papers, Burton Historical Collection, Detroit Public Library, Detroit, Mich.; Horsman, *Matthew Elliott*, 96–105.

72. James Madison in Jonathan Elliot, ed., *The Debates in the Several State Conventions, on the Adoption of the Federal Constitution* . . . (Washington, 1854), III, 384, 413-415; Richard Henry Lee to Edmund Pendleton, May 22, 1788, John Lamb Papers, NYHS. See also Oliver Ellsworth in Elliot, ed., *Debates*, II, 197; Charles Pinckney, "Observations on the Plan of Government . . . ," Max Farrand, ed., *The Records of the Federal Convention of 1787* (rev. ed., New Haven, 1937), III, 118-119.

73. William Vans Murray to Tench Coxe, Sept. 20, 1794, Tench Coxe Papers, HSP; *Gazette of the U.S.* (Phila.), Aug. 2, Sept. 6, Dec. 22, 1794. See also New York *Minerva*, Sept. 30, 1794; Oliver Wolcott, Jr. to Oliver Wolcott, Aug. 16, 1794, *MAWA*, I, 157; Washington to Burges Ball, Sept. 25, 1794, *WGW*, XXXIII, 506.

74. To Washington, Sept. 9, 1792, *PAH*, XII, 346. See also Hamilton to Edward Carrington, May 26, 1792, *ibid.*, XI, 426-445.

75. Sawvel, ed., *Anas of Jefferson*, 183.

76. To Elias Boudinot, Aug. 1, 1794, John William Wallace Papers, HSP. See also Alexander Addison to Henry Lee, Nov. 23, 1794, Isaac Craig Papers, Carnegie Library of Pittsburgh, Pittsburgh, Pa. For Federalist views of the opposition and politics, see Hamilton to ———, May 18, 1793, Stephen Higginson to Hamilton, July 26, 1793, Rufus King to Hamilton, Aug. 3, 1793, Hugh Williamson to Hamilton, May 27, 1794, *PAH*, XIV, 473-476, XV, 127-128, 173, XVI, 436-437; King, memorandum on the opposition, 1793, Rufus King Papers, NYHS; Henry Lee to [Washington?], Sept. 17, 1793, Paul P. Hoffman and John L. Molyneaux, eds., *Lee Family Papers* (microfilm ed., Charlottesville, 1966), reel 7, exposure 856; Hamilton, draft of essay, 1794, Alexander Hamilton Papers, LC; James McHenry to John Bleakley, Feb. 9, 1794, James McHenry Papers, Maryland Historical Society, Baltimore, Md.; Zephaniah Swift to David Daggett, Apr. 17, 1794, Franklin B. Dexter, ed., "Selections from the Letters Received by David Daggett, 1786-1802," *Proceedings of the American Antiquarian Society*, new ser., IV (1887), 372. See also Marshall Smelser, "The Federalist Period as an Age of Passion," *American Quarterly*, X (1958), 391-419; John R. Howe, Jr., "Republican Thought and the Political Violence of the 1790s," *ibid.*, XIX (1967), 147-165; Richard Hofstadter, *The Idea of a Party System: The Rise of Legitimate Opposition in the United States, 1780-1840* (Berkeley and Los Angeles, 1969), ix-x, 7-9, 16-18, 34-35, 84-111. The fear of conspiracy and sedition were more widespread and surfaced earlier than Smelser implies, however, and by 1794 was directly affecting government policy.

77. The background of the rebellion is covered generally by Leland D. Baldwin, *Whiskey Rebels: The Story of a Frontier Uprising* (rev. ed., Pittsburgh, 1962), 23-128. For a review of the literature and an attack on standard assumptions, see Jacob E. Cooke, "The Whiskey Insurrection: A Re-Evaluation," *Pennsylvania History*, XXX (1963), 316-346. The best legislative study of the whiskey tax is William D. Barber, "'Among the Most *Techy Articles of Civil Police*': Federal Taxation and the Adoption of the Whiskey Excise," *WMQ*, XXV (1968), 58-84.

78. Minutes of the meeting, Aug. 21-22, 1792, *PAH*, XII, 308-309n.

79. John Neville to George Clymer, Aug. 23, 1792, *ibid.*, 306n, 310n. The first

incidents of violence had led Neville to conclude that "it will be impossible to carry the law into effect without an armed force" (to Clymer, Nov. 17, 1791, Oliver Wolcott, Jr. Papers, CHS).

80. To Edward Carrington, July 25, 1792, *PAH*, XII, 84.
81. Sept. 3, 1792, *ibid.*, 316–317.
82. Hamilton to Tench Coxe, Sept. 1, 1792, *ibid.*, 310.
83. Sept. 1, 1792, *ibid.*, 310–313.
84. Jay to Hamilton, Sept. 8, 1792, King to Hamilton, Sept. 27, 1792, *ibid.*, 334–335, 493–494.
85. Randolph to Hamilton, Sept. 8, 1792, *ibid.*, 336–340.
86. Washington to Hamilton, Sept. 17, 1792, *ibid.*, 390–392. See also Washington to Hamilton, Sept. 7, 1792, *ibid.*, 331–333.
87. John Gibson to Thomas Mifflin, July 18, 1794, Isaac Craig to Henry Knox, July 18, 1794, Thomas Butler to Knox, July 18, 1794, *Pennsylvania Archives, Second Series* (Harrisburg, 1887–1896), IV, 58–60; Neville to Coxe, July 18, 1794, *Bulletin of the Carnegie Library of Pittsburgh*, XVI (1911), 193–194.
88. "Conference at the President's," Aug. 2, 1794, *Pa. Archives*, IV, 124.
89. There is no record of the July cabinet meeting, but indications that one took place are in Randolph to Washington, Aug. 5, 1794, Washington Papers, LC; Bradford to Boudinot, Aug. 1, 1794, Wallace Papers, HSP. For the arrival of the information from Pittsburgh, the militia law, and administration jitters, see the *General Advertiser* (Phila.), July 25, 1794; *Independent Gazetteer* (Phila.), July 26, 1794; AC, 3C 2S, 1490–1492, 1508–1510; Bradford to Boudinot, Aug. 1, 1794, Wallace Papers, HSP. To buttress their case, Hamilton secured testimony from Francis Mentges, an army colonel who had been in Pittsburgh between July 22 and 25. See the deposition in Hamilton's handwriting, Aug. 1, 1794, Wolcott, Jr. Papers, CHS. Wilson, however, wanted the handwriting of various documents verified. See Hamilton to Tench Coxe, Aug. 1, 1794, *PAH*, XVII, 1.
90. Alexander Dallas to Jared Ingersoll, July 25, 1794, Dallas to the judges, etc. (circular), July 25, 1794, Dallas to John Gibson, July 25, 1794, Dallas to Knox, July 26, 1794, *Pa. Archives*, IV, 66–67. According to the administration's information, county officials had been involved in the rioting. See Neville to Coxe, July 18, 1794, *Bulletin Carnegie Lib. Pittsburgh*, XVI, 194.
91. Knox to Mifflin, May 24, 1794, Knox Papers, MHS; Washington to Knox, June 25, 1794, *WGW*, XXXIII, 410–411. See also Harry Marlin Tinkcom, *The Republicans and Federalists in Pennsylvania, 1790–1801: A Study in National Stimulus and Local Response* (Harrisburg, 1950), 113–131; Kenneth R. Rossman, *Thomas Mifflin and the Politics of the American Revolution* (Chapel Hill, 1952), 232–246.
92. "Conference at the President's," Aug. 2, 1794, *Pa. Archives*, IV, 122–124. According to Dallas, the state officials "were invited" (to William Irvine, Aug. 7, 1794, William Irvine Papers, HSP).
93. See Mifflin to Washington, Aug. 5, 12, 1794, Randolph to Mifflin, Aug. 7, 1794, *ASP, Miscellaneous*, I, 97–103; Dallas to Irvine, Aug. 7, 1794, Irvine Papers, HSP; Bradford to Randolph, Aug. 8, 1794, Pennsylvania Miscellany, Whiskey Rebellion, LC.
94. Both Bradford and Randolph expressed great fears on this point. See

Bradford to Boudinot, Aug. 7, 1794, J. J. Boudinot, ed., *The Life, Public Services, Addresses, and Letters of Elias Boudinot . . .* (Boston, 1896), II, 86–87; Randolph to Thomas Pinckney, Aug. 11, 1794, United States Miscellany, LC.

95. "Memoranda of an Executive Conference," [Aug. 2, 1794], *Pa. Archives*, IV, 70, outlines the agreement.

96. Knox to Washington, Aug. 4, 1794, Washington Papers, LC. See also Hamilton to Washington, Aug. 2, 1794, *PAH*, XVII, 15–19. Both estimated that the insurgents could muster as many as 7,000 armed men.

97. Bradford to Washington, Aug. 1794, Randolph to Washington, Aug. 5, 1794, Washington Papers, LC; Mifflin to Washington, Aug. 5, 1794, *ASP*, *Miscellaneous*, I, 97–99.

98. Randolph to Washington, Aug. 5, 1794, Washington Papers, LC.

99. Wilson to Washington, Aug. 4, 1794, *ASP*, *Miscellaneous*, I, 85.

100. The idea of negotiating was discussed at the August 2 conference ("Memoranda of an Executive Conference," [Aug. 2, 1794], *Pa. Archives*, IV, 70). It was also mentioned by Randolph in his letter to Washington, but there is no ironclad proof that a federal peace commission was agreed upon until August 7 when Bradford actually left on the mission. Preliminary steps were taken by August 5, however, when draft instructions were ready (Randolph to Washington, Aug. 5, 1794, Washington Papers, LC; Hamilton and Knox to Washington, Aug. 5, 1794, *PAH*, XVII, 21). The decision was evidently made final at the cabinet meeting on August 6, since Bradford left Philadelphia on August 7 (minutes of the commissioners, Aug. 7, 1794, Pa. Miscellany, Whiskey Rebellion, LC). The official instructions signed by each cabinet officer, are dated August 7 and are printed in *PAH*, XVII, 22–23.

101. Bradford to Boudinot, Aug. 7, 1794, Boudinot, ed., *Elias Boudinot*, II, 87. For Washington's thinking, see Washington to Charles Mynn Thruston, Aug. 10, 1794, *WGW*, XXXIII, 465, Washington to "Fellow-citizens of the Senate and of the House of Representatives," Nov. 20, 1794, *ASP*, *Miscellaneous*, I, 83–85; Randolph to the commissioners, Sept. 29, 1794, Domestic Letters of the Department of State, General Records of the Department of State, *RG* 59, NA.

102. Proclamation, Aug. 7, 1794, *WGW*, XXXIII, 457–461; Knox to [the Governor of N.J.?], Aug. 7, 1794, Anthony Walton White Papers, Rutgers University Library, New Brunswick, N.J.; Knox to Mifflin, Aug. 7, 1794, *Pa. Archives*, IV, 101–102; minutes of the commissioners, Aug. 7, 1794, Pa. Miscellany, Whiskey Rebellion, LC. There is no record of the August 6 cabinet meeting, but Hamilton and Knox asked for one for that date (Hamilton and Knox to Washington, Aug. 5, 1794, *PAH*, XVII, 21). Since the government acted on August 7 and Bradford left for Pittsburgh that day, the meeting undoubtedly took place and most likely on August 6. Moreover, at the meeting, Washington asked Hamilton to prepare a document citing the opposition and acts of violence against the excise. See Hamilton to Washington, Aug. 5, 6, 16, 1794, *ibid.*, 24–59, 101.

103. Randolph to commissioners, Aug. 7, 1794, Domestic Letters of Department of State, *RG* 59, NA. Another copy of this letter, also dated August 7, is in the Simon Gratz Collection (HSP). Therefore the published version is either

misdated or was purposely backdated by the administration when it sent the document to Congress (Randolph to the commissions, Aug. 5, 1794, *ASP, Miscellaneous*, I, 86–87). The editors of the *PAH* (XVII, 22–23) accept the August 7 date.

104. Bradford to Randolph, Aug. 6, 8, 10, 12, 15, 1794, minutes of the commissioners, Aug. 7–13, 1794, Pa. Miscellany, Whiskey Rebellion, LC; Edward Shippen to Jasper Yeates, Aug. 6, 1794, Gratz Collection, HSP.

105. Yeates and Bradford to Ross, Aug. 14, 1794, minutes of the commissioners, Aug. 15, 1794, commissioners to Randolph, Aug. 17, 1794, Pa. Miscellany, Whiskey Rebellion, LC; Yeates to his wife, Aug. 17, 1794, Jasper Yeates Papers, HSP; Baldwin, *Whiskey Rebels*, 172–182; Raymond Walters, Jr., *Albert Gallatin: Jeffersonian Financier and Diplomat* (New York, 1957), 72–75. Yeates put on a brave front for his wife, but the tension in the letter reveals his mood. Yeates to wife, Aug. 17, 1794, Yeates Papers, HSP.

106. Hugh H. Brackenridge, *Incidents of the Insurrection in the Western Parts of Pennsylvania In the Year 1794* (Philadelphia, 1795), I, 100–101; Baldwin, *Whiskey Rebels*, 187–188. The commissioners' mood can be seen in the tension in Yeates to his wife, Aug. 17, 1794, Yeates Papers, HSP.

107. Commissioners to Randolph, Aug. 17, 1794, Pa. Miscellany, Whiskey Rebellion, LC.

108. Bradford to Washington, Aug. 17, 1794, *ibid*. On August 17, Isaac Craig wrote to Knox saying that the commissioners were convinced that reconciliation was impossible. He asked for something immediate "to excite Confidence in those that remain well effected to Government" (Craig Papers, Carnegie Lib. of Pittsburgh.) Similar fears were voiced by Irvine, one of the state's negotiators (to Dallas, Aug. 17, 1794, *Pa. Archives*, IV, 142–143).

109. For the arrival date, see the endorsement on commissioners to Randolph, Aug. 17, 1794, Pa. Miscellany, Whiskey Rebellion, LC. For the reaction, see Randolph to Washington, Aug. 23, 1794, Miscellaneous Letters of Department of State, *RG* 59, NA; Randolph to commissioners, Aug. 25, 1794, Domestic Letters of Department of State, *RG* 59, NA. For the meeting, see Washington to Randolph, Aug. 23, 1794, WGW, XXXIII, 472. The letter is misdated August 21 in WGW and the manuscript; Saturday, as it was marked, was August 23.

110. *General Advertiser* (Phila.), Aug. 12, 16, 20, 23, 1794; Henry Lee to Washington, Aug. 17, 1794, William Wirt Henry, *Patrick Henry: Life, Correspondence and Speeches* (New York, 1891), II, 539–540. See also Carrington to Edward Heth, Aug. 13, 1794, Whiskey Rebellion, General Records of Internal Revenue Service, *RG* 58, NA.

111. Aug. 8, 1794, Coxe Papers, HSP. For an indication of how the administration reacted to this letter, see Coxe to Thomas Mifflin, Aug. 18, 1794, Coxe to Brackenridge, Aug. 21, 1794, Coxe to Henry Lee, Aug. 29, 1794, Lee to Coxe, Sept. 3, 1794, Brackenridge to Coxe, Sept. 15, 1794, *ibid*. For the approach to Hammond and rumors of an alliance between the British and the rebels, see Hammond to Lord Grenville, Aug. 29, 1794, British State Papers, Ford Transcripts, NYPL; *Gazette of the U.S.* (Phila.), Aug. 24, 1794; *General Advertiser* (Phila.), Aug. 21, 1794; *American Daily Advertiser* (Phila.), Aug. 23, 1794; John Wilkins, Jr. to Randolph, Aug. 14, 1794, Miscellaneous Letters of Department of State, *RG* 59, NA. Evidently the

rumors of overtures to the British had some substance. See Thomas Mc-
Kean to Ingersoll, Aug. 29, 1794, Emmet Collection, NYPL.

112. Henry Lee to Washington, Aug. 17, 1794, Wirt, *Patrick Henry*, II, 539-540.
113. Cabinet notes, Aug. 24, 1794, *PAH*, XVII, 135-137; Randolph to commissioners, Aug. 25, 1794, Domestic Letters of Department of State, *RG* 59,
NA. For Washington's mood of determination and his reasoning, see his
letter to Henry Lee, Aug. 26, 1794, *WGW*, XXXIII, 474-476. For the
military preparations, see Hamilton to Henry Lee (two letters), Aug. 25,
1794, to Samuel Hodgdon, Aug. 25, 27, 1794, to Abraham Hunt, Aug. 27,
1794, to George Gale, Aug. 27, 1794, to Henry Lee, Aug. 27, 1794, *PAH*,
XVII, 142-145, 150-153, 156; John Stagg to Knox, Aug. 30, 1794, Knox
Papers, MHS.
114. Minutes of the commissioners, Aug. 21-23, 1794, commissioners to Randolph, Aug. 21, 23, 29, 1794, Bradford to Hamilton, Aug. 23, 1794, Pa.
Miscellany, Whiskey Rebellion, LC; Yeates to his wife, Aug. 22, 29, 1794,
Yeates Papers, HSP; Bradford to his wife, Aug. 22, 1794, Bradford to Boudinot, Aug. 29, 1794, Wallace Papers, HSP.
115. Commissioners to Randolph, Aug. 30, Sept. 2, 1794, Bradford to [Ran-
dolph?], Aug. 30, 1794, Bradford and Yeates to Randolph, Sept. 5,
1794, Pa. Miscellany, Whiskey Rebellion, LC; Baldwin, *Whiskey Rebels*,
193-197.
116. Bradford and Yeates to Randolph, Sept. 5, 1794, Pa. Miscellany, Whiskey
Rebellion, LC.
117. Minutes of the commissioners, Sept. 1-2, 1794, *ibid.*
118. Bradford and Yeates to Randolph, Sept. 5, 1794, *ibid.* See also the report of
the commissioners, Sept. 24, 1794, *ASP, Miscellaneous*, I, 87-88.
119. The commissioners' letter of August 30 reached Philadelphia on September
7 and the letters of September 2 and September 5 on September 8 (Randolph to Bradford and Yeates, Sept. 8, 1794, Domestic Letters of Department of State, *RG* 59, NA).
120. Randolph to commissioners, Sept. 4, 1794, *ibid.*; Bradford and Yeates to
Randolph, Sept. 5, 1794, Pa. Miscellany, Whiskey Rebellion, LC; Hamilton
to Thomas Sim Lee, Sept. 6, 1794, to Mifflin, Sept. 9, 1794, *PAH*, XVII,
201, 210-211; *General Advertiser* (Phila.), Sept. 4, 1794; Stagg to Knox,
Sept. 11, 1794, Knox Papers, MHS.
121. To Yeates, Sept. 19, 1794, Gratz Collection, HSP. For public opinion, see
General Advertiser (Phila.), Sept. 11, 15, 1794; John Fenno to Joseph
Ward, Sept. 14, 1794, Joseph Ward Papers, Chicago Hist. Soc.; Presley
Neville to Isaac Craig, Sept. 12, 1794, Craig Papers, Carnegie Lib. of Pitts-
burgh; Oliver Wolcott, Jr. to Oliver Wolcott, Sept. 23, 1794, *MAWA*, I, 159;
Hamilton to King, Sept. 17, 1794, to Samuel Smith, Sept. 19, 1794, *PAH*,
XVII, 241-242, 254. Hamilton was the administration's chief publicist. See
Hamilton to Washington, Aug. 5, 21, 1794, "Tully" essays, Aug. 23, 26, 28,
Sept. 2, 1794, *ibid.*, 24-58, 125, 132-135, 148-150, 159-161, 175-180.
There is little evidence about the state of public opinion until *after* September 10, when it became loudly pro-government.
122. To James Monroe, Sept. 25, 1794, James Monroe Papers, LC.
123. Sept. 19, 1794, Gratz Collection, HSP.
124. To Randolph, Sept. 11, 1794, Wallace Papers, HSP. See also John Woods

to Ross, Sept. 12, 1794, Wilkins to Ross, Sept. 11, 12, 1794, Ross to Bradford, Sept. 13, 1794, *ibid.*

125. Sept. 20, 1794, *Pa. Archives*, IV, 281.

126. WGW, XXXIII, 507–509.

127. Hamilton to Mifflin, Oct. 10, 1794, to Lee, Oct. 20, 1794, *PAH*, XVII, 317–318, 331–336; Washington to Lee, Oct. 20, 1794, to Hamilton, Oct. 26, 1794, WGW, XXXIV, 5–9; Dallas to his wife, Oct. 3, 1794, George Mifflin Dallas, *Life and Writings of Alexander James Dallas* (Philadelphia, 1871), 37–38.

128. For the army's march and the occupation, see Baldwin, *Whiskey Rebels*, 220–258.

129. To Angelica Church, Oct. 23, 1794, *PAH*, XVII, 340.

130. "Preservation of Peace with the Indians," Dec. 29, 1794, AC, 3C 2S, 1400–1402.

131. See his marginal notation on Randolph to commissioners, Aug. 7, 1794, *PAH*, XVII, 23.

132. This is speculation. Knox left on August 8, but he had been planning to leave for some time because his speculations in Maine were on the point of ruining him. Knox was not, however, the kind of man to sacrifice his public duty. While not a particularly outstanding administrator, he had been for ten years a patient, regular, and trustworthy Secretary of War. One cannot see him deserting the government on the eve of a military crisis of inestimable proportions—especially after his experience in Shays's Rebellion eight years earlier—unless assured that his absence would not harm the administration. (For a more favorable estimate of Knox's stewardship, see Harry M. Ward, *The Department of War, 1781–1795* [Pittsburgh, 1962].) Neither Hamilton nor Washington had much respect for Knox's administrative abilities. In 1792 several important War Department functions had been shifted to the Treasury, where Hamilton could control them. At some point in the almost continuous meetings of late July and early August, Knox probably expressed his concern over his land speculations and his desire to travel to Maine in person. Because the crisis demanded quick and flexible leadership, Hamilton could well have encouraged the journey. It would give added reason for Hamilton to accompany the troops, which he certainly wanted to do in September, and probably thought of in early August because of Mifflin's reluctance to cooperate and the acknowledged instability of the militia. See Hamilton to Washington, Sept. 19, 1794, Dec. 24, 1795, *PAH*, XVII, 254–255, XIX, 514–515. Washington's very quick reply to Knox's request to leave suggests some kind of prior understanding about the trip. And Washington probably shared Hamilton's doubts about Knox's ability to organize a complex and delicate military operation on short notice. Knox to Washington, Aug. 8, 1794, Washington Papers, LC; Washington to Knox, Aug. 8, 1794, WGW, XXXIII, 461–462.

133. The quotation is from Randolph to Washington, Aug. 5, 1794, Washington Papers, LC. Randolph's statement sounds like a direct quote rather than a paraphrase. He did not name Hamilton specifically as the author. But the implication is overpowering that he meant Hamilton ("the second reason . . . assigned in argument, for calling forth the militia") and the statement

not only has a Hamiltonian ring, but fits his position at the August 2 conference.

134. To Washington, Aug. 5, 1794, Washington Papers, LC. See also Jefferson to Nicholas Lewis, Feb. 9, 1791, *PTJ*, XIX, 263.

135. See Washington to Randolph, Oct. 16, 1794, Washington to Jay, Nov. 1 [-5], 1794, Sixth Annual Address to Congress, Nov. 19, 1794, *WGW*, XXXIII, 4, 17, 34.

136. To Washington, Nov. 11, 1794, *PAH*, XVII, 366.

137. To Richard Peters, Oct. 12, 1794, Richard Peters Papers, HSP. See also William Vans Murray to Coxe, Sept. 20, 1794, Coxe Papers, HSP.

138. To the commissioners, Sept. 29, 1794, Domestic Letters of Department of State, RG 59, NA. The administration did not escape political fire from its opponents. But with the exception of Thomas Jefferson, and then in private, the opposition never questioned the existence of a rebellion. Instead they attacked the excise and Hamilton, arguing that the government had provoked the affair and then that excess force had been used to intimidate all dissenters and militarize the country. See Jefferson to William Branch Giles, Dec. 17, 1794, Jefferson to Madison, Dec. 28, 1794, *WTJ*, VIII, 515, 516; Madison to Jefferson, Nov. 16, 1794, Madison to Monroe, Dec. 4, 1794, James Madison Papers, LC; *General Advertiser* (Phila.), Sept. 5, 9, 11, Nov. 6, 1794; Donald H. Stewart, *The Opposition Press of the Federalist Period* (Albany, 1969), 31, 87-89. There is no evidence that these charges convinced any significant proportion of the public at the time, probably because of the administration's smooth tactics between July and October.

139. Nov. 23, 1795, Charles E. Johnson Collection, N.C. Department Archives and Hist. Judge Alexander Addison, a Federalist who was in Pittsburgh the whole time, made the very same point in a long analysis of the rebellion to Governor Henry Lee (Nov. 23, 1794, Craig Papers, Carnegie Lib. of Pittsburgh): "To quell the disturbances in this country and restore it to peace and government, the measures taken by the President were, in my opinion, the most prudent that could have been devised, and they seem to have been executed with a correspondent propriety and effect: The appointment of Commissioners, by shewing the awakened spirit of publick exertion gave a check to the spirit of revolution in this country, and to the progress of disorder into other parts of the Union. A fair opportunity was given to men of sense and virtue here, who, to guide the current, had seemed to run with it, to step onto, and Chainge its course. And it gave a rallying point to all well disposed men to flock to. The confidence, arising from their supposed strength, now began to abandon the violent; jealousy and distrust crept in among them; and the approach of an army, far superior to all remaining idea of resistance, altogether broke their resolutions, and, as it advanced, subdued their temper." For a stimulating modern discussion of force, phrased in broader terms, see William J. Goode, "The Place of Force in Human Society," *American Sociological Review*, XXXVII (1972), 507-519.

140. To Benjamin Lincoln, Jan. 31, 1790, Knox Papers, MHS. The comment "unless I commanded it" was heavily crossed out by Knox in his draft.

141. Quoted in Merrill Jensen, *The New Nation: A History of the United States During the Confederation, 1781–1789* (New York, 1950), 29.
142. May 11, 1794, Lester J. Cappon, ed., *The Adams-Jefferson Letters* (Chapel Hill, 1959), I, 255.

Chapter 9

HEADNOTE

a. AC, 4C 2S, 1953.

SOURCE NOTES

1. For these programs and their fate, see AC, 3C 1S, 1423–1424, 1428–1429, 1444–1445; Marshall Smelser, *The Congress Founds the Navy, 1787–1798* (Notre Dame, Ind., 1959), ch. IV–VII.
2. Mar. 14, 1794, James Madison Papers, LC. See also William Few to Edward Telfair, Jan. 22, 1793, Edward Telfair Papers, Georgia Historical Society, Savannah, Ga.; Madison to Jefferson, June 1, 1794, Nov. 16, 1794, Madison to Jefferson, June 1, 1794, Nov. 16, 1794, Madison to James Monroe, Dec. 4, 1794, Madison Papers, LC; *General Advertiser* (Phila.), May 22, 1794, Nov. 10, 1794; "Calm Observer," New York *Argus*, May 12, 1795.
3. My figures come from *The Statistical History of the United States from Colonial Times to the Present* (Stamford, Conn., 1965), 711, 719. For expressions of discontent about the size of the budget even earlier, see Francis Preston to William Preston, Jan. 1, 1794, Preston-Joyes Collection, The Filson Club, Louisville, Ky.; AC, 3C 1S, 491.
4. Wayne to Knox, Sept. 20, Nov. 12, Dec. 23, 1794, *WKPM*, 357–358, 362–363, 370–371; Wayne to Knox, Oct. 17, 1794, reports submitted to the House, Records of the United States House of Representatives, RG 233, NA; Wayne to Thomas Hartley, Dec. 22, 1794, Anthony Wayne Papers, HSP.
5. Washington to the Senate, Nov. 25, 1794, Knox to Washington, Nov. 24, 1794, *ASP, MA*, I, 68. For the earlier fight over recruiting see the AC, 3C 1S, 37, 38, 39, 141, 143, 159–163, 167, 248, 251–256, 272, 525–526, 674, 683; acts for completing the military establishment, Dec. 17, 1793, Jan. 23, 1794, bills originating in the House, House Records, RG 233, NA; Francis Preston to William Preston, Jan. 1, 1794, Preston-Joyes Collection, Filson Club; William Findley to Alexander Addison, Apr. 30, 1794, Alexander Addison Papers, Darlington Memorial Library, Univ. of Pittsburgh, Pittsburgh, Pa.; *Centinel of the North-Western Territory* (Cincinnati), July 19, 1794.
6. Dec. 15, 1794, records of committee reports, House Records, RG 233, NA. The third member of the committee was John Nicholas of Virginia (AC, 3C 2S, 968). For Dearborn's career, see Richard Alton Erney, The Public Career of Henry Dearborn (unpub. Ph.D. thesis, Columbia Univ., 1957), 5–20, 26–34.

7. Wayne to Knox, Oct. 17, 1794, reports submitted to the House, House Records, *RG* 233, NA. The letter probably arrived before Congress assembled. The manuscript indicates that it was sent to the House on December 17, suggesting that Knox withheld it until it could have more impact.

8. Dec. 29, 1794, *AC*, 3C 2S, 1400–1402.

9. Report enclosed in Pickering to the Speaker of the House, Jan. 26, 1795, *ASP, IA*, I, 547. Pickering conferred with Knox before drawing up the document (Pickering to Knox, Jan. 22, 1795, Henry Knox Papers, MHS).

10. Jonathan Dayton in *AC*, 3C 2S, 1164. See also *ibid.*, 1164, 1166, 1172.

11. To Ephraim Williams, Feb. 3, 1795, Theodore Sedgwick Papers, MHS. See also Fisher Ames to Theodore Dwight, Feb. 3, 1795, Seth Ames, ed., *Works of Fisher Ames* . . . (Boston, 1854), I, 166; Thomas Hartley to Anthony Wayne, Jan. 7, 29, Feb. 6, 1795, Wayne Papers, HSP.

12. To Ephraim Williams, Feb. 13, 1795, Sedgwick Papers, MHS. Jeremiah Wadsworth lost his temper and made some revealing remarks on the whole subject of military and militia policy. See his speech in the *AC*, 3C 2S, 1221. See also Dwight Foster's journal, Feb. 13, 1795, Dwight Foster Papers, American Antiquarian Society, Worcester, Mass.; Jonathan Trumbull, Jr. to John Trumbull, Feb. 24, 1795, Jonathan Trumbull, Jr. Papers (Hubbard Collection), Connecticut State Library, Hartford, Conn. For Madison's position, see his letter to Jefferson, Feb. 15, 1795, Madison Papers, LC. For an indication of Federalist smugness, see *Gazette of the United States* (Phila.), Mar. 4, 1795.

13. "An Act for continuing and regulating the Military Establishment . . . ," *AC*, 3C 2S, 1515–1516. For the roll calls, see *ibid.*, 1222.

14. See Madison to Jefferson, Feb. 15, 1795, Madison Papers, LC; [John Taylor], *A Definition of Parties* (Philadelphia, 1794), 4; "Calm Observer," N.Y. *Argus*, May 12, 1795.

15. See General James Wilkinson, *Memoirs of My Own Times* (Philadelphia, 1816), II, 108–114. For the Spanish conspiracy, see T. M. Green, *The Spanish Conspiracy* (Cincinnati, 1891); Francis S. Philbrick, *The Rise of the West, 1754–1830* (New York, 1965), 176–184; Thomas P. Abernethy, *The South in the New Nation, 1784–1819* [Wendell Holmes Stephenson and E. Merton Coulter, eds., *A History of the South*, IV] (Baton Rouge, 1961), 46–68; Temple Bodley, introduction to *Reprints of Littell's Political Transactions* . . . [Filson Club Publications, no. 31] (Louisville, 1926); Patricia Watlington, *The Partisan Spirit: Kentucky Politics, 1779–1792* (New York, 1972), 120–125, 139–148, 175–181, 186–187, 196–197; and the editorial note in *PTJ*, XIX, 469–483. A good characterization of Wilkinson is Humphrey Marshall, *History of Kentucky* (Lexington, 1824), I, 165. See also James Ripley Jacobs, *Tarnished Warrior: Major-General James Wilkinson* (New York, 1938), the best but by no means a definitive biography.

16. See John Brown to Harry Innes, Apr. 13, 1792, Harry Innes Papers, LC; Wilkinson to John Armstrong, May 24, 1792, John Armstrong Papers, Indiana Historical Society, Indianapolis, Ind.; John Heckewelder, travel diary, July 14, 1792, Paul A. W. Wallace, *Thirty Thousand Miles with John Heckewelder* (Pittsburgh, 1958), 274.

17. Knox to Wilkinson, Feb. 11, July 17, 1792, James Wilkinson Papers, Chicago Historical Society, Chicago, Ill.; Wilkinson to Wayne, Sept. 12, 1792,

Anthony Wayne Papers, WLCL; Wilkinson to Knox, Nov. 3, 1792, James Wilkinson Letters, Kentucky Historical Society, Frankfurt, Ky.; Wilkinson to Wayne, Nov. 13, 1792, Wayne to Wilkinson, Nov. 18, 1792, Wayne Papers, HSP; Knox to Wayne, Jan. 19, 1793, *WKPM*, 175; Knox to Wilkinson, May 17, 1793, Reuben T. Durrett Collection, Univ. of Chicago Library, Chicago, Ill.

18. Wilkinson to Harry Innes, Oct. 18, 1792, Jan. 5, May 18, June 29, Aug. 20, Oct. 3, 1793, Innes Papers, LC; Wilkinson to Isaac Shelby, Apr. 11, June 24, 1793, Shelby Family Papers, LC; Wilkinson to Shelby, June 21, 1793, Shelby Family Papers, Univ. of Kentucky Library, Lexington, Ky.; Wilkinson to Edward Hand, Aug. 20, 1792, Emmet Collection, NYPL; Wilkinson to John Brown, Aug. 17, 1792, Wilkinson Letters, Ky. Hist. Soc.

19. See the correspondence between Armstrong, and Wayne and Wilkinson, Oct. 1792 through Apr. 1793, and especially Armstrong to Wayne, Mar. 23, 1793, all in the Armstrong Papers, Ind. Hist. Soc. Also see the *Centinel of the North-Western Territory* (Cincinnati), Aug. 30, 1794.

20. June 14, 1793, Innes Papers, LC.

21. Campbell Smith to O. H. Williams, Nov. 16, 1793, Otho H. Williams Papers, Maryland Historical Society, Baltimore, Md. For an indication of Wilkinson's popularity, see John Preston to Francis Preston, Aug. 8, 1793, Preston Papers, College of William and Mary Library, Williamsburg, Va.

22. Thomas Cushing to Jeremiah Wadsworth, Mar. 15, 1794, Joseph Trumbull Papers, Conn. State Lib. Also see Cushing to John Pratt, Nov. 2, 1793, Jan. 13, 1794, John Pratt Collection, Conn. State Lib.

23. Campbell Smith to O. H. Williams, Nov. 16, 1793, Williams Papers, Md. Hist. Soc.; Wayne to Knox, Nov. 15, 1793, Knox Papers, MHS; Armstrong to ———, n.d. [1793], Armstrong Papers, Ind. Hist. Soc.

24. See diary of Dr. John Carmichael (transcript), Sept. 12, 1795, Ohio Historical Society, Columbus, Ohio; diary of Dr. Joseph G. Andrews, Nov. 12, 1795, Peter Force Collection, LC.

25. Erkuries Beatty to John Armstrong, Jan. 5, 1793, Armstrong Papers, Ind. Hist. Soc.

26. Wayne to Knox, Oct. 23, 1793, May 30, 1794, *WKPM*, 278–279, 334–335; Wayne to Knox, Nov. 15, 1793, Knox Papers, MHS. Wayne knew that Wilkinson did not call Armstrong to challenge members of the court or delay proceedings until his witnesses could appear. See Armstrong to Wayne, Feb. 18, Mar. 1, 23, 1793, Armstrong Papers, Ind. Hist. Soc.

27. "Stubborn Facts," *Gazette of the U.S.* (Phila.), June 25, 1794. See also Wilkinson to Jeremiah Wadsworth, Mar. 12, 1794, Joseph Trumbull Collection, Conn. State Lib. For the whispering campaign, see *Centinel of the North-Western Territory* (Cincinnati), Apr. 12, May 17, June 7, 14, 1794; Armstrong to Wayne, June 8, 1794, Miscellaneous Collection, Ohio Hist. Soc.

28. New York *Minerva*, July 23, 1794; Armstrong to Wayne, June 8, 1794, Miscellaneous Collection, Ohio Hist. Soc.; Wayne to Knox, Jan. 25, 1795, Wayne Papers, WLCL.

29. Knox to Wilkinson, July 12, 1794, Knox Papers, MHS; Wilkinson to Wayne, June 8, 1794, Simon Gratz Collection, HSP.

30. Knox to Wilkinson, July 12, 1794, Knox Papers, MHS.
31. Washington to Edmund Randolph, Oct. 6, 1794, WGW, XXXIII, 521. Charles Scott, who commanded the Kentucky volunteers during the campaign, told Knox that Wayne's leadership had been excellent. See Scott to Knox, Apr. 30, 1794, Charles Scott Papers, Univ. of Ky. Lib. For the administration's rebuttal, which included extracts from Scott's letters, see "A Friend to Truth," *Gazette of the U.S.* (Phila.), July 19, 1794.
32. See the diary in the John Pratt Collection, Conn. State Lib. The author of the diary is unknown, but some of it appears to be in Wilkinson's handwriting. And parts of Wilkinson's letter to John Brown (Aug. 28, 1794, M. M. Quaife, ed., "General Wilkinson's Narrative of the Fallen Timbers Campaign," *Mississippi Valley Historical Review*, XVI [1929], 81–90) were obviously copied from the diary.
33. To Innes, Nov. 10, 1794, Innes Papers, LC. For letters to Congress, see Wilkinson to Brown, Aug. 28, 1794, *Miss. Vall. Hist. Rev.*, XVI, 81–90; Wilkinson to Brown, n.d. [after Aug. 1794], Wilkinson Letters, Univ. of Ky. Lib.; Wilkinson to Jeremiah Wadsworth, Dec. 4, 1794, Jeremiah Wadsworth Papers, CHS.
34. Knox to Wayne, Dec. 5, 1794, WKPM, 364; Knox to Wilkinson, Dec. 4, 5, 1794, Innes Papers, LC.
35. Wayne to Knox, Jan. 21, 25, 1795, Wayne Papers, WLCL. See also Wayne to Henry De Butts, Jan. 29, 1795, Wayne Papers, HSP.
36. There is almost no evidence about Wilkinson's activities in 1795, but by early 1796 he was in close communication with Speaker of the House Jonathan Dayton and congressman Josiah Parker. See Dayton to Wilkinson, Apr. 15, 1796, Parker to Wilkinson, May 21, 1796, Wilkinson Papers, Chicago Hist. Soc.; Wilkinson to William Henry Harrison, Apr. 2, 1796, William Henry Harrison Papers, LC. Wilkinson also used Senator John Brown, his old Kentucky colleague. Several of Wilkinson's men had contacts in Congress. Harrison, for example, was the son-in-law of John Cleves Symmes, who had intimate connections with New Jersey politicians. Campbell Smith was related to congressman William Smith (Md.). And Wilkinson used every contact he could, even if the politician was a Federalist. See Thomas Cushing to Dwight Foster, Nov. 17, 1796, Mellen Chamberlain Collection, Boston Public Library, Boston, Mass.
37. See Washington to Pickering, Oct. 7, Nov. 20, 1795, Washington to Hamilton, Oct. 29, 1795, Seventh Annual Address to Congress, Dec. 8, 1795, WGW, XXXIV, 330, 352, 366–367, 390; Pickering to the Speaker of the House with enclosures, Dec. 12, 1795, records of reports of the Secretary of War, House Records, RG 233, NA; AC, 4C 1S, 133–134. These documents are printed as two separate reports submitted to the Senate in ASP, MA, I, 108–110 and ASP, IA, I, 583–584.
38. Memoirs, Albert Gallatin Papers, NYHS. Manning J. Dauer, *The Adams Federalists* (Baltimore, 1953), 290–297, shows that Republicans were actually a majority of the House. See also Rudolph M. Bell, *Party and Faction in American Politics: The House of Representatives, 1789–1801* (Westport, Conn., 1973), 255–256.
39. See Smelser, *Congress Founds the Navy*, 77–84.

40. *AC*, 4C 1S, 241, 905–913; Findley to Addison, Jan. 8, 1796, Addison Papers, Univ. of Pittsburgh Lib.; Robert Goodloe Harper to his constituents, Mar. 9, 1796, Elizabeth Donnan, ed., "Papers of James A. Bayard, 1796–1815," American Historical Association, *Annual Report, 1913* (Washington, 1915), II, 15.

41. Pickering to the Committee on the Military Establishment, Feb. 3, 1796, *ASP, MA*, I, 112–113; Pickering to Washington, Jan. 30, 1796, George Washington Papers, LC. For the makeup of the committee and its appointment, see *AC*, 4C 1S, 151–154.

42. For McHenry's appointment, see Washington to McHenry, Jan. 20, 1796, *WGW*, XXXIV, 423–424; McHenry to Washington, Jan. 21, 24, 1796, Washington Papers, LC; Hugh Williamson to McHenry, Jan. 27, 1796, William Vans Murray to McHenry, Jan. 28, 1796, Bernard C. Steiner, *The Life and Correspondence of James McHenry* (Cleveland, 1907), 164–165, 166–168; William Vans Murray to McHenry, Jan. 27, 1796, James McHenry Papers, LC. The appointments problem in 1795 and 1796 is covered in Stephen G. Kurtz, *The Presidency of John Adams: The Collapse of Federalism* (Philadelphia, 1957), 239–277.

43. McHenry to the Committee, enclosed in McHenry to Abraham Baldwin, Mar. 14, 1796, *ASP, MA*, I, 114–115. There is no evidence that Wayne made a formal presentation but undoubtedly he made his views known. See Wilkinson to William Henry Harrison, Apr. 2, 1796, William Henry Harrison Papers, LC; Wayne, estimate of ordnance and stores, Feb. 22, 1796, estimate of troops, n.d., Northwest Territory Collection, Ind. Hist. Soc.

44. Baldwin committee report with enclosure, Mar. 25, 1796, *ASP, MA*, I, 112–115.

45. The debate is in *AC*, 4C 1S, 905–913, 1264, 1281, 1293. Other relevant statements by Sedgwick and Gallatin are in *ibid.*, 901–902.

46. Chauncey Goodrich to Oliver Wolcott, Sr., May 20, 1796, Oliver Wolcott, Sr. Papers, CHS.

47. Dayton to Wilkinson, Apr. 15, 1796, Wilkinson Papers, Chicago Hist. Soc.; Wilkinson to Harry Innes, Apr. 16, 1796, Innes Papers, LC; Wilkinson to William Winston, Apr. 22, 1796, Isaac Joslin Cox, ed., "Selections from the Torrence Papers, V," *Quarterly Publication of the Historical and Philosophical Society of Ohio*, IV (1909), 95; John Hamtramck to Winston, Apr. 20, 1796, John Mills to Winston, Apr. 22, 1796, Winston to Hamtramck, May 3, 1796, Wilkinson to Winston, May 5, 1796, Torrence Collection, Cincinnati Hist. Soc.; William Henry Harrison to Wilkinson, May 13, 1796, William Henry Harrison Miscellaneous Collection, Ind. Hist. Soc.

48. *AC*, 4C 1S, 84, 96, 98, 1418–1423; Josiah Parker to Wilkinson, May 21, 1796, Wilkinson Papers, Chicago Hist. Soc.

49. "The Truth," *Aurora* (Phila.), May 19, 1796; "Perseverance" [Major Thomas Cushing], June 4, 1796, Wilkinson Papers, Chicago Hist. Soc.

50. *AC*, 4C 1S, 102, 103, 105, 110, 111, 1418–1423, 1428–1430, 1462, 2926–2931; Samuel Hodgdon to Isaac Craig, June 10, 1796, Intendant of Military Stores Letterbook, United States Army Collection, LC; Josiah Parker to Wilkinson, May 21, 1796, "Perseverance" [Major Thomas Cushing], June 4, 1796, Wilkinson Papers, Chicago Hist. Soc.

51. Howard White, *Executive Influence in Determining Military Policy in the United States* [*University of Illinois Studies in the Social Sciences*, XII] (Urbana, 1925), 126-127. One Republican congressman claimed the administration did not push very hard for its 5,000-man force, because it was waiting "for a new house of Representatives who will be more submissive" (Aaron Kitchell to Ebenezer Elmer, May 3, 1796, Gratz Collection, HSP).

52. For the 1796 act, see Francis Paul Prucha, *American Indian Policy in the Formative Years: The Indian Trade and Intercourse Acts, 1790-1834* (Cambridge, 1962).

53. To follow this fight, see the AC, 4C 2S, 1545, 1551, 1553, 1554, 1567-1568, 1569-1570, 1572, 1573, 1817-1818, 1872-1873, 1944-1963, 1966-1982, 2066-2074, 2079-2089, 2092-2094, 2095, 2328, 2330-2332, 2352, 2955; report of Jan. 13, 1797, Records of Select Committee Reports, House Records, RG 233, NA; Samuel Hodgdon to Isaac Craig, March 3, 1797, Samuel Hodgdon Letterbook, LC; Sedgwick to Ephraim Williams, Feb. 1, 1797, Sedgwick Papers, MHS; James McHenry to Charles Lee, Feb. 24, 1797, James McHenry Papers, WLCL; Lee to McHenry, Feb. 25, 1797, McHenry to Washington, Feb. 25, 1797, Washington Papers, LC.

54. Wilkinson to William Winston, Apr. 22, 1796, Cox, ed., "Torrence Papers, V," *Quar. Publication Hist. Phil. Soc. Ohio*, IV, 95. See also Wilkinson to Harry Innes, Apr. 16, 1796, Innes Papers, LC; Wilkinson to Isaac Shelby, June 16, 1796, Isaac Shelby Papers, Filson Club.

55. To William Winston, Apr. 22, 1796, Cox, ed., "Torrence Papers, V," *Quar. Publication Hist. Phil. Soc. Ohio*, IV, 95.

56. Washington to McHenry, July 1, 1796, WGW, XXXV, 108 109; McHenry to Pickering, July 5, 1796, McHenry Papers, WLCL; McHenry to Hamilton, July 4, 1796, Hamilton to McHenry, July 15, 1796, PAH, XX, 245, 252-253; McHenry to William Vans Murray, July 16, 1796, Chamberlain Collection, Boston Public Lib.

57. To Harry Innes, Sept. 4, 1796, Innes Papers, LC. Wilkinson was prepared to use all his political contacts; see Thomas Cushing to Dwight Foster, Nov. 17, 1796, Chamberlain Collection, Boston Public Lib.

58. Capt. Thomas Lewis to Wayne, Dec. 2, 1796, Northwest Territory Collection, Ind. Hist. Soc.

59. Charles Lee, memorandum, Nov. 22, 1796, James McHenry Papers, LC. The peacetime army operated under Articles of War passed in 1776 and amended in 1777 and 1786. See JCC, V, 788-807, VII, 264-266, XXX, 316-322.

60. See AC, 4C 2S, 1966-1969.

61. McHenry to Wayne, Aug. 27, 1796, WKPM, 510-511; "List of Officers" enclosed in McHenry to Wayne, Aug. 27, 1796, Wayne, orders of Oct. 26, 1796, Isaac J. Cox, ed., "Selections from the Torrence Papers, VIII," *Quar. Publication Hist. Phil. Soc. Ohio*, XIII (1918), 83-96.

62. "Rules . . . relative to . . . posts . . . ," Mar. 28, 1797, "Rules . . . recruiting service," n.d. [prior to Apr. 13, 1797], Adams Family Papers, MHS; "Regulations . . . of Fuel and Straw . . . ," Dec. 25, 1797, Denny-O'Hara Papers, Western Pennsylvania Historical Society, Pittsburgh, Pa. Because of the

fire in the War Department in 1800, the official records were destroyed. When John Adams entered office in 1797, however, McHenry sent him (Apr. 13, 1797, Adams Papers, MHS) over 150 pages of documents "relative to the most important objects in the department of War." These documents furnish the best picture of the military establishment at any point before 1800, and provide much of the evidence for this and following interpretations.

63. McHenry to Washington, July 16, 1796, McHenry Papers, WLCL; McHenry to John Harris, Nov. 11, 1796, instructions to various Indian agents, Aug. 29, Sept. 8, 9, 1796, Adams Papers, MHS.

64. See McHenry to Adams with enclosures, Nov. 22, 1797, Pickering to Adams, Dec. 7, 1797, Charles Lee to Pickering, Dec. 6, 1797, William Simmons to Adams, Dec. 11, 1797, Oliver Wolcott, Jr. to Adams, Dec. 13, 1797, John Adams to [Simmons?], n.d. [Dec. 1797], Adams Papers, MHS; McHenry to Simmons, Dec. 28, 1797, McHenry Papers, WLCL.

65. McHenry to Wilkinson, Mar. 22, 1797, Alexander Hamilton Papers, LC; James Wilkinson to John Wilkins, Mar. 16, 1797, Apr. 22, 1797, "Letters from General Wayne and General Wilkinson to the Quartermaster General," *Michigan Pioneer Historical Society, Collections*, XXXV (1907), 620– 621, 622–623.

66. John Steele, opinion on contracts, n.d., John Steele Papers, North Carolina Department of Archives and History, Raleigh, N.C.; contracts between James O'Hara and Oliver Wolcott, Jr., June 1, 1796, Aug. 29, 1798, Solomon Sibley Papers, Burton Historical Collection, Detroit Public Library, Detroit, Mich. To understand the logistical system in the late 1790s, from the top on down, see Intendant of Military Stores Letterbook, U.S. Army Collection, LC; John Wilkins, Jr., Letterbook, Burton Hist. Collection, Detroit Public Lib.; James O'Hara Letterbook, Ind. Hist. Soc.; Denny-O'Hara Papers, Western Pennsylvania Hist. Soc.; Solomon Sibley Papers, James Henry Papers, James O'Hara Papers, and the Samuel Henley Papers, all in the Burton Hist. Collection, Detroit Public Lib.

67. McHenry, draft of a circular on army regulations, 1797, Wilkinson to McHenry, Jan. 18, 1797, Hamtramck, comments on regulations, Jan. 1798, McHenry Papers, WLCL; Wilkinson, general orders, May 22, 1797, Letters received by the Secretary of War, unregistered series, Records of the Office of Secretary of War, RG 107, NA.

68. Capt. Zebulon Pike to Wayne, Aug. 22, 1796, Northwest Territory Collection, Ind. Hist. Soc.; anonymous to Timothy Pickering, n.d. (received July 7, 1797), Timothy Pickering Papers, MHS; Andrew Ellicott to Pickering, Nov. 14, 1797, John Adams to Wilkinson, Feb. 4, 1798, Wilkinson, *Memoirs*, II, 170–171, 155; Wilkinson to Adams, Dec. 26, 1797, Adams Papers, MHS; report of examination of John D. Chisholm by Rufus King, Dec. 5, 1797, F. J. Turner, ed., "Documents on the Blount Conspiracy, 1795–1797," *American Historical Review*, X (1905), 602.

69. McHenry to Wilkinson, Jan. 1798, McHenry Papers, WLCL.

70. Washington to Pickering, Sept. 16, 1795, WGW, XXXIV, 465; Pickering to Washington, Jan. 26, 1796, Bartholomew Dandridge to Pickering, Jan. 28, 1796, Pickering Papers, MHS; Smelser, *Congress Founds the Navy*, ch. VI–

VII. For an assessment of the works at Springfield and West Point at this time, see Duke De La Rochefoucault-Liancourt, *Travels Through the United States* . . . (London, 1799), II, 208, 241. In 1793 the administration decided not to propose an academy so as not to stimulate more antimilitary suspicion. But in 1796, with the army reduced and the Indian war over, the President proposed it to Congress. See cabinet notes, Nov. 23, 28, 1793, Franklin B. Sawvel, ed., *The Complete Anas of Thomas Jefferson* (New York, 1903), 180–181; Eighth Annual Address to Congress, Dec. 7, 1796, WGW, XXXV, 317; AC, 4C 2S, 1520–1521; McHenry to Washington, Oct. 8, 1796, Adams Papers, MHS; Stephen E. Ambrose, *Duty, Honor, Country: A History of West Point* (Baltimore, 1966), 10–23.

71. This is the interpretation of Francis Paul Prucha, *The Sword of the Republic: The United States Army on the Frontier, 1783–1846* (New York, 1969). But see also Roger L. Nichols, "The Army and the Indians 1800–1830: A Reappraisal: The Missouri Valley Example," *Pacific Historical Review*, XLI (1972), 151–168.

Chapter 10

HEADNOTE

a. June 1798, AC, 5C 2S, 2024–2025.

SOURCE NOTES

1. Jefferson to Adams, June 15, 1813, Lester J. Cappon, ed., *The Adams-Jefferson Letters* . . . (Chapel Hill, 1959), II, 331.
2. Adams to Jefferson, June 30, 1813, *ibid.*, 346–347.
3. The quotations are from James Morton Smith, *Freedom's Fetters: The Alien and Sedition Laws and American Civil Liberties* (Ithaca, 1956), 14, 21. Other examples can be found in Alexander DeConde, *The Quasi-War: The Politics and Diplomacy of the Undeclared War with France, 1797–1801* (New York, 1966), 94; John D. Stevens, "Congressional History of the 1798 Sedition Law," *Journalism Quarterly*, XLIII (1966), 256; Richard E. Ellis, *The Jeffersonian Crisis: Courts and Politics in the Young Republic* (New York, 1971), 278–279; Leonard W. Levy, "Freedom in Turmoil: the Sedition Act Era," in Levy's *Judgements: Essays on American Constitutional History* (Chicago, 1972), 159–168. For the historiography of the Federalists (emphasizing the partisanship of historians), see George M. Curtis, III, American Historians and the Federalists (unpub. M.A. thesis, Univ. of Kansas, 1963). Federalist fears of the opposition are discussed in Marshall Smelser's "The Jacobin Phrenzy: Federalism and the Menace of Liberty, Equality, and Fraternity," *Review of Politics*, XIII (1951), 457–482 and "The Federalist Period as an Age of Passion," *American Quarterly*, X (1958), 391–417. Few historians have taken Federalist views of the opposition seriously, even Smelser. Two recent exceptions are John R. Howe, Jr.,

"Republican Thought and the Political Violence of the 1790s," *ibid.*, XIX (1967), 147–165 and Richard Hofstadter, *The Idea of a Party System: The Rise of Legitimate Opposition in the United States, 1780–1840* (Berkeley and Los Angeles, 1969), ch. 1–3. In the last decade and a half, there have been several studies that avoid Federalist-Jeffersonian partisanship and attempt to understand the Federalists on their own terms. Most, however, are either biographies or studies of state and local politics. None deal directly with the national party in the 1790s or Federalist motives in 1798.

4. The leading modern interpretation is Stephen G. Kurtz, *The Presidency of John Adams: The Collapse of Federalism, 1795–1800* (Philadelphia, 1957), especially ch. 14 ("The Bete Noire of Federalism"). Kurtz generally absolves Adams and his supporters from charges of militarism, but he comes down hard on Hamilton. See also Manning J. Dauer, *The Adams Federalists* (Baltimore, 1953), ch. 12 ("The Aim of Federalist Domestic Policy"); Levy, "Sedition Act Era," 165; Lawrence S. Kaplan, *Colonies into Nation: American Diplomacy, 1763–1801* (New York and London, 1972), 276–283.

5. There are several flaws in the standard interpretation. Both the interpretations of paranoia and that of a conspiracy to eradicate the Republicans (as explanations of Federalist motives in passing the Alien and Sedition Acts, and the military program) tend to lump extremists like Hamilton, Pickering, and Uriah Tracy with moderates like Adams, Jay, Marshall, James Iredell, and others. The interpretation does not explain why men of such proven political intelligence and accomplishment succumbed to hysteria or conspiracy, why it happened in 1798 and not earlier, and why all these men were so united in supporting the legislation (despite differences over key provisions) in 1798. There is no explanation of why the Federalists became paranoid and Republicans retained their balance.

6. June 27, 1788, *Documentary History of the Constitution of the United States, 1787–1870* (Washington, 1894–1905), IV, 757. Madison told Hamilton (June 27, 1788, *PAH*, V, 91–92) the same thing.

7. See Madison to Jefferson, Aug. 10, Sept. 21, 1788, *PTJ*, XIII, 497–499, 624–626; James McHenry to Washington, July 27, 1788, Madison to Washington, Aug. 11, 1788, Madison to James Madison, Sr., Sept. 6, 1788, Richard Peters to Washington, Sept. 17, 1788, Washington to Henry Lee, Sept. 22, 1788, Washington to Madison, Sept. 23, 1788, Edward Carrington to Madison, Oct. 19, Nov. 9, 1788, Madison to Edmund Pendleton, Oct. 20, 1788, Washington to Benjamin Lincoln, Oct. 26, 1788, Madison to George Turberville, Nov. 2, 1788, *Documentary History of the Constitution*, IV, 821, V, 16, 46, 52–53, 65, 91–92, 94, 103–106, 110; Jonathan Dayton to John Cleves Symmes, Oct. 22, 1788, John Cleves Symmes Papers (Miami Purchase), Cincinnati Historical Society, Cincinnati, Ohio.

8. Kenneth Russell Bowling, Federalists and Antifederalists after Ratification: The First Congressional Election (unpub. M.A. thesis, Univ. of Wisconsin, 1964), ch. 3–5; Linda Grant De Pauw, "The Anticlimax of Antifederalism: The Abortive Second Convention Movement, 1788–1789," *Prologue*, II (1970), 98–114.

9. To Gabriel Manigault, June 7, 1789, Ulrich B. Phillips, ed., "South Carolina Federalist Correspondence, 1789–1797," *American Historical Review*,

XIV (1909), 776. See also Paine Wingate to John Pickering, Apr. 27, 1789, Charles E. L. Wingate, *Life and Letters of Paine Wingate* (Medford, Mass., 1930), II, 298; T. Lowther to James Iredell, May 9, 1789, Griffith J. McRee, *Life and Correspondence of James Iredell* (New York, 1858), II, 258; Madison to George Nicholas, July 5, 1789, Harry Innes Papers, LC; Kenneth Russell Bowling, Politics in the First Congress, 1789–1791 (unpub. Ph.D. thesis, Univ. of Wisconsin, 1968), 10, 248–250.

10. There were other reasons as well for Madison's campaign for a Bill of Rights. See Bowling, First Congress, ch. 5.

11. For the nature of the opposition party in 1790 and 1791 see *ibid., passim*; Richard Buel, Jr., *Securing the Revolution: Ideology in American Politics, 1789–1815* (Ithaca and London, 1972), 17–27, 94–96.

12. John Quincy Adams to John Adams, Apr. 5, 1790, Worthington Chauncey Ford, ed., *Writings of John Quincy Adams* (New York, 1913–1917), I, 50; John Adams to Jefferson, July 29, 1791, Cappon, ed., *Adams-Jefferson Letters*, I, 249; Fisher Ames to George R. Minot, Nov. 30, 1791, Seth Ames, ed., *Works of Fisher Ames* . . . (Boston, 1854), I, 103. For party activity in 1791, see Noble E. Cunningham, Jr., *The Jeffersonian Republicans: The Formation of Party Organization, 1789–1801* (Chapel Hill, 1957), 9–19.

13. Alfred F. Young, *The Democratic Republicans of New York: The Origins, 1763–1797* (Chapel Hill, 1967), 194–201.

14. To George R. Minot, Mar. 8, 1792, Ames, ed., *Fisher Ames*, I, 114–115. See also Hamilton to Washington, Sept. 9, 1792, *PAH*, XII, 349.

15. Ralph Izard to Thomas Pinckney, Oct. 13, 1792, Pinckney Family Papers, LC. For examples of use of the term to label the opposition, see Charles Adams to Abigail Adams, Oct. 8, 1792, John Adams to Abigail Adams, Dec. 7, 10, 29, 1792, Adams Family Papers, MHS; Charles Carroll of Carrollton to Hamilton, Oct. 22, 1792, *PAH*, XII, 607–608; Thomas Hartley to Tench Coxe, June 24, 1792, Tench Coxe Papers, HSP. For the elections, see Cunningham, *Jeffersonian Republicans*, 33–45; Young, *Democratic Republicans of N.Y.*, ch. 15; Carl E. Prince, *New Jersey's Jeffersonian Republicans: The Genesis of an Early Party Machine, 1789–1817* (Chapel Hill, 1967), 11–12.

16. For a review of the historiography, see Bowling, First Congress, 1–5. See also Buel, *Securing the Revolution*, 1.

17. Bowling, First Congress, ch. 8.

18. Harry Marlin Tinkcom, *The Republicans and Federalists in Pennsylvania, 1790–1801: A Study in National Stimulus and Local Response* (Harrisburg, 1950), 52–53, 71; Young, *Democratic Republicans of N.Y.*, 340–341, 568, 575–582; L. Marx Renzulli, Jr., *Maryland: The Federalist Years* (Rutherford, N.J., 1972), ch. 3. See also Patricia Watlington, *The Partisan Spirit: Kentucky Politics, 1779–1792* (New York, 1972), 226–233; Jackson Turner Main, *Political Parties before the Constitution* (Chapel Hill, 1973), 357–359, 365–366, 405–407. The most recent historiographical study also sees the continuity in factional groupings in the 1780s and 1790s. See H. James Henderson, "The First Party System," Alden T. Vaughan and George Athan Billias, eds., *Perspectives on Early American History: Essays in Honor of Richard B. Morris* (New York, 1973), 325–371.

19. See the list of 100 Antifederalists in Bowling, First Congress, 371–374; Norman K. Risjord, "The Virginia Federalists," *Journal of Southern History*, XXXIII (1967), 487–488.
20. E. James Ferguson, "The Nationalists of 1781–1783 and the Economic Interpretation of the Constitution," *Journal of American History*, LVI (1969), 241–261; Young, *Democratic Republicans of N.Y.*, 578–582. The best statement of this relationship is Ellis, *Jeffersonian Crisis*; ch. XVI–XVII.
21. Hamilton to Adams, June 25, 1792, *PAH*, XI, 559; Charles Adams to Abigail Adams, Oct. 8, 1792, Adams Papers, MHS; George Cabot to Theophilus Parsons, Oct. 3, 1792, Theophilus Parsons, *Memoir of Theophilus Parsons* (Boston, 1859), 469.
22. To Abigail Adams, Dec. 10, 1792, Adams Papers, MHS.
23. To Dwight, Jan. 23, 1792, Ames, ed., *Fisher Ames*, I, 110–111. See also Ames to George R. Minot, Nov. 30, 1791, May 3, 1792, Feb. 20, 1793, *ibid.*, 103–106, 118–119, 128–129; Theodore Sedgwick to Theophilus Parsons, Jan. 16, 1792, Parsons, *Memoir of Parsons*, 467–468; Abigail Adams to Mary Cranch, Apr. 20, 1792, Stewart Mitchell, ed., *New Letters of Abigail Adams, 1788–1801* (Boston, 1947), 83; Abigail Adams to her daughter, Feb. 11, 1793, Charles Francis Adams, ed., *Letters of Mrs. Adams . . .* (4th ed., Boston, 1848), 360–361; Washington to Jefferson, Aug. 23, 1792, WGW, XXXII, 130.
24. See Hamilton to Edward Carrington, May 26, 1792, *PAH*, XI, 441, 444; Ames to Minot, May 3, 1792, Ames, ed., *Fisher Ames*, I, 119; Oliver Wolcott, Sr. to his son, Mar. 25, 1793, *MAWA*, I, 91; [William Loughton Smith], *The Politics and Views of a Certain Party Displayed* (n.p., 1792), 27–32; Ralph Izard to Thomas Pinckney, Nov. 6, 1792, Pinckney Family Papers, LC.
25. Hamilton, "Objections and Answers . . . ," enclosed in Hamilton to Washington, Aug. 18, 1792, *PAH*, XII, 253. The Republican side of the suspicion cycle is covered excellently in Lance Banning, "Republican Ideology and the Triumph of the Constitution, 1789 to 1793," *WMQ*, XXXI (1974), 167–188.
26. To Edward Carrington, May 26, 1792, *PAH*, XI, 439. In 1789, Fisher Ames called Madison "very much Frenchified in his politics" (Irving Brant, *James Madison* [Indianapolis, 1941–1961], III, 249).
27. Hamilton to ———, May 18, 1793, *PAH*, XIV, 474.
28. William L. Smith to Edward Rutledge, Feb., 1794, George C. Rogers, ed., "The Letters of William Loughton Smith . . . ," *South Carolina Historical Magazine*, LXX (1969), 55.
29. See Hamilton to ———, May 18, 1793, Stephen Higginson to Hamilton, July 26, 1793, Rufus King to Hamilton, Aug. 3, 1793, *PAH*, XIV, 473–476, XV, 127–128, 172–173; Rufus King, memorandum on the opposition, 1793, Rufus King Papers, NYHS; Washington to Henry Lee, July 21, 1793, WGW, XXXIII, 23–24; Henry Lee to [Washington?], Sept. 17, 1793, Paul P. Hoffman and John L. Molyneaux, eds., Lee Family Papers (microfilm ed., Charlottesville, 1966), reel 7, exposure 856. For the Genet crisis in general, see Alexander DeConde, *Entangling Alliance: Politics and Diplo-*

macy under George Washington (Durham, N.C., 1958), ch. VI-IX; Harry Ammon, *The Genet Mission* (New York, 1973). For party activities, see Donald H. Stewart, *The Opposition Press of the Federalist Period* (Albany, 1969), 151-168; Cunningham, *Jeffersonian Republicans*, 55-60.

30. Eugene Perry Link, *Democratic-Republican Societies, 1790-1800* (New York, 1942), 10-15, 19, 21, 24-25, 30, 115, 160, 187-192; Buel, *Securing the Revolution*, 97-105.

31. DeConde, *Entangling Alliance*, 235-256.

32. *Ibid.*, 87-100; Charles Downer Hazen, *Contemporary American Opinion of the French Revolution* (Baltimore, 1897), 152-162, 208-278; Rufus King, memorandum on the opposition, 1793, King Papers, NYHS; Collin McGregor to James Miller, Aug. 8, 1793, Collin McGregor Letterbook, NYPL; H. LeRoy to Rufus King, Mar. 19, 1794, *LCRK*, I, 554; Uriah Tracy to Ephraim Kirby, Feb. 24, 1794, Ephraim Kirby Papers, Duke Univ. Library, Durham, N.C.

33. "15 Republicans and boys of Liberty to exterpate Torys" to William L. Smith, 1794, in George C. Rogers, Jr., *Evolution of a Federalist: William Loughton Smith of Charleston (1758-1812)* (Columbia, 1962), 262.

34. Thomas Blount to John Gray Blount, Feb. 13, 1794, Alice Barnwell Keith and William H. Masterson, eds., *The John Gray Blount Papers* [Publication of the North Carolina Department of Archives and History] (Raleigh, 1952-1965), II, 361.

35. See King, memorandum on the opposition, 1793, King Papers, NYHS; Washington to Henry Lee, July 21, 1793, *WGW*, XXXIII, 24; Stephen Higginson to Hamilton, July 12, 1794, Francis Corbin to Hamilton, July 20, 1794, *PAH*, XVI, 592-594, 611-613.

36. George Cabot to Theophilus Parsons, Aug. 12, 1794, Parsons, *Memoir of Parsons*, 471. One of the chief themes in Buel, *Securing the Revolution*, is the Federalist fear that republican institutions and liberty could not survive. Gordon Wood, *The Creation of the American Republic, 1776-1787* (Chapel Hill, 1969), ch. X-XII especially, points out similar fears in the 1780s. I agree with Buel, but as this chapter argues, I believe these fears evolved and sharpened over the 1790s, rather than lying stable in the background. See Banning, "Republican Ideology," *WMQ*, XXXI, 174 ff.

37. Henry Lee to [Washington?], Sept. 17, 1793, Lee Family Papers, r. 7, exp. 856; Rufus King, memorandum on the opposition, 1793, King Papers, NYHS; Francis Corbin to Hamilton, July 20, 1794, *PAH*, XVI, 611-613.

38. Henry Lee to [Washington?], Sept. 17, 1793, Lee Family Papers, r. 7, exp. 856.

39. William Bradford to Elias Boudinot, Aug. 1, 1794, John William Wallace Papers, HSP; "Tully" [Hamilton], *Gazette of the United States* (Phila.), Sept. 2, 1794; Hamilton to Governor Thomas Sim Lee, Sept. 17, 1794, *PAH*, XVII, 242-243.

40. "Extract of a Letter from a gentleman in Macpherson's battalion . . . ," *Aurora* (Phila.), Nov. 22, 1794. Also see Noah Webster to Oliver Wolcott, Nov. 1, 1795, Oliver Wolcott, Jr. Papers, CHS; William Vans Murray to McHenry, 1795, James McHenry Papers, LC.

41. *Gazette of the U.S.* (Phila.), Aug. 2, 1794. See also *ibid.*, Dec. 22, 1794,

Feb. 9, 1795; Oliver Wolcott, Jr. to his father, Aug. 16, 1794, *MAWA*, I, 157; Henry Lee to James Iredell, Jan. 21, 1795, McRee, *James Iredell*, II, 436; Charles Nisbet to Ashbel Green, Oct. 14, 1794, Founders Collection, Dickinson College Library, Carlisle, Pa.

42. New York *Minerva*, Sept. 30, 1794, Jan. 24, 1795; *Gazette of the U.S.* (Phila.), Sept. 6, Dec. 22, 1794. See also William Vans Murray to Tench Coxe, Sept. 20, 1794, Coxe Papers, HSP.

43. Oliver Wolcott, Jr. to his father, Sept. 23, 1794, *MAWA*, I, 159.

44. See Hamilton to Washington, Aug. 5, 1794, to Thomas Fitzsimons, Nov. 27, 1794, *PAH*, XVII, 24–58, 394; *Gazette of the U.S.* (Phila.), Dec. 11, 1794; Ralph Izard to Ralph Wormeley, Dec. 7, 1794, Ralph Izard Papers, South Caroliniana Library, Univ. of South Carolina, Columbia, S.C.; Link, *Democratic-Societies*, 145–148; Washington to Burges Ball, Sept. 25, 1794, Sixth Annual Address to Congress, Nov. 19, 1794, *WGW*, XXXIII, 506–507, XXXIV, 29. For the 1794 House debate, see "Preface to the Cornell Paperbacks Edition," James Morton Smith, *Freedom's Fetters . . .* (Ithaca, 1966), xiii–xv.

45. Draft of a newspaper article, 1794, Alexander Hamilton Papers, LC; William Cobbett, "Account of the Insurrection . . . ," "A Bone to Knaw for the Democrats, Part II," William Cobbett, *Porcupine's Works . . .* (London, 1801), I, 295–296, 304–308, II, 133.

46. Zephaniah Swift to David Daggett, Nov. 4, 1794, Franklin B. Dexter, ed., "Selections from the Letters Received by David Daggett, 1786–1802," *Proceedings of the American Antiquarian Society*, new ser., IV (1887), 373. See also Washington to John Jay, Dec. 18, 1794, to Edmund Pendleton, Jan. 22, 1795, *WGW*, XXXIV, 62, 98–99; John Adams to Abigail Adams, Nov. 8, 1794, Adams Papers, MHS; Jonathan Trumbull, Jr. to John Trumbull, Nov. 10, 1794, Jonathan Trumbull, Jr. Papers (Hubbard Collection), Connecticut State Library, Hartford, Conn.

47. To James McHenry, Dec. 16, 1794, Bernard C. Steiner, *The Life and Correspondence of James McHenry* (Cleveland, 1907), 156.

48. To Christopher Gore, Dec. 17, 1794, Ames, ed., *Fisher Ames*, I, 156. For the history of the appointments crisis, see Kurtz, *Presidency of John Adams*, 239–277.

49. For a sampling of reaction to the Jay Treaty fight and the Randolph affair, see Cobbett, "Account of the Insurrection . . . ," "Popular Proceedings Relative to the British Treaty," *Porcupine's Works*, I, 295–296, 304–308, II, 241; John Adams to Abigail Adams, Dec. 24, 1795, Pickering to J. Q. Adams, Sept. 10, 1795, Adams Papers, MHS; Timothy Williams to Pickering, July 17, 1795, Pickering to Washington, July 27, 1795, to Higginson, Aug. 8, 1795, Timothy Pickering Papers, MHS; Jeremiah Wadsworth to Hamilton, July 11–12, 1795, Hamilton, "The Defence No. I," July 22, 1795, Wolcott to Hamilton, July 28, 30, 1795, *PAH*, XVIII, 460, 484–486, 509, 527; Oliver Wolcott, Jr., to his wife, July 26, 1795, to his father, Aug. 10, 1795, *MAWA*, I, 217, 218–224; J. Q. Adams to Pickering, Nov. 15, 1795, Ford, ed., *Writings of J. Q. Adams*, I, 427–428; Washington, marginal notes on James Monroe, *View of the Conduct of the Executive* (Philadelphia, 1797), xxxvi, in George Washington Papers (Ephemera), LC; Buel,

Securing the Revolution, 70–71; Jerald A. Combs, *The Jay Treaty: Political Battleground of the Founding Fathers* (Berkeley, Los Angeles and London, 1970), ch. 10–11. The Randolph affair and the Secretary's politics is covered in Irving Brant, "Edmund Randolph, Not Guilty!" *WMQ*, VII (1950), 179–198; John Garry Clifford, "A Muddy Middle of the Road: The Politics of Edmund Randolph, 1790–1795," *Virginia Magazine of History and Biography*, LXXX (1972), 286–311.

50. *Aurora* (Phila.), Feb. 27, 1796. The N.Y. *Minerva*, Sept. 3, 1796, noted the foreign birth of "Gallatin, Findley, Swanwick, &c." See also Jonathan Trumbull, Jr. to John Trumbull, Apr. 16, 1796, Trumbull, Jr. Papers (Hubbard Collection), Conn. State Lib. For Republican involvement with Collot, see Wolcott, Jr., memoranda, May 19, 21, 1796, *MAWA*, I, 351.

51. N.Y. *Minerva*, Oct. 8, Dec. 1, 1796; William L. Smith to Ralph Izard, Nov. 8, 1796, Phillips, ed., "S.C. Federalist Correspondence," *American Hist. Rev.*, XIV, 785. James McHenry to William Vans Murray, with Murray's notes, Nov. 19, 1796, William Vans Murray Papers, LC; Oliver Wolcott, Sr. to Oliver Wolcott, Jr., Nov. 21, 1796, *MAWA*, I, 397; Benjamin Goodhue to Stephen Goodhue, Dec. 31, 1796, Benjamin Goodhue Papers, EI.

52. To David Stuart, Jan. 8, 1797, *WGW*, XXXV, 358–359.

53. See Chauncey Goodrich to Wolcott, Sr., Feb. 21, 1796, Oliver Wolcott, Sr. Papers, CHS; N.Y. *Minerva*, May 31, 1796; Izard to Jacob Read, Oct. 12, 1795, Izard Papers, Univ. of S.C. Lib. In 1796, references to the Republicans as the French party became more frequent.

54. To Hamilton, July 29, 1795, *WGW*, XXXIV, 264. See also Stephen Higginson to Pickering, Aug. 29, 1795, J. Franklin Jameson, ed., "Letters of Stephen Higginson, 1783–1804," in Jameson *et al.*, *Report of the Historical Manuscripts Commission of the American Historical Association (1896)* (Washington, 1897), 794.

55. Abigail Adams to John Adams, Feb. 10, 1795, Adams Papers, MHS; Fisher Ames to Christopher Gore, Dec. 17, 1794, to Timothy Dwight, Mar. 9, 1796, Ames, ed., *Fisher Ames*, I, 156–157, 188; Ames to Wolcott, Jr., July 9, 1795, *MAWA*, I, 210–211; Washington to Gouverneur Morris, Mar. 4, 1796, to John Jay, May 8, 1796, *WGW*, XXXIV, 483, XXXV, 37; John Fenno to Joseph Ward, June 5, 1796, Joseph Ward Papers, Chicago Historical Society, Chicago, Ill.; Rachel Bradford to Samuel Bayard, Nov. 26, 1795, J. J. Boudinot, ed., *The Life, Public Services, Addresses, and Letters of Elias Boudinot, LL.D.* (Boston and New York, 1896), II, 114.

56. Jefferson to James Monroe, July 10, 1796, *WTJ*, VII, 89. Federalists agreed. See George Cabot to ———, Feb. 2, 1796, Stan V. Henkels, *A Description . . . of Autograph Letters . . .* [catalogue 817] (Philadelphia, 1898), 65; John Quincy Adams to Joseph Pitcairn, Aug. 11, 1796, Joseph Pitcairn Letters, Cincinnati Hist. Soc.

57. For the birthday celebration, see Carroll and Ashworth, *Washington*, VII, 432–433; James Iredell to his wife, Feb. 24, 1797, Charles E. Johnson Collection, North Carolina Department of Archives and History, Raleigh, N.C. Adams's inauguration is described in Carroll and Ashworth, *Washington*, VII, 436–437 and Page Smith, *John Adams* (Garden City, N.Y., 1962), II, 917–920.

58. *Gazette of the U.S.* (Phila.), July 2, 1796.

59. Harry Ammon, *James Monroe: The Quest for National Identity* (New York, 1971), 131–156; Marvin R. Zahniser, *Charles Cotesworth Pinckney: Founding Father* (Chapel Hill, 1967), 140–149; Samuel Flagg Bemis, *John Quincy Adams and the Foundations of American Foreign Policy* (New York, 1949), 50–53.

60. Apr. 4, 1796, Ford, ed., *Writings of J. Q. Adams*, I, 481–488. See also J. Q. Adams to John Adams, June 6, 1796, *ibid.*, 491–492.

61. To Joseph Pitcairn, Jan. 31, 1797, *ibid.*, II, 96.

62. To the Secretary of State, Feb. 1, 1797, *ibid.*, 99.

63. To John Adams, Feb. 3, 1797, *ibid*, 103–105. See also his letters to Joseph Hall, Feb. 9, 1797, to John Adams, Mar. 18, 1797, *ibid.*, 113–114, 142.

64. To John Adams, Apr. 3, 1797, *ibid.*, 155–157.

65. See, for example, "The Times XXIII," N.Y. *Minerva*, Mar. 15, 1797.

66. Adams evidently showed the letters to others. See Benjamin Goodhue to Stephen Goodhue, June 6, 1797, Goodhue Papers, EI. The April 3 letter to John Adams appeared as an "extract from a man in Holland" in the July 1, 1797, N.Y. *Minerva*. Some Republicans even accepted this interpretation of French motives. See Senator Henry Tazewell to Richard Cocke, June 7, 1797, Henry Tazewell Papers, College of William and Mary Library, Williamsburg, Va.

67. William Vans Murray to James McHenry, July 14, 1797, McHenry Papers, LC; Murray to McHenry, Aug. 7, 1797, Steiner, *James McHenry*, 246; Charles Cotesworth Pinckney to William Smith, July 16, 1797, Autograph Collection, Philip H. and A. S. W. Rosenbach Foundation, Philadelphia, Pa.; Oliver Wolcott, Jr. to his father, Mar. 29, 1797, *MAWA*, I, 482; Uriah Tracy to Samuel Dana, Apr. 1, 1797, Theodore Foster to Welcome Arnold, May 29, 1797, Simon Gratz Collection, HSP; Pickering to J. Q. Adams, Apr. 8, 1797, Pickering Papers, MHS; N.Y. *Minerva*, Apr. 21, July 4, 1797; Washington to Benjamin Goodhue, Oct. 15, 1797, WGW, XXXVI, 48.

68. Apr. 24, 1796, *WTJ*, VII, 75.

69. N.Y. *Minerva*, May 2, June 10, 1797. For the Mazzei letter affair, see Dumas Malone, *Jefferson and His Time* (Boston, 1948–date), III, 302–306.

70. For the Collot mission, see DeConde, *Entangling Alliance*, 446–453; George W. Kyte, "A Spy on the Western Waters: The Military Intelligence Mission of General Collot in 1796," *Mississippi Valley Historical Review*, XXXIV (1947), 427–442; Durand Echeverria, "General Collot's Plan for a Reconaissance of the Ohio and Mississippi Valleys, 1796," *WMQ*, IX (1952), 512–520.

71. See Thomas P. Abernethy, *The South in the New Nation* (Baton Rouge, 1961), 204–216; Zebulon Pike to Anthony Wayne, Aug. 22, 1796, Northwest Territory Collection, Indiana Historical Society, Indianapolis, Ind.; Anthony Wayne to James McHenry, July 8, 28, Oct. 28, 1796, *WKPM*, 495–497, 506, 536–537.

72. For the information on Wilkinson, see anonymous to John Adams, May 5, 1797, Adams Papers, MHS; R. Newman to McHenry, June 17, 18, 1797, Northwest Territory Collection, Ind. Hist. Soc.; Andrew Ellicott to Picker-

ing, Nov. 14, 1797, Washington Papers, LC. The counterspy was Felix de St. Hilaire. See his correspondence with McHenry, Apr.–July 1797, and especially Hilaire to McHenry, received June 7, 1797, and McHenry to Hilaire, sent June 11, 1797, James McHenry Papers, Maryland Historical Society, Baltimore, Md. For other attempts to keep track of western spies, see Pickering to Winthrop Sargent, June 30, 1797, Pickering Papers, MHS; William Henry Harrison to McHenry, Aug. 13, 1797, McHenry Papers, LC. A general indication of the information reaching the War Department in 1797 is in M. Howard Mattsson-Boze, James McHenry, Secretary of War, 1796–1800 (unpub. Ph.D. thesis, Univ. of Minnesota, 1965), ch. IV.

73. To James Iredell, July 12, 1797, McRee, *James Iredell*, II, 515. For the Blount conspiracy, see William H. Masterson, *William Blount* (Baton Rouge, 1954), 302–323.

74. N.Y. *Minerva*, July 21, Aug. 19, 1797; Pickering to Andrew Ellicott, July 28, 1797, Domestic Letters of the Department of State, General Records of the Department of State, RG 59, NA; James Benjamin Wilbur, *Ira Allen: Founder of Vermont, 1751–1814* (Boston and New York, 1928), II, ch. XXIV–XXV; Chilton Williamson, *Vermont in Quandary: 1763–1825* (Montpelier, 1949), ch. 15.

75. See the list of evidence on Spanish attempts to incite the Indians in the James McHenry Papers, box 2, WLCL; Pickering to the Governors of N.C., S.C., Tenn., and Ga., Aug. 3, 1797, to Andrew Ellicott, July 28, 1797, Domestic Letters of Department of State, RG 59, NA; McHenry to commanding officers (circular), July 14, 1797, Isaac Craig Papers, Carnegie Library of Pittsburgh, Pittsburgh, Pa.

76. Memoranda on Collot, May 19, 1796, May 21, 1796, MAWA, I, 351.

77. "Report of Examination of Chisolm by Rufus King," Dec. 5, 1797, F. J. Turner, "Documents on the Blount conspiracy, 1795–1797," *American Hist. Rev.*, X (1905), 602. For others involved in Kentucky, see Arthur Preston Whitaker, ed., "Harry Innes and the Spanish Intrigue: 1794–1795," *Miss. Vall. Hist. Rev.*, XV (1928), 236–248; John Carl Parrish, "The Intrigues of Doctor James O'Fallon," *ibid.*, XVII (1930), 230–263.

78. To Samuel Bayard, July 15, 1797, Boudinot, *Elias Boudinot*, II, 126. See also Roger Griswold to Matthew Griswold, July 5, 1797, Wolcott-Griswold-Williams-Woodbridge-Rogers Family Papers, Univ. of Virginia Library, Charlottesville, Va.

79. To John Adams, Apr. 25, 1797, MAWA, I, 510.

80. Apr. 5, 1797, PAH, XXI, 21. See also Knox to John Adams, Mar. 19, 1797, WJA, VIII, 532–534; Jefferson to Madison, May 18, 1797, WTJ, VIII, 288–289.

81. For these developments, see DeConde, *Quasi-War*, 28–35; Stewart, *Opposition Press*, 281–288; Ammon, *James Monroe*, 157–162; Broadus Mitchell, *Alexander Hamilton* (New York, 1957–1962), II, 405–421.

82. Ames to Sedgwick, Dec. 14, 1797, Sedgwick Papers, MHS. Both sides remarked on the calm in Congress. See Washington to Pickering, Dec. 11, 1797, WGW, XXXVI, 105–106; Albert Gallatin to James Nicholson, Dec. 8, 1797, Albert Gallatin Papers, NYHS; William Barry Grove to James Hogg, Dec. 18, 1797, Henry McGilbert Wagstaff, ed., *Letters of William Barry*

Grove [James Sprunt Historical Publications, IX] (Chapel Hill, 1910), 64; Jefferson to John Eppes, Dec. 21, 1797, to John Taylor, Dec. 23, 1797, to James Monroe, Dec. 27, 1797, *WTJ*, VIII, 346, 348, 350.

83. For the rumors and the mood in Congress, see Abigail Adams to J. Q. Adams, Jan. 3, 1798, Adams Papers, MHS; Jonathan Dayton to William Vans Murray, Jan. 8, 1798, Gratz Collection, HSP; Roger Griswold to Matthew Griswold, Jan. 14, 1798, Griswold Family Papers, Yale Univ. Library, New Haven, Conn.; *Aurora* (Phila.), Jan. 22, 27, 1798.

84. *Porcupine's Gazette*, Jan. 31, 1798 in Cobbett, *Porcupine's Works*, VIII, 68–69; Henry Tazewell to Richard Cocke, Feb. 10, 1798, Henry Tazewell Papers, College of William and Mary Lib.; Abigail Adams to Mary Cranch, Feb. 15, 21, 1798, Mitchell, ed., *New Letters*, 132–133, 135; *Aurora* (Phila.), Feb. 16, 1798; Thomas Blount to John Gray Blount, Feb. 16, 1798, Keith and Masterson, eds., *Blount Papers*, III, 209–210; James Monroe to Jefferson, Feb. 25, 1798, Stanislaus Murray Hamilton, ed., *The Writings of James Monroe* (New York, 1898–1903), III, 209–210; Roger Griswold to Matthew Griswold, Feb. 20, 1798, Wolcott-Griswold-Williams-Woodbridge-Rogers Papers, Univ. of Va. Lib.

85. To [J. Q. Adams?], Jan 3, 1798, Adams Papers, MHS. For general reaction to the XYZ disclosures, see John William Kuehl, The Quest for Identity in an Age of Insecurity: The XYZ Affair and American Nationalism (unpub. Ph.D. thesis, Univ. of Wisconsin, 1968), ch. III.

86. Sedgwick to Peter Van Schaack, Jan. 24, 1798, Sedgwick Papers, MHS.

87. Dwight Foster to his wife, Mar. 10, 1798, Dwight Foster Papers, American Antiquarian Society, Worcester, Mass.

88. William Cranch to J. Q. Adams, Mar. 5, 1798, Adams Papers, MHS. See also Roger Griswold to Matthew Griswold, Feb. 27, 1798, Griswold Family Papers, Yale Univ. Lib.; Griswold to [Matthew Griswold?], Apr. 6, May 24, 1798, Wolcott-Griswold-Williams-Woodbridge-Rogers Papers, Univ. of Va. Lib.

89. To J. Q. Adams, Apr. 13, 21, 1798, Adams Papers, MHS. See also Dwight Foster's journal, Apr. 13, 1798, Foster Papers, American Antiquarian Society.

90. See, for example, Benjamin Goodhue to Stephen Goodhue, Apr. 14, 1798, Goodhue Papers, EI; John Eager Howard to Knox, May 15, 1798, Knox Papers, MHS; Uriah Tracy to Jeremiah Wadsworth, May 17, 1798, Governor Joseph Trumbull Collection, Conn. State Lib.; Pickering to King, June 2, 27, 1798, *LCRK*, II, 329, 351; James Lloyd to Washington, June 6, 1798, Washington Papers, LC.

91. Pickering to J. Q. Adams, Apr. 10, 1798, Adams Papers, MHS; Ebenezer Adams to Dwight Foster, May 20, 1798, Mellen Chamberlain Collection, Boston Public Library, Boston, Mass.

92. Abigail Adams to Mary Cranch, Apr. 13, 1798, Apr. 26, 1798, Mitchell, ed., *New Letters*, 156, 164–165; Roger Griswold to his wife, Apr. 17, 1798, Griswold-Nevins-Perkins Papers, Univ. of Va. Lib.; Henrietta Liston to her uncle, May 3, 1798, Bradford Perkins, ed., "A Diplomat's Wife in Philadelphia: Letters of Henrietta Liston, 1796–1800," *WMQ*, XI (1954), 616.

93. The addresses are in the Petition Book, Records of the United States House

of Representatives, *RG* 233, NA; Petitions and Memorials, 5C, Records of the United States Senate, *RG* 46, NA; and Adams Papers, MHS. The President's replies and other comments are in *WJA*, IX, 182–231; Abigail Adams to Thomas Adams, May 1, 1798, Adams Papers, MHS; Robert Liston to Lord Grenville, May 20, 1798, British State Papers, Ford Transcripts, NYPL; Pickering to David Humphreys, June 2, 1798, Pickering Papers, MHS; William Bingham to Rufus King, June 5, 1798, *LCRK*, II, 331; John Adams to Washington, June 22, 1798, Gratz Collection, HSP; DeConde, *Quasi-War*, 81.

94. George Cabot to Oliver Wolcott, Jr., Apr. 30, 1798, Adams Papers, MHS.
95. Apr. 6, 1798, *LCRK*, II, 297.
96. See Thomas Pinckney to Washington, May 16, 1798, Washington Papers, LC; Wolcott, Jr. to Hamilton, May 18, 1798, Wolcott, Jr. Papers, CHS; Abigail Adams to J. Q. Adams, May 26, 1798, to Cotton Tufts, June 29, 1798, Francis Dana to John Adams, May 27, 1798, Adams Papers, MHS; Ames to Pickering, June 4, July 10, 1798, Ames, ed., *Fisher Ames*, I, 226–227, 235; William Bingham to King, June 5, 1798, *LCRK*, II, 331.
97. Higginson to Pickering, June 9, 1798, Jameson, ed., "Letters of Higginson," 808. For these arguments, see also Ames to Pickering, June 4, July 10, 1798, Ames, ed., *Fisher Ames*, I, 226–227, 232–235; Ames to Wolcott, Jr., June 8, 1798, *MAWA*, II, 52; Francis Dana to John Adams, May 27, 1798, Adams Papers, MHS. British ambassador Robert Liston clearly laid out Federalist thinking on a declaration of war in a letter to Lord Grenville, July 14, 1798, British State Papers, Ford Transcripts, NYPL. Senator Henry Tazewell told Jefferson (July 5, 1798, Thomas Jefferson Papers, LC) that "so soon as a Majority can be secured War will be openly declared. This would not be done, if Treason could be got at without a declaration of War. . . ."
98. King to Hamilton, May 12, 1798, *PAH*, XXI, 458. See also King to Hamilton, July 31, 1798, *LCRK*, II, 374–375; King to Jay, Apr. 9, 1798, John Jay Papers, Columbia Univ. Library, New York, N.Y.; J. Q. Adams to Abigail Adams, May 4, June 27, 1798, Ford, ed., *Writings of J. Q. Adams*, II, 284, 324. In May, Republicans had used rumors of the American negotiators being received by the Directory to delay Provisional Army legislation. See *AC*, 5C 2S, 1771–1772.
99. Stewart, *Opposition Press*, 294–310; Abigail Adams to J. Q. Adams, May 26, 1798, Adams Papers, MHS; Roger Griswold to [Matthew Griswold?], May 24, 1798, Wolcott-Griswold-Williams-Woodbridge-Rogers Papers, Univ. of Va. Lib.
100. See, for example, Alexander Addison in *An Infallible Cure, for Political Blindness . . .* (Richmond, 1798), 7, 15, 17; Wolcott, Jr., report, 1798, *MAWA*, II, 83; Abigail Adams to Mercy Warren, Apr. 25, 1798, *Warren-Adams Letters . . .* [Massachusetts Historical Society, *Collections*, LXXII–LXXIII] (Boston, 1917–1925), II, 337–338; Pickering to Jacob Mayer, June 27, 1798, Pickering Papers, MHS; Daniel Brooks, Nathaniel Smith, Harrison Gray Otis, and Robert Goodloe Harper in *AC*, 5C 2S, 1698, 1736, 1751, 1961–1962, 1988–1989, 1992.
101. To Mercy Warren, Apr. 21, 1798, *Warren-Adams Letters*, II, 338.
102. Abigail Adams to Cotton Tufts, June 29, 1798, Adams Papers, MHS.

103. Alexander Addison in *An Infallible Cure*, 32; Hamilton to Washington, May 19, 1798, *PAH*, XXI, 467.

104. To Jeremiah Wadsworth, June 16, 1798, Joseph Trumbull Collection, Conn. State Lib. See also Roger Griswold to [Matthew Griswold?], May 24, 1798, to his wife, June 6, 1798, Wolcott-Griswold-Williams-Woodbridge-Rogers Papers, Univ. of Va. Lib.

105. Vernon Stauffer, *New England and the Bavarian Illuminati* (New York, 1918); William Cobbett, "Detection of a Conspiracy . . . ," May 1798, *Porcupine's Works*, VIII, 199–229; Washington to McHenry, Mar. 27, 1798, *WGW*, XXXVI, 191–192; Harper in *AC*, 5C 2S, 1530.

106. William Barry Grove to James Hogg, Mar. 23, 1798, Wagstaff, ed., *Letters of Grove*, 75; John Rutledge, Jr. to Bishop Smith, Apr. 1, 1798, John Rutledge, Jr. Papers, Southern Historical Collection, Univ. of N.C. Library, Chapel Hill, N.C.; DeConde, *Quasi-War*, 84–85.

107. "A Friend to America & Truth" to ———, Apr. 1798, Adams Papers, MHS; Abigail Adams to her sister, May 10, 1798, Mitchell, ed., *New Letters*, 170–171; Hilary Baker to William McPherson, May 4, 1798, United States Letters, Rutgers Univ. Library, New Brunswick, N.J.

108. *Aurora* (Phila.), May 7, 1798. For the fires, see *ibid.*, Apr. 17, May 2, June 11, 30, 1798; Roger Griswold to his wife, Apr. 17, 1798, Griswold-Nevins-Perkins Papers, Univ. of Va. Lib.; diary entries, Apr. 16, May 14, 27, 1798, Mahlon Dickerson Diary, New Jersey Historical Society, Newark, N.J.

109. Joseph L. Wilson *et al.*, eds. *Book of the First Troop Philadelphia City Cavalry, 1774–1914* (Philadelphia, 1915), 59; *Aurora* (Phila.), May 10, 23, 1798; Abigail Adams to her sister, May 10, 1798, Mitchell, ed., *New Letters*, 171–172; DeConde, *Quasi-War*, 79, 81–84.

110. To John Ambler, May 9, 1798, Henry Tazewell Papers, LC.

111. For the Logan and Bache affairs, see Smith, *Freedom's Fetters*, 101–111, 193–200; Frederick B. Tolles, *George Logan of Philadelphia* (New York, 1953), 148–158. For other Federalist reactions, see John Wilkes Kittera, Harrison Gray Otis, John Allen, and Robert Goodloe Harper in *AC*, 5C 2S, 2016, 2017, 2024, 2094–2099, 2134, 2165–2166; Francis Dana to Abigail Adams, June 23, 1798, Adams Papers, MHS; Roger Griswold to Matthew Griswold, June 20, 1798, Griswold Family Papers, Yale Univ. Lib.

112. *Porcupine's Gazette*, June 1798, *Porcupine's Works*, VIII 246–247.

113. Stevens T. Mason to Jefferson, July 6, 1798, quoted in Smith, *Freedom's Fetters*, 111.

114. To Matthew Griswold, June 20, 1798, Griswold Family Papers, Yale Univ. Lib. See also Link, *Democratic-Republican Societies*, 146–148; George Rogers Clark to Edmond Genet, Apr. 28, 1794, Edmund C. Burnett, ed., "George Rogers Clark to Genet, 1794," *American Hist. Rev.*, XVIII (1913), 781–783.

115. See Robert R. Palmer, *The Age of Democratic Revolution: A Political History of Europe and America, 1760–1800* (Princeton, 1959–1964), II ("The Struggle").

116. Francis Sergeant Childs, *French Refugee Life in the United States: An American Chapter of the French Revolution* (Baltimore, 1940), especially 63–66, ch. VIII. See also Edward C. Carter II, "A Wild Irishman Under

Every Federalist's Bed: Naturalization in Philadelphia, 1789–1806," *Pa. Mag. Hist. Biog.*, XCIV (1970), 331–346.

117. Robert Brooke, memorandum of conversation in Lawrence Brooke to St. George Tucker, May 17, 1798, Tucker-Coleman Papers, College of William and Mary Lib.

118. Clark to Samuel Fulton, June 3, 1798, to ———, Sept. 10, 1798, in James A. James, *The Life of George Rogers Clark* (Chicago, 1929), 511–513. There is a vast difference between common usage of the term "treason" and its legal definition, since in the United States the crime has been defined by the courts in very narrow terms. See James Willard Hurst, *The Law of Treason in the United States: Collected Essays* (Westport, Conn., 1971), especially ch. 5–6.

119. Bernard Bailyn, "The Origins of American Politics," *Perspectives in American History*, I, (1967), especially 32–34, 78–79, 96–99, 104–121; Hofstadter, *Idea of a Party System*, ch. 1–3 *passim*.

120. Howe, "Republican Thought," *American Quarterly*, XIX, 155–164; James M. Banner, Jr., *To the Hartford Convention: The Federalists and the Origins of Party Politics in Massachusetts, 1789–1815* (New York, 1970), 32–34; Douglass Adair, "Fame and the Founding Fathers," Edmund P. Willis, ed., *Fame and the Founding Fathers* (Bethlehem, Pa., 1967), 27–52.

Chapter 11

HEADNOTE

a. To William Vans Murray, Mar. 20, 1798, Worthington Chauncey Ford, ed., *Writings of John Quincy Adams* (New York, 1913–1917), II, 272–273.

SOURCE NOTES

1. To James Hogg, Apr. 3, 1794, Kemp P. Battle, ed., *Letters of Nathaniel Macon, John Steele, and William Barry Grove* [James Sprunt Historical Monograph, No. 3] (Chapel Hill, 1902), 94.

2. See Hamilton to Washington, Mar. 8, 1794, *PAH*, XVI, 31–36; Sedgwick to Ephraim Williams, Mar. 10, 1794, Theodore Sedgwick Papers, MHS; Rufus King to Christopher Gore, Mar. 10, 1794, *LCRK*, I, 550; William Hindman to Joseph Nicholson, Mar. 16, 1794, Joseph H. Nicholson Papers, LC; Washington to Edmund Randolph, Apr. 15, 1794, *WGW*, XXXIII, 329–330; Fisher Ames and Jonathan Dayton in *AC*, 3C 1S, 736, 736–737.

3. *AC*, 3C 1S, 485. For the fortification and allied legislation, see *ASP, MA*, I, 64–65; *AC*, 3C 1S, 447–451, 479–480, 1423–1424; Marshall Smelser, *The Congress Founds the Navy, 1787–1798* (Notre Dame, Ind., 1959), 48–69.

4. *AC*, 3C 1S, 499–504. Sedgwick undoubtedly had discussed his plan with Hamilton and other Federalist leaders, since Hamilton proposed almost exactly the same plan to the President on March 8 and a meeting of Federalist senators on March 10 decided to propose such a system, along

with other defense measures, to the President. See *PAH*, XVI, 132–136n. Sedgwick himself claimed privately that "The President most completely and explicitly approves of this project, but I am not certain his extreme caution will permit him to bring it forward." To Ephraim Williams, Mar. 10, 1794, Sedgwick Papers, MHS.

5. Stanislaus Murray Hamilton, ed., *The Writings of James Monroe* (New York, 1898–1903), I, 287. See also Madison to Jefferson, Mar. 14, 1794, James Madison Papers, LC; Jefferson to Madison, Apr. 3, 1794, William C. Rives Collection, LC; *General Advertiser* (Phila.), May 22, 1794.

6. To Jefferson, June 1, 1794, Madison Papers, LC. The legislative battle can be followed in *AC*, 3C 1S, 499–504, 504–508, 528, 558, 603, 632, 647, 709–710, 734–739; committee report, Mar. 27, 1794, *ASP, MA*, I, 67; Grove to Steele, Apr. 2, 1794, Battle, ed., *Letters of Macon, Steele, and Grove*, 109; Paine Wingate to Josiah Bartlett, Apr. 2, 1794, Charles E. L. Wingate, *Life and Letters of Paine Wingate* (Medford, Mass., 1930), II, 428; Washington to Tobias Lear, May 6, 1794, *WGW*, XXXIII, 356; Thomas Blount to John Gray Blount, May 30, 1794, Alice Barnwell Keith and William H. Masterson, eds., *The John Gray Blount Papers* [Publications of the North Carolina Department of Archives and History] (Raleigh, 1952–1965), II, 401–402; *General Advertiser* (Phila.), May 22, 1794; *Gazette of the United States* (Phila.), May 22, 1794. Analysis of the roll call (*AC*, 3C 1S, 738–739) shows that Federalists from the South and Middle states joined Republicans in defeating the measure.

7. To Ephraim Williams, Mar. 10, 1794, Sedgwick Papers, MHS.

8. To William Loughton Smith, Apr. 5, 1797, *PAH*, XXI, 21. For other calls for defense, see Uriah Tracy to Samuel Dana, Apr. 1, 19, 1797, Theodore Foster to Welcome Arnold, May 29, 1797, Simon Gratz Collection, HSP; George Cabot to Oliver Wolcott, Jr., Apr. 6, 1797, Wolcott to Washington, Apr. 19, 1797, *MAWA*, I, 522, 496.

9. May 11, 1797, *PAH*, XXI, 83. See also Hamilton to Pickering, Mar. 22, 1797, Hamilton to McHenry, Apr. 29, 1797, with "Answer to questions . . . ," Pickering to Hamilton, Apr. 29, 1797, *PAH*, XX, 546, XXI, 61–71; McHenry, memorandum on defensive force, Apr. 8, 1797, Pickering to Adams, May 1, 1797, Adams Family Papers, MHS; Wolcott to Adams, Apr. 25, 1797, *MAWA*, I, 510–511.

10. Wolcott to Hamilton, Mar. 31, 1797, to Washington, Apr. 19, 1797, George Cabot to Wolcott, Apr. 6, 1797, *MAWA*, I, 486, 496, 522; Charles Lee to William L. Lee, Apr. 4, 1797, Edmund Jennings Lee Papers, Virginia Historical Society, Richmond, Va.

11. Mar. 22, 1797, Hamilton Papers, LC.

12. Address to Congress, May 16, 1797, *WJA*, IX, 115–117.

13. *AC*, 5C 1S, 13, 15–18, 20–22, 239–247; McHenry to Smith, 1797, Smith Papers, LC.

14. *AC*, 5C 1S, 20–22, 25; provisional army bill, Original Senate Bills, 5C 1S, Records of the United States Senate, *RG* 46, NA; Jefferson to Madison, June 22, 1797, *WTJ*, VIII, 315.

15. *AC*, 5C 1S, 281, 282–283, 292–294, 332, 336–339, 341, 3685–3686, 3687, 3687–3688, 3689–3692.

16. Jefferson to Edward Rutledge, June 24, 1797, *WTJ*, VIII, 317. See also Jefferson to Madison, June 22, 1797, *ibid.*, 315; Thomas Blount to John Sevier, June 23, 1797, Emmet Collection, NYPL; Sedgwick to Ephraim Williams, June 23, 1797, Sedgwick Papers, MHS.

17. To Samuel Dana, Apr. 19, 1797, Gratz Collection, HSP. Tracy told Sedgwick before Congress met that "if the House of Representatives will do nothing . . . , I am clear for Separating the Union immediately" (Mar. 29, 1797, Sedgwick Papers, MHS).

18. To Peter Van Schaack, June 16, 1797, Sedgwick Papers, MHS.

19. To Richard Cocke, June 7, 1797, Henry Tazewell Papers, College of William and Mary Library, Williamsburg, Va.

20. For the caucus, see Manning J. Dauer, *The Adams Federalists* (Baltimore, 1953), 146-147; Raymond Walters, Jr., *Albert Gallatin: Jeffersonian Financier and Diplomat* (New York, 1957), 106-107; Dumas Malone, *Jefferson and His Time* (Boston, 1948-date), III, 374-375; AC, 5C 2S, 1319-1320; Albert Gallatin, *The Oregon Question* (New York, 1846), in Henry Adams, ed., *The Writings of Albert Gallatin* (Philadelphia, 1879), III, 553; Jefferson to Monroe, Mar. 21, 1798, *WTJ*, VIII, 389; William Hindman to King, Apr. 12, 1798, *LCRK*, II, 314.

21. For the legislative history of these bills, see AC, 5C 2S, 527, 528, 531, 543, 549, 551, 1333-1334, 1380-1383, 1394-1402, 1414, 1427-1439, 3725-3726, 3726-3727; *ASP, MA*, I, 119-120, 123.

22. See AC, 5C 2S, 542, 544, 545, 1402-1412, 1415-1426, 1426-1427, 3723-3724; Robert Liston to Lord Grenville, May 2, 1798, British State Papers, Ford Transcripts, NYPL.

23. McHenry to Samuel Sewall, Apr. 9, 1798, *ASP, MA*, I, 120-123. Compare McHenry's suggestions to Hamilton's in Hamilton to Pickering, Mar. 17, 1798, *PAH*, XXI, 364-366. The differences between Hamilton and McHenry are of size only, as Dauer (*Adams Federalists*, 147) argues. John Adams's position on the military program is explained below. McHenry submitted Hamilton's ideas to the President (see his undated observations in the James McHenry Papers, vol. I of photostats, LC, which by internal evidence appears to have been written in March 1798 and meant for Adams). The President evidently modified the number of ships and troops.

24. AC, 5C 2S, 540, 542, 543, 544, 546. The bill is in Original Senate Bills, 5C 2S, Senate Records, RG 46, NA.

25. AC, 5C 2S, 1425.

26. Section 1, "A Bill . . . ," Original Senate bills, 5C 2S, Senate Records, RG 46, NA.

27. AC, 5C 2S, 1640.

28. William Claiborne in *ibid.*, 1653.

29. *Ibid.*, 1760.

30. *Ibid.*, 1745.

31. *Ibid.*, 1746, 1753.

32. *Ibid.*, 1698.

33. To Andrew Jackson, Apr. 27, 1798, John Spencer Bassett, ed., *Correspondence of Andrew Jackson* (Washington, 1926-1933), I, 47. See also Henry Tazewell to John Ambler, May 9, 1798, Henry Tazewell Papers, LC;

Gallatin to James W. Nicholson, May 18, 1798, Albert Gallatin Papers, NYHS; *Aurora* (Phila.), May 11, 1798.

34. Samuel Sitgreaves in *AC*, 5C 2S, 1738.

35. *Ibid.*, 1730.

36. Cabot to Wolcott, Jr., Apr. 30, 1798, Adams Papers, MHS.

37. To Hamilton, June 9, 1798, *PAH*, XXI, 501–506.

38. The quotations are from *ibid.*; Abigail Adams to Mary Cranch, May 26, 1798, Stewart Mitchell, ed., *New Letters of Abigail Adams, 1788–1801* (Boston, 1947), 179; Harper to Hamilton, Apr. 27, 1798, Hamilton, ed., *Writings of Hamilton*, VI, 282; Cabot to Wolcott, Apr. 30, 1798, Adams Papers, MHS. See also William Barry Grove to McHenry, Aug. 20, 1798, McHenry Papers, LC; Sedgwick to King, Apr. 9, 1798, *LCRK*, II, 313; Hamilton, "The Stand VII," Apr. 9, 1798, *WAH*, VI, 310–318; Knox to John Adams, June 26, 1798, Dudley W. Knox, ed., *Naval Documents Related to Quasi-war between the United States and France* (Washington, 1935–1938), I, 139–140; Benjamin Stoddert to Wolcott, Nov. 24, 1798, Oliver Wolcott, Jr. Papers, CHS; Roger Griswold to [Matthew Griswold?], May 18, 1798, Wolcott-Griswold-Williams-Woodbridge-Rogers Family Papers, Univ. of Virginia Library, Charlottesville, Va.

39. To McHenry, June 15, 1798, McHenry Papers, LC.

40. James Ash to McHenry, Aug. 24, 1798, Bernard C. Steiner, *The Life and Correspondence of James McHenry* (Cleveland, 1907), 333.

41. To Hamilton, June 9, 1798, *PAH*, XXI, 504–505.

42. Compare the final law in *AC*, 5C 2S, 3729–3733, with the Senate bill in Original Senate Bills, 5C 2S, Senate Records, *RG* 46, NA. For its passage through Congress and the debate, see *AC*, 5C 2S, 542, 543, 544, 546, 559, 560, 561, 1525–1545, 1561, 1594, 1631–1707, 1725–1772; committee report, May 4, 1798, records of select committees, 4C 2S to 6C 2S, Records of the United States House of Representatives, *RG* 233, NA; Jefferson to Madison, May 17, 1798, *WTJ*, VII, 420; Liston to Grenville, May 2, 1798, British State Papers, Ford Transcripts, NYPL. For the reaction of the Federalist leadership, see Wolcott to Hamilton, May 18, 1798, Wolcott, Jr. Papers, CHS; Hamilton to Wolcott, June 5, 1798, Pickering to Hamilton, June 9, 1798, *PAH*, XXI, 485–487, 501–506.

43. Section 5, *AC*, 5C 2S, 3730. See also Harper to Hamilton, Apr. 27, 1798, *PAH*, XXI, 449.

44. See Hamilton to Washington, May 19, June 2, 1798, Washington to Hamilton, May 27, 1798, *PAH*, XXI, 466–468, 479–480, 470–474; Pickering to Washington, July 6, 1798, George Washington Papers, LC.

45. Pickering to Hamilton, June 9, 1798, *PAH*, XXI, 506.

46. See Sedgwick to King, Dec. 12, 1799, *LCRK*, III, 155; Sedgwick to Peter Van Schaack, Jan. 15, 1800, Sedgwick Papers, MHS.

47. *AC*, 5C 2S, 581, 582, 583, 584, 591, 593, 1867, 1868–1869, 1871–1873, 1877, 1916–1917.

48. *Ibid.*, 2084. Compare Harper's resolutions to Hamilton to Wolcott, June 5, 1798, *PAH*, XXI, 485–487.

49. To Andrew Jackson, July 20, 1798, Bassett, ed., *Correspondence of Jackson*, I, 52.

50. July 10, 1798, Seth Ames, ed., *Works of Fisher Ames . . .* (Boston, 1854), I,

233–234. For the caucus and question of declaring war, see Alexander DeConde, *The Quasi-War: The Politics and Diplomacy of the Undeclared War with France, 1797–1801* (New York, 1966), 103–108. DeConde dates the caucus (p. 343) at July 2, but Henry Tazewell (to Jefferson, July 5, 1798, Thomas Jefferson Papers, LC) indicated that it took place on Sunday, July 1. See also Sedgwick to King, July 1, 1798, *LCRK*, II, 352–353; Liston to Grenville, July 14, 1798, British State Papers, Ford Transcripts, NYPL; Robert C. Alberts, *The Golden Voyage: The Life and Times of William Bingham, 1752–1804* (Boston, 1969), 341.

51. To King, Dec. 12, 1799, *LCRK*, III, 155.
52. For the passage of the New Army legislation, see AC, 5C 2S, 605, 609, 611, 613, 614, 2084, 2088–2093, 2114, 2128, 2129–2132, 3785–3787. There is no record that the House considered the rest of Hamilton's program except the ships. I interpret the New Army law as a compromise substitute because it was introduced by Samuel Smith and supported by most of the Republican leadership. Gallatin and Smith explained Republican support on the grounds of fears of invasion, black insurrection, and Toussaint. See *ibid.*, 6C 1S, 268, 324–325.
53. See Adams to Elbridge Gerry, Feb. 13, 1797, *WJA*, VIII, 523–524; Hamilton to Pickering, Aug. 29, 1798, Timothy Pickering Papers, MHS; Stephen G. Kurtz, *The Presidency of John Adams: The Collapse of Federalism, 1795–1800* (Philadelphia, 1957), 192–196, 204–207; Page Smith, *John Adams* (Garden City, N.Y., 1962), II, 907–908.
54. See Adams to Gerry, Feb. 13, 1797, "Boston Patriot Letter XIII," 1809, *WJA*, VIII, 523, IX, 288–289. Upon reading Hamilton's military plans, shown to Adams directly by Senator Tracy, the President in his own words "was utterly astonished. I said 'this man [Hamilton] is stark mad, or I am.'" See Adams to Harrison Gray Otis, May 9, 1823, Adams Papers, MHS.
55. Smith, *John Adams*, II, 950–951; Samuel Eliot Morison, *Harrison Gray Otis, 1765–1848: The Urbane Federalist* (Boston, 1969), 128–130.
56. Jan. 9, 1797, Adams Papers, MHS.
57. May 3, 1798, *ibid.*
58. "Boston Patriot Letter XIII," 1809, *WJA*, IX, 290.
59. Harper to Hamilton, Apr. 27, 1798, *PAH*, XXI, 449.
60. "Boston Patriot Letter II," 1809, *WJA*, IX, 243.
61. Aug. 23, 1805, John A. Shutz and Douglass Adair, eds., *The Spur of Fame: Dialogues of John Adams and Benjamin Rush, 1805–1813* (San Marino, Cal., 1966), 36. In 1809, Adams claimed that "such was the influence of Mr. Hamilton in Congress, that, without any recommendation from the President, they passed a bill to raise an army, not a large one, indeed, but enough to overturn the then Federal government." See "Boston Patriot Letter XIII," *WJA*, IX, 290. For Adams's messages in 1797 and 1798, see *ibid.*, 111–127, 156–157. Adams claimed (to James Lloyd, Jan. 1815, *ibid.*, X, 111) that he had been a navalist since 1775.
62. Pickering to Washington, July 6, 1798, Washington Papers, LC; Pickering to Charles Cotesworth Pinckney, May 27, 1800, Henry Adams, ed., *Documents Relating to New-England Federalism, 1800–1815* (Boston, 1877), 332n; Timothy Pickering, *Review of the Correspondence between the Hon. John Adams . . . and . . . Wm. Cunningham . . .* (Salem, 1824), 160–161.

According to Senator Benjamin Goodhue, the Senate always expected Hamilton to be named first after Washington, and it provided for an Inspector General with Hamilton specifically in mind. See Goodhue to Pickering, Sept. 17, 1798, Pickering Papers, MHS.

63. Adams to Washington, June 22, 1798, *WJA*, VIII, 573. See also Adams to John Langdon, Feb. 27, 1812, *Letters by Washington . . . and Others . . . to John Langdon . . .* (Philadelphia, 1880), 16; Abigail Adams to J. Q. Adams, July 14, 1798, Adams Papers, MHS; Abigail Adams to her sister, July 3, 1798, Mitchell, ed., *New Letters*, 199; McHenry to Washington, June 26, July 3, 1798, McHenry Papers, LC; John Fenno to Joseph Ward, July 28, 1798, Joseph Ward Papers, Chicago Historical Society, Chicago, Ill.

64. Abigail Adams to ———, July 10, 1798, Adams Papers, MHS. See also Pickering to Washington, July 6, 1798, Washington Papers, LC; Smith, *John Adams*, II, 972–973. Adams purposely titled Washington "Commander-in-Chief." See Stevens T. Mason to Jefferson, July 6, 1798, Jefferson Papers, LC. Adams told Benjamin Rush that he (Adams) would not appoint Hamilton to a generalcy. See Tench Coxe to Rush, Oct. 12, 1800, Tench Coxe Papers, HSP.

65. Adams to Washington, June 22, 1798, *WJA*, VIII, 572–573; Tazewell to Jefferson, July 5, 1798, Stevens T. Mason to Jefferson, July 6, 1798, Jefferson Papers, LC; *Journal of the Executive Proceedings of the Senate of the United States . . .* (Washington, 1828), I, 284.

66. Washington to McHenry, July 5, 1798, WGW, XXXVI, 318–319. See also Washington to Adams, July 4, Sept. 25, 1798, to McHenry, July 4, 1798, to Pickering, July 11, 1798, *ibid.*, 304–312, 453–456, 312–315, 324.

67. Washington to Hamilton, May 27, 1798, Hamilton to Washington, June 2, 1798, *PAH*, XXI, 470–474, 479–480.

68. Washington Papers, LC.

69. See Adams to McHenry, July 6, 1798, to Washington, July 7, 1798, *WJA*, VIII, 573–575; McHenry to Adams, July 12, 1798, Washington Papers, LC; Washington to Pickering, July 11, 1798, "Proposed Arrangement of . . . Officers," July 14, 1798, "Answers to Queries of the Secretary of War," July 14, 1798, Washington to Hamilton, July 14, 1798, to Knox, July 16, 1798, WGW, XXXVI, 323–326, 333–335, 346–347; Pickering to John Jay, July 28, 1798, John C. Hamilton, *History of the Republic . . . as traced in the Writings of Alexander Hamilton . . .* (New York, 1850–1851), VI, 329–330.

70. Washington to Hamilton, July 14, 1798, WGW, XXXVI, 329–334. See also Washington to Knox, July 16, Aug. 9, 1798, to Pickering, Sept. 9, 1798, *ibid.*, 346–347, 397–398, 432; Pickering to Jay, July 28, 1798, Hamilton, ed., *Writings of Hamilton*, VI, 329–330; McHenry to Washington, July 18, 1798, Washington Papers, LC.

71. McHenry to Washington, July 18, 1789, Washington Papers, LC; McHenry to Washington, Sept. 19, 1798, Jared Sparks, ed., *The Writings of George Washington . . . ,* XI (Boston, 1855), 542; Pickering to King, Sept. 18, 1798, LCRK, II, 419; Steiner, *James McHenry*, 313–314. Washington's list is in Washington to Hamilton, July 14, 1798, WGW, XXXVI, 331. See also Smith, *John Adams*, II, 978.

72. *Senate Executive Journal*, I, 292; McHenry to Washington, Sept. 19, 1798, Sparks, ed., *Writings of Washington*, XI, 542–543.

73. *Senate Executive Journal*, I, 292. For the Smith affair, see McHenry to Washington, July 18, 1798, Hamilton to Washington, Dec. 13, 1798, Washington Papers, LC; Pickering to Hamilton, July 18, 1798, Hamilton, ed., *Writings of Hamilton*, VI, 327–328; Pickering to Jay, July 20, 1798, Benjamin Goodhue to Pickering, Sept. 17, 1798, Pickering Papers, MHS; Tracy to Jeremiah Wadsworth, July 19, 1798, Joseph Trumbull Collection, CHS; Robert Troup to King, July 24, 1798, Rufus King Papers, NYHS; William North to Benjamin Walker, July 24, 1798, Ferdinand Dreer Collection, HSP; Pickering to King, Aug. 29, 1798, *LCRK*, II, 404; Pickering to his son, May 27, 1800, Timothy Pickering Papers, EI; Pickering to William Loughton Smith, May 28, 1800, Smith Papers, LC; Smith, *John Adams*, II, 978–979.
74. Knox to Adams, June 26, 1798, Knox, ed., *Quasi-War Naval Documents*, I, 139–141.
75. Some recent accounts of this episode are Smith, *John Adams*, II, 972–974, 978–979, 980–983; John Alexander Carroll and Mary Wells Ashworth, *George Washington* [completing the biography by Douglas Southall Freeman] (New York, 1957), 529–534; Broadus Mitchell, *Alexander Hamilton: The Revolutionary Years* (New York, 1970), 328–338; Kurtz, *Presidency of John Adams*, 324–329; Gerald H. Clarfield, *Timothy Pickering and American Diplomacy, 1795–1800* (Columbia, Mo., 1969), 165–179; Bernhard Knollenberg, "John Adams, Knox, and Washington," *Proceedings of the American Antiquarian Society*, LVI (1946), 228–238.
76. Hamilton to McHenry, July 30, 1798, Hamilton, ed., *Writings of Hamilton*, V, 139. See also McHenry to Hamilton, July 25, 1798, *ibid.*, 137; Pickering to Charles Adams, July 25, 1798, Pickering Papers, MHS; Hamilton to McHenry, July 22, 1798, McHenry Papers, LC; John Fenno to Joseph Ward, July 28, 1798, Ward Papers, Chicago Hist. Soc.; Hamilton to Washington, July 29–Aug. 1, 1798, *WAH*, X, 302.
77. McHenry to Adams, Aug. 4, 1798, Steiner, *James McHenry*, 321. See also Wolcott to Hamilton, Aug. 7, 1798, Hamilton Papers, LC.
78. Adams to McHenry, Aug. 14, 1798, *WJA*, VIII, 580.
79. Aug. 20, 1798, Adams Papers, MHS.
80. Adams to McHenry, Aug. 29, 1798, *WJA*, VIII, 587–588.
81. McHenry to Washington, Aug. 25, 1798, McHenry Papers, LC; McHenry to Washington, Sept. 7, 1798, Pickering to Washington, Sept. 13, 18, 1798, Washington Papers, LC; Pickering to Washington, Sept. 1, 1798, McHenry to Washington, Sept. 19, 1798, Sparks, ed., *Writings of Washington*, XI, 540–547. For the cabinet strategy and relations with Adams, see Adams to McHenry, Aug. 14, 29, 1798, *WJA*, VIII, 580, 587–588; Pickering to Hamilton, Aug. 21–22, 23, 1798, Hamilton, ed., *Writings of Hamilton*, VI, 343–346, 351–352; McHenry to Adams, Sept. 6, 1798, Pickering to Adams, Sept. 6, 1798, Adams Papers, MHS.
82. Sept. 17, 1798, Adams Papers, MHS. A printed version with minor errors is in *MAWA*, II, 93–99.
83. Sept. 19, 1798, Hamilton Papers, LC.
84. Hamilton to McHenry, Sept. 8, 1798, McHenry to Hamilton, Sept. 10, 1798, Hamilton, ed., *Writings of Hamilton*, VI, 355–356.
85. Washington to Pickering, Sept. 9, 1798, Washington to McHenry, Sept. 16,

26, Oct. 1, 1798, Washington to Hamilton, Sept. 24, 1798, to Adams, Sept. 25, 1798, *WGW*, XXXVI, 431–433, 447–449, 463–464, 476–477, 452, 453–462.

86. Adams to Wolcott [marked "never to be sent"], Sept. 24, 1798, Adams Papers, MHS.

87. *WGW*, XXXVI, 453–462. Nearly thirty years later, Timothy Pickering remembered the letter as "Washington's final and decisive interference." See "Intimation of Documents . . . [for] writing the Life of General Hamilton," July 25, 1827, Hamilton-McLane Papers, LC. For Adams's thinking, see Adams to Wolcott [marked "never to be sent"], Sept. 24, 1798, Cabot to Adams [marked "not to be answered"], Sept. 29, 1798, McHenry to Adams, Sept. 21, 1798, Adams Papers, MHS; Adams to McHenry, Sept. 30, 1798, McHenry Papers, LC.

88. Oct. 22, 1798, *WJA*, VIII, 612–613. For the closing of the rank affair, see Adams to Washington, Oct. 9, 1798, *ibid.*, 600–601; Wolcott to Hamilton, Oct. 10, 1798, Hamilton Papers, LC; McHenry to the cabinet, Oct. 12, 1798, McHenry Papers, WLCL; McHenry to Adams, Oct. 15, 1798, Adams Papers, MHS; McHenry to Washington, Oct. 16, 1798, Washington Papers, LC.

89. To Mary Cranch, Mar. 27, 1798, Mitchell, ed., *New Letters*, 148.

Chapter 12

HEADNOTE

a. Conversation with George Logan recorded in Thomas Jefferson's memorandum, Jan. 14, 1799, Thomas Jefferson Papers, LC. For dating this conversation, see Frederick B. Tolles, *George Logan of Philadelphia* (New York, 1953), 175–176.

SOURCE NOTES

1. For the arms purchases, see the contract between Eli Whitney and Wolcott, June 14, 1798, Letters Received by the Secretary of War, unregistered series, Records of the Office of the Secretary of War, RG 107, NA; Rufus King to Joseph Pitcairn, July 19, Sept. 10, Oct. 8, 19, 1798, Joseph Pitcairn Letters, Cincinnati Historical Society, Cincinnati, Ohio. For the coast fortifications program, see the correspondence in April, May, and June in the Adams Family Papers, reel 396, MHS; Ebenezer Stevens Papers, vol. I, NYHS. McHenry let affairs in the western army slide until January 1799. See McHenry to Wilkinson, Jan. 31, 1799, Alexander Hamilton Papers, LC.

2. McHenry to Adams, Aug. 4, 1798, Adams Papers, MHS; McHenry to Washington, Aug. 25, Oct. 2, 1798, George Washington Papers, LC.

3. To Washington, Aug. 25, 1798, Washington Papers, LC. See also McHenry to John Brooks, July 31, 1798, to Knox, July 31, 1798, to Adams, Aug. 4, 1798, Adams Papers, MHS.

4. McHenry to James Ross, June 22, 1798, James McHenry Papers, WLCL; Robert Troup to Rufus King, July 10, 1798, Rufus King Papers, NYHS; John Caldwell, draft of report on possible volunteer companies, July 19, 1798, James McHenry Papers, LC; Abigail Adams to Thomas Adams, July 20, 1798, John Adams to McHenry, Oct. 25, 1798, Adams Papers, MHS; Harper, "Letter . . . ," July 23, 1798, *Select Works of Robert Goodloe Harper* . . . (Baltimore, 1814), 271; Abraham Shepherd to Thomas Worthington, Sept. 9, 1798, Thomas Worthington Papers, Ohio Historical Society, Columbus, Ohio; "To Volunteer Companies, who . . . intend offering their Services . . . ," Nov. 1, 1798, Broadside Collection, Maryland Historical Society, Baltimore, Md.

5. Eleanor Parke Custis to McHenry, July 26, 1798, Bernard C. Steiner, *The Life and Correspondence of James McHenry* (Cleveland, 1907), 356–359.

6. John Rutledge, Jr. to Bishop Robert Smith, July 17, 1798, McHenry to Rutledge, July 30, 1798, John Rutledge, Jr. Papers, Southern Historical Collection, Univ. of North Carolina Library, Chapel Hill, N.C.; Tracy to Jeremiah Wadsworth, July 28, Aug. 17, Sept. 15, 1798, Joseph Trumbull Collection, Connecticut State Library, Hartford, Conn.; Aaron Ogden to Jonathan Dayton, Aug. 29, 1798, Jonathan Dayton Miscellany, New Jersey Historical Society, Newark, N.J.

7. McHenry to Washington, Aug. 25, 1798, Washington Papers, LC; Washington to McHenry, Sept. 3, 14, Oct. 15, 1798, WGW, XXXVI, 423–424, 441, 488–489; McHenry to Davie, Sept. 12, 1798, William R. Davie Papers, North Carolina Department of Archives and History, Raleigh, N.C.

8. McHenry to Wolcott, Sept. 3, 1798, Adams Papers, MHS; Washington to McHenry, Oct. 1, 1798, WGW, XXXVI, 478.

9. McHenry to Washington, Oct. 2, 1798, Washington Papers, LC; Troup to King, Oct. 2, 1798, *LCRK*, II, 428–429.

10. Hamilton to McHenry, Aug. 19, 1798, WAH, X, 309.

11. Adams to McHenry, Aug. 29, 1798, WJA, VIII, 587–588; Washington to Hamilton, Aug. 9, 1798, to McHenry, Aug. 10, Sept. 14, 1798, WGW, XXXVI, 394, 402–404, 441–443.

12. I am in basic agreement with the interpretation advanced by M. Howard Mattsson-Boze, James McHenry, Secretary of War, 1796–1800 (unpub. Ph.D. thesis, Univ. of Minnesota, 1965), ch. VIII, although Mattsson-Boze (pp. 273–276) is harder on McHenry than I am. It is significant that both of us, studying the War Department rather than listening to the complaints of Federalist leaders, find McHenry's personal weaknesses and administrative incompetence overrated and overemphasized.

13. Jefferson to Madison, Mar. 15, 1798, WTJ, VIII, 384–385; Harper to Hamilton, Apr. 27, 1798, PAH, XXI, 449; William North to John Jay, June 6, 1798, Henry P. Johnston, ed., *The Correspondence and Public Papers of John Jay* (New York, 1890–1893), IV, 242. See also Jacob Read to Ralph Izard, June 5, 1798, Ralph Izard Papers, South Caroliniana Library, Univ. of South Carolina, Columbia, S.C.

14. Hamilton to Washington, July 29, 1798, to McHenry, July 30, 1798, WAH, X, 302, VI, 483–485; Hamilton to Wolcott, Aug. 6, 1798, to Sedgwick, Aug. 29, 1798, Hamilton Papers, LC.

15. Washington to Hamilton, Aug. 9, 1798, to McHenry, Aug. 10, Sept. 14, Oct. 1, 1798, *WGW*, XXXVI, 394–395, 402–404, 441–442, 477–479; Hamilton to McHenry, Oct. 9, 1798, McHenry Papers, LC; Hamilton to Washington, Oct. 29, 1798, *WAH*, VI, 486; Wolcott to Hamilton, Aug. 7, 1798, Hamilton Papers, LC; Wolcott to Hamilton, Oct. 10, 1798, *MAWA*, II, 101; Tracy to McHenry, Oct. 8, 1798, Steiner, *James McHenry*, 351; Sedgwick to Marshall, Oct. 23, 1798, John Marshall Papers, LC; McHenry to Adams, Oct. 15, Nov. 25, 1798, Adams Papers, MHS.

16. McHenry to Washington, Oct. 16, 1798, Washington Papers, LC; McHenry to Charles Cotesworth Pinckney, Oct. 30, 1798, Adams Papers, MHS.

17. Tracy to Jeremiah Wadsworth, Jan. 2, 1799, Joseph Trumbull Collection, Conn. State Lib.; Sedgwick to Hamilton, Feb. 7, 1799, Wolcott to Hamilton, Apr. 1, 1799, Hamilton Papers, LC; Washington to McHenry, Mar. 25, 1798, *WGW*, XXXVII, 163–164; Troup to King, Apr. 19, 1799, Sedgwick to King, July 26, 1799, *LCRK*, II, 596, 69–71; Mattsson-Boze, James McHenry, 278.

18. To McHenry, July 27, 1799, *WJA*, IX, 4–5. For Adams's position, see Stephen Higginson to Wolcott, Mar. 26, 1799, Sedgwick to Wolcott, May 8, 1799, *MAWA*, II, 230, 239; McHenry to Washington, Apr. 10, 1799, Washington Papers, LC.

19. To McHenry, July 7, 1799, *WJA*, VIII, 662.

20. Oct. 10, 1798, *MAWA*, II, 101.

21. Sept. 30, 1798, *WGW*, XXXVI, 474.

22. To McHenry, Feb. 6, 1799, *WAH*, VII, 63–64.

23. John C. Miller, *Alexander Hamilton: Portrait in Paradox* (New York, 1959), 479–480; Gaillard Hunt, "Office-Seeking during the Administration of John Adams," *American Historical Review*, II (1897), 243–244; Adams to McHenry, July 6, 1798, "Boston Patriot Letter XVII," 1809, *WJA*, VIII, 574, IX, 301. For other information on the meetings and appointment of officers, see Washington to McHenry, Oct. 21, 1798, Jan. 28, 1799, *WGW*, XXXVI, 504–505, XXXVII, 113–114; McHenry to Washington, Nov. 10, 14 (with enclosures), 1798, Washington Papers, LC; McHenry to William L. Smith, Nov. 30, 1798, William Loughton Smith Papers, LC.

24. Tracy to Jonathan Trumbull, Jr., Dec. 13, 1798, Jonathan Trumbull, Jr. Papers, CHS; McHenry to Pickering, Dec. 18, 1798, Miscellaneous Letters of the Department of State, General Records of the Department of State, *RG* 59, NA; McHenry to Washington, Dec. 28, 1798, Jan. 10, Mar. 31, 1799, Washington Papers, LC; McHenry to Hamilton, Jan. 21, Mar. 21, 1799, Hamilton Papers, LC; Washington to Davie, Dec. 28, 1798, to McHenry, Jan. 28, Mar. 25, 1799, *WGW*, XXXVII, 73, 160–161; Pinckney to McHenry (extracts), Jan. 17, Feb. 10, 1799, McHenry Papers, WLCL; McHenry to Adams, Mar. 16, 1799, Adams Papers, MHS.

25. McHenry to Washington, Nov. 10, 14, 1798, Wolcott to McHenry, Nov. 16, 1798, Benjamin Stoddert to Wolcott, Nov. 22, 1798, Washington Papers, LC; queries to Hamilton and Pinckney, Nov. 10, 1798, Washington to Hamilton and Pinckney, Nov. 12, 1798, Washington to McHenry (drafted by Hamilton and Lear), Dec. 13, 1798, *WGW*, XXXVII, 14–17, 21–22, 32–45; Hamilton, answers to queries, n.d. [Nov. 1798], memorandum of

western army ammunition and clothing, Nov. 2, 1798, [Hamilton] to [McHenry], Nov. 1798, Hamilton Papers, LC. Originally Hamilton tried to distinguish reform and the raising of the army (see Hamilton to McHenry, Oct. 9, 1798, McHenry Papers, LC), but by December the two goals had become inseparable.

26. Washington to McHenry [drafted by Hamilton], Dec. 13, 1798, *WAH*, VII, 31.
27. See the sources cited in notes 24 and 25 above and Abigail Adams to John Adams, Jan. 12, 1799, Adams Papers, MHS.
28. Dec. 19, 1798, John C. Hamilton, *History of the Republic . . . as traced in the Writings of Alexander Hamilton . . .* (New York, 1850–1851), V, 183.
29. For congressional action, see the reorganization act, Jan.–Feb. 1799, Original Senate Bills, 5C 3S, Records of the United States Senate, *RG* 46, NA; McHenry to Adams, Dec. 24, 1798, enclosed in Adams to Congress, Dec. 31, 1798, *ASP, MA*, I, 124–129; various military laws, *AC*, 5C 3S, 3614–3629, 3929–3931, 3963–3970; Hamilton to Otis, Dec. 27, 1798, to McHenry, Jan. 21, 1799, *WAH*, X, 325–326, VII, 58–59; Gunn to Hamilton, Dec. 19, 1798, Jan. 23, 1799, Hamilton to Gunn, Dec. 22, 1798, McHenry to Hamilton, Jan. 10, 11, 22, 1799, Hamilton to McHenry, Jan. 15, 16, Feb. 21, 1799, Hamilton, "An Act to Regulate the Medical Establishment," Feb. 25, 1799, Hamilton, ed., *Writings of Hamilton*, V, 182–183, 184–185, 188–189, 190–191, 194–195, 218–221; Otis to Hamilton, Dec. 21, 1798, Samuel Eliot Morison, *The Life and Letters of Harrison Gray Otis, Federalist, 1765–1848* (Boston and New York, 1913), I, 159; Hamilton to Sedgwick, Feb. 2, 1799, Theodore Sedgwick Papers, MHS.
30. Washington to McHenry, Dec. 13, 1798, *WGW*, XXXVII, 46.
31. Washington to McHenry, Dec. 16, 1798, *ibid.*, 60–62; McHenry to Hamilton, Dec. 18, 1798, Hamilton Papers, LC; McHenry to Washington, Dec. 28, 1798, Washington Papers, LC; Hamilton to McHenry, Jan. 24, 1799, *WAH*, VII, 59–61; McHenry to Hamilton, Feb. 4, 1799, Hamilton, ed., *Writings of Hamilton*, V, 199–208.
32. June 7, 1799, *WAH*, VII, 90. See also Hamilton to Washington, May 3, 1799, *ibid.*, 77–78; Samuel Livermore to Hamilton, Feb. 22, 1799, Hamilton to Pinckney, Mar. 7, 1799, McHenry to Hamilton, Mar. 13, 18, 1799, Hamilton to McHenry, Mar. 10, Apr. 30, 1799, McHenry Papers, LC; McHenry to Hamilton, Mar. 18, 21, Apr. 4, 1799, McHenry to Caleb Swan, Apr. 3, 1799, Hamilton to Washington, Mar. 27, 1799, Hamilton, general orders, May 15, 1799, Washington Papers, LC; McHenry, circulars, Apr. 1, 3, 1799, Broadside Collection, Md. Hist. Soc.; Tracy to McHenry, June 10, 24, 1799, Steiner, *James McHenry*, 392–393; Hamilton to McHenry, Mar. 15, 16, 19, 1799, Hamilton, ed., *Writings of Hamilton*, V, 234–235, 236–237. An outline history of the New Army, which covers recruiting as well as other aspects, is William H. Gaines, Jr., "The Forgotten Army: Recruiting for a National Emergency (1799–1800)," *Virginia Magazine of History and Biography*, LVI (1948), 267–279.
33. McHenry to Washington, May 2, 19, 1799, Washington Papers, LC; Sedgwick to Wolcott, May 8, 1799, *MAWA*, II, 239; Sedgwick to King, July 26, 1799, *LCRK*, III, 69–70. For Adams's other tactics, see Sedgwick to Hamil-

ton, Feb. 7, 1799, McHenry to Hamilton, Feb. 8, 1799, Hamilton Papers, LC; Hamilton to Washington, Feb. 16, 1799, *WAH*, VII, 68; Adams to McHenry, May 7, July 7, 19, 1799, *WJA*, VII, 640–641, 662, 666; McHenry to Adams, July 12, 1799, Adams Papers, MHS.

34. Pinckney to McHenry, May 29, 1799, Washington Papers, LC; Pinckney to Hamilton, June 10, July 29, 1799, James Read to Hamilton, Sept. 12, 1799, William North to Hamilton, Jan. 9, 1800, Hamilton Papers, LC; Adams to McHenry, June 19, 1799, *WJA*, VIII, 659–670.

35. Hamilton to McHenry, Sept. 21, 1799, Hamilton to Washington, May 18, 1799, *WAH*, VII, 145–146, 174–179; McHenry to Hamilton, Mar. 8, Sept. 28, Nov. 16, 1799, Hamilton to Swan, Sept. 23, 1799, Thomas Parker to Hamilton, Oct. 6, 1799, Hamilton Papers, LC.

36. To McHenry, June 14, 1799, Steiner, *James McHenry*, 390.

37. To McHenry, June 17, 1799, *ibid.*, 393–394.

38. Circular to Lt. Cols., Sept. 7, 1799, Hamilton Papers, LC. For the supply troubles, see Tench Francis to McHenry, Mar. 12, 1799, McHenry to Hamilton, Apr. 11, May 3, July 10, 1799, Hamilton to McHenry, Sept. 2, 1799, Thomas Parker to Hamilton, Sept. 18, 1799, Timothy Taylor to Hamilton, Sept. 22, 1799, William Bentley to Hamilton, Sept. 25, 1799, Richard Hennewell to Hamilton, Oct. 19, 1799, Hamilton Papers, LC; Hamilton to McHenry, May 2, July 22, 1799, McHenry Papers, LC; Hamilton to Washington, May 3, 1799, Hamilton to McHenry, May 27, Aug. 19, 1799, *WAH*, VII, 77–78, 88–89, 108–109. For a description of the supply system, see McHenry to Hamilton, Sept. 20, 1799, Hamilton to Aaron Ogden, Apr. 15, 1800, Hamilton Papers, LC.

39. "Remarks on the Brigade . . . ," enclosed in North to Hamilton, Apr. 20, 1800, Hamilton Papers, LC. See also the inspection returns enclosed in *ibid.*, LXXIV, 11814. With 8,448 authorized rank and file, the New Army actually enlisted only 3,399. See McHenry to Hamilton, Mar. 7, 1800, *ibid.* For the lack of training in the Harpers Ferry regiments, see Pinckney to McHenry, Feb. 10, 1800, *ibid.*

40. William S. Smith to Hamilton, May 2, 1800, *ibid.* The operational history of one regiment, the 8th in Virginia, can be followed in the orderly books, Sept. 19, 1799 to June 7, 1800, Philip Lightfoot Papers, College of William and Mary Library, Williamsburg, Va.

41. To McHenry, Mar. 25, 1799, *WGW*, XXXVII, 159.

42. See Washington to McHenry, Dec. 13, 1798, to Thomas Parker, Oct. 27, 1799, *ibid.*, 40–41, 411; Hamilton to McHenry, July 12, 1799, Hamilton to Nathan Rice, Aug. 22, 1799, to Aaron Ogden, Aug. 22, 1799, Hamilton Papers, LC; Hamilton to William S. Smith, Oct. 4, 1799, Sol Feinstone Collection, American Philosophical Society, Philadelphia, Pa.; Hamilton to James Miller, Oct. 8, 1799, Lloyd Wadell Smith Collection, Morristown National Historical Park, Morristown, N.J.

43. To Philip Lightfoot, May 26, 1799, Lightfoot Papers, College of William and Mary Lib.; Parker to Garnett Peyton, May 26, 1799, Preston Family Papers, The Filson Club, Louisville, Ky.

44. Regimental Orders, Nov. 3, 1799, Orderly Books, Lightfoot Papers, College of William and Mary Lib.

45. To Jonathan Trumbull, Jr., Jan. 2, 1799, Trumbull, Jr. Papers, CHS. See also Tracy to Jeremiah Wadsworth, Jan. 29, 1799, Joseph Trumbull Collection, Conn. State Lib.

46. To Dayton, 1799, *WAH*, X, 329–336.

47. To Sedgwick, *ibid.*, 341–342.

48. For the Virginia and Kentucky resolutions, see Dumas Malone, *Jefferson and His Time* (Boston, 1948–date), III, 395–415; Adrienne Koch and Harry Ammon, "The Virginia and Kentucky Resolutions: An Episode in Jefferson's and Madison's Defense of Civil Liberties," *WMQ*, V (1948), 147–176.

49. To William Vans Murray, Mar. 30, 1799, Worthington Chauncey Ford, ed., *Writings of John Quincy Adams* (New York, 1913–1917), II, 398. For other Federalist reaction of a similar nature, see Roger Griswold to Matthew Griswold, Dec. 9, 1798, Wolcott-Griswold-Williams-Woodbridge-Rogers Family Papers, Univ. of Virginia Library, Charlottesville, Va.; William L. Smith to McHenry, Feb. 2, 1799, McHenry Papers, LC; Stephen G. Kurtz, *The Presidency of John Adams: The Collapse of Federalism, 1795–1800* (Philadelphia, 1957), 356–358; Frank Maloy Anderson, "Contemporary Opinion of the Virginia and Kentucky Resolutions," *American Historical Review*, V (1899–1900), 45–63, 225–252; and the documents cited in note 58 below.

50. Richard R. Beeman, *The Old Dominion and the New Nation, 1788–1801* (Lexington, Ky., 1972), 201–204, describes these measures, the rumors that resulted, and the Federalist reaction. Beeman believes that Virginia did not intend to resist the Alien and Sedition Acts with force, but to reform its militia and defend the state. I do not find the argument convincing; Virginians must have known how such action would look, and that the timing of such legislation, so soon after the Virginia Resolutions, would be peculiar.

51. To Archibald Stuart, Feb. 13, 1799, to Edmund Pendleton, Feb. 14, 1799, *WTJ*, IX, 44, 46.

52. For the rebellion, see W. W. H. Davis, *The Fries Rebellion . . .* (Doylestown, Pa., 1899; repr. New York, 1969); Peter Levine, "The Fries Rebellion: Social Violence and the Politics of the New Nation," *Pennsylvania History*, XL (1973), 241–258.

53. To Sedgwick, Feb. 2, 1799, *WAH*, X, 342.

54. To Jeremiah Wadsworth, Jan. 29, 1799, Joseph Trumbull Collection, Conn. State Lib.

55. To King, July 9, 1798, *LCRK*, II, 362; Pickering to J. Q. Adams, July 9, 1798, Adams Papers, MHS; Pickering to David Humphreys, July 16, 1798, Timothy Pickering Papers, MHS.

56. Sedgwick to King, Dec. 12, 1799, *LCRK*, III, 155; Sedgwick to Peter Van Schaack, Jan. 15, 1800, Sedgwick Papers, MHS; Hamilton to McHenry, Mar. 14, 1799, Steiner, *James McHenry*, 377; Hamilton to Dayton, 1799, *WAH*, X, 329–336.

57. To ———, Feb. 18, 1799, Sedgwick Papers, MHS. For the congressional debate and the Eventual Army statute, see AC, 5C 3S, 3022–3044, 3934–3936.

58. To Jeremiah Wadsworth, Jan. 29, 1799, Joseph Trumbull Collection,

Conn. State Lib. See also William Barry Grove to McHenry, Aug. 20, 1798, Samuel Chase to McHenry, Jan. 19, 1799, Bernard C. Steiner, ed., "Maryland Politics in 1799, Being Letters from the Correspondence of James McHenry," *Publications of the Southern History Association*, X (1906), 100–101, 151; Daniel Dewey to Sedgwick, Feb. 6, 1799, Sedgwick Papers, MHS.

59. Hamilton to Jay, Apr. 24, 1798, to Washington, June 2, 1798, *PAH*, XXI, 447, 479–480.

60. Jefferson to Benjamin Rush, Jan. 16, 1811, quoted in Douglass Adair, "Fame and the Founding Fathers," in Edmund P. Willis, ed., *Fame and the Founding Fathers* (Bethlehem, Pa., 1967), 37.

61. June 2, 1798, *PAH*, XXI, 479.

62. See Miller, *Alexander Hamilton*, 495–500; Broadus Mitchell, *Alexander Hamilton* (New York, 1957–1962), II, 442–448. See King to Hamilton, July 31, 1798, Hamilton to Miranda, Aug. 22, 1798, Hamilton to King, Oct. 2, 1798, King Papers, NYHS.

63. To McHenry, July 29, 1799, McHenry Papers, LC. See Joseph W. Cox, *Champion of Southern Federalism: Robert Goodloe Harper of South Carolina* (Port Washington, N.Y., 1972), 118–119, 135. For eighteenth-century fame, see Adair, "Fame," in Willis, ed., *Fame and the Founding Fathers*, 29–32, 34–40, 44, 49. Even Adams, as un-military as any politician of the era, had to acknowledge (in old age) to the cadets at West Point that "Military glory is esteemed the first and greatest of glories." Aug. 1821, *WJA*, X, 419.

64. See Jefferson to Edmund Pendleton, Apr. 22, 1799, *WTJ*, IX, 65.

65. Hamilton to King, Jan. 5, 1800, *WAH*, X, 358–359.

66. Adams was convinced that Hamilton aspired to the Presidency or to ultimate power. See Adams to Thomas Adams, Jan. 14, 1801, Adams Papers, MHS; Adams to Benjamin Rush, Dec. 4, 1805, Jan. 25, 1806, John A. Schutz and Douglass Adair, eds., *The Spur of Fame: Dialogues of John Adams and Benjamin Rush, 1805–1813* (San Marino, Cal., 1966), 45, 48.

67. To Pickering, Aug. 6, 1799, *WJA*, IX, 11.

68. James Wilkinson, *Memoirs of My Own Times* (Philadelphia, 1816), I, 437–468; Wilkinson to Hamilton, Sept. 6, Oct. 31, Nov. 21, 1799, to McHenry, Sept. 16, 17, Oct. 12, Nov. 23, 30, Dec., Dec. 19, 1799, Hamilton to Washington, Sept. 9, 1799, Hamilton, circular to officers, Aug. 27, 1799, Hamilton Papers, LC. See also his manuals and papers on tactics and other military affairs in vols. LXXX–LXXXII and Hamilton to Pinckney, Dec. 2, 1799, Pinckney to Hamilton, Dec. 12, 1799, Lewis Tousard to Hamilton, Feb. 25, 1800, *ibid*.

69. For Hamilton's mood, see Henry Lee to Hamilton, Mar. 5, 1800, Hamilton to King, Jan. 5, 1800, to George Izard, Feb. 27, 1800, to Sedgwick, Feb. 27. 1800, to Henry Lee, Mar. 7, 1800, *ibid*. For the question of Hamilton's promotion, see in addition, Troup to King, Jan. 1, 1800, King Papers, NYHS; Alexander Hamilton, *Letter from Alexander Hamilton, Concerning . . . John Adams . . .* (New York, 1800), 3, 45–46; [James Cheetham], *Answer to Alexander Hamilton's Letter . . .* (New York, 1800), 14–15.

Chapter 13

HEADNOTE

a. To James Lloyd, Feb. 11, 1815, WJA, X, 118-119.

SOURCE NOTES

1. To Washington, Feb. 21, 1799, Autograph Collection, Philip H. and A. S. W. Rosenbach Foundation, Philadelphia, Pa.
2. Higginson to Pickering, Mar. 3, 1799, J. Franklin Jameson, ed., "Letters of Stephen Higginson, 1783-1804," *Report of the Historical Manuscripts Commission of the American Historical Association, 1896* (Washington, 1897), 820.
3. To Cabot, Feb. 21, 1799, Timothy Pickering Papers, MHS.
4. Troup to King, Apr. 19, 1799, LCRK, II, 596. For the nomination and reaction, see Stephen G. Kurtz, *The Presidency of John Adams: The Collapse of Federalism, 1795-1800* (Philadelphia, 1957), ch. 15-17; Alexander DeConde, *The Quasi-War: The Politics and Diplomacy of the Undeclared War with France, 1797-1801* (New York, 1966), ch. V; Page Smith, *John Adams* (Garden City, N.Y., 1962), II, 999-1003; Peter P. Hill, *William Vans Murray, Federalist Diplomat: The Shaping of Peace with France, 1797-1801* (Syracuse, 1971), 103-143; Stephen G. Kurtz, "The French Mission of 1799-1800: Concluding Chapter in the Statecraft of John Adams," *Political Science Quarterly,* LXXX (1965), 543-557; Jacob E. Cooke, "Country Above Party: John Adams and the 1799 Mission to France," Edmund P. Willis, ed., *Fame and the Founding Fathers* (Bethlehem, Pa., 1967), 53-77. For the Senate reaction and the meeting with Adams, see in addition Robert Liston to Lord Grenville, Feb. 22, 1799, British State Papers, Ford Transcripts, NYPL; Sedgwick to Hamilton, Feb. 25, 1799, Alexander Hamilton Papers, LC; Richard E. Welch, Jr., *Theodore Sedgwick, Federalist: A Political Portrait* (Middletown, Conn., 1965), 185-190; Robert C. Alberts, *The Golden Voyage: The Life and Times of William Bingham, 1752-1804* (Boston, 1969), 350-355.
5. To James Lloyd, Feb. 6, 1815, WJA, X, 115.
6. "Boston Patriot Letters IX, XII, XIV," 1809, *ibid.,* IX, 268, 278-281, 294; Kurtz, "French Mission of Adams," *Political Science Quarterly,* LXXX, 548-549.
7. To Rush, Apr. 22, 1812, John A. Schutz and Douglass Adair, eds., *The Spur of Fame: Dialogues of John Adams and Benjamin Rush, 1805-1813* (San Marino, Cal., 1966), 214.
8. Carl Prince's forthcoming book on the federal civil service in the 1790s explores Adams's use of the patronage.
9. To Lloyd, Mar. 30, 1815, WJA, X, 149.
10. To Rush, Nov. 11, 1807, Schutz and Adair, eds., *Spur of Fame,* 99. The battle over Smith is covered in Chapter 11, above. For the importance Adams placed on the refusal to appoint Burr and Muhlenberg, see Adams

to Rush, Sept. 30, 1805, *ibid.*, 41–42; Adams to McHenry, July 6, 1798, "Boston Patriot Letter XVII," 1809, Adams to Lloyd, Feb. 11, 14, 17, 1815, *WJA*, VIII, 574, IX, 301, X, 119–124.

11. Sedgwick to Hamilton, Feb. 7, 1799, Hamilton Papers, LC.

12. To Attorney General Charles Lee, Mar. 29, 1799, *WJA*, VIII, 629.

13. Adams to William Cunningham, Mar. 20, 1809, E. M. Cunningham, *Correspondence between the Hon. John Adams . . . and the late Wm. Cunningham . . .* (Boston, 1823), 107–108. Adams raised the question of a new mission in a letter to Pickering, Oct. 20, 1798, *WJA*, VII, 609.

14. For optimistic predictions, see James Rutledge, Jr. to John Grimke, John Grimke Papers, South Carolina Historical Society, Charleston, S.C.; Peter Brown to James Iredell, Aug. 11, 1798, Charles E. Johnson Collection, North Carolina Department of Archives and History, Raleigh, N.C.; Cabot to King, Aug. 18, 1798, Hamilton to King, Aug. 22, 1798, *LCRK*, II, 397. 658–659. Pickering's role can be seen in Pickering to Rufus Putnam, Aug. 2, 1798, Rufus Putnam Papers, Marietta College Library, Marietta, Ohio; Pickering to James Ross, Aug. 6, 1798, to Jay, Aug. 6, 1798, to Abraham Hunt, Aug. 9, 1798, to Isaac Tichenor, Aug. 9, 1798, to Joseph Habersham, Dec. 10, 1798, Pickering Papers, MHS; Pickering, "Copies of Ross's edition . . . distributed . . . ," Jan. 1, 1799, Miscellaneous Letters of the Department of State, General Records of the Department of State, *RG* 59, NA; John William Kuehl, The Quest for Identity in an Age of Insecurity: The XYZ Affair and American Nationalism (unpub. Ph.D. thesis, Univ. of Wisconsin, 1968), 104–112.

15. For Federalist explanations, see McHenry to William L. Smith, Oct. 20, 1798, Wolcott to Smith, Nov. 29, 1798, William Loughton Smith Papers, LC; Noah Webster to King, Nov. 1, 1798, *LCRK*, II, 455; Pickering to King, Dec. 14, 1798, Pickering Papers, MHS; Washington to Patrick Henry, Jan. 15, 1799, *WGW*, XXXVII, 88. Election results are covered in Manning J. Dauer, *The Adams Federalists* (Baltimore, 1953), 233–237; Lisle A. Rose, *Prologue to Democracy: The Federalists in the South, 1789–1800* (Lexington, Ky., 1968), 169–187, 193–204; Carl E. Prince, *New Jersey's Jeffersonian Republicans: The Genesis of an Early Party Machine, 1789–1817* (Chapel Hill, 1967), 31–32; Harry Marlin Tinkcom, *The Republicans and Federalists in Pennsylvania, 1790–1801: A Study in National Stimulus and Local Response* (Harrisburg, 1950), 184–189; Delbert Harold Gilpatrick, *Jeffersonian Democracy in North Carolina, 1789–1816* (New York, 1931), ch. III; John W. Kuehl, "Southern Reaction to the XYZ Affair," *Register Kentucky Historical Society*, LXX (1972), 21–49, and "The XYZ Affair and American Nationalism: Republican Victories in the Middle Atlantic States," *Maryland Historical Magazine*, LXVII (1972), 1–20; L. Marx Renzulli, Jr., *Maryland: The Federalist Years* (Rutherford, N.J., 1972), 203–208.

16. To James Monroe, Jan. 23, 1799, *WTJ*, IX, 11. See also Gallatin to his wife, Jan. 18, 1799, Henry Adams, *The Life of Albert Gallatin* (Philadelphia, 1879), I, 226.

17. Jefferson to Archibald Stuart, Feb. 13, 1799, *WTJ*, IX, 44; Kurtz, *Presidency of John Adams*, 366. Examples of the petitions can be seen in entries for Jan.–Feb. 1799, House Petition Book, 5C 3S, Records of the United States House of Representatives, *RG* 233, NA; Address of Essex County,

N.J., Jan. 7, 1799, Senate Petitions, 5C 3S, Records of the United States Senate, *RG* 46, NA.

18. Sedgwick to Hamilton, Feb. 7, 1799, Hamilton Papers, LC. See also Adams to McHenry, July 27, 1799, *WJA*, IX, 4–5.

19. To Lloyd, Jan. 1815, *WJA*, X, 113. See also Adams to Mercy Warren, Aug. 19, 1807, Charles Francis Adams, ed., "Correspondence between John Adams and Mercy Warren . . . ," Massachusetts Historical Society, *Collections*, 5th ser., IV (Boston, 1878), 470–471.

20. Feb. 22, 1799, Adams Family Papers, MHS.

21. Mar. 3, 1799, *ibid.* Additional evidence about Adams's motivation is in John Quincy Adams, *Parties in the United States*, ed. Charles Truc Adams (New York, 1941), 30.

22. *Aurora* (Phila.), July 3, 1799.

23. *Ibid.*, Aug. 5, 1799.

24. *Ibid.*, Sept. 24, 1799.

25. Kurtz, *Presidency of John Adams*, 364.

26. To Matthew Griswold, Dec. 20, 1799, Wolcott-Griswold-Williams-Woodbridge-Rogers Family Papers, Univ. of Virginia Library, Charlottesville, Va. For the mood and events in the capital, see Sedgwick to King, Dec. 12, 29, 1799, Hamilton to King, Jan. 5, 1800, *LCRK*, III, 154–155, 162–163, 173–174; Wolcott to Ames, Dec. 29, 1799, *MAWA*, II, 314–317; Sedgwick to ———, Dec. 21, 29, Theodore Sedgwick Papers, MHS; Troup to King, Jan. 1, 1800, Rufus King Papers, NYHS; Otis to his wife, Jan 11, 1800, Samuel Eliot Morison, *The Life and Letters of Harrison Gray Otis, Federalist, 1765–1848* (Boston and New York, 1913), I, 179; Patrick J. Furlong, "John Rutledge, Jr. and the Election of a Speaker of the House in 1799," *WMQ*, XXIV (1967), 432–436.

27. AC, 6C 1S, 227–228; Liston to Grenville, Feb. 2, 1800, British State Papers, Ford Transcripts, NYPL.

28. AC, 6C 1S, 307.

29. *Ibid.*, 352. The debate can be followed in *ibid.*, 247–369.

30. To his wife, Morison, *Harrison Gray Otis*, I, 179.

31. Randolph to Adams, Jan. 11, 1800, Abigail Adams to J. Q. Adams, Feb. 8, 1800, Adams Papers, MHS.

32. AC, 6C 1S, 296–300, 370, 372–374, 377–388, 426–507; Jefferson to Mary Eppes, Jan. 17, 1800, *WTJ*, IX, 93; Jefferson to Martha Randolph, Jan. 21, 1800, Jefferson Papers, Coolidge Collection, MHS; *ASP, Miscellaneous*, I, 195–202.

33. To Grenville, Feb. 2, 1800, British State Papers, Ford Transcripts, NYPL.

34. To Ames, Dec. 29, 1799, *MAWA*, II, 317.

35. Sedgwick to King, Dec. 29, 1799, *LCRK*, III, 162. For the Hamiltonian position, see Sedgwick to King, Dec. 12, 1799, Jan. 5, 1800, *ibid.*, 154–155, 173–174; Ames to Pickering, Oct. 19, Nov. 5, 1799, Seth Ames, ed., *The Works of Fisher Ames* . . . (Boston, 1854), I, 258, 260; Chauncey Goodrich to Wolcott, Nov. 18, 1799, Oliver Wolcott, Jr. Papers, CHS; Cabot to Wolcott, Dec. 16, 1799, Jan. 16, 1800, Ames to Wolcott, Jan. 12, 1800, *MAWA*, II, 312, 320–322.

36. To Ames, Dec. 29, 1799, *MAWA*, II, 317.

37. To Edmund Pendleton, Apr. 22, 1799, *WTJ*, IX, 65.

38. St. George Tucker to James Monroe, Dec. 29, 1799, James Monroe Papers, LC.
39. "An Act to prevent the Interference . . . ," Mar. 14, 1800, Engrossed House Bills, 6C 1S, House Records, RG 233, NA. See also AC, 6C 1S, 108, 151, 522–523, 527, 625, 626, 656.
40. To Ames, Dec. 29, 1799, MAWA, II, 314.
41. AC, 6C 1S, 369; Caleb Swan to James Findlay, Jan. 11, 1800, Torrence Collection, Cincinnati Historical Society, Cincinnati, Ohio. Three Federalists (two from the South) and three Republicans voted against their party. For Federalist strategy, see McHenry to his nephew, Oct. 22, 1799, James McHenry Papers, Maryland Historical Society, Baltimore, Md.; Wolcott to Ames, Dec. 29, 1799, MAWA, II, 314–317; Sedgwick to King, Dec. 12, 29, 1799, LCRK, III, 154–155, 162–163. Marshall outlined his position in AC, 6C 1S, 251–255; Marshall to Charles Dabney, Jan. 20, 1800, Charles W. Dabney Papers, Southern Historical Collection, Univ. of North Carolina Library, Chapel Hill, N.C.
42. To Wolcott, Jan. 16, 1800, MAWA, II, 322.
43. To C. C. Pinckney, Jan. 28, 1800, James McHenry Papers, WLCL. For the report and passage of the bill, see Otis to McHenry (typescript), Jan. 1, 1800, Research Note File, Independence National Historical Park, Philadelphia, Pa.; McHenry to Hamilton, Jan. 6, 16, Feb. 18, 1800, Hamilton Papers, LC; McHenry to John Rutledge, Jr., Jan. 7, 1800, John Rutledge, Jr. Papers, Southern Hist. Collection, Univ. of N.C. Lib.; Otis committee report with enclosure, Jan. 13, 1800, ASP, MA, I, 132; AC, 6C 1S, 374–375, 376, 389–404, 425, 1438. For the moderates' position, see David Stone to [John Haywood?], Jan. 10, 1800, Ernest Haywood Collection; Marshall to Dabney, Jan 20, 1800, Dabney Papers; Rutledge to Robert Smith, Jan. 28, 1800, Rutledge, Jr. Papers; Robert Williams to ———, Feb. 10, 1800, Cameron Family Papers, all in the Southern Hist. Collection, Univ. of N.C. Lib.
44. Feb. 27, 1800, WAH, X, 362.
45. For events in the election prior to April 1800, see Noble E. Cunningham, Jr., *The Jeffersonian Republicans: The Formation of Party Organization, 1789–1801* (Chapel Hill, 1957), 144–154, 166–182; Donald H. Stewart, *The Opposition Press of the Federalist Period* (Albany, 1969), 622–623; Dauer, *Adams Federalists*, 246–249; Kurtz, *Presidency of John Adams*, 387–388, 392–393. For Jefferson's early platform, see Jefferson to Elbridge Gerry, Jan. 26, 1799, WTJ, IX, especially 17–18.
46. Jan. 31, 1800, Massachusetts Historical Society, *Proceedings*, XLIII (1909–1910), 653.
47. To William L. Smith, May 7, 1800, Pickering Papers, MHS. See also Troup to King, Mar. 9, 1800, LCRK, III, 208–209; Peter Jay to John Jay, May 3, 1800, John Jay Papers, Columbia Univ. Library, New York, N.Y.; Cunningham, *Jeffersonian Republicans*, 176–185; Charles A. Beard, *Economic Origins of Jeffersonian Democracy* (New York, 1915), 382–387; John C. Miller, *Alexander Hamilton: Portrait in Paradox* (New York, 1959), 511–514; Sidney I. Pomerantz, *New York: An American City, 1783–1803; A Study of Urban Life* (2d ed., Port Washington, N.Y., 1965), 125–130; William Bruce Wheeler, Urban Politics in Nature's Republic: The Develop-

ment of Political Parties in the Seacoast Cities in the Federalist Era (unpub. Ph.D. thesis, Univ. of Virginia, 1967), 300–321.

48. To Sedgwick, May 10, 1800, *WAH*, X, 375. For the caucus, see Kurtz, *Presidency of John Adams*, 392, 394; Dauer, *Adams Federalists*, 249–250; Miller, *Alexander Hamilton*, 514–516; Marvin R. Zahniser, *Charles Cotesworth Pinckney: Founding Father* (Chapel Hill, 1967), 214–216.

49. Mar. 11, 19, 1800, Adams Papers, MHS. Adams learned of the caucus immediately. See Adams to Joseph Lyman, Apr. 20, 1809, to Lloyd, Feb. 17, 1815, *WJA*, IX, 620, X, 125. The Republicans also knew about the plan to elect Pinckney. See Gallatin to Tench Coxe, May 14, 1800, Tench Coxe Papers, HSP.

50. McHenry sent Adams a verbatim account of the conversation on May 31, 1800 (Adams Papers, MHS). M. Howard Mattsson-Boze, James McHenry, Secretary of War, 1796–1800 (unpub. Ph.D. thesis, Univ. of Minnesota, 1965), 259–260, accepts McHenry's account as accurate. See also McHenry to John McHenry, May 21, 1800, Wolcott to McHenry, Aug. 26, 1800, *MAWA*, II, 347–348, 410–412; McHenry to John Carroll, May 16, 1800, to James Winchester, June 3, 1800, McHenry Papers, WLCL. Adams's biographer claims that the old man, surrounded by intrigue and enemies, simply lost his temper in an otherwise routine interview (Smith, *John Adams*, II, 1027–1028). But Adams's summons, its timing in relation to other events, and the President's questions and charges suggest without doubt that Adams meant to force McHenry out of the cabinet then and there. Adams's rage may not have been calculated, but it did serve as a useful guise under which to force the resignation of a kind and friendly man for whom Adams had no hatred. McHenry was known as the weakest personality in the cabinet, the symbol not only of Hamilton's penetration of the administration, but of the New Army as well. McHenry had to go quickly, but since Adams had no pretext, he had to goad the Secretary into resignation. Undoubtedly Adams did not foresee how difficult and unpleasant the interview would be. As a result, he did not use the same tactic on Pickering, a stronger and more dangerous adversary. See also Noble E. Cunningham, Jr., "Election of 1800," Arthur M. Schlesinger, Jr. *et al.*, eds., *History of American Presidential Elections, 1789–1968* (New York, 1971), I, 112–113.

51. Sedgwick to Hamilton, May 13, 1800, John C. Hamilton, ed., *History of the Republic . . . as Traced in the Writings of Alexander Hamilton . . .* (New York, 1850–1851), VI, 442; Joseph Hopkinson to Henry Glen, May 26, 1800, American Papers, Bancroft Collection, NYPL.

52. William Duane to ———, Apr. 17, 1800, Worthington C. Ford, ed., "Letters of William Duane," Massachusetts Historical Society, *Proceedings*, 2d ser., XX (1907), 260; Pickering to Benjamin Goodhue, May 26, 1800, Goodhue Family Papers, New York Society Library, New York, N.Y.; Liston to Grenville, May 29, 1800, British State Papers, Ford Transcripts, NYPL; McHenry to James Winchester, June 3, 1800, McHenry Papers, WLCL.

53. To his son, May 27, 1800, Timothy Pickering Papers, EI. See also Pickering to C. C. Pinckney, May 25, 1800, Henry Adams, ed., *Documents Relating to New-England Federalism, 1800–1815* (Boston, 1877), 332–337.

54. McHenry to his nephew, May 20, 1800, *MAWA*, II, 347–348; McHenry to

John Carroll, May 16, 1800, to James Winchester, June 3, 1800, McHenry Papers, WLCL; Benjamin Goodhue to Pickering, May 19, 1800, Pickering to David Humphreys, May 28, 1800, to Herman Stump, May 30, 1800, Pickering Papers, MHS; Pickering to William L. Smith, May 28, 1800, Smith Papers, LC; Pickering to King, May 28, 1800, Goodhue to Pickering, June 2, 1800, *LCRK*, III, 248–249, 263–265; Pickering to his son, May 27, 1800, Pickering Papers, EI; Pickering to Goodhue, May 26, 1800, Goodhue Family Papers, N.Y. Society Lib.; Pickering to C. C. Pinckney, May 25, 1800, Adams, ed., *Documents*, 332–337.

55. James Gunn to John Rutledge, Jr., May 12, 1800, Rutledge, Jr. Papers, Southern Hist. Collection, Univ. of N.C. Lib.; Sedgwick to Hamilton, May 13, 1800, Hamilton, ed., *Writings of Hamilton*, VI, 442; Cabot to King, May 29, 1800, *LCRK*, III, 249; James A. Bayard to Hamilton, June 8, 1800, Hamilton Papers, LC. No such deal of course existed. See Adams to Stoddert, Oct. 15, 1811, Stoddert to Adams, Oct. 27, 1811, *WJA*, X, 3–7.

56. To James Winchester, June 3, 1800, McHenry Papers, WLCL.

57. Adams to the cabinet, May 20, 1800, cabinet to Adams, May 20, 1800, Adams, "Proclamation Granting Pardon . . . ," May 21, 1800, Adams to Charles Lee, May 21, 1800, *WJA*, IX, 57–61, 178–179. Adams's son indicated at the time that the firings were aimed at Hamilton. "He [Hamilton] felt the blow, which was perhaps not accidentally aimed." Thomas Boylston Adams to Joseph Pitcairn, July 30, 1800, "Letters of Thomas Boylston Adams," *Quarterly Publication of the Historical and Philosophical Society of Ohio*, XII (1917), 38. See also J. Q. Adams, *Parties in United States*, 31.

58. Kurtz, *Presidency of John Adams*, 393–408. Republicans interpreted the cabinet explosion as part of a bid for re-election. See Nathaniel Ames diary, May 16, 1800, Charles Warner, ed., *Jacobin and Junto or Early American Politics as viewed in the Diary of Dr. Nathaniel Ames, 1758–1822* (Cambridge, 1931), 150.

59. Interview memorandum, May 5, 1800, in McHenry to Adams, May 31, 1800, Adams Papers, MHS.

60. Adams's view of the Hamiltonians is covered above. But also see Thomas B. Adams to Joseph Pitcairn, July 30, 1800, Joseph Pitcairn Letters, Cincinnati Hist. Soc.

61. See *American Daily Advertiser* (Phila.), Mar. 11, 12, Apr. 4, 18, May 7, 1800.

62. David Stone to [John Haywood?], May 13, 1800, William H. Hill to John Haywood, May 15, 1800, Haywood Collection, Southern Hist. Collection, Univ. of N.C. Lib.; *AC*, 6C 1S, 691, 692, 704, 713–715, 1530–1531; Liston to Grenville, May 28, 1800, British State Papers, Ford Transcripts, NYPL; Adams to McHenry, May 15, 1800, *WJA*, IX, 56.

63. May 15, 1800, Elizabeth Donnan, ed., "Papers of James A. Bayard, 1796–1815," *Annual Report of the American Historical Association, 1913* (Washington, 1915), II, 103–104.

64. To Monroe, May 15, 1800, James Monroe Papers, NYPL.

65. Hamilton to McHenry, July 2, 1800, *WAH*, VII, 224–225. For Hamilton's mood and activities, see Hamilton to McHenry, May 19, 1800, to Caleb Swan, May 26, 1800, *ibid.*, 217–218, 218–220; McHenry to Hamilton, May 16, 1800, to W. S. Smith, Nathan Rice, and C. C. Pinckney, May 17, 1800, to McHenry, May 29, 1800, Hamilton Papers, LC; Abigail Adams to T. B.

Adams, July 12, 1800, T. B. Adams to Abigail Adams, July 19, 1800, Adams Papers, MHS.

66. June 14, 1800, Adams Papers, MHS.

67. *Aurora* (Phila.), July 23, 1800, quoted in Stewart, *Opposition Press*, 586.

68. W. Barton to Tench Coxe, Feb. 13, 1799, Coxe Papers, HSP. For the use of the issue, see John Beckley to Coxe, Jan 24, 1800, *ibid.*; Stewart, *Opposition Press*, 441–444, 490, 500, 518, 523, 550–551, 565, 586–587, 594; Cunningham, *Jeffersonian Republicans*, 211–217, 221; Cunningham, "Election of 1800," Schlesinger *et al.*, eds., *Presidential Elections*, I, 118–126; James T. Callender, *The Prospect Before Us* (Richmond, 1800–1801), II, 122; Coxe to Jefferson, Jan. 10, 1801, Letters of Application and Recommendation During the Administration of Thomas Jefferson, General Records of the Department of State, *RG* 59, NA; Beckley to Ephraim Kirby, Aug. 6, 1800, Ephraim Kirby Papers, Duke Univ. Library, Durham, N.C.

69. To Wolcott, June 27, 1800, *MAWA*, II, 375. See also Hamilton to Wolcott, July 1, 1800, Goodhue to Wolcott, July 10, 1800, *ibid.*, 376, 379; Harper to Hamilton, June 5, 1800, Hamilton to Jonathan Wilmer, July 1, 1800, Rutledge, Jr. to Hamilton, July 17, 1800, Hamilton Papers, LC; Hamilton to Bayard, Aug. 6, 1800, *WAH*, X, 383–387. A good example of Hamilton's efforts with these leaders, and the response, is Arthur Fenner to ————, Dec. 14, 1800, George Champlin Mason, *Reminiscences of Newport* (Newport, 1884), 112–115.

70. Hamilton to Pickering, May 14, 1800, *WAH*, X, 377.

71. To McHenry, Aug. 27, 1800, James McHenry Papers, LC.

72. To Wolcott, July 22, 1800, *MAWA*, II, 385. A copy of part of the letter is in the Hamilton Papers, LC.

73. Ames to King, Aug. 19–26, 1800, *LCRK*, III, 297.

74. Ames to Wolcott, Aug. 3, 1800, *MAWA*, II, 396.

75. To Ames, Aug. 10, 1800, *ibid.*, 401–405. For other New England information, see Hamilton to Wolcott, July 1, Aug. 3, 1800, to Charles Carroll, July 1, 1800, to Bayard, Aug. 6, 1800, *WAH*, X, 377–380, 383–387.

76. To Wolcott, Aug. 3, 1800, *WAH*, X, 383–384. See also Hamilton to Adams, Aug. 1, 1800, to McHenry, Aug. 27, 1800, *ibid.*, 382, 388–389.

77. Cabot to Hamilton, Aug. 21, 1800, Hamilton Papers, LC.

78. To Hamilton, Aug. 26, 1800, Ames, ed., *Fisher Ames*, I, 282. See also Cabot to Wolcott, Aug. 23, 1800, Wolcott to Hamilton, Sept. 3, Oct. 2, 1800, *MAWA*, II, 406, 416–417, 431.

79. To Wolcott, Sept. 26, 1800, *WAH*, X, 389.

80. "The Public Conduct and Character of John Adams . . . ," 1800, *ibid.*, VII, 348.

81. Sept. 26, 1800, *ibid.*, X, 390.

82. To King, Nov. 9, 1800, *LCRK*, III, 331. Slightly different interpretations of Hamilton's action and motives are in Miller, *Alexander Hamilton*, 519–524; Broadus Mitchell, *Alexander Hamilton* (New York, 1957–1962), II, 474–484,

83. Mitchell, *Alexander Hamilton*, II, 484–487; Noah Webster, *A Letter to General Hamilton . . .* (Philadelphia, 1800); [James Cheetham], *Answer to Alexander Hamilton's Letter . . .* (New York, 1800), especially 5–6, 14–16; Troup to King, Nov. 9, Dec. 14, 1800, *LCRK*, III, 331, 340.

84. To T. B. Adams, July 12, 1800, Adams Papers, MHS. See also John Adams

to T. B. Adams, July 14, 1800, Abigail Adams to J. Q. Adams, Sept. 1, 1800, *ibid.*

85. To Jay, Nov. 24, 1800, *WJA*, IX, 90–91. For Adams's views and his campaign, see Adams to Abigail Adams, Nov. 15, 1800, to T. B. Adams, Jan. 14, 1801, [Adams?] to [T. B. Adams?], Jan. 16, 1801, Adams to J. Q. Adams, Jan. 29, 1801, Adams Papers, MHS; Kurtz, *Presidency of John Adams*, 397–403. For a differing interpretation, see Smith, *John Adams*, II, 1036–1052.

86. Anonymous to Adams, Mar. 11, 1800, Adams Papers, MHS. The best general analyses of the election are Kurtz, *Presidency of John Adams*, 402–408; Cunningham, "Election of 1800," Schlesinger *et al.*, eds., *Presidential Elections*, I, 101–134. For the election in New York, see note 47 above. Adams could have won if he had carried South Carolina, but the party split was not the deciding factor in his defeat there. South Carolina Federalists, including Charles Cotesworth Pinckney, worked hard for the ticket and to the end stuck by the national caucus's public decision to support Adams and Pinckney equally. See Zahniser, *Charles Cotesworth Pinckney*, 213–233. Adams may have been hurt at the polls in the state by the controversy over a letter he had written impugning Thomas Pinckney. See Rose, *Federalists in the South*, 267–282.

87. To J. Q. Adams, Jan. 29, 1801, Adams Papers, MHS.

88. To Lloyd, Feb. 6, 1815, *WJA*, X, 116. See also Adams to Harrison Gray Otis, May 9, 1823, Adams Papers, MHS; Lynn Hudson Parsons, "Continuing Crusade: Four Generations of the Adams Family View Alexander Hamilton," *New England Quarterly*, XXXVII (1964), 43–49, 56–58.

89. To Washington, Aug. 5, 1794, George Washington Papers, LC. Thomas Jefferson made the same point, ironically on the excise tax in 1791: "There are certainly persons in all the departments who are for driving too fast. Government being founded on opinion, the opinion of the public, even when it is wrong, ought to be respected to a certain degree. The prudence of the President [Washington] is an anchor of safety to us." To Nicholas Lewis, Feb. 9, 1791, *PTJ*, XIX, 263.

90. To William Vans Murray, Jan. 27, 1801, Worthington Chauncey Ford, ed., *Writings of John Quincy Adams* (New York: 1913–1917), II, 494–495.

91. Theodore Sedgwick, Jr. to Theodore Sedgwick, Jan. 16, 1800, Sedgwick Papers, MHS.

92. See the sources cited in Chapter 14, notes 14 and 55.

93. To Lloyd, Jan. 1815, *WJA*, X, 113.

Chapter 14

HEADNOTES

a. AC, 3C 1S, 736.

b. To Jefferson, Mar. 14, 1794, James Madison Papers, LC.

SOURCE NOTES

1. *AC*, 6C 1S, 305.
2. Anonymous, *A Definition of Parties* (Philadelphia, 1794), 4.
3. James T. Callender, *The Prospect Before Us* (Richmond, 1800–1801), II, 24.
4. To Jefferson, Mar. 14, 1794, Madison Papers, LC.
5. To Jefferson, Feb. 15, 1795, *ibid*.
6. Individual Jeffersonian statements would be too numerous to list here, but they are cited at appropriate places in the chapters above. Jeffersonian interpretations on nearly every subject can be found in Donald H. Stewart, *The Opposition Press of the Federalist Period* (Albany, 1969). Also see, in addition to the pamphlets cited in notes 2 and 3 above, A Citizen [William Findley], *A Review of the Revenue System . . .* (Philadelphia, 1794); James T. Callender, *Sedgwick & Co., or A Key to the Six Per Cent Cabinet* (Philadelphia, 1798); "A Calm Observer," New York *Argus*, May 12, 1795. The best historiographical study of the Federalists is George M. Curtis, III, American Historians and the Federalists (unpub. M.A. thesis, Univ. of Kansas, 1963), although Curtis deals only briefly with post World War II interpretations. Some of the more influential modern historians on the subject of Federalist militarism are Merrill Jensen, *The New Nation: A History of the United States During the Confederation, 1781–1788* (New York, 1950), 67–79; Stephen G. Kurtz, *The Presidency of John Adams: The Collapse of Federalism, 1795–1800* (Philadelphia, 1957), ch. 14; Leland D. Baldwin, *Whiskey Rebels: The Story of a Frontier Uprising* (rev. ed., Pittsburgh, 1968), 110–112; Joseph Charles, *The Origins of the American Party System* (Chapel Hill, 1956), 59–64.
7. For a similar argument on this point, see Richard Buel, Jr., *Securing the Revolution: Ideology in American Politics, 1789–1815* (Ithaca and London, 1972), 127–128.
8. To George R. Minot, May 3, 1793, Seth Ames, ed., *Works of Fisher Ames . . .* (Boston, 1854), I, 118–119.
9. Journal, Feb. 17, 1795, Dwight Foster Papers, American Antiquarian Society, Worcester, Mass.
10. To Hamilton, Sept. 17, 1792, *PAH*, XII, 390–392.
11. *Parties in the United States*, ed. Charles True Adams (New York, 1941), 25.
12. See Alfred Vagts, *A History of Militarism* (rev. ed., London, 1959); Gerhard Ritter, *The Sword and the Scepter: The Problem of Militarism in Germany*, trans. Heinz Norden (Coral Gables, Fla., 1969), vol. I.
13. James Sullivan. *Observations upon the Government of the United States of America* (Boston, 1791), 10.
14. For Adams's support of a military academy, and his attempt in 1800 to get one going by executive action alone, see Adams to the Senate and House, Jan. 14, 1800, with enclosures, *ASP, MA*, I, 133–141; Adams to Samuel Dexter, May 24, 1800, Dexter to Adams, July 16, Aug. 4, 1800, Adams Family Papers, MHS; Adams to Dexter, July 25, 1800, *WJA*, IX, 65. In addition, Adams authorized a thorough inspection trip by Senator Tracy of the garrisons and forts on the frontier, and encouraged the development of the arsenals to make the United States self-sufficient in munitions. See

Adams to McHenry, May 24, 1800, Adams Papers, MHS; Adams, speech to Congress, Nov. 22, 1800, *WJA*, IX, 146; Tracy to McHenry, Nov. 28, 1800, James McHenry Papers, LC.

15. To Moss Kent, Jan. 12, 1815, Max Farrand, ed., *The Records of the Federal Convention of 1787* (rev. ed., New Haven, 1937), III, 420.

16. A *Letter on the Subject of an Established Militia, and Military Establishment* . . . (New York, 1784), 16.

17. See Knox's militia plan, Jan 18, 1790, AC, 1C 2S, 2089–2090.

18. *Ibid.*, 3C 1S, 736.

19. *Ibid.*, 5C 2S, 1640.

20. This interpretation of the social and psychological basis of Federalism is Richard Buel's (*Securing the Revolution*, 75–85).

21. My figures on the military establishment come from documents or reports submitted to Congress, Jan. 29, Mar. 10, Apr. 27, 1802, Feb. 14, 1803, *ASP, Naval Affairs*, I, 83, 84–86, 103, 110, and Feb. 13, 1805, *ASP, MA*, I, 174–184. See also Uriah Tracy to McHenry, Nov. 28, 1800, McHenry Papers, LC.

22. The concept of military potential and vulnerability is John Shy's, in "The American Military Experience: History and Learning," *Journal of Interdisciplinary History*, I (1971), 205–228. See also Frederick W. Marks III, *Independence on Trial: Foreign Affairs and the Making of the Constitution* (Baton Rouge, 1973), ch. I.

23. Appropriations and expenditures are from Harry M. Ward, *The Department of War, 1781–1795* (Pittsburgh, 1962), 103; *The Statistical History of the United States from Colonial Times to the Present* (Stamford, Conn., 1965), 719.

24. Quoted in Charles J. Stillé, *Major-General Anthony Wayne and the Pennsylvania Line in the Continental Army* (1893, repr. Port Washington, N.Y., 1968), 324–325.

25. For the passwords in the two armies, see Milo M. Quaife, ed., "A Picture of the First United States Army: The Journal of Captain Samuel Newman," *Wisconsin Magazine of History*, II (1918), 40–73; Anthony Wayne General Orders, United States Military Academy Library, West Point, N.Y. (quotations from Oct. 20, 1792, Apr. 17, 1793). Wayne's leadership can be seen in Richard Clark Knopf, Anthony Wayne and the Founding of the United States Army (unpub. Ph.D. thesis, Ohio State Univ., 1960), especially ch. 4–7.

26. Most of these administrative changes can be followed in Ward, *Department of War*, 84, 103; Jennings B. Sanders, *Evolution of the Executive Departments of the Continental Congress, 1774–1789* (Chapel Hill, 1935), 107; William H. Glasson, *Federal Military Pensions in the United States* (New York, 1918), 54–61; Clement Biddle, *The Philadelphia Directory* (Philadelphia, 1791), 161; James Hardie, comp., *The Philadelphia Directory and Register* (Philadelphia, 1793), 168; *American Daily Advertiser* (Phila.), Feb. 20, 1792; Leonard D. White, *The Federalists: A Study in Administrative History* (New York, 1948), 145–150, 343–344, 360–361, 375–382; report on War Department personnel enclosed in Knox to the Speaker of the House,

Jan. 3, 1793, Records of Reports from Executive Departments, 1C 2S to 2C 2S, Records of the United States House of Representatives, *RG* 233, NA.

27. White, *Federalists*, 145-146, 361-363. For an indication of the variety of officers and individuals used by the War Department in these years, see the schedules of moneys advanced by the Treasury for the military establishment to Jan. 1, 1797 (submitted to the House, Feb. 17, 1798), *ASP, Finance*, I, 507-551. The problems of accounting, paperwork, and internal War Department organization can be seen in Oliver Wolcott, Jr. to Samuel Hodgdon, Oct. 2, 1794, William Irvine Papers, HSP.

28. An indication of the complexity of the supply system and the flow of paper can be seen in the manuscript collections cited in chapter 9, note 66, above.

29. See above, pages 187-188; McHenry to Washington, July 16, 1796, James McHenry Papers, WLCL.

30. See McHenry to Adams, Nov. 22, 1797, Charles Lee to Pickering, Dec. 6, 1797, Pickering to Adams, Dec. 7, 1797, Wolcott to Adams, Dec. 13, 1797, John Adams memorandum, Dec. 1797, Adams Papers, MHS. Another dispute with the Accountant broke out in 1800. See McHenry to his successor, May 29, 1800, Northwest Territory Papers, Indiana Historical Society, Indianapolis, Ind.

31. White, *Federalists*, 147.

32. *Ibid.*

33. See Francis Paul Prucha, *American Indian Policy in the Formative Years: The Indian Trade and Intercourse Acts, 1790-1834* (Cambridge, 1962), 52-55, 61-63, 67, 144-145, 189-193.

34. Jonathan Williams in AC, 5C 2S, 1543.

35. For professionalism in the military then and now, see J. R. Western, "Professionalism in Armies, Navies, and Diplomacy" in Alfred Cobban, *The Eighteenth Century* (New York, 1969), 181-216; Samuel P. Huntington, *The Soldier and the State: The Theory and Politics of Civil-Military Relations* (Cambridge, 1957), ch. 1.

36. See Ralph Izard to his wife, Jan. 2, 1795, Jacob Read to McHenry, Oct. 22, 1798, Read to Ralph Izard, June 5, 1798, Ralph Izard Papers, South Caroliniana Library, Univ. of South Carolina, Columbia, S.C.; William Loughton Smith to McHenry, Aug. 4, 1798, McHenry Papers, WLCL; Allen Johnson and Dumas Malone, eds., *Dictionary of American Biography* (New York, 1928-1936), IX, 523.

37. See Armstrong's 1785-1790 notebook, Nov. 1785, Feb., Mar. 1787, Armstrong to Francis Johnston, Sept. 5, 1788, to William Alexander, Sept. 6, 1788, Indentures with soldiers, Jan. 1, Mar. 3, 1789, Francis Johnston to Armstrong, Oct. 12, 1791, Mar. 1, 1792, John Armstrong Papers, Ind. Hist. Soc.

38. See David Mayo to Hamtramck, Oct. 20, 1799, Articles of Agreement with Robert Abbott, Aug. 24, 1799, John F. Hamtramck Papers, Burton Historical Collection, Detroit Public Library, Detroit, Mich.

39. Johnson and Malone, eds., *Dictionary of American Biography*, XIV, 4. For his Quartermaster activities, see the James O'Hara Letterbook, Ind. Hist. Soc.; Denny-O'Hara Papers, Western Pennsylvania Historical Society,

Pittsburgh, Pa.; Solomon Sibley Papers, Burton Hist. Collection, Detroit Public Lib. Of course such activity was not uncommon. Secretary of War Pickering, Intendent of Military Stores Hodgdon, and Commissioner of the Revenue Coxe were in partnership speculating in lands also. See the Tench Coxe Papers for 1795, HSP.

40. John Cleves Symmes to Jonathan Dayton (transcript), Aug. 15, 1791, John Cleves Symmes Papers (Miami Purchase), Cincinnati Historical Society, Cincinnati, Ohio; garrison orderly book (copy to Armstrong), Feb. 13, 1792, Armstrong Papers, Ind. Hist. Soc.; Jefferson to Washington, Mar. 28, 1792, Miscellaneous Letters of the Department of State, General Records of the Department of State, RG, 59, NA; F. Clever Bald, *Detroit's First American Decade, 1796 to 1805* (Ann Arbor, 1948), 112–119; David Strong to Mc-Henry, Jan. 23, 1799, McHenry to Hamilton, Apr. 11, 1799, with Proclamation of Wilkinson, July 12, 1797, Alexander Hamilton Papers, LC.

41. To John Gray Blount, Nov. 7, 1797, Alice Barnwell Keith and William H. Masterson, eds., *The John Gray Blount Papers* [Publications of the North Carolina Department of Archives and History] (Raleigh, 1952–1965), III, 176.

42. Wayne to Erkuries Beatty, Jan. 10, 1793, Northwest Territory Collection, Ind. Hist. Soc.; Caleb Swan to Armstrong, Feb. 6, 1793, Armstrong to Knox, Mar. 5, 1793, Armstrong Papers, Ind. Hist. Soc.

43. Minutes of a meeting of officers, Jan. 7–8, 1795, Isaac Guion Papers, Southern Historical Collection, Univ. of North Carolina, Chapel Hill, N.C.; AC, 3C 1S, 1491; Mrs. Richard Butler to Samuel Smith, Nov. 4, 1793, Darlington Memorial Library, University of Pittsburgh, Pittsburgh, Pa.

44. To John Buell, Oct. 15, 1800, Jacob Kingsbury Papers, Burton Hist. Collection, Detroit Public Lib. See also John Pratt Papers for the 1790s, Connecticut State Library, Hartford, Conn.

45. See, for example, John Mills to William Winston, Apr. 22, 1796, The Torrence Collection, Cincinnati Hist. Soc.; William H. Harrison to Wilkinson, May 13, 1796, William H. Harrison Miscellaneous Collection, Ind. Hist. Soc.; Kingsbury to Buell, Oct. 15, 1800, Kingsbury Papers, Burton Hist. Collection, Detroit Public Lib.; William North to John Hamtramck, Feb. 23, 1801, John Francis Hamtramck Papers, Duke Univ. Library, Durham, N.C.

46. Feb. 23, 1801, Hamtramck Papers, Duke Univ. Lib. For instances of angling for rank and partisan politics among officers, see John Stagg to Henry Burbeck, May 3, 1793, Henry Burbeck Papers, NYPL; William Burrows to Jonathan Williams, Oct. 23, 1800, Jan. 7, 1801, Jonathan Williams Papers, United States Military Academy Library, West Point, N.Y.

47. See Chapter 3, above; E. James Ferguson, "The Nationalists of 1781–1783 and the Economic Interpretation of the Constitution," *Journal of American History*, LVI (1969), 241–261.

48. For the issues in the states, see Jackson Turner Main, *Political Parties before the Constitution* (Chapel Hill, 1973). H. James Henderson, "The Structure of Politics in the Continental Congress," in Stephen G. Kurtz

and James H. Hutson, eds., *Essays on the American Revolution* (Chapel Hill, 1973), 157–198, sees factionalism present all through Congress's history, but his evidence tends to reveal that the alignments were transitory and mostly regional. For interpretations of politics in this era similar to my own, see Lee Benson, *Turner and Beard: American Historical Writing Reconsidered* (Glencoe, Ill., 1960), 214–228; Richard E. Ellis, *The Jeffersonian Crisis: Courts and Politics in the Young Republic* (New York, 1971), ch. XVI–XVII; and Lance Banning, "Republican Ideology and the Triumph of the Constitution, 1789 to 1793," WMQ, XXXI (1974), 167–188.

49. To Jefferson, Feb. 15, 1795, Madison Papers, LC.

50. The change in Republican understanding of Federalist motives and the party's new public position can be seen in Madison to Jefferson, Mar. 14, June 1, 1794, Feb. 15, 1795, *ibid.*; Monroe to Jefferson, Mar. 16, 1794, Stanislaus Murray Hamilton, ed., *The Writings of James Monroe* (New York, 1898–1903), I, 286–287; *General Advertiser* (Phila.), May 22, 1794; "A Calm Observer," N.Y. *Argus*, May 12, 1795.

51. My understanding of the tactical and strategic changes in warfare at this time comes from Robert S. Quimby, *The Background of Napoleonic Warfare: The Theory of Military Tactics in Eighteenth Century France* (New York, 1957), ch. XIII; Cyril Falls, *The Art of War From the Age of Napoleon to the Present Day* (New York, 1961), ch. 1; R. R. Palmer, "Frederick the Great, Guibert, Bulow: From Dynastic to National War," in Edward Mead Earle, ed., *Makers of Modern Strategy: Military Thought from Machiavelli to Hitler* (Princeton, 1941), 49–74; Peter Paret, *Yorck and the Era of Prussian Reform, 1807–1815* (Princeton, 1966), ch. I–II.

52. To Timothy Pickering, Aug. 18, 1798, Timothy Pickering Papers, MHS. See also statements by Republicans Joseph McDowell, Nathaniel Macon, and Joseph B. Varnum, AC, 5C 2S, 1535, 1673, 1737, 1740.

53. Jan. 26, 1799, WTJ, IX, 18; First Inaugural Address, Mar. 4, 1801, James D. Richardson, ed., *A Compilation of Messages and Papers of the Presidents, 1789–1897* (Washington, 1896–1899), I, 323.

54. See Jefferson's notes on cabinet meetings, Nov. 23, 28, 1793, Franklin B. Sawvel, ed., *The Complete Anas of Thomas Jefferson* (New York, 1903), 180–181; "Memorandum of matters to be communicated to Congress," Nov. 1793, Eighth Annual Address to Congress, Dec. 7, 1796, WGW, XXXIII, 160–161, XXXV, 317.

55. To McHenry, July 18, 1800, MAWA, II, 382. For the development of the Adams administration's plans for an academy, and its actions on the subject, see Hamilton to Louis Du Portail, July 23, 1798, McHenry to Hamilton, Mar. 1, 1800, Hamilton to McHenry, May 31, 1800, Alexander Hamilton Papers, LC; Hamilton to McHenry, Nov. 23, 1799, WAH, VII, 180–186; McHenry's reports submitted to Congress, Jan. 14, Feb. 13, 1800, ASP, MA, I, 133–135, 142–144; Adams to Dexter, July 25, 1800, WJA, IX, 65; McHenry to Washington, Oct. 8, 1796, Dexter to Adams, July 16, Aug. 4, Nov. 13, 1800, Adams Papers, MHS.

56. AC, 6C 1S, 634, 690–691.

57. The standard studies of the founding of the military academy are Edward S. Holden, "Origins of the United States Military Academy, 1777–1802," *The*

Centennial of the United States Military Academy at West Point, New York 1802–1902 (Washington, 1904), I, 201–222; James Ripley Jacobs, *The Beginning of the U.S. Army, 1783–1812* (Princeton, 1947), ch. 11; Sidney Forman, *West Point: A History of the United States Military Academy* (New York, 1950), ch. 1, and "Why the United States Military Academy was Established in 1802," *Military Affairs*, XXIX (1965), 16–28; Edgar Denton, The Formative Years of the United States Military Academy, 1775–1833 (unpub. Ph.D. thesis, Syracuse Univ., 1964), ch. 1; Stephen E. Ambrose, *Duty, Honor, Country: A History of West Point* (Baltimore, 1966), ch. 1.

Essay on Sources

In range and sheer bulk, the source material for reconstructing the beginning of the military establishment is enormous. The following discussion is meant only to indicate which were my most important sources, in part how they were approached (and thus how this book was researched), and some of the possibilities which exist for future historians of the military establishment and of politics in the last two decades of the eighteenth century. Because the sources for political history are far better known and have been worked many times, the emphasis here is on military material.

Manuscripts

MILITARY

The fire at the War Department in 1800 destroyed nearly all official army records, but those were only a part of the written material which was generated by the military in the decade and a half before Jefferson's election. Personal correspondence and records of all kinds have survived, and in such quantity that the history of the army and the military establishment generally is surprisingly rich and complete.

Papers for all three Secretaries of War exist. The Henry Knox Papers (MHS) proved to be the most disappointing because they contain mostly personal material, and by far the greatest portion relate to Knox's land speculations. However the Timothy Pickering Papers (MHS and smaller collections elsewhere) and the James McHenry collections (LC, WLCL, and Maryland Historical Society) contain a great deal of relevant correspondence on every War Department activity. Although many of McHenry's papers were sold at a Parke-Bernet auction in 1944, substantial portions of that sale have found their way into the Northwest Territory

Collections at the WLCL and the Indiana Historical Society. And some of that material deals with military problems before McHenry became Secretary. In addition, the papers of the government itself, in the 1780s the Papers of the Continental Congress (NA), and afterwards the George Washington Papers (LC), the Adams Family Papers (MHS), and the Records of the House of Representatives and the Senate (RG 233 and 46, NA), illustrate the development of policy at the highest level, the reasoning behind those policies, and much of the internal operations of the military establishment.

Similarly, especially rich papers survive from the commanding generals of the army in this era. The detailed Josiah Harmar Papers (WLCL) are without question the best source for the army from 1784 through 1790. They should be supplemented and continued into 1791 with Arthur St. Clair's papers (Peter Force Transcripts, LC and Ohio State Library), and after 1791 with the papers of Anthony Wayne (HSP, WLCL, and Detroit Public Library). Much from these collections has of course been published, but a great deal remains in manuscript. For the 1798–1800 period, the Washington Papers and the Alexander Hamilton Papers (LC) are filled, the Hamilton collection containing about as much material for those years as for the entire Treasury period. The only exception to the documentation is the papers of James Wilkinson, who probably knew better than to allow many of his letters to survive. His correspondence exists in small collections (Chicago Historical Society, University of Kentucky Library, Detroit Public Library, and elsewhere) and in the papers of his associates in the army and in Kentucky mentioned below.

Papers of army officers of lesser rank also survive, although for the 1780s and 1790s they are thinner and less revealing than for later periods in the army's history. The best by far is the John Armstrong Papers (Indiana Historical Society), which has never been exploited by historians. Also good is the John Pratt Collection (Connecticut State Library). Smaller but occasionally excellent are the Nicholas Fish Papers (LC), the Torrence Collection (Cincinnati Historical Society), the Preston-Joyes Collection (Filson Club, Louisville), and the Philip Lightfoot Papers (College of William and Mary Library), the latter important for the Quasi-war years. Many other collections, like the William Henry Harrison Papers (LC) or the Jacob Kingsbury Papers (Detroit Public Library) are sparse for the 1790s. But, as was true throughout the research for this book, a good army letter or document was often found in miscellaneous or autograph collections, or in the papers of political leaders. And in some respects, better for army life generally in this period are the diaries, journals, and reminiscences, many of which have been published, especially for the campaigns against the Indians. One notable manuscript, however, is Erkuries Beatty's diary (NYHS), only part of which has been printed.

Two great unused sources, however, and ones that include material

about enlisted personnel, are the interviews conducted during the nineteenth century by Lyman C. Draper and recorded in his papers (State
Historical Society of Wisconsin) along with a fund of other good army
and political material. In fact, historians Jared Sparks and Benson Lossing also interviewed eighteenth-century figures about their political and
military experiences, and notes on the interviews in at least Sparks's case
remain (Harvard University Library). George Bancroft (papers at NYPL),
as well as other nineteenth-century historians and antiquarians, corresponded with personages from the Revolution, or their descendants, and
the letters are often quite revealing.

For the logistical system of the army, fort construction, Indian
affairs, and other subjects, a variety of collections in addition to those
already named are available. For the coast artillery, one of the best is the
Ebenezer Stevens Papers (NYHS). War Department Indian activities are
chronicled exceptionally well in the Henry O'Reilly Papers (NYHS) and
the small David Henley Papers (Duke University Library). At the Burton
Historical Collection of the Detroit Public Library, there are orderly
books of Wilkinson, Wayne, and St. Clair, and papers of James O'Hara,
Samuel Henley, Solomon Sibley, James Henry, and John Wilkins, Jr., all
of which concern contracts and supplies in the 1790s, and contain ledgers
and invoice books as well as correspondence. Contractors' papers can
also be found for the 1780s and early 1790s in the William Duer Papers
(NYHS) and Otho H. Williams Papers (Maryland Historical Society). Six
boxes of miscellaneous army records—invoices, vouchers, returns,
inventories, and the like—plus a dozen volumes of accounts, receipts,
and forage books for various posts are in the Torrence Collection already
mentioned. Quartermaster records abound: a James O'Hara letterbook
(Indiana Historical Society), the Denny-O'Hara Papers (Western Pennsylvania Historical Society), which includes Denny's orderly book as
Harmar's adjutant, plus the immense Isaac Craig Papers (Carnegie
Library of Pittsburgh). The latter contains so much loose paper and
correspondence that an historian interested in the economic development of the Ohio Valley could probably trace every axe and barrel of
whiskey that went to the army for a five-year period. And at the top of the
logistical system there are the papers of Tench Coxe while Purveyor of
Public Supplies (NA), and Intendant of Military Stores Samuel Hodgdon's Letterbooks, 1795–1798, in the U.S. Army Papers (LC).

Many collections, personal papers as well as those pertaining to
logistics, contain lists, storekeeper accounts, paymaster records, and unit
orderly books. But in addition, such records exist, along with rosters,
musters, and the like in miscellaneous or "U.S. Army" collections at such
repositories as the Filson Club, the United States Military Academy
Library, the NYPL, and the LC. From such records the internal history
of the military establishment could be written.

Papers concerning the militia and volunteer military activities have rarely been published and never searched thoroughly by historians. Without looking specifically for this material, I found informative documents on frontier operations in the James Young Love and Thomas Love Papers (Filson Club), the Charles Scott Papers (University of Kentucky Library), the Archibald Woods Papers (College of William and Mary Library), and of course in the Draper Collection. In addition, one can find documents on the eastern militia for the Whiskey Rebellion and the partial mobilizations in 1794 and 1798 in the Joseph Jones Papers (Duke University Library), the Anthony Walton White Papers (Rutgers University Library), the Harmar Papers, and if the Governor's Papers (North Carolina Department of Archives and History) are typical, in the official records of many of the state governments.

POLITICAL

The manuscripts pertaining to political history have been used and described often enough by scholars to need little discussion here. For this book, all the known collections on microfilm and at the most promising manuscript repositories from Massachusetts to South Carolina and west to Wisconsin were searched for material. Naturally the Washington Papers and the Adams Family Papers proved exceptionally rich, as did the well-worked papers of such leaders as Alexander Hamilton, James Madison, and Thomas Jefferson (all at LC), Rufus King (NYHS), William Irvine (HSP), Theodore Sedgwick (MHS), Albert Gallatin (NYHS), and Oliver Wolcott, Jr. (CHS), to name only a few. Always important too, were the large autograph collections such as the Simon Gratz and Ferdinand Dreer Collections (both at HSP), and the Emmet Collection (NYPL). The newly opened Tench Coxe Papers (HSP) contained excellent political material.

I also attempted from the beginning to search out less well-known collections in the belief that for most of this era, the military was probably a secondary issue in national politics. Sometimes, while I discovered only a few items, they were crucial. Historians should not neglect such collections as the Benjamin Goodhue Papers (EI), the Thacher Papers (Boston Public Library), the Dwight Foster Papers (American Antiquarian Society), the Henry Tazewell Papers (College of William and Mary Library), or the large number of smaller collections at the Library of Congress, like the papers of Henry Tazewell, William Loughton Smith, and Elbridge Gerry. In general, however, I was disappointed by the dearth of large collections for southern Federalists, the Charles E. Johnson collection of James Iredell material (North Carolina Department of Archives and History) and the Pinckney Family Papers (LC) being exceptions. There is also extremely good political information in the reports of British diplomats in the 1790s (British State Papers, Ford Transcripts, NYPL).

On special topics, certain collections were especially useful. The history of the Newburgh conspiracy could not be written without the Robert Morris Papers (LC). The Harry Innes and Shelby Family Papers (both at LC), the microfilmed Winthrop Sargent Papers (MHS), and the correspondence of John Cleves Symmes (LC and Cincinnati Historical Society) which Beverley W. Bond, Jr., did not publish were all necessary for understanding the Indian war. Nor could I have fully documented the administration's response to the Whiskey Rebellion without the John William Wallace Papers (HSP) and the two volumes of Pennsylvania Miscellany, Whiskey Rebellion (LC), a special archive maintained evidently on purpose by Washington and the cabinet. The papers of various southern representatives in the Southern Historical Collection (University of North Carolina Library) illuminated the inner politics of the Sixth Congress. And on a variety of different topics, the two series, Miscellaneous and Domestic Letters of the Department of State (RG 59, NA), proved invaluable.

The sources for political history in this era are known to be rich, but the range and size of the material is less well understood. The massive *National Union Catalogue of Manuscript Collections* (Ann Arbor, 1962–date) is a much improved finding guide over the individual effort by the late Philip M. Hamer, ed., *A Guide to Archives and Manuscripts in the United States* (New Haven, 1961). But because manuscript repositories do not themselves know the contents of their own collections, the subject indices in the *National Union Catalogue* are weak. Therefore, unless one's research pertains to individuals who were famous enough to be named in the short descriptions of each collection, the *Catalogue* provides very crude and incomplete listings. What is needed are chronological guides to manuscripts (such as some repositories, the Historical Society of Pennsylvania being one example, maintain) so that all available manuscript collections for each decade of American history could be listed together. Perhaps the National Historic Publications Commission might underwrite detailed listings and evaluations by experienced scholars of the manuscripts for particular periods. Also helpful would be a published master listing of all calendars of manuscript collections, those available only in typescript at the repositories as well as those in print.

One other group of sources proved very helpful. Historians for too long have neglected maps, prints, other illustrations, and even visits to historical sites as a way of gaining insight into research problems. Visits to Congress Hall in Philadelphia heightened my understanding of the bitterness of politics in the 1790s. And had I discovered earlier the Abraham Bradley map of the United States for 1796 (Prints Division, NYPL), my sense of the spatial and temporal relationships in the 1790s would have been enhanced greatly.

Newspapers and Pamphlets

Newspapers proved to be of much less value than private correspondence, but they did provide critical information on several points. And in general the newspapers gave a sense of what topics were discussed in public, what party leaders wanted the public to see, and how Federalist thinking in private compared to their public rhetoric. For the 1780s I paged several sheets in different parts of the country and for the 1790s, the party organs in Philadelphia (*Gazette of the United States*, *National Gazette*, *General Advertiser*, and *Aurora*), as well as Noah Webster's New York *Minerva*.

In some instances, newspapers helped immensely. For example, they revealed how much and what kind of information about the Newburgh conspiracy became public, when, and where; public awareness of the West; the arguments over the Constitution and over the Indian war; public opinion and policy making; the information that the Washington administration possessed about the Whiskey Rebellion, and when that information reached Philadelphia; the struggle between Wayne and Wilkinson over command of the army; reaction to the army in the Quasi-war; and other specifics. Occasionally the newspapers provided facts, or, through a published article, altered my perception of evidence.

Pamphlets and other contemporary published materials were also used, again mostly to gauge public understanding of events. Occasionally there was a major find, like Peter Edes's collection of Boston Massacre orations (Boston, 1785), or a bill or act in Congress, debate on military or political issues, or good information in the interpretations advanced by partisans of both parties in the 1790s, such as the well-known writings of William Cobbett and James T. Callender, and such tracts as William Loughton Smith's *The Politics and Views of a Certain Party Displayed* (n.p., 1792) and William Findley's *A Review of the Revenue System* . . . (Philadelphia, 1794). Less often, a diatribe or apologia furnished specific facts, like Hugh H. Brackenridge's *Incidents of the Insurrection in the Western Parts of Pennsylvania in the Year 1794* (Philadelphia, 1795).

Printed Documents

MILITARY

Printed correspondence was fully as important to this book as letters in manuscript. The *Journals of the Continental Congress*, *Annals of Congress*, and *American State Papers* (full citations on pages xix–xx) revealed the actions and thinking of Congress, the executive branch, and the forging of nearly every piece of legislation that created the military establishment. Both of the latter sources must be used carefully, however, because the nineteenth-century editors of the *Annals* used only a portion of the available newspaper accounts of debates. (If Congresses in the 1960s and 1970s are willing to fund a complete documentary history of the First Congress, one would think they would underwrite a complete and reliable new edition of debates for the eighteenth and early nineteenth centuries.) The *State Papers* series consists mostly of documents sent by the executive to Congress, and the Washington administration occasionally backdated material or selected for submission that which would make the most favorable impact. Also, the editors sometimes separated the documents—or even a single report—in order to insert the parts into the appropriate series.

State public collections proved marginal, with the outstanding exception of *Pennsylvania Archives*, *Second Series* (Harrisburg, 1887–1896), volume IV, which concerns the Whiskey Rebellion and the Indian war, and Sherwin McRae, ed., *Calendar of Virginia State Papers* . . . (Richmond, 1875–1893).

Very little of the Secretary of War's correspondence is printed as such except for Bernard C. Steiner, *The Life and Correspondence of James McHenry* (Cleveland, 1907). But much is available in the papers of the commanding generals, such as Gayle Thornbrough, ed., *Outpost on the Wabash, 1787–1791* . . . *[Indiana Historical Society Publications, XIX]* (Indianapolis, 1957), William Henry Smith, ed., *The St. Clair Papers* . . . (Cincinnati, 1882), and Richard C. Knopf, ed., *Anthony Wayne, A Name in Arms* . . . *The Wayne-Knox-Pickering-McHenry Correspondence* (Pittsburgh, 1960). The latter apparently prints documents only from the Wayne Papers at the Historical Society of Pennsylvania.

There are also a large number of officers' diaries, letters, and journals in printed form. Best for the army in the 1780s and for Harmar's campaign are William Denny, ed., "The Military Journal of Major Ebenezer Denny," *Memoirs of the Historical Society of Pennsylvania*, VII (1860), 205–492, Consul Wright Butterfield, ed., *Journal of Capt. Jonathan Heart* . . . (Albany, 1885), and nineteenth-century magazines and histories such as Charles Cist, ed., *The Cincinnati Miscellany* . . . (Cincinnati, 1845–1846), S. P. Hildreth, *Pioneer History* . . . (Cincinnati, 1848), and Neville B. Craig, *The Olden Time* (Pittsburgh, 1846–1848). The most informative and well known is the Denny journal. However an impressionistic comparison of the printed version with the manuscript in the Denny-O'Hara Papers shows enough discrepancies to warrant a new edition.

For the 1790s there are a large number of journals and diaries. Most interesting for St. Clair's campaign are "Winthrop Sargent's Diary . . . [of] St. Clair's Expedition . . . ," *Ohio Archeological and Historical Quarterly*, XXXIII (1924), 237–273, and Beverley W. Bond, Jr., "Memoirs of Benjamin Van Cleve," *Quarterly Publication of the Historical and Philo-*

sophical Society of Ohio, XVII (1922), 1–71. For Wayne's campaign, see the sources cited in chapter 8, footnote 71.

POLITICAL

For political history and special topics, I consulted all the collections of printed documents I could find for the period. The sources cited on pages xix–xx (showing footnote abbreviations) were the most helpful. Edmund C. Burnett's *Letters of Members of the Continental Congress*, although indispensable, was extremely frustrating. Burnett often omitted important portions of letters, did not print letters if the congressman was not actually present at a session, and of course published no incoming correspondence. Fortunately the new edition being prepared by Paul H. Smith at the Library of Congress will add material and upgrade the series. Although the papers of the Founding Fathers—Jefferson, Hamilton, Adams, Monroe, Washington, and the like—were critical, those dated prior to World War II should be used with care. For example, Charles R. King's *Life and Correspondence of Rufus King* omits large parts of letters and on occasion without the telltale ellipses.

In addition, there are collections of letters of congressmen and others in the know which were extremely important: Seth Ames, ed., *Works of Fisher Ames* . . . (Boston, 1854); Kemp P. Battle, ed., *Letters of Nathaniel Macon, John Steele, and William Barry Grove* [James Sprunt Historical Monograph, no. 3] (Chapel Hill, 1902); Stewart Mitchell, ed., *New Letters of Abigail Adams, 1788–1801* (Boston, 1947); and a host of others. Diaries and journals were also significant. For example, Franklin B. Sawvel, ed., *The Complete Anas of Thomas Jefferson* (New York, 1903) and Charles A. Beard, ed., *The Journal of William Maclay* . . . (New York, 1927) are funds of information and insight into the mood in the capital. For western affairs, one of the best was Paul A. W. Wallace, *Thirty Thousand Miles with John Heckewelder* (Pittsburgh, 1958). For Canadian events, readers should begin with Brig. General E. A. Cruikshank, ed., *The Correspondence of Lieut. Governor John Graves Simcoe* (Toronto, 1923–1931). Of course, one of the chief sources for letters and correspondence from personal manuscript collections are the publications of the historical societies, the richest and most extensive for my research being the Massachusetts Historical Society, *Collections*, in various series.

But there is also a vast amount of material printed in more out of the way places. First are the nineteenth-century biographies. Some have already been mentioned, but in addition, the following were very useful: Griffith J. McRee, *Life and Correspondence of James Iredell* (New York, 1858); Octavius Pickering and Charles Upham, *The Life of Timothy Pickering* (Boston, 1863–1867); J. J. Boudinot, *The Life, Public Services,*

Addresses, and Letters of Elias Boudinot, LL.D. (Boston and New York, 1896); and William Wirt Henry, *Patrick Henry: Life, Correspondence, and Speeches* (New York, 1891). Sometimes, biographies in this style have continued into the twentieth century, one of the finest and most revealing being Charles E. L. Wingate, *Life and Letters of Paine Wingate* (Medford, Mass., 1930).

Other sources, used rarely by historians, are the nineteenth-century historical magazines and newspapers which included primary material, and the manuscript and autograph catalogues. Very often in the process of attracting buyers, manuscript dealers printed portions of letters (and still do) which then disappear into private hands. As a result, important documents can be used only in extract form from the sale catalogues. The best are those of Stan Henkels, Parke-Bernet Galleries, Walter and Mary Benjamin, and Charles Hamilton. The most complete collection of catalogues is at the New York Public Library. Last, some of the best published documents are in twentieth-century historical journals. Much of this material can be uncovered using the well-known *Writings on American History* series, but it should be consulted well after research is underway so that key names can be recognized in the various indices. The primary material in nineteenty-century newspapers, magazines, and the autograph catalogues is scattered, however, and not until some bibliographer goes to work, or some project is put together, can the individual scholar be certain of locating all the available sources.

Secondary Sources

MILITARY

There exists a surprisingly large literature on the peacetime military in late eighteenth-century America, but it varies greatly in quality and leaves much for further research. Inevitably, the general works on military policy and practice neglect the army in the 1780s and 1790s under the assumption that it was pathetically small and the establishment crude and unfinished. Professional military officers from Emory Upton, *The Military Policy of the United States* [62d Congress 2d session, Senate Document no. 494] (Washington, 1912) to John McAuley Palmer, *Washington, Lincoln, Wilson: Three War Statesmen* (Garden City, N.Y., 1930), and beyond have skimmed over these years. Palmer has some depth, but he focused mostly on Washington's "Sentiments," and like most officers, he was more interested in affecting military policy than in understanding the past. Modern works like C. Joseph Bernardo and Eugene H. Bacon, *American Military Policy: Its Development Since 1775* (2d ed., Harrisburg, 1961), Samuel P. Huntington, *The Soldier and the State: The*

Theory and Politics of Civil-Military Relations (Cambridge, 1957), and the brilliant Walter Millis, *Arms and Men: A Study of American Military History* (New York, 1956) are also weak in terms of coverage. Better, but still spotty because of the dearth of monographic literature which goes beyond operations, is Russell F. Weigley's comprehensive *History of the United States Army* (New York and London, 1967). Marcus Cunliffe's excellent *Soldiers & Civilians: The Martial Spirit in America, 1775–1865* (Boston, 1968) depicts military thinking and the cultural milieu of military affairs, but he too passes lightly over the last two decades of the eighteenth century.

The background of colonial and Revolutionary military affairs is covered generally in two fine surveys by Douglas Edward Leach, *Arms for Empire: A Military History of the British Colonies in North America, 1607–1763* (New York and London, 1973) and Don Higginbotham, *The War of American Independence: Military Attitudes, Policies, and Practice, 1763–1789* (New York and London, 1971), both in the *Macmillan Wars of the United States*, edited by Louis Morton, and both containing notes and bibliographies which serve as guides to more specialized studies. For the English background, one must also consult Lois G. Schwoerer's new *"No Standing Armies!": The Antiarmy Ideology in Seventeenth-Century England* (Baltimore, 1974) and J. R. Western, *The English Militia in the Eighteenth Century: The Story of a Political Issue, 1660–1802* (London and Toronto, 1965). The melding of English and American military attitudes and affairs is handled deftly by John Shy, *Toward Lexington: The Role of the British Army in the Coming of the American Revolution* (Princeton, 1965).

On military policy after the Revolution, Howard White, *Executive Influence in Determining Military Policy in the United States [University of Illinois Studies in the Social Sciences, XII]* (Urbana, 1924), although dated in its assumptions about politics, should be consulted more often by military historians. Far better, although thinly researched, is Richard H. Frazer, The Foundations of American Military Policy, 1783–1800 (unpublished Ph.D. thesis, University of Oklahoma, 1959). On institutional developments, Harry M. Ward, *The Department of War, 1781–1795* (Pittsburgh, 1962) is thoroughly documented but extremely weak on analysis and interpretation. On the politics of military affairs, John K. Mahon, "Pennsylvania and the Beginnings of the Regular Army," *Pennsylvania History*, XXI (1954), 33–44, and Bernard Donahoe and Marshall Smelser, "The Congressional Power to Raise Armies: The Constitutional and Ratifying Conventions, 1787–1788," *Review of Politics*, XXXII (1971), 202–211 are both limited in scope. Arthur A. Ekirch, Jr., *The Civilian and the Military* (New York, 1956) is superficial. The best study of military thought by far is Russell F. Weigley, *Towards an American Army: Military Thought from Washington to Marshall* (New York and

London, 1962), but Weigley covers only Washington and Hamilton, and while the essays are cogent and sound, they leave much out. A good narrative of military policy during Jefferson's administration is Richard Alton Erney, The Public Life of Henry Dearborn (unpublished Ph.D. thesis, Columbia University, 1957), but it is dated now, and Erney's ends up a brief and breathless survey and should be used more as a guide to further research.

For the militia in the colonial period, the best studies are in unpublished Ph.D. dissertations. The most helpful and perceptive were David Richard Millar, The Militia, the Army and Independency in Colonial Massachusetts (Cornell University, 1967); Richard Henry Marcus, The Militia of Colonial Connecticut, 1639-1775: An Institutional Study (University of Colorado, 1965); Frederick Stokes Aldridge, Organization and Administration of the Militia System of Colonial Virginia (American University, 1964), and Archibald Hanna, Jr., New England Military Institutions, 1693-1750 (Yale University, 1950). On post-revolutionary militia, Jim Dan Hill, *The Minute Man in Peace and War: A History of the National Guard* (Harrisburg, 1964) is a survey and badly biased in favor of the Guard. Far better is John K. Mahon, *The American Militia: Decade of Decision, 1789-1800* [*University of Florida Monographs, Social Sciences*, VI] (Gainesville, 1960). Still needed, however, is research into the attempt to reform the militia in the 1780s, musters and training, the mobilizations and operations on the frontier and in the East in 1794 and 1798, the volunteer companies, and the social character and semi-military uses of the militia in this period.

The largest literature concerns military operations in the West. Two excellent surveys, with good bibliographies, are James Ripley Jacobs, *The Beginning of the U.S. Army, 1783-1812* (Princeton, 1947) and Francis Paul Prucha, *The Sword of the Republic: The U.S. Army on the Frontier, 1783-1846* (New York and London, 1969). More specialized are Jack Jule Gifford's fine study, The Northwest Indian War, 1784-1795 (unpublished Ph.D. thesis, University of California—Los Angeles, 1964); Alan S. Brown, "The Role of the Army in Western Settlement, Josiah Harmar's Command, 1785-1790," *Pennsylvania Magazine of History and Biography*, XLIII (1969), 161-178; and William H. Gaines, Jr., "The Forgotten Army: Recruiting for a National Emergency (1799-1800)," *Virginia Magazine of History and Biography*, LVI (1948), 267-279, the only adequate study in print of the Quasi-war army. William H. Guthman's *March to Massacre: A History of the First Seven Years of the United States Army, 1784-1791* (New York, 1975) appeared too late to be of use, but it should be consulted first for details on the operations and internal history of the First Regiment.

More work needs to be done, however—for example, the founding of West Point from a political and military standpoint is not adequately covered in Edgar Denton, The Formative Years of the United States Military Academy, 1775-1833 (unpublished Ph.D. thesis, Syracuse University, 1964) or in the published sources cited in Chapter 14, footnote 57. The operation of the arsenals is barely sketched out for the 1790s in Merritt Roe Smith, The Harpers Ferry Armory and the "New Technology" in America, 1794-1854 (unpublished Ph.D. thesis, Pennsylvania State University, 1971). Until William Skelton completes his study of the army officer corps, 1783-1860, for the 1780s and 1790s one still has to rely on Norman Caldwell's three descriptive articles, "The Frontier Army Officer, 1794-1814," "The Enlisted Soldier at the Frontier Post, 1790-1814," and "Civilian Personnel at the Frontier Military Post (1790-1814)," Mid-America, XXXVII (1955), 101-128, 195-204, XXXVIII (1956), 101-119. Only certain aspects of veterans affairs are covered in Dixon Wector's excellent but neglected When Johnny Comes Marching Home (Boston, 1944); Wallace Evan Davies, Patriotism on Parade: The Story of Veterans and Hereditary Organizations in America, 1783-1900 (Cambridge, 1955); William H. Glasson, Federal Military Pensions in the United States (New York, 1918); and the article by Sidney Kaplan, "Veteran Officers and Politics in Massachusetts, 1783-1787," WMQ, IX (1952), 29-57. All of these studies concern revolutionary veterans, not those from the peacetime army.

Still needed are good biographies covering the full careers of Harmar and St. Clair, and the postwar career of Wayne. The army in the Quasi-war deserves a book-length study, beyond what has been done here and which penetrates below the War Department and high command level so well discussed in M. Howard Mattsson-Boze, James McHenry, Secretary of War, 1796-1800 (unpublished Ph.D. thesis, University of Minnesota, 1965). There is nothing at all on tactics in the United States, or the development of the artillery, cavalry, or coast artillery from a technical standpoint. More important, there is no adequate exploration of the impact of European military events and ideas on the American military establishment after the Revolution.

POLITICAL

The literature on the political history of the 1780s and 1790s is gigantic but well known; and although new monographs, histories, and articles appear every year, no list or survey would be useful here. A good guide to the historiography and to pre-1950 literature is George M. Curtis III, American Historians and the Federalists (unpublished M.A. thesis, University of Kansas, 1963). For bibliographies of the 1780s and 1790s, readers should start with Richard B. Morris, "The Confederation Period and the American Historian," WMQ, XIII (1956), 139-156, and William Nisbet Chambers, Political Parties in a New Nation: The American

Experience, 1776–1809 (New York, 1963). For this book, I checked virtually every work of political history and found almost all of them helpful to one degree or another. Even when I disagreed, my reactions to various interpretations, combined with my own reading of the sources, resulted in a better understanding of the nature of political life in the period and its relationship to military issues. For my purposes, the best works were Merrill Jensen, *The New Nation: A History of the United States During the Confederation, 1781–1789* (New York, 1950); E. James Ferguson, *The Power of the Purse: A History of Public Finance, 1776–1790* (Chapel Hill, 1961); Jackson Turner Main, *The Antifederalists: Critics of the Constitution, 1781–1788* (Chapel Hill, 1961); Kenneth Russell Bowling, Politics in the First Congress, 1789–1791 (unpublished Ph.D. thesis, University of Wisconsin, 1968); Noble E. Cunningham, Jr., *The Jeffersonian Republicans: The Formation of Party Organization, 1789–1801* (Chapel Hill, 1957); Richard Buel, Jr., *Securing the Revolution: Ideology in American Politics, 1789–1815* (Ithaca and London, 1972); Manning J. Dauer, *The Adams Federalists* (Baltimore, 1953); Stephen G. Kurtz, *The Presidency of John Adams: The Collapse of Federalism, 1795–1800* (Philadelphia, 1957); James Morton Smith, *Freedom's Fetters: The Alien and Sedition Laws and American Civil Liberties* (Ithaca, 1956); and some of the topical studies discussed below.

State studies did not prove particularly useful except for information on some specific points or interpretations, for example: Harry Marlin Tinkcom, *The Republicans and Federalists in Pennsylvania, 1790–1801: A Study in National Stimulus and Local Response* (Harrisburg, 1950), on relations between Pennsylvania and the Washington administration in 1794; and various studies for the congressional elections in 1798–1799 and the election of 1800. Three specific works were especially helpful: Alfred F. Young, *The Democratic Republicans of New York: The Origins, 1763–1797* (Chapel Hill, 1967), for its implications for the national political scene, the rise of the Republican party, and party formation generally; Patricia Watlington, *The Partisan Spirit: Kentucky Politics, 1779–1792* (New York, 1972), for untangling the subject and the people; and James M. Banner, Jr., *To the Hartford Convention: The Federalists and the Origins of Party Politics in Massachusetts, 1789–1815* (New York, 1970), for elements of Federalist ideology.

Biographies proved useful primarily for political information and confirmation on specific points, since almost none of them provided any facts or insight into military thinking or affairs. Significantly, and indicative of how military affairs are neglected for this as well as other eras, even those biographies of the chief characters in this book are shamefully weak on the military side of careers after 1783. See, for example, relevant portions (or omissions) in Douglas Southall Freeman, *et al.*, *George Washington: A Biography* (New York, 1948–1957); James Thomas Flexner, *George Washington* (Boston, 1965-1972); Broadus Mitchell, *Alexander Hamilton* (New York, 1957-1962); Richard E. Welch, Jr., *Theodore Sedgwick, Federalist: A Political Portrait* (Middletown, Conn., 1965); and although accurate and interpretatively sound, Page Smith, *John Adams* (Garden City, N.Y., 1962), which also buries one of Adams's greatest political crises in a plethora of other information. To cite one last example, Dumas Malone, *Jefferson and His Time* (Boston, 1948-date) does not discuss the founding of West Point despite the implications for Jefferson's politics, Presidency, and thinking on education.

A variety of special monographs and articles proved invaluable. On the Constitution, most of the secondary literature was marginal since it approached the Constitution from the standpoint of legal precedent and constitutional history rather than the realities of politics, events, and political philosophy in the Revolutionary era. Notable exceptions are Gordon Wood, *The Creation of the American Republic* (Chapel Hill, 1969); William M. Wiecek, *The Guarantee Clause of the U.S. Constitution* (Ithaca and London, 1972); Charles A. Lofgren, "War-Making Under the Constitution: The Original Understanding," *Yale Law Journal* LXXXI (1972), 672-702; and the histories of ratification. The best interpretative study of the convention for my purposes was Merrill Jensen, *The Making of the American Constitution* (Princeton, 1964).

Congressional affairs during the last two decades of the eighteenth century are only beginning to be studied in depth. Edmund C. Burnett's *The Continental Congress* (New York, 1941) proved of little or no use to me. Due to a dearth of secondary accounts, for an entire twenty-year period I had to write a legislative history for every military resolution or law passed. (H. James Henderson's *Political Parties in the Continental Congress, 1774-1789* [New York, 1974] appeared too late for my purposes.) Virtually every law or resolution in this period could be studied further. For example, even Francis Paul Prucha in his excellent *American Indian Policy in the Formative Years: The Indian Trade and Intercourse Acts, 1790-1834* (Cambridge, 1962) could not plumb the political, military, and intellectual underpinnings of the legislation in enough depth. I am probably guilty also, since in a book that turned out to be so large, I had to shorten my treatment of individual pieces of legislation.

Nor has the inner history of the Washington and Adams administrations really been unmasked, beyond foreign affairs and the Hamiltonian program. Administration history has been surveyed in Leonard D. White's pioneering *The Federalists: A Study in Administrative History* (New York, 1948), but the number of special topics and questions remaining is immense. Donald H. Stewart, *The Opposition Press of the Federalist Period* (Albany, 1969) is short on interpretation but furnishes a veritable catalogue of Republican thought and rhetoric in the 1790s. In the form of an analytic intellectual history, it should be duplicated for the

Federalists since neither party has been subjected to analysis as to their thought (except for a few of the top leaders). Chapter 1 of David Hackett Fischer's *The Revolution of American Conservatism: The Federalist Party in the Era of Jeffersonian Democracy* (New York, 1965) is the unrivalled discussion of Federalist social and political attitudes today, although sections of James M. Banner's study of the Massachusetts Federalists mentioned above is also very good. Linda K. Kerber, *Federalists in Dissent: Imagery and Ideology in Jeffersonian America* (Ithaca and London, 1970) covers a later period. In any event, a thorough study for each party is needed, focusing on substance as opposed to the rhetoric so well dissected by Marshall Smelser in his articles, "The Jacobin Phrenzy: Federalists and the Menace of Liberty, Equality, and Fraternity," *Review of Politics*, XIII (1951), 457–482, "The Jacobin Phrenzy: The Menace of Monarchy, Plutocracy, and Anglophilia, 1789–1798," *ibid.*, XXI (1959), 239–258, and "The Federalist Period as an Age of Passion," *American Quarterly*, X (1958), 391–417; John R. Howe, Jr., "Republican Thought and the Political Violence of the 1790s," *ibid.*, XIX (1967), 147–165; and Richard Hofstadter, *The Idea of a Party System: The Rise of Legitimate Opposition in the United States, 1780–1840* (Berkeley and Los Angeles, 1969).

Foreign relations during the period has been richly mined. Frederick W. Marks III, *Independence on Trial: Foreign Affairs and the Making of the Constitution* (Baton Rouge, 1973) captures the mood and thinking of the 1780s, but most helpful to me were the general studies of the 1790s by Alexander DeConde, *Entangling Alliance: Politics and Diplomacy under George Washington* (Durham, N.C., 1958) and *The Quasi-War: The Politics and Diplomacy of the Undeclared War with France, 1797–1801* (New York, 1966). Also helpful were books which deal with the West: Samuel Flagg Bemis's *Jay's Treaty: A Study in Commerce and Diplomacy* (rev. ed., New Haven and London, 1962) and *Pinckney's Treaty: America's Advantage from Europe's Distress, 1783–1800* (rev. ed., New Haven, 1960); A. L. Burt, *The United States, Great Britain, and British North America from the Revolution to . . . the War of 1812* (New Haven, 1940); Charles R. Ritcheson, *Aftermath of Revolution: British Policy Toward the United States, 1783–1795* (Dallas, Tex., 1969); and Arthur Preston Whitaker, *The Spanish-American Frontier: 1783–1795* (Boston, 1927). More specialized works were not as useful, although a model study is Harry Ammon, *The Genet Mission* (New York, 1973).

On Indian policy and affairs, there is good material on nearly every aspect except the thinking of the Washington administration. Walter H. Mohr's workmanlike *Federal Indian Relations, 1774–1788* (Philadelphia, 1933) has been supplemented but not replaced by Reginald Horsman, *Expansion and American Indian Policy, 1783–1812* (East Lansing, Mich., 1967) and Randolph Chandler Downes, *Council Fires on the*

Upper Ohio . . . (Pittsburgh, 1940). There are several studies illuminating the British side of the Indian war, but the best are by Horsman, in article form and his *Matthew Elliott: British Indian Agent* (Detroit, 1964). The Indian side of the war, however, has gone essentially untouched, even in such a recent study as Bert Anson, *The Miami Indians* (Norman, Okla., 1970). The best analysis of what happened to the northern Indians at this time from a cultural and political standpoint, well worth duplicating for the Ohio and Indiana tribes as a group, is Anthony F. C. Wallace, *The Death and Rebirth of the Seneca* (New York, 1970). And of course critical to understanding the thinking generally on Indian affairs is Bernard W. Sheehan's beautifully crafted *Seeds of Extinction: Jeffersonian Philanthropy and the American Indian* (Chapel Hill, 1973).

Finally, there are a variety of events and personalities in the 1780s and 1790s that deserve further research. Although most are probably suitable for articles and would require a thorough combing of the sources, manuscript and printed, the effort would be rewarding. Some of these events were so important that more work could well revise our understanding of the entire period. One excellent example is Kenneth R. Bowling's forthcoming study of Charles Thomson. As fine as is Leland Baldwin's *Whiskey Rebels: The Story of a Frontier Uprising* (rev. ed., Pittsburgh, 1962), it remains essentially a work of the late 1930s, marred by Turnerian assumptions and Jeffersonian biases. And one of the next important steps forward in studying the late eighteenth century may be psycho-history, done carefully, with balance, and with compassion. As much as one might dispute Fawn Brodie's *Thomas Jefferson: An Intimate History* (New York, 1974), some effort of that sort was long overdue. And historians have generally applauded older works along the same lines, as I do here, such as Adrienne Koch, *Power, Morals, and the Founding Fathers: Essays in the Interpretation of the American Enlightenment* (Ithaca, 1961), and the brilliant Douglass Adair, "Fame and the Founding Fathers," in Edmund P. Willis, ed., *Fame and the Founding Fathers* (Bethlehem, Pa., 1967), 27–52.

Index